THE GLOSSARY OF
SUSTAINABILITY
CIRCULAR
ECONOMY

I0436243

Compiled & Edited By:
Dr.Padmaja Saha

Rhythm

Independent
Publication

THE GLOSSARY OF SUSTAINABILITY CIRCULAR ECONOMY

Compiled & Edited By:
Dr.Padmaja Saha

ISBN:9798861503730

9798861503730

Published by:
Rhythm Independent Publication,
Jinkethimmanahalli, Varanasi, Bengaluru, Karnataka, India - 560036

For all types of correspondence, send your mails to the provided address above.

The information presented herein has been collated from a diverse range of sources, comprehensive perspective on the subject matter.

3D Printing For Sustainable Manufacturing

3D printing for sustainable manufacturing refers to the use of additive manufacturing techniques to produce products and components in a way that minimizes the environmental impact. It involves the layer-by-layer construction of objects using various materials, such as plastics, metals, and ceramics, based on digital designs.

This manufacturing method offers several benefits in terms of sustainability. Firstly, it enables the use of less raw material compared to traditional manufacturing methods, as it only adds material where it is needed. This reduces waste and promotes resource efficiency. Additionally, 3D printing allows for the production of complex geometries and intricate designs, making it possible to optimize the weight and performance of products, leading to the reduction of material consumption.

Moreover, 3D printing can contribute to the circular economy by enabling the recycling and reusing of materials. It allows for the creation of products from recycled plastics or metals, reducing the need for new raw materials and diverting waste from landfills. The technology also facilitates the repair and replacement of specific components without the need to discard the whole product, extending its lifespan and reducing overall waste generation.

Furthermore, the localized nature of 3D printing can reduce transportation-related emissions. Instead of shipping products or components from distant manufacturing facilities, they can be produced on-demand and closer to the point of consumption. This not only decreases carbon emissions but also offers opportunities for local job creation and economic development.

3D-Printed Prosthetics For Sustainability

3D-printed prosthetics for sustainability refer to the use of 3D printing technology to create and produce prosthetic limbs in an environmentally friendly and socially responsible manner.

This approach to prosthetic limb production aims to address two key aspects of sustainability. First, it focuses on reducing the environmental impact associated with traditional manufacturing processes. With 3D printing, prosthetics can be created using additive manufacturing techniques, which minimize waste by only using the materials necessary for the specific design. This reduces the consumption of raw materials and energy compared to traditional prosthetic production methods, which often involve subtractive processes and generate significant waste.

Second, 3D-printed prosthetics contribute to social sustainability. By utilizing this technology, prosthetics can be produced at a lower cost, making them more accessible to individuals who may not have had the means to afford traditional prosthetics. This increases social equity and ensures the provision of essential healthcare services to a wider population, regardless of socioeconomic status.

In conclusion, 3D-printed prosthetics for sustainability enable the creation of prosthetic limbs using environmentally-friendly manufacturing processes and improve accessibility to affordable healthcare solutions. By addressing both environmental and social aspects of sustainability, this approach contributes to a more sustainable and equitable society.

3D-Printed Sustainable Homes

3D-printed sustainable homes are eco-friendly housing structures constructed using 3D printing technology and designed with a focus on reducing environmental impact and promoting sustainability. The process involves using a large-scale 3D printer that extrudes layers of a sustainable building material, such as recycled plastic or bio-based materials, to create the walls, floors, and other components of the home.

These homes offer several benefits in terms of sustainability. Firstly, the use of sustainable materials reduces the demand for traditional construction materials such as concrete and steel, which are known for their high carbon footprint. Additionally, 3D printing technology allows for precise control over the amount of material used, minimizing waste and reducing the overall environmental impact.

Moreover, 3D-printed sustainable homes can have a smaller carbon footprint throughout their lifespan compared to traditional homes. The use of energy-efficient designs, such as improved insulation and passive solar strategies, can significantly reduce energy consumption for heating and cooling. Furthermore, these homes can be designed to incorporate renewable energy systems, such as solar panels or wind turbines, to generate clean and renewable power on-site, further reducing reliance on non-renewable energy sources.

In conclusion, 3D-printed sustainable homes utilize innovative technology and eco-friendly materials to create housing structures that are both environmentally friendly and energy-efficient. By minimizing waste, reducing carbon emissions, and utilizing renewable energy sources, these homes contribute to a more sustainable future for the construction industry and help address the pressing challenges of climate change.

Adaptive Reuse Architecture

Adaptive reuse architecture, in the context of sustainability, refers to the practice of repurposing existing buildings or structures for new purposes without significant alterations or demolition. It involves creatively adapting and transforming existing spaces to meet contemporary needs while considering environmental, social, and economic aspects.

This approach contributes to sustainability by minimizing the consumption of resources and reducing waste associated with demolishing and constructing new buildings. By reusing existing structures, the embodied energy and materials invested in their original construction are preserved and utilized, reducing the overall carbon footprint of the project. This also helps to conserve natural resources, such as land and raw materials, that would otherwise be required for new construction.

Adaptive Reuse Of Industrial Spaces

Adaptive reuse of industrial spaces is a sustainable practice that involves repurposing existing industrial buildings or infrastructure for new and different purposes, while minimizing waste and environmental impact. This approach aims to breathe new life into underutilized or abandoned industrial sites, transforming them into functional and valuable assets that benefit the community and the environment.

By repurposing industrial spaces, we can reduce the need for new construction, which in turn helps to conserve resources and limit the generation of construction waste. Additionally, adaptive reuse promotes the preservation of historical and cultural heritage tied to these industrial sites, preventing their demolition and loss of collective memory.

Instead of demolishing old industrial buildings, adaptive reuse looks for opportunities to restore and retrofit them to meet the needs of the present, such as converting warehouses into residential lofts, factories into office spaces, or power plants into cultural centers. This approach not only extends the lifespan of the existing infrastructure but also reduces the environmental impact associated with constructing new buildings.

Adaptive reuse of industrial spaces also contributes to sustainable urban development by revitalizing urban areas, promoting economic growth, and creating new community spaces. By repurposing these sites, we can develop sustainable mixed-use neighborhoods that integrate residential, commercial, and recreational functions, reducing the need for long commutes and fostering a sense of community.

Advanced Nuclear Reactors

Advanced nuclear reactors are a sustainable form of energy technology that offer significant advancements over traditional nuclear power plants. These reactors utilize innovative designs and technologies to enhance the safety, efficiency, and environmental performance of nuclear energy.

One key feature of advanced nuclear reactors is their ability to utilize a wider range of fuel sources compared to conventional reactors. While traditional reactors primarily rely on enriched uranium, advanced reactors can use a variety of fuels, including depleted uranium, thorium, and even nuclear waste. This fuel flexibility not only helps to reduce waste and increase resource efficiency but also enables the utilization of abundant and underutilized fuel sources.

Furthermore, advanced nuclear reactors incorporate passive safety features that minimize the risk of accidents and mitigate the potential impact of any incidents. These safety features do not rely on human intervention or external power sources, making them highly reliable and robust. Additionally, advanced reactors can operate at lower pressures and temperatures, reducing the likelihood of catastrophic incidents such as core meltdowns.

The sustainability of advanced nuclear reactors is further enhanced through their ability to produce significantly less long-lived radioactive waste. These reactors can either reduce the volume and toxicity of waste generated or utilize nuclear waste as fuel, effectively recycling the material. This helps to minimize the long-term environmental impact of nuclear power generation.

With their advanced features and improved sustainability, advanced nuclear reactors have the potential to play a significant role in the future energy landscape by providing a reliable and environmentally friendly source of electricity.

Advanced Wastewater Treatment

Advanced wastewater treatment refers to the technologically advanced methods and processes employed to remove additional pollutants from wastewater that have not been effectively removed through conventional treatment methods. This approach is an essential component of sustainable wastewater management systems, as it ensures the protection of the environment and human health by minimizing the release of harmful substances into water bodies and ecosystems.

The primary objective of advanced wastewater treatment is to achieve a higher level of pollutant removal, specifically targeting contaminants such as nutrients, heavy metals, pharmaceuticals, and persistent organic pollutants (POPs). These pollutants can have detrimental effects on ecosystems, water quality, and public health if not adequately treated before discharge.

Advanced treatment processes typically involve a combination of physical, chemical, and biological techniques, such as membrane filtration, activated carbon adsorption, ion exchange, advanced oxidation processes, and biological nutrient removal. These methods are designed to specifically target and break down or remove the difficult-to-treat compounds present in wastewater.

In addition to pollutant removal, advanced wastewater treatment also aims to promote the reuse of treated wastewater, further enhancing sustainability. By producing high-quality reclaimed water, advanced treatment processes offer opportunities for non-potable reuse in agricultural irrigation, industrial processes, and groundwater recharge. This reduces the demand on freshwater resources and provides a more circular approach to water management.

In conclusion, advanced wastewater treatment plays a crucial role in ensuring sustainable water management by removing additional pollutants from wastewater and promoting the reuse of treated water. These technological advancements help protect the environment, preserve water resources, and safeguard public health.

Aeroponics (Soilless Agriculture)

Aeroponics, also known as soilless agriculture, is a sustainable method of plant cultivation that eliminates the need for traditional soil-based growing systems. This innovative approach involves suspending plant roots in a misted environment, where they receive essential nutrients directly from the air and water mist.

Aeroponics offers numerous sustainability benefits. Firstly, it conserves water compared to conventional agricultural practices. By misting plants with water and nutrients at regular intervals, aeroponics minimizes water waste and ensures optimal water usage for each plant. This water efficiency is particularly crucial in arid regions where water scarcity is a pressing issue.

Secondly, aeroponics minimizes the need for pesticides and chemical fertilizers. The controlled environment of aeroponic systems reduces the risk of plant diseases and pest infestations, eliminating the need for harmful chemical interventions. This leads to healthier and safer produce, promoting the well-being of both consumers and the environment.

Thirdly, aeroponics allows for year-round cultivation regardless of weather conditions or seasonal restrictions. In indoor aeroponic systems, plants can be grown in climate-controlled environments, ensuring a consistent and reliable food supply throughout the year. This feature reduces dependence on long-distance transportation and enables local food production, reducing carbon emissions associated with food transportation.

Overall, aeroponics demonstrates a sustainable alternative to traditional agriculture by reducing water consumption, minimizing the use of pesticides and fertilizers, and enabling year-round cultivation. By harnessing the power of technology and innovation, aeroponics has the potential to revolutionize agricultural practices, contributing to a more sustainable and resilient food system.

Affordable Eco-Hotel Architecture

Affordable eco-hotel architecture refers to the design and construction of hotel buildings that prioritize sustainability while maintaining a budget-friendly approach. This architectural concept aims to create environmentally friendly and energy-efficient hospitality structures that minimize the impact on the natural resources and promote a sustainable way of living.

These eco-hotels incorporate various sustainable features to reduce their carbon footprint. The design incorporates green building practices, such as the use of locally sourced and renewable materials, efficient insulation to minimize energy loss, and incorporating natural lighting and ventilation systems to reduce the need for artificial lighting and air conditioning. The architecture also includes rainwater harvesting systems, greywater recycling, and the efficient use of water resources through low-flow fixtures and appliances.

Furthermore, affordable eco-hotel architecture focuses on creating spaces that blend harmoniously with the surrounding environment by integrating green spaces, rooftop gardens, and landscaping with native plants. The architectural design also prioritizes the use of renewable energy sources, such as solar panels or wind turbines, to power the hotel's operations.

By adopting affordable eco-hotel architecture, the hospitality industry can contribute significantly to global sustainability efforts. These sustainable buildings not only reduce operational costs for hotel owners but also provide a comfortable and eco-friendly experience for guests. Affordable eco-hotel architecture showcases a commitment to environmental responsibility and sets an example for other industries to follow in creating a sustainable future.

Affordable Eco-Hotel Design

An affordable eco-hotel design refers to the creation of a sustainable hotel establishment that is both cost-effective and environmentally friendly. It involves incorporating various design principles and strategies to minimize the hotel's ecological footprint while keeping costs affordable for guests and hotel owners.

These designs typically focus on reducing energy consumption, water usage, and waste generation throughout the hotel's operations. This can be achieved through the implementation of energy-efficient technologies, such as LED lighting, low-flow plumbing fixtures, and smart energy management systems. Additionally, renewable energy sources, such as solar panels or wind turbines, may be integrated into the hotel's infrastructure to further reduce reliance on fossil fuels.

The design also takes into consideration the use of sustainable building materials and practices. For example, utilizing locally sourced materials reduces transportation emissions and supports the local economy. Incorporating recycled or upcycled materials, such as reclaimed wood or repurposed furniture, can also contribute to a more eco-friendly hotel design.

Furthermore, an affordable eco-hotel design incorporates measures to promote environmental awareness and guest engagement. This may include providing recycling bins in guest rooms, offering incentivized programs for guests to conserve resources, and educating staff and guests about sustainable practices.

In summary, an affordable eco-hotel design focuses on creating a hotel establishment that balances environmental responsibility with affordability. By adopting sustainable design principles, incorporating energy-efficient technologies, utilizing eco-friendly materials, and promoting guest engagement, these hotels strive to minimize their impact on the environment while providing a budget-friendly accommodation option.

Affordable Eco-Housing Design

An affordable eco-housing design refers to a sustainable and cost-effective approach to constructing residential buildings that minimize negative environmental impacts while providing affordable housing solutions.

This design approach incorporates various principles of sustainability, including energy efficiency, use of renewable resources, waste reduction, and consideration of the local environment. By considering these factors, affordable eco-housing designs aim to promote environmental sustainability, social equity, and economic viability.

Affordable Eco-Residential Complexes

An affordable eco-residential complex refers to a sustainable housing development that is designed and built with environmental considerations and affordability in mind. These complexes aim to provide environmentally friendly and energy-efficient housing options for individuals or families with limited financial resources.

The main goal of affordable eco-residential complexes is to reduce the negative impact on the environment and promote sustainable living practices. This is achieved through various strategies, including but not limited to the use of renewable energy sources, energy-efficient building systems, and the implementation of recycling and waste management programs.

Agricultural Drones

Agricultural drones refer to unmanned aerial vehicles (UAVs) that are specifically designed for use in the field of agriculture. These drones are equipped with various sensors and cameras that enable them to collect data and imagery of crops and farmland. They are used to monitor crops, assess crop health, detect pests and diseases, and improve overall farm management.

From a sustainability perspective, agricultural drones have the potential to greatly benefit the agricultural industry. By providing farmers with valuable insights and information about their crops, these drones can help optimize resource use and reduce environmental impact. Through the use of sensors and advanced imaging technology, they can identify areas of over or under watering, nutrient deficiencies, and crop stress. This enables farmers to implement targeted interventions, such as adjusting irrigation and fertilization practices, leading to more efficient resource utilization.

Agricultural Waste Management

Agricultural waste management refers to the practice of effectively handling and minimizing the negative environmental impacts of waste generated from agricultural activities, with the aim of promoting sustainable agricultural practices.

This process involves the efficient collection, treatment, and utilization of agricultural waste materials such as crop residues, animal manure, and agrochemicals to minimize their potential adverse effects on the environment while maximizing their potential benefits to agricultural systems.

Agricultural Waste-To-Energy

Agricultural waste-to-energy refers to the process of converting unused agricultural by-products or residues into a usable form of energy, such as electricity or heat, with the aim of promoting sustainability in the agricultural sector.

This approach to energy generation not only helps address the problem of agricultural waste disposal but also contributes to the overall goal of sustainability by reducing greenhouse gas emissions and fostering a circular economy.

Agricultural Water Conservation

Agricultural water conservation refers to the practice of using water resources efficiently and effectively in agricultural activities to minimize water wastage and preserve the sustainability of water sources. It involves the implementation of techniques and strategies that promote responsible water management and ensure long-term availability of water for agricultural purposes.

By adopting agricultural water conservation practices, farmers can optimize their water usage by reducing runoff, evaporation, and inefficient irrigation methods. This can be achieved through the implementation of various techniques such as drip irrigation, precision agriculture, and crop rotation. Drip irrigation systems deliver water directly to the plant roots, minimizing water loss through evaporation and ensuring that plants receive the right amount of water without excess. Precision agriculture utilizes advanced technologies like sensors and GPS to measure soil moisture levels and deliver water precisely where and when it is needed, avoiding over-watering and preventing water waste.

In addition to efficient irrigation methods, agricultural water conservation also involves soil management practices that improve water retention capabilities. Techniques like mulching and cover cropping help in reducing evaporation, retaining moisture in the soil, and preventing erosion. These practices not only reduce the need for irrigation but also enhance soil health and fertility.

Agricultural water conservation plays a crucial role in achieving sustainable agricultural practices. By conserving water resources, farmers can contribute to the preservation of ecosystems, maintain water quality, and ensure the availability of water for future generations. This practice not only benefits the environment but also helps farmers in managing their resources more effectively and reducing operational costs.

Agricultural Water Purification

Agricultural water purification is the sustainable process of treating and filtering water used in agricultural activities to remove impurities and contaminants, ensuring its quality meets the required standards for irrigation, livestock consumption, and other farming needs.

The practice of agricultural water purification is crucial for promoting sustainability in the agricultural sector. As water scarcity becomes a growing concern, it is essential to utilize water resources efficiently and responsibly. By purifying water, farmers can optimize the use of available water sources, reduce water wastage, and minimize the negative environmental impact associated with agricultural activities.

Agroecological Farm Design

An agroecological farm design refers to the intentional planning and management of farming systems that prioritize sustainability, ecological balance, and resilience. It is a holistic approach that takes into consideration the interconnections between various components of the farm, including crops, livestock, soil, water, and biodiversity.

The design of an agroecological farm aims to mimic natural ecosystems, drawing inspiration from their functioning and diversity. Instead of relying on external inputs such as synthetic fertilizers and pesticides, agroecological farms promote the use of ecological processes and practices to enhance soil fertility, control pests, and manage diseases. These practices include crop rotation, intercropping, cover cropping, and integrated pest management.

The design of an agroecological farm also emphasizes the conservation and enhancement of biodiversity, recognizing the importance of natural ecosystems for long-term sustainability. It promotes the creation of habitats that support beneficial insects, birds, and other animals, as well as the preservation of native plant species. Agroecological farms often include elements such as hedgerows, windbreaks, and ponds to provide habitat and resources for wildlife.

Furthermore, agroecological farm design takes into account the social and economic aspects of farming. It strives to create farming systems that are economically viable, socially just, and culturally appropriate. This includes considerations such as fair working conditions, equitable distribution of resources, and support for local communities.

In summary, agroecological farm design is a sustainable approach to farming that integrates ecological principles, biodiversity conservation, and social considerations. It seeks to create farming systems that are resilient, regenerative, and harmonious with the surrounding environment.

Agroecological Farm Layout

An agroecological farm layout refers to the design and arrangement of agricultural systems that prioritize environmental sustainability, social equity, and economic viability. It is a holistic approach that seeks to integrate diverse elements of the farm ecosystem to optimize productivity while minimizing negative impacts on the environment.

The agroecological farm layout takes into account ecological principles and seeks to mimic natural processes to create a self-sustaining and resilient farming system. This includes designing crop rotations that promote biodiversity, minimizing chemical inputs, managing soil health through organic practices, and using conservation techniques to preserve water resources.

Furthermore, the layout considers the social dimension of farming, promoting fair and equitable labor practices, fostering community engagement, and enhancing local food systems. It encourages farmer-to-farmer knowledge sharing, fosters partnerships with consumers, and supports local markets.

This approach to farm layout recognizes that sustainable agriculture requires careful consideration of the farm as an ecosystem and involves a deep understanding of the interactions between plants, animals, soil, water, and human beings. It seeks to achieve a balance between productivity and sustainability by optimizing resource use, reducing waste, and enhancing natural processes that support ecosystem services.

Agroecology

Agroecology is an interdisciplinary approach to agriculture that seeks to optimize the productivity, sustainability, and resilience of agricultural systems while minimizing negative environmental and social impacts. It combines ecological principles with social and economic factors to promote the long-term viability of food production and rural livelihoods.

Agroecology recognizes the interconnectedness of natural processes and human activities within agricultural systems. It emphasizes the importance of biodiversity, soil health, and ecosystem services in maintaining agricultural productivity and sustainability. By supporting ecological processes such as nutrient cycling, biological pest control, and pollination, agroecology reduces reliance on synthetic inputs and minimizes the potential for negative environmental impacts such as pollution and soil degradation.

Furthermore, agroecology takes into account social and economic dimensions, considering the needs and aspirations of farmers, consumers, and local communities. It promotes participatory

7

approaches that involve farmers in decision-making processes, encourages knowledge exchange and innovation, and aims to enhance social equity and resilience in farming communities.

Through its holistic and systemic approach, agroecology aligns with the principles of sustainability. By optimizing the use of natural resources, minimizing chemical inputs, and maintaining ecological balance, agroecology contributes to the long-term viability of agricultural systems and the well-being of both people and the planet.

Agroforestry Landscape Design

Agroforestry landscape design is a sustainable approach to land management that integrates the cultivation of trees, crops, and livestock. It aims to create productive and resilient landscapes that support both environmental and social well-being.

By designing agroforestry landscapes, farmers and land managers strategically plan the arrangement of trees, crops, and livestock to optimize interactions and benefits between components. This design approach takes into account environmental factors such as soil types, topography, climate, and water availability, as well as economic and social considerations.

The benefits of agroforestry landscape design are numerous. Trees planted in agroforestry systems provide shade and windbreaks, reducing soil erosion and water evaporation while improving microclimates for crops and livestock. They also act as natural habitat for wildlife, promoting biodiversity and ecological balance. Furthermore, the integration of trees with crops can enhance soil fertility, reduce nutrient runoff, and improve water quality.

Agroforestry landscape design also offers economic advantages. The diverse range of products, including timber, fruits, nuts, fibers, and medicinal plants, provides multiple income streams for farmers. Additionally, agroforestry systems can increase the resilience of agricultural production by buffering against climate change impacts, diversifying income sources, and reducing market risks.

Overall, agroforestry landscape design is a holistic and sustainable approach that seeks to optimize productivity while enhancing environmental conservation, biodiversity, and social well-being. It recognizes the interconnectedness of various components within an ecosystem and aims to create landscapes that are both productive and resilient in the long term.

Agroforestry System Design

Agroforestry system design is a sustainable approach to land management that combines the cultivation of trees, crops, and/or livestock in a mutually beneficial and integrated manner. It aims to optimize the use of natural resources, enhance biodiversity, and promote ecological stability while providing economic, social, and environmental benefits.

This system is rooted in the principles of sustainability and resource conservation. By strategically planning the arrangement, composition, and management of trees, crops, and animals, agroforestry systems can help mitigate climate change, improve soil health and fertility, conserve water, and protect against soil erosion. The diverse vegetation of these systems provides habitat for wildlife and fosters biodiversity, contributing to increased ecosystem resilience.

Agroforestry can contribute to food security and poverty reduction by diversifying farmers' income sources and enhancing productivity. The intercropping of trees and crops, for example, can protect crops from wind damage, provide shade, and improve soil fertility through the cycling of nutrients. Livestock integration in agroforestry systems also presents opportunities for sustainable livestock production by providing shade, forage, and shelter for animals.

Furthermore, the use of agroforestry practices reduces the reliance on synthetic inputs such as chemical fertilizers and pesticides, thus minimizing the negative impacts on soil, water, and air quality. Agroforestry systems are also integral to climate change adaptation and mitigation efforts, as they sequester carbon, enhance carbon storage in the soil, and contribute to the reduction of greenhouse gas emissions.

In conclusion, agroforestry system design is a sustainable land management approach that combines trees, crops, and/or livestock to optimize resource use, enhance biodiversity, and provide economic and environmental benefits. It is a holistic approach that aligns with the principles of sustainability and contributes to the resilience of ecosystems and the livelihoods of communities.

Agroforestry

Agroforestry is a sustainable land management system that combines the cultivation of trees with other agricultural practices. It involves the deliberate integration of trees and shrubs into farming systems, where they coexist with crops and livestock.

This approach promotes ecological, social, and economic benefits through the synergistic interactions between trees, crops, and animals. Agroforestry systems are designed to mimic natural ecosystems, creating a diverse and resilient environment that enhances biodiversity, conserves natural resources, and improves soil health.

Agroforestry plays a crucial role in promoting sustainable agricultural practices and mitigating the negative impacts of conventional farming methods. By incorporating trees into agricultural landscapes, agroforestry systems provide multiple ecosystem services such as climate regulation, carbon sequestration, water filtration, and erosion control.

Furthermore, the inclusion of trees in agroforestry systems enhances the productivity and resilience of agricultural productions. The shade provided by trees can protect crops from extreme weather conditions, while their root systems improve soil structure, nutrient cycling, and water-holding capacity. This helps reduce the need for synthetic fertilizers and pesticides, contributing to a more environmentally friendly and sustainable farming approach.

Additionally, agroforestry systems also generate additional sources of income for farmers. Trees can serve as a source of timber, fuelwood, fruits, nuts, or medicinal products, diversifying their revenue streams and enhancing their livelihoods.

In conclusion, agroforestry provides a sustainable and holistic approach to agriculture, integrating trees with traditional farming practices. It offers numerous environmental, social, and economic benefits, making it a valuable strategy for promoting sustainability in the agricultural sector.

Air Quality Monitoring Sensors

Air quality monitoring sensors are devices designed to measure and monitor the levels of pollutants and other harmful substances present in the air. These sensors play a significant role in environmental sustainability by providing accurate and timely data about the air quality in a specific location or region.

The main objective of air quality monitoring sensors is to assess and analyze the quality of the air we breathe, identify potential sources of pollution, and evaluate the effectiveness of pollution control measures. By collecting data on various pollutants such as particulate matter, nitrogen dioxide, ozone, carbon monoxide, and volatile organic compounds, these sensors enable scientists, researchers, and policymakers to make informed decisions for improving air quality and mitigating the adverse impacts of pollution on human health and the environment.

Algae-Based Biofuels

Algae-based biofuels are a form of renewable energy derived from the cultivation and processing of algae. Algae, which are microscopic photosynthetic organisms, have the ability to convert sunlight and carbon dioxide into biomass through photosynthesis. This biomass can be harvested and processed to produce biofuels such as biodiesel, bioethanol, and biogas.

Algae-based biofuels hold great potential in the context of sustainability due to several reasons. Firstly, they offer a carbon-neutral or even carbon-negative alternative to fossil fuels. As algae grow, they absorb carbon dioxide from the atmosphere, effectively offsetting the carbon emissions produced when the biofuels are burned. This makes algae-based biofuels a more environmentally friendly option and helps to mitigate climate change.

Furthermore, algae can be cultivated using non-arable land, such as deserts or wastewater treatment facilities, without competing with food crops for resources. This reduces the pressure on agricultural land and preserves biodiversity by avoiding deforestation or habitat destruction associated with the cultivation of traditional biofuel feedstocks like corn or soybeans.

In addition, algae-based biofuels have the potential to address the issue of energy security. As algae can be grown in diverse regions, they offer a decentralized and distributed energy source, reducing dependence on fossil fuel imports and enhancing energy independence.

Algae-Based Carbon Capture

Algae-based carbon capture is a sustainable method of reducing carbon dioxide (CO_2) emissions from the atmosphere by using algae to absorb and store CO_2. Algae are photosynthetic organisms that can effectively convert CO_2 into biomass through the process of photosynthesis. This process not only helps to mitigate greenhouse gas emissions, but also has the potential for various additional environmental benefits.

Algae-based carbon capture systems are designed to harness the natural ability of algae to absorb CO_2 and convert it into organic matter. These systems typically involve the cultivation of algae in specialized containment units, such as photobioreactors or open ponds. The algae are provided with the necessary nutrients, sunlight, and CO_2, allowing them to grow and photosynthesize. As they photosynthesize, the algae take in CO_2 and release oxygen, effectively reducing the amount of CO_2 in the surrounding environment.

Once the algae have absorbed the CO_2, they can be harvested and processed to extract the captured carbon. This carbon-rich biomass can then be utilized in a variety of ways, such as producing biofuels, animal feed, or even biodegradable plastics. By converting CO_2 into valuable products, algae-based carbon capture not only reduces greenhouse gas emissions but also contributes to the development of a circular economy and the transition towards a more sustainable future.

Algae-Based Carbon Sequestration

Algae-based carbon sequestration refers to the process of using algae to capture and store carbon dioxide (CO_2) from the atmosphere, thereby mitigating climate change and promoting sustainability. Algae, a group of photosynthetic organisms, have the ability to absorb large amounts of CO_2 during their growth. This CO_2 is then converted into biomass through photosynthesis, with the algae using sunlight and nutrients to create organic matter.

By harnessing this natural process, algae-based carbon sequestration offers a promising solution for reducing greenhouse gas emissions. It utilizes the rapid growth rate and high carbon fixation capacity of algae to sequester CO_2 from various sources such as industrial emissions, power plants, and even directly from the air. This technology has the potential to capture significant amounts of CO_2, potentially offsetting some of the emissions generated by human activities.

Algae-Based Renewable Energy

Algae-based renewable energy refers to the sustainable production of energy using algae as a feedstock. Algae, both macroalgae (seaweeds) and microalgae, are photosynthetic organisms that convert sunlight and carbon dioxide into biomass through the process of photosynthesis. This biomass can be used to produce a variety of renewable energy sources, including biofuels, biogas, and bioelectricity.

Algae-based renewable energy offers several environmental benefits. Firstly, algae can be grown in a wide range of environments, including wastewaters, ponds, and open ocean, without taking up valuable agricultural land. This reduces the competition for land resources between food and energy production. Secondly, algae capture and utilize carbon dioxide, helping to mitigate greenhouse gas emissions and combat climate change. Thirdly, algae can be cultivated using wastewater or nutrients derived from agricultural runoff, providing an opportunity for nutrient recycling and reducing pollution in water bodies. Lastly, algae-based renewable energy has the potential to reduce dependence on fossil fuels and contribute to energy security.

However, there are still challenges to overcome in the large-scale implementation of algae-based renewable energy. The cultivation of algae requires optimal environmental conditions, such as sunlight, nutrients, and water quality, which can be challenging to maintain consistently. Additionally, the extraction and conversion of algae biomass into energy products can be technically and economically demanding. Research and development efforts are ongoing to optimize algae cultivation and processing techniques, improve efficiency, and reduce costs to make algae-based renewable energy more viable and competitive with other energy sources.

Algae-Based Sustainable Materials

Algae-based sustainable materials are materials that are derived from algae, a diverse group of photosynthetic organisms. These materials are considered sustainable because they offer numerous environmental benefits and have the potential to reduce our dependency on non-renewable resources.

One of the key advantages of algae-based sustainable materials is their ability to be produced in a renewable and resource-efficient manner. Algae can be grown using non-arable land, saltwater, and wastewater, therefore minimizing the need for valuable resources such as freshwater and agricultural land. This makes algae-based materials a promising alternative to traditional materials that often rely on the extraction and processing of finite resources.

Furthermore, algae-based materials have a low carbon footprint. Algae absorb carbon dioxide during photosynthesis, helping to mitigate greenhouse gas emissions. In some cases, algae-based materials can even sequester more carbon than is emitted during their production, making them carbon-negative. This positive environmental attribute contributes to the mitigation of climate change and the transition towards a low-carbon economy.

In addition to their sustainability credentials, algae-based materials also possess desirable properties that make them suitable for various applications. These materials can be used in the production of bioplastics, biofuels, textiles, building materials, and even food products. They offer versatility, biodegradability, and can be tailored to specific requirements. As such, algae-based materials have the potential to contribute to the development of a sustainable and circular economy.

Algae-Based Wastewater Filtration

Algae-based wastewater filtration refers to a sustainable process that utilizes algae to remove pollutants and nutrients from wastewater. This method harnesses the natural abilities of algae to absorb and metabolize contaminants, thereby improving the quality of water discharged into the environment. In this process, wastewater containing pollutants such as nitrogen, phosphorus, heavy metals, and organic compounds is treated with algae. The presence of these contaminants stimulates the growth of algae, which then absorb and convert them into biomass. The biomass can be harvested and further processed for various applications, such as biofuels, animal feed, or fertilizers, contributing additional sustainability benefits. Algae-based wastewater filtration offers several advantages over conventional treatment methods. Firstly, it reduces the reliance on energy-intensive and costly chemical treatments. Algae have a high growth rate and can thrive in a wide range of environmental conditions, making them a cost-effective and accessible solution. Additionally, the process is environmentally friendly as it helps to mitigate the harmful effects of nutrient pollution on aquatic ecosystems. The excessive presence of nutrients in water bodies, particularly nitrogen and phosphorus, can lead to eutrophication, causing harmful algal blooms and oxygen depletion. By incorporating algae-based filtration, nutrients are captured and recycled, preventing their release into natural water sources. Moreover, this sustainable wastewater treatment method also contributes to carbon sequestration and climate change mitigation. Algae absorb carbon dioxide during photosynthesis, helping to reduce greenhouse gas emissions and their impact on global warming. In conclusion, algae-based wastewater filtration is an effective, sustainable solution for treating and reclaiming water resources. It not only removes pollutants and nutrients from wastewater but also offers opportunities for resource recovery and environmental stewardship.

11

Algae-Based Wastewater Remediation

Algae-based wastewater remediation refers to the process of using algae to clean and purify polluted wastewater, in order to mitigate the environmental impact and promote sustainable water management. This practice utilizes the natural ability of certain types of algae to absorb and remove contaminants from water sources, such as heavy metals, nutrients, organic compounds, and pathogens.

Algae-based wastewater remediation systems typically involve the cultivation of algae in specially designed ponds or tanks, where they are exposed to wastewater containing pollutants. Through a process known as bioremediation, the algae extract nutrients and chemicals from the water as they grow, ultimately causing the water to be purified. The captured contaminants can be utilized as a valuable resource for various applications, such as biofuel production or fertilizer manufacturing, further enhancing the sustainability of the process.

Compared to traditional wastewater treatment methods, algae-based remediation offers several advantages in terms of sustainability. Firstly, algae are capable of removing a wide range of pollutants, including harmful substances that are more difficult to eliminate using conventional techniques. Additionally, algae-based systems operate in a more energy-efficient manner, requiring less electricity and generating fewer greenhouse gas emissions. Moreover, the use of algae can contribute to the reduction of water scarcity, as it allows for the recycling and reclamation of water resources.

In conclusion, algae-based wastewater remediation is a sustainable solution that utilizes the natural properties of algae to effectively clean polluted water sources. By harnessing the potential of this renewable resource, we can promote the conservation of water, reduce pollution, and move towards a more environmentally-friendly future.

Algae-Based Wastewater Treatment

Algae-based wastewater treatment is a sustainable solution that utilizes algae to treat and purify wastewater while minimizing its environmental impact. This method harnesses the natural ability of algae to remove pollutants and nutrients from water, effectively restoring its quality and reducing the release of harmful substances into the environment.

By employing a two-step process, algae-based wastewater treatment offers an environmentally friendly alternative to traditional treatment methods. Firstly, wastewater is directed into a shallow pond or tank where it is exposed to sunlight and nutrients. This stimulates the growth of algae, which acts as a natural filter, absorbing contaminants such as nitrogen, phosphorus, and heavy metals from the water. The algae also consume carbon dioxide during photosynthesis, contributing to the reduction of greenhouse gas emissions.

Once the algae have absorbed the pollutants, the second step involves separating the algae from the treated water. This can be achieved through sedimentation or filtration methods. The clean water that emerges from this process can then be safely discharged or reused for various purposes, such as irrigation or industrial processes.

Algae-based wastewater treatment systems have several advantages from a sustainability perspective. Firstly, they require significantly less energy compared to conventional wastewater treatment plants, reducing the carbon footprint associated with the process. Additionally, by removing nutrients from the water, algae-based systems help prevent eutrophication and the ensuing negative impacts on aquatic ecosystems. This method also has the potential for biomass harvesting, where the algae can be used to produce biofuels, animal feed, or other valuable products, further contributing to a circular and sustainable economy.

Algal Biofuel Production

Algal biofuel production refers to the process of cultivating, harvesting, and converting algae into a renewable source of energy in a sustainable manner. It involves using photosynthetic microorganisms, such as algae, to harness solar energy and converting it into biofuels that can be used as a substitute for fossil fuels.

As a sustainable alternative to traditional fossil fuels, algal biofuel production has several advantages. Firstly, algae are highly efficient in terms of photosynthesis, meaning they can capture and convert solar energy into biomass at a much higher rate than traditional crop-based biofuel feedstocks. This efficiency allows for a higher yield of biofuels per unit area of cultivation.

Furthermore, algae can be grown in a variety of environments, including wastewater and saline water, which are unsuitable for traditional agriculture. This reduces the competition for arable land and freshwater resources, making algal biofuel production a more sustainable option.

Additionally, algal biofuel production has the potential to reduce greenhouse gas emissions. While the combustion of biofuels still releases carbon dioxide, the overall carbon footprint of algal biofuels can be significantly lower compared to fossil fuels. Algae can sequester large amounts of carbon dioxide during their growth, offsetting the emissions produced during their conversion into biofuels.

In conclusion, algal biofuel production is a sustainable approach to energy production that utilizes photosynthetic microorganisms to convert solar energy into biofuels. Its high efficiency, ability to grow in diverse environments, and potential for greenhouse gas reduction make it a promising renewable energy solution.

Alliance For Water Stewardship (AWS)

The Alliance for Water Stewardship (AWS) is an international standard and certification program that promotes sustainable water management practices by providing a framework for organizations to effectively manage and protect shared water resources.

The AWS standard is based on a holistic approach to water stewardship, considering the social, environmental, and economic aspects of water management. It provides a set of criteria and indicators that guide organizations in assessing their water-related risks, impacts, and dependencies. By implementing the AWS standard, organizations can identify and address potential water risks, minimize negative impacts on the environment and communities, and optimize water use efficiency.

The AWS certification process involves an independent verification of an organization's compliance with the standard. It evaluates the organization's water performance, governance, engagement with stakeholders, and ongoing improvement efforts. Achieving AWS certification demonstrates a commitment to responsible water management and helps organizations gain recognition for their sustainable practices.

By adopting the AWS standard, organizations contribute to the sustainability of water resources on a local and global scale. They contribute to the preservation of water quality, the protection of ecosystems and biodiversity, and the equitable distribution of water among diverse users. Additionally, organizations that engage in AWS certification join a network of water stewards who share knowledge, best practices, and innovative solutions to address water challenges collectively.

Alliance For A Green Revolution In Africa (AGRA)

The Alliance for a Green Revolution in Africa (AGRA) is an organization dedicated to promoting sustainable agricultural practices and ensuring food security in Africa. AGRA works towards achieving its goals by supporting smallholder farmers and improving their access to resources, knowledge, and markets.

AGRA focuses on four key areas: improving productivity and production, increasing market access and competitiveness, promoting sustainable agricultural systems, and fostering policy and institutional reforms. By addressing these areas, AGRA aims to ensure that African smallholder farmers are equipped with the necessary tools and resources to increase their agricultural productivity and income, while also safeguarding the environment and natural resources.

Aquaponic Farm Architecture

13

Aquaponic farm architecture refers to the design and structure of a sustainable farming system that combines aquaculture (raising fish) and hydroponics (growing plants without soil) in a symbiotic environment. The architecture of an aquaponic farm is specifically designed to maximize resource efficiency, minimize waste, and provide a self-sustaining ecosystem that supports both fish and plants.

In an aquaponic farm, the architecture includes various components such as fish tanks, grow beds, water circulation systems, and filtration systems. These components are carefully designed to create a closed-loop system where the waste produced by the fish serves as nutrients for the plants, and the plants naturally filter and clean the water for the fish.

The architectural design of an aquaponic farm takes into account factors such as optimal water flow, lighting, temperature control, and space utilization. The layout and arrangement of the different components are planned to optimize natural sunlight exposure, facilitate efficient water circulation, and provide a suitable environment for both the fish and plants to thrive.

Aquaponic farm architecture plays a crucial role in promoting sustainability by reducing the use of water and land compared to traditional farming methods. The closed-loop system eliminates the need for chemical fertilizers and pesticides, resulting in reduced environmental pollution and water contamination. Additionally, the symbiotic relationship between fish and plants helps maintain a balanced ecosystem and reduces the overall ecological footprint of the farm.

In conclusion, aquaponic farm architecture encompasses the design and layout of a sustainable farming system that integrates aquaculture and hydroponics. This innovative approach to farming promotes resource efficiency, minimizes waste, and creates a self-sustaining ecosystem that supports the growth of both fish and plants while reducing the environmental impact.

Aquaponic Farm Layout

An aquaponic farm layout refers to the strategic arrangement and organization of components within an aquaponics system, designed to promote sustainable practices and maximize resource efficiency. This layout encompasses the placement of fish tanks, grow beds, water filtration systems, and other essential elements, with the aim of creating a harmonious and efficient symbiotic relationship between plants and fish.

The sustainability aspect of an aquaponic farm layout is manifested through several key principles. Firstly, the layout encourages resource conservation by utilizing the closed-loop system, in which fish waste provides nutrients for plant growth, and plants, in turn, filter and purify the water for the fish. This symbiotic cycle minimizes water usage and nutrient losses, ensuring the overall system operates in a highly efficient and sustainable manner.

Secondly, the farm layout promotes biodiversity and ecological balance. By integrating various types of plants and fish species, the aquaponics system mimics a natural ecosystem, fostering a diverse and self-regulating environment. This approach reduces the need for chemical inputs, such as pesticides or fertilizers, and enhances the resilience of the farm against pests and diseases.

Additionally, the aquaponic farm layout emphasizes space optimization and scalability. By utilizing vertical space and employing efficient arrangement techniques, such as staggered grow beds or multi-level systems, the layout maximizes the production capacity of the farm while minimizing land and energy requirements. This scalability not only enhances the economic viability of aquaponics but also allows for the potential conversion of underutilized urban spaces into productive and sustainable farming areas.

Artificial Photosynthesis

Artificial photosynthesis, in the context of sustainability, refers to the process of replicating the natural photosynthesis that occurs in plants using artificial means. Photosynthesis, a fundamental biological process, converts sunlight, water, and carbon dioxide into oxygen and glucose, providing energy for living organisms and sustaining the Earth's ecosystem.

The concept of artificial photosynthesis aims to harness this process to generate clean and renewable energy while reducing the emission of greenhouse gases. By utilizing sunlight, water, and carbon dioxide, researchers are developing technologies that can mimic the efficient energy conversion of plants and produce valuable fuels, such as hydrogen or hydrocarbons, as well as other chemical compounds.

This innovative approach holds tremendous potential for addressing the challenge of sustainable energy production. Unlike fossil fuels, the energy generated through artificial photosynthesis is clean, emission-free, and renewable. It offers a promising pathway for reducing dependence on non-renewable resources and mitigating the adverse effects of climate change.

Moreover, artificial photosynthesis also contributes to the sustainable management of resources. It can help tackle the issue of carbon dioxide accumulation in the atmosphere by actively capturing and utilizing this greenhouse gas as a raw material in the production of energy and valuable chemicals. This process has the additional benefit of reducing the net carbon emissions, thus aiding in the fight against global warming.

B Corporation

B Corporation is a type of for-profit company that prioritizes sustainable practices and social and environmental impact in addition to financial gains. B Corps are certified by B Lab, a non-profit organization that evaluates and verifies a company's performance in these areas.

These companies are legally required to consider the impact of their decisions on workers, customers, suppliers, community, and the environment. They must meet specific performance standards, demonstrate transparency by making their social and environmental practices available to the public, and amend their corporate bylaws to include their commitment to social and environmental responsibility.

Bamboo As A Sustainable Material

Bamboo is a highly sustainable material that offers numerous environmental benefits and can be utilized as a renewable resource in a wide range of applications. It is a type of grass that grows rapidly, typically reaching maturity within 3-5 years, making it one of the fastest-growing plants on the planet. This rapid growth rate allows for sustainable harvesting practices, as bamboo can be easily replenished without depleting natural resources.

One of the key sustainability advantages of bamboo is its ability to absorb carbon dioxide and release oxygen into the atmosphere. Compared to most trees, bamboo is significantly more efficient in carbon sequestration, making it a valuable tool in mitigating climate change. Additionally, bamboo has a vast root system that helps prevent soil erosion, providing crucial support for maintaining healthy ecosystems.

Furthermore, the cultivation of bamboo requires minimal water and no pesticides or fertilizers, reducing the negative impact on water resources and minimizing pollution compared to other crops. Additionally, bamboo can thrive on marginal lands that are unsuitable for other agricultural purposes, further minimizing the competition for fertile soil and preserving biodiversity.

In terms of its application as a sustainable material, bamboo possesses exceptional strength and durability. It can be used in construction, furniture production, paper manufacturing, and even as a substitute for traditional materials such as wood and plastic. Due to its quick growth and versatility, bamboo products have the potential to replace less sustainable alternatives, contributing to a more sustainable and eco-friendly society.

Bamboo Construction Design

Bamboo construction design refers to the utilization of bamboo as a primary material in the creation of sustainable structures, taking into account the principles of environmental responsibility, social equity, and economic viability.

With its fast growth rate, renewability, and strength comparable to steel, bamboo has gained recognition as an eco-friendly construction material. In sustainable bamboo construction design,

15

it is used in various forms, such as poles, boards, and panels, to create structural frames, walls, roofs, and floors.

The sustainability of bamboo construction design lies in its numerous environmental benefits. Bamboo plays a crucial role in mitigating climate change as it absorbs high amounts of carbon dioxide and releases oxygen into the atmosphere. Due to its regenerative nature, bamboo can be harvested without causing permanent damage to the environment, making it a more sustainable alternative to traditional construction materials like timber and steel.

Moreover, bamboo has a low energy requirement during its growth, harvest, and processing stages compared to other materials. This makes it an energy-efficient choice that reduces the carbon footprint associated with construction. Additionally, bamboo construction design often incorporates passive design strategies to enhance energy efficiency, such as optimizing natural lighting, ventilation, and thermal insulation.

From a social perspective, bamboo construction can contribute to sustainable development by generating livelihood opportunities for local communities. Cultivating and harvesting bamboo can provide income and employment, especially in rural areas where bamboo resources are abundant. Furthermore, bamboo construction design embraces the cultural heritage and craftsmanship of communities that have traditionally worked with bamboo, preserving their knowledge and skills.

In conclusion, bamboo construction design is a sustainable approach that harnesses the unique qualities of bamboo to create environmentally responsible, socially equitable, and economically viable structures that contribute to a more sustainable built environment.

Bamboo Construction Materials

Bamboo construction materials are sustainable building materials that are made from bamboo, a fast-growing woody grass. These materials are Eco-friendly and have gained popularity due to their numerous environmental benefits.

Bamboo is a renewable resource that grows much faster than conventional timber, making it a highly sustainable material choice. It can reach full maturity within 3 to 5 years, whereas hardwood trees can take several decades to grow to a similar size. This rapid growth rate means that bamboo can be harvested without causing significant environmental damage or deforestation.

In addition to its sustainable growth cycle, bamboo has several other eco-friendly properties. It absorbs more carbon dioxide and releases more oxygen into the atmosphere than most other plants, helping to reduce greenhouse gas emissions. Bamboo also has a strong root system that helps to prevent soil erosion and improve water quality.

Bamboo construction materials are versatile and can be used for a variety of sustainable building applications. These materials can be used in the construction of houses, furniture, flooring, roofing, and even as a substitute for steel reinforcement in concrete structures. Bamboo has a high tensile strength and is lightweight, making it an ideal alternative to traditional construction materials.

Overall, bamboo construction materials offer a sustainable and environmentally friendly solution to the challenges faced by the construction industry. Their renewable nature, rapid growth, and eco-friendly properties make them an excellent choice for sustainable building projects, supporting the goal of creating a more sustainable and greener future.

Bee-Friendly Garden Layouts

Bee-friendly garden layouts can be defined as sustainable garden designs that prioritize the well-being and conservation of bees. These layouts aim to provide a conducive environment for bees to thrive by incorporating various elements that support their habitat and foraging needs.

The key principle of a bee-friendly garden layout is to include a diverse range of native plants that bloom at different times throughout the year. This ensures a continuous and abundant source of nectar and pollen for bees. Additionally, incorporating a variety of flower shapes and colors can attract different bee species with specific preferences.

Another important element of a bee-friendly garden layout is the avoidance of pesticides and herbicides. These chemicals can have harmful effects on bees, including impairing their navigation abilities and weakening their immune systems. Instead, natural pest control methods and organic gardening practices are used to maintain a healthy garden ecosystem.

In order to provide nesting sites for bees, bee-friendly gardens may incorporate features such as bee hotels, nesting boxes, or areas of undisturbed soil. These provide shelter for solitary bees, which make up the majority of bee species. It is also essential to ensure that there is a source of clean water available for bees to drink and for maintaining humidity in the garden.

Bee-friendly garden layouts promote the conservation and well-being of bees, which are vital pollinators for both wild plants and agricultural crops. By creating a sustainable garden that supports the needs of bees, individuals can contribute to the overall health of ecosystems and help ensure the future survival of these important pollinators.

Bee-Friendly Landscape Design

Bee-friendly landscape design is a sustainable approach to gardening and landscaping that aims to support and protect bee populations. This type of design focuses on creating a habitat that is conducive to the needs of bees and other pollinators.

The key principles of bee-friendly landscape design involve planting a variety of flowering plants that provide a continuous source of nectar and pollen throughout the year. This includes selecting plants with different blooming periods and a diverse range of flower shapes and colors to attract a variety of bee species.

Avoiding the use of chemical pesticides and herbicides is another important aspect of bee-friendly design. These chemicals can harm bees directly or indirectly by contaminating their food sources. Instead, natural pest control methods such as companion planting and introducing beneficial insects are encouraged.

Bee-friendly landscapes also include providing suitable nesting sites for bees. This can be achieved through the inclusion of bee hotels, which are structures that provide spaces for solitary bees to lay their eggs. Additionally, leaving areas of bare soil or providing natural materials like fallen branches and twigs can create nesting opportunities for ground-nesting bees.

In conclusion, bee-friendly landscape design plays a crucial role in promoting the health and well-being of bee populations. By providing a diverse and pesticide-free habitat, we can support the important work of pollinators and contribute to the sustainability of our ecosystems.

Bio-Based Chemicals Production

Bio-based chemicals production refers to the process of manufacturing chemicals using renewable resources such as plants, agricultural waste, and other biological materials. These chemicals are synthesized through various sustainable methods that minimize the use of fossil fuels and non-renewable resources.

One of the key objectives of bio-based chemicals production is to substitute traditionally petroleum-based chemicals with environmentally friendly alternatives. By utilizing biomass as feedstock, this process helps reduce greenhouse gas emissions, dependence on fossil fuels, and depletion of natural resources. It contributes towards the transition to a more sustainable and circular economy.

Bio-Based Materials

Bio-based materials refer to products made from renewable biological resources such as plants, trees, and agricultural and forest residues. These materials are utilized as alternatives to conventional materials derived from fossil fuels, contributing to the transition to a more sustainable and circular economy.

The production of bio-based materials aims to minimize environmental impacts by reducing greenhouse gas emissions, decreasing dependence on nonrenewable resources, and promoting the efficient use of natural resources. By using renewable feedstocks, such as crops or biomass, these materials have the potential to reduce the carbon footprint associated with their manufacturing process.

One key aspect of bio-based materials is their ability to biodegrade or be composted, enabling their integration into a circular economy model. This means that at the end of their useful life, bio-based materials can be returned to the environment without causing long-term harm. In contrast, materials derived from fossil fuels, such as plastics, can persist in the environment for hundreds of years, contributing to pollution and waste accumulation.

The applications of bio-based materials are diverse and extend across various industries, including packaging, construction, textiles, automotive, and electronics. For example, bio-based plastics can be used to produce biodegradable packaging materials, reducing the environmental impact associated with single-use plastics. In the construction sector, bio-based materials like timber and engineered wood products provide sustainable alternatives to traditional construction materials like concrete and steel.

Biodegradable 3D Printing Materials

Biodegradable 3D printing materials refer to the substances that can be used in additive manufacturing processes and break down naturally over time, minimizing their environmental impact. These materials are designed to decompose into basic components, such as water, carbon dioxide, and biomass, through natural processes such as microbial activity or exposure to sunlight.

By utilizing biodegradable 3D printing materials, industries can contribute to a more sustainable future by reducing the amount of waste generated and the consumption of non-renewable resources. Traditional 3D printing materials, such as plastics derived from petroleum, can take hundreds of years to decompose, leading to long-term pollution and resource depletion.

As the demand for 3D printed objects increases, the development of biodegradable materials becomes crucial for sustainable manufacturing. These materials can encompass a wide range of substances, including biopolymers derived from renewable resources like cornstarch or cellulose. Some biodegradable 3D printing materials can even be derived from waste products, further reducing their environmental footprint.

The use of biodegradable 3D printing materials aligns with the principles of circular economy. After a product's useful life, it can be composted or returned to the environment as harmless compounds, closing the loop and minimizing waste generation. This approach supports the transition towards a more sustainable and regenerative manufacturing system.

Biodegradable And Compostable Packaging

Biodegradable and compostable packaging refers to packaging materials that are designed to break down naturally and contribute to the environment's sustainability. These packaging solutions are created with the intention of minimizing the negative impact of traditional packaging materials on the planet.

Biodegradable packaging materials are made from substances that can be broken down by natural processes, such as the action of bacteria, fungi, and other microorganisms. When these materials decompose, they are transformed into simpler compounds and become part of the Earth's natural nutrient cycles. This process helps to prevent the accumulation of waste in landfills, as biodegradable packaging can break down into non-toxic components over time.

Compostable packaging, on the other hand, refers to materials that can undergo composting along with organic waste. Composting is a controlled process that involves the decomposition of organic materials, such as food waste and yard trimmings, into nutrient-rich compost. Compostable packaging materials are specifically designed to be broken down during this process, leaving behind no toxic residue. This means that they can be safely used as a soil amendment, enriching the soil and supporting plant growth.

In summary, biodegradable and compostable packaging materials offer sustainable alternatives to traditional packaging options. By utilizing these eco-friendly materials, we can reduce waste accumulation, decrease reliance on non-renewable resources, and support the overall health of our environment.

Biodegradable Cleaning Products

Biodegradable cleaning products are sustainable cleaning solutions that are designed to break down naturally and quickly in the environment, minimizing their impact on ecosystems and human health. These products are formulated using ingredients that are derived from renewable resources and are free from harmful chemicals, toxins, and synthetic fragrances.

Biodegradable cleaning products are specifically designed to degrade into simpler substances through the action of natural microorganisms such as bacteria and fungi. This natural breakdown process is facilitated by the presence of enzymes that help break down organic compounds. Unlike conventional cleaning products, which can persist in the environment for long periods of time, biodegradable cleaning products biodegrade within a relatively short period, reducing their carbon footprint and preventing long-term pollution.

Biodegradable Clothing Patterns

Biodegradable clothing patterns refers to the designs and fabrication techniques used to create garments that are environmentally friendly and can naturally decompose without causing harm to the ecosystem. The concept of biodegradable clothing is rooted in sustainability, aiming to reduce the negative impact of the fashion industry on the environment.

These patterns are often made from organic and natural fibers, such as bamboo, hemp, organic cotton, and linen, which are biodegradable materials. Unlike conventional clothing made from synthetic fibers, biodegradable clothing patterns are designed to break down naturally over time, returning to the earth without leaving behind toxic residues or microplastics.

The production of biodegradable clothing involves environmentally conscious practices, such as using non-toxic dyes, minimizing water and energy consumption, and reducing waste. Additionally, these patterns often focus on creating garments with timeless styles and durable construction, promoting longevity and reducing the need for frequent replacements.

By opting for biodegradable clothing patterns, individuals can contribute to a more sustainable and circular economy. When these garments reach the end of their life cycle, they can be composted or returned to the earth, where they will naturally decompose and nourish the soil. This process helps to minimize textile waste and reduce the carbon footprint associated with the fashion industry.

Biodegradable Cutlery

Biodegradable cutlery refers to a type of utensils that are designed to decompose naturally and return to the environment without causing harm or pollution. These utensils are made from organic materials such as plant starch, bamboo, wood, or other biodegradable polymers, instead of traditional non-biodegradable materials like plastic.

The use of biodegradable cutlery aligns with the principles of sustainability as it contributes to reducing the amount of plastic waste generated and the associated negative environmental impacts. Plastic cutlery takes thousands of years to decompose, leading to significant pollution of landfills and water bodies. In contrast, biodegradable cutlery breaks down naturally in a much shorter timeframe, reducing the long-term environmental burden.

Furthermore, the production of biodegradable cutlery often requires fewer fossil fuels and chemicals compared to plastic cutlery manufacturing. This contributes to a lower carbon footprint and less air and water pollution during production. Additionally, many biodegradable utensils are made from renewable resources, such as bamboo, which can be harvested sustainably without

19

depleting natural resources.

By opting for biodegradable cutlery, individuals and businesses can actively support sustainable practices, reduce plastic waste, and minimize their environmental impact. Whether used in homes, restaurants, or events, the use of biodegradable cutlery can help transition towards a more eco-friendly and responsible way of consuming while promoting a circular economy.

Biodegradable Fashion Design

Biodegradable fashion design refers to the concept of creating clothing and accessories using materials that can naturally decompose in the environment, without causing harm or pollution. This practice aligns with sustainability principles by reducing waste, minimizing the use of non-renewable resources, and promoting ecological balance.

By using biodegradable materials such as organic cotton, hemp, bamboo, and bioplastics derived from renewable resources, fashion designers can create garments that have a significantly lower environmental impact compared to traditional clothing made from synthetic fabrics like polyester and nylon. These synthetic materials take hundreds of years to break down and often release harmful chemicals during decomposition.

Furthermore, biodegradable fashion design extends beyond just the choice of materials. It also encompasses various sustainable practices throughout the entire production process, including ethical sourcing, eco-friendly dyeing and printing methods, and minimizing energy consumption and waste generation.

Biodegradable fashion design contributes to a more circular economy, where products are designed with their end-of-life in mind. When these biodegradable garments are discarded or no longer in use, they can degrade naturally and return nutrients back into the soil, closing the loop of the fashion industry's material lifecycle.

Overall, biodegradable fashion design is a crucial step towards creating a more sustainable and environmentally conscious fashion industry. By embracing biodegradable materials and sustainable practices, fashion designers can make a positive impact, reducing their ecological footprint and promoting a more circular and regenerative fashion economy.

Biodegradable Food Container Design

A biodegradable food container is a design that aims to reduce the environmental impact of food packaging by using materials that can naturally break down and be absorbed back into the environment. This type of container is made from organic and renewable materials, such as plant fibers, that can decompose over time.

By utilizing biodegradable materials, these containers offer several sustainability benefits. Firstly, they minimize the use of non-renewable resources, such as petroleum-based plastics, which require energy-intensive processes to produce. This reduces the overall carbon footprint associated with the production of the containers. Secondly, as biodegradable containers can break down naturally, they prevent waste buildup in landfills. This is essential for preventing pollution and reducing the strain on limited landfill space.

Biodegradable Food Container Designs

A biodegradable food container refers to a type of packaging that is designed to easily break down and decompose into natural elements after it is discarded. These containers are made from organic and sustainable materials that can be broken down by microorganisms or other natural processes, such as composting.

The purpose of using biodegradable food containers is to reduce the environmental impact associated with traditional disposable packaging options, such as plastic or Styrofoam. By choosing biodegradable materials, we can minimize the accumulation of non-biodegradable waste in landfills and oceans, and promote a more sustainable approach to packaging and waste management.

Biodegradable Food Packaging

Biodegradable food packaging refers to the use of materials that can decompose naturally in the environment without leaving any harmful residues. It is a sustainable alternative to traditional non-biodegradable packaging materials that significantly contribute to pollution and waste accumulation.

The concept of biodegradable food packaging aligns with the principles of sustainability, as it aims to reduce the environmental impact of packaging materials throughout their lifecycle. Biodegradable packaging materials are typically made from plant-based sources, such as cornstarch, sugarcane fiber, or wood pulp, which are renewable and have a lower carbon footprint compared to fossil fuel-based plastics.

When biodegradable food packaging is discarded, it undergoes a process called biodegradation, where microorganisms break down the material into simpler compounds, such as water, carbon dioxide, and biomass. This process occurs naturally in various environments, including industrial composting facilities, home composts, and even in soil or water bodies. Unlike non-biodegradable packaging, biodegradable materials do not persist in the environment for hundreds of years, reducing the amount of waste that ends up in landfills or oceans.

The use of biodegradable food packaging supports the transition towards a circular economy, where resources are kept in use for as long as possible and waste is minimized. By choosing biodegradable packaging options, businesses and consumers can contribute to the reduction of plastic pollution and the conservation of natural resources. However, it is essential to ensure that biodegradable packaging is disposed of properly, either through composting facilities or waste management systems that support its biodegradation.

Biodegradable Materials

Biodegradable materials are substances that are capable of breaking down and decomposing naturally over time, through the action of microorganisms such as bacteria, fungi, and other living organisms present in the environment. These materials can be derived from both natural sources, such as plants and animals, as well as synthetic sources.

In the context of sustainability, biodegradable materials are highly valued and widely encouraged due to their ability to alleviate the negative environmental impacts associated with the accumulation of non-biodegradable waste. When biodegradable materials are disposed of in soil, water, or other suitable environments, they undergo a process called biodegradation, where they are broken down into simpler compounds. This process not only reduces the volume of waste in landfills and oceans but also minimizes greenhouse gas emissions and the depletion of non-renewable resources.

Biodegradable Packaging Design

Biodegradable packaging design refers to the development and implementation of sustainable packaging materials that can naturally decompose and return to the environment without causing harm or leaving any residue. It focuses on using materials derived from renewable sources, such as plants, that can break down through natural biological processes.

The goal of biodegradable packaging design is to reduce the environmental impact associated with traditional packaging materials, such as plastics, that have significant negative consequences, including pollution and landfill waste. By using biodegradable materials, packaging can avoid long-lasting effects on ecosystems and contribute to a circular economy by minimizing resource consumption and waste generation.

Biodegradable Packaging Materials

Biodegradable packaging materials are materials that are capable of breaking down and decomposing into natural elements over time, through the action of microorganisms, such as bacteria or fungi. These materials are designed to minimize environmental impact by reducing the amount of waste generated and the duration of their presence in ecosystems.

Biodegradable packaging materials are made from renewable resources and can include various types of materials, such as plant-based plastics, paper, cardboard, and natural fibers. These materials are often used as alternatives to traditional packaging materials, such as non-recyclable plastics, which can persist in the environment for hundreds of years.

Biodegradable Packaging

Biodegradable packaging refers to the use of materials that can naturally decompose and break down into smaller components over time, through the action of microorganisms and environmental factors, such as humidity, temperature, and light. This type of packaging is designed to reduce the negative impact on the environment and promote sustainability.

Biodegradable packaging is made from organic matter, such as plant-based materials or polymers derived from natural sources like cornstarch, sugarcane, or cellulose. These materials are capable of being broken down into simpler compounds by bacteria, fungi, and other microorganisms found in the soil or water, without leaving harmful residues behind. The decomposition process of biodegradable packaging occurs within a relatively short time frame, usually within a few months to a few years, depending on the specific material and the surrounding environmental conditions.

Biodegradable Plastics Production

Biodegradable plastics production refers to the process of manufacturing plastic materials that are designed to break down and decompose naturally, returning to the environment in a safe and non-harmful manner. Unlike traditional plastics, which can persist in the environment for hundreds of years, biodegradable plastics are specifically engineered to degrade over a shorter period of time, minimizing their impact on ecosystems and human health.

Sustainability is a key consideration in the production of biodegradable plastics. These materials are typically made from renewable resources, such as plant-based polymers, rather than petroleum-based sources that contribute to climate change and resource depletion. Additionally, the production process for biodegradable plastics often requires less energy and emits fewer greenhouse gases compared to traditional plastics production.

The biodegradation of these plastics is facilitated by microorganisms, which break down the polymer chains into smaller fragments that can be consumed by bacteria and other natural processes. This degradation occurs when the plastic is exposed to specific environmental conditions, such as sunlight, heat, and moisture. The resulting byproducts of biodegradation are typically water, carbon dioxide, and biomass, which can be assimilated into natural systems without causing harm.

While biodegradable plastics offer a more sustainable alternative to conventional plastics, it is important to note that the term "biodegradable" does not necessarily imply complete and rapid decomposition in all environments. The rate of biodegradation varies depending on factors such as temperature, humidity, and the presence of microorganisms. Therefore, proper disposal and management of biodegradable plastics is crucial to ensure that they are given the necessary conditions to break down effectively and do not contribute to pollution.

Biodegradable Plastics Recycling

Biodegradable plastics recycling refers to the process of reclaiming and reusing biodegradable plastic materials in a manner that is sustainable and environmentally-friendly. Biodegradable plastics are plastics that can break down and decompose into natural elements, such as water, carbon dioxide, and biomass, through the action of microorganisms in the environment.

The recycling of biodegradable plastics is an essential component of sustainable waste management practices. By collecting and processing biodegradable plastics, we can divert these materials from landfills and incineration, reducing the amount of waste that accumulates in our environment and limiting the release of greenhouse gases associated with traditional plastic production and disposal.

In the recycling process, biodegradable plastics are typically sorted and separated from other waste materials. They are then processed through various techniques, such as thermal or enzymatic degradation, to break down the molecular structure of the plastic and facilitate its decomposition. The resulting materials can be used in the production of new biodegradable plastic products or converted into other forms of renewable energy.

The recycling of biodegradable plastics not only helps conserve natural resources but also reduces the reliance on fossil fuels and mitigates the environmental impacts associated with plastic pollution. By closing the loop and integrating biodegradable plastics into the circular economy, we can promote a more sustainable and regenerative approach to plastic production and consumption, minimizing the negative consequences of plastic waste on ecosystems and human health.

Biodegradable Plastics

Biodegradable plastics are a type of polymer materials that are designed to break down and decompose naturally in the environment. Unlike traditional plastics that can persist in the environment for hundreds or even thousands of years, biodegradable plastics are specifically engineered to go through a process of degradation and disintegration, ultimately returning to the earth as organic matter.

These plastics are considered a more sustainable alternative to conventional plastics because of their ability to biodegrade. The term "biodegradable" refers to the ability of a material to be broken down by microorganisms such as bacteria and fungi, resulting in the conversion of the material into natural elements like carbon dioxide, water, and biomass. This natural decomposition process occurs within a relatively short period of time, typically ranging from a few months to a few years.

Biodegradable Product Development

A biodegradable product is a sustainable material that has the ability to decompose naturally in the environment without leaving behind harmful residue or negatively impacting the ecosystem. It is designed to minimize waste and pollution by breaking down into smaller components through the action of microorganisms, such as bacteria and fungi. This natural decomposition process ensures that the product does not accumulate in landfills or water bodies, reducing the strain on these ecosystems.

Biodegradable products are typically made from renewable resources, such as plant-based materials or organic compounds, and are produced using sustainable manufacturing practices. They are designed to have a reduced environmental footprint throughout their lifecycle, from raw material extraction to disposal. The development of biodegradable products aims to address the growing concerns regarding the pollution caused by non-biodegradable materials, such as plastics.

Biodegradable Straws

Biodegradable straws are environmentally-friendly alternatives to traditional plastic straws that are designed to break down and decompose naturally over time. These straws are made from renewable resources such as plant-based materials like cornstarch, bamboo, or paper, and are specifically engineered to have a minimal impact on the environment.

Unlike conventional plastic straws which can take hundreds of years to decompose, biodegradable straws undergo a natural process called biodegradation. This means that microorganisms present in the environment can break down the molecular structure of the straw, converting it into simpler substances that can be absorbed back into the natural ecosystem. By allowing the straws to degrade, they can minimize the amount of waste that ends up in landfills and oceans, thus reducing the negative impact on wildlife and marine life.

Biodegradable Sunscreen

Biodegradable sunscreen is a type of sunscreen that is designed to break down naturally and harmlessly in the environment, specifically in water bodies, without causing pollution or long-term damage. It is an increasingly popular choice for individuals seeking to reduce their environmental impact and promote sustainability.

Traditional sunscreens often contain chemicals that can be detrimental to marine life and ecosystems when they enter the water through swimming, snorkeling, or other water activities. These chemicals, known as oxybenzone and octinoxate, have been found to contribute to coral bleaching and can disrupt hormone balances in marine organisms. Biodegradable sunscreens, on the other hand, are formulated with natural, organic ingredients that degrade over time and pose minimal risk to marine life.

One of the key characteristics of biodegradable sunscreen is its ability to break down into smaller, harmless components through natural processes like oxidation and microbial decomposition. This allows the sunscreen to be absorbed by natural organisms and ecosystems without negatively impacting their health or balance. Furthermore, biodegradable sunscreens are often free from harmful synthetic chemicals, parabens, and nanoparticle-sized minerals that can accumulate in the environment and potentially harm plants, animals, and humans.

Another benefit of biodegradable sunscreen is that it typically comes in eco-friendly and recyclable packaging, reducing waste and promoting responsible consumption. Many biodegradable sunscreen brands also prioritize sustainability in their production processes, using renewable energy sources, minimizing water usage, and supporting ethical labor practices.

Biodiversity International

Biodiversity International refers to an organization committed to advancing sustainable development by focusing on the critical challenge of biodiversity loss.

Sustainability, in the context of Biodiversity International, can be defined as the capability to maintain and preserve the diversity of life forms and their ecological processes while meeting the needs of present and future generations. It recognizes that biodiversity is not only essential for the survival and well-being of humans but also plays a fundamental role in maintaining ecosystem stability and resilience.

Biodiversity Monitoring And Conservation Tools

Biodiversity monitoring and conservation tools refer to a range of methods, techniques, and approaches used to assess and protect the variety and abundance of living organisms in a given ecosystem. These tools are employed to collect data on the state and trends of biodiversity, analyze patterns and changes, and guide conservation efforts in order to ensure the long-term sustainability of ecosystems and the services they provide.

Monitoring tools may include various surveys, sampling protocols, and remote sensing technologies that allow researchers and managers to gather information on species composition, population size, distribution patterns, and ecological interactions. These tools help to assess the health and functionality of ecosystems, identify threatened species and habitats, and detect changes over time. By monitoring biodiversity, scientists can gain insights into the impacts of human activities, climate change, and other stressors, helping to inform conservation strategies and management decisions.

Conservation tools, on the other hand, encompass a range of practices and interventions aimed at preserving, restoring, and managing biodiversity and its associated ecosystems. These tools may involve protected area design and management, habitat restoration, species reintroduction, and the implementation of sustainable land and resource use practices. Conservation tools are informed by biodiversity monitoring data, scientific research, and local knowledge and are designed to mitigate threats to biodiversity, maintain ecosystem resilience, and promote ecological balance.

In summary, biodiversity monitoring and conservation tools are critical components of sustainable development efforts, as they enable us to track the status and trends of biodiversity, identify conservation priorities, and implement effective measures to safeguard ecosystems and their invaluable contributions to human well-being.

Biogas Production From Organic Waste

Biogas production from organic waste is a sustainable process that involves the anaerobic decomposition of organic materials, such as food scraps, agricultural residues, and animal manure, to generate renewable energy in the form of biogas. Biogas is a mixture of methane (CH4) and carbon dioxide (CO2), along with trace amounts of other gases, such as hydrogen sulfide (H2S) and ammonia (NH3).

This process takes place in biogas reactors or digesters, which create conditions favorable to the growth of anaerobic bacteria. These bacteria break down the organic matter in the waste by releasing enzymes, which convert complex organic compounds into simpler compounds. The bacteria then consume these simpler compounds and produce biogas as a byproduct.

The biogas produced from the anaerobic digestion process can be used as a renewable energy source for various applications. It can be used for cooking, heating, and electricity generation, providing a sustainable alternative to fossil fuels and reducing greenhouse gas emissions. Additionally, the residual material left after the digestion process, known as digestate, can be used as a nutrient-rich fertilizer in agriculture, further enhancing the sustainability of the biogas production process.

Overall, biogas production from organic waste contributes to a circular economy by converting waste materials into valuable resources. It offers multiple environmental benefits, including the reduction of methane emissions from waste decomposition, the displacement of fossil fuel consumption, and the diversion of organic waste from landfills. By harnessing the potential of organic waste, biogas production plays a crucial role in achieving sustainable development goals and transitioning towards a low-carbon economy.

Biomimetic Architecture

Biomimetic architecture refers to the design and construction of buildings and structures that imitate or are inspired by the principles, strategies, and forms found in nature.

When it comes to sustainability, biomimetic architecture offers numerous benefits. By studying and emulating natural systems, architects and builders can create structures that are not only environmentally friendly but also energetically efficient, resilient, and adaptable.

Biomimetic Building Structures

Biomimetic building structures are architectural designs that emulate and integrate principles from the natural world, specifically from biological systems and processes. This approach seeks to create sustainable and efficient buildings by applying the wisdom of nature to the built environment.

Inspired by the intricate design and adaptation found in organisms and ecosystems, biomimetic building structures aim to mimic nature's strategies for energy efficiency, resource utilization, and resilience. By observing and understanding how organisms regulate temperature, capture and store water, and optimize material use, architects and engineers can derive innovative solutions to improve the sustainability performance of buildings.

For instance, a biomimetic building may incorporate features that resemble the efficient airflow system of termite mounds to naturally ventilate and regulate temperature, reducing the need for mechanical cooling and heating. Similarly, a structure could be designed to mimic the efficient water filtration and storage mechanisms seen in plants, enabling rainwater harvesting and minimizing water waste.

By emulating nature's time-tested solutions, biomimetic building structures can contribute to a more sustainable future. These designs not only reduce the environmental impact of buildings during their lifecycle but also enhance the well-being of occupants by creating healthier and more productive indoor environments.

Biomimicry-Inspired Design

Biomimicry-inspired design refers to the practice of drawing inspiration from nature's processes, functions, and structures to create sustainable and innovative solutions to design challenges. It is based on the understanding that nature has already evolved sophisticated and efficient designs over billions of years, making it the ultimate designer.

By studying and emulating biological systems, biomimicry-inspired design seeks to find sustainable answers to human problems while minimizing the negative impact on the environment. This approach recognizes that nature has developed efficient systems for energy production, resource utilization, waste management, and adaptation to changing conditions.

The principles of biomimicry-inspired design encourage designers to observe and analyze how nature solves similar challenges, adapt those strategies to human needs, and integrate them into the design process. This can involve learning from the ways plants capture and store energy, how animals move efficiently, or how organisms communicate and cooperate within ecosystems.

Through biomimicry-inspired design, innovative and sustainable solutions can be developed across various fields such as architecture, engineering, product design, and materials science. By imitating nature's time-tested designs, it is possible to create more energy-efficient buildings, develop new materials that mimic the strength and flexibility of natural materials, and enhance the overall resilience and sustainability of our systems and technologies.

Biophilic Architecture

Biophilic architecture is a sustainable design approach that incorporates elements and principles of nature within the built environment in order to enhance the well-being of occupants and promote environmental sustainability. It involves creating spaces that connect people with nature, fostering a sense of harmony, tranquility, and health.

By integrating natural elements such as plants, water features, natural lighting, and views of nature, biophilic architecture aims to create a deeper connection and engagement with the natural world. This connection has proven psychological and physiological benefits, including reduced stress, improved cognitive function, increased productivity, and overall well-being.

Biophilic Design In Architecture

Biophilic design in architecture refers to the practice of incorporating elements of nature into the built environment in order to create sustainable and positive living spaces. It is a design approach that recognizes the innate human connection to nature and aims to enhance well-being, productivity, and overall quality of life.

This design philosophy holds that by incorporating natural materials, views of nature, and the use of natural light and ventilation, buildings can promote a sense of calm, rejuvenation, and increased productivity. It seeks to mimic the patterns, colors, and textures found in the natural world, creating spaces that are visually appealing and evoke a sense of connection to nature.

Biophilic design also takes into consideration the importance of biodiversity and habitat preservation. It aims to create habitats that support and enhance local ecosystems, promoting the integration of green spaces, gardens, and other natural elements into the built environment. This not only contributes to the ecological sustainability of the area but also provides opportunities for interaction with local flora and fauna.

By integrating biophilic design principles into architectural practices, sustainability is enhanced on multiple levels. The use of natural lighting and ventilation reduces the need for artificial lighting and mechanical ventilation systems, leading to energy savings. The incorporation of green spaces and vegetation helps to reduce heat island effects, improve air quality, and mitigate stormwater runoff. Additionally, by providing connections to nature within the built environment, biophilic design promotes well-being and mental health, leading to more sustainable and resilient communities.

Biophilic Design Principles

Biophilic design principles refer to the integration of nature and natural elements within built environments in order to create sustainable and visually appealing spaces. This design approach aims to connect people with nature, promoting physical and mental wellbeing while also reducing environmental impact.

Biophilic design principles follow a set of guidelines that incorporate nature in various forms, such as incorporating natural lighting, views of nature, natural materials, and vegetation. By bringing nature into the built environment, these principles seek to mimic the positive effects that being in nature has on humans, including reducing stress, enhancing creativity, and improving cognitive function.

Biophilic Office Environments

Biophilic office environments refer to workspaces that incorporate elements of nature and natural materials to create a more eco-friendly and sustainable office environment.

The concept of biophilia, which was coined by biologist Edward O. Wilson, suggests that humans have an innate connection with nature and a need to be in contact with it. Biophilic design seeks to fulfill this need by bringing natural elements and patterns into the built environment.

Biophilic Office Furnishings

Biophilic office furnishings refer to furniture and design elements that incorporate natural materials, patterns, and colors in order to create a work environment that promotes well-being, productivity, and sustainability. This concept is based on the idea that humans have an innate connection to nature, and by incorporating natural elements into the office, we can create a more harmonious and healthier workspace.

The use of biophilic office furnishings supports sustainability efforts in several ways. Firstly, these furnishings often utilize sustainable and renewable materials such as wood, bamboo, and natural fabrics, reducing the reliance on non-renewable resources. Additionally, incorporating natural materials in the office reduces the carbon footprint associated with the manufacturing and transportation of synthetic materials.

Furthermore, biophilic office furnishings contribute to the overall sustainability of the workspace by improving indoor air quality. Many synthetic materials used in traditional office furnishings release volatile organic compounds (VOCs) which can be harmful to human health and the environment. In contrast, natural materials used in biophilic furnishings have been shown to have lower VOC emissions, creating a healthier and more sustainable indoor environment.

By embracing biophilic office furnishings, organizations can create an eco-friendly and sustainable workspace that prioritizes the well-being of employees. The incorporation of natural elements not only enhances the aesthetic appeal of the office but also promotes a sense of calm, creativity, and focus, resulting in increased productivity and employee satisfaction. Overall, biophilic office furnishings are a sustainable solution for creating a healthier and more environmentally friendly workspace.

Biophilic Office Furniture

Biophilic office furniture refers to the design and inclusion of furniture items in an office space that are inspired by nature and promote a connection with the natural environment. This concept is rooted in the principles of biophilia, which recognizes the innate human need to be connected with nature for psychological and physiological well-being.

From a sustainability standpoint, biophilic office furniture offers numerous benefits. Firstly, the use of natural materials such as wood, bamboo, and recycled materials in the manufacturing of furniture reduces the reliance on non-renewable resources. This helps to preserve the environment and reduces the carbon footprint associated with furniture production.

Secondly, biophilic office furniture often incorporates elements such as plants, green walls, and natural patterns, which contribute to the overall aesthetic appeal of the office while also

27

improving indoor air quality. Plants help to filter pollutants and release oxygen, creating a healthier working environment for employees.

In addition, biophilic office furniture fosters a connection with nature, which has been shown to boost productivity, creativity, and overall well-being. This can result in increased employee satisfaction and engagement, leading to higher job performance and retention rates.

In conclusion, biophilic office furniture plays a pivotal role in sustainable office design by incorporating natural elements, reducing reliance on non-renewable resources, improving indoor air quality, and enhancing employee well-being. By embracing this concept, organizations can create healthier and more sustainable workspaces for their employees.

Biophilic Workspace Design

Biophilic workspace design refers to the intentional incorporation of elements from the natural world into work environments with the aim of improving sustainability. It recognizes the inherent human need to connect with nature and aims to create workspaces that support workers' physical, mental, and emotional well-being while minimizing negative environmental impacts.

This design approach takes inspiration from nature to create a more sustainable and conducive work environment. It may include features such as natural light, views of greenery, indoor plants, and natural materials like wood and stone. These elements not only enhance the aesthetic appeal of the workspace but also provide tangible benefits for the individuals working within it.

From a sustainability perspective, biophilic workspace design can contribute to reduced energy consumption by maximizing the use of natural light and reducing the need for artificial lighting. It can also incorporate sustainable materials and practices in construction and interior design, such as using recycled or eco-friendly materials and implementing efficient HVAC systems.

Furthermore, biophilic workspace design can have positive impacts on workers' well-being and productivity. Studies have shown that exposure to nature and natural elements in the workplace can reduce stress, enhance creativity and concentration, and increase overall job satisfaction. By designing work environments that prioritize workers' health and well-being, organizations can create a more sustainable and productive workforce.

Bioswale Landscape Design

A bioswale is a landscape design feature that promotes sustainable stormwater management.

It is a shallow, vegetated channel or depression that is designed to collect, filter, and manage stormwater runoff from impervious surfaces, such as roofs, parking lots, and roads. The main purpose of a bioswale is to reduce the quantity of stormwater entering the local stormwater system, prevent flooding, and improve water quality.

Bioswales are typically constructed with a gentle slope to encourage the flow of water, and they are lined with vegetation, such as grasses, shrubs, and trees. The plants in the bioswale help to slow down the flow of stormwater and enhance infiltration, allowing the water to slowly percolate into the soil. As the stormwater passes through the bioswale, the vegetation and soil filter out pollutants and sediment, helping to improve the quality of the water before it reaches nearby streams, rivers, or other bodies of water.

In addition to managing stormwater, bioswales also provide several other environmental benefits. They create habitat for wildlife, enhance biodiversity, and improve air quality by absorbing carbon dioxide and releasing oxygen. Bioswales can also reduce the urban heat island effect by providing shade and cooling the surrounding environment.

Overall, bioswales are a sustainable landscape design solution for managing stormwater runoff. They help to mitigate the negative impacts of urbanization on the water cycle and create more resilient and environmentally-friendly communities.

Bioswale Landscape Planning

28

Bioswale landscape planning refers to the design and implementation of green infrastructure that effectively manages stormwater runoff and promotes sustainable urban development.

Bioswales are long, narrow channels or depressions in the ground specifically designed to capture and filter rainwater. They typically feature vegetation, such as grasses and native plants, along with engineered fill media and specially designed soil mixes. These features allow the bioswales to capture, retain, and treat stormwater, reducing the burden on combined sewer systems and preventing pollutants from entering natural water bodies.

Bioswale landscape planning incorporates various sustainable principles and practices. It focuses on reducing stormwater runoff volume and velocity by directing it into bioswales instead of directly into sewer systems. This reduces the risk of flooding and helps recharge groundwater sources. Additionally, bioswales slow down the flow of stormwater, allowing time for pollutants to settle and be naturally filtered by the vegetation and soil. This natural filtration process improves water quality and reduces the load on wastewater treatment facilities.

Furthermore, bioswale landscape planning promotes the use of native plants, which have deep root systems that enhance water absorption and retention. Native plants also provide habitat for pollinators, support biodiversity, and contribute to the overall aesthetic value of the landscape. These green spaces create opportunities for urban residents to connect with nature and enjoy improved air quality, reduced heat island effects, and enhanced overall well-being.

Blue Planet Foundation

The Blue Planet Foundation is a non-profit organization dedicated to advancing clean energy sustainability in Hawaii and beyond. Founded in 2007, its mission is to end the use of fossil fuels by transitioning to 100% renewable energy sources. By implementing innovative policies, advocating for clean energy investments, and engaging with communities, the foundation aims to create a more sustainable future for generations to come.

Blue Planet Foundation works on various fronts to achieve its goals. Through research and policy analysis, the organization identifies key barriers and proposes solutions to accelerate the adoption of renewable energy technologies. It collaborates with government agencies, businesses, and communities to develop and implement progressive policies and programs that promote clean energy adoption. Additionally, the foundation conducts educational campaigns, public outreach initiatives, and media campaigns to raise awareness about the benefits of renewable energy and the urgent need for its widespread integration. By mobilizing individuals and organizations, the Blue Planet Foundation creates a powerful force for change, advocating for clean energy policies that reduce greenhouse gas emissions, combat climate change, and drive economic growth.

Business For Social Responsibility (BSR)

Business for Social Responsibility (BSR) is an organization that promotes sustainability in business practices. It provides guidance and support to companies, helping them integrate social and environmental considerations into their operations and decision-making processes.

BSR works with a diverse network of companies, governments, and other stakeholders to address pressing sustainability challenges. It offers consulting services, facilitates collaboration and knowledge sharing, and develops tools and resources to assist businesses in their sustainability efforts.

Carbon Disclosure Project (CDP)

The Carbon Disclosure Project (CDP) is an international non-profit organization that works to disclose and manage greenhouse gas emissions and climate change-related risks and opportunities.

CDP collects and reports environmental data from thousands of companies around the world, providing investors and businesses with a comprehensive understanding of the risks and opportunities associated with climate change and environmental sustainability. Through its annual disclosure process, CDP encourages companies to publicly disclose their greenhouse gas emissions, climate-related risks, and sustainability strategies.

CDP's main focus is on encouraging companies to reduce their carbon footprint, mitigate climate risks, and transition to a low-carbon economy. It provides a platform for companies to measure, manage, and report their environmental impact, allowing investors to assess climate-related risks in their portfolios and make informed investment decisions. CDP also works with policymakers and governments to establish regulations and policies that promote sustainable practices and address climate change issues.

By promoting transparency and accountability, CDP plays a crucial role in driving sustainable business practices and fostering climate change mitigation efforts. It helps companies identify and address their environmental impacts, engage with stakeholders, and contribute to the global goal of reducing greenhouse gas emissions and building a resilient and sustainable future. CDP's efforts contribute to a more sustainable and environmentally responsible business landscape, helping companies and investors navigate the challenges and opportunities presented by climate change.

Carbon Trust

The Carbon Trust is a sustainability-focused organization with the mission to accelerate the transition to a low-carbon, sustainable economy. Established in the year 2001 in the United Kingdom, it provides expert advice, support, and certification services to help organizations reduce their carbon emissions and improve their resource efficiency.

In order to fulfill its objectives, the Carbon Trust works with businesses, governments, and the public sector to develop and implement sustainable strategies, technologies, and practices. It offers a range of services including carbon footprint assessments, energy efficiency solutions, renewable energy implementation, and sustainable supply chain initiatives. The organization also provides training and guidance to help companies improve their overall environmental performance.

One of the key initiatives of the Carbon Trust is its certification schemes, which include the Carbon Trust Standard and the Carbon Trust Offsets. The Carbon Trust Standard recognizes organizations that have successfully reduced their carbon emissions and adopted sustainable practices, giving them a distinctive mark of environmental leadership. Carbon Trust Offsets, on the other hand, allow companies to compensate for their unavoidable emissions by investing in high-quality carbon reduction projects.

The Carbon Trust plays a crucial role in driving sustainability efforts worldwide by promoting innovation, supporting the development of low-carbon technologies, and influencing policy decisions. By helping businesses and organizations reduce their environmental impact and improve their resource efficiency, the Carbon Trust contributes to the overall goal of building a more sustainable and resilient future.

Carbon Capture And Storage (CCS)

Carbon capture and storage (CCS) is a sustainable process aimed at reducing the emissions of carbon dioxide (CO_2) from large-scale industrial sources such as power plants and factories. This technology involves the capture, transportation, and long-term storage of CO_2 underground, preventing it from being released into the atmosphere and contributing to climate change.

The process starts with the capture of CO_2 from the flue gases produced by fossil fuel combustion or certain industrial processes. This can be achieved through several methods, including post-combustion capture, pre-combustion capture, and oxy-fuel combustion. Once captured, the CO_2 is compressed and transported, typically via pipelines or ships, to suitable storage sites.

The storage of CO_2 is usually done in deep underground geological formations, such as depleted oil and gas fields or saline aquifers. This involves injecting the CO_2 into the storage sites and ensuring its long-term confinement, preventing it from leaking back into the atmosphere. Various monitoring techniques are employed to verify the integrity and safety of the storage sites.

CCS plays a crucial role in mitigating climate change by significantly reducing CO2 emissions from industrial activities. It enables the continued use of fossil fuels while minimizing their environmental impact. By preventing CO2 from entering the atmosphere, CCS helps in achieving emissions reduction targets and limiting global warming. Furthermore, the storage of CO2 underground also has the potential to enhance oil and gas recovery from depleted fields, offering additional economic benefits.

In conclusion, carbon capture and storage is a sustainable solution that contributes to the reduction of greenhouse gas emissions and plays an essential role in achieving long-term climate goals. It enables the sustainable use of fossil fuels while mitigating their impact on the environment and helps to ensure a more sustainable and low-carbon future.

Carbon Capture And Utilization Technology

Carbon capture and utilization (CCU) technology is a sustainable approach that aims to reduce greenhouse gas emissions and mitigate climate change by capturing carbon dioxide (CO2) from industrial processes or directly from the atmosphere, and then converting it into useful products or storing it permanently.

The first step of CCU technology involves capturing CO2, typically from power plants or industrial facilities, before it is released into the atmosphere. Various methods are used to capture CO2, including solvent-based absorption, adsorption, and membrane separation. Once captured, the CO2 can be compressed and transported via pipelines or shipped for further processing.

The captured CO2 can then be utilized in a variety of ways to create valuable products or services. One common utilization method is carbonation, where CO2 is reacted with minerals to produce materials like concrete or aggregates. Another approach is carbon-based fuel synthesis, where CO2 is converted into synthetic natural gas or other forms of fuel. Additionally, CO2 can be used in the production of chemicals, polymers, or even animal feed.

By converting CO2 into useful products, CCU technology not only reduces emissions but also helps to displace the use of fossil fuels or other carbon-intensive materials. This contributes to sustainable development by promoting a circular economy and reducing reliance on non-renewable resources.

In addition to its utilization potential, CCU technology also offers the option of permanently storing the captured CO2 underground in geological formations or deep saline aquifers, preventing its re-entry into the atmosphere. This process, known as carbon capture and storage (CCS), provides a long-term solution for emissions reduction.

Carbon Capture Storage (CCS)

Carbon capture and storage (CCS) is a sustainable technology that aims to mitigate climate change by capturing carbon dioxide (CO2) emissions from industrial processes and power generation, and storing it underground in geological formations.

CCS plays a crucial role in reducing greenhouse gas emissions and achieving global climate targets. It is designed to prevent CO2, a major contributor to global warming, from being released into the atmosphere, thus helping to combat climate change. By capturing and storing CO2, CCS helps to minimize the impact of human activities on the environment.

Carbon Farming

Carbon farming is a sustainable land management practice aimed at sequestering carbon dioxide from the atmosphere and mitigating climate change. It involves implementing agricultural techniques that enhance the ability of plants and soils to capture and store carbon, thus reducing the concentration of greenhouse gases in the atmosphere.

One key aspect of carbon farming is increasing the organic matter content in soil through practices such as cover cropping, crop rotation, and the use of animal manure or compost. These practices enhance soil health, increase nutrient availability, and improve water retention, while also promoting the sequestration of carbon. Additionally, carbon farming emphasizes the preservation and restoration of natural ecosystems, like forests and wetlands, which act as carbon sinks.

By adopting carbon farming practices, farmers and land managers can effectively reduce greenhouse gas emissions and enhance the resilience of agricultural systems to climate change. Carbon farming contributes to sustainable and regenerative agriculture by promoting biodiversity, conserving water resources, and improving the long-term productivity of farmland. Moreover, it offers economic benefits through the potential sale of carbon credits and the creation of new market opportunities for sustainably produced agricultural products.

In conclusion, carbon farming plays a crucial role in achieving global climate goals and ensuring the long-term sustainability of agricultural systems. Through the holistic management of land and ecosystems, carbon farming contributes to climate change mitigation, adaptation, and the overall resilience of our planet.

Carbon Footprint Calculators

A carbon footprint calculator is a tool used to estimate the amount of greenhouse gas emissions produced by an individual, organization, or product. It calculates the total carbon dioxide (CO_2) and other greenhouse gases emitted during various activities, such as transportation, energy usage, and waste production. The purpose of a carbon footprint calculator is to raise awareness about the environmental impact of these activities and to encourage individuals and organizations to take measures to reduce their carbon emissions. The calculator uses mathematical algorithms and input data, such as energy consumption, travel distance, and consumption patterns, to estimate the carbon emissions associated with these activities. It takes into account factors such as the type of energy used, the fuel efficiency of vehicles, and the carbon intensity of different products. The calculated results are typically expressed in terms of equivalent metric tons of CO_2 emitted per year or per activity. By assessing their carbon footprint, individuals and organizations can gain a better understanding of their contribution to climate change and identify areas where they can make changes to reduce their impact. This may include adopting energy-efficient practices, using renewable energy sources, reducing waste, and making environmentally conscious choices in transportation and purchasing habits. Carbon footprint calculators are valuable tools in promoting sustainability by making individuals and organizations aware of their environmental impact and encouraging them to take steps to reduce their carbon emissions. They serve as a starting point for individuals and organizations to evaluate their current practices and make informed decisions to minimize their contribution to climate change. Carbon footprint calculators are widely available online and can be accessed through various websites and sustainability organizations.

Carbon Offset Marketplace Platforms

A carbon offset marketplace platform refers to an online platform that facilitates the buying and selling of carbon offsets. It operates within the context of sustainability, aiming to reduce greenhouse gas emissions and mitigate climate change.

Through these platforms, individuals, organizations, and businesses can purchase carbon offsets, which are credits representing a reduction in or removal of greenhouse gas emissions from a verified project. These projects can include renewable energy, reforestation, energy efficiency, and other initiatives that help to offset carbon emissions. Carbon offset marketplace platforms provide a transparent and trustworthy marketplace where buyers can choose from a variety of offset projects, ensuring that their investments are supporting sustainable and impactful initiatives. These platforms often have robust verification processes in place to ensure the legitimacy and effectiveness of the carbon offsets being sold. By participating on these platforms, buyers can effectively neutralize or "offset" their own carbon footprint. For example, individuals or companies can calculate their emissions from activities such as traveling or energy consumption and then purchase an equivalent amount of carbon offsets to counterbalance their carbon impact. Furthermore, these platforms contribute to the overall shift towards a low-carbon economy by incentivizing and supporting sustainable projects that reduce greenhouse gas emissions. They create opportunities for project developers to raise funds and expand their operations, driving innovation and investment in renewable energy and environmental initiatives. In summary, carbon offset marketplace platforms play a vital role in promoting sustainability by providing a marketplace for the buying and selling of carbon offsets, allowing individuals and businesses to take action towards reducing their carbon footprint and supporting projects that help mitigate climate change.

Carbon Offset Marketplaces

A carbon offset marketplace is a platform that facilitates the trading of carbon offsets, which are a way for organizations to compensate for their greenhouse gas emissions. These marketplaces provide a space for buyers and sellers to connect and engage in transactions that result in the reduction or removal of carbon dioxide or other greenhouse gases from the atmosphere.

On a carbon offset marketplace, organizations that produce greenhouse gas emissions can purchase carbon offsets from projects that have implemented sustainable practices or technologies to reduce emissions. These projects can include renewable energy installations, reforestation initiatives, or methane capture projects, among others.

The marketplace plays a crucial role in ensuring the credibility and integrity of the carbon offsets being traded. It verifies the emissions reductions achieved by the projects and ensures that they adhere to recognized standards and methodologies. Additionally, marketplaces often provide tools and resources to help organizations calculate their emissions and determine how many offsets they need to purchase to achieve carbon neutrality.

By participating in a carbon offset marketplace, organizations can effectively offset their emissions by supporting projects that are actively working to reduce greenhouse gases. This mechanism helps to promote sustainability and the transition to a low-carbon economy by incentivizing the development and implementation of sustainable practices globally.

Carbon Offset Projects

Carbon offset projects refer to initiatives that aim to mitigate greenhouse gas emissions by supporting activities that reduce or remove an equivalent amount of carbon dioxide or other greenhouse gases from the atmosphere. These projects are an integral part of sustainability efforts as they contribute to the overall goal of reducing the net carbon emissions and addressing climate change.

Carbon offset projects can take various forms, including renewable energy projects, forest conservation or reforestation initiatives, methane capture and utilization projects, and energy efficiency improvements, among others. These projects work by either preventing the release of greenhouse gases into the atmosphere or actively removing them through natural or technological means.

Carbon Offset Verification Services

Carbon offset verification services refer to organizations or agencies that provide independent and credible verification of carbon offset projects. These services play a crucial role in ensuring that carbon offset projects are genuine, accurately measure their emissions reductions, and meet established standards and criteria.

Verification services typically follow internationally recognized protocols and methodologies to assess the credibility and effectiveness of carbon offset projects. They conduct rigorous evaluations and audits to verify project-specific data, calculations, and documentation, such as emission baselines, monitoring plans, and offset certificates.

The verification process involves on-site visits, interviews with project developers and stakeholders, and detailed analysis of project documentation. The goal is to confirm that the carbon offset project has effectively reduced or removed a specific amount of greenhouse gas emissions and has generated real, measurable, and additional environmental benefits.

By conducting independent verification, these services help in building trust and transparency within the carbon offset market. Their assessments provide confidence to buyers and investors that the carbon offsets they purchase or invest in are legitimate and have a tangible impact on reducing greenhouse gas emissions. Verification services also assist project developers in identifying and addressing any gaps or shortcomings in their projects, thereby improving overall project quality and credibility.

In summary, carbon offset verification services are crucial for ensuring the integrity and reliability of carbon offset projects. Their independent evaluations help guarantee that emission reductions claimed by these projects are accurate, credible, and contribute to global efforts towards mitigating climate change.

Carbon-Negative Agriculture

Carbon-negative agriculture refers to a sustainable farming practice that goes beyond carbon neutrality, actively removing more carbon dioxide (CO_2) from the atmosphere than it emits. This approach aims to restore ecosystems, improve soil health, and sequester carbon through various regenerative farming techniques.

One key element of carbon-negative agriculture is the use of regenerative practices, such as cover cropping, crop rotation, and minimal tilling. These techniques help increase organic matter in the soil, which enhances its carbon storage capacity. By minimizing soil disturbance and keeping the land covered with vegetation throughout the year, carbon-negative agriculture promotes the sequestration of atmospheric carbon into the soil.

Another important aspect of carbon-negative agriculture is the integration of renewable energy sources into farming operations. This includes utilizing solar panels, wind turbines, and biogas systems to power machinery and reduce reliance on fossil fuels. By generating clean energy on-site, farmers can lower their carbon footprint and contribute to the overall reduction of greenhouse gas emissions.

Furthermore, carbon-negative agriculture encourages the adoption of agroforestry practices, such as planting trees and establishing forested areas within or alongside agricultural fields. Trees are powerful carbon sinks, absorbing and storing significant amounts of CO_2 from the atmosphere. Introducing agroforestry into farming systems offers additional carbon sequestration opportunities while promoting biodiversity and enhancing ecosystem resilience.

Overall, carbon-negative agriculture prioritizes the restoration and regeneration of ecosystems, aiming to not only reduce carbon emissions but actively remove CO_2 from the atmosphere. By combining regenerative farming techniques, renewable energy integration, and agroforestry practices, this approach contributes to mitigating climate change, improving soil health, and promoting long-term sustainability in the agricultural sector.

Carbon-Negative Building Materials

Carbon-negative building materials are construction materials that have a net negative carbon footprint throughout their entire life cycle, meaning they remove more carbon dioxide from the atmosphere than they emit during their production, transportation, use, and disposal. These materials play a vital role in sustainable construction practices, as they help to mitigate the effects of climate change by actively reducing greenhouse gas emissions.

One of the key characteristics of carbon-negative building materials is their ability to sequester or absorb carbon dioxide. They achieve this by utilizing carbon capture and storage (CCS) technologies or by incorporating carbon-rich materials such as biomass, recycled carbon-based materials, or waste products. By sequestering carbon, these materials effectively remove carbon dioxide from the atmosphere, contributing to the reduction of greenhouse gas concentrations.

Carbon-Neutral Agriculture

Carbon-neutral agriculture refers to a sustainable farming approach that aims to eliminate or offset the emission of greenhouse gases generated from agricultural activities. It seeks to achieve a net-zero carbon footprint by reducing, capturing, or offsetting the amount of carbon dioxide and other greenhouse gases released into the atmosphere.

The concept of carbon-neutral agriculture recognizes that conventional agricultural practices contribute significantly to climate change. These practices release greenhouse gases through various channels such as livestock production, deforestation, excessive use of synthetic fertilizers, and heavy machinery emissions. Carbon-neutral agriculture promotes the adoption of alternative methods and technologies to minimize these emissions and mitigate their impact on the environment.

To achieve carbon-neutrality, farmers employ a range of strategies. These may include optimizing soil management techniques, such as composting and cover cropping, to enhance carbon sequestration in agricultural soils. Additionally, implementing agroforestry practices, such as planting trees on farms, can also help sequester carbon dioxide from the atmosphere. Farmers may also invest in renewable energy sources, such as solar panels or wind turbines, to power their operations and reduce the reliance on fossil fuels.

Furthermore, carbon-neutral agriculture often involves the use of precision farming techniques to maximize resource efficiency and minimize emissions. This includes precision application of fertilizers and pesticides, as well as smart irrigation systems that reduce water consumption. Additionally, promoting biodiversity and integrating natural habitats within agricultural landscapes can support ecological balance and contribute to carbon sequestration.

Carbon-Neutral Building Materials

Carbon-neutral building materials refer to construction materials or products that have been manufactured with minimal or no carbon emissions throughout their production lifecycle, including raw material extraction, manufacturing processes, transportation, and waste management.

These materials are designed to significantly reduce or eliminate the total amount of greenhouse gas emissions associated with their production and use. By using carbon-neutral building materials, architects, builders, and homeowners can contribute to mitigating climate change and promoting sustainable development.

Carbon-Neutral Data Centers

A carbon-neutral data center refers to a facility that operates with minimal or zero carbon emissions, effectively reducing its environmental impact. The term "carbon-neutral" signifies that the data center's overall carbon footprint is offset or balanced by using renewable energy sources and implementing energy-efficient practices.

Carbon-neutral data centers play a crucial role in addressing the sustainability challenges associated with the rapid growth of the digital infrastructure. Traditional data centers consume vast amounts of electricity, contributing significantly to greenhouse gas emissions and exacerbating climate change.

Carbon-neutral data centers strive to achieve a net-zero carbon emissions status by adopting various strategies. These strategies include sourcing renewable energy, such as solar or wind power, to power the facility. Implementing energy-efficient measures, such as advanced cooling systems, efficient server utilization, and optimized infrastructure, also contribute to minimizing the energy consumption and subsequent emissions.

Additionally, carbon-neutral data centers may invest in carbon offset projects to compensate for any remaining emissions. These projects involve supporting clean energy initiatives, reforestation efforts, or investing in technologies that capture and store carbon dioxide from the atmosphere.

By embracing carbon neutrality, data centers reduce their contribution to global warming, conserve natural resources, and promote sustainable development. They serve as models for the industry, setting the standard for responsible and environmentally conscious practices. As digital infrastructure continues to expand, the adoption of carbon-neutral data centers becomes increasingly crucial in mitigating the environmental impact and ensuring sustainable operations.

Carbon-Neutral Event Space Design

A carbon-neutral event space design refers to a sustainable and environmentally friendly approach to designing and operating event venues with the goal of minimizing or offsetting carbon emissions. The design focuses on reducing energy consumption and utilizing renewable energy sources in order to create a space that has a minimal impact on the environment.

Such a design incorporates various strategies to achieve carbon neutrality. This may include using energy-efficient lighting systems, such as LED lights, and optimizing the use of natural light to reduce electricity consumption. Implementing insulation and efficient heating, ventilation, and air conditioning (HVAC) systems can further reduce energy consumption and associated carbon emissions.

Additionally, a carbon-neutral event space design prioritizes the use of renewable energy sources, such as solar panels or wind turbines, to power the venue. This helps to eliminate or significantly reduce reliance on fossil fuels and the associated greenhouse gas emissions. Furthermore, sustainable materials and practices are employed during construction to minimize the carbon footprint of the event space.

To offset any remaining carbon emissions, the design may also incorporate initiatives such as carbon offset programs or partnerships with organizations involved in reforestation efforts. By doing so, the event space design ensures that any carbon emissions generated during its operation are balanced out by activities that remove or reduce an equivalent amount of carbon dioxide from the atmosphere, achieving carbon neutrality.

Carbon-Neutral Fuels

Carbon-neutral fuels are sustainable energy sources that produce no net carbon dioxide emissions when used as a fuel. These fuels are considered environmentally friendly and contribute to the reduction of greenhouse gases in the atmosphere.

Carbon neutrality refers to the balancing of carbon dioxide emissions with carbon removal or offsetting. Carbon-neutral fuels achieve this balance by either being produced from renewable resources or by capturing and storing the carbon dioxide that is emitted during their use.

Renewable carbon-neutral fuels, such as biofuels, are derived from organic matter such as plants or microorganisms. These fuels are produced through processes like fermentation or biomass conversion, where carbon dioxide is absorbed during the growth of the feedstock. When these fuels are burned, the carbon dioxide released is equal to the amount that was previously absorbed, resulting in no net emissions.

Alternatively, carbon capture and storage technologies can be used with fossil fuel-based carbon-neutral fuels. This involves capturing the carbon dioxide emissions from the fuel combustion and storing them deep underground, preventing their release into the atmosphere. While the fuel itself may still generate carbon dioxide, the overall emissions are balanced by the amount that is captured and stored, resulting in a net zero or carbon-neutral outcome.

Carbon-Neutral Shipping

Carbon-neutral shipping refers to a sustainable method of transporting goods that involves minimizing or offsetting the carbon emissions generated throughout the entire shipping process. It aims to achieve a net-zero carbon footprint by reducing greenhouse gas emissions and investing in initiatives that absorb or mitigate an equivalent amount of carbon dioxide.

The first step towards carbon-neutral shipping involves reducing emissions through various strategies, such as optimizing shipping routes and consolidating shipments to minimize the number of trips. This can be achieved by utilizing advanced technologies, adopting fuel-efficient vessels, and implementing sustainable practices within the logistics chain, including packaging and warehousing.

To offset the remaining emissions that cannot be avoided, carbon-neutral shipping relies on investing in projects that remove or prevent an equivalent amount of carbon dioxide from entering the atmosphere. These projects often involve renewable energy production, reforestation, and the promotion of sustainable agriculture practices. By supporting these initiatives, shipping companies can compensate for the emissions produced during transportation and contribute to the overall reduction of greenhouse gas levels.

Carbon-neutral shipping aligns with the principles of sustainability by not only reducing environmental impact but also supporting the transition to a low-carbon economy. It provides an opportunity for businesses to take responsibility for their carbon emissions and actively contribute to the preservation of the planet's resources. By adopting carbon-neutral shipping practices, industries can lead the way towards more sustainable and environmentally conscious supply chains.

Overall, carbon-neutral shipping plays a vital role in mitigating climate change and promoting sustainable development. By considering the entire lifecycle of shipping and incorporating emission reduction and offsetting measures, it helps to create a more environmentally friendly and socially responsible global shipping industry.

Carbon-Offset Public Transportation

Carbon-offset public transportation refers to the practice of reducing greenhouse gas emissions from public transportation systems by investing in projects that offset or compensate for carbon emissions generated by these systems.

Public transportation plays a crucial role in promoting sustainability and mitigating climate change. However, it still produces carbon emissions, mainly in the form of carbon dioxide (CO_2), which contribute to global warming. Carbon-offsetting in public transportation aims to neutralize these emissions by funding projects that reduce or remove an equivalent amount of greenhouse gases from the atmosphere.

These offsetting projects can take various forms and include initiatives such as reforestation and afforestation projects, renewable energy installations, energy efficiency improvements, and methane capture from landfills or farms. By investing in these projects, public transportation agencies and operators can counterbalance their carbon emissions and contribute to the overall reduction of greenhouse gas levels in the atmosphere.

The concept of carbon-offset public transportation aligns with the principles of sustainable development and the goals of the Paris Agreement, which emphasize the need to limit global warming to well below 2 degrees Celsius above pre-industrial levels. It allows public transportation systems to prioritize environmental stewardship and take responsibility for their carbon footprint while still providing efficient and accessible transportation options for communities.

Carbon-Offset Travel Experiences

A carbon-offset travel experience refers to a sustainable travel practice aimed at mitigating the environmental impact of a journey by compensating for the greenhouse gas emissions produced during the trip. This concept is based on the understanding that travel, particularly by airplane, contributes significantly to the release of carbon dioxide and other pollutants, leading to climate change and environmental degradation.

The process of carbon offsetting involves calculating the carbon footprint of a travel activity, which includes emissions from transportation, accommodation, and other related factors. To compensate for these emissions and achieve carbon neutrality, travelers can participate in various offsetting programs or initiatives. These programs invest in projects that reduce or remove greenhouse gas emissions elsewhere, such as renewable energy projects, reforestation efforts, or energy efficiency initiatives.

By supporting carbon offset projects, travelers essentially neutralize the negative environmental impact of their travel. This allows them to enjoy their travel experience while taking responsibility for their contribution to climate change. Carbon-offset travel experiences promote sustainability by encouraging individuals and organizations to minimize their carbon footprints through conscious choices and offsetting their unavoidable emissions.

Moreover, carbon-offset travel experiences can contribute to sustainable development by supporting local communities and biodiversity conservation. Many offset projects prioritize social and environmental co-benefits, aiming to create positive impacts beyond carbon reduction.

Carbon-Positive Agriculture

Carbon-positive agriculture refers to farming practices that actively remove more carbon dioxide (CO_2) from the atmosphere than they emit, thereby helping to mitigate climate change and contribute to overall sustainability. This approach focuses on adopting techniques and strategies that enhance soil carbon sequestration, reduce greenhouse gas emissions, and promote the use of renewable resources.

One key aspect of carbon-positive agriculture is the implementation of regenerative farming practices. These include minimizing or eliminating the use of synthetic fertilizers and pesticides, which release CO_2 during their production, and instead using organic methods that promote soil health and biodiversity. By allowing plants to grow in natural, nutrient-rich conditions, regenerative agriculture helps plants absorb more carbon from the atmosphere and store it in the soil. This serves as a carbon sink, effectively removing CO_2 from the air.

Another important component of carbon-positive agriculture is the integration of sustainable land management techniques. This involves practices such as agroforestry, which combines the cultivation of trees with traditional agriculture to maximize carbon sequestration. By incorporating trees into agricultural systems, farmers can enhance carbon storage in both above-ground biomass and in the soil. Additionally, diverse crop rotation and intercropping methods can improve soil health, minimize erosion, and optimize carbon capture.

Overall, carbon-positive agriculture represents a proactive and sustainable approach to farming that aims to reduce the carbon footprint of agricultural activities. By implementing practices that actively remove CO_2 from the atmosphere and promote soil carbon sequestration, farmers can contribute to climate change mitigation and strengthen the overall resilience of agricultural systems.

Carbon-Positive Farming

Carbon-positive farming refers to agricultural practices that aim to reduce greenhouse gas emissions in order to have a net positive impact on the environment. This approach focuses on sequestering more carbon dioxide from the atmosphere than is released during farming activities. By implementing sustainable techniques and utilizing regenerative practices, carbon-positive farming aims to create a carbon sink, ultimately helping to mitigate climate change.

The key objective of carbon-positive farming is to achieve carbon neutrality or even carbon negativity by implementing various strategies. These include optimizing soil health, minimizing the use of synthetic fertilizers and pesticides, and adopting agroforestry practices. By increasing organic matter in the soil through techniques such as cover cropping, composting, and crop rotation, farmers can enhance carbon sequestration, effectively removing carbon dioxide from the atmosphere and storing it in the soil. Additionally, incorporating trees and perennial crops into agricultural systems can further enhance carbon capture and storage.

Carbon-positive farming not only aims to reduce greenhouse gas emissions, but also strives to create a resilient and sustainable agricultural system. By promoting biodiversity, conserving water resources, and reducing soil erosion, this approach helps to maintain ecosystem health and enhance the overall sustainability of farming practices. Furthermore, carbon-positive farming can have additional benefits such as improving soil fertility, increasing crop yield, and enhancing food security.

Carbon-Sequestering Agriculture

Carbon-sequestering agriculture is a sustainable farming practice that aims to mitigate climate change by capturing and storing carbon dioxide (CO_2) from the atmosphere into the soil, plants, and other biological materials. This method promotes a more balanced carbon cycle by

38

absorbing more carbon than the agricultural activities emit, thus helping to reduce greenhouse gas concentrations and combat global warming.

By adopting carbon-sequestering agriculture techniques, farmers can increase the carbon content in their soils, enhancing their fertility and productivity. These practices include using cover crops, crop rotations, and agroforestry systems, which promote the growth of plant biomass and the subsequent sequestration of carbon through photosynthesis. Additionally, adopting conservation tillage methods, such as no-till or reduced tillage, minimizes soil disturbance and prevents the release of stored carbon into the atmosphere.

Carbon sequestration in agriculture provides multiple environmental benefits. It improves soil health and structure, enhancing its water retention capacity and reducing erosion. Moreover, by sequestering carbon, this agricultural approach helps to offset carbon emissions from other sectors, contributing to overall net-negative emissions. It also promotes biodiversity by creating habitat for various organisms and supporting beneficial soil microorganisms. Additionally, carbon-sequestering agriculture can have co-benefits for rural communities by diversifying income streams, enhancing food security, and promoting sustainable land management practices.

Carbon-Sequestering Building Designs

Carbon-sequestering building designs are architectural and engineering approaches that aim to reduce the carbon footprint of buildings and enhance their ability to capture and store carbon dioxide (CO2) from the atmosphere. These designs are an integral part of sustainable development strategies, as they help mitigate climate change and support the transition towards a low-carbon economy.

There are several key principles and techniques employed in carbon-sequestering building designs. One such approach is the use of sustainable materials with low embodied carbon, such as recycled or reclaimed materials, as well as those sourced from renewable resources. This reduces the amount of CO2 emissions associated with the production and transportation of building materials.

Another important aspect is energy efficiency. By incorporating features such as effective insulation, high-performance windows, and efficient HVAC (heating, ventilation, and air conditioning) systems, carbon-sequestering buildings minimize energy consumption and subsequent greenhouse gas emissions. Additionally, renewable energy sources, such as solar panels or wind turbines, can be integrated into the design to further reduce dependence on fossil fuels.

In terms of carbon capture, buildings can be designed to include green roofs and vertical gardens that promote the growth of vegetation. Plants naturally absorb CO2 through photosynthesis and convert it into oxygen, effectively sequestering carbon. Similarly, living walls and indoor plants improve air quality and contribute to carbon sequestration.

Overall, carbon-sequestering building designs prioritize sustainable practices and materials, energy efficiency, and the integration of natural elements to reduce greenhouse gas emissions and promote carbon capture. By implementing these strategies, buildings can actively contribute to combatting climate change and achieving a more sustainable future.

Carbon-Sequestering Building Materials

Carbon-sequestering building materials refer to construction materials that capture and store carbon dioxide (CO2) emissions from the atmosphere throughout their lifespan. These materials play a crucial role in promoting sustainability and mitigating climate change by reducing greenhouse gas emissions.

Typically, carbon-sequestering building materials are made from renewable resources or utilize waste products in their production. Examples include wood, bamboo, hemp, and recycled aggregates. These materials have the ability to absorb carbon dioxide during their growth or manufacturing process, acting as carbon sinks and offsetting emissions.

By incorporating carbon-sequestering building materials into construction projects, the building industry can contribute to a net reduction in CO2 emissions. This is achieved by not only preventing the release of carbon dioxide during material production but also by actively capturing and storing carbon dioxide from the atmosphere. As a result, these materials help to lower the carbon footprint of buildings.

Moreover, carbon-sequestering building materials can also enhance indoor air quality and provide better insulation, leading to reduced energy consumption. This further contributes to sustainability efforts by reducing the need for fossil fuel-based energy sources and lowering overall greenhouse gas emissions.

Carbon-Sequestering Landscape Design

Carbon-sequestering landscape design refers to the intentional planning and arrangement of natural features within the built environment to maximize the capture and storage of carbon dioxide from the atmosphere. This design approach aims to mitigate greenhouse gas emissions and combat climate change by harnessing the natural processes of plant photosynthesis and soil carbon storage.

This design strategy involves the strategic placement and selection of vegetation, such as trees, shrubs, and groundcover, that have high carbon sequestration potential. These carbon-absorbing plants remove carbon dioxide from the air during photosynthesis and store it in their biomass and root systems. Additionally, carbon-sequestering landscape design encourages the establishment of diverse plant communities that can enhance ecosystem resilience and biodiversity.

Furthermore, carbon-sequestering landscape design incorporates the use of sustainable land management practices, such as organic fertilization, mulching, and soil erosion control, to support healthy plant growth and carbon storage in the soil. By optimizing soil health and fertility, this design approach enhances the capacity of soils to store carbon for extended periods.

Overall, carbon-sequestering landscape design seeks to enhance the ability of urban and suburban areas to act as carbon sinks, effectively removing and storing carbon dioxide from the atmosphere. By integrating nature into the built environment and considering the carbon sequestration potential of plants and soils, this design approach contributes to the sustainability and resilience of ecosystems, while also addressing the urgent challenge of climate change.

Carbon-Sequestering Landscape Layouts

Carbon-sequestering landscape layouts refer to the strategic arrangement and design of elements within a given landscape with the objective of maximizing carbon sequestration or the removal of carbon dioxide from the atmosphere through natural processes. This approach aims to mitigate climate change by reducing greenhouse gas concentrations and promoting the storage of carbon in various ecosystems.

Such landscape layouts prioritize the incorporation of vegetation, including trees, shrubs, and other plants, as well as organic matter into the design. By utilizing a diverse range of vegetation types and ensuring their proper growth and maintenance, carbon-sequestering landscape layouts facilitate the photosynthetic process, during which plants absorb carbon dioxide and store it as carbon in their biomass and soils.

Center For Climate And Energy Solutions (C2ES)

The Center for Climate and Energy Solutions (C2ES) is an independent, nonprofit organization focused on promoting sustainability in the face of climate change and advancing clean energy solutions.

C2ES serves as a leading resource for policymakers, businesses, and the public, offering research and analysis, policy guidance, and collaborative initiatives to address the complex challenges of climate change. The organization engages with stakeholders at local, national, and international levels to foster a coordinated approach to sustainability.

Center For Sustainable Energy (CSE)

The Center for Sustainable Energy (CSE) is an organization dedicated to promoting and accelerating the transition to a sustainable energy future. CSE operates as an independent nonprofit with a mission to support clean and renewable energy solutions that are environmentally responsible, economically viable, and socially equitable.

At the core of CSE's work is the recognition that sustainability encompasses various aspects, including environmental, economic, and social factors. The organization aims to address these dimensions and create a balanced energy system that meets the needs of the present without compromising the ability of future generations to meet their own needs.

Center For Sustainable Shale Development (CSSD)

The Center for Sustainable Shale Development (CSSD) is an organization dedicated to promoting sustainable practices in the shale energy industry. The CSSD works collaboratively with industry, environmental organizations, and other stakeholders to develop and implement a set of performance standards for shale development.

The CSSD's performance standards are designed to address the environmental, social, and economic impacts of shale development, with the goal of minimizing these impacts and ensuring the long-term sustainability of the industry. The standards cover a range of issues, including water and air quality, community engagement, and resource conservation.

Ceres

Ceres is a non-profit organization that works with influential investors and companies to promote sustainable practices and solutions for global sustainability challenges. Founded in 1989, Ceres aims to accelerate the transition to a more sustainable economy by mobilizing the business community to take action on climate change, water scarcity, and deforestation, among others.

Ceres believes that sustainable business practices are key to addressing the urgent environmental and social issues facing the world today. The organization utilizes a unique approach that focuses on engaging investors, companies, and policymakers to drive positive change. Through collaborative initiatives, Ceres works to improve corporate disclosure, enhance integration of sustainability into business strategies, and advocate for stronger policies and regulations that support sustainability and resilience.

Circular Business Strategies

Circular business strategies refer to sustainable economic models that prioritize resource efficiency, waste reduction, and the reuse, recycling, and repurposing of materials. This approach aims to break away from the linear economy, which follows a "take-make-dispose" pattern, and instead adopts a closed-loop system.

In circular business strategies, products and materials are designed with longevity in mind, promoting durability, repairability, and upgradeability. This extends the lifespan of goods and reduces the need for constant production and consumption. Additionally, materials used in products are carefully selected to ensure they can be easily extracted, separated, and recycled at the end of their life cycle.

Furthermore, circular business strategies prioritize the use of renewable energy sources and the elimination of hazardous substances in production processes. By implementing sustainable practices throughout the entire value chain, businesses can reduce their environmental impact, conserve natural resources, and mitigate climate change.

Transitioning to circular business strategies can have numerous benefits, such as cost savings through improved resource efficiency, reduced waste management expenses, and the creation of new job opportunities in sectors related to recycling and repurposing. Moreover, it fosters innovation and encourages collaboration between businesses, policymakers, and consumers to drive sustainable development and create a more resilient and regenerative economy.

Circular Economy Advocacy Groups

Circular economy advocacy groups are organizations or coalitions that promote the concept and adoption of a circular economy as a means of achieving sustainability. The circular economy is a regenerative economic system aimed at minimizing waste and maximizing resource efficiency. It is based on the principles of designing out waste and pollution, keeping products and materials in use for as long as possible, and regenerating natural systems.

Advocacy groups play a crucial role in driving the transition towards a circular economy by advocating for policy changes, raising awareness, and facilitating collaborations among various stakeholders. These groups work to influence governments, businesses, and individuals to embrace circular practices and shift away from the traditional linear "take-make-dispose" model.

Through their advocacy efforts, these groups highlight the environmental, social, and economic benefits of adopting circular economy principles. They emphasize the importance of reducing greenhouse gas emissions, conserving natural resources, creating green jobs, and fostering social inclusivity. Moreover, they often collaborate with businesses and policymakers to develop innovative solutions, such as eco-design, product leasing, sharing platforms, and recycling initiatives.

Circular economy advocacy groups also serve as knowledge hubs, providing resources, research, and best practices to inspire and guide individuals and organizations. They organize events, workshops, and conferences to facilitate knowledge exchange and networking opportunities. Additionally, they may collaborate with educational institutions to integrate circular economy concepts into curricula and promote capacity building.

In summary, circular economy advocacy groups play a crucial role in advocating for and promoting the adoption of circular economy principles and practices. Through their efforts, they drive change, raise awareness, facilitate collaboration, and provide resources to support the transition towards a regenerative and sustainable economic model.

Circular Economy Advocacy

A circular economy is a concept that promotes sustainable development by redefining the traditional linear economic model of "take-make-waste" into one that aims to reduce waste and resource consumption.

In a circular economy, resources are managed and used efficiently throughout their lifecycle, ensuring their maximum value is maintained for as long as possible. This involves designing products for durability and reparability, and promoting the reuse, remanufacturing, and recycling of materials to extend their lifespan.

The concept of circular economy also focuses on the regeneration of natural systems, aiming to minimize environmental impact and preserve ecosystems. It emphasizes the use of renewable energy sources and the reduction of carbon emissions, as well as the efficient management of water resources.

Moreover, circular economy advocates for a shift in consumer behavior, promoting responsible consumption and encouraging individuals to choose products that are environmentally friendly and ethically sourced.

By embracing a circular economy, societies can achieve sustainable development goals, including the reduction of waste and pollution, the conservation of natural resources, and the creation of new job opportunities in green industries. Ultimately, this approach aims to create a more resilient and inclusive economy that operates within the boundaries of the planet, ensuring a sustainable future for generations to come.

Circular Economy Awareness Campaigns

A circular economy awareness campaign is a targeted effort to increase knowledge and understanding about the concepts and benefits of a circular economy, with the goal of promoting sustainable and responsible consumption and production patterns.

A circular economy aims to minimize waste by maximizing the utilization of resources throughout their life cycles, creating a closed-loop system where materials, products, and components are constantly circulated and reused. It is an alternative to the traditional linear economy model, which follows a "take-make-dispose" approach.

These awareness campaigns seek to educate and engage individuals, businesses, and communities in adopting circular economy principles and practices. They often involve various communication channels such as online platforms, social media, workshops, seminars, and events.

The campaigns focus on raising awareness about the environmental, social, and economic benefits of a circular economy. They highlight how a transition to circularity can reduce resource depletion, minimize pollution, create new business opportunities, foster innovation, and enhance social well-being.

These awareness campaigns also emphasize the role of individuals and businesses in driving the transition to a circular economy. They provide information on sustainable consumption and production practices, waste reduction, recycling, and the importance of supporting circular businesses and initiatives.

Overall, circular economy awareness campaigns play a crucial role in encouraging behavioral change, shaping attitudes, and mobilizing action towards a more sustainable and regenerative economic model. By increasing awareness and understanding, these campaigns help create a culture that embraces circularity and inspires collective efforts towards a healthier and more resilient planet.

Circular Economy Best Practices

A circular economy refers to an economic system that aims to create sustainable development by minimizing resource consumption and waste generation. It is based on the principles of designing out waste and pollution, keeping products and materials in use for as long as possible, and regenerating natural systems.

This economic model seeks to shift away from the traditional linear economy, where resources are extracted, processed, and disposed of after use, towards a more circular and regenerative approach. In this system, products are designed to be durable, repairable, and recyclable, promoting the reuse of materials and reducing the need for virgin resources.

Circular Economy Business Models

A circular economy business model refers to a sustainable approach that aims to minimize waste and maximize resource efficiency through the continual use and recycling of materials. It is a departure from the traditional linear economy, which follows a "take-make-dispose" pattern, leading to the depletion of resources and generation of large amounts of waste.

In a circular economy, products and materials are designed to be reused, repaired, or recycled, ensuring that valuable resources are kept in circulation for as long as possible. This approach reduces the extraction of raw materials and minimizes the environmental impact associated with their production, processing, and disposal. By closing the material loop, a circular economy aims to create a regenerative system that operates within the boundaries of the planet's resources.

Circular Economy Case Studies

A circular economy is an economic system that aims to keep resources in use for as long as possible, extracting value from them while minimizing waste and the consumption of new resources. It promotes a regenerative approach where products, materials, and resources are kept in circulation through strategies such as reusing, recycling, and refurbishing.

In the context of sustainability, a circular economy is driven by the principle of decoupling economic growth from resource consumption and environmental degradation. It recognizes that the traditional linear economy, which relies on a "take-make-dispose" model, is unsustainable and results in the depletion of finite resources, increasing waste generation, and greenhouse gas emissions.

By implementing circular economy practices, businesses and societies can transition towards a more sustainable and resilient model. This approach allows for the preservation of natural resources, the reduction of waste, and the minimization of environmental impacts. Additionally, it presents economic opportunities, such as the development of new technologies, job creation, and cost savings through resource efficiency.

Several case studies demonstrate the successful implementation of circular economy principles. For example, the Dutch company Philips has shifted from selling lighting products to providing lighting services, creating a "circular lighting" business model. This approach allows customers to lease lighting solutions rather than purchasing them, encouraging reuse and recycling of components. This innovative model reduces waste and promotes energy efficiency.

Another case study is the Danish company Novozymes, which produces enzymes used in various industries. Novozymes implemented a "circular mindset" throughout its operations, optimizing energy and resource use, reducing waste, and designing products for circularity. This approach not only benefits the environment but also enhances the company's competitiveness in the market.

Circular Economy Circularity Metrics

A circular economy is an economic system that aims to minimize waste and maximize the use of resources by promoting the reuse, recycling, and regeneration of products, materials, and components. It is built on the principle of closing the loop of resource consumption and production, in order to achieve long-term sustainability.

Circularity metrics refer to the quantitative measures used to assess the progress and effectiveness of a circular economy. These metrics provide insights into the extent to which a system or organization is circular and can help identify areas for improvement. They help monitor and evaluate resource flows and the efficiency of circular processes, contributing to the overall goal of achieving a more sustainable and circular economy.

Circular Economy Conferences

A circular economy conference is a formal gathering of individuals, organizations, and policymakers focused on promoting sustainability and advancing the principles of circular economy.

The concept of a circular economy aims to reduce waste, preserve resources, and minimize environmental impact by transitioning from a linear "take-make-dispose" model to one that emphasizes reuse, recycling, and regeneration. This shift is crucial for achieving a more sustainable and resilient global economy.

At circular economy conferences, participants engage in discussions, workshops, and presentations to share knowledge, insights, and best practices related to circular economy principles. These events provide an opportunity for stakeholders from various sectors, including business, government, academia, and civil society, to network, collaborate, and collectively address the challenges and opportunities associated with sustainable resource management.

Key topics typically covered at such conferences include resource efficiency, product design for circularity, waste reduction and recycling strategies, innovative business models, policy development, and the role of technology in enabling a circular economy. Speakers and experts share case studies, research findings, and success stories, highlighting practical examples of circular economy implementation and showcasing the potential benefits for both the environment and the economy.

Ultimately, circular economy conferences play a vital role in fostering dialogue, driving innovation, and catalyzing action towards a more sustainable future. By bringing together diverse perspectives and expertise, these events contribute to the collective effort of transitioning to a circular economy that enables long-term prosperity while protecting the planet.

Circular Economy Consulting Firms

Circular economy consulting firms are businesses that provide expertise and guidance to help organizations transition from a linear economy to a circular economy, with a focus on sustainability.

A circular economy is an economic system that aims to minimize waste and maximize the use of resources. Unlike the traditional linear economy, which follows a "take-make-dispose" model, a circular economy promotes the idea of designing out waste and pollution, keeping products and materials in use for as long as possible, and regenerating natural systems.

Circular economy consulting firms work with clients from various sectors to develop strategies and implement practices that support the principles of a circular economy. They may offer services such as:

- Assessing current business models and identifying opportunities for circularity

- Providing guidance on product design and material selection to optimize resource efficiency and recyclability

- Helping organizations develop closed-loop supply chains and establish partnerships for waste reduction and resource recovery

- Assisting with the implementation of sustainable production and consumption practices

- Conducting lifecycle assessments and offering recommendations for improving environmental performance

By engaging with circular economy consulting firms, organizations can better understand the potential benefits of transitioning to a circular economy and receive tailored guidance on how to achieve their sustainability goals. These firms play a crucial role in driving the adoption of circular business models, promoting resource efficiency, and contributing to a more sustainable future.

Circular Economy Consulting

A circular economy consulting refers to a sustainability-focused advisory service that helps businesses and organizations transition from a linear economic model to a circular one. In a linear economy, resources are extracted, processed, used, and disposed of, leading to resource depletion and waste accumulation. On the other hand, a circular economy aims to maximize resource use efficiency by promoting the continual circulation and repurposing of materials.

By providing circular economy consulting, experts assist clients in adopting and implementing strategies and practices that support the principles of a circular economy. This may involve analyzing the client's current operations, identifying areas for improvement, and developing customized plans to optimize resource utilization and minimize waste generation throughout the product life cycle.

Circular Economy Courses

A circular economy is a sustainable economic model that aims to minimize waste and maximize the use of resources by reducing, reusing, and recycling materials. It promotes a closed-loop system where products and materials are designed to have a longer lifespan and to be easily disassembled and recycled.

In a circular economy, the traditional linear model of "take-make-dispose" is replaced with a holistic approach that considers the entire lifecycle of products. This means that products are not only designed with durability in mind but also with the ability to be repaired, remanufactured, or recycled at the end of their life.

Circular Economy Data Analysis Tools

45

A circular economy data analysis tool is a software or system that enables the collection, organization, and analysis of data related to the circular economy in the context of sustainability. It allows businesses, organizations, and governments to measure and monitor their progress towards achieving circularity by providing insights and metrics on resource recycling, waste reduction, and value retention.

These tools help identify opportunities for improvement and inform decision-making processes by providing comprehensive and reliable data on key circular economy indicators. They can analyze data from various sources, such as waste management, material flows, product lifecycles, and supply chains, to assess the environmental, social, and economic impacts of circular actions.

By using circular economy data analysis tools, stakeholders can track their performance, set targets, and benchmark against industry standards and best practices. This enables them to identify inefficiencies and implement strategies to optimize resource use, minimize waste generation, and maximize resource recovery and reuse.

Furthermore, circular economy data analysis tools facilitate transparency and accountability in sustainability reporting by enabling the creation of standardized reports and disclosure of key performance indicators. This allows stakeholders to communicate their circular economy efforts and achievements to customers, investors, and the wider public.

In summary, circular economy data analysis tools play a crucial role in driving the transition towards a circular economy by providing data-driven insights, facilitating decision-making processes, and promoting accountability and transparency in sustainability reporting.

Circular Economy Data Analytics

A circular economy is a concept in sustainability that aims to minimize waste and maximize the utilization of resources by closing the loop of production and consumption. It is based on the idea of shifting from a linear "take-make-waste" model to a circular model that focuses on the regeneration of materials and resources.

Data analytics plays a crucial role in enabling and optimizing a circular economy. It involves the collection, analysis, and interpretation of data to gain insights and make informed decisions regarding resource management, waste reduction, and process efficiency.

By leveraging data analytics, organizations can identify inefficiencies in their value chains, such as areas of resource wastage or potential for material reuse. They can then apply data-driven strategies to improve the design and production processes, reducing waste generation and environmental impact.

Data analytics also enables better monitoring and tracking of resource flows, allowing organizations to optimize the use of resources and identify opportunities for recycling and reclamation. It can help in identifying patterns and trends in consumption and waste generation, enabling targeted interventions and the development of more sustainable business models.

In conclusion, data analytics is a powerful tool in the context of a circular economy as it enables organizations to make informed decisions, optimize resource utilization, and minimize waste. By leveraging data-driven insights, businesses and policymakers can contribute to the transition towards a more sustainable and regenerative economic model.

Circular Economy Education

A circular economy is a sustainable economic model focused on minimizing waste and maximizing the use of resources. It aims to create a closed-loop system where materials are continuously reused, repurposed, or recycled, rather than being disposed of after a single use.

In a circular economy, products and materials are designed to be restorative and regenerative, promoting the long-term health and well-being of both society and the environment. This involves the implementation of strategies such as waste prevention, product longevity, efficient resource use, and the adoption of renewable energy sources.

Circular Economy Educational Initiatives

A circular economy educational initiative refers to programs, courses, and awareness campaigns designed to educate individuals, organizations, and communities about the principles and practices of a circular economy in the context of sustainability.

The goal of circular economy educational initiatives is to promote a shift away from the traditional linear economy model, which follows a "take-make-dispose" pattern, towards a circular economy model, which aims to keep resources in use for as long as possible, extract maximum value from them while in use, and then recover and regenerate products and materials at the end of their life cycle.

Circular Economy Educational Programs

A circular economy educational program is a comprehensive and structured learning initiative that aims to foster understanding and promote action towards a sustainable and regenerative economic model. Grounded in the principles of sustainability, a circular economy educational program equips learners with the knowledge, skills, and mindset needed to contribute to the transition towards a more resource-efficient and less wasteful society.

The primary focus of a circular economy educational program is to empower individuals with a deep understanding of the interconnectedness of economic activities, environmental conservation, and social well-being. Through various learning methods such as lectures, workshops, case studies, and practical exercises, participants gain insights into the principles, practices, and benefits of a circular economy.

These programs typically cover a wide range of topics, including but not limited to waste reduction, recycling, product design for durability and repair, resource recovery, and sustainable consumption patterns. They explore how to transform linear production and consumption systems into circular ones that prioritize waste prevention, resource efficiency, and the reuse and recycling of materials.

Furthermore, a circular economy educational program fosters a holistic understanding of sustainable business models, policy frameworks, and technological innovations that support the transition to a circular economy. Participants are encouraged to think critically, and to develop innovative and scalable solutions that address the complex challenges posed by unsustainable production and consumption practices.

In summary, a circular economy educational program is a crucial tool for creating a future workforce that is well-equipped to devise and implement sustainable solutions, contributing to a more resilient, inclusive, and environmentally friendly society.

Circular Economy Educational Resources

A circular economy is a sustainable economic system that aims to minimize waste and maximize the use of resources by promoting the principles of reduce, reuse, and recycle. It operates on the concept of closed-loop systems, where products and materials are reused or recycled at the end of their life cycle, rather than being discarded as waste.

In a circular economy, the emphasis is on designing products with longevity and durability, as well as promoting repairability and upgradability. This approach encourages the reuse of products and components, extending their lifespan and reducing the need for new production. Additionally, materials are kept in circulation for as long as possible through recycling processes.

Circular Economy Entrepreneurship

A circular economy entrepreneurship refers to the business practices that aim to create a sustainable economy by minimizing the use of resources, reducing waste, and promoting the reuse and recycling of materials. It involves adopting innovative and efficient strategies that focus on generating value from resources instead of depleting them.

In a circular economy, the traditional linear "take-make-dispose" model is replaced by a closed-loop system. This means that products and materials are designed to be continuously cycled and reused, reducing the need for extracting new resources and preventing the accumulation of waste. Circular economy entrepreneurship embraces the principles of sustainability, resource efficiency, and waste reduction to create a regenerative economic and environmental system.

Circular Economy Forums

A circular economy forum is a platform or gathering where individuals, organizations, and stakeholders come together to discuss and promote sustainable practices and solutions that contribute to the development of a circular economy.

A circular economy is an economic model that aims to eliminate waste and promote the continual use and regeneration of resources. It is based on the principles of designing out waste and pollution, keeping products and materials in use as long as possible, and regenerating natural systems. The transition to a circular economy involves rethinking traditional linear models of production and consumption and embracing a more holistic and regenerative approach.

In a circular economy forum, participants engage in dialogue, share knowledge and best practices, and collaborate on initiatives that promote the principles of a circular economy. Discussions may focus on a wide range of topics, such as eco-design, resource efficiency, waste management, recycling and upcycling, sustainable business models, and innovative technologies.

By bringing diverse stakeholders together, circular economy forums foster collaboration and the exchange of ideas, leading to the identification of opportunities, challenges, and potential solutions for transitioning to a more circular and sustainable economy. These forums play a crucial role in driving collective action, encouraging innovation, and promoting the adoption of circular economy principles at various levels, from policy-making to business strategies and everyday practices.

Circular Economy Guidelines

A circular economy refers to an economic system that aims to minimize resource consumption and waste generation while maximizing the use of resources through a continuous cycle of reuse, repair, recycling, and regeneration. This sustainable approach promotes the notion of "closing the loop" by designing products and processes that ensure materials and resources remain in circulation for as long as possible.

In a circular economy, products are designed with durability, recyclability, and eco-friendly materials in mind. The focus is on shifting from a linear, take-make-dispose model to a closed-loop system that reduces the extraction of new resources and the generation of waste. Key principles of a circular economy include:

- Extending the lifespan of products through repair, refurbishment, and sharing platforms

- Recovering materials and components from discarded products through recycling and upcycling

- Promoting renewable energy sources and reducing greenhouse gas emissions

- Encouraging collaboration and innovation among stakeholders from various sectors, including businesses, policymakers, and consumers.

The transition toward a circular economy presents significant opportunities for sustainable development, including the creation of new business models, job opportunities, and environmental benefits. By adopting a circular approach, businesses and society can simultaneously address environmental challenges, reduce resource dependency, and foster economic growth. Moreover, a circular economy promotes the concept of a regenerative and restorative system that respects planetary boundaries, ultimately contributing to the long-term well-being of both humans and the environment.

Circular Economy Impact Assessment Tools

A circular economy impact assessment tool refers to a method or framework used to evaluate the environmental, social, and economic effects of implementing circular economy practices. It aims to measure the overall sustainability impacts and potential benefits of transitioning from a linear economy model to a circular one.

By employing such tools, businesses, organizations, and policymakers can assess the potential benefits and trade-offs associated with circular economy initiatives. These tools focus on quantifying the impacts of resource circulation, waste reduction, and the adoption of sustainable practices. They consider a broad range of factors, such as greenhouse gas emissions, resource consumption, waste generation, employment generation, and economic growth.

Circular Economy Impact Assessment

The circular economy is an approach towards economic development that aims to maximize the value and utility of resources while minimizing waste and negative environmental impacts. It is a model that seeks to decouple economic growth from the consumption of finite resources, promoting sustainability and resilience.

In a circular economy, products, materials, and resources are kept in use for as long as possible through various strategies such as recycling, refurbishment, remanufacturing, and sharing platforms. The goal is to create a closed-loop system where materials are continuously cycled back into the economy, reducing the need for virgin resources and preventing the accumulation of waste.

Circular Economy Impact Measurement

A circular economy impact measurement refers to the systematic assessment and evaluation of the environmental, social, and economic effects of implementing circular economy practices. The concept of a circular economy emphasizes the need to move away from the traditional linear approach of take-make-dispose and instead adopt a more sustainable model that focuses on preserving resources, reducing waste, and maximizing the value of materials throughout their lifecycle.

In the context of sustainability, measuring the impact of a circular economy helps to quantify the benefits and drawbacks of implementing circular practices. This includes evaluating the reduction in resource consumption and waste generation, the mitigation of environmental pollution, the promotion of sustainable production and consumption patterns, and the creation of new economic opportunities such as job creation and innovation.

Circular Economy Indicators

A circular economy is an economic system that aims to eliminate waste and promote the continual use of resources through a closed-loop system. It focuses on reducing resource consumption, extending product lifespan, and minimizing the amount of waste generated.

Circular economy indicators are metrics used to measure the progress and effectiveness of implementing circular economy principles. These indicators provide valuable information on the environmental, social, and economic aspects of the circular economy, allowing policymakers, businesses, and individuals to track sustainability performance and make informed decisions.

Some common circular economy indicators include:

1. Material and resource efficiency: This indicator measures the amount of materials used per unit of output or value-added. It helps assess the efficiency of resource use and identify opportunities for improvement.

2. Waste generation and recycling rates: These indicators provide insights into the amount of waste generated and the percentage of waste that is recycled or reused. They help gauge the effectiveness of waste management strategies and the progress towards a circular system.

3. Product lifespan and durability: This indicator measures the lifespan of products and their ability to withstand multiple cycles of use. It highlights the importance of designing products that are long-lasting and can be easily repaired, refurbished, or remanufactured.

4. Carbon and environmental footprint: These indicators quantify the greenhouse gas emissions and environmental impact associated with production, consumption, and waste disposal. They help identify areas for carbon and environmental footprint reduction and guide efforts towards more sustainable practices.

By monitoring and tracking circular economy indicators, stakeholders can identify areas of improvement, set targets, and implement strategies to transition towards a more sustainable and circular economic model.

Circular Economy Initiatives

A circular economy is a sustainability initiative that aims to design out waste and pollution, keep products and materials in use, and regenerate natural systems. Unlike the traditional linear economy, which follows a "take-make-dispose" model, a circular economy focuses on closing the loop by prioritizing the reduction, reuse, recycling, and recovery of materials and products.

At the core of a circular economy is the concept of "closing the loop," which means that resources are used more efficiently and for longer periods, creating a continuous cycle of use and reuse. This is achieved through various strategies:

- Designing products and services with a focus on durability, reparability, and recyclability, ensuring that they can be easily disassembled, repaired, and recycled at the end of their life. - Implementing strategies to extend the lifespan of products, such as sharing platforms or leasing arrangements, encouraging consumers to use products for longer rather than buying new ones. - Establishing efficient waste management systems that prioritize recycling and recovery of materials rather than landfilling or incineration. - Promoting the use of renewable resources and energy, reducing the extraction and consumption of finite resources. - Emphasizing the importance of collaboration and cooperation between different stakeholders, including governments, businesses, and consumers, to create a more sustainable and circular economy.

Circular Economy Innovation Challenges

A circular economy innovation challenge refers to the process of identifying and addressing the barriers and opportunities related to transitioning from a linear economy based on resource consumption and waste generation to a circular economy focused on sustainability. This challenge involves generating new ideas and solutions that redefine and optimize the use of resources, reduce waste, and promote sustainable practices.

It requires a systemic and holistic approach to find innovative solutions at all stages of the product lifecycle, including design, production, distribution, consumption, and disposal. The challenge is to develop and implement business models, technologies, and policies that enable the circular flow of materials, energy, and information, while minimizing environmental impacts.

Circular Economy Innovation Contests

A circular economy innovation contest is an organized event or competition that aims to encourage and promote sustainable solutions to resource management, waste reduction, and environmental preservation. The primary objective of such contests is to foster the development of innovative ideas, products, or services that adhere to the principles of circular economy.

In a circular economy, the focus is on designing products, systems, and business models that minimize waste and utilize resources efficiently. This approach aims to decouple economic growth from resource depletion, reducing the negative impacts on the environment while creating new economic opportunities. Circular economy innovation contests serve as platforms for individuals, companies, and organizations to showcase their creative approaches towards achieving these goals.

Participants in these contests propose innovative ideas that address various sustainability challenges, such as recycling and upcycling materials, reusing products, extending the lifespan of products through repair and refurbishment, implementing sharing or collaborative consumption models, or designing regenerative systems. The proposed solutions should prioritize resource conservation, carbon neutrality, and promote a shift from the linear 'take-make-dispose' model to a circular and regenerative approach.

Through these contests, participants have the opportunity to receive recognition, support, and funding for their innovative ideas, which can then be implemented in real-world settings. Circular economy innovation contests contribute to the advancement of sustainable development by fostering creativity, collaboration, and awareness around the importance of circular economy principles. They encourage stakeholders from all sectors to think critically and holistically about how to transform current resource management practices towards a more sustainable and prosperous future.

Circular Economy Keynote Speakers

A circular economy keynote speaker is an expert or influencer who is knowledgeable about the principles, strategies, and practices of a circular economy in the context of sustainability. They deliver keynote speeches to educate, inspire, and motivate individuals, organizations, and communities to transition from a linear economy to a circular economy.

In a circular economy, the goal is to design out waste and maximize the value of resources by keeping them in use for as long as possible. The concept is based on the principle of closed-loop systems, where products, materials, and resources are reused, repurposed, remanufactured, or recycled to create a continuous cycle of value. This shift from the traditional linear "take-make-dispose" model contributes to sustainable development, resource efficiency, waste reduction, and the minimization of environmental impact.

>

Circular Economy Knowledge Sharing Platforms

A circular economy knowledge sharing platform is a web-based platform that promotes collaboration and knowledge exchange among individuals and organizations with a common goal of advancing sustainability in the context of circular economy.

These platforms facilitate the sharing of information, experiences, best practices, and expertise related to circular economy principles and practices. They aim to foster a community of like-minded individuals and organizations who are committed to developing and implementing sustainable solutions that minimize resource use, reduce waste, and promote the reuse, recovery, and recycling of materials.

Users of circular economy knowledge sharing platforms can access a wide range of resources, including case studies, research papers, reports, toolkits, and guidance materials. They can also participate in online discussions, forums, and webinars to interact with experts and peers, ask questions, and share insights.

Through these platforms, individuals and organizations can learn from each other, collaborate on projects and initiatives, and identify opportunities for partnerships. They can also stay updated on the latest trends, innovations, and policy developments in the field of circular economy.

In summary, circular economy knowledge sharing platforms play a crucial role in promoting knowledge dissemination, collaboration, and learning in support of sustainable practices and the transition towards a circular economy.

Circular Economy Knowledge Sharing

A circular economy is an economic system that aims to minimize waste and maximize the use of resources. It is based on principles of sustainability and seeks to create a closed-loop system where materials and products are kept in circulation for as long as possible.

In a circular economy, the emphasis is on reducing resource consumption and minimizing environmental impact. This is achieved through strategies such as recycling, reusing, and remanufacturing. Instead of the traditional linear model of take-make-dispose, a circular economy promotes a regenerative approach where materials are continuously recycled and reused, creating a more sustainable and resilient system.

Circular Economy Metrics

A circular economy is an economic system aimed at minimizing waste and maximizing resource efficiency. It is founded on the principles of designing out waste and pollution, keeping products and materials in use, and regenerating natural systems.

Circular economy metrics are a set of measurable indicators that assess the performance and progress of a company, organization, or economy in transitioning towards a circular economy. These metrics provide quantitative data on various aspects of circularity, such as resource consumption, waste generation, recycling rates, and product lifecycles.

One key metric in a circular economy is the percentage of recycled or reused materials in production processes. This measures how effectively resources are kept in circulation and diverted from landfill or incineration. It reflects the ability of an organization or economy to close the material loop and reduce the extraction of finite resources.

Another important metric is the product lifespan or durability. By tracking the average lifespan of products, businesses can determine how long their products remain in use before disposal. Longer lifespans reduce the need for frequent replacements and contribute to resource conservation.

The circular economy metrics also encompass indicators of waste generation and management. Metrics such as total waste produced, waste per unit of output, and the proportion of waste that is recycled or recovered provide insights into how efficiently an organization deals with waste and its potential for resource reutilization.

Furthermore, circular economy metrics assess the adoption of circular business models, such as product-as-a-service or sharing platforms. These models promote resource efficiency by emphasizing access over ownership, encouraging product repair and refurbishment, and facilitating product-sharing among users.

Circular Economy Online Resources

A circular economy is a sustainable economic system that aims to minimize waste and maximize resource efficiency. It is driven by the principles of designing out waste and pollution, keeping products and materials in use, and regenerating natural systems.

In a circular economy, resources are used in a closed loop, where products are designed to be reused, repaired, remanufactured, or recycled instead of being disposed of as waste. This shift away from the traditional linear economy, which follows a take-make-dispose model, is crucial for addressing the environmental challenges we face today.

Circular Economy Optimization Software

A circular economy optimization software is a technological tool that helps businesses and organizations to enhance sustainability and efficiency in their operations by applying principles of the circular economy. The circular economy is an economic model that aims to minimize waste generation and maximize resource utilization by keeping products, materials, and resources in continuous cycles of use, thereby reducing the reliance on raw materials and reducing environmental impacts.

The software uses advanced algorithms and data analysis techniques to enable organizations to optimize their resource usage, product design, production processes, and supply chains. It provides insights and recommendations on how to achieve greater resource efficiency, minimize waste generation, reduce energy consumption, and improve overall environmental performance. By digitalizing and modeling various aspects of the circular economy, the software allows businesses to simulate different scenarios, evaluate the potential impacts, and make informed decisions to drive sustainability improvements.

Circular Economy Partnerships

A circular economy partnership refers to a collaborative and mutually beneficial relationship between organizations, governments, and communities that aims to promote sustainability and reduce waste through the implementation of circular economy principles.

In a circular economy, the traditional linear model of "take-make-dispose" is replaced with a more regenerative approach that focuses on resource efficiency, reuse, recycling, and the creation of new value from waste materials. Circular economy partnerships are formed to harness the power of collective action and cooperation to achieve the goals of a circular economy.

These partnerships involve the sharing of knowledge, expertise, and resources among participating entities to develop innovative and sustainable solutions. For example, businesses can collaborate with recycling facilities to ensure that their products or materials are properly recycled and incorporated back into the production cycle, closing the loop and minimizing waste.

Government bodies can also play a crucial role in facilitating circular economy partnerships by providing policy support, incentives, and regulations that promote sustainable practices and create a favorable environment for circular business models to thrive.

Furthermore, circular economy partnerships can extend beyond organizational boundaries and engage local communities to drive social and environmental change. By involving community members, such partnerships can ensure that local needs and aspirations are considered in the development and implementation of circular economy initiatives.

In conclusion, circular economy partnerships are collaborative endeavors that enable organizations, governments, and communities to work together towards the common goal of achieving sustainability by embracing the principles of a circular economy.

Circular Economy Performance Metrics

A circular economy is an economic system that aims to eliminate waste and regenerate resources in order to create a sustainable and self-sustaining ecosystem. In this context, circular economy performance metrics refer to the measures used to assess the effectiveness and progress of implementing circular economy principles within a given system or organization.

These metrics evaluate various aspects of circularity, such as resource efficiency, waste reduction, and the extent to which materials and products are kept in circulation. They provide quantitative indicators that help track and analyze the performance of initiatives and activities designed to transition towards a circular economy.

Circular Economy Policies

A circular economy is a systemic approach to economic development designed to benefit businesses, society, and the environment. It aims to reduce waste, extend the lifespan of products and materials, and promote the use of renewable resources. Circular economy policies are a set of regulations, strategies, and initiatives implemented by governments or organizations to foster the transition towards a circular economy.

These policies typically focus on three main principles: reducing, reusing, and recycling. They encourage eco-design and innovative product and system design to minimize waste generation and resource consumption. They also promote the development of circular business models, such as product-as-a-service or sharing platforms, to maximize the utilization of resources and minimize their impact on the environment.

Circular economy policies often involve the implementation of extended producer responsibility (EPR) schemes, which oblige producers to take responsibility for the entire lifecycle of their products, including recycling and disposal. They also encourage the establishment of eco-industrial parks and networks, where different companies can exchange waste or by-products to create new value chains.

Furthermore, circular economy policies promote awareness and education regarding sustainable consumption and production patterns, aiming to shift societal behavior towards more responsible choices. They leverage financial incentives and fiscal measures to encourage businesses and individuals to adopt circular practices, such as tax incentives for recycling or fees for landfilling waste.

Circular Economy Principles

A circular economy is an economic system aimed at minimizing waste, reducing resource consumption, and maximizing the use of materials, products, and resources. It is an alternative to the traditional linear economy, which follows a "take-make-dispose" model, resulting in large volumes of waste and pollution.

In a circular economy, the principles revolve around designing products with a focus on durability, repairability, and recyclability. This allows for the circulation of materials and resources within the economy, reducing the need for extracting and producing virgin resources.

One key principle of a circular economy is to promote the reuse and regeneration of products and materials. This involves implementing strategies such as refurbishment, remanufacturing, and product sharing. By extending the lifespan of products and enabling multiple uses, the circular economy can significantly reduce the demand for new resources.

Another principle is to prioritize recycling and resource recovery. This involves implementing efficient recycling systems that allow materials to be recovered and reintroduced into the production cycle. By maximizing the recovery of valuable resources, the circular economy minimizes the need for raw material extraction and reduces environmental degradation.

Additionally, the circular economy emphasizes the importance of renewable energy sources and eco-design. By transitioning to renewable energy, the reliance on fossil fuels is reduced, leading to a lower carbon footprint. Eco-design focuses on creating products and systems that consider the entire lifecycle, from production to disposal, and aim to minimize negative environmental impacts.

Circular Economy Publications

A circular economy is a sustainable economic system that aims to minimize waste, maximize resource efficiency, and promote the use of renewable resources. It is based on the principles of reducing, reusing, and recycling materials and products to create a closed-loop system where the value of resources is maintained for as long as possible.

In a circular economy, products are designed to be long-lasting, repairable, and easy to disassemble and recycle. Materials from end-of-life products are recovered, processed, and used as inputs for new products, reducing the need for virgin resources. This approach not only reduces the environmental impact of resource extraction and waste disposal but also offers economic benefits by creating new business models based on the recovery and reuse of materials.

Circular Economy Regulations

A circular economy is a regenerative system that aims to minimize waste and maximize the efficient use of resources. It is an alternative to the traditional linear economy, where goods are produced, used, and then discarded as waste.

In a circular economy, products and materials are designed and produced with the intention of being used for as long as possible. When they reach the end of their useful life, they are recovered, repaired, or recycled to create new products or materials. This approach keeps resources in use for longer periods, reduces the need for raw materials extraction, and decreases the generation of waste.

Circular Economy Research Papers

A circular economy is a sustainable economic system that aims to minimize waste and maximize the use of resources. In this context, research papers on circular economy examine various strategies and approaches to transition from a linear economy, based on the take-make-dispose model, to a regenerative system that promotes closed-loop flows of materials and energy.

These research papers focus on analyzing the principles, practices, and potential impacts of circular economy strategies in different industries and sectors. They explore concepts such as design for circularity, resource recovery, product life extension, and shifting towards a service-based economy. The papers often assess the economic, environmental, and social implications of adopting circular economy principles and evaluate the effectiveness of specific policies and interventions.

Circular Economy Research

A circular economy is an economic system that aims to maximize the value and utilization of resources throughout their entire life cycle, in order to create sustainable growth and reduce negative environmental impacts.

In a circular economy, the traditional linear approach of "take, make, and dispose" is replaced with a regenerative approach. Resources are kept in use for as long as possible, through strategies such as reuse, repair, remanufacture, and recycling. This not only reduces waste and pollution but also minimizes the extraction of new raw materials and the production of new goods.

Circular Economy Seminars

A circular economy seminar is an educational event focused on promoting sustainable practices within the economy. The seminar aims to facilitate discussions and presentations on the concept of a circular economy, which is a regenerative approach to resource management.

In a circular economy, resources are used efficiently, waste and pollution are minimized, and materials are continually cycles back into the production process. This shift from the traditional linear economy, where resources are extracted, used, and then discarded, aims to create a more sustainable and resilient economic system.

Circular Economy Software Solutions

A circular economy software solution refers to a computer-based program or system that facilitates and supports the implementation of circular economy practices. Circular economy is a sustainable approach aimed at reducing waste, preserving resources, and minimizing environmental impact while promoting economic growth.

Such software solutions are designed to help organizations adopt and execute circular economy strategies by providing tools, analysis, and monitoring capabilities. These solutions enable businesses to track and optimize their resource usage, manage waste and emissions, promote recycling and reusing initiatives, and drive the overall transition from the linear "take-make-dispose" model to a more circular and regenerative one.

Circular Economy Stakeholder Engagement

A circular economy stakeholder engagement refers to the process of involving and collaborating with individuals, organizations, and communities who are affected by, or have an interest in, the transition towards a sustainable and circular economy.

This engagement aims to gather input, feedback, and insights from various stakeholders to inform and shape policies, strategies, and initiatives that promote sustainable practices and minimize waste across all stages of the product lifecycle. Stakeholders may include government agencies, businesses, non-profit organizations, academic institutions, consumers, and local communities.

Circular Economy Standards

A circular economy is a system that aims to minimize waste and maximize the efficient use of resources. It is based on the principles of sustainability and seeks to create a closed-loop system where materials and products are recycled and reused instead of being disposed of after their initial use.

In a circular economy, the emphasis is on designing products with a focus on their entire lifecycle, from production to disposal. This involves considering the materials used, the manufacturing process, and the end-of-life options for the product. The goal is to keep materials and resources in use for as long as possible through recycling, remanufacturing, and refurbishment.

Circular Economy Startups

A circular economy startup is a sustainable business that aims to eliminate waste and promote the efficient use of resources by closing the loop of production and consumption. In a circular economy, products and materials are designed to have a long lifespan, with the intention of keeping them in use for as long as possible through reuse, repair, and recycling.

These startups prioritize the reduction of waste and pollution by implementing sustainable practices throughout their operations. They often adopt innovative business models that encourage circularity, such as product-as-a-service or resource-sharing platforms. Instead of following a linear "take-make-dispose" approach, circular economy startups focus on creating value through the continuous circulation of resources.

Circular Economy Sustainability Assessments

A circular economy sustainability assessment is a formal evaluation that measures the environmental, social, and economic performance of a specific business, product, or process in relation to the principles of a circular economy.

The circular economy is an alternative model to the traditional linear economy in which resources are extracted, used, and then discarded as waste. In contrast, a circular economy aims to maximize the value and utilization of resources by circulating them within the economy for as long as possible through strategies such as recycling, reuse, and repair. Sustainability assessments in the context of a circular economy evaluate how well a company or system is aligning with these principles.

These assessments typically consider multiple dimensions of sustainability. Environmental factors include the use of renewable energy, reduction of greenhouse gas emissions, and minimization of resource extraction. Social factors may include considerations of fair working conditions, social equity, and community engagement. Economic factors assess the financial efficiency and viability of circular practices.

By conducting circular economy sustainability assessments, businesses and organizations can identify areas for improvement and make informed decisions about strategies for transitioning towards a more circular and sustainable economy. These assessments can also help to identify potential risks and opportunities related to environmental and social impacts, as well as economic competitiveness. Ultimately, the goal of a circular economy sustainability assessment is to promote sustainable practices that maximize resource efficiency, minimize waste, and contribute to a more resilient and equitable economy for present and future generations.

Circular Economy Symposiums

A circular economy symposium is an event or conference that focuses on the principles and practices of a circular economy in the context of sustainability. It brings together experts, professionals, scholars, policymakers, and individuals who are interested in advancing the concept and application of a circular economy.

During a circular economy symposium, various aspects of the circular economy are discussed, including its definition, principles, challenges, and opportunities. The symposium provides a platform for exchanging knowledge, ideas, and experiences related to designing and implementing circular economy strategies at both local and global levels.

The symposium typically features presentations, panel discussions, workshops, and networking sessions. Experts from different fields, such as economics, environmental science, business, design, and engineering, present their research and findings on circular economy models, innovations, and best practices. The audience gets a chance to learn about successful case studies, ongoing projects, and emerging trends in the field.

Moreover, the symposium facilitates collaboration and partnership among various stakeholders, including businesses, government agencies, non-governmental organizations, and academic institutions. It serves as a catalyst for driving sustainable development by promoting resource efficiency, waste reduction, recycling, and the reuse of materials.

In conclusion, a circular economy symposium is a platform for promoting and advancing the principles and practices of a circular economy in the context of sustainability. It brings together a diverse range of stakeholders to share knowledge, experiences, and ideas, with the aim of accelerating the transition towards a more sustainable and resilient future.

Circular Economy Technology Advancements

A circular economy is a system that aims to minimize waste and maximize the use of resources through strategies such as recycling, reusing, and remanufacturing. It shifts away from the traditional linear economy model of "take-make-dispose" towards a more sustainable and regenerative approach.

Technology plays a crucial role in driving advancements in the circular economy. With the rapid pace of technological innovations, new and improved solutions are being developed to enhance resource efficiency, reduce environmental impacts, and promote sustainability across various industries.

One key area of technological advancement in the circular economy is in the development of recycling technologies. Advanced recycling techniques, such as chemical recycling and biodegradable materials, are being explored to enable the recovery of valuable resources from waste streams. These technologies help to close the loop by transforming waste into new products, reducing the need for virgin materials and minimizing the environmental footprint.

Another important technology advancement in the circular economy is in the area of product design and manufacturing. The adoption of techniques like modular design, product disassembly, and remanufacturing processes enable products to be easily repaired, upgraded, or refurbished instead of being discarded. This extends the lifespan of products, reduces waste generation, and promotes a more sustainable consumption pattern.

Furthermore, digital technologies and data analytics play a significant role in optimizing resource management and supply chain efficiency. By leveraging data, businesses can identify areas for improvement, enhance traceability, and enable better decision-making in material sourcing, production planning, and waste management. This leads to a more holistic and transparent approach to resource utilization.

Circular Economy Technology Development

A circular economy is a system that aims to eliminate waste and promote the continual use of resources through closed-loop production and consumption processes. It is a sustainable approach that focuses on reducing resource consumption, minimizing waste generation, and maximizing resource efficiency.

In a circular economy, products are designed to be durable, repairable, and recyclable, allowing them to be used for a longer period. The concept encourages the reuse, repair, and recycling of products and materials to create a closed-loop system where waste is minimized, and resources are kept in circulation for as long as possible.

Technology plays a vital role in the development and implementation of circular economy practices. It enables the design of more sustainable products, the optimization of resource use, and the efficient management of waste streams. Some of the key technologies used in the circular economy include:

1. Renewable Energy Systems: Clean and renewable energy sources, such as solar and wind power, are essential for reducing reliance on non-renewable resources and minimizing greenhouse gas emissions.

2. Advanced Recycling Technologies: Innovative recycling technologies enable the recovery of valuable materials from waste streams, allowing them to be reintroduced into the production cycle.

3. Digital Technologies: Internet of Things (IoT), artificial intelligence (AI), and data analytics can optimize resource use, supply chain management, and product life cycle assessments, leading to more efficient and sustainable processes.

The development and adoption of these technologies contribute to the transition towards a circular economy by promoting resource conservation, minimizing environmental impacts, and enhancing overall sustainability.

Circular Economy Toolkits

A circular economy toolkit refers to a set of resources, guidelines, and methodologies designed to facilitate the transition from a linear, unsustainable economic model to a more sustainable and regenerative one. It is a comprehensive collection of tools and frameworks that aims to enable businesses, governments, and communities to implement circular economy principles and practices.

The circular economy, in the context of sustainability, is an alternative to the traditional linear model of production and consumption, which follows a take-make-waste approach. In a circular economy, resources are continuously cycled back into the production process, reducing waste generation, preserving natural resources, and minimizing environmental impacts.

A circular economy toolkit encompasses a range of elements, including awareness-raising materials, educational resources, practical guidance, case studies, and policy frameworks. It offers a systematic and integrated approach to address the challenges and opportunities associated with transitioning to a circular economy.

The toolkit provides stakeholders with the necessary knowledge, tools, and support to implement circular economy principles across various sectors and contexts. It includes strategies for resource optimization, waste reduction, product design for longevity and recyclability, materials reuse and recycling, remanufacturing, and the development of new business models that prioritize sustainability.

Furthermore, a circular economy toolkit fosters collaboration and knowledge sharing among different actors, encouraging dialogue, partnerships, and the exchange of best practices. It facilitates the identification of innovative solutions, the assessment of environmental and social impacts, and the exploration of new economic opportunities.

In conclusion, a circular economy toolkit is a valuable resource for driving the adoption of circular economy practices and promoting sustainable development at local, regional, and global levels.

Circular Economy Training Sessions

A circular economy is a sustainable economic system that aims to minimize waste and maximize the use of resources. It is based on the principles of designing out waste and pollution, keeping products and materials in use for as long as possible, and regenerating natural systems.

In a circular economy, the traditional linear model of production and consumption, which involves extracting raw materials, manufacturing products, and disposing of them after use, is transformed into a closed-loop system. This means that resources are reused, repaired, or recycled, and waste is minimized.

Circular Economy Webinars

A circular economy refers to an economic system that aims to minimize waste and enhance resource efficiency by reducing, reusing, and recycling materials. It seeks to move away from the traditional linear model of "take-make-dispose" towards a more sustainable approach where materials are continually used and kept within the economy for as long as possible.

In a circular economy, products and materials are designed with the intention of being easily repaired, remanufactured, or repurposed once they reach the end of their lifecycle, rather than being discarded as waste. This requires a shift in the way businesses and consumers think about production and consumption, as well as the implementation of innovative practices and technologies.

Circular Economy Workshops And Seminars

A circular economy workshop or seminar is a formal gathering of individuals and experts with the aim of discussing and promoting the principles and practices of a circular economy in the context of sustainability. The workshop or seminar provides a platform for exchanging ideas and experiences, fostering collaboration, and inspiring action towards a more sustainable and circular economy.

During a circular economy workshop or seminar, various topics related to sustainability and circularity are typically addressed. These include but are not limited to: the concept and principles of a circular economy, the benefits and challenges associated with transitioning to a circular economy, case studies and examples of successful circular economy initiatives, strategies and tools for implementing circular economy principles in different sectors and industries, and policy and regulatory frameworks that support the transition to a circular economy.

Circular Economy Workshops

A circular economy workshop is a sustainability-focused event or program that aims to educate and engage participants on the principles and implementation of a circular economy.

In a circular economy, resources are used in a way that eliminates waste and promotes the continual use and reuse of materials, components, and products. The workshop provides a platform for participants to learn about the various strategies and approaches that can be applied to close the loop in the production and consumption cycle.

The workshop typically includes presentations, discussions, and interactive activities that explore topics such as resource efficiency, waste reduction, product design for circularity, and innovative business models. Participants are encouraged to think creatively and critically about the current linear economic model and its negative impacts on the environment and society.

Through the workshop, participants gain a deeper understanding of the potential benefits and challenges of transitioning to a circular economy. They are equipped with knowledge and tools to identify opportunities for circularity in their own industries and communities. The workshop may also provide practical guidance on how to implement circular economy principles, such as through case studies and best practice examples.

Overall, a circular economy workshop serves as a catalyst for change by fostering awareness and inspiring action towards a more sustainable and regenerative economic system.

Circular Fashion Design

Circular fashion design refers to the approach of designing and producing clothing and accessories with the aim of minimizing waste, reducing the consumption of natural resources, and promoting sustainability throughout the entire lifecycle of a product. This concept is an essential part of the circular economy framework, which aims to create a regenerative and restorative system by eliminating the concept of waste and continually cycling materials and resources.

In circular fashion design, the focus is not only on creating durable and high-quality garments but also on extending the lifespan of products. This is achieved through different strategies such as using renewable and recyclable materials, designing for disassembly and repairability, and promoting responsible consumption and product longevity. The ultimate goal is to create a closed-loop system where products are designed to be easily disassembled, repaired, and eventually transformed into new products or materials, thereby reducing the need for extracting virgin resources and generating waste.

Circular Fashion Industry

The circular fashion industry refers to an approach in the fashion sector that aims to minimize waste, pollution, and resource consumption by promoting the reuse, recycling, and regeneration of materials and garments throughout their lifecycle. It is a sustainable alternative to the traditional linear fashion model, which follows a "take-make-dispose" pattern.

In the circular fashion industry, the focus is on creating a closed-loop system where materials and products are continuously kept in use, thereby reducing the need for extracting new resources and minimizing environmental impact. This is achieved through various strategies such as:

- Designing products for durability, repairability, and adaptability, ensuring they last longer and can be easily maintained or transformed.

- Implementing recycling and upcycling processes to convert post-consumer garments and textile waste into new fabrics and products.

- Establishing take-back programs, where consumers can return their used clothing and accessories for reselling, redistribution, or remanufacturing.

- Promoting sharing and rental initiatives, allowing individuals to access and use fashion items temporarily instead of owning them outright.

- Embracing innovative technologies like 3D printing and digital design to reduce material waste and optimize production processes.

The circular fashion industry also emphasizes the importance of transparency and ethical practices throughout the supply chain, ensuring fair wages, safe working conditions, and responsible sourcing of materials. By adopting this sustainable approach, the industry aims to break free from its heavy reliance on scarce resources, harmful production practices, and excessive waste generation, ultimately contributing to a more environmentally friendly and socially conscious fashion system.

Circular Fashion Marketplaces

A circular fashion marketplace is an online platform that facilitates the buying and selling of second-hand or upcycled clothing and accessories. It operates on the principles of sustainability, aiming to create a closed-loop system in the fashion industry by promoting the reuse, recycling, and repurposing of garments.

From both environmental and social perspectives, circular fashion marketplaces play a crucial role in driving sustainable practices. By enabling the sale of pre-owned items, these platforms contribute to reducing the demand for new clothing production, which can be highly resource-intensive and generate excessive waste. They promote the concept of extending a garment's lifespan, ensuring that it remains in use for as long as possible, thereby minimizing its environmental impact.

In addition to promoting the reuse of clothing, circular fashion marketplaces also provide opportunities for upcycling and remanufacturing. They connect consumers with designers and artisans who transform old or damaged garments into new, fashionable products. By giving these items a second life, they divert materials from landfills and reduce the demand for virgin resources.

Furthermore, circular fashion marketplaces contribute to the ethical and social aspects of sustainability. They empower individuals to participate in the circular economy by selling their own unwanted clothing or by purchasing second-hand items at affordable prices. This supports a more equitable and inclusive fashion industry, as it allows people of varying financial backgrounds to access quality clothing and reduces the reliance on exploitative fast-fashion practices that often disregard worker rights.

Circular Fashion Rental Platforms

A circular fashion rental platform is a sustainable alternative to traditional fashion consumption models, which promotes the reuse and circulation of clothing items instead of their disposal. It operates on a rental business model, allowing customers to borrow clothes and accessories for a specific period of time, typically ranging from a few days to several weeks.

These platforms contribute to sustainability by reducing the demand for new clothes and minimizing the environmental and social impacts associated with fast fashion. By extending the life cycle of garments, they help to conserve resources, reduce waste, and decrease pollution caused by the production and disposal of clothing. By encouraging the use of pre-owned items, they also reduce the consumption of raw materials and the energy needed to manufacture new garments.

Circular Product Certification

Circular product certification refers to a formal recognition system that verifies and validates products based on their adherence to sustainability principles and circular economy practices. This type of certification aims to promote and encourage the design, production, use, and disposal of products in a way that minimizes environmental impact, conserves resources, and maximizes value retention.

The certification process involves thorough assessment and evaluation of a product's lifecycle, taking into account factors such as its materials, production methods, energy efficiency, durability, repairability, recyclability, and overall environmental footprint. It also considers the product's potential for being reused, remanufactured, or recycled to create new products or materials, thus closing the loop and minimizing waste generation.

Circular product certification typically sets specific criteria and performance standards that products must meet to receive certification. These criteria are often developed based on internationally recognized sustainability frameworks or standards, such as the Ellen MacArthur Foundation's Circular Economy Standards or ISO 14021 for environmental labeling. Certification bodies or third-party assessors conduct audits and inspections of product design, manufacturing processes, and supply chains to ensure compliance with these criteria.

By certifying products as circular, manufacturers and brands gain credibility and assurance that their products align with sustainable and circular economy principles. Consumers, businesses, and other stakeholders can confidently choose certified products, knowing that they contribute to resource conservation, waste reduction, and the transition towards a more sustainable and circular future.

Circular product certification plays a crucial role in driving the adoption of circular economy practices across various industries, fostering innovation, and rewarding sustainable product design and production.

Circular Product Lifecycle Design

A circular product lifecycle design is an approach that aims to minimize environmental impacts and promote sustainability throughout the entire lifespan of a product. It involves designing and producing products in a way that considers their entire lifecycle, from raw material extraction to disposal, and seeks to reduce waste, conserve resources, and maximize value.

At the core of circular product lifecycle design is the concept of a circular economy, which emphasizes closing the loop of material and energy flows. This means designing products that can be easily repaired, remanufactured, or recycled, ensuring that valuable materials are kept in circulation for as long as possible. By doing so, the need for extracting new resources is reduced, leading to lower environmental impacts and a more sustainable use of finite resources.

Furthermore, circular product lifecycle design promotes the adoption of eco-design principles, which consider the environmental aspects of a product throughout its entire lifespan. This includes minimizing the use of toxic materials, optimizing energy efficiency, and designing for disassembly, making it easier to separate and recycle different components at the end of a product's life.

By embracing circular product lifecycle design, companies can not only reduce their ecological footprint but also reap economic benefits. By adopting a more sustainable approach, companies can optimize their use of resources, reduce waste management costs, and tap into new business opportunities associated with the development of circular economy strategies.

Circular Product Lifecycle

A circular product lifecycle refers to a sustainable approach to the entire lifecycle of a product, aiming to minimize environmental impact and maximize resource efficiency. Unlike the traditional linear model, where products follow a "take-make-dispose" pattern, a circular product lifecycle seeks to close the loop, ensuring that materials and resources are continuously reused, recycled, or repurposed.

In a circular product lifecycle, the design and manufacturing phase takes into consideration the product's end-of-life possibilities, aiming to create products that are easy to repair, recycle, and disassemble. This includes using eco-friendly materials, reducing waste, and designing for durability and reusability.

After the product is used, it enters the next stage of the lifecycle, which involves proper disposal, recycling, or repurposing. Here, the focus is on diverting waste from landfill and finding alternative uses for materials. This can include refurbishing, remanufacturing, or upcycling the product or its components, reintroducing them back into the market as new products or materials.

The circular product lifecycle is driven by the principles of sustainability, aiming to minimize resource extraction, energy consumption, and greenhouse gas emissions. By adopting this approach, businesses can reduce their environmental footprint, promote a more resilient and circular economy, and contribute to the long-term well-being of the planet.

Circular Product Take-Back

The circular product take-back is a sustainable practice that aims to promote the responsible management of products throughout their entire lifecycle. It involves the return and recovery of end-of-life products from consumers, which are then recycled, refurbished, or used for other purposes instead of being disposed of as waste.

This practice contributes to the principles of the circular economy, where resources are kept in use for as long as possible and waste generation is minimized. By implementing a circular product take-back system, companies can reduce their environmental impact, conserve valuable resources, and create economic opportunities.

Circular Supply Chain Design

A circular supply chain design is a sustainable approach to managing the flow of resources, products, and information within a network of interconnected organizations. It aims to minimize waste and maximize resource efficiency by creating a closed-loop system where products and materials are continuously recycled and reused rather than disposed of at the end of their life cycle.

This design promotes the principles of sustainability by reducing the environmental impacts associated with traditional linear supply chains, such as resource depletion, pollution, and greenhouse gas emissions. By incorporating circularity into the supply chain, organizations can minimize their reliance on virgin raw materials, decrease the consumption of energy and water, and contribute to the preservation of ecosystems.

Circular Supply Chain Management

Circular supply chain management refers to a sustainable approach that aims to minimize waste, maximize resource efficiency, and close the loop of product lifecycles. It involves the continuous flow and recovery of materials and products across different stages of the supply chain, diminishing the need for virgin resources and reducing the environmental impact of production and consumption.

In a circular supply chain, products and materials are designed, produced, used, and disposed of in a way that minimizes resource extraction, waste generation, and environmental pollution. This is achieved through various strategies such as product design for durability, reparability, and recyclability, as well as the adoption of material recovery and recycling processes.

The circular supply chain management approach emphasizes the importance of collaboration and information sharing among different stakeholders involved in the supply chain, including manufacturers, suppliers, distributors, and customers. It requires proactive engagement and coordination to ensure the efficient flow of materials and products, as well as the proper management of waste and by-products.

By implementing circular supply chain management practices, businesses can contribute to the transition towards a more sustainable and circular economy. This approach offers numerous benefits, including the reduction of resource scarcity, greenhouse gas emissions, and waste generation. It also promotes economic growth and competitiveness by creating new business opportunities, improving resource efficiency, and fostering innovation.

Circular Waste Management Strategies

Circular waste management strategies refer to the practices and approaches employed to minimize waste generation, promote recycling, and maximize resource efficiency in a sustainable manner. The concept follows a circular economy model, which aims to reduce waste, extend the lifespan of products, and close the loop of product lifecycles.

These strategies involve the implementation of various measures at different stages of the waste management process. At the production stage, the emphasis is on designing products with longer lifecycles, using renewable materials, and promoting repairability and upgradability. This minimizes the generation of waste and encourages product longevity.

During the consumption phase, circular waste management strategies focus on reducing waste accumulation. This includes encouraging responsible consumption habits, promoting the sharing economy, and discouraging single-use items. Recycling and composting are essential components of these strategies, as they help divert waste from landfills and enable the recovery of valuable resources.

Furthermore, circular waste management strategies emphasize efficient waste collection and sorting methods. This includes implementing separate waste streams for different materials, such as plastics, paper, glass, and organic waste. By ensuring proper sorting, these strategies enhance the recyclability and reusability of materials.

In conclusion, circular waste management strategies play a crucial role in creating a sustainable future. By valuing resources, minimizing waste generation, and promoting recycling, these strategies aim to create a closed-loop system that reduces the environmental impact of waste disposal and maximizes the use of valuable resources.

Circular Waste Management Systems

A circular waste management system refers to a sustainable approach to managing waste that aims to minimize the use of resources and reduce the impact on the environment. It involves a holistic and integrated approach to waste management, where waste is viewed as a valuable resource that can be reused, recycled, or repurposed.

In a circular waste management system, the focus is on designing and implementing strategies that promote waste prevention, as well as the recovery and reuse of materials and resources. This involves the implementation of practices such as waste segregation, recycling, composting, and energy recovery. It also emphasizes the importance of reducing the generation of waste through product design, extended producer responsibility, and the promotion of sustainable consumption patterns.

This approach to waste management recognizes the interconnectedness between the economy, society, and the environment. It acknowledges that traditional linear waste management systems, which are based on the "take-make-dispose" model, are not sustainable in the long run. Instead, a circular approach aims to close the loop by continually cycling resources back into the production process, reducing the need for virgin materials and minimizing waste generation.

Beyond environmental benefits, a circular waste management system also offers economic opportunities. It can create jobs, stimulate innovation, and contribute to the development of a more resource-efficient and resilient economy. Moreover, it can help reduce the reliance on finite resources, improve resource security, and mitigate the environmental impacts associated with waste disposal.

Circular Waste-To-Compost Facilities

Circular waste-to-compost facilities are sustainable infrastructure systems that aim to reduce waste and promote the production of compost. In these facilities, organic waste materials such as food scraps, yard trimmings, and agricultural residues are processed through a series of composting techniques to convert them into nutrient-rich compost that can be used as a soil amendment.

These facilities follow a circular approach to waste management by diverting organic waste from landfills and incineration, which contribute to greenhouse gas emissions and environmental pollution. Instead, the waste is segregated, treated, and transformed into valuable compost that can replenish soil health and support agricultural practices.

By implementing circular waste-to-compost facilities, communities can achieve several sustainability goals. Firstly, the reduction of organic waste in landfills reduces methane emissions, a potent greenhouse gas that contributes to climate change. Secondly, producing compost from organic waste minimizes the need for synthetic fertilizers, thereby reducing the reliance on fossil fuel-based inputs and the associated carbon emissions. Thirdly, the utilization of compost in agriculture enhances soil fertility, promotes healthy plant growth, and reduces the need for chemical pesticides and herbicides, leading to more sustainable farming practices.

Circular waste-to-compost facilities can also contribute to a localized circular economy by creating job opportunities in waste management, promoting eco-friendly practices, and closing the nutrient loop in local food systems. Overall, these facilities play a crucial role in the transition towards a more sustainable and regenerative approach to waste management, fostering a circular economy that minimizes waste, conserves resources, and promotes environmental stewardship.

Circular Waste-To-Energy Facilities

Circular waste-to-energy facilities are sustainable infrastructure systems that convert waste materials into energy through a circular economy approach, aiming to minimize environmental impact and promote resource efficiency.

These facilities employ advanced technologies to convert various types of waste, such as biomass, organic waste, and non-recyclable waste, into clean and renewable energy sources, such as electricity, heat, and biofuels. The circular approach refers to the utilization of waste as a valuable resource in a closed loop system, where waste is diverted from landfill and transformed into energy, reducing the need for fossil fuel-based energy production.

Key components of circular waste-to-energy facilities include waste sorting and separation processes, pre-treatment of feedstock, advanced conversion technologies (e.g., thermal or biological processes), energy recovery systems, and emissions control systems. These facilities operate with a focus on maximizing energy output while minimizing environmental impacts, ensuring sustainable waste management practices.

By harnessing the energy potential of waste, circular waste-to-energy facilities contribute to the reduction of greenhouse gas emissions, mitigate climate change, and reduce reliance on fossil fuel-based energy sources. Moreover, these facilities play a crucial role in waste management, diverting waste from landfills and reducing the need for conventional waste disposal methods that contribute to environmental pollution.

In conclusion, circular waste-to-energy facilities represent a sustainable solution for waste management and energy production, aligning with the principles of a circular economy and contributing to the transition towards a more sustainable and resource-efficient future.

Circular Waste-To-Energy Solutions

Circular waste-to-energy solutions are sustainable techniques that aim to convert waste materials into useful energy while minimizing environmental impact. This concept promotes a circular economy approach where waste is no longer viewed as disposable but as a valuable resource that can be recycled and repurposed.

These solutions involve the use of advanced technologies to efficiently extract energy from different types of waste, such as organic materials, plastics, and biomass. The waste is first segregated and processed to remove any non-combustible or hazardous components. Then, it undergoes a thermal treatment process, such as combustion, gasification, or pyrolysis, which converts the waste into thermal energy or electricity.

Utilizing waste-to-energy solutions not only helps in reducing the amount of waste sent to landfills but also addresses the increasing demand for energy in a sustainable manner. These systems contribute to the reduction of greenhouse gas emissions by reducing the need for fossil fuels and promoting the use of renewable energy sources. Additionally, the residue generated from the process, such as ash or slag, can often be used in construction materials or as a fertilizer, further closing the waste loop.

Implementing circular waste-to-energy solutions requires a comprehensive approach that involves waste management infrastructure, technological advancements, and policy support. By embracing these solutions, societies can transition towards a more sustainable and resource-efficient future, where waste is no longer a burden but a valuable resource for energy production.

Circular Waste-To-Renewable Energy Solutions

Circular waste-to-renewable energy solutions refer to sustainable systems that aim to transform waste materials into usable forms of energy, closing the loop of the resource cycle. It involves the conversion of various types of waste, such as organic waste, agricultural residues, or even industrial byproducts, into renewable sources of energy, including bioenergy, biogas, or electricity.

These solutions are an integral part of the circular economy framework, which promotes the efficient use of resources and the reduction of waste generation. By diverting waste from landfills or incineration facilities and utilizing it as a feedstock for energy production, circular waste-to-renewable energy solutions mitigate environmental degradation, reduce greenhouse gas emissions, and contribute to a more sustainable and resilient energy system.

Circular Waste-To-Renewable Energy Systems

Circular waste-to-renewable energy systems refer to sustainable processes that involve the conversion of waste materials into renewable energy sources. These systems aim to reduce waste generation, minimize resource depletion, and mitigate the negative environmental impacts associated with conventional waste management practices.

By adopting a circular approach, waste materials such as organic waste, agricultural residues, and municipal solid waste are diverted from traditional disposal methods, such as landfilling or incineration, and are instead utilized to generate renewable forms of energy. This waste-to-energy conversion process typically involves advanced technologies such as anaerobic digestion, thermal conversion, and biomass gasification.

Circular Water Conservation Measures

Circular water conservation measures refer to strategies and practices aimed at minimizing water wastage, optimizing water use efficiency, and recycling water resources within a sustainability framework. The concept of circular water conservation recognizes that water is a finite resource that needs to be managed in a holistic and cyclical manner to ensure its long-term availability and quality.

These measures encompass a range of actions, including reducing water consumption through efficient technologies and practices, promoting water reuse and recycling, and adopting innovative water management approaches. Examples of circular water conservation measures include collecting and storing rainwater for irrigation or toilet flushing, implementing water-efficient appliances and fixtures, treating and reusing wastewater for non-potable purposes such as industrial processes or landscape irrigation, and integrating water-sensitive design principles in urban planning.

Circular Water Conservation Systems

Circular water conservation systems are sustainable approaches to conserving and efficiently utilizing water resources. These systems aim to create a closed-loop water cycle that minimizes water wastage and maximizes water reuse within a given community or facility.

At the heart of circular water conservation systems is the concept of circularity, which is based on the principles of reduce, reuse, and recycle. These systems ensure that water is treated as a valuable resource and not as a disposable commodity. Instead of relying solely on traditional linear water management practices that involve extraction, use, and disposal, circular systems focus on turning wastewater into a valuable resource.

In a circular water conservation system, wastewater is collected, treated, and purified to remove impurities, pathogens, and contaminants. This treated water, also known as reclaimed water or recycled water, can then be utilized for various non-potable purposes, such as irrigation, industrial processes, toilet flushing, and street cleaning. By reusing reclaimed water, the demand for fresh water decreases, reducing the strain on natural water sources.

In addition to reclaiming and reusing water, circular systems also emphasize water efficiency through the implementation of water-saving technologies and practices. These may include low-flow fixtures, rainwater harvesting systems, greywater recycling, and water-efficient appliances. By reducing water consumption, circular water conservation systems contribute to preserving freshwater ecosystems, mitigating water scarcity, and promoting overall sustainability.

Circular Water Purification Measures

Circular water purification measures refer to a set of sustainability-focused strategies and techniques aimed at preserving and efficiently utilizing water resources. These measures are designed to create a closed-loop system where water is continuously treated and reused, reducing the reliance on freshwater sources and minimizing waste.

One key aspect of circular water purification measures is the implementation of advanced water treatment technologies. This involves the use of innovative filtration systems, such as membrane filtration, reverse osmosis, and activated carbon filtration, to remove impurities, contaminants, and pollutants from wastewater and other water sources. By adopting these technologies, water can be purified to a high standard, making it suitable for various non-potable applications, such as irrigation, industrial processes, and toilet flushing.

Another crucial component of circular water purification measures is the implementation of water reuse and recycling systems. This involves collecting, treating, and reusing wastewater and other water sources within the same area or facility. By collecting and treating wastewater on-site, water can be redirected back into the system for secondary uses, reducing the demand for freshwater sources.

In addition to technological solutions, circular water purification measures also incorporate sustainable water management practices. This includes implementing water-efficient technologies and practices, such as rainwater harvesting, graywater recycling, and water-efficient fixtures, to reduce overall water consumption and minimize water waste.

Circular Water Purification Systems

Circular water purification systems are sustainable technologies that aim to efficiently treat and manage wastewater while minimizing environmental impact and promoting resource conservation. These systems use an integrated approach to water treatment and reuse, taking into account the entire water cycle and utilizing various physical, chemical, and biological processes.

The main objective of circular water purification systems is to close the water loop by recovering, treating, and reusing water resources in a sustainable and cost-effective manner. These systems prioritize the reduction of water consumption, pollution prevention, and the recovery of valuable resources from wastewater.

By adopting circular water purification systems, communities can achieve multiple benefits. Firstly, it helps to alleviate water scarcity by reducing the reliance on freshwater sources. Secondly, it minimizes the discharge of untreated or poorly treated wastewater into natural ecosystems, protecting water quality and biodiversity. Thirdly, these systems facilitate the recovery of nutrients, such as nitrogen and phosphorus, from wastewater, which can be used as valuable resources for agricultural purposes.

Furthermore, circular water purification systems contribute to the reduction of energy consumption and greenhouse gas emissions, as they often employ innovative technologies such as anaerobic digestion and membrane filtration. This not only reduces the environmental footprint but also improves the overall efficiency of the water treatment process.

In conclusion, circular water purification systems play a vital role in achieving sustainable water management. By integrating various treatment processes and promoting the reuse of water resources, these systems help conserve precious freshwater supplies, protect ecosystems, and create a more sustainable future.

Circularity Assessment

Circularity assessment refers to the evaluation of a system, process, or product in terms of its ability to operate within the principles of a circular economy, with the aim of minimizing resource use, waste generation, and environmental impact. Circular economy is an alternative to the traditional linear economy, where resources are extracted, used, and disposed of, resulting in a high level of waste and resource depletion.

The assessment involves analyzing the entire lifecycle of a product or system, including raw material extraction, production, distribution, use, and end-of-life management. It examines the extent to which resources are being used efficiently, waste is being minimized, and materials are being recycled or reused. This assessment helps to identify areas for improvement and guide the transition towards a more sustainable and circular system.

Circularity Auditing

Circularity auditing refers to the evaluation and assessment of the circularity of a system or process in the context of sustainability. It involves the examination of the inputs, outputs, and overall resource flows within a system to determine its level of circularity. The goal of circularity auditing is to identify areas for improvement and to optimize the efficiency and effectiveness of resource use.

Through circularity auditing, organizations can gain insights into their current resource consumption patterns and identify opportunities for implementing circular economy principles. This evaluation process enables companies to identify wasteful practices, reduce resource consumption, and minimize environmental impacts. By understanding the circularity of a system, organizations can identify ways to design out waste, keep materials and products in use, and regenerate natural systems.

Circularity Education

Circularity education is a form of education that focuses on promoting sustainable and regenerative practices within our economic systems. It aims to shift the traditional linear approach of "take-make-dispose" towards a circular model that encourages the reuse, recycle, and repurpose of resources.

By providing individuals with the knowledge and skills necessary to understand the concepts and principles behind circularity, this form of education empowers them to contribute to a more sustainable future. It emphasizes the importance of reducing waste, minimizing resource consumption, and designing products with a focus on durability and recyclability.

The objective of circularity education is to create a mindset shift among individuals, businesses, and communities, instilling a deeper understanding of the interconnectedness between our actions and the environment. It encourages critical thinking and problem-solving skills to identify innovative solutions that support the circular economy principles.

This type of education can be integrated into various educational levels, from schools to universities and vocational training. It covers a range of topics including waste management, product design, supply chain management, and sustainable business practices. By equipping learners with the necessary knowledge and competencies, circularity education enables them to make informed decisions and actively participate in efforts to create a more sustainable and regenerative society.

Furthermore, circularity education also aims to foster collaboration and collective action among learners by emphasizing the importance of partnerships and engaging stakeholders from different sectors. Through this collaborative approach, circularity education seeks to create a systemic change towards a more sustainable and circular economy.

Circularity In Electronics Industry

Circularity in the electronics industry refers to a sustainable approach that aims to minimize waste, maximize resource efficiency, and promote the reuse, repair, and recycling of electronic products and components. It involves closing the loop of the product lifecycle, shifting away from the traditional linear model of "take, make, and dispose" towards a more circular and regenerative system. In this context, circularity emphasizes the need to design electronic products with durability, modularity, and recyclability in mind. This means creating devices that are more easily repairable, upgradeable, and standardized, enabling longer lifetimes and reducing the need for premature disposal. It also involves the responsible sourcing of materials, prioritizing those with low environmental impact and high recyclability. Furthermore, circularity promotes the establishment of effective collection and recycling systems for electronic waste. This includes the development of proper infrastructure and the implementation of efficient processes to ensure that discarded electronics are safely collected, treated, and either refurbished or recycled. By doing so, valuable materials can be recovered, reducing the extraction of raw resources and minimizing the associated environmental and social impacts. Circularity in the electronics industry is also closely related to the concept of the sharing economy. Promoting the sharing or leasing of electronic products and facilitating second-hand markets encourages extended product use and reduces the overall demand for new devices. This approach helps to reduce the environmental footprint associated with manufacturing new electronics while also providing more affordable options for consumers. Overall, circularity in the electronics industry aims to create a more sustainable and responsible system that minimizes waste, promotes resource efficiency, and aligns with the principles of the circular economy. By closing the loop, the industry can contribute to a more sustainable future, addressing the challenges posed by electronic waste and resource depletion.>

Circularity In Fashion Industry

Circularity in the fashion industry refers to the idea of creating a closed-loop system, where resources and materials are continuously recycled, reused, or repurposed, in order to minimize waste and reduce the environmental impact of the industry.

The concept of circularity focuses on shifting away from the traditional linear model of production and consumption, which follows a "take-make-dispose" approach. Instead, it promotes a more sustainable and regenerative approach, where products are designed to be durable, repairable, and made from recyclable or biodegradable materials.

Circularity In The Aerospace Industry

Circularity in the aerospace industry refers to the paradigm shift towards a sustainable and regenerative approach to design, production, and operation of aerospace systems and services. It aims to create a closed-loop system where resources are continuously recycled and waste is minimized, ultimately reducing the industry's environmental footprint.

This concept of circularity aligns with the principles of the circular economy, focusing on three main pillars: reduce, reuse, and recycle. In the aerospace industry, this means designing products and processes that prioritize resource efficiency, durability, and reparability. By implementing a circular economy model, the industry can minimize the extraction and consumption of raw materials, optimize the use of existing resources, and mitigate waste generation.

Circularity In The Automotive Industry

Circularity in the automotive industry refers to the implementation of sustainable practices and principles aimed at reducing waste, minimizing resource consumption, and promoting the reuse, repair, and recycling of materials throughout the entire lifecycle of vehicles.

This concept is centered around the idea of creating a closed-loop system, where materials and components are continuously circulated within the industry, rather than being discarded as waste. It involves strategies such as designing vehicles for disassembly and recyclability, utilizing renewable and recyclable materials, and implementing efficient manufacturing processes.

Circularity In The Biotechnology Sector

Circularity in the biotechnology sector refers to the concept of utilizing resources in a closed-loop system to minimize waste, reduce environmental impact, and promote sustainable practices.

In this context, circularity aims to optimize the use of resources throughout the life cycle of biotechnological products and processes. It involves designing and implementing strategies that enable the recovery, reuse, and recycling of materials, energy, and waste. By adopting circular approaches, the biotechnology sector can contribute to a more sustainable future by reducing its reliance on finite resources, minimizing pollution, and lowering greenhouse gas emissions.

Circularity In The Chemical Industry

Circularity in the chemical industry refers to the concept of creating a closed-loop system where resources and materials are continuously recycled and reused, minimizing waste generation and reducing the reliance on finite resources. This approach aims to promote sustainable practices, reduce environmental impact, and enhance the industry's overall efficiency.

In a circular chemical industry, products and materials are designed to be recyclable, renewable, and biodegradable. This involves adopting innovative processes and technologies that enable the recovery, regeneration, and repurposing of valuable resources. By implementing circularity principles, the industry can eliminate or minimize the extraction of raw materials from the environment, reduce the consumption of energy and water, and minimize the release of harmful substances into ecosystems.

Circularity In The Construction Sector

Circularity in the construction sector refers to the adoption of sustainable practices that aim to minimize waste, maximize resource efficiency, and promote the continuous use and reuse of materials throughout the entire life cycle of buildings and infrastructure.

By embracing circularity, the construction industry strives to reduce its environmental impact and contribute to the attainment of long-term sustainability goals. This involves a shift from the prevailing linear model, which is characterized by the extraction of raw materials, manufacturing, construction, use, and eventual disposal. Instead, a circular approach focuses on the principles of reduce, reuse, and recycle, prioritizing the preservation of resources and the prevention of waste.

Circularity In The Electronics Sector

Circularity in the electronics sector refers to the practice of designing, producing, using, and disposing of electronic devices in a way that maximizes resource efficiency, minimizes waste generation, and promotes the reuse, repair, and recycling of products throughout their life cycle. It is a concept rooted in the principles of sustainability, aiming to minimize the negative environmental impacts of electronics while optimizing their economic and social benefits.

At its core, circularity in the electronics sector entails a shift away from the traditional linear model of production and consumption, which involves the extraction of raw materials, manufacturing of products, use by consumers, and disposal in landfills or incineration. Instead, it promotes a closed-loop system where products are designed for durability, modularity, and recyclability, enabling the recovery and reintegration of valuable materials back into the production cycle.

Circularity In The Energy Industry

Circularity in the energy industry refers to the concept of creating a sustainable and regenerative system that minimizes waste and optimizes resource utilization throughout the entire energy value chain. It involves designing and implementing strategies that aim to close the loop on energy production, consumption, and waste disposal, focusing on the principles of reduce, reuse, and recycle.

In a circular energy system, renewable energy sources are utilized to generate power, such as solar, wind, hydro, and geothermal energy, which have minimal environmental impact compared to fossil fuels. The emphasis is on harnessing these clean energy sources efficiently and effectively to meet the energy needs of society while minimizing the carbon footprint.

Energy efficiency plays a crucial role in circularity, as it aims to maximize the output from energy sources while minimizing the input required. This can be achieved through the adoption of energy-efficient technologies, improved infrastructure, and optimizing energy consumption patterns. By reducing the overall energy demand, circularity in the energy industry can contribute to the sustainability goals by lessening the strain on natural resources and reducing greenhouse gas emissions.

Circularity In The Food Industry

Circularity in the food industry refers to the implementation of sustainable practices in the production, consumption, and disposal of food, with the aim of minimizing waste and maximizing resource efficiency. It involves the concept of closing the loop in the food system, where all the waste generated from production and consumption is treated as a valuable resource and reintegrated back into the system.

At its core, circularity in the food industry focuses on reducing the linear model of "take-make-dispose" and instead embraces a circular model where the byproducts and waste from one process become inputs for another. This approach aims to eliminate the concept of waste by turning food waste, packaging waste, and other byproducts into valuable resources.

Circularity In The Manufacturing Sector

Circularity in the manufacturing sector refers to the practice of closing the loop in the production and consumption processes by minimizing waste and maximizing the reuse, recycling, and regeneration of resources. It is a key principle of sustainability that aims to create a more efficient and environmentally conscious manufacturing industry.

In a circular manufacturing system, products are designed to be durable, repairable, and recyclable. Materials and resources are used efficiently, and waste is minimized. Instead of following a linear production model where resources are extracted, used, and disposed of, circularity promotes a closed-loop approach where materials are kept in use for as long as possible.

By implementing circularity in the manufacturing sector, companies can reduce their environmental impact and decrease reliance on finite resources. They can minimize the extraction of raw materials, reduce energy consumption, and lower greenhouse gas emissions associated with production. Circular manufacturing also opens up opportunities for new business models, such as take-back programs, remanufacturing, and product-as-a-service offerings.

Furthermore, circularity in the manufacturing sector promotes economic growth and job creation by fostering innovation and the development of sustainable technologies. It encourages collaboration and integration across different industries, promoting a more holistic and resilient manufacturing ecosystem.

Circularity In The Mining Sector

Circularity in the mining sector refers to the principles and practices that aim to minimize resource extraction and waste generation, while maximizing the reuse, recycling, and restorative activities within the sector. It is an approach that aligns with the concept of sustainability by promoting the efficient use of resources and reducing the environmental impact associated with mining activities.

In a circular mining economy, the traditional linear model of extraction, production, consumption, and disposal is transformed into a closed-loop system where materials and resources are continuously circulated and utilized. This requires the adoption of strategies and technologies that prioritize resource efficiency, waste reduction, and the recovery and recycling of valuable materials.

Implementing circularity in the mining sector involves several key elements. Firstly, it requires the implementation of sustainable mining practices that focus on reducing the environmental impact of mining operations and improving resource efficiency. This includes measures such as minimizing waste generation, optimizing energy and water use, and rehabilitating and restoring mined areas.

Additionally, circularity involves the promotion of responsible and sustainable sourcing of materials, including the use of recycled or secondary raw materials. This reduces the reliance on primary material extraction and minimizes the associated environmental and social impacts.

Furthermore, circularity in the mining sector entails the development of innovative technologies and processes that enable the extraction and recovery of valuable minerals and materials from waste and by-products. This includes the exploration and utilization of new extraction techniques and the implementation of advanced separation and refining technologies.

Overall, circularity in the mining sector is a crucial aspect of sustainable development as it aims to balance the economic benefits of resource extraction with the environmental and social considerations. It enables the mining sector to contribute to a more sustainable and resource-efficient economy by maximizing the value of resources, reducing waste, and minimizing the overall environmental footprint.

Circularity In The Pharmaceutical Industry

Circularity in the pharmaceutical industry refers to the implementation of sustainable practices that promote resource efficiency and reduce environmental impact throughout the life cycle of pharmaceutical products. It involves the adoption of a circular economy approach, which aims to

71

minimize waste generation, maximize the use of renewable resources, and promote the reuse, recycling, and recovery of materials and by-products.

Pharmaceutical circularity encompasses various strategies and initiatives, such as eco-design, green procurement, extended producer responsibility, and the development of closed-loop systems. Eco-design involves designing pharmaceutical products with a focus on reducing their environmental footprint, such as using recyclable packaging materials or minimizing the use of hazardous substances. Green procurement refers to the sourcing of sustainable and environmentally-friendly materials, components, and services, while extended producer responsibility entails manufacturers taking responsibility for the entire life cycle of their products, including their disposal and recycling.

Circularity in the pharmaceutical industry is crucial for achieving sustainable development goals and addressing environmental challenges. By promoting resource efficiency and reducing waste generation, circular practices help conserve natural resources, reduce greenhouse gas emissions, and minimize pollution. Moreover, the adoption of circularity can contribute to the development of a resilient and sustainable healthcare system, ensuring the availability of safe and effective medicines while minimizing the industry's environmental impact.

Overall, pharmaceutical circularity is a fundamental pillar of sustainable development in the industry, aiming to prioritize eco-friendly practices, minimize waste, and promote the efficient use of resources throughout the life cycle of pharmaceutical products.

Circularity In The Renewable Energy Industry

Circularity in the renewable energy industry refers to the concept of closing the loop in resource use, maximizing the efficiency and longevity of materials, and minimizing waste and environmental impacts throughout the lifecycle of renewable energy systems. This approach aligns with the principles of sustainability by reducing the reliance on finite resources, promoting a regenerative and restorative economy, and mitigating the negative effects of climate change.

In the context of renewable energy, circularity involves designing, producing, and managing energy systems in a way that prioritizes the reuse, recycling, and repurposing of materials. This means moving away from the linear "take-make-dispose" model and embracing a circular economy framework, where resources are kept in use for as long as possible, their value is maintained through continuous loops of reuse, and waste is minimized.

By implementing circular practices in the renewable energy industry, various benefits can be achieved. Firstly, it helps to reduce the demand for raw materials, as existing resources are reused or recycled. This reduces the environmental impact associated with resource extraction, such as land degradation and water pollution.

Secondly, circularity promotes energy efficiency by ensuring that materials and components are used to their fullest potential. This includes extending the lifespan of renewable energy systems through maintenance, repair, and refurbishment, as well as repurposing or remanufacturing components for new applications.

Circularity In The Telecommunications Sector

Circularity in the telecommunications sector refers to the implementation of sustainable practices that aim to minimize resource consumption and waste generation throughout the lifecycle of telecommunications products and services.

It encompasses the adoption of circular economy principles, which prioritize the reduction, reuse, and recycling of materials, as well as the extension of product lifecycles. This approach seeks to shift away from the linear "take-make-dispose" model that characterizes many industries and instead embraces a more regenerative and environmentally friendly system.

Circularity Training Programs

A circularity training program, in the context of sustainability, refers to a structured and educational initiative aimed at promoting and facilitating the adoption of circular economy

72

principles and practices. The program focuses on equipping individuals, organizations, and communities with the knowledge, skills, and tools necessary to transition from a linear consumption model to a circular one.

The training program typically covers various aspects related to sustainability and circularity, including the understanding of the circular economy concept, the identification of circular business models, the implementation of sustainable production and consumption practices, and the mitigation of waste and resource depletion. It may also delve into topics such as eco-design, product life extension, resource recovery, and the creation of closed-loop systems.

This type of training program aims to raise awareness about the environmental and social benefits of the circular economy, such as the reduction of waste generation, the conservation of natural resources, the creation of new economic opportunities, and the promotion of social equity. It seeks to inspire and empower individuals and organizations to rethink their current practices and embrace more sustainable and regenerative approaches.

Through a combination of theoretical knowledge, practical exercises, case studies, and collaborative projects, participants in a circularity training program gain a deeper understanding of the circular economy principles and learn how to apply them in their respective contexts. By acquiring the necessary skills and mindset, they become change agents who can drive the transition toward a more sustainable and circular future.

Clean Energy States Alliance (CESA)

The Clean Energy States Alliance (CESA) is an organization that promotes the adoption and implementation of clean and sustainable energy technologies and practices at the state level in the United States.

CESA works with state governments, private sector partners, and other stakeholders to accelerate the transition to a clean energy future. The organization provides technical assistance, conducts research, offers educational resources, and facilitates collaboration among states to promote the development and deployment of renewable energy, energy efficiency, and other clean energy solutions.

By focusing on state-level action, CESA recognizes the important role that states play in driving the shift towards cleaner and more sustainable energy sources. States have the authority to set renewable energy standards, establish incentives and policies, and implement programs that support the adoption of clean energy technologies. Through its initiatives and programs, CESA aims to support states in developing and implementing effective strategies to reduce greenhouse gas emissions, enhance energy security, and create economic opportunities in the clean energy sector.

CESA also serves as a platform for knowledge-sharing and collaboration among states, allowing them to learn from each other's successes and challenges. By facilitating the exchange of information and expertise, CESA enables states to accelerate their clean energy efforts and achieve their sustainability goals.

Clean Energy For America

Clean Energy for America is a sustainable approach to powering our country that includes the utilization of renewable and non-polluting sources of energy. It aims to reduce our dependence on fossil fuels and minimize the negative impacts these fuels have on the environment, while promoting economic growth and job creation in the clean energy sector.

Clean Energy For EU Islands Initiative

The Clean Energy for EU Islands Initiative is a sustainable development initiative aimed at promoting the transition of European islands towards clean and renewable energy sources. The initiative recognizes that islands face unique challenges in terms of energy supply, as they are often dependent on imported fossil fuels and have limited access to traditional grid infrastructure.

The main objective of the initiative is to support and accelerate the efforts of EU islands in becoming self-sufficient in energy through the use of renewable energy sources such as solar, wind, and hydro power. By reducing reliance on fossil fuels, the initiative aims to promote environmental sustainability, mitigate climate change, and improve the overall quality of life for island communities.

Clean Coal Technology

Clean coal technology, in the context of sustainability, refers to a collection of technologies and methods aimed at reducing the environmental impact of coal-based energy generation. It focuses on minimizing the release of pollutants, including carbon dioxide (CO_2), sulfur dioxide (SO_2), nitrogen oxides (NOx), and particulate matter.

The development of clean coal technology is driven by the need to address the negative consequences of using coal as a primary energy source, including air pollution, greenhouse gas emissions, and health risks. By implementing various strategies, clean coal technology seeks to limit these impacts and improve the overall sustainability of coal-based energy production.

One key aspect of clean coal technology is the deployment of advanced combustion techniques like fluidized bed combustion and Integrated Gasification Combined Cycle (IGCC). These methods help to improve the energy efficiency of coal combustion, reduce emissions, and allow for the capture and storage of CO_2 to prevent it from entering the atmosphere.

Another important component of clean coal technology is the use of pollution control technologies such as electrostatic precipitators, scrubbers, and selective catalytic reduction systems. These systems remove or convert pollutants like SO_2, NOx, and particulate matter before they are released into the air.

Additionally, clean coal technology involves the exploration and utilization of alternative coal resources like coalbed methane and coal-to-liquids conversion processes. These approaches not only enhance the efficiency of coal utilization but also contribute to diversifying energy sources and reducing reliance on fossil fuels.

Clean Cooking Technologies

Clean cooking technologies refer to the use of energy-efficient and low-emission cooking stoves and fuels that aim to reduce the negative impacts of traditional cooking methods on the environment and human health. These technologies are designed with sustainability in mind, as they address multiple interconnected issues, including deforestation, indoor air pollution, climate change, and gender equality.

In many developing countries, traditional cooking methods involve the burning of solid fuels like wood, charcoal, crop waste, or coal in inefficient stoves. This not only contributes to high levels of indoor air pollution but also leads to deforestation, as unsustainable harvesting practices are often employed to meet the growing demand for fuelwood. The use of traditional stoves and fuels also exacerbates climate change, as it releases significant amounts of greenhouse gases into the atmosphere.

Clean cooking technologies, on the other hand, offer sustainable alternatives. Improved cookstoves, for example, are designed to burn fuel more efficiently, reducing fuel consumption and harmful emissions. These stoves often have features like insulated designs and chimneys that help to minimize heat loss and direct smoke outside the cooking area, improving indoor air quality. Additionally, utilizing cleaner cooking fuels such as liquefied petroleum gas (LPG), biogas, or ethanol can further reduce emissions and deforestation.

Clean cooking technologies play a vital role in achieving sustainable development goals, especially those related to health, energy access, and climate change mitigation. They contribute to improved respiratory health for households by reducing indoor air pollution, particularly benefiting women and children who are more exposed to harmful smoke. Moreover, the adoption of clean cooking technologies helps to alleviate energy poverty and enhance energy access, as it reduces the time and effort required for collecting fuelwood. By transitioning to cleaner fuels and stoves, communities also contribute to mitigating climate change by reducing their carbon footprint and preserving forests.

Clean Energy Innovation

Clean energy innovation refers to the development and implementation of new technologies, practices, and approaches that focus on reducing environmental impact and increasing sustainability in the production and use of energy.

It entails the creation and advancement of renewable energy sources such as solar, wind, hydro, and geothermal power, as well as the improvement of energy efficiency in sectors such as transportation, buildings, and industry. Clean energy innovation aims to reduce the reliance on fossil fuels and decrease greenhouse gas emissions, thus mitigating climate change and promoting a more sustainable future.

Clean Energy Microfinance

Clean energy microfinance is a financial mechanism that aims to provide small-scale, affordable, and sustainable energy solutions to low-income individuals and communities. It involves offering microloans to facilitate the purchase, installation, and maintenance of clean energy technologies, such as solar panels, biogas digesters, and improved cookstoves.

The primary objective of clean energy microfinance is to promote energy access, poverty alleviation, and environmental sustainability. By targeting underserved populations who lack access to reliable and affordable energy sources, it helps reduce energy poverty, improve living conditions, and enhance overall well-being. Additionally, it contributes to environmental sustainability by mitigating greenhouse gas emissions and reducing reliance on fossil fuel-based energy systems.

Clean Energy Partnerships

Clean energy partnerships refer to collaborations and alliances between multiple stakeholders, including governments, businesses, and organizations, with the goal of promoting sustainable and renewable energy sources. These partnerships aim to accelerate the transition from fossil fuels to cleaner alternatives, such as solar, wind, hydro, geothermal, and bioenergy.

These partnerships recognize the urgent need to address climate change and reduce greenhouse gas emissions to mitigate the adverse impacts on our planet. By working together, the involved parties can pool resources, share knowledge and expertise, and implement innovative solutions to increase the uptake of clean energy technologies.

The key objectives of clean energy partnerships are to foster research and development in renewable energy, improve energy efficiency, promote policy reforms, and create favorable market conditions for clean energy investments. Through coordination and cooperation, these partnerships can facilitate the deployment of renewable energy projects on a larger scale, making them more cost-effective and accessible to a broader population.

Furthermore, clean energy partnerships often prioritize inclusive and equitable approaches, aiming to ensure that all communities have access to affordable and reliable clean energy solutions. This focus on social and environmental sustainability is crucial for a just energy transition that leaves no one behind.

In conclusion, clean energy partnerships play a vital role in advancing the global sustainability agenda by fostering collaboration, promoting renewable energy technologies, and facilitating the transition to a low-carbon future. Through these partnerships, we can work collectively to mitigate climate change, promote energy independence, and create a more sustainable and resilient planet for future generations.

Clean Energy Policy

Clean energy policy refers to a set of guidelines, regulations, and initiatives implemented by governments or organizations to promote the use of renewable and sustainable energy sources while reducing reliance on fossil fuels and minimizing environmental impact. The objective of clean energy policy is to facilitate the transition to a low-carbon economy, mitigate climate change, and ensure long-term energy security.

This policy encompasses various measures to incentivize the adoption and development of clean energy technologies such as solar, wind, hydro, geothermal, and biomass. It often includes financial incentives, grants, tax credits, and subsidies to promote the generation, distribution, and consumption of clean energy. Additionally, clean energy policy aims to enhance energy efficiency, encourage technological innovation, and support research and development in renewable energy.

Clean Energy Research

Clean energy research refers to the systematic investigation and examination of sustainable energy sources, technologies, and practices with the intention of reducing greenhouse gas emissions, minimizing environmental impact, and promoting long-term energy security. It involves the exploration, development, and improvement of renewable resources such as solar, wind, hydro, geothermal, and bioenergy, as well as the efficient utilization of energy through energy conservation and efficiency measures.

The goal of clean energy research is to accelerate the transition from fossil fuels to cleaner and more sustainable alternatives, in order to mitigate the adverse effects of climate change, enhance energy independence, and create a sustainable future. Through comprehensive studies, experiments, and analysis, researchers aim to better understand the potential of various clean energy sources and technologies, assess their feasibility, and identify ways to overcome technical, economic, and policy barriers to their widespread adoption.

Clean Energy Startups

Clean energy startups refer to newly established companies that focus on developing and providing sustainable energy solutions to address the environmental challenges associated with conventional, fossil fuel-based energy sources.

These startups aim to revolutionize the energy sector by introducing innovative technologies and business models that reduce greenhouse gas emissions, minimize pollution and waste, and promote the efficient use of renewable energy resources, such as solar, wind, hydro, geothermal, and biomass.

Clean Energy Storage Solutions

Clean energy storage solutions are technologies or systems that enable the efficient and sustainable storage of renewable energy. These solutions play a crucial role in addressing the intermittent nature of renewable energy sources, such as solar and wind power, by storing excess energy during times of low demand and making it available when demand is high or there is no direct source of generation.

One of the key challenges facing the widespread adoption of renewable energy is the issue of energy intermittency. Unlike traditional fossil fuel-based power generation, which can provide a consistent and stable supply of electricity, renewable energy sources are dependent on weather conditions and daylight availability. Therefore, energy storage solutions are needed to address the fluctuations in energy generation and consumption.

Clean energy storage technologies can be categorized into various types, including battery storage, pumped hydro storage, compressed air energy storage, and hydrogen fuel cells. These technologies allow for the efficient capture, conversion, and release of energy, thereby ensuring a reliable and continuous supply of renewable power.

The adoption of clean energy storage solutions is crucial for the transition to a more sustainable energy system. By enabling the integration of renewable energy sources into the grid, these technologies help reduce greenhouse gas emissions, improve energy security, and promote the development of a more resilient and decentralized power infrastructure.

In conclusion, clean energy storage solutions are essential for the successful integration and utilization of renewable energy. These technologies provide a means to overcome the limitations of intermittent energy sources and contribute to the overall sustainability of our energy system.

Clean Energy Technology

Clean energy technology refers to the use of renewable energy sources and the development of efficient and sustainable methods to produce and consume energy. It encompasses a range of technologies, practices, and systems that aim to minimize negative environmental impacts while meeting the growing global energy demands.

The primary focus of clean energy technology is to replace traditional, fossil fuel-based energy sources with cleaner alternatives such as solar, wind, hydro, geothermal, and biomass. These renewable energy sources have inherently low or zero emissions of greenhouse gases, reducing the carbon footprint and contributing to the mitigation of climate change.

Clean energy technologies also include advanced and energy-efficient systems for power generation, transportation, and industrial processes. This entails improving energy efficiency, reducing energy waste, and enhancing the use of smart grids, energy storage systems, and electric vehicles.

The adoption and deployment of clean energy technologies play a crucial role in achieving sustainability goals. By supporting the transition to a low-carbon economy, they contribute to the conservation of natural resources, reduction of air and water pollution, and preservation of ecosystems. Additionally, they promote energy independence, stimulate economic growth, and create job opportunities in the renewable energy sector.

In summary, clean energy technology encompasses a wide range of renewable energy sources and energy-efficient systems that aim to reduce environmental impact while meeting energy demands sustainably. Its implementation is essential for achieving a more sustainable and resilient future.

Clean Meat (Lab-Grown)

Clean meat, also known as lab-grown meat or cultured meat, refers to meat that is produced in a laboratory setting through a process known as cellular agriculture. Unlike conventional meat, which is obtained by raising and slaughtering animals, clean meat is produced by cultivating animal cells in a controlled environment. This innovative approach to meat production has emerged as a sustainable solution to address the environmental and ethical concerns associated with traditional livestock farming.

Clean meat offers several sustainability benefits. Firstly, it significantly reduces the environmental footprint of meat production. Livestock farming is a major contributor to greenhouse gas emissions, deforestation, water pollution, and biodiversity loss. In contrast, clean meat production requires fewer resources, such as land, water, and feed, resulting in lower carbon emissions and land use. This sustainable production process also eliminates the need for antibiotics and growth hormones, reducing the risk of antimicrobial resistance and enhancing food safety.

Clean Transportation Initiatives

Clean transportation initiatives refer to sustainable efforts aimed at reducing the environmental impact of transportation systems. These initiatives strive to promote more efficient and less polluting transportation options, such as the use of renewable energy sources, public transportation, cycling, and walking.

The transportation sector is a significant contributor to greenhouse gas emissions and air pollution. To address these environmental challenges, clean transportation initiatives focus on implementing strategies that minimize carbon emissions, improve air quality, and reduce dependence on fossil fuels.

A key aspect of clean transportation initiatives is the promotion of public transportation systems.

Investing in high-quality public transportation networks encourages people to use alternative modes of transportation, reducing the number of private vehicles on the road. Additionally, initiatives to improve infrastructure for cycling and walking aim to create safe and convenient options for short-distance travel, further reducing the reliance on cars.

Another important component of clean transportation initiatives is the advancement of electric vehicles (EVs) and the development of charging infrastructure. By transitioning from traditional internal combustion engine vehicles to EVs, greenhouse gas emissions and air pollution can be significantly reduced. Supportive infrastructure, including charging stations, is essential to facilitate the widespread adoption of EVs.

In conclusion, clean transportation initiatives play a crucial role in promoting sustainable transportation systems. By encouraging the use of public transportation, active modes of transportation, and electric vehicles, these initiatives aim to reduce pollution, improve air quality, and mitigate climate change effects associated with transportation.

Clean Water Access Projects

Clean water access projects are initiatives that aim to provide communities with sustainable access to safe and clean drinking water. These projects are crucial for achieving the goal of water security and ensuring the well-being of individuals and the overall sustainability of the environment.

Sustainability is at the core of these projects, as they focus on implementing long-term solutions that meet the water needs of present and future generations. This involves addressing multiple aspects, including water quality, quantity, and availability, while considering the environmental, social, and economic dimensions.

These projects typically involve the development and implementation of various strategies and technologies to improve water infrastructure, such as constructing wells, water supply systems, and water treatment facilities. Additionally, they may include capacity-building activities that educate and empower communities to manage and maintain their water resources effectively.

Sustainable water access projects also prioritize the consideration of local context and community participation. They engage with stakeholders, including local governments, community leaders, and water users, to ensure that the projects meet the specific needs and aspirations of the communities involved.

By providing clean water access, these projects contribute significantly to various aspects of sustainability. They improve public health by reducing waterborne diseases and improving sanitation practices. They also enhance socio-economic development by freeing up time spent on water collection and allowing individuals, particularly women and children, to pursue education and income-generating activities.

In conclusion, clean water access projects play a crucial role in ensuring sustainable development and water security. Through their focus on long-term solutions, community involvement, and consideration of local context, they contribute to improving the overall well-being of communities and the sustainability of water resources.

Clean Water Filtration Systems

Clean water filtration systems refer to sustainable technologies designed to remove impurities, contaminants, and pollutants from water sources, ensuring the provision of safe and potable water for various purposes. These systems play a pivotal role in addressing water scarcity, promoting environmental conservation, and improving public health.

With sustainability being a primary ethos, clean water filtration systems prioritize the efficient use of resources, including energy and water, while minimizing waste and environmental impacts. They typically employ advanced filtration techniques such as activated carbon, reverse osmosis, or ultraviolet disinfection to remove chemicals, bacteria, viruses, sediment, and other harmful substances from water.

Climate Reality Project

The Climate Reality Project is an organization dedicated to addressing the urgent issue of climate change and promoting sustainability. Founded by former Vice President Al Gore, the project aims to raise awareness about the reality of climate change and empower individuals and communities to take action.

The Climate Reality Project conducts trainings and initiatives worldwide to educate and engage people on the impacts of climate change and the importance of transitioning to a sustainable, low-carbon future. Through its global network of Climate Reality Leaders, the organization seeks to bridge the gap between scientific knowledge and public understanding, encouraging people to become climate advocates in their own communities.

Climate Risk Assessment Tools

Climate risk assessment tools refer to a set of instruments or methodologies used to evaluate and analyze the potential risks and vulnerabilities associated with climate change and its impacts on various sectors and systems, particularly in the context of sustainability. These tools help in understanding the likelihood and magnitude of climate-related risks to inform decision-making processes and develop strategies to mitigate and adapt to those risks.

The primary objective of climate risk assessment tools is to assist policymakers, businesses, and organizations in making informed choices and taking proactive measures to address climate risks. These tools typically involve the collection and analysis of relevant data, such as climate projections, historical weather patterns, and socio-economic indicators, to identify areas and assets that are most susceptible to climate change impacts.

The outputs of climate risk assessments provide valuable information on the potential consequences of climate change, including risks related to extreme weather events, sea-level rise, changes in precipitation patterns, and shifts in temperature. By assessing these risks, decision-makers can identify potential vulnerabilities, prioritize actions, allocate resources, and develop adaptation and mitigation strategies to build resilience and reduce the negative impacts of climate change.

Climate risk assessment tools are multidisciplinary in nature, integrating scientific knowledge, modeling capabilities, and socio-economic analysis. They contribute to a comprehensive understanding of climate-related risks, enable the development of robust policies and strategies, and facilitate the integration of climate change considerations into sustainability planning and decision-making processes.

Climate-Resilient Crop Varieties

Climate-resilient crop varieties refer to plant breeds that are specifically developed and cultivated to withstand and adapt to the challenges posed by climate change and related environmental vulnerabilities. These varieties are designed to mitigate the adverse impacts of changing climatic conditions such as extreme temperatures, erratic rainfall patterns, increased frequency of droughts and floods, and the spread of pests and diseases.

By employing traditional breeding techniques, genetic modification, or a combination of both, climate-resilient crop varieties have characteristics that enable them to maintain productivity, nutritional value, and overall crop quality under stress conditions. These varieties possess traits like heat and drought tolerance, resistance to pests and diseases, and the ability to efficiently utilize water and nutrients. The selection and development process of these varieties also take into consideration the specific needs and conditions of different regions, ensuring that they are well-adapted to local climate conditions.

Climate-Responsive Agriculture Technology

Climate-responsive agriculture technology refers to innovative tools, practices, and systems that are designed to optimize agricultural productivity while minimizing the negative environmental impacts associated with farming.

These technologies focus on adapting agricultural practices to the specific climate conditions of a particular region. They aim to enhance climate resilience, improve resource efficiency, and reduce greenhouse gas emissions in order to support the long-term sustainability of agricultural systems.

Closed-Loop Aquaponics

Closed-loop aquaponics is a sustainable agricultural system that combines aquaculture (the cultivation of fish or other aquatic organisms) with hydroponics (the cultivation of plants in water). In this system, the waste produced by the fish is converted into nutrients for the plants, which in turn filter the water for the fish.

This closed-loop system is environmentally friendly and promotes sustainable practices in several ways. First, it reduces dependency on external inputs such as chemical fertilizers, which are often harmful to the environment. Instead, the fish waste provides the necessary nutrients for plant growth, eliminating the need for additional fertilizers.

Second, closed-loop aquaponics conserves water by recycling and reusing it in a closed system. The water used for the plants is continuously filtered and returned to the fish tanks, reducing the need for frequent water changes. This not only saves water but also prevents the release of potentially harmful chemicals into local waterways.

Third, this system minimizes the risk of disease and pests through natural biological processes. The fish waste provides vital nutrients for the plants, creating a balanced ecosystem that naturally controls pests and diseases. This reduces the need for chemical pesticides and antibiotics, supporting a healthier and more sustainable approach to agriculture.

Closed-Loop Production

Closed-loop production, in the context of sustainability, refers to a circular approach to manufacturing and resource management that aims to minimize waste, reduce environmental impact, and promote long-term sustainability. It involves the continuous recycling and reuse of materials throughout the production process, creating a closed loop where resources are conserved and waste is minimized.

In a closed-loop production system, products are designed with the intention of easy disassembly and material recovery. This allows for the extraction of valuable resources from end-of-life products, which can then be used to create new products or feed back into the production cycle. By implementing closed-loop production practices, businesses can reduce the extraction of natural resources and decrease reliance on virgin materials, contributing to the preservation of ecosystems and the reduction of carbon emissions associated with resource extraction and processing.

Beyond the environmental benefits that closed-loop production provides, it also offers economic advantages. By reusing materials, businesses can reduce production costs and increase efficiency. Additionally, closed-loop systems often require less energy and water, leading to further cost savings. The closed-loop approach also encourages innovation and the development of new, sustainable technologies and materials.

In conclusion, closed-loop production is a key strategy for achieving sustainability in manufacturing and resource management. By implementing this approach, businesses can minimize waste generation, conserve resources, reduce environmental impact, and create economic opportunities for a more sustainable future.

Closed-Loop Recycling

Closed-loop recycling is a sustainable process that involves the collection and reprocessing of waste materials into new products, which can then be recycled again at the end of their life cycle. This process aims to minimize the consumption of finite resources and reduce environmental pollution.

In closed-loop recycling, the materials that are collected for recycling are sorted, cleaned, and processed to remove any contaminants or impurities. The cleaned materials are then transformed into new products through various manufacturing processes. These new products have the same quality and functionality as those made from virgin materials, but with lower environmental impact.

Closed-Loop Systems

A closed-loop system, in the context of sustainability, refers to a system designed to minimize resource consumption, eliminate waste, and promote the efficient use of resources. It is a system where the outputs of a process are reused or recycled within the system, rather than being discarded as waste.

In a closed-loop system, materials or products are viewed as valuable resources that can be reused, repaired, or recycled, rather than being treated as disposable. This approach aims to reduce the reliance on finite resources, minimize environmental impact, and foster a more sustainable economy.

Community Garden Planning

A community garden is a piece of land that is collectively cultivated and maintained by a group of individuals within a community with the aim of promoting sustainable practices and fostering social connections.

The main goal of a community garden is to provide a space where people can grow organic fruits, vegetables, herbs, and flowers in an environmentally friendly manner without the use of harmful chemicals or pesticides. By utilizing sustainable gardening practices such as composting, rainwater harvesting, and companion planting, community gardens reduce the overall environmental impact associated with traditional agricultural methods.

In addition to promoting sustainable food production, community gardens also have social benefits. They bring people of different backgrounds and ages together, creating opportunities for social interactions, cultural exchange, and shared learning. These gardens often serve as vibrant hubs where community members can gather, work together, and support one another.

Community gardens play a vital role in enhancing food security and resilience within communities. They enable individuals and families to access fresh, nutritious produce, especially in urban areas where access to healthy food may be limited. Moreover, these gardens empower individuals to become active participants in their own food production, helping them develop valuable skills and knowledge about sustainable gardening practices.

In summary, community gardens promote sustainability by providing shared spaces where individuals can cultivate their own food in an environmentally responsible way. These gardens not only contribute to food security but also foster social connections and empower individuals to be active participants in creating more sustainable and resilient communities.

Community Solar Initiatives

Community solar initiatives are sustainable energy programs that aim to increase access to renewable energy for individuals who are unable to install solar panels on their own properties. In a community solar project, a large solar array is installed in a centralized location, such as a field or rooftop, and multiple participants can then subscribe to the project and receive credits for the energy produced by their portion of the solar array.

These initiatives promote sustainability by providing an alternative to traditional fossil-fuel based energy sources and reducing greenhouse gas emissions. By pooling resources and sharing the benefits of solar energy, community solar projects allow individuals and communities to contribute to a cleaner and greener future. They enable more people to take advantage of renewable energy, regardless of their income or property ownership, promoting energy equity and democratizing access to clean power.

Community Solar Power Projects

Community Wind Farms

Community wind farms refer to the development and operation of wind energy projects by local communities, typically owned and controlled by the residents, farmers, or businesses within the community. These wind farms harness the power of wind through the use of wind turbines, generating renewable energy that can be used to meet the electricity needs of the community or sold back to the grid.

These projects are driven by the principles of sustainability, seeking to create environmental, social, and economic benefits for the community. From an environmental perspective, community wind farms contribute to reducing greenhouse gas emissions and mitigating climate change by displacing the need for fossil fuel-based electricity generation. By harnessing the power of wind, a clean and abundant resource, these projects promote the transition to a low-carbon energy system.

In terms of social benefits, community wind farms empower local residents by providing an opportunity for community involvement and active participation in renewable energy production. The development of these projects often involves consultations and engagement with community members, ensuring that their perspectives and needs are taken into account. This enhances community resilience and cohesion, fostering a sense of ownership and pride in contributing to a sustainable future.

Economically, community wind farms can have a positive impact by creating local jobs during construction, operation, and maintenance phases. The revenue generated from the sale of electricity can be reinvested in the community, supporting local economies and initiatives. Additionally, community ownership allows for the retention of economic benefits within the community, as opposed to profits being directed solely to external corporations.

Community Wind Power Projects

Community wind power projects are collaborative initiatives that involve local communities in the development, ownership, and operation of wind energy facilities. These projects aim to promote sustainability by harnessing the power of wind to generate renewable energy, reducing reliance on fossil fuels and mitigating the negative impacts of climate change.

Unlike conventional wind energy projects that are typically owned by large corporations or utilities, community wind power projects give local residents, businesses, and organizations the opportunity to have a direct stake in the development and benefits of the project. This involvement can take various forms, including community ownership, cooperative structures, or partnerships between local stakeholders and developers.

By engaging the community in wind power projects, these initiatives foster a sense of ownership and responsibility among residents, leading to increased support for renewable energy in the region. Community wind power projects not only contribute to the diversification of the energy mix but also provide economic, environmental, and social benefits.

Economically, community wind power projects can help stimulate local economies by creating jobs, attracting investments, and generating long-term revenue streams through power sales. Moreover, they contribute to energy independence and price stability by reducing dependence on imported fossil fuels and volatile market prices.

From an environmental perspective, community wind power projects offer a clean and sustainable alternative to fossil fuels. Wind energy is a renewable resource that produces no pollutant emissions or greenhouse gases during operation, thus helping to mitigate climate change and improve air quality.

Furthermore, community wind power projects have social benefits, as they can enhance community resilience, promote education and awareness about renewable energy, and support local priorities and initiatives. These projects often involve consultation and collaboration with local stakeholders, ensuring that the benefits are shared equitably and addressing any potential concerns or conflicts.

Community-Based Renewable Energy

Community-Based Solar Power

Community-based solar power is a sustainable energy initiative that involves the installation and operation of solar panels in a community, with the aim of generating clean and renewable electricity for the benefit of its members. This approach to solar power encourages local participation and cooperative decision-making, ultimately promoting environmental and social sustainability.

By bringing solar power projects to communities, this decentralized energy model enables residents to collectively invest in and benefit from renewable energy generation. Community-based solar power projects often take the form of shared solar installations, where the electricity produced is distributed among multiple households, businesses, or organizations. This allows community members who may not have suitable rooftops or financial resources to still access the benefits of solar energy.

Not only does community-based solar power promote sustainable energy practices, but it also fosters a sense of ownership, empowerment, and social equity within the community. By participating in these projects, individuals can reduce their reliance on fossil fuels, decrease energy costs, and contribute to the overall reduction of greenhouse gas emissions.

Furthermore, community-based solar power offers various economic and environmental advantages. It creates local job opportunities, enhances energy resilience and security, and contributes to the transition towards a low-carbon society. Additionally, these initiatives can promote education and awareness about renewable energy, inspiring communities to embrace cleaner and more sustainable ways of generating electricity.

Community-Based Wind Power

Community-based wind power refers to a sustainable approach to harnessing wind energy within a localized community. It involves the development, ownership, and operation of wind turbines by community members or organizations rather than by large energy corporations.

This approach promotes renewable energy generation and contributes to the overall sustainability and resilience of the community. Community-based wind power projects empower local residents to actively participate in the clean energy transition and reduce their dependence on fossil fuels.

Community-Oriented Public Spaces

Community-oriented public spaces are physical areas that are intentionally designed and created to promote social interaction, cultural expression, and collective engagement among community members. These spaces play a crucial role in enhancing sustainability by fostering a sense of belonging, promoting social cohesion, and facilitating the exchange of ideas and resources within a community.

These public spaces are vital for the well-being and resilience of communities, as they offer a platform for individuals of diverse backgrounds and interests to come together, build relationships, share knowledge, and collectively address local challenges. By providing opportunities for active participation, these spaces empower community members to take ownership of their environment and actively contribute to the sustainable development of their neighborhoods.

Community-Oriented Urban Development

Community-oriented urban development refers to a sustainable approach that prioritizes the well-being and engagement of local communities in the planning, design, and implementation of urban projects. It acknowledges the importance of community input and participation in shaping the future of cities, with the goal of creating inclusive and livable environments.

At its core, community-oriented urban development aims to address the social, economic, and environmental needs of residents, while promoting equity and resilience. It goes beyond traditional top-down approaches, where decisions are made solely by government or private entities, by involving community members in decision-making processes. This collaborative approach allows for a greater sense of ownership and empowerment among residents, leading to more sustainable outcomes.

Community-Oriented Urban Planning

Community-oriented urban planning is a holistic approach to urban development that prioritizes the well-being and participation of local communities while promoting sustainable practices to enhance the quality of life for all residents. This planning strategy recognizes that communities are the primary stakeholders in urban areas and seeks to actively engage them in decision-making processes.

The key principles of community-oriented urban planning include inclusivity, collaboration, and long-term sustainability. Inclusivity ensures that all community members, regardless of socioeconomic background or demographic characteristics, have an equal opportunity to participate in shaping their neighborhoods. Collaboration emphasizes the importance of involving various stakeholders, such as residents, local businesses, non-governmental organizations, and government agencies, in the planning process to ensure diverse perspectives are considered.

The goal of community-oriented urban planning is to create livable, healthy, and sustainable communities. It takes into account social, economic, and environmental factors to achieve a balance between the needs of the present and future generations. This approach promotes the development of mixed-use neighborhoods that integrate housing, parks, schools, and other amenities within walkable distances to reduce automobile dependence and encourage active transportation modes.

Furthermore, community-oriented urban planning focuses on prioritizing green infrastructure, such as green spaces, urban forests, and sustainable water management systems, to enhance environmental resilience and mitigate the negative impacts of climate change. By engaging and empowering local communities, this planning approach fosters a sense of ownership and shared responsibility for the well-being and sustainability of urban areas.

Community-Supported Agriculture (CSA)

Community-supported agriculture (CSA) is a sustainable agricultural model that fosters a direct relationship between farmers and local communities, aiming to address social, economic, and environmental challenges. CSA initiatives involve individuals or families, referred to as shareholders or members, who invest in a farm by purchasing a share or subscription in advance.

By participating in a CSA program, shareholders provide financial support to farmers, which helps cover the costs of production and operating expenses. In return, they receive a regular supply of fresh, seasonal produce directly from the farm. This mutually beneficial arrangement ensures farmers have a reliable market for their crops and consumers have access to locally grown, sustainably produced food.

This sustainable farming approach promotes ecological stewardship by reducing the carbon footprint associated with long-distance transportation and packaging of food. It also encourages biodiversity and soil health through organic and regenerative farming practices that minimize the use of synthetic chemicals, preserve natural resources, and support wildlife habitats.

In addition to environmental benefits, CSA fosters community engagement and empowerment. By connecting consumers with the source of their food, CSA programs educate individuals about the challenges faced by farmers, the importance of sustainable agriculture, and the benefits of consuming fresh, seasonal produce. This direct relationship builds trust and transparency, as shareholders have the opportunity to visit the farm, engage in farm activities, and build personal connections with the farmers.

Overall, CSA promotes a holistic and sustainable approach to food production and consumption by fostering a resilient and mutually supportive relationship between farmers and local communities. By participating in CSA initiatives, individuals contribute to the preservation of local agriculture, the reduction of environmental impacts, and the cultivation of a more sustainable and resilient food system.

Compact Eco-Friendly Housing

Compact eco-friendly housing refers to smaller dwellings that are designed and built with a focus on sustainability and environmental consciousness. These houses are intentionally crafted to have a smaller ecological footprint compared to traditional housing options. The concept of compact eco-friendly housing aligns with the principles of sustainable development, which aim to meet the needs of the present generation without compromising the ability of future generations to meet their own needs.

Compact eco-friendly housing utilizes innovative design strategies and technologies to optimize space and minimize resource consumption. These houses often incorporate energy-efficient appliances, lighting, and insulation, as well as renewable energy systems like solar panels or wind turbines. Additionally, sustainable building materials with low embodied energy, such as recycled or locally sourced materials, are commonly used in the construction of compact eco-friendly houses.

One of the key advantages of compact eco-friendly housing is its reduced ecological impact. The smaller size of these dwellings requires less land and resources, resulting in minimized deforestation, reduced urban sprawl, and preserved green spaces. Moreover, compact housing promotes a more efficient use of resources, as it typically requires less energy for heating, cooling, and maintenance.

From a social perspective, compact eco-friendly housing can contribute to affordable and equitable housing solutions. By providing smaller, more affordable options, these houses can help address housing affordability issues in urban areas where land and housing costs are high. Furthermore, the concept of compact living encourages a sense of community and social connection, as it often involves shared spaces and amenities.

In conclusion, compact eco-friendly housing offers an environmentally conscious and socially sustainable alternative to traditional housing. Through its smaller size, energy-efficiency, and use of sustainable materials, these dwellings minimize their ecological footprint while promoting affordability and community engagement.

Compact Eco-Friendly Offices

A compact eco-friendly office refers to a workspace that is designed, constructed, and operated in a sustainable manner, with the aim of minimizing negative environmental impacts while promoting employee well-being and productivity. It embodies the principles of sustainability by focusing on resource efficiency, waste reduction, and the use of renewable energy sources.

Compactness, in the context of eco-friendly offices, refers to the efficient use of space to minimize the office's physical footprint. This involves optimizing the layout and design to maximize productivity while minimizing energy consumption and material waste. The use of open spaces, shared workstations, and modular furniture are common strategies employed in compact office designs.

Eco-friendly offices prioritize the use of sustainable materials, such as recycled or low-impact materials, in their construction and furnishings. They also emphasize energy efficiency through the installation of energy-saving appliances, LED lighting, and smart building systems that monitor and control energy usage. Utilizing natural lighting and ventilation, as well as implementing insulation and shading techniques, help to further reduce energy consumption.

The concept of sustainability extends beyond physical aspects and encompasses the well-being of employees. Compact eco-friendly offices prioritize the creation of a healthy work environment by considering factors such as indoor air quality, acoustics, ergonomic furniture, and access to green spaces. Employee engagement in sustainable practices, such as recycling and reducing paper waste, is also encouraged through the provision of adequate facilities and awareness campaigns.

In summary, compact eco-friendly offices are designed to optimize space, conserve resources, and promote employee well-being. By integrating sustainable practices into the office environment, these spaces contribute to a greener future while ensuring a productive and healthy work environment for employees.

Compact Green Office Layouts

Compact green office layouts refer to the design and organization of office spaces that prioritize sustainability and efficiency in a confined area. This concept aims to optimize the use of available space while minimizing the ecological footprint of the office environment.

By adopting a compact green office layout, businesses can minimize the consumption of resources such as energy, water, and materials. This can be achieved through various design strategies, such as maximizing natural light and ventilation to reduce the need for artificial lighting and air conditioning. Additionally, using energy-efficient appliances and equipment, as well as implementing effective waste management systems, contribute to the overall sustainability of the office layout.

The compact aspect of these layouts is advantageous both economically and environmentally. It allows for a more efficient use of office space, reducing real estate costs and minimizing the impact on the surrounding environment. Compact green office layouts often prioritize collaborative workspaces, flexible seating arrangements, and multipurpose areas to optimize the use of limited space and enhance productivity.

Moreover, these layouts can promote employee well-being and satisfaction. By incorporating elements of biophilic design, such as indoor plants, natural materials, and access to outdoor views, the office environment becomes more aesthetically pleasing and conducive to productivity. Implementing ergonomic furniture and considering sound control measures also contribute to a healthier and more comfortable workspace.

Overall, compact green office layouts offer a sustainable and efficient approach to office design, ensuring the optimal use of space, resources, and employee well-being. By considering these principles, businesses can create environmentally friendly workplaces that positively impact both the planet and the people who inhabit them.

Compact Green Office Spaces

Compact green office spaces refer to office environments that are designed and built with sustainable principles and practices in mind, while also maximizing the efficient use of space. These spaces aim to minimize their environmental impact, conserve resources, and foster a healthy and productive working environment.

By incorporating sustainable design elements, such as energy-efficient lighting, heating, and cooling systems, compact green office spaces are able to minimize energy consumption and reduce greenhouse gas emissions. They often utilize renewable energy sources, such as solar panels or wind turbines, to further decrease their carbon footprint. Additionally, they may incorporate natural ventilation and daylighting strategies to reduce the need for artificial lighting and mechanical ventilation, thus saving energy and promoting occupant comfort.

Water conservation is another key aspect of compact green office spaces. They may incorporate features such as low-flow fixtures and water-efficient landscaping to minimize water usage and reduce strain on local water resources. Furthermore, these spaces prioritize waste management practices and promote recycling and composting to minimize waste sent to landfills.

Compact green office spaces also prioritize the use of eco-friendly materials and sustainable construction practices. This may include using recycled or reclaimed materials, selecting non-toxic and low-VOC (volatile organic compound) products, and minimizing construction waste through efficient project management.

In summary, compact green office spaces combine sustainable design principles, energy efficiency, water conservation, waste reduction, and eco-friendly materials to create environmentally responsible and resource-efficient work environments. By embracing these concepts, businesses can not only reduce their environmental footprint but also create healthier and more productive spaces for their employees.

Compact Greenhouses

A compact greenhouse is a sustainable structure designed to maximize plant growth by creating an enclosed environment that allows for the controlled cultivation of plants. It is typically small in size and built using materials with a minimal environmental impact.

The primary goal of a compact greenhouse is to create a microclimate that extends the growing season and protects plants from adverse weather conditions. By capturing and retaining solar radiation, the greenhouse creates a warm and sheltered environment that allows plants to thrive. This results in increased crop yield and production, making compact greenhouses an efficient and sustainable option for food production.

Compostable Food Packaging

Compostable food packaging refers to a type of packaging material that is designed to be environmentally sustainable and can be broken down into natural elements through the process of composting. Composting is a natural process where organic waste decomposes into nutrient-rich soil, which can be used to support plant growth.

Compostable food packaging is typically made from renewable resources such as plant-based materials, including cornstarch, sugarcane, and bamboo. These materials are chosen for their ability to biodegrade and return to the earth without leaving harmful residues or toxins. When disposed of in the proper composting facilities, compostable food packaging can break down within a relatively short period of time, contributing to a closed-loop system that promotes sustainability.

Compostable Packaging

Compostable packaging refers to the use of materials that can be broken down and converted into nutrient-rich compost through natural decomposition processes. It is a sustainable alternative to conventional packaging options, such as plastic, that contribute to environmental pollution and waste accumulation.

Compostable packaging materials are typically derived from renewable resources, such as plants or agricultural waste, and are designed to mimic the natural biological cycles. These materials undergo a controlled degradation process, facilitated by microorganisms, moisture, and oxygen, ultimately resulting in the production of compost that can enrich the soil when used as a fertilizer. The decomposition of compostable packaging occurs without leaving behind toxic residues or harmful pollutants, making it an environmentally friendly choice.

By opting for compostable packaging, businesses and consumers can significantly reduce their carbon footprint and minimize the negative impact on the environment. Composting the packaging materials diverts waste from landfills, where they would generate methane, a potent greenhouse gas that contributes to climate change. Additionally, composting helps improve soil health and fertility, supports biodiversity, and reduces the need for synthetic fertilizers and pesticides.

While compostable packaging offers numerous benefits in terms of sustainability, it is essential to ensure proper disposal and processing. Compostable materials should be sent to specialized composting facilities or home composting systems to ensure optimal conditions for composting. Mixing compostable packaging with regular waste or recycling can hinder the decomposition process and negate its eco-friendly advantages. Therefore, awareness and education regarding the proper handling and disposal of compostable packaging play a crucial role in ensuring its effectiveness as a sustainable solution.

Compostable Product Design

Compostable product design refers to the intentional creation of products that can be biodegraded through composting, contributing to the sustainable management of waste and reducing the environmental impact.

Compostable products are designed with materials that are easily broken down by microorganisms in composting facilities, resulting in nutrient-rich compost or organic matter. These products are typically made from natural materials such as plant fibers, starches, or cellulose, and do not contain synthetic or harmful chemicals that could persist in the environment. Compostable product design takes into account the entire lifecycle of the product, ensuring that it aligns with the principles of the circular economy and minimizing waste generation.

Composting Initiatives

Composting initiatives are sustainable practices aimed at the decomposition of organic matter into nutrient-rich compost. Composting is a natural process that converts kitchen scraps, yard waste, and other organic materials into a valuable soil amendment.

These initiatives play a crucial role in sustainability by diverting organic waste from landfills, reducing methane emissions, and conserving natural resources. Through composting, organic waste is transformed into a beneficial product that can be used to enrich soil, improve plant growth, and decrease the need for chemical fertilizers.

Composting Solutions

Composting solutions refer to sustainable techniques aimed at the decomposition of organic waste materials into nutrient-rich soil amendment known as compost. Composting is a natural process that mimics the decomposition of organic matter in nature, utilizing microorganisms such as bacteria, fungi, and insects to break down the waste materials.

Composting is an essential component of sustainable waste management as it diverts organic waste from landfills, reducing greenhouse gas emissions and preventing the release of harmful leachate into the environment. By recycling organic waste into compost, composting solutions contribute to the circular economy and promote resource efficiency.

Composting Toilet Architecture

A composting toilet is a sustainable sanitation system that converts human waste into nutrient-rich compost through the process of decomposition. Unlike traditional flush toilets that rely on a complex network of infrastructure and water supply, composting toilets operate in a self-contained manner, making them ideal for areas with limited access to water or sewage systems. The architecture of a composting toilet is designed to facilitate the biological breakdown of waste materials. It typically consists of three main components: a toilet bowl or seat, a ventilation system, and a composting chamber. The toilet bowl or seat allows users to deposit their waste, while the ventilation system helps control odor and promote aerobic decomposition. The composting chamber is where the waste is stored and transformed into compost. Composting toilets rely on the natural processes of bacteria, fungi, and other microorganisms to break down organic matter. These microorganisms thrive in an oxygen-rich environment, which is why ventilation is a critical aspect of the design. Adequate ventilation ensures a sufficient supply of oxygen, preventing the accumulation of harmful gases and facilitating the decomposition process. The composting chamber of a composting toilet is typically designed to accommodate both solid and liquid waste. Solid waste, such as feces and toilet paper, is mixed with a bulking agent, such as sawdust or coconut coir, to absorb moisture and provide carbon for the composting process. Liquid waste is directed to a separate compartment or drainage system to prevent excess moisture in the composting chamber. As the waste in the composting chamber decomposes, it goes through different stages of transformation. Initially, thermophilic bacteria generate heat, raising the temperature of the chamber and promoting rapid decomposition. Over time, mesophilic bacteria take over and continue breaking down the waste, resulting in compost that is safe and suitable for use in gardening or agriculture. The architecture of composting toilets embraces sustainability by reducing water consumption, preventing pollution of water sources, and producing valuable compost for soil enrichment. Composting toilets are particularly beneficial in rural areas, off-grid residences, and environmentally sensitive regions, as they provide a hygienic and eco-friendly alternative to traditional flush toilets.

Composting Toilet Design

A composting toilet is a sustainable sanitation system that converts human waste into fertilizer through the natural process of decomposition. It is designed to mimic the natural decomposition environment found in compost piles, allowing for the safe and efficient breakdown of organic waste.

Composting toilets consist of two separate chambers: a toilet bowl and a composting chamber. When a person uses the toilet bowl, the waste is deposited into the composting chamber instead of being flushed away with water. In the composting chamber, the waste is mixed with a bulking agent such as sawdust or coconut coir, which helps maintain the balance of carbon and nitrogen and eliminates odor.

Within the composting chamber, beneficial microorganisms and bacteria break down the waste aerobically, or in the presence of oxygen. This aerobic decomposition process eliminates harmful pathogens and reduces the volume of waste through natural composting. The end product is a nutrient-rich compost material that can be safely used as fertilizer for plants and gardens.

The design of composting toilets promotes sustainability in several ways. Firstly, they save a significant amount of water by eliminating the need for traditional flush toilets. This reduction in water usage helps conserve water resources, which is particularly important in areas experiencing water scarcity.

Moreover, composting toilets address the issue of nutrient pollution by safely recycling human waste into valuable compost. Instead of releasing untreated waste into water bodies or relying on energy-intensive sewage treatment plants, composting toilets allow for the on-site treatment and reuse of human waste in a closed-loop system.

Composting Toilets

A composting toilet is a sustainable alternative to conventional flush toilets that uses biological processes to transform human waste into compost. It operates by separating liquid and solid waste, allowing for the decomposition of solid waste into nutrient-rich compost that can be safely used as a fertilizer. This environmentally-friendly solution significantly reduces the need for water, prevents pollution of water sources, and promotes the recycling of nutrients.

Composting toilets function by creating an aerobic environment that facilitates the break-down of organic matter. The solid waste is mixed with bulking agents such as sawdust or wood chips to enhance airflow and absorb moisture. Through the process of composting, microorganisms present in the waste break down the organic material, converting it into humus-like compost. The composting process is often supported by mechanical systems, such as fans or heaters, to regulate temperature and airflow.

Composting toilets offer numerous benefits in terms of sustainability and environmental conservation. By eliminating the need for water, they significantly reduce water usage and conserve this precious natural resource. Additionally, the resulting compost can be used as a nutrient-rich fertilizer, closing the nutrient cycle and reducing the reliance on chemical fertilizers. Composting toilets also help protect water sources from contamination, as they prevent the release of untreated waste into the environment. Furthermore, they can be employed in off-grid or remote locations, where conventional sanitation systems are challenging to implement.

In conclusion, composting toilets are a sustainable sanitation option that promotes resource conservation, reduces water usage, and protects water sources. By transforming human waste into compost, they contribute to the circular economy and reduce the dependency on chemical fertilizers. Their environmentally-friendly design and suitability for various locations make them an attractive solution for sustainable sanitation.

Conservation Alliance

The Conservation Alliance is an organization committed to the protection and preservation of natural landscapes and wildlife habitats in North America. It aims to facilitate cooperation among businesses and conservation groups to ensure the long-term sustainability of these environments.

Through its membership program, the Conservation Alliance brings together outdoor industry companies that share a common concern for the health and integrity of wild places. Member companies contribute annual dues to support a fund that is used to provide grants to grassroots conservation organizations. These grants are instrumental in funding projects that safeguard and restore important habitats, threatened species, and recreational access.

Conservation International

Conservation International is an environmental organization that is dedicated to promoting the sustainable use of natural resources and protecting the biodiversity of our planet.

The organization works towards ensuring that ecosystems are protected and restored in a way that maintains their ability to support life in the long term. Conservation International recognizes that human activities, such as deforestation and pollution, are threatening the health of our planet and the well-being of future generations. Therefore, it advocates for the adoption of practices that minimize negative impacts on the environment and promote sustainability.

Conservation Land Trust

A Conservation Land Trust is a legal entity that acquires and manages land for the purpose of protecting and preserving the natural environment. It operates based on the principles of sustainability, working to maintain and restore ecosystems, conserve biological diversity, and protect natural resources for future generations.

The primary goal of a Conservation Land Trust is to safeguard sensitive and ecologically valuable areas from development and degradation. These areas may include forests, wetlands, wildlife habitats, or other unique ecosystems that are home to endangered species or exhibit significant ecological importance.

Through land acquisition, a Conservation Land Trust aims to create a network of protected lands, often referred to as preserves or conservation areas. These lands are managed with the intention of promoting biodiversity, enabling natural processes and ecological functions to occur, and providing opportunities for scientific research, education, and low-impact recreation.

Conservation Land Trusts typically work with government agencies, private landowners, and other conservation organizations to identify and secure land parcels that are of key ecological value. They may negotiate land purchases, accept donations or bequests, and implement conservation easements or agreements that restrict future development and ensure the long-term protection of the land.

By establishing and maintaining protected areas, Conservation Land Trusts contribute to the overall sustainability of the planet by safeguarding vital ecosystems and natural resources. They play a crucial role in mitigating the loss of biodiversity, protecting wildlife habitats, and preserving the ecological services that these areas provide, such as clean air, water, and climate regulation.

Conservation Stewards Program

The Conservation Stewards Program is a sustainability-driven initiative that aims to empower individuals with the knowledge and skills necessary to actively contribute to the protection and restoration of natural ecosystems and biodiversity. Through this program, participants are trained to become effective stewards of the environment, working towards a more sustainable future.

The program focuses on providing participants with a comprehensive understanding of the principles and practices of conservation, as well as the tools and techniques needed to address environmental challenges. By taking part in various educational activities, workshops, and hands-on experiences, individuals develop a deep appreciation for the interconnectedness of ecological systems and learn how their actions can positively impact the environment.

Conservation Stewards are encouraged to play an active role in their communities, collaborating with local organizations, government agencies, and fellow participants to implement sustainable strategies and initiatives. They may be involved in projects such as habitat restoration, species monitoring, climate change adaptation, and environmental education. Through these efforts, Conservation Stewards contribute to the protection of natural resources, the preservation of biodiversity, and the overall enhancement of ecological resilience.

Moreover, the Conservation Stewards Program emphasizes the importance of fostering a sense of responsibility and stewardship towards the environment, promoting sustainable practices in all aspects of life. Participants are encouraged to make environmentally-conscious choices in their daily lives, advocate for sustainable policies, and inspire others to join the movement towards a more sustainable and resilient future for all.

Conservation Strategy Fund

The Conservation Strategy Fund (CSF) is a nonprofit organization focused on advancing sustainable development and conservation through economic analysis and policy development. Their mission is to empower decision-makers with the tools and knowledge necessary to protect and sustain natural resources.

CSF works on a global scale, collaborating with governments, NGOs, and local communities to develop innovative approaches to conservation. They use economic analysis to identify the costs and benefits associated with different conservation strategies, helping decision-makers prioritize and implement the most effective policies. CSF also provides training and capacity building to ensure that local stakeholders have the skills and knowledge to participate in sustainable development efforts.

Cradle-To-Cradle Certification

The Cradle-to-Cradle (C2C) certification is a sustainability framework that evaluates and assesses products based on their environmental impact and design strategies. This certification encompasses a comprehensive approach to sustainability, considering both the materials used in production and the product's potential for reuse or recycling.

At its core, C2C certification focuses on the concept of closing the loop in the product lifecycle. It promotes the idea that products should create a positive impact on the environment throughout their life cycle, from extraction and manufacturing to use and disposal. This is achieved by incorporating principles of circular economy and regenerative design.

The C2C certification evaluates products based on five key categories: material health, material reutilization, renewable energy and carbon management, water stewardship, and social fairness. Each category has specific criteria that products must meet to achieve certification, ensuring a holistic assessment of sustainability performance.

One of the main principles of C2C certification is the elimination of harmful substances in the product's composition. Products with hazardous materials are not eligible for certification. Instead, the focus is on using safe and non-toxic materials that can be recycled or biodegraded without harming the environment.

C2C-certified products are also expected to be designed for disassembly, enabling easy separation of different components for recycling or reuse. This supports the shift towards a circular economy, where resources are kept in use for as long as possible.

In conclusion, the Cradle-to-Cradle certification is a rigorous sustainability framework that evaluates products based on their environmental and social impact. It encourages the use of safe and recyclable materials, promotes circularity, and aims to create a positive contribution to the environment throughout a product's lifecycle.

Cradle-To-Cradle Design

Cradle-to-cradle design is a sustainability concept that aims to create products and systems which, instead of being discarded after use, can be recycled or used as raw materials for future products. It focuses on the idea of a continuous cycle of resources, where waste is eliminated through innovative design and materials.

The cradle-to-cradle approach encourages manufacturers to design products with the goal of avoiding waste entirely. This involves considering the entire lifecycle of a product, from its creation to its ultimate disposal, and finding ways to make each stage as sustainable as possible.

Key principles of cradle-to-cradle design include using materials that are safe and healthy for both humans and the environment, maximizing the use of renewable energy sources, and designing products to be easily disassembled and recycled. This approach promotes the use of materials that can be infinitely recycled without losing their quality or usefulness.

By adopting cradle-to-cradle design principles, companies can reduce their environmental impact and contribute to a circular economy, where resources are continuously reused and waste is minimized. This approach also encourages innovation and collaboration, as companies must work together to create sustainable supply chains and develop new technologies and materials.

In conclusion, cradle-to-cradle design is a sustainable approach that emphasizes the importance of creating products and systems that can be endlessly recycled or reused. By eliminating waste and considering the entire lifecycle of a product, this design philosophy supports a more sustainable and circular economy.

Cradle-To-Gate Analysis

Cradle-to-gate analysis is a sustainability assessment tool that measures the environmental impacts of a product or process from the extraction of raw materials (the cradle) to the manufacturing or production stage (the gate). This analysis aims to provide a comprehensive understanding of the resource use, energy consumption, and emissions associated with the production of a particular product or process, highlighting the potential environmental implications.

Cradle-to-gate analysis considers the entire life cycle of a product or process, including the extraction, processing, and transportation of raw materials, as well as the manufacturing or production stage. It examines various aspects such as water usage, energy consumption, greenhouse gas emissions, waste generation, and ecological impacts. By assessing the complete life cycle, cradle-to-gate analysis enables the identification of hotspots and potential areas for improvement in terms of environmental performance.

This sustainability assessment tool supports decision-making processes by providing stakeholders with crucial information about the environmental impacts associated with different stages of production. It helps identify ways to optimize resource efficiency, minimize environmental footprint, and promote the use of more sustainable materials and processes. Cradle-to-gate analysis can provide insights into the potential environmental benefits of alternative production methods, materials, or technologies, contributing to the development of more sustainable practices.

Overall, the cradle-to-gate analysis is a valuable approach for evaluating and improving the environmental performance of products and processes, supporting the transition toward a more sustainable and resource-efficient economy.

Decentralized Energy Generation

Decentralized energy generation refers to the production of electricity or heat using small-scale energy systems that are located close to the point of consumption, as opposed to relying on large centralized power plants and long-distance transmission lines. This approach aims to minimize energy losses during transmission and distribution while promoting sustainability and resilience in the energy sector.

In the context of sustainability, decentralized energy generation offers several benefits. Firstly, it reduces the environmental impact associated with long-distance transmission and distribution of energy by decreasing energy losses and the need for extensive infrastructure. By generating energy closer to where it is consumed, decentralized systems can also utilize local renewable resources, such as solar, wind, or biomass, promoting the use of clean and sustainable energy sources.

Furthermore, decentralized energy generation enhances energy resilience. In the event of a disruption or failure in the centralized grid, decentralized systems can continue to operate, providing energy security to local communities. These systems enable greater energy independence, allowing communities to generate their own power and reduce their reliance on external sources. This aspect contributes to the overall resilience and stability of the energy sector, particularly in the face of climate change, natural disasters, or other emergencies.

In conclusion, decentralized energy generation represents a sustainable and resilient approach to meeting energy needs. By minimizing energy losses, utilizing local renewable resources, and enhancing energy resilience, decentralized systems play a crucial role in reducing environmental impacts and promoting long-term sustainability in the energy sector.

Decentralized Renewable Energy Systems

Decentralized renewable energy systems refer to energy production systems that utilize renewable sources of energy (such as solar, wind, or hydropower) and are distributed across various small-scale locations, rather than centralized in a single large power plant. These systems are designed to provide sustainable and environmentally friendly energy solutions that can contribute to the reduction of greenhouse gas emissions and help mitigate climate change.

The decentralization of renewable energy systems promotes several key sustainability benefits. Firstly, by utilizing renewable sources, these systems significantly reduce reliance on fossil fuels, which are finite resources with detrimental environmental impacts. Additionally, decentralized systems often involve smaller-scale installations, which can have a lower environmental footprint compared to large centralized power plants. These systems can be integrated into existing infrastructure, such as rooftops or unused land, minimizing the need for additional land development.

Furthermore, the localization of energy production allows for improved energy access and energy security. Communities and households can generate their own electricity, reducing dependence on unreliable or centralized grids. This is particularly beneficial in remote or under-served areas, where access to electricity may be limited. Decentralized renewable energy systems empower individuals and communities to take control of their energy supply, leading to greater resilience and self-sufficiency.

In conclusion, decentralized renewable energy systems play a crucial role in promoting sustainability by harnessing renewable sources of energy, reducing reliance on fossil fuels, minimizing environmental impacts, and increasing energy access and security within communities.

Decentralized Waste Management

Decentralized waste management refers to a sustainable approach in which waste is managed at the local level, eliminating the need for central collection and disposal systems. This decentralized system aims to minimize the negative environmental impact of waste generation and promote the efficient use of resources, while also improving the well-being of communities and reducing their dependence on external waste management services.

In this decentralized model, waste is sorted and processed closer to its source, typically within the community or even at individual households. This approach encourages waste reduction, recycling, and reuse, as it allows for better management and control of different types of waste streams. By reducing the distance that waste needs to travel, decentralized waste management reduces transportation-related emissions and the associated environmental and social costs.

93

Decentralized Wastewater Treatment

Decentralized wastewater treatment refers to a sustainable approach in managing and treating wastewater at the local level, away from centralized sewer systems. It involves the use of smaller, more flexible treatment systems that are implemented closer to the source of wastewater generation, such as individual households, communities, or small businesses.

This approach offers several sustainability benefits. Firstly, by treating wastewater on-site, it reduces the need for long-distance transport to centralized treatment plants, decreasing the associated energy consumption and greenhouse gas emissions. Additionally, it minimizes the risk of system failure or overload in the event of extreme weather events or natural disasters, ensuring the continued safe and efficient treatment of wastewater. Moreover, decentralized systems can be tailored to meet specific local needs, allowing for more efficient and effective treatment processes.

Decentralized Water Purification

Decentralized water purification refers to the process of treating and purifying water on a small-scale, local level, typically at the point of use or near the source of water. It involves the implementation of purification systems that are sustainable, cost-effective, and efficient in removing contaminants from water, making it safe for consumption and various other uses.

This approach to water purification aligns with the principles of sustainability as it addresses several key aspects. First and foremost, it reduces the dependence on centralized water treatment plants and long-distance distribution networks, minimizing energy consumption and transportation-related carbon emissions. By purifying water closer to the point of use, it mitigates the need for extensive infrastructure, which is costly, resource-intensive, and often difficult to maintain in remote areas or densely populated regions.

Moreover, decentralized water purification promotes resilience and independence by providing localized solutions that can be tailored to specific needs and risks. Communities, industries, and households can adapt their purification systems to treat water contaminated with specific pollutants or pathogens prevalent in their surroundings, ensuring a reliable supply of clean water even in times of natural disasters, emergencies, or water scarcity.

This approach also fosters community engagement and capacity-building, empowering individuals to take responsibility for their water quality and encouraging sustainable water management practices. By increasing awareness and knowledge regarding water treatment, decentralized purification systems can help safeguard water resources, reduce pollution, and protect ecosystem health.

Decentralized Water Recycling

Decentralized water recycling is a sustainable approach to managing water resources that involves the local treatment and reuse of wastewater for non-drinking purposes. It is a process that takes place on a smaller scale, typically at the community or individual level, as opposed to centralized water treatment plants.

This decentralized system aims to mitigate water scarcity and reduce the environmental impact caused by excessive water consumption and wastewater discharge. By treating and reusing wastewater locally, communities can decrease their reliance on freshwater sources and minimize the strain on existing water infrastructure.

Decentralized Water Treatment Plants

A decentralized water treatment plant refers to a compact and self-contained system that is designed to treat and purify water on a smaller scale, typically serving a specific community or a cluster of buildings. Unlike centralized water treatment plants that serve large populations, decentralized plants offer a more localized and sustainable approach to addressing water quality and availability challenges.

These plants utilize innovative and environmentally friendly technologies to remove impurities, such as bacteria, viruses, chemicals, and pollutants, from the water. This ensures that the treated water meets stringent quality standards, making it safe for various uses, including drinking, cooking, and sanitation.

Decentralized water treatment plants are characterized by their adaptability and versatility. They can be designed to suit the specific needs and conditions of the community they serve, whether it is a rural village, a remote settlement, or an urban neighborhood. The modularity of these systems allows for easy scalability, meaning that additional units can be added or removed as the population or water demand changes.

From a sustainability perspective, decentralized water treatment plants offer several advantages. Firstly, they reduce reliance on long-distance transportation of water, which not only reduces energy consumption but also minimizes the associated carbon emissions. Secondly, by treating water locally, these plants contribute to water conservation by minimizing water losses during transmission. Thirdly, the use of advanced water treatment technologies in these plants helps to conserve natural resources and protect ecosystems by minimizing the discharge of harmful pollutants into rivers, lakes, and other bodies of water.

In conclusion, decentralized water treatment plants play a vital role in ensuring sustainable water management by providing clean and safe water in an efficient, cost-effective, and environmentally friendly manner.

Decentralized Water Treatment Systems

Decentralized water treatment systems are sustainable solutions that are designed to address the challenge of providing clean and safe water in areas that lack centralized water infrastructure. These systems offer a decentralized approach to water treatment, which means that they are capable of purifying water at the point of use, without the need for extensive network infrastructure.

By utilizing decentralized water treatment systems, communities can reduce their dependence on larger centralized facilities, which can be costly to maintain and vulnerable to disruptions in case of natural disasters or system failures. These systems are typically installed closer to the source of water supply or within the community itself, ensuring safe and reliable access to clean water for everyone.

Decentralized Water Treatment

Decentralized water treatment refers to a sustainable approach towards managing and purifying water resources at a local level, without reliance on centralized water treatment facilities. It involves the implementation of various decentralized technologies and practices to treat water closer to the point of use, ensuring improved access to clean and safe water while minimizing negative environmental impacts.

This approach focuses on decentralizing water treatment systems, deviating from traditional centralized methods that require extensive infrastructure, energy, and resources. Decentralized water treatment systems can be implemented in small communities, households, or specific sources of water, such as rivers or lakes.

Decentralized water treatment methods often utilize sustainable and resource-efficient technologies, such as constructed wetlands, biofilters, membrane filtration, and solar disinfection. These decentralized systems have several advantages, including reduced transmission losses, lower energy consumption, increased water reuse, and improved resilience to natural disasters or system failures.

By decentralizing water treatment practices, communities can reduce their dependence on large-scale infrastructure, lower the carbon footprint associated with water treatment, and enhance local water security. Additionally, decentralized water treatment promotes community engagement and empowerment, enabling individuals and organizations to actively participate in the management and conservation of their water resources.

In summary, decentralized water treatment is a sustainable approach that emphasizes local-level water purification using efficient technologies. This decentralized approach enhances access to clean and safe water, reduces environmental impacts, and fosters community involvement in water resource management.

Desalination Desiccants

Desalination desiccants are substances used in the desalination process to remove moisture from the air or gas streams, thereby increasing the efficiency of the desalination system while also reducing the environmental impact.

Desalination is the process of removing salt and other impurities from seawater or brackish water to produce fresh water for drinking, irrigation, or industrial use. This process is crucial in areas where fresh water is scarce or limited. However, desalination is an energy-intensive process that often leads to the emission of greenhouse gases and other pollutants.

Desiccants, on the other hand, are materials with a high affinity for water vapor. By using desiccants in the desalination process, moisture in the air or gas streams is adsorbed by the desiccant material, thus decreasing the energy required to remove moisture from the water during desalination. This not only increases the overall efficiency of the desalination process but also reduces the amount of energy and resources needed.

By incorporating desalination desiccants into the desalination systems, the sustainability of the process is improved. Desiccants help reduce the energy consumption and associated greenhouse gas emissions, making desalination a more environmentally friendly and sustainable solution for providing fresh water in water-stressed regions. Additionally, the use of desalination desiccants can enhance the longevity and performance of desalination equipment by preventing corrosion and fouling caused by moisture in the air or gas streams. This leads to reduced maintenance and replacement costs, further contributing to the economic and environmental sustainability of the desalination process.

Desalination Membrane Technology

Desalination membrane technology is an innovative and sustainable solution to address the increasing global water scarcity problem. It involves the use of specialized membranes to remove salt and other impurities from seawater, brackish water, or even wastewater, making it suitable for human consumption or irrigation.

The process of desalination involves two main types of membrane technologies: reverse osmosis (RO) and electrodialysis. In reverse osmosis, the saline water is forced through a semi-permeable membrane at high pressure, separating the salt molecules from the water molecules. This allows clean water to pass through while the salt and impurities are retained and later discharged. On the other hand, electrodialysis uses ion-selective membranes and an electric field to separate ions from the water, effectively desalinating it.

Desalination membrane technology offers several advantages in terms of sustainability. Firstly, it provides a reliable and abundant source of clean water, reducing the pressure on freshwater resources and easing water scarcity issues. This is especially crucial in regions with limited access to freshwater or facing drought conditions, as it reduces dependence on unsustainable water extraction methods.

Moreover, desalination membrane technology is energy-efficient compared to traditional desalination processes, such as thermal desalination. Advances in membrane materials and design have significantly reduced the energy requirements for desalination, minimizing its environmental impact.

In conclusion, desalination membrane technology is a sustainable solution to address water scarcity by providing a reliable source of clean water and reducing energy consumption. Its use can help in meeting the increasing global water demand while minimizing the exploitation of freshwater resources.

Desalination Technology

Desalination technology refers to the process of removing salts and impurities from seawater or brackish water to produce fresh water that is suitable for human and ecological use. This technology plays a crucial role in ensuring sustainable water management and addressing the growing global water crisis.

The desalination process typically involves two main methods: distillation and membrane separation. In distillation, seawater is heated to create steam, which is then condensed to produce fresh water, leaving behind the salt and other impurities. Membrane separation, on the other hand, utilizes semi-permeable membranes to filter out the salts and contaminants, allowing only pure water molecules to pass through.

Desalination technology offers several advantages in the context of sustainability. Firstly, it provides an alternative freshwater source, mitigating water scarcity in areas with limited access to freshwater resources. This is particularly crucial in arid regions or coastal areas where traditional freshwater sources are scarce.

Furthermore, desalination technology can reduce reliance on freshwater withdrawals from rivers, lakes, and other vulnerable ecosystems, preserving natural water resources and protecting aquatic biodiversity. By utilizing seawater or brackish water, desalination helps alleviate the pressure on freshwater ecosystems and supports sustainable water usage practices.

Desert Greening Projects

Desert greening projects refer to initiatives aimed at restoring and rehabilitating arid and semi-arid regions by increasing vegetation cover and improving the overall ecological balance. These projects focus on combating desertification, a process whereby fertile land loses its productivity and transforms into desert-like conditions, primarily due to human activities and climate change.

Desert greening projects employ various techniques and strategies to promote sustainable development and mitigate the adverse effects of desertification. They often involve the implementation of soil conservation measures, such as terracing and contour farming, to prevent soil erosion and retain moisture. Additionally, these projects encompass afforestation and reforestation efforts, which involve the planting of native vegetation species to enhance soil fertility, promote water infiltration, and encourage biodiversity.

Furthermore, desert greening projects may incorporate the use of innovative technologies to combat water scarcity, such as drip irrigation systems and water harvesting techniques. These technologies aim to optimize water usage and enable the survival and growth of vegetation in arid regions. In some cases, these projects also involve the establishment of green infrastructure, such as windbreaks and shelterbelts, to mitigate wind erosion and provide favorable conditions for plant growth.

Overall, desert greening projects play a crucial role in promoting sustainability by restoring degraded lands, enhancing ecosystem resilience, and supporting local communities. By increasing vegetation cover and improving soil quality, these initiatives contribute to carbon sequestration, mitigate climate change, and provide ecosystem services such as erosion control, water regulation, and habitat creation. Through their focus on rehabilitation and regeneration, desert greening projects contribute to the preservation and long-term sustainability of arid and semi-arid environments.

Desert Reforestation Techniques

Desert reforestation techniques refer to sustainable practices employed to restore and conserve vegetation in arid and semi-arid regions. These techniques aim to mitigate desertification, enhance biodiversity, promote soil stabilization, and improve local ecosystems' resilience. Through strategic interventions, such as water management, soil restoration, and planting native species, desert reforestation seeks to reestablish a healthy balance between nature and human activities in these fragile ecosystems.

The process of desert reforestation involves several key components. Initially, the identification and assessment of degraded areas in the desert landscape are crucial in order to determine where reforestation efforts should be focused. Subsequently, water management techniques, such as drip irrigation and rainwater harvesting systems, are utilized to provide the necessary moisture for plant growth. To ensure long-term sustainability, water-efficient irrigation practices are implemented to minimize water wastage.

Soil restoration is another vital aspect of desert reforestation. This involves the use of organic matter, mulching, and other soil enrichment techniques to improve the soil's fertility and structure, promoting better growth conditions for plants. In addition, the selection of appropriate plant species plays a crucial role in reforestation success. Indigenous and drought-resistant plants naturally adapt to the harsh desert environment, increasing survivability and reducing the need for excessive water and maintenance.

Desert reforestation techniques also focus on community involvement, raising awareness, and engaging local populations in the conservation and restoration efforts. This fosters a sense of ownership, empowers the local communities, and ensures the long-term success and sustainability of the reforestation projects. Consequently, desert reforestation techniques not only combat desertification and restore ecosystems but also contribute to the socioeconomic well-being of the communities living in these fragile environments.

Design For Disassembly

Design for disassembly is a sustainable design approach that focuses on creating products or systems that can be easily taken apart at the end of their life cycle, with the purpose of facilitating reuse, recycling, or repair of their components or materials.

The concept of design for disassembly stems from the recognition that many products today are designed without considering their end-of-life fate, leading to inefficient resource use and significant environmental impacts. By contrast, design for disassembly aims to extend the lifespan of products and minimize waste generation by enabling efficient disassembly processes.

The key principles of design for disassembly involve designing products with clear separation points and minimizing the use of adhesives, fasteners, or materials that hinder disassembly. Additionally, modular design strategies are often employed, allowing for the easy removal of individual components or subsystems. Standardized interfaces and labeling systems can further enhance disassembly, as they facilitate the identification and sorting of materials for recycling or reprocessing.

Implementing design for disassembly requires the collaboration of various stakeholders, including designers, manufacturers, and recyclers. It necessitates considering the entire life cycle of a product, from its initial design stages to its end-of-life management. By incorporating design for disassembly principles into product development, manufacturers can reduce the ecological footprint of their products, conserve resources, and contribute to the circular economy.

Digital Agriculture

Digital agriculture refers to the use of technology and data in the field of agriculture to improve sustainability practices and enhance productivity. It involves the integration of digital tools, such as sensors, drones, and artificial intelligence, with traditional farming techniques to optimize resource use, reduce environmental impact, and promote the efficient production of food.

In the context of sustainability, digital agriculture plays a crucial role in addressing the challenges faced by the agricultural sector. By harnessing the power of data and technology, farmers can make informed decisions about various aspects of their operations, including irrigation, fertilization, and pest management. This enables them to minimize the use of water, energy, and chemicals, thereby reducing the negative impact on the environment.

Furthermore, digital agriculture allows for real-time monitoring and analysis of crop conditions, enabling farmers to identify and respond to potential issues promptly. By detecting signs of disease, nutrient deficiencies, or pest infestations at an early stage, farmers can take appropriate action to prevent crop losses and minimize the need for chemical interventions.

Additionally, digital agricultural practices can contribute to increased productivity and resource efficiency. Through precision farming techniques, farmers can optimize the allocation of resources, such as fertilizers and pesticides, based on the specific requirements of different areas within their fields. This targeted approach improves yield while minimizing input waste.

In conclusion, digital agriculture offers tremendous opportunities for sustainable farming practices. By combining technological advancements with ecological considerations, it enables farmers to achieve higher yield, reduce resource consumption, and minimize environmental harm, thus contributing to the long-term viability of the agricultural sector.

Digital Twin Technology For Sustainability

A digital twin is a virtual replica of a physical object, process, or system that uses real-time data and advanced technologies, such as internet of things (IoT) sensors, artificial intelligence (AI), and machine learning (ML), to simulate and model its behavior.

In the context of sustainability, digital twin technology can play a crucial role in enabling the efficient and effective management of resources and promoting sustainable practices. By creating a digital twin of a physical asset, such as a building, a city, or an industrial process, organizations and governments can monitor, analyze, and optimize its performance and operations.

For example, in the case of a smart city, a digital twin can integrate data from various sources, such as energy consumption, waste management, transportation, and air quality sensors, to provide a holistic view of the city's sustainability performance. This enables city planners and policymakers to identify areas for improvement, optimize resource allocation, and implement targeted interventions to reduce environmental impact.

The use of digital twin technology for sustainability also extends to industries such as manufacturing, energy, and agriculture. By creating a digital twin of a production line or a power plant, organizations can gain insights into energy consumption patterns, identify inefficiencies, and optimize resource utilization to minimize waste and emissions. In agriculture, digital twins can simulate crop growth, predict yield, and optimize resource allocation, thereby promoting sustainable farming practices.

In conclusion, digital twin technology enables the development of virtual representations that can be used to optimize the performance and sustainability of physical assets, processes, and systems. By harnessing real-time data and advanced technologies, organizations and governments can make informed decisions, implement targeted interventions, and drive positive environmental and social outcomes.

Distributed Renewable Energy Grids

Distributed renewable energy grids refer to interconnected systems that utilize sustainable energy sources, such as solar, wind, hydro, geothermal, and biomass, to generate electricity and deliver it to end-users. Unlike centralized power grids, which rely heavily on fossil fuels and are susceptible to blackouts and transmission losses, distributed renewable energy grids promote decentralized energy generation, increased reliability, and reduced environmental impact.

These grids consist of distributed energy resources (DERs) that are located in close proximity to the energy consumers they serve. DERs include residential and commercial solar panels, wind turbines, small-scale hydroelectric systems, and on-site energy storage devices. By harnessing energy from various renewable sources, these systems can provide a more resilient and sustainable alternative to traditional power grids.

Distributed Renewable Energy Storage

Distributed renewable energy storage refers to the decentralized and localized storage of renewable energy resources, such as solar and wind power, in various locations to enhance sustainability and resilience in the energy sector. This approach aims to store excess energy generated from renewable sources during times of low demand and make it available when demand is high or when renewable energy generation is limited.

In the context of sustainability, distributed renewable energy storage plays a crucial role in enabling the efficient integration of intermittent renewable resources into the grid. By storing surplus renewable energy at the local level, this form of energy storage helps to address the mismatch between energy generation and demand, ensuring a consistent and reliable energy supply.

Distributed Wind Power Generation

Distributed wind power generation refers to the production of renewable energy through the use of wind turbines that are located in close proximity to where the electricity is consumed. Unlike traditional centralized power generation, which relies on large-scale wind farms located far from population centers, distributed wind power generation brings the generation of electricity closer to the end users.

This decentralized approach to wind power offers several sustainability benefits. First and foremost, it reduces transmission losses by minimizing the distance over which electricity needs to be transmitted. By generating electricity on-site or in nearby communities, the efficiency of energy transmission is improved, resulting in less wasted energy and a lower carbon footprint.

E-Waste Collection Programs

E-waste collection programs are initiatives designed to promote the proper disposal and recycling of electronic waste (e-waste) in an environmentally responsible manner. E-waste refers to any discarded electronic devices or equipment, including computers, mobile phones, televisions, and refrigerators, among others.

These collection programs aim to address the growing concern of electronic waste accumulation and its negative impact on the environment and human health. They encourage individuals, businesses, and communities to participate in the recycling and disposal of their outdated or unused electronic devices, rather than discarding them in regular waste streams.

By providing designated drop-off points or partnering with recycling facilities, these programs facilitate the safe and proper disposal of e-waste. This ensures that valuable materials, such as metals, plastics, and glass, are recovered and recycled, reducing the need to extract and process virgin resources.

In addition to reducing the environmental impact, e-waste collection programs also help to minimize the potential health hazards associated with the improper handling and disposal of electronic devices. Many electronic devices contain hazardous substances, including lead, mercury, cadmium, and brominated flame retardants, which can leach into soil and water if not disposed of correctly. By promoting proper disposal methods, these programs aim to protect both human health and the environment.

Overall, e-waste collection programs play a crucial role in addressing the challenges posed by electronic waste. They contribute to sustainable practices by recycling valuable resources, minimizing pollution, and safeguarding public health. By raising awareness and providing convenient and responsible avenues for e-waste disposal, these programs support the transition to a more circular and sustainable economy.

E-Waste Recycling And Management Solutions

E-waste recycling and management solutions refer to the processes and practices implemented to properly dispose of electronic waste in an environmentally responsible manner. Electronic waste, or e-waste, includes discarded electronic devices such as computers, mobile phones, televisions, and other electronic appliances.

These solutions aim to address the issue of e-waste, which poses significant environmental and health risks if not managed properly. E-waste often contains hazardous substances like lead, mercury, cadmium, and brominated flame retardants, which can contaminate soil, water, and air if not disposed of correctly.

E-waste recycling and management solutions typically involve several key steps. First, collection methods are established to gather e-waste from manufacturers, consumers, and businesses. This can include designated drop-off locations, recycling events, or the implementation of take-back programs by electronic manufacturers.

Once collected, e-waste is sorted, categorized, and processed to separate hazardous materials from reusable components. Recycling technologies are employed to extract valuable materials like metals, plastics, and glass, which can then be used in the manufacturing of new electronic products.

Proper disposal of hazardous substances is a significant aspect of e-waste management solutions. Hazardous materials are safely managed through specialized treatment and disposal methods to prevent contamination and minimize environmental and health risks.

E-waste recycling and management solutions also focus on raising awareness and educating the public about the importance of responsible e-waste disposal. This includes promoting the benefits of recycling, advocating for legislation and regulations, and encouraging product design that facilitates easier and safer recycling.

E-Waste Recycling Initiatives

E-waste recycling initiatives are sustainable programs aimed at reducing the environmental impact of electronic waste. Electronic waste, or e-waste, refers to discarded electronic devices such as computers, smartphones, and televisions. These devices often contain hazardous materials, including heavy metals and toxic chemicals, which can pose significant risks to human health and the environment if not properly managed.

E-waste recycling initiatives promote the responsible disposal and recycling of electronic waste to prevent it from ending up in landfills or being illegally dumped. These programs aim to recover valuable resources from e-waste, such as metals and plastics, through processes like dismantling, sorting, and processing. By extracting these materials, e-waste recycling initiatives reduce the need for mining raw materials and manufacturing new electronic products, thereby conserving natural resources and reducing energy consumption.

In addition to resource conservation, e-waste recycling initiatives help minimize the release of hazardous substances into the environment. Electronic devices contain toxic materials like lead, mercury, and brominated flame retardants, which can contaminate soil, water, and air if not properly managed. By recycling e-waste, these harmful substances can be safely contained and disposed of, preventing their potential negative impacts on ecosystems and human health.

E-Waste Recycling Kiosks

E-waste recycling kiosks are dedicated stations where individuals can dispose of electronic waste in an environmentally friendly manner. These kiosks are strategically placed in public locations such as shopping centers, schools, and office complexes to encourage convenient and responsible disposal of electronic devices that have reached the end of their useful lives.

By providing a designated space for e-waste recycling, these kiosks promote sustainability and reduce the negative environmental impacts associated with improper disposal of electronic devices. Electronic waste, also known as e-waste, includes items such as old computers, mobile phones, televisions, and other electronic appliances that are no longer functional or needed.

Electronic devices often contain hazardous materials such as lead, mercury, and cadmium, which can cause harm to human health and the environment if not properly disposed of. E-waste recycling kiosks aim to minimize the release of these pollutants by ensuring that electronic devices are recycled or disposed of safely and responsibly.

When individuals deposit their e-waste in these kiosks, the devices are collected by specialized recycling companies. These companies dismantle the devices, separate the various

101

components, and extract valuable materials such as precious metals and plastics. These materials can then be reused or repurposed in the manufacturing of new electronic devices, reducing the need for virgin raw materials and conserving natural resources.

E-waste recycling kiosks play an essential role in promoting a circular economy by closing the loop on the lifecycle of electronic devices. They provide individuals with a convenient and accessible solution for disposing of their electronic waste, while also contributing to the conservation of resources and the reduction of harmful environmental impacts.

E-Waste Recycling Technologies

E-waste recycling technologies refer to the processes and methods used to reduce the environmental impact of electronic waste, often referred to as e-waste. E-waste includes discarded electronic devices such as computers, mobile phones, televisions, and other electronic appliances.

Sustainability is a key factor when it comes to e-waste recycling technologies. These technologies aim to minimize the negative effects of e-waste on the environment, human health, and natural resources. By recycling and reusing the materials found in electronic devices, these technologies contribute to resource preservation and minimize the need for raw material extraction.

E-waste recycling technologies typically involve several steps. First, e-waste needs to be collected and sorted to identify the types of devices and materials present. This is followed by dismantling, where the devices are taken apart to separate the different components and materials. Hazardous substances such as mercury and lead are removed and treated separately to avoid their release into the environment.

The next step involves the actual recycling processes, which can vary according to the materials and components present in the e-waste. These processes may include mechanical shredding, separation by density or magnetism, and chemical treatments to recover valuable metals such as gold, silver, copper, and palladium. The recovered materials can then be used as secondary raw materials in the production of new electronic devices.

In conclusion, e-waste recycling technologies play a crucial role in ensuring the sustainability of our electronic consumption. By reducing the environmental impact of e-waste and promoting the efficient use of resources, these technologies contribute to a more environmentally friendly and sustainable future.

Earth Island Institute

The Earth Island Institute is an organization that focuses on promoting sustainability and environmental protection. It works towards protecting the Earth's natural resources and advocating for sustainable solutions to various environmental challenges. The institute aims to develop and implement initiatives that lead to a more sustainable and resilient planet.

Through research, education, and advocacy, the Earth Island Institute strives to raise awareness about environmental issues and mobilize individuals and communities to take action. It supports a wide range of projects and campaigns that address critical issues such as climate change, biodiversity loss, pollution, and deforestation.

Earth Policy Institute

The Earth Policy Institute is a non-profit organization dedicated to providing research and analysis on global environmental and sustainability issues. Their work focuses on creating a sustainable future through the development of policies and strategies that address the complex challenges facing our planet. The Institute conducts in-depth research and produces publications and reports that explore various topics, such as climate change, renewable energy, population growth, and food scarcity. Their objective is to raise awareness and provide solutions to global sustainability issues by presenting data-driven analysis and proposing innovative policies. Through their research and publications, the Earth Policy Institute aims to inform and influence policymakers, businesses, and the general public. They provide evidence-based information and recommend policies that promote sustainable practices, such as transitioning to renewable energy sources, reducing greenhouse gas emissions, and implementing conservation measures. The organization also advocates for the adoption of sustainable development practices at the local, national, and international levels. They work to build partnerships and collaborations with governments, businesses, and organizations to promote sustainable policies and initiatives. Overall, the Earth Policy Institute serves as a valuable resource for policymakers, researchers, and individuals interested in environmental sustainability. Their research and advocacy efforts contribute to the global dialogue on sustainability and help shape policies and actions that can lead to a more sustainable future for our planet.>

Earthjustice

Earthjustice is an environmental law organization that works tirelessly to protect the Earth and promote sustainability. With a focus on the legal aspect of environmental issues, Earthjustice utilizes the power of the law to advocate for and defend the rights of the environment, communities, and future generations.

Through its strategic litigation, Earthjustice aims to ensure a just and sustainable planet for all, fighting against environmental degradation, pollution, and climate change. This organization works on a wide range of issues, including protection of natural resources, preservation of biodiversity, defense of wildlife habitats, and promotion of clean energy solutions.

Earthworks

Earthworks refers to activities that involve the manipulation and alteration of natural landforms and landscape features, often for the purpose of construction or land management. These activities can include excavations, grading, filling, and reshaping of the terrain.

In the context of sustainability, earthworks play a crucial role in managing and conserving resources, minimizing environmental impacts, and promoting ecological balance. Sustainable earthworks are guided by principles that aim to reduce the consumption of non-renewable resources, preserve biodiversity, and enhance ecosystem functions.

Eco-Conscious Architecture

Eco-conscious architecture refers to the practice of designing and constructing buildings in a way that minimizes their negative impact on the environment and promotes sustainability. It involves a holistic approach that considers the entire lifecycle of a building, from its conception to its eventual demolition or repurposing.

The primary goal of eco-conscious architecture is to reduce the consumption of non-renewable resources and decrease greenhouse gas emissions. This is achieved through various strategies, such as incorporating renewable energy sources, optimizing energy efficiency, utilizing environmentally friendly materials, and implementing water conservation measures.

Renewable energy sources, such as solar panels and wind turbines, are often integrated into the design of eco-conscious buildings to generate electricity and reduce dependence on fossil fuels. Energy efficiency is achieved through improved insulation, advanced HVAC systems, and smart building technologies that monitor and control energy usage.

In terms of materials, eco-conscious architecture prioritizes the use of sustainable and recycled materials that have a lower environmental impact compared to conventional alternatives. This includes utilizing locally sourced materials to reduce carbon emissions associated with transportation. Additionally, eco-conscious architects focus on optimizing the durability and lifespan of a building, reducing the need for frequent repairs and replacements.

Water conservation is another essential aspect of eco-conscious architecture. Buildings can incorporate rainwater harvesting systems, gray water recycling, and efficient plumbing fixtures to minimize water waste. Additionally, landscape design can prioritize native and drought-resistant plants to reduce irrigation requirements.

Eco-conscious architecture also emphasizes the importance of creating healthy indoor

103

environments. This involves using low-emission materials, designing for optimal natural lighting and ventilation, and considering the well-being of occupants by promoting access to nature and incorporating biophilic design principles.

In conclusion, eco-conscious architecture is a design approach that prioritizes sustainability and environmental responsibility. By integrating energy-efficient technologies, sustainable materials, water conservation measures, and considerations for occupant health, eco-conscious architecture aims to minimize the ecological footprint of buildings and contribute to a more sustainable future.

Eco-Conscious Building Materials

Eco-conscious building materials are materials used in the construction industry that are produced and utilized in a manner that minimizes their negative impact on the environment and promotes sustainability. These materials are chosen based on their ability to reduce energy consumption, limit waste generation, and minimize the depletion of natural resources.

The primary objective of eco-conscious building materials is to create a built environment that is both socially responsible and environmentally friendly. This means that these materials are sourced, manufactured, and used in a way that reduces carbon emissions, water consumption, and pollution throughout their lifecycle. Additionally, eco-conscious building materials prioritize the health and well-being of building occupants by emphasizing the use of non-toxic, low-emission materials that improve indoor air quality.

Examples of eco-conscious building materials include recycled steel, reclaimed wood, bamboo, and cork flooring. These materials are chosen for their high levels of recycled content or their ability to be sustainably harvested. Additionally, eco-conscious building materials often incorporate energy-efficient technologies such as insulation made from recycled materials, solar panels, and high-performance windows, which help to reduce heating, cooling, and electricity demands.

In summary, eco-conscious building materials aim to minimize the ecological footprint of the construction industry by using materials and technologies that promote sustainability, resource efficiency, and environmental responsibility. Their utilization contributes to the creation of healthier, more energy-efficient buildings with reduced impacts on ecosystems and human health.

Eco-Conscious Building Retrofits

Eco-conscious building retrofits refer to the process of making sustainable improvements or modifications to existing structures in order to reduce their environmental impact. These retrofits often aim to improve energy efficiency, conserve resources, minimize waste, and enhance indoor environmental quality.

By implementing eco-conscious building retrofits, buildings can become more environmentally friendly and contribute to the sustainability of our planet. These retrofits involve various strategies and technologies that focus on reducing energy consumption and greenhouse gas emissions. Examples of eco-conscious retrofits include the installation of energy-efficient lighting systems, upgrading insulation and windows to improve thermal performance, implementing renewable energy systems such as solar panels, and optimizing heating, ventilation, and air conditioning (HVAC) systems.

In addition to energy efficiency measures, eco-conscious building retrofits may also involve sustainable water management practices. This can include the installation of water-saving fixtures, rainwater harvesting systems, and graywater recycling systems to reduce water consumption and minimize strain on local water resources.

Furthermore, eco-conscious retrofits prioritize the use of sustainable and recyclable materials, as well as the reduction of construction waste. This may involve utilizing locally sourced materials, implementing recycling programs, and employing green construction practices to minimize the carbon footprint associated with building renovations.

Overall, eco-conscious building retrofits play a crucial role in advancing sustainability in the built environment. By implementing these retrofit strategies, buildings can significantly reduce their negative environmental impact, conserve resources, and create healthier and more comfortable spaces for building occupants.

Eco-Conscious Construction Materials

Eco-conscious construction materials are sustainable building materials that are produced and used in a way that minimizes negative environmental impacts throughout their life cycle. These materials are sourced, manufactured, and disposed of in a manner that promotes ecological balance and reduces strain on the natural resources.

Eco-conscious construction materials are characterized by several key considerations and qualities. Firstly, they are derived from renewable or recycled sources, minimizing the depletion of finite resources and reducing waste. Examples include reclaimed wood, recycled plastic, and renewable cork. Secondly, these materials have a low carbon footprint, meaning that their production and transportation result in minimal greenhouse gas emissions. This can be achieved through efficient manufacturing processes, the use of alternative energy sources, and locally sourced materials to reduce transportation distances. Additionally, eco-conscious construction materials promote energy efficiency and conservation. They are designed to enhance the insulation and overall energy performance of the building, reducing the need for artificial heating, cooling, and lighting. This can be achieved through the use of sustainable insulation materials, such as cellulose or sheep's wool. Furthermore, these materials prioritize the health and well-being of occupants. They are non-toxic, free from harmful chemicals, and have low volatile organic compound (VOC) emissions, creating a healthier indoor environment. Examples include natural paints, adhesives, and sealants. Lastly, eco-conscious construction materials aim to promote waste reduction and recycling. They are designed for easy disassembly and recyclability at the end of their useful life, contributing to a circular economy and minimizing landfill waste. In summary, eco-conscious construction materials are sustainable building materials that prioritize environmental responsibility, energy efficiency, occupant health, and waste reduction. They play a vital role in creating environmentally friendly and sustainable buildings.

Eco-Conscious Consumer Products

Eco-conscious consumer products are goods or services that are designed, manufactured, and marketed with environmental sustainability in mind. These products are developed to minimize their impact on the environment throughout their entire lifecycle, from production to disposal.

When it comes to production, eco-conscious consumer products are typically made using environmentally friendly materials and processes. This includes using renewable resources, reducing waste and emissions, and avoiding the use of toxic chemicals. Additionally, these products often aim to have a lower carbon footprint by minimizing energy consumption and utilizing renewable energy sources during manufacturing.

Furthermore, eco-conscious consumer products are intended to be used in a sustainable manner. This means they are designed to be durable and long-lasting, reducing the need for frequent replacements and thus reducing overall waste. They may also offer features that encourage energy efficiency or resource conservation during use.

Finally, disposal of eco-conscious consumer products is considered in their design. They are often designed to be recyclable, allowing for the recovery and reuse of materials at the end of their lifecycle. Some products may even be compostable, further reducing the environmental impact of their disposal.

In summary, eco-conscious consumer products are goods or services that prioritize environmental sustainability throughout their entire lifecycle. From production to use to disposal, these products aim to minimize their impact on the environment, making them a more responsible choice for environmentally conscious consumers.

Eco-Conscious Design

Eco-conscious design refers to the implementation of sustainable and environmentally-friendly principles in the design process. It involves considering the impacts of design choices on the Earth's resources and ecosystems, as well as the well-being of individuals and communities.

In an eco-conscious design approach, designers aim to minimize the negative environmental and social impacts of their creations by focusing on a range of factors. This includes using materials and resources that are renewable, recyclable, or biodegradable, as well as reducing waste and pollution throughout the product lifecycle.

Furthermore, eco-conscious design emphasizes energy efficiency and the use of renewable energy sources. Designers strive to create products that require less energy to produce, use, and dispose of, in order to reduce greenhouse gas emissions and combat climate change.

Additionally, eco-conscious design incorporates considerations of social equity and human well-being. Designers prioritize the use of non-toxic materials and ensure that their products are safe and healthy for both the end-users and the workers involved in the production process.

Eco-conscious design also involves a shift towards more sustainable and responsible consumption patterns. Designers encourage users to make conscious choices by providing information on sustainable alternatives, promoting durability and reparability, and encouraging the reuse and recycling of products.

Eco-Conscious Energy Sources

Eco-conscious energy sources refer to renewable and sustainable energy options that are environmentally friendly and have minimal negative impacts on the planet. These energy sources aim to reduce carbon emissions, conserve natural resources, and minimize pollution levels, ultimately contributing to the overall goal of sustainability.

Renewable energy sources such as solar, wind, hydro, and geothermal power are considered eco-conscious due to their ability to replenish naturally and their low or zero carbon emissions during operation. Solar energy, for example, harnesses the power of the sun using photovoltaic (PV) cells or solar thermal collectors to convert sunlight into electricity or heat, respectively. Wind energy, on the other hand, utilizes turbines to convert wind power into electricity. Hydroelectric power takes advantage of the gravitational force of flowing water to generate electricity, while geothermal energy taps into the heat beneath the Earth's surface for heating and electricity production.

In addition to these well-known renewable energy sources, other eco-conscious options include biomass energy and tidal power. Biomass energy utilizes organic matter such as wood, agricultural residues, or dedicated energy crops to produce heat or electricity. Tidal power, on the other hand, captures the energy from the natural rise and fall of the tides to drive turbines and generate electricity.

By shifting towards eco-conscious energy sources, society can greatly reduce its reliance on fossil fuels and minimize the negative impact of traditional energy generation on the environment. These sustainable alternatives offer a promising pathway towards a greener and more sustainable future, as they help combat climate change, reduce air and water pollution, protect natural habitats, and promote long-term resource conservation.

Eco-Conscious Fashion Lines

An eco-conscious fashion line refers to a collection of clothing and accessories that prioritize sustainability and environmental responsibility throughout the production process. These fashion lines aim to minimize the negative impact on the planet, including reducing waste, conserving resources, and using eco-friendly materials.

Eco-conscious fashion lines typically follow several key principles to achieve sustainability. They prioritize the use of natural, organic, or recycled materials, such as organic cotton, hemp, or recycled polyester. By opting for these materials, they reduce the demand for resource-intensive fabrics and minimize the use of chemicals in production.

In addition to material choices, eco-conscious fashion lines also focus on ethical manufacturing practices. They value fair wages and safe working conditions for their employees. By supporting responsible manufacturing processes, they ensure that workers are treated fairly and that their rights are respected.

Furthermore, these fashion lines aim to reduce waste by implementing strategies such as upcycling and recycling. Upcycling involves transforming discarded materials or products into new garments or accessories, while recycling refers to the process of converting waste materials into reusable materials.

Eco-conscious fashion lines also strive for transparency in their supply chains. They work to trace the origins of their materials and ensure that they are sourced ethically and sustainably. By doing so, these fashion lines promote accountability and encourage consumers to make informed choices.

Overall, eco-conscious fashion lines play a crucial role in promoting sustainability in the fashion industry. Through their commitment to reducing environmental impact, prioritizing ethical practices, and embracing innovation, these fashion lines inspire change and pave the way for a more sustainable future.

Eco-Conscious Transportation Initiatives

Eco-conscious transportation initiatives refer to collective efforts and strategies aimed at reducing the environmental impact of transportation systems and promoting sustainability. These initiatives focus on developing and implementing environmentally friendly and low-carbon transportation alternatives, as well as encouraging individuals and organizations to adopt more sustainable travel practices.

Eco-conscious transportation initiatives encompass a wide range of measures and approaches, including the promotion of public transportation systems, the development of efficient and clean energy vehicles, the improvement of infrastructure to support walking and cycling, the implementation of carpooling and ridesharing programs, and the integration of technology to optimize transportation networks.

By prioritizing the reduction of greenhouse gas emissions, air pollution, and congestion caused by traditional transportation modes, eco-conscious initiatives strive to mitigate the negative environmental impact associated with commuting and traveling. These sustainable transportation efforts aim to create a more vibrant and livable environment by improving air quality, reducing noise pollution, enhancing public health, and fostering social equity.

In addition to minimizing environmental harm, eco-conscious transportation initiatives can have several positive impacts on the economy and society. They can create green jobs, reduce dependence on fossil fuels, decrease traffic congestion, enhance access to transportation for marginalized communities, and encourage healthy lifestyles through active modes of transportation, such as walking and cycling. Moreover, these initiatives can contribute to the achievement of global climate targets and facilitate the transition to a more sustainable and resilient future.

Eco-Conscious Transportation Networks

Eco-conscious transportation networks refer to integrated systems of transportation that are designed and managed with a focus on minimizing negative impacts on the environment and promoting sustainability. These networks prioritize the use of clean and energy-efficient modes of transportation, such as walking, cycling, public transportation, and electric vehicles, while reducing reliance on fossil fuel-powered vehicles.

Eco-conscious transportation networks aim to reduce carbon emissions, air pollution, and traffic congestion, as well as conserve natural resources and improve overall quality of life. They involve the implementation of various strategies and initiatives, including the development of alternative transportation infrastructure, the promotion of public transportation systems, the encouragement of active modes of travel like walking and cycling, and the adoption of cleaner fuel technologies.

These networks often involve the integration of different modes of transportation, making it easier for individuals to choose sustainable options for their commutes and daily travel. They may include the provision of dedicated bicycle lanes and pedestrian paths, the expansion of public transit services, the establishment of shared mobility services like bike-sharing and carpooling, and the creation of electric vehicle charging infrastructure.

By promoting eco-conscious transportation networks, communities and cities can reduce their carbon footprint, improve air quality, and create more livable and inclusive spaces. This not only benefits the environment but also improves public health, encourages physical activity, and enhances accessibility and mobility for all residents.

Eco-Conscious Transportation Policies

Eco-conscious transportation policies refer to a set of measures and regulations implemented by governments, organizations, and individuals to promote sustainable transportation practices that minimize environmental impact. These policies aim to address the negative consequences associated with traditional transportation systems, such as greenhouse gas emissions, air pollution, traffic congestion, and resource depletion.

Eco-conscious transportation policies emphasize the use of alternative modes of transportation that are less harmful to the environment, such as public transit, cycling, and walking. These policies often involve the development and improvement of transportation infrastructure, such as the construction of bike lanes, pedestrian-friendly pathways, and the expansion of public transportation networks. They also encourage the adoption of fuel-efficient vehicles and the use of clean and renewable energy sources in transportation.

Additionally, eco-conscious transportation policies promote behavioral changes that foster sustainable transportation practices. This includes promoting carpooling, ride-sharing, and telecommuting to reduce the number of vehicles on the road. They may also involve implementing congestion pricing, parking policies, and land use planning strategies that prioritize transit-oriented development and discourage private vehicle usage.

The overall goal of eco-conscious transportation policies is to create a more sustainable and environmentally friendly transportation system that supports economic growth, enhances public health and well-being, reduces carbon emissions, and preserves natural resources for future generations.

Eco-Conscious Transportation Solutions

Eco-conscious transportation solutions refer to strategies and initiatives that aim to reduce the negative environmental impact of transportation systems on the planet. As sustainability becomes increasingly important in combating climate change and protecting the Earth's resources, eco-conscious transportation solutions focus on addressing issues such as greenhouse gas emissions, air pollution, congestion, and inefficient use of energy.

These solutions encompass a wide range of practices and technologies that promote sustainable transportation options. Examples include:

1. Public transportation: Encouraging the use of buses, trains, trams, and subways reduces the number of individual cars on the road, decreasing congestion and emissions.

2. Cycling and walking infrastructure: Investing in bike lanes, pedestrian-friendly pathways, and facilities like bike-sharing programs promotes active transportation and reduces dependency on fossil-fuel-powered vehicles.

3. Electric vehicles: Supporting the adoption of electric cars, bikes, and public transportation vehicles reduces reliance on fossil fuels, curbing greenhouse gas emissions and improving air quality.

4. Carpooling and ride-sharing: Facilitating and incentivizing carpooling and ride-sharing

services reduces the number of vehicles on the road and optimizes travel efficiency.

5. Efficient urban planning: Designing cities and communities with mixed-use zoning, compact development, and access to amenities reduces the need for long-distance travel and encourages more sustainable transportation options.

Implementing eco-conscious transportation solutions not only helps tackle climate change but also improves air quality, enhances public health, reduces traffic congestion, and creates more vibrant and livable cities. By prioritizing sustainable transportation practices, communities and individuals can contribute to a healthier and more sustainable future.

Eco-Conscious Transportation

Eco-conscious transportation refers to the use of modes of transport that have minimal negative impact on the environment, with a focus on reducing greenhouse gas emissions, conserving energy and resources, and promoting sustainable practices. This approach aims to address the environmental challenges associated with traditional forms of transportation, such as air pollution, carbon emissions, and traffic congestion.

Eco-conscious transportation includes various alternative options that are more sustainable, such as walking, biking, and using public transportation. These modes of transport have lower carbon footprints compared to fuel-powered vehicles, as they produce little to no emissions. Additionally, they promote physical activity, reduce traffic congestion, and alleviate the demand for parking spaces.

Another key aspect of eco-conscious transportation is the utilization of fuel-efficient technologies and renewable energy sources. Electric vehicles (EVs) and hybrid cars, for example, significantly reduce greenhouse gas emissions and dependence on fossil fuels. Furthermore, the development and implementation of charging stations and infrastructure for EVs play a crucial role in making sustainable transportation more accessible and convenient.

In addition to encouraging the use of sustainable transportation options, eco-conscious transportation also focuses on creating infrastructure and policies that support these alternatives. This includes the construction of bike lanes and pedestrian-friendly pathways, improvement of public transportation systems, and the integration of smart transportation technologies.

By adopting eco-conscious transportation practices, individuals, communities, and governments contribute to mitigating the negative impacts of traditional transportation on the environment, enhancing public health, and fostering sustainable development.

Eco-Conscious Urban Planning

Eco-conscious urban planning refers to the practice of creating and designing cities and urban areas that prioritize environmental sustainability, resource efficiency, and the well-being of both the natural environment and the people who live in these areas. It involves taking into account the ecological, economic, and social factors when making decisions about the development and management of urban spaces.

Eco-conscious urban planning aims to minimize the negative impact of urbanization on the environment and maximize the benefits for both current and future generations. It involves incorporating principles of sustainable development, such as reducing greenhouse gas emissions, conserving natural resources, promoting renewable energy sources, and implementing green infrastructure policies.

This type of urban planning involves a holistic approach that considers various aspects, such as land use, transportation, infrastructure, and building design. It encourages compact and walkable communities to reduce the dependence on cars and promote public transportation, cycling, and walking. It also emphasizes the importance of preserving and enhancing green spaces, including parks, gardens, and urban forests, which provide numerous environmental and social benefits.

Eco-conscious urban planning recognizes the interconnectedness of different urban systems and advocates for integrated and sustainable solutions. It takes into account the local context, cultural heritage, and community input to ensure that the planning process is inclusive and responsive to the needs and aspirations of the residents.

Eco-Friendly HVAC Systems

Eco-friendly HVAC systems, or environmentally friendly heating, ventilation, and air conditioning systems, aim to reduce the environmental impact associated with the operation of HVAC systems. These systems are designed to be energy-efficient, minimize greenhouse gas emissions, and conserve natural resources.

Eco-friendly HVAC systems incorporate various technologies and design strategies that adhere to sustainability principles. These may include:

- Energy efficiency: Eco-friendly HVAC systems utilize advanced technologies, such as variable speed compressors and fans, to optimize energy consumption. These systems are designed to achieve higher energy efficiency ratios (EER) and seasonal energy efficiency ratios (SEER). They also often incorporate energy recovery ventilation (ERV) systems to reduce energy loss during ventilation. - Use of renewable energy sources: Eco-friendly HVAC systems can integrate renewable energy sources, such as solar panels or geothermal heat pumps, to reduce reliance on fossil fuels and minimize greenhouse gas emissions. - Smart controls and automation: Smart controls and automation enable efficient operation and temperature control of HVAC systems. These systems can adjust settings based on occupancy, weather conditions, and indoor air quality, optimizing energy usage and reducing unnecessary heating and cooling. - Sustainable refrigerants: Eco-friendly HVAC systems use low-global warming potential (GWP) refrigerants that have a minimal impact on climate change. These refrigerants are designed to replace traditional hydrochlorofluorocarbons (HCFCs) and hydrofluorocarbons (HFCs) that contribute to ozone layer depletion and global warming. - Proper system sizing and maintenance: Eco-friendly HVAC systems are sized and maintained correctly to ensure optimal performance and minimize energy waste. Regular maintenance, including cleaning filters and checking for leaks, is essential to keep these systems operating efficiently. - Indoor air quality considerations: Eco-friendly HVAC systems incorporate features to enhance indoor air quality, such as filtration systems that remove pollutants and allergens from the air. This helps ensure a healthier and more comfortable indoor environment.

Eco-Friendly Batteries

Eco-friendly batteries are rechargeable power sources that are designed with features that minimize negative impacts on the environment and promote sustainability. These batteries are manufactured using environmentally friendly materials and technologies that reduce resource consumption, waste generation, and greenhouse gas emissions throughout their lifecycle.

One key characteristic of eco-friendly batteries is their ability to be recharged multiple times, reducing the need for the frequent disposal of single-use batteries. This not only saves resources but also helps prevent hazardous chemicals found in traditional batteries, such as lead, mercury, and cadmium, from entering landfills and polluting soil and water sources.

Eco-friendly batteries also prioritize energy efficiency, allowing for longer-lasting and more efficient energy storage. This reduces overall energy consumption and extends the lifespan of the battery, further minimizing waste and the need for frequent replacement.

In addition to their rechargeability and energy efficiency, eco-friendly batteries often utilize materials that are less harmful to the environment. For example, some eco-friendly batteries use lithium-ion technology, which is more environmentally friendly compared to other battery chemistries. Lithium-ion batteries have a lower environmental impact, require fewer raw materials, and have the potential for recycling and recovering valuable metals.

Overall, eco-friendly batteries play a crucial role in promoting sustainability by reducing waste, conserving resources, and minimizing environmental harm. Through their design and manufacturing processes, these batteries strive to align with the principles of the circular economy, wherein resources are used efficiently and waste is minimized, contributing to a greener and more sustainable future.

Eco-Friendly Beauty And Personal Care

Eco-friendly beauty and personal care refers to products and practices that are designed to minimize the negative impact on the environment and promote sustainability. These products are made using natural and organic ingredients that are non-toxic and biodegradable, and are packaged in eco-friendly materials that can be easily recycled or reused.

Eco-friendly beauty and personal care is rooted in the principles of sustainability, which is the ability to meet present needs without compromising the ability of future generations to meet their own needs. The production and use of conventional beauty and personal care products often involve the extraction and use of finite resources, such as petroleum and synthetic chemicals, which contribute to pollution, greenhouse gas emissions, and waste.

Eco-friendly beauty and personal care seeks to minimize these impacts by using renewable resources, such as plant-based ingredients, and avoiding the use of harmful chemicals, such as parabens and phthalates. These products are often produced using sustainable farming and manufacturing practices, which prioritize resource conservation, waste reduction, and fair labor practices.

In addition to using eco-friendly ingredients, packaging is also an important aspect of eco-friendly beauty and personal care. Conventional beauty and personal care products are often packaged in single-use plastic containers that end up in landfills or oceans. Eco-friendly packaging, on the other hand, uses materials that are recyclable, biodegradable, or compostable, such as glass, aluminum, or paper.

By choosing eco-friendly beauty and personal care products, consumers can make a positive impact on the environment by reducing waste, minimizing pollution, and supporting sustainable practices. These products not only benefit the planet, but they also promote the health and well-being of individuals by using natural and safe ingredients that are free from harmful chemicals.

Eco-Friendly Building Design Services

Eco-friendly building design services refer to the practice of designing and constructing buildings that are environmentally responsible and sustainable throughout their lifecycle. This approach takes into consideration the impact of the building on the environment, society, and economy, aiming to minimize resource consumption, reduce waste generation, and promote the use of renewable energy sources.

These services focus on integrating sustainable design principles into every aspect of the building, including site selection, energy efficiency, water conservation, indoor environmental quality, and materials selection. They strive to create buildings that are energy-efficient, with reduced carbon footprints and lower energy consumption. This is achieved through the use of energy-efficient building materials, efficient heating, ventilation, and air conditioning systems, and the adoption of renewable energy systems such as solar panels.

Furthermore, eco-friendly building design services prioritize water conservation by implementing rainwater harvesting systems, graywater reuse, and low-flow fixtures. They also aim to improve indoor environmental quality by utilizing natural ventilation, maximizing natural light, and using non-toxic and sustainable materials. This not only enhances the health and well-being of the building occupants but also reduces the environmental impact of the building.

By employing eco-friendly building design services, construction projects contribute to the sustainable development goals by reducing greenhouse gas emissions, conserving natural resources, and promoting a healthier and more sustainable built environment. These services play a crucial role in creating buildings that are not only aesthetically appealing but also socially responsible and environmentally friendly, ensuring a more sustainable future for generations to come.

Eco-Friendly Building Insulation

111

Eco-friendly building insulation refers to the materials and techniques used to insulate buildings in a sustainable and environmentally friendly manner. It involves the use of insulation materials that have a low impact on the environment throughout their entire life cycle, from extraction or production to disposal or recycling.

These insulation materials are typically made from renewable or recycled resources and have minimal greenhouse gas emissions and energy consumption in their production processes. They are designed to reduce heat transfer and improve energy efficiency in buildings, resulting in lower energy consumption for heating and cooling purposes.

Eco-Friendly Building Materials Recycling

Eco-friendly building materials recycling refers to the process of collecting, sorting, and reusing construction and demolition waste in a sustainable manner. It involves diverting materials from landfills and incineration facilities and repurposing them for new construction projects or other applications.

The objective of eco-friendly building materials recycling is to reduce the environmental impact of the construction industry by promoting the responsible management of waste. By recycling materials such as concrete, wood, metal, glass, and plastics, the need for virgin resources and energy-intensive manufacturing processes is minimized.

This practice contributes to sustainability in several ways. Firstly, it conserves valuable natural resources by reducing the demand for raw materials. This helps to preserve ecosystems and protects biodiversity. Secondly, it reduces the amount of waste that ends up in landfills, minimizing the release of harmful pollutants and greenhouse gases into the environment. Additionally, recycling construction materials can save energy since it typically requires less energy to process recycled materials than to produce new ones.

Eco-friendly building materials recycling is an integral part of the circular economy model, which aims to reduce waste generation and promote resource efficiency. Through effective waste management strategies, construction companies can minimize their environmental footprint and contribute to a more sustainable built environment.

Eco-Friendly Building Materials

Eco-friendly building materials are sustainable construction products that aim to reduce the environmental impact associated with the building industry. These materials are typically made from renewable resources, have a low carbon footprint, and can be recycled or reused after their intended use.

The use of eco-friendly building materials contributes to sustainable development by minimizing the depletion of natural resources and reducing harmful emissions throughout the entire life cycle of a building. These materials are designed to be energy efficient, durable, and non-toxic, ensuring a healthy indoor environment for occupants.

Eco-Friendly Building Practices

Eco-friendly building practices, in the context of sustainability, refer to the construction and design methods that prioritize minimizing the negative impact on the environment throughout the entire lifecycle of a building. These practices aim to conserve resources, reduce pollution, and promote a healthier and more sustainable built environment.

Eco-friendly building practices encompass various aspects, including materials sourcing, energy efficiency, water conservation, waste management, and indoor environmental quality. To be considered eco-friendly, a building project typically incorporates the following principles:

1. Sustainable materials: Usage of renewable, locally sourced, and low-impact materials that have minimal environmental footprints in their production, transportation, and disposal.

2. Energy efficiency: Incorporation of energy-efficient design strategies, such as proper insulation, high-performance windows, energy-efficient lighting, and the use of renewable energy

sources, to reduce energy consumption and greenhouse gas emissions.

3. Water conservation: Implementation of water-efficient fixtures, rainwater harvesting systems, greywater recycling, and landscaping techniques that reduce water consumption and minimize the strain on local water resources.

4. Waste management: Adoption of strategies to minimize construction waste, promote recycling and reuse of materials, and effective management of waste generated during the building's operation and maintenance.

5. Indoor environmental quality: Focus on providing a healthy and comfortable indoor environment through proper ventilation, use of non-toxic materials, daylighting, and incorporation of indoor plants that enhance air quality.

By adhering to eco-friendly building practices, the construction industry can contribute significantly to sustainable development goals, reduce carbon emissions, preserve natural resources, and create healthier and more resilient communities.

Eco-Friendly Carpooling Apps

Eco-friendly carpooling apps are digital platforms that facilitate the sharing of rides among individuals with the aim of reducing carbon emissions and promoting sustainable transportation options. These apps provide a convenient and efficient way for people to connect and share car rides, thereby minimizing the number of cars on the road and reducing traffic congestion.

In line with sustainability goals, eco-friendly carpooling apps promote the principles of carpooling, which include the effective utilization of vehicles, reducing fuel consumption, and decreasing air pollution. These apps typically allow users to search for nearby commuters heading in the same direction, enabling them to share rides and split the costs associated with travel.

By encouraging carpooling, these apps contribute to reducing the carbon footprint in several ways. Firstly, they help optimize the occupancy of vehicles, ensuring that fewer empty seats are on the road. Secondly, carpooling reduces the overall number of cars on the road, leading to decreased traffic congestion and improved air quality. Furthermore, by reducing the demand for individual car travel, these apps promote the use of public transportation and alternative modes of transportation, such as biking or walking.

Overall, eco-friendly carpooling apps play a vital role in promoting sustainable transportation by fostering a sense of shared responsibility among individuals for reducing their impact on the environment. By making it easier and more accessible for people to share rides, these apps contribute to a more sustainable and eco-friendly future by reducing carbon emissions, mitigating traffic congestion, and supporting the use of alternative transportation options.

Eco-Friendly Cleaning And Sanitation Products

Eco-friendly cleaning and sanitation products, also known as sustainable cleaning products, are cleaning agents that are produced and used in a manner that minimizes their impact on the environment and maximizes their sustainability. These products are designed to reduce the use of harmful chemicals, conserve resources, and promote the well-being of people and the planet.

Eco-friendly cleaning and sanitation products are typically made from natural, biodegradable ingredients that are derived from renewable sources. These ingredients are non-toxic and do not release harmful pollutants or contribute to air, water, and soil pollution. They are also free from synthetic fragrances, dyes, and other additives that can pose risks to human health and the environment. In addition to their composition, eco-friendly cleaning and sanitation products are formulated to be highly efficient and effective in their cleaning and sanitizing properties. They are designed to remove dirt, grime, and germs without the need for excessive scrubbing or the use of harsh chemicals. This not only reduces the amount of water and energy required for cleaning but also minimizes the exposure of people and the environment to potentially harmful substances. Furthermore, eco-friendly cleaning and sanitation products are packaged and distributed using sustainable practices. They are often sold in recyclable or compostable packaging, and efforts are made to reduce waste and promote recycling throughout the product life cycle. Overall, eco-friendly cleaning and sanitation products play a crucial role in reducing the environmental impact of cleaning and hygiene practices. By choosing these products, individuals and organizations can contribute to a healthier and more sustainable future for the planet.

Eco-Friendly Composting Solutions

Eco-friendly composting solutions are sustainable methods of converting organic waste materials into nutrient-rich compost, while minimizing negative environmental impacts. Composting is an essential practice in achieving a circular economy and reducing greenhouse gas emissions.

Composting involves the natural decomposition of organic matter, such as food scraps, yard waste, and agricultural residues, by microorganisms. Eco-friendly composting solutions ensure that this decomposition process is carried out in a controlled and environmentally responsible manner.

These solutions typically focus on optimizing the composting process through proper management techniques. This can include managing the carbon-to-nitrogen ratio, maintaining appropriate moisture levels, ensuring adequate aeration, and controlling the temperature. By maintaining these conditions, eco-friendly composting solutions accelerate the decomposition process, resulting in faster compost production.

Eco-friendly composting solutions also prioritize the diversion of organic waste from landfills, where it would otherwise generate harmful greenhouse gases. By diverting organic waste to composting facilities, these solutions reduce methane emissions and contribute to climate change mitigation.

In addition to reducing greenhouse gas emissions, eco-friendly composting solutions also offer numerous environmental benefits. Compost can improve soil health, enhance water retention capacities, reduce the need for chemical fertilizers, and promote biodiversity. By returning organic nutrients to the soil, composting supports sustainable agriculture and reduces the reliance on synthetic inputs.

Overall, eco-friendly composting solutions play a critical role in promoting sustainability by responsibly managing organic waste, reducing greenhouse gas emissions, and enhancing soil health. By adopting these solutions, individuals, businesses, and communities can contribute to a more circular and environmentally conscious economy.

Eco-Friendly Construction Materials

Eco-friendly construction materials are materials that are chosen and utilized in building projects with the aim of reducing the negative environmental impact and promoting sustainability. These materials are carefully selected to minimize resource consumption, limit waste generation, and decrease pollution during their entire lifecycle.

The primary focus of eco-friendly construction materials is to lower the carbon footprint associated with construction activities. This begins with the sourcing of raw materials, where sustainable options such as recycled or renewable materials are preferred. These materials are carefully extracted or manufactured using processes that minimize energy consumption and harmful emissions.

Furthermore, eco-friendly construction materials prioritize durability and longevity to minimize the need for frequent replacements. This reduces resource consumption and waste generation over time. Additionally, these materials aim to minimize maintenance requirements and promote energy efficiency during usage, leading to reduced energy consumption and lower environmental impact.

In addition to the choice of materials, the construction process itself plays a crucial role in sustainability. Eco-friendly construction materials are often designed for easy installation, reducing construction time and energy use. They also facilitate the adoption of sustainable construction practices, such as improved insulation, rainwater harvesting, and renewable energy integration.

Overall, eco-friendly construction materials contribute to sustainable development by minimizing resource depletion, waste generation, and environmental pollution throughout their lifecycle. They prioritize the principles of reduce, reuse, and recycle to ensure the preservation of natural resources for future generations.

Eco-Friendly Construction Practices

Eco-friendly construction practices refer to the use of sustainable materials and techniques to reduce the environmental impact of building projects. These practices are designed to minimize waste, conserve energy and water, and promote the health and well-being of both occupants and the surrounding ecosystem.

One key aspect of eco-friendly construction is the use of green building materials. These materials are typically sourced from renewable or recycled sources, such as bamboo, reclaimed wood, or recycled concrete. They are chosen for their low embodied energy, which refers to the amount of energy required to extract, process, manufacture, transport, and install the materials. By using green materials, builders can reduce greenhouse gas emissions and minimize the depletion of natural resources.

Another important aspect of eco-friendly construction is energy efficiency. This involves designing buildings with well-insulated walls and roofs, efficient heating and cooling systems, and energy-saving appliances and fixtures. By reducing the reliance on fossil fuel-based energy sources, eco-friendly buildings help to mitigate climate change and reduce air pollution.

Water conservation is also a key focus of eco-friendly construction. This can be achieved through the use of low-flow plumbing fixtures, rainwater harvesting systems, and graywater recycling. By minimizing water consumption, builders can help preserve freshwater resources and reduce the strain on local water supplies.

In addition, eco-friendly construction practices also prioritize indoor air quality and occupant comfort. This can be achieved through proper ventilation, the use of non-toxic paints and finishes, and the avoidance of materials that emit volatile organic compounds (VOCs). By creating healthier indoor environments, these practices contribute to the overall well-being of the occupants.

Eco-Friendly Construction

Eco-friendly construction refers to the practice of building structures using materials and methods that have minimal impact on the environment. It is a sustainable approach to construction that aims to reduce the overall carbon footprint and promote the efficient use of resources.

The main principles of eco-friendly construction include using renewable and recyclable materials, minimizing waste generation, and optimizing energy efficiency. Renewable materials such as bamboo, cork, and straw are commonly used in eco-friendly construction as they have a lower environmental impact compared to traditional building materials like concrete and steel.

Furthermore, eco-friendly construction also emphasizes the use of energy-efficient technologies and design strategies. This can include the installation of solar panels, high-quality insulation, and energy-efficient lighting systems. By reducing energy consumption, eco-friendly construction helps to mitigate the effects of climate change and reduce reliance on non-renewable energy sources.

In addition to material selection and energy efficiency, water conservation is another important aspect of eco-friendly construction. Implementing water-saving technologies such as low-flow fixtures and rainwater harvesting systems can help reduce water consumption and promote sustainable water management.

Overall, eco-friendly construction aims to create buildings that are not only environmentally responsible but also promote the well-being of occupants. This can be achieved through the use of non-toxic materials, good indoor air quality, and the integration of natural lighting and ventilation. By adopting eco-friendly construction practices, we can contribute to a sustainable future and minimize the negative impacts of construction on the environment.

Eco-Friendly Consumer Product Ratings

Eco-friendly consumer product ratings refer to a system of evaluating and classifying consumer products based on their environmental impact and sustainability. These ratings aim to provide consumers with information about the environmental performance of products, enabling them to make informed and sustainable purchasing decisions.

The purpose of eco-friendly consumer product ratings is to encourage and promote environmentally friendly products by creating a transparent and standardized measure of their sustainability. These ratings typically consider various criteria, such as resource usage, energy efficiency, carbon footprint, waste management, and use of hazardous substances. By quantifying the environmental impact of products, eco-friendly consumer product ratings enable consumers to compare different brands and make choices in favor of those with lower negative impacts on the environment.

Eco-friendly consumer product ratings are typically assigned by independent organizations or governmental bodies that specialize in sustainable product assessments. These organizations use rigorous methodologies and scientific data to evaluate products and assign ratings based on their environmental performance. The ratings are often displayed using a standardized symbol or label, making it easy for consumers to identify and select eco-friendly products.

Eco-friendly consumer product ratings play a crucial role in creating a market demand for sustainable products and encouraging manufacturers to adopt environmentally friendly practices. By providing information on the environmental impact of products, these ratings promote greater awareness and accountability, ultimately leading to a more sustainable and environmentally conscious society.

Eco-Friendly Energy Sources

Eco-friendly energy sources refer to renewable and sustainable energy alternatives that minimize the negative impact on the environment, while also ensuring long-term availability. These energy sources are derived from natural resources that are naturally replenished or have a minimal impact on the environment during their extraction and conversion.

One such eco-friendly energy source is solar energy, which harnesses sunlight and converts it into electricity through the use of photovoltaic cells or solar thermal collectors. Solar power is renewable, abundant, and has zero greenhouse gas emissions, making it an ideal alternative to fossil fuels.

Another eco-friendly energy source is wind energy, which captures the kinetic energy of the wind and converts it into electricity using wind turbines. Wind power is also renewable, abundant, and emits no pollutants or greenhouse gases during operation. However, the installation of wind turbines may have some environmental impacts on local ecosystems and bird migration patterns.

Hydropower, derived from the energy of flowing or falling water, is another eco-friendly energy source. It is generated by capturing the force of rivers, tides, or ocean waves and converting it into electricity through hydroelectric power plants or tidal generators. Although hydropower is renewable and emits low greenhouse gases, its construction can have significant environmental and social impacts, such as the alteration of local ecosystems and displacement of communities.

Geothermal energy is a sustainable energy source that taps into the Earth's natural heat. It involves extracting heat energy from deep underground and converting it into electricity or using it directly for heating and cooling purposes. Geothermal power plants have minimal emissions and provide a continuous and reliable source of energy. However, the exploration and extraction of geothermal resources can have localized environmental impacts.

In summary, eco-friendly energy sources are essential for achieving sustainability goals by reducing greenhouse gas emissions, promoting energy independence, and minimizing the depletion of finite fossil fuel resources. These renewable alternatives provide a way forward in building a cleaner and greener future.

Eco-Friendly Energy-Efficient HVAC Systems

An eco-friendly energy-efficient HVAC system refers to a heating, ventilation, and air conditioning system that is designed and operated in a manner that minimizes its negative impact on the environment while maximizing energy efficiency. This type of system is constructed using sustainable materials and technologies that reduce greenhouse gas emissions, conserve natural resources, and prioritize energy conservation.

Eco-friendly energy-efficient HVAC systems often incorporate various features and practices to achieve their sustainability goals. These may include the use of renewable energy sources, such as solar or geothermal power, to reduce reliance on fossil fuels. Additionally, they employ advanced insulation and sealing techniques to minimize energy loss and improve thermal efficiency.

These systems are also designed with intelligence and automation, utilizing sensors and smart controls to optimize performance and minimize energy consumption. They may include zone control capabilities, allowing individual temperature settings in different areas or rooms to avoid unnecessary heating or cooling. Furthermore, eco-friendly energy-efficient HVAC systems prioritize the use of non-toxic and environmentally friendly refrigerants to minimize harm to the ozone layer and lessen the overall carbon footprint.

Overall, an eco-friendly energy-efficient HVAC system plays a crucial role in sustainable building practices by reducing energy consumption, lowering greenhouse gas emissions, and promoting long-term environmental preservation. By investing in these systems, individuals and businesses can contribute to a more sustainable future while enjoying improved indoor comfort and lower utility bills.

Eco-Friendly Event Planning Services

Eco-friendly event planning services refer to the organization and management of events, such as conferences, weddings, or parties, with a strong focus on minimizing negative environmental impacts and promoting sustainability. These services aim to create events that are environmentally responsible, socially conscious, and economically viable.

By adopting eco-friendly practices, event planners strive to reduce waste generation and energy consumption, use renewable resources, and promote the conservation of natural resources. They seek to minimize carbon emissions, water usage, and the use of harmful chemicals and materials throughout the event planning process.

Key principles followed by eco-friendly event planning services include:

1. Sustainable sourcing: The use of locally sourced and organic ingredients for catering, as well as eco-friendly materials for decorations and event supplies.

2. Waste management: Implementing comprehensive recycling and waste reduction programs, such as composting food waste and encouraging attendees to use reusable items.

3. Energy efficiency: Utilizing energy-efficient lighting, heating, and cooling systems, as well as renewable energy sources whenever possible.

4. Transportation and mobility: Encouraging the use of public transportation, carpooling, or cycling to reduce carbon emissions and reliance on private vehicles.

5. Community engagement: Partnering with local businesses, suppliers, and organizations that share the commitment to sustainability, and actively involving attendees in sustainability initiatives.

Through their eco-friendly event planning services, organizers aim to provide a positive and memorable experience for event attendees, while minimizing any negative impacts on the environment and promoting a sustainable future.

Eco-Friendly Fashion Accessories

Eco-friendly fashion accessories refer to accessories that are made and produced in a sustainable and environmentally friendly manner. These accessories are designed to have minimal negative impact on the environment, both in terms of their production process and their afterlife.

One key aspect of eco-friendly fashion accessories is the use of sustainable materials. These materials can include organic fabrics, recycled materials, and natural fibers. By using sustainable materials, the production of these accessories minimizes the use of non-renewable resources and reduces waste and pollution.

In addition to the materials used, eco-friendly fashion accessories are also produced with a focus on ethical and fair trade practices. This means that the workers involved in the production process are treated fairly and paid a living wage. These accessories are often handcrafted, which supports local artisans and traditional craftsmanship.

Furthermore, eco-friendly fashion accessories are designed with durability in mind. They are made to last, reducing the need for frequent replacements and ultimately decreasing waste. When the lifespan of these accessories does come to an end, they can often be recycled or repurposed, ensuring that they do not end up in landfills.

Overall, eco-friendly fashion accessories are an important part of the sustainable fashion movement. They not only allow individuals to express their style and personality but also contribute to the protection and preservation of the environment and the well-being of communities involved in their production.

Eco-Friendly Furniture Rental Platforms

An eco-friendly furniture rental platform refers to a sustainable business model that allows individuals, businesses, or organizations to rent furniture for temporary use, rather than purchasing new furniture that may contribute to environmental degradation. These platforms aim to minimize waste, reduce consumption, and promote the circular economy by providing a convenient and cost-effective alternative to traditional furniture ownership.

By opting for eco-friendly furniture rental, customers can lower their environmental footprint by avoiding the production, transportation, and disposal of new furniture. The platform typically offers a range of high-quality, well-maintained furniture options that are carefully selected for their durability, functionality, and style. This ensures that customers can enjoy a comfortable and aesthetically pleasing space while minimizing the negative impact on the environment.

The sustainability aspect of these platforms extends beyond the furniture itself. They often prioritize environmentally friendly practices throughout their operations, including using eco-friendly packaging materials, optimizing delivery routes to reduce carbon emissions, and implementing responsible waste management practices.

Eco-friendly furniture rental platforms also play a role in promoting a more sustainable and conscious lifestyle. By encouraging the reuse and sharing of resources, they contribute to a more efficient use of materials and resources, reducing the demand for new furniture production. Additionally, these platforms may collaborate with sustainable manufacturers or offer refurbished and upcycled furniture options to further extend the lifespan of furniture and reduce waste generation.

Eco-Friendly Home Automation Systems

Eco-friendly home automation systems are innovative technologies that aim to maximize energy efficiency and minimize environmental impact within residential spaces. These systems integrate various devices and appliances, enabling homeowners to remotely control and optimize their energy usage, leading to reduced energy consumption and lower carbon emissions.

By automating and monitoring various aspects of the home, such as heating, cooling, lighting, and appliances, eco-friendly home automation systems provide homeowners with a sustainable approach to managing their energy consumption. These systems typically utilize smart sensors, timers, and programmable settings to ensure efficient and effective energy usage.

Eco-Friendly Home Energy Audits

An eco-friendly home energy audit is a comprehensive assessment of a residential property's energy usage and efficiency, conducted with the goal of identifying opportunities for energy savings and reducing environmental impact. This evaluation is typically performed by a qualified professional, such as an energy auditor or sustainability consultant, using a systematic approach to examining the various components and systems within the home that contribute to energy consumption.

The purpose of an eco-friendly home energy audit is to help homeowners understand their current energy consumption patterns and identify areas where energy efficiency can be improved. Through a detailed analysis of insulation levels, heating and cooling systems, appliances, lighting, and other factors, the audit provides actionable recommendations for reducing energy waste and improving overall sustainability.

Eco-Friendly Home Energy Management

Eco-friendly home energy management refers to the practice of utilizing sustainable and efficient technologies and strategies to minimize energy consumption and reduce environmental impact in residential buildings.

This approach involves implementing various measures such as energy-efficient appliances, insulation, and smart home automation systems to optimize energy usage within a household. By actively monitoring and controlling energy consumption, homeowners can make informed decisions about their energy usage and take steps to reduce waste.

Eco-friendly home energy management encompasses several key principles:

First, it focuses on reducing energy consumption by employing energy-efficient technologies. This includes using appliances with high energy ratings, such as ENERGY STAR certified products, as well as selecting LED lighting and energy-efficient heating, ventilation, and air conditioning (HVAC) systems.

Second, it emphasizes the importance of renewable energy sources. Homeowners can integrate solar panels or small wind turbines into their homes to generate clean, sustainable energy and reduce reliance on fossil fuels.

Third, it promotes the adoption of smart home automation systems that enable energy monitoring and control. These systems allow homeowners to monitor their energy usage in real-time, identify energy-intensive appliances or behaviors, and adjust energy settings accordingly.

In addition, eco-friendly home energy management encourages the use of insulation and weatherization techniques to improve energy efficiency. Proper insulation reduces heat transfer, minimizing energy loss through walls, roofs, and windows.

Overall, adopting eco-friendly home energy management practices is crucial for reducing carbon emissions, achieving energy independence, and contributing to a sustainable future.

Eco-Friendly Home Energy Storage Solutions

An eco-friendly home energy storage solution refers to a sustainable system that allows homeowners to store excess energy generated by renewable sources, such as solar panels or wind turbines, for later use. This helps to reduce dependence on the electrical grid and promotes a more environmentally conscious way of consuming and managing energy.

119

These solutions typically involve the use of batteries or other energy storage devices that can store the surplus energy during periods of low demand or high production. The stored energy can then be used during peak demand times or when the renewable energy source is not actively generating power.

By implementing an eco-friendly home energy storage solution, homeowners can not only reduce their reliance on fossil-fuel-based energy but also lower their carbon footprint. This is because storing and using self-generated renewable energy avoids the need to draw electricity from power plants that contribute to greenhouse gas emissions.

Furthermore, these systems can also enable homeowners to take advantage of time-of-use pricing, where electricity rates vary based on the time of day. By storing and using energy during periods of lower pricing, homeowners can potentially save on their electricity bills.

Eco-Friendly Home Improvement Apps

An eco-friendly home improvement app is a mobile application designed to help users make sustainable choices when renovating or improving their homes. These apps provide information, resources, and tools that enable individuals to reduce their environmental impact and create greener living spaces.

With the growing concern over climate change and the need for sustainable living, eco-friendly home improvement apps play a crucial role in promoting environmentally-conscious practices. These apps offer a wide range of features and functionalities that address various aspects of sustainability, such as energy conservation, water efficiency, waste reduction, and the use of eco-friendly materials.

One key feature of these apps is the provision of green product information. Users can access comprehensive databases that contain details about environmentally-friendly materials, such as sustainable paints, flooring options, insulation, and appliances. This helps them make informed decisions when purchasing supplies, ensuring that their choices align with sustainability goals.

Eco-friendly home improvement apps also provide guidance on energy-saving techniques and practices. They offer tips and tutorials on how to optimize energy usage, such as installing smart thermostats, energy-efficient lighting, and insulation. Some apps even offer energy calculators that estimate the potential savings from implementing specific eco-friendly measures, enabling users to track their progress and make adjustments accordingly.

In addition to energy conservation, water efficiency is another critical aspect of sustainable home improvement. These apps often include water-saving tips, product recommendations, and even irrigation system controllers that help users monitor and reduce water consumption. This promotes responsible water usage and supports efforts to conserve this precious resource.

Furthermore, eco-friendly home improvement apps emphasize waste reduction and recycling. They may provide information about local recycling centers, tips for reducing construction waste, and recommendations for donating or repurposing unwanted materials. By encouraging responsible waste management, these apps help minimize the environmental impact of home improvement projects.

Eco-Friendly Home Insulation Materials

Eco-friendly home insulation materials are environmentally sustainable materials that are used to improve the energy efficiency and thermal performance of buildings. These materials are designed to minimize the negative impact on the environment and contribute to the long-term sustainability of our planet.

There are various types of eco-friendly home insulation materials available, each with its own unique set of characteristics and benefits. Some common examples include:

1. Recycled materials: These insulation materials are made from recycled waste products such as newspapers, cardboard, denim, and glass. By utilizing recycled materials, these products help reduce the demand for new raw materials and prevent waste from ending up in landfills.

2. Natural fibers: Insulation materials made from natural fibers such as wool, cotton, hemp, and cellulose are considered eco-friendly. These materials are renewable, biodegradable, and have low embodied energy, meaning they require less energy to produce compared to synthetic materials.

3. Plant-based foams: Plant-based foams, such as those made from soy or castor oil, are a sustainable alternative to traditional petroleum-based foams. These foams have lower global warming potential and carbon emissions, making them more environmentally friendly.

4. Aerogel: Aerogel is a highly effective and eco-friendly insulation material that is made from silica or other inorganic materials. It has excellent thermal performance and is extremely lightweight, reducing transportation energy during installation.

Eco-friendly home insulation materials not only help reduce energy consumption and greenhouse gas emissions, but also improve indoor air quality, reduce noise transmission, and increase the overall comfort of a building. By choosing these sustainable alternatives, homeowners can contribute to a greener future and create healthier living environments.

Eco-Friendly Household Appliances

Eco-friendly household appliances refer to electronic devices or machines designed to minimize their negative impact on the environment throughout their lifecycle, from production to disposal. These appliances aim to reduce energy consumption, water usage, and waste generation, while promoting sustainability and environmental responsibility.

One key characteristic of eco-friendly household appliances is their energy efficiency. They are designed and manufactured to consume less electricity or fuel compared to their conventional counterparts, without compromising their functionality. Energy-efficient appliances help reduce greenhouse gas emissions and dependence on non-renewable energy sources, contributing to the global effort to mitigate climate change.

In addition to energy efficiency, eco-friendly appliances often incorporate other environmentally-friendly features. For example, water-saving appliances limit water consumption through innovative technologies, such as efficient water flow systems or sensor-based controls. This not only saves water but also reduces the energy required to heat or cool it, further lowering the appliance's environmental footprint.

Furthermore, eco-friendly appliances prioritize materials and manufacturing processes that minimize resource depletion and pollution. They may be made from recycled or renewable materials and have a reduced number of hazardous substances. Additionally, design considerations may focus on improving product lifespan and recyclability, allowing for easier disassembly and recycling at the end of the appliance's useful life.

Overall, eco-friendly household appliances play a crucial role in promoting sustainable living practices and reducing the environmental impact of residential activities. Their energy efficiency, water-saving features, and eco-conscious design contribute to a more sustainable future by conserving resources, reducing pollution, and mitigating climate change.

Eco-Friendly Household Cleaning Apps

An eco-friendly household cleaning app is a digital tool designed to promote sustainable cleaning practices in households. These apps typically provide comprehensive information, guidance, and resources to help individuals make environmentally conscious choices when it comes to cleaning their homes.

These apps often feature tips and tricks on how to use fewer harsh chemicals, reduce water wastage, and minimize environmental impact. They may include step-by-step instructions for making homemade cleaning solutions using natural and non-toxic ingredients such as vinegar, baking soda, and lemon juice. By encouraging the use of these eco-friendly alternatives, these apps contribute to reducing the overall consumption of chemical-based cleaning products that can harm both human health and the environment.

In addition, eco-friendly household cleaning apps may offer educational content on sustainable cleaning practices and their environmental benefits. They may provide information on the negative effects of traditional cleaning products, such as air and water pollution, and emphasize the importance of choosing biodegradable, non-toxic options. Some apps may even feature product reviews and recommendations for eco-friendly cleaning brands and suppliers.

Furthermore, these apps may include features for tracking cleaning routines and schedules, allowing users to set reminders for regular cleaning tasks and manage their cleaning supplies more efficiently. By promoting organization and planning, these apps help users avoid unnecessary waste and overconsumption.

In summary, eco-friendly household cleaning apps aim to empower individuals to adopt sustainable cleaning practices by providing them with information, resources, and tools to make more environmentally friendly choices. Through education, guidance, and organization, these apps contribute to reducing the ecological footprint of households and promoting a cleaner, healthier environment.

Eco-Friendly Household Products

Eco-friendly household products refer to items that are designed and manufactured with the goal of minimizing their negative impact on the environment throughout their lifecycle. These products are made using sustainable resources, have reduced energy consumption during production, and are designed to be easily recyclable or biodegradable after their intended use.

Eco-friendly household products encompass a wide range of everyday items that are used in households, including cleaning products, personal care items, and home appliances. These products are typically made using natural, non-toxic ingredients and materials that are sourced responsibly and do not contribute to deforestation or habitat destruction. They are also often packaged in minimal, recyclable, or biodegradable materials to further minimize waste and pollution.

The sustainability of eco-friendly household products extends beyond their production and packaging. These products are also designed to be energy-efficient during use, helping to reduce carbon emissions and conserve natural resources. For example, energy-saving light bulbs require less electricity to produce the same amount of light, and water-saving faucets and showerheads limit water consumption without compromising functionality.

By choosing eco-friendly household products, individuals can contribute to a more sustainable lifestyle and reduce their ecological footprint. These products not only help protect the environment by conserving natural resources and reducing pollution, but they also promote healthier living by minimizing exposure to harmful chemicals and toxins. Furthermore, supporting businesses that prioritize sustainability encourages and motivates other companies to adopt more environmentally friendly practices.

Eco-Friendly Household Water Filtration

Eco-friendly household water filtration refers to the use of sustainable methods and technologies to purify and treat household water, ensuring it is free from contaminants while minimizing harm to the environment.

The process of eco-friendly household water filtration typically involves a combination of physical, chemical, and biological methods to remove impurities and improve water quality. These methods may include sediment filtration, activated carbon filtration, reverse osmosis, ultraviolet (UV) disinfection, and ozone treatment.

Eco-friendly household water filtration systems are designed with sustainability in mind. They aim to minimize the use of harmful chemicals and reduce waste generation compared to traditional water treatment methods. These systems often use renewable energy sources, such as solar power, to power the filtration process.

By adopting eco-friendly household water filtration, individuals can contribute to the preservation of natural resources, reduce their carbon footprint, and protect human and environmental health.

These filtration systems help to conserve water by treating and reusing wastewater for non-potable purposes, such as irrigation or toilet flushing.

In conclusion, eco-friendly household water filtration combines sustainable methods and technologies to provide clean and safe water for daily use. By implementing these filtration systems, individuals can play a part in promoting a more sustainable and environmentally friendly approach to water treatment.

Eco-Friendly Industrial Cleaning Solutions

Eco-friendly industrial cleaning solutions are sustainable cleaning products and practices that aim to minimize the negative impact on the environment and human health while effectively cleaning and maintaining industrial facilities.

These cleaning solutions are designed with the principles of sustainability in mind, focusing on reducing the use of hazardous chemicals, minimizing water and energy consumption, and prioritizing the use of renewable resources. They are formulated to be biodegradable, non-toxic, and free from substances that contribute to air and water pollution.

By using eco-friendly industrial cleaning solutions, businesses can make significant contributions to environmental preservation. The reduced use of harmful chemicals not only decreases the risk of contaminating ecosystems but also protects the health of workers and surrounding communities. Additionally, minimizing water and energy consumption helps conserve natural resources and reduces greenhouse gas emissions.

These solutions are not only safer for the environment but also offer several practical benefits. They are effective in removing dirt, grease, and other contaminants from industrial surfaces, ensuring the cleanliness, hygiene, and longevity of equipment and infrastructure. Furthermore, eco-friendly cleaning solutions often have lower life cycle costs and are approved by regulatory agencies for meeting sustainability standards.

In summary, eco-friendly industrial cleaning solutions are sustainable alternatives that prioritize environmental protection, human health, and the long-term economic viability of industrial cleaning practices. By adopting these solutions, businesses can achieve their cleaning goals while minimizing their ecological footprint and contributing to a more sustainable future.

Eco-Friendly Insecticides

Eco-friendly insecticides are chemical compounds or substances that are used to control and eliminate insects in a sustainable and environmentally friendly manner. These insecticides are designed to minimize harm to the ecosystem, including non-target organisms, water sources, and the overall biodiversity of the area.

Eco-friendly insecticides aim to reduce the negative impact on the environment and human health compared to traditional insecticides. They are formulated using natural or organic ingredients, such as plant extracts, essential oils, microorganisms, or minerals. These ingredients are biodegradable and pose minimal risk to non-target organisms and the environment.

The use of eco-friendly insecticides aligns with the principles of sustainability by promoting a balanced ecosystem and protecting beneficial insects, such as pollinators and predators, that play a vital role in maintaining ecological equilibrium. They also reduce the risk of water contamination and soil pollution, which can have long-term detrimental effects on biodiversity and human health.

Furthermore, eco-friendly insecticides typically have a shorter residual life and lower toxicity levels, reducing the risk of accumulation in the environment. This decreases the potential for long-term ecological disturbances and allows for a safer and more sustainable approach to pest management.

Eco-Friendly Interior Design

123

Eco-friendly interior design refers to the practice of creating interior spaces that are designed and constructed with sustainability in mind. This approach involves using environmentally friendly materials and incorporating energy-efficient and resource-efficient design principles.

Eco-friendly interior design aims to minimize the negative impact on the environment by reducing energy consumption, conserving natural resources, and promoting the use of renewable materials. It goes beyond surface-level changes and focuses on creating a space that is not only visually appealing but also environmentally responsible.

In terms of materials, eco-friendly interior design prioritizes the use of sustainable and recycled materials. This may include using reclaimed wood, bamboo, cork, or natural stone. These materials are renewable, require less energy to produce, and have a lower carbon footprint compared to traditional materials.

Additionally, eco-friendly interior design incorporates energy-efficient lighting systems, such as LED bulbs, that consume less energy and have a longer lifespan. It also emphasizes the use of efficient appliances, such as ENERGY STAR certified products, to minimize energy consumption.

The design layout and space planning in eco-friendly interior design focus on maximizing natural light and ventilation to reduce the need for artificial lighting and cooling. This can be achieved through the strategic placement of windows and skylights, as well as the use of light-colored or reflective surfaces to enhance natural lighting. This approach not only reduces energy usage but also promotes a healthier and more comfortable living environment.

By adopting eco-friendly interior design practices, individuals and businesses can contribute to sustainable development by reducing their carbon footprint, conserving natural resources, and promoting a healthier and more environmentally friendly lifestyle.

Eco-Friendly Landscape Architecture

Eco-friendly landscape architecture refers to the practice of designing outdoor spaces that minimize harm to the environment and promote sustainability. It encompasses various strategies and techniques aimed at reducing the ecological footprint of landscapes while enhancing their aesthetic and functional qualities.

One key aspect of eco-friendly landscape architecture is the use of native plants and vegetation. Native species are well adapted to the local climate and require less water, fertilizers, and pesticides compared to non-native species. By incorporating native plants, landscape architects can create landscapes that are not only visually appealing but also support local biodiversity and require minimal maintenance.

In addition to plant selection, eco-friendly landscape architecture also focuses on efficient water management. This includes implementing rainwater harvesting systems, designing permeable surfaces to allow water infiltration, and using irrigation systems that minimize water wastage. By minimizing water use and maximizing water efficiency, eco-friendly landscapes can conserve this precious resource and reduce the need for energy-intensive water treatment and transportation.

The use of sustainable materials and construction techniques is another important aspect of eco-friendly landscape architecture. This involves choosing environmentally friendly materials such as recycled or locally sourced products, as well as employing construction methods that minimize waste and pollution. By incorporating sustainable materials and practices, landscape architects can contribute to reducing the environmental impact of landscape development and maintenance.

Overall, eco-friendly landscape architecture aims to create outdoor spaces that are not only visually appealing but also harmonious with the natural environment. By incorporating native plants, efficient water management, and sustainable materials, landscape architects can design landscapes that contribute to the conservation of natural resources, enhance biodiversity, and promote a more sustainable future.

Eco-Friendly Landscape Design

Eco-friendly landscape design refers to the practice of creating outdoor spaces that prioritize sustainability and minimize harm to the environment. It takes into account the overall ecological balance, water conservation, energy efficiency, and the use of native plants and materials.

Eco-friendly landscape design focuses on reducing negative impacts on the environment, such as decreasing water consumption, minimizing the use of pesticides and synthetic fertilizers, and reducing waste. It is designed to promote biodiversity, enhance natural ecosystems, and provide habitat for wildlife. This type of design also aims to create spaces that are aesthetically pleasing, functional, and comfortable for users.

Eco-Friendly Landscaping Design Services

Eco-friendly landscaping design services are sustainable practices aimed at creating and maintaining outdoor spaces that minimize negative environmental impacts while maximizing ecological benefits.

These services involve the use of environmentally friendly materials, techniques, and strategies to conserve resources, reduce pollution, and promote biodiversity. They prioritize the health and well-being of both the ecosystem and the individuals utilizing the space.

Eco-Friendly Landscaping Equipment

Eco-friendly landscaping equipment refers to a range of tools, machinery, and devices used in landscaping activities which are designed to minimize negative environmental impacts and promote sustainability. These equipment are specifically designed to reduce or eliminate greenhouse gas emissions, noise pollution, and other environmental pollutants commonly associated with conventional landscaping practices.

This type of equipment includes but is not limited to: battery-powered or electric lawn mowers, trimmers, and leaf blowers; manual or reel mowers; environmentally-friendly fertilizers and pesticides; rainwater collection systems; and organic composting equipment. By opting for eco-friendly landscaping equipment, individuals and professionals in the landscaping industry contribute to the overall reduction of carbon emissions and protect the surrounding ecosystem.

Eco-Friendly Landscaping Services

Eco-friendly landscaping services refer to the use of sustainable practices and materials to design, create, and maintain outdoor spaces that promote environmental health and preserve natural resources.

These services prioritize the use of organic fertilizers, natural pest control methods, and native plants that require minimal water and maintenance. The goal is to minimize the use of chemicals, reduce water consumption, and conserve energy throughout the landscaping process.

By employing eco-friendly landscaping services, property owners can minimize their carbon footprint, contribute to the preservation of biodiversity, and create a healthier and more sustainable environment.

Some key features of eco-friendly landscaping services include:

- Water conservation: These services employ techniques such as drip irrigation and rainwater harvesting to reduce water waste and ensure efficient water use.

- Soil health: Eco-friendly landscaping focuses on improving soil structure and fertility through practices such as composting and the use of organic matter.

- Native plants: By using native plants, eco-friendly landscaping services enhance the biodiversity of the area and minimize the need for excessive watering or chemical fertilizers.

125

- Integrated pest management: Instead of relying on chemical pesticides, eco-friendly landscaping services prioritize the use of biological controls, beneficial insects, and other natural methods to manage pests sustainably.

In summary, eco-friendly landscaping services promote sustainable practices that help conserve water, reduce chemical usage, and support the overall well-being of the environment. By choosing these services, individuals can create beautiful outdoor spaces while minimizing the negative impact on the planet.

Eco-Friendly Lawn Care Services

Eco-friendly lawn care services are sustainable practices focused on the maintenance and preservation of healthy lawns and landscapes while minimizing negative environmental impacts. These services prioritize the use of organic, non-toxic, and environmentally friendly products and techniques, aiming to support biodiversity, conserve water, reduce pollution, and promote soil health.

Eco-friendly lawn care professionals employ a range of strategies to achieve sustainable results. They prioritize soil health by utilizing organic fertilizers, compost, and natural soil amendments to promote nutrient-rich soils that support healthy plant growth. They employ manual or electric-powered lawn maintenance equipment, minimizing noise and air pollution compared to gas-powered alternatives.

In addition, these services implement water conservation practices by encouraging proper lawn watering techniques, such as deep and infrequent watering to promote deep root growth, preventing water wastage. Rainwater harvesting and efficient irrigation systems, such as drip irrigation or smart controllers, may also be employed to further reduce water usage.

Integrated pest management (IPM) is another key aspect of eco-friendly lawn care. Instead of relying on chemical pesticides, IPM practices involve identifying and monitoring pests, practicing proper lawn maintenance, using mechanical or biological pest control methods (such as nematodes or beneficial insects), and only resorting to targeted pesticide treatments when necessary.

By adopting these sustainable practices, eco-friendly lawn care services prioritize the long-term health of lawns and landscapes, minimizing the use of harmful chemicals and reducing waste and pollution. Through their commitment to sustainability, they help create and maintain beautiful outdoor spaces that are safe, healthy, and beneficial for both humans and the environment.

Eco-Friendly Office Furniture

Eco-friendly office furniture refers to furniture that is designed and manufactured with the goal of minimizing its environmental impact throughout its lifecycle, from production to disposal. It is a sustainable alternative to conventional furniture, as it reduces resource consumption, minimizes waste generation, and promotes the use of renewable materials.

Eco-friendly office furniture typically incorporates sustainable materials, such as FSC-certified wood, bamboo, or recycled materials, which help to reduce deforestation and promote responsible sourcing. Additionally, it uses non-toxic finishes and adhesives, reducing indoor air pollution and creating a healthier working environment for employees.

Eco-Friendly Office Supplies

Eco-friendly office supplies are products that are designed and manufactured with a focus on sustainability, reducing negative impacts on the environment throughout their lifecycle. These supplies are made from renewable or recycled materials and are produced using methods that conserve natural resources and minimize waste and pollution.

Eco-friendly office supplies help to promote a more sustainable workplace by reducing the consumption of natural resources, decreasing greenhouse gas emissions, and minimizing the amount of waste sent to landfills. These supplies often have a lower carbon footprint compared to their conventional counterparts, as they utilize materials that require less energy to produce and generate fewer greenhouse gas emissions during manufacturing.

Examples of eco-friendly office supplies include recycled paper and notebooks made from post-consumer waste, pens and pencils made from sustainably sourced wood or bamboo, refillable ink cartridges, energy-efficient LED desk lamps, and biodegradable or compostable packaging materials. These products are typically marked with eco-labels or certifications to help consumers easily identify them as environmentally-friendly options.

By choosing eco-friendly office supplies, businesses can demonstrate their commitment to sustainability and contribute to a healthier planet. In addition to reducing environmental impacts, these supplies can also have financial benefits, such as lower operating costs and increased energy efficiency. Overall, incorporating eco-friendly office supplies into everyday operations is an important step in creating a greener, more sustainable workplace.

Eco-Friendly Paint And Coatings

Eco-friendly paint and coatings refer to products that are designed and manufactured with the aim of reducing their environmental impact throughout their lifecycle. These products are specifically formulated to minimize harmful chemicals and pollutants, conserve resources, and promote sustainability.

These paints and coatings are characterized by several key attributes that make them eco-friendly. Firstly, they have a low or zero volatile organic compound (VOC) content, which means they emit fewer or no harmful chemicals into the air during application and drying. VOCs contribute to air pollution and can have adverse effects on human health and the environment.

Secondly, eco-friendly paints and coatings are typically made from renewable or recycled materials, reducing the demand for virgin resources and decreasing waste. This includes using plant-based or water-based binders instead of traditional petroleum-based ones. Additionally, sustainable pigments derived from natural sources may be used to reduce the reliance on synthetic and toxic colorants.

Furthermore, these products prioritize energy efficiency and reduce the carbon footprint associated with their production and application. This involves implementing energy-saving manufacturing processes, utilizing sustainable packaging, and promoting proper waste management and recycling practices.

In summary, eco-friendly paint and coatings are environmentally responsible alternatives that minimize harm to human health and the planet. They aim to minimize the use of harmful chemicals, reduce waste generation, conserve resources, and promote a sustainable and greener future for the paint and coatings industry.

Eco-Friendly Personal Transportation Devices

An eco-friendly personal transportation device refers to a mode of transportation that is designed to minimize its impact on the environment and promote sustainability. These devices are typically powered by clean and renewable energy sources, such as electricity or solar power, and offer an alternative to traditional vehicles that run on fossil fuels.

By using eco-friendly personal transportation devices, individuals can reduce their carbon footprint and contribute to the preservation of the environment. These devices often have lower emissions and noise pollution compared to conventional vehicles, making them ideal for crowded urban areas where air quality is a concern.

Eco-Friendly Pest Management Services

Eco-friendly pest management services refer to the use of sustainable and environmentally friendly methods to control and eradicate pests. These services aim to minimize the negative impact on the ecosystem, humans, and non-target organisms, while effectively managing pest populations.

Eco-friendly pest management focuses on prevention, monitoring, and intervention strategies that prioritize the use of non-toxic and natural pest control methods. This includes the implementation of Integrated Pest Management (IPM) techniques, which involve the careful selection and combination of cultural, biological, physical, and chemical control measures to achieve long-term pest management goals.

Instead of relying primarily on chemical pesticides, eco-friendly pest management services emphasize the use of alternative approaches, such as biological controls and cultural practices. Biological controls involve the introduction of natural enemies, such as predators, parasites, or pathogens, to control pest populations. Cultural practices include modifying the environment, such as removing pest habitats or implementing crop rotation, to reduce pest infestations.

Furthermore, these services prioritize the use of low-impact pesticides that are less harmful to the environment and human health. They also promote the use of pest-resistant crop varieties, proper waste management practices, and education on sustainable pest control techniques to prevent pest outbreaks.

In summary, eco-friendly pest management services strive to achieve sustainable and effective pest control through the adoption of non-toxic and environmentally friendly practices. By minimizing reliance on chemical pesticides and integrating various control strategies, these services help to maintain the ecological balance, protect human health, and promote long-term pest management solutions.

Eco-Friendly Pet Products

An eco-friendly pet product refers to a sustainable and environmentally conscious item specifically designed and manufactured for pets, such as dogs, cats, or small mammals. These products are created with the aim of minimizing negative impacts on the ecosystem and promoting a more sustainable lifestyle for both pets and their owners.

Eco-friendly pet products are typically made from organic or recycled materials, reducing the demand for new resources and minimizing waste. For example, pet beds may be constructed from recycled plastic bottles or organic cotton, while toys may be made from natural fibers or sustainably sourced wood. Additionally, these products are often free from harmful chemicals, such as BPA or phthalates, which can be hazardous to pets and the environment.

Furthermore, eco-friendly pet products can extend to food and accessories. Sustainable pet food options may include ingredients sourced from local and organic farms, utilizing sustainable farming practices that minimize the use of pesticides and reduce carbon emissions. Accessories, such as collars and leashes, may be crafted from biodegradable materials or upcycled fabrics, reducing the environmental impact of traditional synthetic alternatives.

In summary, eco-friendly pet products are designed with a commitment to sustainability, ensuring that pets can enjoy high-quality and safe products while minimizing their carbon footprint. By choosing these products, pet owners can contribute to a more environmentally friendly and responsible pet care routine, supporting a healthier planet for both pets and humans.

Eco-Friendly Product Design Tools

Eco-friendly product design tools refer to tools, techniques, or methods used in the design process of products that prioritize sustainability. These tools help designers create products that have a reduced impact on the environment throughout their lifecycle.

Sustainability in product design is achieved by considering the entire lifecycle of a product, from its raw material extraction, manufacturing, use, and disposal. Eco-friendly product design tools support this approach by facilitating the integration of environmental, social, and economic considerations into the design process.

These tools often include software applications or platforms that enable designers to assess and minimize the environmental impacts of a product. They allow for the modeling and simulation of different design options, taking into account factors such as energy consumption, waste

128

generation, and material selection.

Additionally, eco-friendly product design tools may provide databases or resources that help designers make informed decisions regarding sustainable materials, manufacturing processes, and end-of-life recycling or disposal options.

By using eco-friendly product design tools, designers can identify opportunities to optimize their designs for sustainability. They can explore alternative materials, design for disassembly or recyclability, and incorporate energy-efficient features.

In summary, eco-friendly product design tools play a crucial role in promoting sustainable practices by enabling designers to incorporate environmental considerations into the product design process. They help minimize the environmental footprint of products and support the transition towards a more sustainable and circular economy.

Eco-Friendly Public Transit Initiatives

Eco-friendly public transit initiatives refer to various strategies and actions implemented by governments, organizations, and communities to promote sustainable and environmentally-friendly transportation options for the public. These initiatives aim to reduce the environmental impact of transportation systems, improve air quality, combat climate change, and enhance overall sustainability.

One key aspect of eco-friendly public transit initiatives is the promotion and development of modes of transportation that have lower carbon emissions compared to private vehicle usage. This includes the expansion and improvement of public transportation systems such as buses, trains, trams, and subways, which can accommodate larger numbers of passengers and reduce the number of individual cars on the road.

In addition to promoting sustainable modes of transportation, these initiatives often involve implementing infrastructure improvements and technological advancements. This can include the creation or enhancement of bicycle lanes and pedestrian-friendly pathways, the introduction of electric or hybrid buses and trains, and the integration of smart technologies that optimize traffic flow and reduce congestion.

Eco-friendly public transit initiatives also prioritize accessibility and affordability, making sustainable transportation options available to as many people as possible. Inclusivity measures may involve providing discounted or free fares for low-income individuals, improving accessibility for people with disabilities, and prioritizing underserved communities with limited transportation options.

Overall, eco-friendly public transit initiatives play a crucial role in promoting sustainable mobility, reducing greenhouse gas emissions, and fostering healthier and more livable communities. By prioritizing environmentally-friendly transportation options and investing in infrastructure improvements, governments and organizations can contribute to a more sustainable future for both local and global communities.

Eco-Friendly Public Transportation Apps

Eco-friendly public transportation apps are mobile applications designed to provide individuals with sustainable and environmentally friendly transportation options. These apps aim to promote the use of public transportation as a means of reducing carbon emissions, congestion, and overall environmental impact associated with traditional private vehicle usage.

By aggregating data from various public transportation systems, eco-friendly public transportation apps offer users real-time information on bus, train, tram, and subway schedules, routes, and current availability. Additionally, these apps often integrate other features such as trip planning, ticket purchasing, and fare payment options, making it easier for individuals to make informed decisions and seamlessly navigate public transportation networks.

Through the use of eco-friendly public transportation apps, users can minimize their reliance on private cars, leading to a decrease in greenhouse gas emissions and air pollution. Increased utilization of public transportation can also alleviate traffic congestion, resulting in smoother traffic flow and reduced fuel consumption.

Moreover, eco-friendly public transportation apps contribute to the creation of more sustainable and livable cities. By promoting public transportation as a convenient and reliable alternative to private vehicles, these apps support the development of more efficient transportation systems, better land use planning, and the preservation of green spaces.

Overall, eco-friendly public transportation apps play a crucial role in fostering a shift towards sustainable mobility by empowering individuals to make environmentally conscious transportation choices and contributing to the creation of greener, healthier, and more resilient communities.

Eco-Friendly Public Transportation Systems

An eco-friendly public transportation system refers to a network of transportation options that are designed and operated with the principles of sustainability in mind. These systems prioritize the use of clean and efficient energy sources, minimize pollution and emissions, and promote the conservation of resources and the well-being of the environment.

Eco-friendly public transportation systems typically include various modes of transportation such as buses, trains, trams, subways, and ferries. These modes are powered by renewable energy sources, such as electricity, biofuels, or hydrogen, which significantly reduce greenhouse gas emissions and other harmful pollutants compared to fossil fuel-powered vehicles. Additionally, these systems often incorporate innovative technologies and design features to further reduce energy consumption and minimize environmental impact.

Beyond the choice of energy sources, eco-friendly public transportation systems consider various sustainability factors. They prioritize the efficient use of resources by optimizing routes, schedules, and vehicle occupancy to minimize energy consumption and reduce congestion. They also integrate infrastructure and design elements that promote walking, cycling, and other non-motorized modes of transportation, reducing the reliance on motorized vehicles and improving overall sustainability.

In summary, eco-friendly public transportation systems are vital to sustainable urban development. By reducing emissions, conserving resources, and promoting active and sustainable modes of transportation, these systems contribute to mitigating climate change, improving air quality, and enhancing the overall well-being of communities.

Eco-Friendly Renewable Energy Tariffs

Eco-friendly renewable energy tariffs are pricing plans offered by energy providers that encourage the use of sustainable and environmentally friendly sources of energy. These tariffs aim to combat climate change and reduce reliance on fossil fuels by promoting the use of renewable energy sources such as solar, wind, hydro, and geothermal power.

By opting for an eco-friendly renewable energy tariff, consumers support the production and distribution of clean energy. These tariffs are typically backed by renewable energy certificates or guarantees of origin, ensuring that the energy supplied to the consumer comes from renewable sources. This helps to reduce greenhouse gas emissions and minimize the environmental impact of energy generation.

Eco-Friendly Restaurant Practices

Eco-friendly restaurant practices refer to the environmentally conscious and sustainable actions implemented by a restaurant to minimize its negative impact on the environment and promote a more sustainable future.

These practices encompass a wide range of strategies and initiatives that address various aspects of the restaurant's operations, including energy usage, water conservation, waste reduction, sourcing of ingredients, and waste disposal. By adopting eco-friendly practices, restaurants aim to minimize their carbon footprint and contribute to the conservation of resources and overall environmental health.

Eco-Friendly Shipping And Logistics Platforms

An eco-friendly shipping and logistics platform refers to a sustainable system that aims to minimize the environmental impact of transporting goods and managing supply chains. It encompasses various practices, technologies, and strategies that enhance efficiency, reduce waste and emissions, and promote the use of renewable energy sources.

Such platforms prioritize the integration of eco-friendly measures in every stage of the shipping and logistics process. This includes optimizing transportation routes to reduce mileage and fuel consumption, implementing advanced tracking systems for real-time monitoring and planning, and utilizing eco-efficient vehicles and transportation modes.

Eco-friendly shipping and logistics platforms also emphasize the adoption of sustainable packaging materials and techniques. This includes using recyclable, biodegradable, and compostable materials, as well as reducing packaging size and weight to minimize resource consumption and waste generation.

In addition, these platforms promote collaboration and transparency among stakeholders, such as shippers, carriers, and consumers. They facilitate the exchange of information and data to enhance visibility, traceability, and decision-making, fostering a responsible and accountable supply chain.

Ultimately, eco-friendly shipping and logistics platforms strive to achieve a balance between economic growth, social responsibility, and environmental preservation. By implementing sustainable practices, they aim to mitigate the adverse impact of transportation and logistics activities, contribute to climate change mitigation, and promote the transition towards a more sustainable and circular economy.

Eco-Friendly Shipping Containers

Eco-friendly shipping containers are a sustainable solution for transporting goods across the world. These containers are designed with the goal of minimizing their environmental impact throughout their lifespan.

Firstly, eco-friendly shipping containers are typically made from recycled materials, such as used steel or aluminum. By using recycled materials, the demand for new raw materials is reduced, conserving natural resources and reducing energy consumption. This also helps to divert waste from landfills, contributing to waste reduction efforts.

Additionally, these containers are built to be durable and long-lasting. This ensures that they can be used for multiple trips, minimizing the need for new containers to be manufactured. The extended lifespan of eco-friendly shipping containers also means a reduced carbon footprint associated with the production and transportation of new containers.

Eco-friendly shipping containers are also designed to be energy-efficient. They are equipped with insulation and ventilation systems that help regulate the temperature inside, reducing the need for excessive energy consumption for heating or cooling. Some containers are even fitted with renewable energy sources, such as solar panels, to power their internal systems.

Furthermore, these containers can be repurposed and recycled at the end of their life cycle. They can be easily converted into various structures, such as offices, homes, or even community spaces. This not only avoids adding them to the waste stream but also encourages the adaptive reuse of materials, promoting a circular economy.

In conclusion, eco-friendly shipping containers offer a sustainable solution for global trade. By using recycled materials, prolonging their lifespan, and promoting energy efficiency, these containers contribute to reducing the environmental impact of the shipping industry.

Eco-Friendly Shipping Practices

Eco-friendly shipping practices refer to the methods and approaches used in the transportation of goods that minimize negative impacts on the environment and promote sustainability. These practices aim to reduce the carbon footprint, conserve energy and natural resources, protect ecosystems, and mitigate pollution associated with shipping activities.

One important aspect of eco-friendly shipping practices is the use of alternative fuels and energy sources. This includes the adoption of cleaner and more fuel-efficient technologies, such as hybrid or electric-powered vessels, as well as the use of renewable energy options such as wind or solar power. By reducing the reliance on fossil fuels and minimizing greenhouse gas emissions, these practices contribute to mitigating climate change and improving air quality.

Another key component is the optimization of shipping routes and logistics. This involves minimizing empty or half-loaded trips, implementing efficient packaging and loading methods, and utilizing advanced technologies to streamline operations. By maximizing cargo capacity and reducing unnecessary travel distances, eco-friendly shipping practices help conserve fuel and decrease transportation-related emissions.

Additionally, eco-friendly shipping practices embrace the principles of circular economy and waste reduction. This involves implementing strategies to reduce packaging waste, promote the reuse and recycling of materials, and minimize the generation of hazardous substances and pollutants. Through proper waste management and pollution prevention measures, these practices aim to protect marine ecosystems, water quality, and biodiversity.

In summary, eco-friendly shipping practices prioritize environmental responsibility in the transportation of goods. By adopting cleaner technologies, optimizing logistics, and reducing waste, these practices contribute to a more sustainable and resilient shipping industry.

Eco-Friendly Solar Panels

Eco-friendly solar panels are energy-efficient devices designed to harness sunlight and convert it into electricity or heat, while minimizing negative environmental impacts. These panels are a sustainable choice for power generation as they produce renewable energy, reduce carbon emissions, and have a low ecological footprint.

Solar panels consist of photovoltaic (PV) cells made from semiconductor materials, such as silicon, that allow electrons to move when sunlight strikes them. The movement of these electrons generates an electric current, which can be used to power various appliances and devices.

Eco-friendly solar panels play a significant role in promoting sustainability by utilizing clean, renewable energy from the sun. By using solar power, we reduce reliance on fossil fuels, such as coal or natural gas, which contribute to climate change and air pollution. Solar energy is abundant, freely available, and does not produce greenhouse gas emissions during operation.

Furthermore, solar panels have a long lifespan, typically around 25 to 30 years, and require minimal maintenance. This longevity ensures a prolonged period of energy generation with minimal impact on the environment. Additionally, the materials used in solar panels, such as glass, aluminum, and silicon, can be recycled, reducing waste and minimizing resource extraction.

In conclusion, eco-friendly solar panels are a sustainable solution for clean energy generation. They harness the power of sunlight to produce electricity, reduce reliance on fossil fuels, and minimize negative environmental impacts. By embracing solar energy, we can contribute to a greener future, combat climate change, and preserve the planet for future generations.

Eco-Friendly Supply Chain Management

Eco-friendly supply chain management refers to the practice of integrating sustainable and environmentally responsible principles into the entire process of sourcing, manufacturing, distributing, and disposing of products. It aims to minimize the negative impact of supply chain activities on the environment, while also maximizing social and economic benefits.

This approach involves assessing and addressing the environmental impact of various supply chain activities, such as transportation, packaging, and waste management. It includes the use of renewable energy sources, reducing greenhouse gas emissions, optimizing logistics to minimize fuel consumption, and implementing eco-friendly packaging materials. Additionally, eco-friendly supply chain management focuses on enhancing resource efficiency, promoting recycling and waste reduction, and ensuring fair and ethical treatment of workers throughout the supply chain.

Eco-Friendly Transportation Apps

An eco-friendly transportation app refers to a mobile application that promotes sustainable modes of transport and encourages users to make environmentally conscious choices when it comes to commuting or traveling. These apps aim to reduce carbon emissions, alleviate traffic congestion, and minimize the overall ecological footprint associated with transportation.

Typically, eco-friendly transportation apps provide users with a range of features and functionalities that support sustainable mobility. These may include:

1. Real-Time Public Transit Information: Users can access up-to-date information about bus, train, tram, or subway schedules, enabling them to plan their journeys efficiently and rely on public transportation instead of private vehicles.

2. Carpooling and Ride-Sharing Services: These apps often facilitate ride-sharing or carpooling arrangements, connecting individuals who are headed in the same direction. By optimizing the occupancy of vehicles, they help reduce the number of cars on the road, minimizing traffic congestion and emissions.

3. Bike and Scooter Sharing: Eco-friendly transportation apps may integrate with bike-sharing or scooter-sharing platforms, allowing users to easily locate and rent these sustainable modes of transport for short-distance trips.

4. Electric Vehicle (EV) Charging Stations: As the adoption of electric vehicles increases, these apps may provide information on the availability and location of EV charging stations, helping users plan their routes accordingly.

5. Carbon Footprint Tracking: Some apps enable users to track and monitor their carbon footprint based on their transportation choices. By providing insights into emissions generated by different modes of transport, users can make more informed decisions that align with their sustainability goals.

Overall, eco-friendly transportation apps strive to transform the way people move by encouraging the use of greener alternatives and fostering a more sustainable transportation ecosystem.

Eco-Friendly Transportation Design

Eco-friendly transportation design refers to the development and implementation of sustainable transportation systems that minimize negative impacts on the environment and promote the efficient use of resources. It aims to reduce greenhouse gas emissions, air and noise pollution, and dependence on non-renewable energy sources.

This design approach considers various aspects such as vehicle technology, infrastructure, and travel behavior to create transportation systems that are environmentally responsible, socially equitable, and economically viable.

Eco-Friendly Transportation Fleets

Eco-friendly transportation fleets refer to a collection of vehicles that are designed and operated with the aim of minimizing their negative impact on the environment. These fleets are specifically focused on reducing carbon emissions, promoting sustainable energy sources, and adopting efficient transportation practices.

By utilizing eco-friendly transportation fleets, organizations and communities can contribute to the overall sustainability goals and reduce their carbon footprint. This is achieved through various means, such as:

1. Embracing alternative fuel sources: Eco-friendly transportation fleets prioritize the use of cleaner and renewable energy sources, such as electric vehicles (EVs) or vehicles running on biofuels. This reduces reliance on fossil fuels and helps mitigate air pollution and greenhouse gas emissions.

2. Adopting fuel-efficient technologies: Incorporating fuel-saving technologies, such as hybrid engines or vehicles with improved aerodynamics, helps maximize fuel efficiency. By minimizing fuel consumption, eco-friendly transportation fleets reduce both cost and pollution emissions.

In summary, eco-friendly transportation fleets play a crucial role in promoting sustainable mobility. By prioritizing alternative fuels and fuel-efficient technologies, these fleets minimize the negative environmental impact associated with transportation. Their adoption contributes to the broader goal of mitigating climate change, improving air quality, and advancing overall sustainability.

Eco-Friendly Transportation Infrastructure

Eco-friendly transportation infrastructure can be defined as a sustainable system that promotes the use of environmentally friendly modes of transportation and supports the reduction of overall carbon emissions, energy consumption, and adverse environmental impacts associated with transportation activities. It encompasses the design, construction, and maintenance of transportation networks, facilities, and services that prioritize the use of clean and efficient transportation modes, such as walking, cycling, public transit, and electric vehicles. Such infrastructure aims to provide safe, accessible, and efficient transportation options while minimizing negative environmental externalities. It typically involves the implementation of various technologies and practices that align with the principles of sustainable development and conservation of natural resources. This can include the construction of bike lanes and pedestrian-friendly sidewalks, the integration of green spaces and urban forests within transport corridors, the development of electric vehicle charging stations, and the deployment of intelligent transport systems to optimize traffic flow and reduce congestion. Additionally, eco-friendly transportation infrastructure also involves the establishment of policies and regulations that promote sustainable transportation practices. This can include incentivizing the use of low-emission vehicles, implementing carbon pricing mechanisms, and creating legislation that encourages the adoption of alternative transportation modes. By embracing eco-friendly transportation infrastructure, communities and cities can enhance their overall quality of life, improve public health, reduce air and noise pollution, mitigate climate change impacts, and foster more sustainable and equitable urban environments.

Eco-Friendly Transportation Logistics Solutions

Eco-friendly transportation logistics solutions refer to the implementation of sustainable practices in the transportation industry to reduce environmental impact and promote long-term sustainable development. These solutions aim to optimize the movement of goods and people while minimizing energy consumption, greenhouse gas emissions, and other negative environmental effects.

Eco-friendly transportation logistics solutions incorporate various strategies and technologies to achieve sustainable transportation, including:

1. Efficient route planning: By utilizing advanced routing and optimization algorithms, logistics companies can minimize the distance traveled, reducing fuel consumption and emissions. This includes considering factors like traffic patterns, delivery schedules, and vehicle capacity to optimize routes.

2. Modal shift: Encouraging the use of environmentally friendly modes of transportation, such as rail or waterways, can significantly reduce carbon emissions compared to traditional road transportation. Shifting goods from trucks to trains or ships for long-distance travel can

significantly decrease fuel consumption and congestion.

3. Alternative fuels and vehicles: Implementing alternative fuels, such as biofuels, hydrogen, or electricity, and using low-emission vehicles, such as hybrid or electric vehicles, can reduce the carbon footprint of transportation activities. Additionally, investing in vehicle technology advancements, like aerodynamic design and lightweight materials, can further enhance fuel efficiency.

4. Collaboration and consolidation: Sharing logistics networks and resources among multiple organizations can optimize vehicle utilization and reduce empty miles. Consolidating shipments and utilizing shared distribution centers can also minimize the number of vehicles on the road, resulting in reduced emissions and costs.

Eco-friendly transportation logistics solutions play a crucial role in achieving sustainable development by mitigating the environmental impact of transportation activities. By adopting these practices, businesses can contribute to environmental preservation and the creation of a greener and more sustainable transportation industry.

Eco-Friendly Transportation Logistics

Eco-friendly transportation logistics refers to the practice of organizing and managing the movement of goods and people in a manner that reduces environmental impact and promotes sustainability.

This approach involves implementing strategies and using technologies that minimize carbon emissions, energy consumption, and waste generation throughout the transportation process. This includes optimizing routes to reduce unnecessary distance traveled, using alternative fuels or electric vehicles to lower greenhouse gas emissions, and employing efficient loading and packaging methods to reduce material waste.

Eco-friendly transportation logistics also involves considering the entire lifecycle of transportation, from sourcing raw materials to the end of a product's life. This includes assessing the environmental impact of suppliers and choosing those with sustainable practices, as well as promoting the reuse, recycling, or responsible disposal of transportation-related materials.

Furthermore, eco-friendly transportation logistics incorporates innovative approaches and technologies that reduce the environmental footprint of transportation. This can include the use of intelligent transportation systems, such as traffic management tools, to optimize routes and reduce congestion, as well as the integration of renewable energy sources, such as solar or wind power, to power vehicles and infrastructure.

By adopting eco-friendly transportation logistics practices, businesses and organizations can minimize their carbon footprint, improve air quality, and contribute to overall environmental sustainability. These practices not only benefit the environment but also have the potential to reduce transportation costs and improve operational efficiency in the long run.

Eco-Friendly Transportation Options

Eco-friendly transportation options refer to modes of transportation that have minimal negative impact on the environment and contribute to sustainable development. These options aim to reduce greenhouse gas emissions, air pollution, noise pollution, and other environmental pollutants, while also promoting energy efficiency and conservation.

One example of eco-friendly transportation is cycling. Bicycles do not emit any pollution during operation, unlike vehicles powered by fossil fuels. They also promote physical health and well-being, reducing the need for motorized transportation and improving air quality. Another example is walking, which is a carbon-neutral mode of transportation that requires no energy other than human effort.

Public transportation systems, such as buses and trains, are also considered eco-friendly options. These modes of transportation can accommodate a significant number of passengers and help reduce the number of individual vehicles on the road, thus decreasing traffic

135

congestion and emissions. Additionally, electric vehicles (EVs) and hybrid vehicles are becoming increasingly popular eco-friendly transportation options. EVs produce zero tailpipe emissions and can be charged using renewable energy sources, whereas hybrid vehicles combine an internal combustion engine with an electric motor, reducing fuel consumption and emissions.

Overall, eco-friendly transportation options play a vital role in mitigating climate change, promoting sustainable urban development, and improving public health. By prioritizing these modes of transportation and investing in infrastructure to support them, societies can move towards a more sustainable and environmentally-friendly future.

Eco-Friendly Transportation Planning

Eco-friendly transportation planning refers to the process of developing and implementing transportation systems that minimize negative impacts on the environment and promote sustainability. It aims to reduce greenhouse gas emissions, air and noise pollution, and resource consumption associated with transportation activities, while ensuring efficient movement of people and goods.

This planning approach prioritizes the integration of sustainable transport modes, such as walking, cycling, and public transportation, into urban and regional networks. It also emphasizes the use of cleaner and more fuel-efficient vehicles, including electric and hybrid technologies, as well as the promotion of carpooling and ridesharing to reduce the number of single-occupancy vehicles on the road.

Eco-friendly transportation planning involves careful consideration of land use patterns, transport infrastructure design, and policy development. It includes strategies to encourage compact and mixed-use development, which reduce the need for long-distance travel and enable better accessibility to daily necessities, workplaces, and recreational areas. This planning approach also involves the provision of infrastructure and facilities to support sustainable mobility options, such as bike lanes, pedestrian walkways, and well-connected public transit systems.

By adopting eco-friendly transportation planning principles, communities can foster a shift towards low-carbon and sustainable mobility, which not only reduces environmental impacts but also improves public health, enhances social equity, and boosts economic growth. This approach aligns with the broader goals of achieving sustainable development and combating climate change, as transportation is a significant contributor to global greenhouse gas emissions.

Eco-Friendly Transportation Systems

Eco-friendly transportation systems refers to sustainable modes of transportation that minimize negative impacts on the environment, reduce greenhouse gas emissions, conserve natural resources, and promote social equity. These systems aim to address the challenges associated with traditional transportation systems, such as reliance on fossil fuels, air pollution, traffic congestion, and excessive energy consumption.

Eco-friendly transportation systems include various options that prioritize environmental and social considerations. One such option is the use of electric vehicles (EVs) that are powered by renewable energy sources such as solar or wind power. EVs produce zero tailpipe emissions and have lower energy consumption compared to conventional internal combustion engine vehicles.

Eco-Friendly Travel And Tourism Apps

Eco-friendly travel and tourism apps refer to mobile applications that promote and facilitate sustainable travel practices. These apps offer tools and resources to help travelers make environmentally conscious decisions when planning, booking, and experiencing their trips.

By using eco-friendly travel and tourism apps, users can access valuable information on sustainable accommodations, transportation options, and local attractions that prioritize conservation, community support, and eco-friendly practices. These apps often provide users with recommendations on eco-conscious activities, tours, and dining options, helping them make responsible choices that minimize their carbon footprint during their travels.

In addition, eco-friendly travel and tourism apps may include features that track and offset users' carbon emissions, providing a clear understanding of the environmental impact of their journeys and offering solutions to mitigate it. These apps may also provide educational content on sustainable travel practices, raising awareness about the importance of preserving natural resources and protecting local cultures and ecosystems.

Overall, eco-friendly travel and tourism apps are essential tools for modern travelers who prioritize sustainability and want to make a positive impact on the environment. By promoting eco-conscious choices and providing resources to support sustainable travel, these apps contribute to the overall goal of creating a more sustainable tourism industry and preserving natural and cultural heritage for future generations.

Eco-Friendly Urban Design

Eco-friendly urban design refers to the practice of creating and maintaining urban environments that are sustainable, resource-efficient, and environmentally conscious. It involves the planning and development of cities and towns that prioritize the well-being of both the inhabitants and the planet.

Eco-friendly urban design takes into consideration various factors such as energy consumption, waste management, transportation systems, green spaces, and water and air quality. It aims to minimize the negative impact of urbanization on the natural environment while enhancing the quality of life for residents.

One of the key aspects of eco-friendly urban design is promoting sustainable transportation options. This includes creating walkable and bike-friendly neighborhoods, developing efficient public transportation systems, and integrating alternative modes of transportation like electric vehicles. By reducing reliance on private cars, eco-friendly urban design helps decrease air pollution and carbon emissions.

In addition, eco-friendly urban design prioritizes the conservation and preservation of natural resources. This involves the use of energy-efficient building materials and techniques, incorporating renewable energy sources such as solar panels, and implementing smart building designs that maximize natural lighting and ventilation. It also emphasizes the conservation of water through the use of rainwater harvesting systems and the protection of natural habitats.

The integration of green spaces is another important aspect of eco-friendly urban design. By incorporating parks, gardens, and green roofs, cities can improve air quality, reduce the urban heat island effect, and provide recreational spaces for residents. These green areas also support biodiversity and create a healthier and more enjoyable urban environment.

Eco-Friendly Urban Development

Eco-friendly urban development refers to the planning, design, and construction of urban areas that prioritize sustainable practices, with the aim of reducing negative impacts on the environment and promoting a high quality of life for residents. This type of development takes into account a range of factors, including energy efficiency, waste management, transportation systems, and green spaces, to create environmentally-friendly and socially-responsible cities.

Key features of eco-friendly urban development include the incorporation of renewable energy sources, such as solar panels and wind turbines, to power buildings and reduce reliance on fossil fuels. Additionally, sustainable construction materials and techniques, such as utilizing recycled materials or implementing green building certifications, are used to minimize the carbon footprint of urban infrastructure.

Waste management is another important aspect of eco-friendly urban development. This involves implementing recycling programs, encouraging composting, and reducing the generation of waste through efficient consumption and production practices. By diverting waste from landfills and promoting a circular economy, cities can significantly reduce their environmental impact.

Transportation systems play a crucial role in eco-friendly urban development, with an emphasis on promoting public transportation, walking, and cycling as sustainable alternatives to car use. Well-connected and accessible public transit networks, along with infrastructure that prioritizes pedestrians and cyclists, reduce congestion and air pollution while increasing the livability of cities.

Finally, eco-friendly urban development includes the creation and preservation of green spaces, such as parks, gardens, and urban forests. These areas provide numerous benefits, including carbon sequestration, improved air quality, and enhanced biodiversity, while offering residents spaces for recreation, relaxation, and connection with nature.

Eco-Friendly Urban Planning Initiatives

Eco-friendly urban planning initiatives refer to the set of sustainable practices and strategies employed in the development and management of urban areas. These initiatives aim to create environmentally conscious cities that minimize their ecological footprint, promote resource efficiency, and prioritize the health and well-being of residents and ecosystems.

Such initiatives encompass a variety of actions, including the preservation and restoration of natural habitats, the reduction of greenhouse gas emissions, the promotion of renewable energy sources, and the enhancement of public transportation systems. Additionally, eco-friendly urban planning initiatives focus on the implementation of sustainable building design and construction practices, the integration of green spaces and urban agriculture into the urban fabric, and the establishment of walkable and bike-friendly neighborhoods.

By incorporating these principles into urban development, cities can mitigate the impacts of climate change, contribute to the conservation of natural resources, improve air and water quality, enhance biodiversity, and create healthier and more livable environments for their residents. Furthermore, eco-friendly urban planning initiatives foster social equity and inclusivity by ensuring equal access to green spaces, public transportation, and basic services.

In conclusion, eco-friendly urban planning initiatives play a crucial role in promoting sustainable and resilient cities. By adopting a holistic approach that addresses environmental, social, and economic aspects, these initiatives aspire to create urban environments that are not only environmentally friendly but also socially inclusive and economically viable.

Eco-Friendly Urban Planning

Eco-friendly urban planning refers to the strategic and sustainable design, development, and management of urban areas with a focus on minimizing ecological footprint, conserving resources, and enhancing the overall quality of life for its residents. It encompasses a range of practices and principles that aim to create environmentally responsible cities while promoting economic viability and social equity.

This approach to urban planning takes into consideration various factors such as energy consumption, waste management, transportation systems, water conservation, green space allocation, and the use of renewable resources. It prioritizes the reduction of greenhouse gas emissions, pollution, and the depletion of natural resources, while simultaneously enhancing ecological resilience and biodiversity within urban landscapes.

Eco-friendly urban planning promotes the integration of sustainable infrastructure and technologies, such as efficient public transportation systems, renewable energy sources, green building design, and the implementation of recycling and waste reduction programs. It emphasizes the development of compact, mixed-use neighborhoods that encourage walkability and reduce dependence on private vehicles. It also encourages the preservation of green spaces, parks, and urban forests for recreation, air purification, and temperature regulation.

Moreover, eco-friendly urban planning recognizes the importance of community engagement and participation in decision-making processes, in order to ensure that diverse perspectives are considered and local needs are met. It fosters social cohesion, equitable access to resources and services, and the inclusion of vulnerable populations in the planning and development process.

Eco-Friendly Urban Streetscapes

Eco-friendly urban streetscapes can be defined as urban landscapes that are designed, developed, and managed in a sustainable manner to minimize negative impacts on the environment and promote harmony between human activities and the natural world.

These streetscapes are characterized by various features and elements that contribute to their eco-friendliness. For example, they often include green infrastructure such as street trees, planters, and green roofs, which help to reduce stormwater runoff, improve air quality, and mitigate the urban heat island effect. Additionally, eco-friendly urban streetscapes prioritize the use of environmentally friendly materials, such as recycled or locally sourced materials, and often incorporate renewable energy technologies to power street lighting or other infrastructure.

Furthermore, these streetscapes are designed to prioritize sustainable transportation options and promote active modes of mobility, such as walking, cycling, and public transit. Pedestrian and cyclist-friendly infrastructure, such as wide sidewalks, dedicated bike lanes, crosswalks, and bike-sharing programs, are integrated into the streetscape to encourage non-motorized transportation and reduce reliance on private vehicles.

Overall, eco-friendly urban streetscapes aim to create vibrant, livable, and sustainable urban environments that enhance the quality of life for residents while minimizing environmental impacts. By integrating nature with the built environment and promoting sustainable transportation options, these streetscapes contribute to the overall sustainability and resilience of cities, helping to create healthier, greener, and more equitable communities.

Eco-Friendly Urban Transportation Design

Eco-friendly urban transportation design refers to the development and implementation of transportation systems and vehicles that aim to minimize their negative impact on the environment while meeting the mobility needs of urban inhabitants.

This design approach focuses on sustainability by addressing environmental, social, and economic concerns. It involves the integration of various elements such as energy efficiency, reduced emissions, alternative fuels, and resource conservation.

One key aspect of eco-friendly urban transportation design is promoting the use of public transportation systems. Efficient and well-connected bus, tram, and subway networks can significantly reduce the number of private cars on the road, thereby decreasing air pollution, traffic congestion, and carbon emissions. Additionally, the introduction of electric buses or even hydrogen-powered public transport can further contribute to a cleaner urban environment.

Another component of eco-friendly transportation design is the promotion of non-motorized modes of transport such as walking and cycling. The provision of safe and accessible pedestrian walkways and cycling infrastructure encourages people to choose these modes for short-distance travel, reducing the dependence on motorized vehicles and promoting physical activity.

Eco-friendly urban transportation design also emphasizes the need for vehicle electrification and the use of renewable energy sources. Electric cars and bikes, powered by clean energy, offer lower emissions and reduced noise pollution compared to traditional fossil fuel-powered vehicles. Implementing charging infrastructure and supporting the development of renewable energy systems can further enhance the sustainability of urban transportation.

Eco-Friendly Urban Transportation Planning

Eco-friendly urban transportation planning refers to the process of designing and implementing sustainable transportation systems within urban areas. It involves the development of strategies, policies, and initiatives that prioritize the use of environmentally friendly modes of transportation, such as walking, cycling, public transit, and electric vehicles, while minimizing the negative environmental impacts associated with urban mobility.

This planning approach aims to create a balance between the growing demand for transportation services and the need to reduce greenhouse gas emissions, air pollution, congestion, and noise levels in cities. It considers the integration and optimization of various modes of transport, as well as the improvement of infrastructure, accessibility, and safety for pedestrians and cyclists.

By promoting eco-friendly transportation options, urban transportation planning seeks to achieve several objectives:

1. Reduce carbon emissions: By encouraging the use of low-emission vehicles and promoting sustainable modes of transport, cities can contribute to mitigating climate change and improving air quality.

2. Enhance public health: Increasing active modes of transport, such as walking and cycling, can help improve public health by promoting physical activity and reducing sedentary behavior.

3. Improve mobility and accessibility: By providing efficient and affordable transportation options, urban transportation planning aims to enhance mobility for all residents, including those with limited access to private vehicles.

4. Reduce traffic congestion: Implementing comprehensive transportation strategies can help alleviate traffic congestion, leading to shorter travel times, improved road safety, and increased productivity.

In conclusion, eco-friendly urban transportation planning plays a vital role in creating sustainable, accessible, and efficient urban environments. Through the prioritization of eco-friendly modes of transport and the adoption of innovative solutions, cities can minimize environmental impacts while improving the quality of life for their inhabitants.

Eco-Friendly Vehicle Aesthetics

Eco-friendly vehicle aesthetics refers to the visual design elements and features of a vehicle that contribute to its environmental sustainability. These aesthetics are aimed at minimizing the negative impact on the environment by enhancing the efficiency and eco-friendliness of the vehicle design.

The aesthetics of eco-friendly vehicles focus on several key aspects:

1. Aerodynamic Design: Eco-friendly vehicles are designed with streamlined shapes and smooth surfaces to minimize drag and improve fuel efficiency. These designs reduce air resistance, allowing the vehicle to require less energy to move, resulting in reduced carbon emissions.

2. Lightweight Materials: The use of lightweight materials, such as aluminum or carbon fiber, helps reduce the overall weight of the vehicle. Lighter vehicles require less energy to propel, leading to improved fuel efficiency and reduced emissions.

3. Energy-Efficient Lighting: Eco-friendly vehicles often incorporate energy-efficient lighting systems, such as light-emitting diodes (LEDs). These lighting systems consume less power than traditional bulbs, contributing to energy conservation and reduced greenhouse gas emissions.

4. Sustainable Interior Materials: The use of sustainable and recyclable materials in the interior design of eco-friendly vehicles is another important aesthetic consideration. This may include the use of recycled plastic, natural fibers, or eco-friendly fabrics, all aimed at reducing the environmental impact of the vehicle's production and use.

In conclusion, eco-friendly vehicle aesthetics encompass a range of design elements and features that enhance the sustainability of vehicles. These aesthetics prioritize aerodynamic design, lightweight materials, energy-efficient lighting, and the use of sustainable interior materials. By incorporating these design principles, eco-friendly vehicles aim to minimize their impact on the environment, reduce fuel consumption, and lower carbon emissions.

Eco-Friendly Vehicle Design

140

An eco-friendly vehicle design refers to the creation and development of automobiles that prioritize sustainability and minimize negative environmental impacts throughout their lifecycle. Such vehicles aim to reduce greenhouse gas emissions, dependence on fossil fuels, and other pollutants associated with traditional vehicles. The design process encompasses multiple aspects, including materials, production methods, fuel efficiency, and overall energy consumption.

One fundamental element of eco-friendly vehicle design is the use of alternative energy sources. This includes electric vehicles (EVs) powered by rechargeable batteries and hydrogen fuel cell vehicles (FCVs) using hydrogen gas. These energy sources produce zero direct emissions, making them more environmentally friendly than internal combustion engines. Additionally, EVs and FCVs can be charged or refueled using renewable energy sources, further reducing their carbon footprint.

In addition to alternative energy sources, eco-friendly vehicle design emphasizes lightweight materials that minimize energy consumption during driving. This includes the use of advanced composites, aluminum, or carbon fiber instead of traditional steel. Lighter vehicles require less energy to accelerate and operate, leading to improved fuel efficiency and reduced emissions.

Eco-friendly vehicle designs also prioritize the use of recycled or recyclable materials to minimize waste and resource consumption. This includes incorporating recycled plastics, natural fibers, and bio-based materials in vehicle components and interiors. Designers also consider end-of-life solutions, such as facilitating vehicle disassembly and providing for ease of recycling or reuse of components.

Overall, eco-friendly vehicle design focuses on integrating sustainable principles to create automobiles that are energy-efficient, emit low or zero emissions, and minimize their environmental impact throughout their lifecycle. By promoting the use of alternative energy sources, lightweight materials, and recyclable components, these designs contribute to a more sustainable transportation system and help mitigate the effects of climate change.

Eco-Friendly Waste Disposal Solutions

Eco-friendly waste disposal solutions refer to methods or approaches that are designed to minimize environmental impact and promote sustainability during the management and disposal of waste materials. These solutions aim to reduce the amount of waste generated, maximize resource recovery and recycling, and minimize the release of pollutants into the environment.

One eco-friendly waste disposal solution is recycling, which involves collecting, sorting, and processing waste materials to manufacture new products. By recycling materials such as paper, plastic, glass, and metal, the need for extracting and processing virgin resources is reduced, resulting in energy savings and reduced greenhouse gas emissions.

Another eco-friendly waste disposal solution is composting, which involves the decomposition of organic waste materials such as food scraps and yard trimmings in a controlled environment. Composting not only diverts organic waste from landfills, reducing methane emissions, but also produces nutrient-rich compost that can be used to enhance soil health and promote sustainable agriculture.

Waste-to-energy technologies are also considered eco-friendly waste disposal solutions. These technologies convert waste materials into heat, electricity, or fuel through processes such as incineration, gasification, or anaerobic digestion. By harnessing the energy content of waste, these technologies reduce the reliance on fossil fuels and provide a renewable source of energy.

Eco-Friendly Waste Disposal Systems

Eco-friendly waste disposal systems refer to sustainable methods and practices aimed at managing and handling waste in a way that minimizes negative environmental impacts and promotes long-term sustainability. These systems focus on reducing, reusing, recycling, and properly disposing of waste materials while taking into consideration the protection of the natural environment and the conservation of resources.

The key principles and components of eco-friendly waste disposal systems include:

1. Waste reduction: This involves minimizing the generation of waste at the source through measures such as product redesign, packaging reduction, and promoting sustainable consumption practices. By reducing the amount of waste produced, fewer resources are consumed, and less waste ends up in landfills or incinerators.

2. Reuse and recycling: Eco-friendly waste disposal systems prioritize the reuse and recycling of materials whenever possible. Reusable items are encouraged to be used again, while recyclable materials are collected, sorted, and processed to create new products. This helps conserve natural resources, reduces energy consumption, and decreases the need for new raw materials.

3. Proper disposal: When waste cannot be reduced, reused, or recycled, eco-friendly waste disposal systems ensure that it is properly treated and disposed of. This can involve techniques such as composting organic waste, using advanced waste treatment technologies, or utilizing landfills that follow strict environmental regulations to minimize the release of pollutants into the environment.

Overall, eco-friendly waste disposal systems play a crucial role in the transition towards a more sustainable and circular economy. By adopting such systems, individuals, businesses, and communities can contribute to minimizing waste generation, conserving resources, and protecting the environment for future generations.

Eco-Friendly Waste Management Systems

An eco-friendly waste management system refers to a set of practices and technologies that aim to minimize the negative impact of waste on the environment and promote sustainability. It involves the efficient collection, separation, recycling, and disposal of waste, with the goal of reducing pollution and conserving resources.

One key aspect of an eco-friendly waste management system is the implementation of recycling and reuse programs. This involves sorting waste at the source and recycling materials such as paper, plastic, glass, and metal instead of sending them to landfills or incinerators. By promoting recycling, valuable resources can be conserved and air and water pollution associated with the production and extraction of raw materials can be reduced.

Additionally, eco-friendly waste management systems often employ composting techniques to divert organic waste from landfills. Composting involves the decomposition of organic matter, such as food scraps and yard waste, into nutrient-rich soil amendments. By composting organic waste, greenhouse gas emissions from landfills are minimized, and the resulting compost can be used to enrich soil and support sustainable agriculture.

Moreover, an eco-friendly waste management system emphasizes the responsible disposal of hazardous and non-recyclable waste. This includes the proper treatment and containment of hazardous materials to prevent contamination of soil and water sources. By implementing effective waste disposal practices, the risks to human health and the environment can be minimized.

In summary, an eco-friendly waste management system is a sustainable approach to handling waste that focuses on minimizing pollution, conserving resources, and promoting the recycling and reuse of materials. By adopting such systems, communities can reduce their environmental footprint and contribute to a more sustainable future.

>

Eco-Friendly Waste Management

Eco-friendly waste management refers to the implementation of practices and strategies that minimize the negative impact of waste on the environment. It involves the efficient handling, disposal, and treatment of waste materials, taking into consideration their potential environmental and social consequences.

Eco-friendly waste management aims to reduce the amount of waste generated, encourage recycling and reuse, and promote responsible waste disposal. It encompasses various activities such as waste segregation, composting, recycling, and the use of alternative energy sources.

One of the key principles of eco-friendly waste management is the adoption of the 3Rs: Reduce, Reuse, and Recycle. This involves reducing the amount of waste produced by opting for sustainable practices, reusing items whenever possible, and recycling materials to extract their value and prevent them from ending up in landfills or polluting the environment.

Another important aspect of eco-friendly waste management is the proper disposal and treatment of hazardous waste. This includes the safe handling and storage of hazardous materials, as well as their treatment through methods such as incineration, neutralization, or biological processes.

In addition to minimizing the negative impact of waste, eco-friendly waste management also aims to maximize the benefits that can be derived from waste. This includes generating renewable energy from organic waste through anaerobic digestion or utilizing waste as a resource for producing new materials.

Eco-Friendly Waste Recycling Technologies

Eco-friendly waste recycling technologies refer to the various methods and processes used to efficiently and sustainably manage and reduce waste. These technologies prioritize the conservation of resources, reduction of pollution, and preservation of the environment.

One commonly used eco-friendly waste recycling technology is mechanical recycling. This method involves the collection, sorting, and processing of waste materials such as plastics, paper, and metals. These materials are then transformed into new products, reducing the need for virgin resources and minimizing waste production.

Another important technology is composting. Composting involves the decomposition of organic waste such as food scraps, yard trimmings, and agricultural residues. Through a controlled process that mimics nature, organic waste is transformed into nutrient-rich compost that can be used as a natural fertilizer, improving soil health and reducing the need for synthetic fertilizers.

In addition to mechanical recycling and composting, advanced technologies such as pyrolysis and anaerobic digestion are gaining traction. Pyrolysis involves heating waste materials in the absence of oxygen, resulting in the production of biochar, bio-oil, and syngas. These can be used as alternative energy sources or as feedstock for various industries. Anaerobic digestion, on the other hand, breaks down organic waste in an oxygen-free environment, producing biogas that can be used for electricity generation or as a source of renewable natural gas.

Overall, eco-friendly waste recycling technologies play a critical role in promoting sustainability by reducing waste generation, conserving resources, and minimizing environmental impacts. By implementing these technologies, we can move towards a circular economy where waste is seen as a valuable resource rather than a burden.

Eco-Friendly Waste-To-Energy Solutions

Eco-friendly waste-to-energy solutions refer to sustainable methods of converting waste materials into usable forms of energy, while minimizing negative environmental impacts.

These solutions aim to address two pressing issues - waste management and energy production - by integrating practices that prioritize resource conservation and pollution prevention. Waste-to-energy technologies encompass a range of processes, including incineration, gasification, pyrolysis, and anaerobic digestion, which enable the recovery of heat, electricity, or biofuels from organic or non-organic waste materials.

By implementing eco-friendly waste-to-energy solutions, societies can achieve multiple environmental and sustainability benefits. Firstly, these technologies help reduce the volume of waste sent to landfills, thereby reducing emissions of greenhouse gases and minimizing the release of pollutants into the air, water, and soil. Secondly, they contribute to the diversification of energy sources and reduce dependence on non-renewable fossil fuels such as coal or oil, thereby mitigating climate change and promoting energy security. Thirdly, waste-to-energy solutions have the potential to generate renewable energy, reducing the need for traditional forms of electricity generation and contributing to the achievement of renewable energy targets.

Overall, eco-friendly waste-to-energy solutions play a crucial role in achieving a circular economy and promoting sustainable development by addressing the interconnected challenges of waste management, climate change, and energy security.

Eco-Friendly Wastewater Treatment Solutions

Eco-friendly wastewater treatment solutions refer to sustainable methods and systems used to purify and manage wastewater while minimizing environmental impact. These solutions aim to address the increasing challenges associated with wastewater treatment, including water scarcity, pollution, and the depletion of natural resources.

The primary goal of eco-friendly wastewater treatment is to treat and reuse wastewater effectively, reducing the strain on freshwater resources and preventing pollution of water bodies. This is achieved through various sustainable practices such as:

1. Biological Treatment: This method utilizes microorganisms to break down organic matter in wastewater, converting it into harmless byproducts like carbon dioxide and water. By harnessing natural biological processes, this treatment option eliminates the need for harmful chemicals or energy-intensive processes.

2. Green Infrastructure: Eco-friendly treatment solutions integrate natural elements like wetlands, vegetation, and constructed wetlands to naturally filter and treat wastewater. These green technologies mimic natural processes and enhance the quality of effluent, while also providing additional ecosystem benefits such as habitat creation and climate resilience.

3. Resource Recovery: Sustainable treatment systems focus on extracting valuable resources from wastewater, such as nutrients like phosphorus and elements like nitrogen. These recovered resources can be reused in agriculture or other industries, reducing the reliance on synthetic fertilizers and minimizing environmental pollution.

Eco-friendly wastewater treatment solutions play a vital role in promoting sustainable development by efficiently managing water resources, reducing pollution, and preserving ecosystems. By adopting these innovative technologies and strategies, we can achieve a more circular and sustainable approach to wastewater management, supporting a healthier environment for current and future generations.

Eco-Friendly Water Conservation Technology

Eco-friendly water conservation technology refers to the use of innovative and sustainable methods, systems, and devices to reduce water wastage and promote the efficient use of water resources. This technology aims to address the increasing global water scarcity and the negative environmental impacts caused by excessive water consumption.

One aspect of eco-friendly water conservation technology is the implementation of water-saving devices. These devices are designed to minimize water consumption in various settings, such as households, industries, and agriculture. Examples of such devices include low-flow faucets, showerheads, and toilets, as well as irrigation systems with smart sensors and controllers that optimize water usage based on weather conditions and plant needs.

Another approach to eco-friendly water conservation technology involves the use of advanced water treatment and recycling systems. These systems treat wastewater and make it suitable for reuse in various non-potable applications, such as irrigation, toilet flushing, and industrial processes. By reducing the demand for freshwater, these technologies help conserve water resources and minimize the pollution of natural water bodies.

Furthermore, eco-friendly water conservation technology encompasses the integration of digital solutions and data-driven approaches. This includes the use of smart technologies, such as IoT

(Internet of Things) devices and sensors, to monitor water usage, detect leaks, and optimize water distribution systems. By providing real-time information and automated control, these technologies enable more efficient and sustainable water management.

Eco-Friendly Water Filtration

Eco-friendly water filtration refers to the process of purifying water in a sustainable manner, with minimal negative impact on the environment.

It involves the use of filtration systems that are designed to reduce or eliminate harmful contaminants from water sources, without contributing to pollution or resource depletion. These systems are typically designed to be energy-efficient, using minimal amounts of electricity or relying on natural processes for filtration.

Eco-Friendly Water Purification Systems

Eco-friendly water purification systems are sustainable technologies that remove impurities and contaminants from water sources, making them safe and suitable for various purposes while minimizing negative environmental impacts. These systems use innovative and environmentally conscious methods to treat and manage water resources, ensuring the protection of ecosystems and promoting long-term sustainable use of water.

By incorporating eco-friendly practices, these water purification systems reduce harmful pollutants, chemical usage, and energy consumption. They aim to minimize the depletion of natural resources and prevent the release of harmful substances into the environment. These systems prioritize the use of renewable energy sources, such as solar or wind power, to operate the purification process, eliminating or reducing reliance on fossil fuels and reducing greenhouse gas emissions.

Eco-friendly water purification systems often employ diverse techniques such as filtration, sedimentation, disinfection, and chemical-free processes like activated carbon absorption or reverse osmosis. These methods help remove bacteria, viruses, heavy metals, chemicals, and other contaminants from water, ensuring its quality and safety.

Moreover, these systems often incorporate sustainable and recyclable materials in their design and construction. They focus on reducing waste generation and increasing resource efficiency by adopting closed-loop systems that minimize water and material wastage.

The implementation of eco-friendly water purification systems contributes to the preservation and restoration of clean water sources, protecting ecosystems, and improving human health. They promote a sustainable water cycle, ensuring clean water availability for current and future generations while reducing the overall environmental footprint.

Eco-Friendly Water-Efficient Appliances

Eco-friendly water-efficient appliances are devices that have been designed and manufactured to reduce water consumption and minimize their environmental impact. These appliances are specifically engineered to operate using less water without compromising their performance or efficiency.

By employing innovative technologies and features, eco-friendly water-efficient appliances help conserve water resources while minimizing energy consumption and reducing carbon emissions. These appliances can include washing machines, dishwashers, showers, faucets, toilets, and irrigation systems, among others.

In terms of sustainability, these appliances play a crucial role in reducing water waste and promoting efficient use of resources. Water scarcity is a growing concern globally, and eco-friendly water-efficient appliances help tackle this issue by addressing the excessive water consumption associated with traditional appliances.

These appliances typically incorporate features such as low-flow showerheads, aerators, and sensors that detect water level and adjust usage accordingly. They may also offer programmable settings or options for water-saving cycles, allowing users to customize their water consumption based on specific needs.

Furthermore, eco-friendly water-efficient appliances not only conserve water but also contribute to energy efficiency. By using less water, they require less energy for heating and transporting the water, leading to reduced energy costs and decreased carbon emissions associated with energy production.

Overall, by choosing eco-friendly water-efficient appliances, individuals and businesses can contribute to sustainable water management, reduce their environmental footprint, and conserve valuable natural resources for future generations.

Eco-Friendly Water-Saving Fixtures

Eco-friendly water-saving fixtures are bathroom and kitchen fixtures that are designed to minimize water consumption while maintaining optimal functionality. These fixtures aim to address the increasing global concern of water scarcity, promote sustainable water management, and reduce water wastage.

These water-saving fixtures typically include faucets, showerheads, toilets, and dishwashers, among others. They are designed with innovative technologies and features that enable efficient water usage without compromising on user experience. For instance, low-flow faucets and showerheads have flow restrictors that limit water flow without sacrificing water pressure, resulting in significant water savings. Similarly, dual-flush toilets provide the option to use less water for liquid waste and more water for solid waste, offering further water conservation benefits.

Furthermore, eco-friendly water-saving fixtures often incorporate additional features such as automatic sensors that detect when water is needed, reducing the likelihood of accidental water wastage. Some fixtures may also include advanced filtration systems that help improve water quality, promoting both sustainability and health.

By using eco-friendly water-saving fixtures, individuals and households can actively contribute to conserving water resources and reducing water consumption. The implementation of these fixtures can have a substantial impact on reducing water usage and associated energy costs, as well as alleviating the strain on freshwater sources.

In summary, eco-friendly water-saving fixtures are sustainable solutions that promote water conservation and sustainable water management. Through innovative design and technology, these fixtures facilitate reduced water consumption without sacrificing functionality or user experience.

Eco-Labeling And Certification Services

Eco-labeling and certification services refer to the process of assessing and labeling products or services that meet specific environmental standards. These standards are developed based on sustainable practices and aim to promote environmentally friendly choices among consumers.

Eco-labels are symbols or logos that indicate a product or service has been certified as meeting these set environmental standards. They provide information to consumers about the sustainability of a product or service and enable them to make informed purchasing decisions. Eco-labels typically cover a range of environmental aspects, such as energy efficiency, water conservation, waste reduction, and emissions reduction.

Certification services play a crucial role in the eco-labeling process. They are responsible for conducting assessments and audits to verify if a product or service meets the required sustainability criteria. Certification bodies follow standardized protocols and criteria set by regulatory bodies or industry associations to ensure credibility and consistency in the certification process.

By obtaining an eco-label, businesses can differentiate themselves in the market and demonstrate their commitment to sustainability. Eco-labels also serve as a marketing tool, as consumers increasingly prioritize environmentally friendly products and services. Additionally, eco-labeling and certification services contribute to fostering sustainable practices across industries by encouraging companies to adopt green initiatives and improve their environmental performance.

Eco-Labeling For Consumer Products

Eco-labeling for consumer products refers to the practice of certifying and labeling products with information about their environmental impact and sustainability. It is a voluntary system that aims to inform consumers about the environmental attributes of a product, allowing them to make more sustainable purchasing decisions.

Eco-labels can provide information on various aspects of a product's environmental performance, such as its energy efficiency, carbon footprint, water usage, waste generation, and use of hazardous substances. These labels often include a standardized symbol or logo that indicates the product meets certain environmental criteria, typically set by an independent third-party organization or certification body.

The purpose of eco-labeling is to promote transparency and accountability in the marketplace, by providing consumers with reliable and easily understandable information about the environmental impacts associated with different products. This enables consumers to choose products that align with their values and sustainability goals, while also incentivizing manufacturers to improve the environmental performance of their products.

By encouraging the production and consumption of more sustainable products, eco-labeling can contribute to the broader goal of sustainable development. It helps raise awareness about environmental issues and fosters a shift towards more responsible and environmentally friendly production and consumption patterns.

Eco-Labeling For Food Products

Eco-labeling for food products can be defined as a system that provides consumers with information about the environmental impacts of specific food items. This labeling allows consumers to make more sustainable choices by considering the ecological footprint associated with the production, packaging, transportation, and disposal of food products.

The purpose of eco-labeling is to promote sustainable agricultural practices, minimize the use of natural resources, reduce pollution, and protect biodiversity. It helps consumers identify products that have undergone environmentally friendly practices throughout their supply chains. By displaying specific eco-labels on packaging, such as organic, fair trade, or carbon neutral certifications, food producers indicate that their products meet certain sustainability criteria.

Eco-labeling typically covers various aspects of sustainability, including greenhouse gas emissions, water usage, waste management, pesticide use, and animal welfare. The labels also provide information about the origin of the product, supporting local and small-scale producers, and fair labor practices. In addition, eco-labeling schemes often require adherence to strict environmental standards, which may involve regular audits and certifications to ensure compliance.

Eco-labels empower consumers to make informed choices aligned with their values and support sustainable food systems. They encourage responsible consumption and promote transparent communication between producers and consumers. By choosing eco-labeled food products, consumers can contribute to the preservation of natural resources, reduce environmental degradation, and support the livelihoods of farmers and producers committed to sustainable practices.

Eco-Labeling Standards

Eco-labeling standards refer to a set of transparent and measurable criteria that are used to assess the environmental and sustainability performance of products, services, or organizations. These standards are typically developed by independent organizations or government bodies and are aimed at guiding consumers and stakeholders in making informed decisions to support environmentally friendly and socially responsible choices.

Eco-labeling standards serve as a certification or labeling mechanism that identifies and validates the environmental claims of a product, service, or organization. They provide a reliable and credible way to communicate the environmental attributes and impact of a product, service, or organization throughout its life cycle, from sourcing of raw materials to disposal. Through clear and consistent labeling, eco-labeling standards help consumers identify products and services that have reduced environmental impact, are energy efficient, promote responsible resource use, and reduce pollution.

The criteria used in eco-labeling standards vary depending on the context and type of product or service being assessed. They may include considerations such as carbon footprint, water usage, waste generation, biodiversity conservation, renewable energy use, and social and ethical responsibility. These criteria are often based on scientific research, life cycle assessment methodologies, and best practices in sustainable production and consumption.

Eco-labeling standards play a crucial role in promoting sustainable development by encouraging innovation, driving market demand for environmentally friendly products and services, and facilitating informed decision-making. By choosing products and services with recognized eco-labels, consumers can contribute to a more sustainable and responsible society and support companies that are committed to minimizing their environmental impact.

Eco-Sensitive Architecture

Eco-sensitive architecture refers to the design and construction of buildings that prioritize sustainability and environmental consciousness. It aims to minimize the negative impact of buildings on the natural environment by utilizing innovative technologies and materials.

This architectural approach emphasizes the use of renewable energy sources, such as solar power, wind energy, and geothermal heating and cooling systems. By relying on these sustainable alternatives, eco-sensitive buildings reduce their dependence on non-renewable energy sources and contribute to lower greenhouse gas emissions.

In addition to energy efficiency, eco-sensitive architecture also focuses on water conservation. It incorporates features such as rainwater harvesting systems, greywater recycling, and efficient plumbing fixtures to minimize water wastage. By adopting these water-saving solutions, eco-sensitive buildings promote responsible use of this valuable resource.

Furthermore, eco-sensitive architecture prioritizes the use of environmentally friendly materials. It encourages the selection of renewable, recycled, and low-impact building materials, reducing the consumption of natural resources and minimizing waste generation during construction and demolition.

The design of eco-sensitive buildings also takes into account the surrounding ecosystem. It aims to seamlessly blend with nature, preserving existing trees and vegetation, and minimizing disruption to the local habitat. By incorporating green spaces, vertical gardens, and rooftop gardens, eco-sensitive architecture promotes biodiversity and enhances the overall quality of the built environment.

In conclusion, eco-sensitive architecture serves as an essential tool in promoting sustainability and mitigating the environmental impact of buildings. By integrating energy efficiency, water conservation, the use of eco-friendly materials, and consideration for the surrounding ecosystem, it contributes to a greener and more sustainable future.

Eco-Sensitive Building Designs

Eco-sensitive building designs refer to architectural and construction practices that prioritize sustainability and environmental responsibility. These designs are focused on reducing the negative impact of buildings on the environment throughout their entire life cycle.

Such designs adhere to principles like energy efficiency, water conservation, waste reduction, and the use of environmentally friendly materials. They aim to minimize the consumption of natural resources, reduce waste generation, and lower greenhouse gas emissions. Eco-sensitive buildings also prioritize the health and well-being of occupants by providing optimal indoor air quality, natural lighting, and thermal comfort.

Energy efficiency plays a crucial role in eco-sensitive building designs. This entails incorporating renewable energy sources, such as solar panels and wind turbines, to generate electricity. It also involves using insulation materials and efficient windows to minimize heat loss or gain, thus reducing the energy needed for heating and cooling.

Water conservation is another key aspect of eco-sensitive building designs. Strategies may include rainwater harvesting, graywater recycling, and the use of low-flow plumbing fixtures to reduce water consumption and minimize strain on water resources.

Additionally, eco-sensitive building designs focus on reducing the ecological footprint by using sustainable materials. This involves selecting materials with low embodied energy, minimizing the use of non-renewable resources, and prioritizing materials that can be recycled or reused at the end of their lifespan.

In summary, eco-sensitive building designs integrate sustainable practices to minimize environmental impact, reduce resource consumption, and create healthy and efficient living spaces.

Ecodesign Principles

Ecodesign principles can be defined as a set of guidelines that aim to integrate sustainability considerations into the design and development process of products, systems, and services. These principles prioritize the reduction of negative environmental impacts throughout the entire lifecycle of a product, from raw material extraction to disposal.

The first principle is the minimization of resource consumption. This involves using fewer materials, energy, and water in the production process, as well as designing products that are lightweight and durable. By reducing resource consumption, ecodesign can help conserve natural resources and minimize pollution associated with extraction and manufacturing.

The second principle is the reduction of waste and emissions. Ecodesign promotes the use of materials and technologies that generate minimal waste and emissions during production, use, and disposal. It also encourages the design of products that can be easily disassembled and recycled at the end of their life, closing the loop and reducing the burden on landfills.

The third principle is the optimization of energy efficiency. Ecodesign focuses on minimizing energy consumption throughout a product's life cycle, from production to use. This involves designing products that are energy efficient during operation, as well as considering the energy consumed in manufacturing, transportation, and disposal.

The fourth principle is the incorporation of renewable and recyclable materials. Ecodesign encourages the use of materials that can be replenished or recycled, reducing reliance on non-renewable resources and minimizing environmental impacts.

Overall, the ecodesign principles play a crucial role in promoting sustainable development by encouraging the integration of environmental considerations into the design and development process. By adopting these principles, designers and businesses can create products, systems, and services that are more environmentally friendly, resource-efficient, and sustainable.

Ecological Park Architecture

An ecological park architecture refers to the design and construction of a park that is designed with the principles of sustainability in mind. It takes into consideration the natural environment, biodiversity, and ecological systems to ensure minimal impact and maximum benefit to the surrounding ecosystem.

The architecture of an ecological park focuses on creating a harmonious balance between the built environment and nature. It incorporates sustainable materials and construction techniques,

149

such as using local and renewable resources, implementing efficient energy systems, and promoting water conservation measures.

The layout and design of an ecological park aim to protect and enhance the existing ecological features of the site. It includes the preservation and restoration of natural habitats, such as wetlands, forests, and grasslands, to support local flora and fauna. The park's design may also incorporate features like green roofs, rainwater harvesting systems, and permeable surfaces to manage stormwater runoff and reduce the impact on local waterways.

Furthermore, an ecological park architecture encourages the use of renewable energy sources, such as solar panels or wind turbines, to power facilities within the park. It promotes the integration of nature into the built environment, with walking and cycling paths, wildlife corridors, and green spaces, providing opportunities for people to connect with and appreciate the natural surroundings.

In conclusion, ecological park architecture emphasizes the sustainable development and management of park landscapes, focusing on enhancing biodiversity, conserving natural resources, and promoting environmentally-friendly practices. It serves as a model for future designs, showcasing how human-made structures can coexist with and contribute to a healthy and thriving ecosystem.

Ecological Park Design

An ecological park is a designated area of land that is designed and managed in a sustainable way to protect and enhance the environmental balance and biodiversity of the surrounding ecosystem. It aims to create a harmonious relationship between humans and nature, providing a space for recreational activities while preserving and restoring natural habitats.

The design of an ecological park considers various factors such as the conservation of natural resources, the promotion of native plant and animal species, and the minimization of environmental impact. It involves utilizing eco-friendly practices throughout the planning, construction, and maintenance processes, as well as educating visitors about the importance of sustainability and ecological stewardship.

Ecological Restoration Projects

Ecological restoration projects refer to initiatives that aim to enhance or rehabilitate ecosystems that have been degraded, damaged, or destroyed. These projects focus on restoring the ecological processes, biodiversity, and overall health and functionality of an ecosystem, with the ultimate goal of achieving sustainability.

Restoration projects can encompass a range of activities, including the restoration of native vegetation, reintroduction or recovery of endangered species, improvement of water quality, and the rehabilitation of degraded habitats. These initiatives are driven by the recognition that human activities, such as deforestation, pollution, and climate change, have caused widespread environmental degradation, leading to the loss of biodiversity and ecosystem services.

Restoration projects typically involve conducting assessments of degraded ecosystems to determine the extent of damage and identify key ecological needs. Based on these assessments, restoration plans are developed, which may include activities such as reforestation, vegetation management, soil erosion control, and the implementation of sustainable management practices.

By restoring ecosystems, these projects contribute to the sustainability of the natural environment and human societies. They help to conserve biodiversity by creating or enhancing habitats for a variety of species, thereby promoting ecological resilience. Ecological restoration also plays a crucial role in mitigating climate change, as healthy ecosystems act as carbon sinks and can contribute to carbon sequestration.

In addition to their environmental benefits, ecological restoration projects often provide social and economic advantages. They can create jobs and income opportunities, particularly in rural communities dependent on natural resources. Restoration efforts also help to safeguard ecosystem services, such as water purification and flood prevention, which are essential for human well-being and sustainable development.

Electric Aviation

Electric aviation refers to the use of electricity as the primary source of power for aircraft, enabling them to operate without relying on fossil fuels. This sustainable aviation solution aims to reduce greenhouse gas emissions, air pollution, and noise pollution associated with traditional aviation, contributing to a more sustainable and environmentally friendly transportation sector.

By utilizing electric motors and batteries, electric aircraft can significantly decrease or completely eliminate the use of fossil fuels, which are major contributors to global warming. The shift towards electric aviation helps to mitigate climate change by reducing carbon dioxide and other harmful emissions that are released into the atmosphere during aircraft operation. This not only benefits the environment but also improves air quality, particularly in densely populated areas near airports.

Electric Bikes (E-Bikes)

Electric bikes (e-bikes) are a sustainable mode of transportation that provide an alternative to conventional bicycles and motorized vehicles. They are equipped with an electric motor that assists the rider while pedaling, allowing them to travel at faster speeds and overcome uphill challenges with less effort.

The primary goal of e-bikes is to promote sustainable mobility and reduce the environmental impact associated with traditional transportation options. By utilizing an electric motor, e-bikes minimize the reliance on fossil fuels and significantly decrease greenhouse gas emissions. This makes them an eco-friendly alternative for commuting, running errands, or leisurely rides.

Furthermore, e-bikes contribute to sustainable urban planning by reducing traffic congestion and parking space demands. Their compact size and maneuverability allow riders to navigate through crowded urban areas, thereby decreasing the need for larger vehicles. Additionally, e-bikes promote a healthier lifestyle by encouraging physical activity and providing a more accessible option for individuals with limited mobility.

In terms of sustainability, e-bikes also offer economic benefits. They typically have lower maintenance costs compared to cars or motorcycles, and the cost of electricity used to charge the battery is significantly lower than the price of gasoline. This makes e-bikes a more cost-effective transportation option for both individuals and communities.

Electric Vehicle (EV) Charging Infrastructure

Electric vehicle (EV) charging infrastructure refers to the network of charging stations and associated equipment that enables the recharging of electric vehicles. It plays a crucial role in promoting the sustainable adoption of electric vehicles by providing convenient and accessible charging options to EV owners.

EV charging infrastructure is an essential component of the transition towards sustainable transportation. As electric vehicles become more prevalent, the establishment of a robust charging network is crucial to address the range anxiety concerns of potential EV owners and ensure their confidence in the availability of charging facilities.

The sustainability aspect of EV charging infrastructure lies in its contribution to reducing greenhouse gas emissions and reliance on fossil fuels. By providing widespread access to charging stations powered by renewable energy sources, such as solar or wind, EV charging infrastructure helps to mitigate the carbon footprint associated with transportation. This infrastructure also supports the integration of renewable energy into the electric grid, facilitating the transition towards a cleaner energy system.

In addition to environmental benefits, EV charging infrastructure has the potential to promote local economic growth and job creation. The installation, operation, and maintenance of charging stations require a skilled workforce, leading to employment opportunities in the green

151

energy sector.

Electric Vehicle Charging Infrastructure

Electric vehicle charging infrastructure refers to the network of charging stations and supporting facilities that enable the charging of electric vehicles (EVs). It plays a crucial role in promoting sustainable transportation by providing convenient and accessible charging options for EV owners.

Electric vehicles are an important component of a sustainable future as they offer several environmental benefits, including lower greenhouse gas emissions and reduced dependence on fossil fuels. However, for EVs to be a viable alternative to conventional vehicles, a robust charging infrastructure is necessary.

The charging infrastructure consists of charging stations that are strategically located in public places, such as parking lots, shopping centers, and along highways. These stations may offer different types of charging options, including level 1 (standard household outlets), level 2 (commercial charging stations), and fast-charging stations. The availability of different types of chargers ensures flexibility and convenience for EV owners, allowing them to choose the most appropriate charging option based on their needs.

In addition to charging stations, the EV charging infrastructure also includes supportive facilities such as charging networks, payment systems, and data management systems. These components enable seamless integration of EV charging into our daily lives by providing real-time information about the availability of charging stations, facilitating payment processes, and optimizing charging networks for efficient use.

Overall, a well-developed electric vehicle charging infrastructure is essential for the widespread adoption of EVs and the achievement of sustainable transportation goals. It not only meets the charging needs of EV owners but also contributes to the reduction of greenhouse gas emissions and the transition towards a cleaner and greener future.

Energy-Efficient HVAC Systems

An energy-efficient HVAC system refers to a heating, ventilation, and air conditioning system that optimizes energy consumption while providing necessary thermal comfort and indoor air quality to occupants. This type of system is designed to reduce energy waste, minimize greenhouse gas emissions, and promote sustainability.

Energy efficiency in HVAC systems can be achieved through various measures, including the use of advanced technologies, effective design strategies, and proper maintenance practices. These systems employ high-efficiency components and utilize advanced controls to regulate temperature, humidity, and ventilation effectively. By efficiently managing energy consumption, these systems can significantly decrease energy costs and reduce the environmental impact associated with heating and cooling buildings.

Energy-Efficient HVAC Upgrades

An energy-efficient HVAC upgrade refers to the installation or replacement of heating, ventilation, and air conditioning systems with more sustainable and environmentally friendly options, aimed at reducing energy consumption and minimizing carbon emissions.

These upgrades typically involve the installation of new HVAC equipment that is designed to operate more efficiently, such as high-efficiency furnaces, heat pumps, and air conditioners. Additionally, energy-efficient HVAC upgrades may also include advancements in system controls, insulation, and ductwork to enhance overall energy performance.

By improving the energy efficiency of HVAC systems, buildings can significantly reduce their energy consumption and associated greenhouse gas emissions. This is crucial in the context of sustainability, as buildings are significant contributors to global energy use and climate change impacts.

Energy-efficient HVAC upgrades offer multiple benefits. Firstly, they help reduce energy costs for building owners and occupants, as more efficient equipment requires less fuel or electricity to operate. Secondly, these upgrades improve indoor comfort and air quality by providing better temperature control and ventilation. Lastly, they contribute to the overall sustainability of the building sector by lowering carbon emissions and reducing reliance on fossil fuels.

In conclusion, energy-efficient HVAC upgrades play a vital role in promoting sustainability by reducing energy consumption and emissions in buildings. These upgrades enhance both economic and environmental performance, making them a crucial component of green building practices.

Energy-Efficient HVAC

Energy-efficient HVAC refers to heating, ventilation, and air conditioning systems that are designed and operated with the primary goal of minimizing energy consumption and reducing environmental impact. These systems utilize advanced technologies and strategies to provide improved comfort while using less energy.

By utilizing energy-efficient HVAC systems, buildings can significantly reduce their energy consumption and subsequent greenhouse gas emissions. This not only contributes to the global efforts in combating climate change but also helps in achieving long-term sustainability goals. These systems often incorporate features such as high-efficiency heat exchangers, variable speed motors, improved insulation, and smart automation to optimize energy performance.

An energy-efficient HVAC system works by efficiently transferring heat or cool air into a space while minimizing energy losses. This can be achieved through various means, such as using thermal insulation, optimizing ductwork design, and employing energy recovery systems to capture and reuse waste heat. Additionally, advanced controls and sensors allow for precise monitoring and adjustment of temperature, humidity, and airflow, ensuring optimal conditions with minimal energy waste.

Overall, energy-efficient HVAC systems play a crucial role in creating sustainable buildings and reducing the carbon footprint associated with heating and cooling. By prioritizing energy efficiency in HVAC design and operation, businesses and individuals can reduce their energy costs, enhance occupant comfort, and contribute to a more sustainable future.

Energy-Efficient Appliances And Fixtures

Energy-efficient appliances and fixtures refer to household or commercial devices and systems that consume less energy compared to their traditional counterparts. These appliances and fixtures are designed and optimized to perform the desired function while minimizing wasted energy and reducing greenhouse gas emissions.

In the context of sustainability, energy efficiency plays a crucial role in reducing our carbon footprint and conserving natural resources. By using energy-efficient appliances and fixtures, we can significantly decrease our energy consumption, which helps combat climate change and contributes to a more sustainable future.

Energy-Efficient Appliances

Energy-efficient appliances are devices that are designed to minimize energy consumption and reduce greenhouse gas emissions. These appliances are built with advanced technologies and features that enable them to perform their functions while using less energy compared to traditional appliances.

Energy efficiency is a crucial aspect of sustainability as it helps to conserve natural resources, reduce the demand for energy production, and decrease the environmental impact associated with energy consumption. Energy-efficient appliances achieve this by utilizing energy-saving techniques such as improved insulation, optimized heating and cooling systems, and better control mechanisms.

One of the primary benefits of energy-efficient appliances is their ability to lower electricity bills

153

for consumers. By using less energy, these appliances reduce the amount of electricity consumed, resulting in reduced energy costs. This cost savings can be significant over the lifetime of the appliance.

In addition to cost savings, energy-efficient appliances also contribute to the reduction of carbon dioxide and other greenhouse gas emissions. Traditional appliances consume large amounts of energy, which often comes from fossil fuel-based power plants. These power plants emit greenhouse gases that contribute to climate change. By using energy-efficient appliances, individuals and society as a whole can reduce their carbon footprint and help mitigate climate change.

Energy-Efficient Building Designs

Energy-efficient building designs are sustainable architectural designs that aim to minimize energy consumption and reduce environmental impact. These designs utilize various strategies and technologies to optimize the use of energy resources, ensuring efficient operation and reducing the overall carbon footprint of the building.

One of the key principles of energy-efficient building designs is using passive design strategies. This involves optimizing the building's orientation, layout, and insulation to minimize the need for external heating or cooling systems. By maximizing natural light and ventilation, passive design strategies help reduce the need for artificial lighting and mechanical ventilation, thus reducing energy consumption.

Additionally, energy-efficient building designs incorporate advanced insulation materials, energy-efficient windows, and efficient heating, ventilation, and air conditioning (HVAC) systems. These components help maintain a comfortable indoor environment while minimizing energy loss. Moreover, renewable energy systems, such as solar panels and geothermal heating, can be integrated into the building design to generate clean energy on-site.

Energy-efficient building designs also prioritize the use of sustainable materials and construction practices. This includes using locally sourced and recycled materials, as well as employing energy-efficient equipment during the construction process. By reducing construction waste and optimizing material usage, these designs contribute to the overall sustainability of the building.

In conclusion, energy-efficient building designs play a crucial role in promoting sustainability by reducing energy consumption and mitigating the environmental impact of buildings. By incorporating passive design strategies, energy-efficient systems, and sustainable construction practices, these designs help create buildings that are environmentally friendly and energy-efficient.

Energy-Efficient Building Insulation Materials

Energy-efficient building insulation materials refer to materials that are used in the construction of buildings to reduce energy consumption and improve overall sustainability. These materials are designed to minimize heat transfer through walls, roofs, and floors, thereby reducing the amount of energy required to cool or heat a building.

Insulation materials with high thermal resistance (R-value) are considered energy-efficient as they greatly reduce the amount of heat that can pass through them. Common examples of energy-efficient building insulation materials include fiberglass batts, cellulose, spray foam, and rigid foam boards. These materials are typically installed in the walls, attic, and floors of a building to create a thermal barrier and prevent the transfer of heat from the inside to the outside or vice versa.

Energy-Efficient Building Materials

Energy-efficient building materials are materials that are designed and constructed in a way that conserves energy and promotes sustainability in the built environment. These materials are specifically chosen or developed to minimize energy consumption during the production, use, and disposal stages of their lifecycle.

Energy efficiency in building materials is achieved through various strategies, including:

However, these materials are specifically chosen or developed to minimize energy consumption during the production, use, and disposal stages of their lifecycle. Energy efficiency in building materials is achieved through various strategies, including: 1. Thermal insulation: Energy-efficient building materials have excellent thermal insulation properties, reducing heat transfer between the interior and exterior of a building. This decreases the need for artificial heating or cooling, resulting in lower energy consumption. 2. High solar reflectance: Building materials with high solar reflectance can effectively reflect sunlight and reduce heat absorption. This helps to maintain comfortable indoor temperatures without relying heavily on air conditioning. 3. Daylighting: Energy-efficient materials allow for effective utilization of natural daylight, reducing the need for artificial lighting during the day. This not only saves energy but also improves occupants' well-being and productivity. 4. Renewable and recycled materials: Using renewable resources, such as sustainably harvested wood or bamboo, reduces the environmental impact associated with material sourcing. Similarly, incorporating recycled materials, such as reclaimed wood or recycled plastic, reduces the extraction of natural resources and promotes waste reduction. 5. Low embodied energy: Energy-efficient building materials have a low embodied energy, meaning the energy required for their production is minimized. This includes reducing energy-intensive manufacturing processes and transportation distances. By incorporating energy-efficient building materials into construction projects, we can significantly reduce energy consumption, lower greenhouse gas emissions, and enhance the overall sustainability of the built environment.>

Energy-Efficient Building Practices

Energy-efficient building practices refer to the design, construction, and operation of buildings that minimize the use of energy resources while maximizing the comfort, health, and productivity of the occupants. These practices aim to reduce the overall energy consumption of a building and decrease its carbon footprint, contributing to the larger goal of sustainability.

Energy-efficient building practices encompass various strategies and technologies that can be applied to both new construction and existing buildings. This includes implementing effective insulation, using high-performance windows and doors, employing efficient heating, ventilation, and air conditioning (HVAC) systems, and incorporating renewable energy sources such as solar panels. Additionally, proper building orientation and efficient lighting systems can reduce energy usage.

By adopting energy-efficient building practices, the demand for non-renewable energy sources is decreased, resulting in lower greenhouse gas emissions and a reduced dependence on fossil fuels. This helps mitigate climate change and promotes a more sustainable future. Moreover, energy-efficient buildings often lead to cost savings for owners and occupants through reduced energy bills.

In conclusion, energy-efficient building practices are essential for achieving sustainability in the built environment. By employing strategies that minimize energy consumption and maximize efficiency, these practices contribute to a healthier and more environmentally responsible way of living and working.

Energy-Efficient Building Retrofits

Energy-efficient building retrofits refer to making significant modifications to existing structures in order to improve their energy efficiency. This is achieved through the implementation of various sustainable design strategies and the incorporation of innovative technologies and systems.

Retrofits typically involve the upgrading or replacement of outdated equipment, such as HVAC systems, windows, and insulation, with more energy-efficient alternatives. Additionally, retrofits may involve the installation of renewable energy sources, such as solar panels or wind turbines, to generate clean energy on-site.

By undertaking energy-efficient building retrofits, the overall environmental impact of the building is reduced, as it requires less energy to operate. This helps to decrease greenhouse gas emissions and combat climate change. Moreover, retrofits can lead to substantial cost savings for building owners and occupants, as energy usage and utility bills decrease.

Furthermore, these retrofits contribute to the overall goal of sustainability by promoting the efficient use of resources. By utilizing energy-efficient technologies, buildings become less dependent on non-renewable energy sources and reduce their reliance on fossil fuels. This not only conserves natural resources but also enhances energy security.

In conclusion, energy-efficient building retrofits play a crucial role in achieving sustainability objectives by reducing energy consumption, decreasing environmental impact, generating cost savings, and promoting resource efficiency. These retrofits are imperative in the transition towards a more sustainable built environment.

Energy-Efficient Building Upgrades

Energy-efficient building upgrades refer to the act of implementing various measures in a building to reduce its energy consumption and increase its overall energy efficiency. These upgrades are aimed at minimizing the environmental impact of the building's operation, reducing energy costs, and improving the comfort and well-being of its occupants.

The upgrades can be applied to both new and existing buildings and may involve the installation of energy-saving technologies, improved insulation, efficient heating, ventilation, and air conditioning (HVAC) systems, and the use of renewable energy sources. Energy-efficient building upgrades can also encompass the optimization of lighting systems, water conservation measures, and the implementation of smart building technologies for better control and monitoring of energy usage.

Such upgrades are an integral part of sustainable development strategies as they contribute to the reduction of greenhouse gas emissions, the preservation of natural resources, and the mitigation of climate change. Additionally, energy-efficient buildings can bring numerous economic benefits, including reduced energy bills, increased property value, and job creation in the green technology sector.

The adoption of energy-efficient building upgrades is crucial in addressing the pressing global challenges of resource depletion and environmental degradation. By implementing these upgrades, societies can move towards a more sustainable future, where buildings are not only functional and aesthetically pleasing but also prioritize the efficient use of energy and resources.

Energy-Efficient Construction

Energy-efficient construction refers to the design, construction, and operation of buildings and infrastructure systems that are optimized to minimize energy consumption and reduce negative impacts on the environment. This approach to construction focuses on employing sustainable and resource-efficient technologies and materials to maximize energy performance and minimize waste.

Energy-efficient construction integrates various strategies and practices to effectively manage energy use throughout the lifecycle of a building. This includes reducing heat transfer through improved insulation, utilizing natural lighting and ventilation to reduce the need for artificial lighting and mechanical cooling, implementing efficient heating, ventilation, and air conditioning (HVAC) systems, and employing renewable energy technologies such as solar panels and geothermal systems to generate on-site electricity.

Additionally, energy-efficient construction emphasizes the use of sustainable building materials with low embodied energy, such as recycled or locally sourced materials, and the implementation of efficient water management systems to reduce water consumption and promote water conservation. Moreover, the design and layout of energy-efficient buildings prioritize factors such as site orientation, shading, and passive solar design principles to optimize thermal comfort and minimize the need for excessive energy consumption.

Overall, energy-efficient construction plays a crucial role in sustainable development by reducing greenhouse gas emissions, minimizing dependence on non-renewable energy sources, and promoting the efficient use of resources. By implementing energy-saving technologies and employing sustainable practices, energy-efficient buildings contribute to a greener and more sustainable built environment, benefiting both the occupants and the larger community through reduced energy costs, improved indoor air quality, and minimized environmental impact.

Energy-Efficient Cooking Stoves

An energy-efficient cooking stove refers to a kitchen appliance designed to minimize the amount of energy required for cooking purposes. These stoves aim to reduce the environmental impact of cooking by efficiently using fuel sources and limiting greenhouse gas emissions, while also promoting sustainability practices.

Energy-efficient cooking stoves are engineered with features and technologies that optimize heat utilization, thereby reducing the overall energy consumption. These stoves often incorporate improved insulation, better combustion systems, and advanced heat distribution mechanisms, allowing for higher heating efficiency and reduced energy wastage. By utilizing fuel more effectively, these stoves can significantly decrease the amount of fuel needed for cooking, which in turn minimizes the depletion of natural resources and lowers greenhouse gas emissions.

Furthermore, energy-efficient cooking stoves can also contribute to a more sustainable kitchen environment by reducing indoor air pollution and promoting healthier cooking practices. Many of these stoves incorporate mechanisms for better ventilation and smoke removal, which improves indoor air quality and prevents respiratory health issues associated with traditional cooking methods.

In summary, energy-efficient cooking stoves play a crucial role in achieving sustainable cooking practices. By optimizing energy utilization, these appliances reduce greenhouse gas emissions, conserve natural resources, and contribute to healthier cooking environments. Investing in energy-efficient cooking stoves not only benefits the environment but also promotes a sustainable and healthier lifestyle for individuals and communities.

Energy-Efficient Cooling Systems

Energy-efficient cooling systems are technological innovations designed to maximize the cooling performance while minimizing the energy consumption. These systems aim to reduce the amount of power required to cool a space, resulting in lower energy bills and reduced greenhouse gas emissions.

These cooling systems employ various strategies to enhance their energy efficiency. They may utilize advanced insulation materials to minimize heat transfer between the indoors and outdoors, reducing the need for excessive cooling. Additionally, they may incorporate smart thermostats and controls, allowing users to optimize cooling settings based on occupancy and external environmental conditions.

Energy-efficient cooling systems often feature high-efficiency compressors and fans, which consume less electricity compared to traditional cooling systems. They may also utilize innovative heat exchangers and advanced heat transfer fluids, optimizing the cooling process while minimizing energy wastage.

Cooling systems that meet energy efficiency criteria help in promoting sustainability by reducing the demand for electricity from power plants, which often rely on fossil fuels for energy generation. By consuming less electricity, these systems contribute to the reduction of carbon emissions and help mitigate the negative environmental impact associated with high energy consumption.

In conclusion, energy-efficient cooling systems are innovative technologies that prioritize cooling performance while minimizing energy consumption. They play a crucial role in promoting sustainability by reducing energy demand, mitigating carbon emissions, and minimizing the environmental impact of cooling processes.

Energy-Efficient Data Centers

An energy-efficient data center is a facility designed and operated with the aim of minimizing its energy consumption and environmental impact. It employs various strategies and technologies to increase energy efficiency and reduce carbon emissions, thereby contributing to overall sustainability goals.

Energy-efficient data centers adopt advanced cooling systems, such as hot/cold aisle containment and free cooling, to reduce the energy required for cooling equipment. They also leverage virtualization and consolidation techniques to optimize server utilization and reduce idle capacity. By using energy-efficient hardware and equipment, such as low-power servers and high-efficiency power supplies, these data centers minimize energy waste and maximize performance per watt. Moreover, they implement power management features and dynamic workload management to ensure efficient resource allocation and utilization.

In addition to technological measures, energy-efficient data centers prioritize sustainable practices in their daily operations. They employ renewable energy sources, such as solar or wind power, to reduce reliance on fossil fuels and minimize greenhouse gas emissions. They also implement comprehensive monitoring and management systems to continuously track energy usage and identify areas for improvement. By regularly assessing their energy performance and implementing energy-saving initiatives, these data centers create a culture of energy efficiency and promote a sustainable approach to data center operations.

In conclusion, energy-efficient data centers are essential for reducing the environmental impact of digital infrastructure. By employing energy-saving technologies and sustainable practices, these facilities contribute to overall sustainability goals by minimizing energy consumption, reducing carbon emissions, and promoting efficient resource utilization.

Energy-Efficient Data Storage

Energy-efficient data storage refers to the use of technologies and practices that minimize energy consumption and maximize resource efficiency in the storage and retrieval of digital data. It focuses on reducing the environmental impact of data storage systems by optimizing energy usage and decreasing carbon emissions.

With the exponential growth of digital data, energy consumption in data centers has become a significant concern. The energy required to power and cool these facilities contributes to carbon emissions and strains the power grid. Energy-efficient data storage aims to mitigate these issues by optimizing hardware components, improving data management strategies, and adopting renewable energy sources.

There are several strategies employed to achieve energy efficiency in data storage. One approach is through hardware optimization, including the use of low-power processors, energy-efficient disk drives, and solid-state storage devices. By selecting components with lower power requirements, data centers can reduce overall energy consumption.

Another aspect of energy-efficient data storage involves effective data management. Technologies such as data deduplication, compression, and tiered storage help eliminate redundant data, reduce storage space requirements, and improve overall system efficiency. Additionally, implementing intelligent caching and data migration techniques can minimize energy usage by prioritizing frequently accessed data and utilizing the most energy-efficient storage resources.

Moreover, the adoption of renewable energy sources plays a crucial role in achieving energy efficiency in data storage. Data centers can implement solar panels, wind turbines, or hydroelectric power to meet their energy needs. By relying on renewable sources, they can minimize their carbon footprint and reduce dependence on fossil fuels.

Energy-Efficient Heating And Cooling Systems

Energy-efficient heating and cooling systems refer to the technologies and practices that aim to minimize the energy consumption associated with maintaining desirable indoor temperatures. These systems are designed to provide thermal comfort while using a reduced amount of energy, thus contributing to sustainability goals.

Energy-efficient heating systems utilize technologies that maximize the efficiency of energy conversion, distribution, and transfer. This includes the use of high-efficiency furnaces, boilers, and heat pumps that convert energy sources such as natural gas, electricity, or renewable fuels into heat with minimal waste. These systems often employ advanced controls and monitoring mechanisms to optimize performance and reduce energy losses.

Similarly, energy-efficient cooling systems utilize technologies that minimize energy consumption while providing effective cooling. This includes the use of high-efficiency air conditioners and heat pumps that maximize the efficiency of energy transfer and minimize heat gain. These systems may employ features like variable-speed compressors, advanced refrigerants, and intelligent controls to improve performance and reduce energy use.

Beyond the technology itself, energy-efficient heating and cooling systems also involve practices that enhance the overall efficiency of the heating and cooling process. This may include insulation improvements, air sealing, proper maintenance, and regular system inspections. By minimizing heat loss or gain and optimizing system performance, these practices further contribute to energy savings and sustainability objectives.

In summary, energy-efficient heating and cooling systems aim to provide thermal comfort while minimizing energy consumption and waste. By employing efficient technologies and implementing best practices, these systems contribute to sustainability efforts by reducing greenhouse gas emissions, conserving energy resources, and promoting a more environmentally friendly approach to indoor climate control.

Energy-Efficient Heating Systems

Energy-efficient heating systems are technologies and practices designed to provide warmth and comfort while minimizing energy consumption and reducing environmental impacts. These systems aim to optimize the use of energy resources by leveraging innovative designs, advanced technologies, and efficient heating methods.

By reducing energy waste and maximizing efficiency, energy-efficient heating systems contribute to sustainability efforts by conserving resources and minimizing greenhouse gas emissions. They help combat climate change by reducing the overall energy demand and reliance on fossil fuels, which are major contributors to carbon dioxide emissions and global warming.

Energy-Efficient Home Appliances

Energy-efficient home appliances are products designed to minimize the amount of energy they consume during operation. These appliances are engineered to be more energy efficient than their standard counterparts, allowing them to perform the same tasks while using less electricity.

By using energy-efficient appliances, individuals can reduce their carbon footprint and help mitigate the effects of climate change. These appliances typically feature advanced technologies and innovative designs that maximize energy savings without compromising performance. Examples of energy-efficient home appliances include refrigerators, washing machines, dishwashers, air conditioners, and heating systems.

Energy-Efficient Home Automation

Energy-efficient home automation refers to the use of advanced technology to optimize energy consumption and enhance sustainability in residential buildings.

This concept involves the integration of various automated systems and devices that monitor, control, and manage energy usage within a home, with the aim of reducing energy waste, improving efficiency, and minimizing environmental impact.

Energy-Efficient Home Designs

159

The term "energy-efficient home designs" refers to architectural and construction practices that aim to minimize the energy consumption of a residential building while maximizing its overall performance and comfort. These designs prioritize sustainability by reducing the amount of energy required for heating, cooling, and electricity, thereby minimizing the building's carbon footprint and environmental impact.

Energy-efficient home designs encompass various aspects of a building's construction, including insulation, window placement, ventilation, and use of renewable energy sources. Effective insulation materials, such as spray foam or cellulose, are commonly used to minimize heat transfer and ensure a consistent indoor temperature, reducing the need for excessive heating or cooling. Similarly, strategic window placement takes advantage of natural sunlight for heating purposes while minimizing heat gain during warmer seasons.

Proper ventilation systems are crucial in energy-efficient home designs to maintain indoor air quality and prevent the need for excessive heating or cooling. Heat recovery ventilation (HRV) or energy recovery ventilation (ERV) systems help retain warmth in the winter and coolness in the summer by transferring heat between the incoming and outgoing air streams.

Furthermore, energy-efficient home designs often incorporate renewable energy sources to supplement or even eliminate reliance on carbon-based energy systems. Solar panels, for example, can harness solar energy to power lighting and appliances, reducing the need for grid electricity and saving both money and resources.

Energy-Efficient Home Insulation

Energy-efficient home insulation refers to the implementation of materials and techniques that minimize heat transfer and improve thermal performance within a residential building, resulting in reduced energy consumption and increased sustainability.

This type of insulation aims to limit the exchange of heat between the interior and exterior of a home, providing better temperature regulation and reducing the need for artificial heating and cooling. By effectively sealing the building envelope, energy-efficient insulation becomes a vital component in sustainable construction and green building practices.

Energy-Efficient Industrial Processes

Energy-efficient industrial processes refer to the use of technologies, practices, and management strategies that optimize the use of energy resources in industrial operations, while minimizing energy waste, reducing greenhouse gas emissions, and promoting sustainability. These processes aim to reduce energy consumption, improve resource efficiency, and lower operational costs, without compromising the output or quality of the products or services produced.

To achieve energy efficiency in industrial processes, various measures can be implemented. These may include the adoption of energy-efficient equipment and machinery, optimizing production processes to reduce energy usage, implementing energy management systems, integrating renewable energy sources into the production process, and improving waste heat recovery systems.

Energy-Efficient Insulation Materials

Energy-efficient insulation materials are materials that are used to reduce heat transfer and improve thermal efficiency in buildings. These materials are designed to provide effective insulation, minimizing energy consumption and reducing greenhouse gas emissions.

Insulation plays a crucial role in sustainable building design and contributes to energy conservation. Energy-efficient insulation materials are typically made from renewable or recycled resources, reducing the environmental impact of their production and disposal. They are designed to have high thermal resistance, preventing heat from escaping through walls, floors, and roofs. By reducing heat transfer, these materials help to maintain a comfortable indoor temperature and minimize the need for heating and cooling, thereby reducing energy usage and associated costs.

160

Furthermore, energy-efficient insulation materials can also improve indoor air quality and comfort by reducing air infiltration and condensation. They provide an effective barrier against moisture, preventing the growth of mold and mildew, and minimizing the risk of respiratory problems. Additionally, these materials are often fire-resistant and non-toxic, ensuring the safety and health of building occupants.

In summary, energy-efficient insulation materials are essential for sustainable building practices. Through their use, buildings can achieve significant energy savings, reduce their carbon footprint, and contribute to a more environmentally friendly and comfortable living environment.

Energy-Efficient Insulation

Energy-efficient insulation refers to a material or system that is designed to reduce the transfer of heat or cold between the interior and exterior of a building, thereby improving its thermal performance and reducing energy consumption. This type of insulation plays a crucial role in sustainability efforts by minimizing the use of energy for heating and cooling, which in turn reduces greenhouse gas emissions and decreases the dependence on non-renewable energy sources.

The primary objective of energy-efficient insulation is to create a thermal barrier that limits the exchange of heat or cold between a building and its surroundings. This is achieved by using materials with high thermal resistance, such as fiberglass, cellulose, or foam insulation, which are commonly installed in walls, floors, roofs, and attics. By preventing the escape of conditioned air, energy-efficient insulation helps maintain a stable indoor temperature, reducing the need for artificial heating or cooling. As a result, less energy is required to maintain a comfortable living or working environment, leading to substantial energy savings.

Energy-Efficient Lighting Design Software

Energy-efficient lighting design software refers to computer programs or applications that are specifically designed to aid in the planning and implementation of lighting systems that maximize energy efficiency. These software tools utilize various algorithms and simulation models to analyze and optimize lighting design parameters, such as the type of light fixtures, their placement, and the control strategies employed.

The primary goal of energy-efficient lighting design software is to reduce energy consumption and minimize environmental impacts by providing designers, architects, and engineers with tools for making informed decisions regarding lighting system design. By accurately simulating lighting conditions and energy usage, these software applications enable professionals to assess the performance of different design configurations and compare energy savings potential, helping them to select the most efficient lighting solutions for a given space.

Energy-Efficient Lighting Systems

Energy-efficient lighting systems refer to lighting technologies that are designed to minimize energy consumption while providing adequate illumination. These systems are a crucial component of sustainable practices as they reduce energy use and greenhouse gas emissions, thereby contributing to environmental conservation and the fight against climate change.

Energy-efficient lighting systems employ advanced technologies and design principles aimed at maximizing energy efficiency. They typically use light-emitting diodes (LEDs) or compact fluorescent lamps (CFLs) instead of traditional incandescent bulbs. LEDs and CFLs use significantly less energy to produce the same amount of light, making them highly efficient alternatives.

In addition to using energy-saving light sources, energy-efficient lighting systems also incorporate various features to further optimize energy consumption. These features may include motion sensors, dimmers, and timers, allowing the system to automatically adjust lighting levels or turn off lights when they are not needed. By reducing unnecessary lighting, these systems conserve energy and extend the lifespan of the light sources.

Implementing energy-efficient lighting systems in residential, commercial, and industrial settings offers multiple benefits. Not only do these systems lower energy bills and decrease electricity demand, but they also contribute to the reduction of carbon dioxide emissions. Moreover, energy-efficient lighting systems often have longer lifespans compared to traditional lighting, resulting in lower maintenance costs and reduced waste generation.

Energy-Efficient Lighting

Energy-efficient lighting refers to the use of lighting technology and design practices that minimize energy consumption and maximize performance while reducing greenhouse gas emissions and negative environmental impacts.

Energy-efficient lighting systems are designed to optimize the use of energy, reduce waste, and enhance sustainability. These systems can encompass various technologies, including LED (Light Emitting Diode) lighting, compact fluorescent lamps (CFL), and high-efficiency fluorescent lighting. Compared to traditional incandescent lighting, energy-efficient lighting options provide significant energy savings, longer lifespans, and greater cost-effectiveness.

By incorporating energy-efficient lighting solutions, individuals, businesses, and organizations can contribute to mitigating climate change and reducing their overall carbon footprint. The energy savings achieved through the use of these lighting systems directly reduce the reliance on fossil-fuel-generated electricity, which is a significant source of greenhouse gas emissions. This reduction in energy consumption also translates into financial savings and promotes energy independence.

Moreover, energy-efficient lighting plays a crucial role in sustainable building design and operation, as lighting accounts for a substantial portion of a building's energy usage. By adopting energy-saving practices such as using motion sensors, dimmers, and timers, lighting systems can be optimized to only operate when necessary, further reducing energy waste.

In conclusion, energy-efficient lighting serves as a sustainable solution for energy conservation and environmental protection. It offers a range of benefits, including reduced energy consumption, lower carbon emissions, cost savings, and improved longevity. Embracing energy-efficient lighting is a fundamental step towards achieving long-term sustainability goals and creating a greener future.

Energy-Efficient Manufacturing

Energy-efficient manufacturing refers to the implementation of strategies and technologies that aim to minimize energy consumption and waste during the production process, while maintaining or improving product quality and output. This approach acknowledges the importance of sustainability and the need to reduce the negative environmental impact of manufacturing activities.

Energy-efficient manufacturing involves the adoption of various measures, such as optimizing equipment and machinery, implementing energy management systems, adopting renewable energy sources, and improving process design and control. By reducing energy consumption, manufacturers can decrease greenhouse gas emissions, alleviate the strain on natural resources, and mitigate the environmental and health risks associated with energy production and consumption.

Energy-Efficient Office Buildings

An energy-efficient office building refers to a structure that is designed, constructed, and operated in a sustainable manner to minimize energy consumption and reduce its environmental impact. These buildings utilize various strategies and technologies to optimize energy efficiency, lower energy demand, and decrease the overall carbon footprint.

Key features of an energy-efficient office building include:

- Passive design principles that maximize natural lighting, optimize natural ventilation, and minimize the need for artificial heating and cooling systems.

162

- High-performance insulation and windows that reduce heat transfer and maintain the desired indoor temperature, thereby reducing the reliance on mechanical heating and cooling systems.

- Energy-efficient lighting systems, such as LED lights, and sensors that automatically control lighting levels based on occupancy and natural light availability.

- Energy-efficient HVAC (heating, ventilation, and air conditioning) systems that use advanced technologies and controls to optimize energy consumption while maintaining comfortable indoor conditions.

- Integration of renewable energy sources, such as solar panels or wind turbines, to generate on-site clean energy and reduce reliance on grid electricity.

- Efficient water management systems that minimize water consumption through technologies like low-flow fixtures, rainwater harvesting, and greywater recycling.

By incorporating these features, energy-efficient office buildings not only contribute to reducing greenhouse gas emissions and combating climate change but also offer several benefits such as lower operating costs, improved indoor comfort and air quality, and enhanced occupant productivity and well-being.

Energy-Efficient Public Transportation

Energy-efficient public transportation refers to the use of sustainable and low-energy consumption modes of transportation for public commuting. It encompasses a range of systems and technologies that aim to reduce energy consumption, decrease greenhouse gas emissions, and improve overall environmental sustainability.

This form of transportation includes various types of vehicles such as electric buses, hybrid trains, and tramways that are designed to minimize fuel consumption and carbon emissions. Energy-efficient public transportation systems also incorporate infrastructure developments like dedicated bus lanes, bike lanes, and smart traffic management systems to optimize efficiency and reduce congestion.

Energy-Efficient Refrigeration

Energy-efficient refrigeration refers to the use of refrigeration systems that consume minimal energy while performing their cooling tasks. It focuses on reducing the energy consumption of refrigeration systems in order to minimize their negative environmental impacts and promote sustainability.

Energy-efficient refrigeration technologies are designed to optimize the cooling process while minimizing energy wastage. This involves using advanced insulation materials, such as high-quality insulation panels, to reduce heat transfer and improve the efficiency of cooling. Additionally, energy-efficient refrigeration systems may incorporate innovative compressor technology, such as variable-speed compressors, which adjust their speed based on the cooling demands, resulting in reduced energy consumption.

Energy efficiency in refrigeration is essential for sustainable development as traditional refrigeration systems can be highly energy-intensive. By adopting energy-efficient refrigeration, businesses and households can significantly reduce their energy consumption, leading to a variety of environmental benefits. These include a decrease in greenhouse gas emissions, reduced reliance on non-renewable energy sources, and lower overall energy costs.

Furthermore, energy-efficient refrigeration contributes to the preservation of natural resources by minimizing the need for additional energy generation and reducing the strain on the power grid. It also promotes the long-term durability and reliability of refrigeration systems, reducing the need for frequent repairs and replacements, which can be resource-intensive.

Energy-Efficient Roofing Materials

Energy-efficient roofing materials are a key component of sustainable construction practices.

163

These materials are designed to minimize heat transfer and reduce energy consumption within buildings by providing effective insulation and reflecting sunlight.

One type of energy-efficient roofing material is reflective roofing. This material has a light-colored or reflective surface that helps to reflect sunlight, reducing the amount of heat absorbed by the building. By minimizing heat absorption, reflective roofing materials can lower the need for air conditioning and reduce energy consumption. Another type of energy-efficient roofing material is insulation. These materials are designed to prevent heat transfer between the building and the outside environment, reducing the need for heating during colder months and cooling during hotter months. Insulation roofing materials help to maintain a comfortable temperature inside the building, reducing the reliance on energy-consuming heating and cooling equipment. Green roofs are also considered energy-efficient roofing materials. These roofs are covered in vegetation, which provides natural insulation and absorbs sunlight. Green roofs can improve a building's energy efficiency by reducing heat transfer, improving air quality, and preventing stormwater runoff. In conclusion, energy-efficient roofing materials play a crucial role in sustainable construction practices. They help to minimize heat transfer, reduce energy consumption, and create more comfortable living and working environments. By utilizing these materials, buildings can become more energy-efficient, reduce greenhouse gas emissions, and contribute to a more sustainable future.

Energy-Efficient Roofing

Energy-efficient roofing refers to the design, materials, and installation techniques used to reduce the amount of energy required to heat, cool, and illuminate a building. It aims to minimize energy waste and maximize energy conservation by optimizing the insulation and reflectivity of the roof.

Energy efficiency is a critical aspect of sustainable construction practices as buildings account for a significant portion of global energy consumption and greenhouse gas emissions. By implementing energy-efficient roofing, the overall energy demand of a building can be reduced, resulting in lower energy costs and a decreased environmental footprint.

Energy-Efficient Traffic Signals

Energy-efficient traffic signals refer to the use of technology and design principles aimed at reducing the energy consumption of traffic signal systems while maintaining their functionality and effectiveness in managing traffic flow. These signals utilize various energy-saving measures to optimize their operation, resulting in a reduced environmental impact and lower energy costs.

One of the primary strategies employed by energy-efficient traffic signals is the use of LED (light-emitting diode) lamps instead of traditional incandescent bulbs. LEDs are highly energy-efficient, converting a greater portion of energy into visible light, reducing wasteful heat production. This significantly decreases power consumption, leading to substantial energy savings. LED traffic signals are also more durable and have a longer lifespan, reducing maintenance and replacement costs.

Additionally, energy-efficient traffic signals often incorporate advanced control systems that intelligently adjust their timing and intensity based on real-time traffic conditions. By using sensors and data analysis, these signals can optimize the allocation of green, yellow, and red phases, reducing unnecessary idling and traffic congestion. This dynamic and adaptive approach not only enhances energy efficiency but also improves overall traffic flow and reduces travel time for vehicles.

Furthermore, energy-efficient traffic signals may utilize solar panels to generate clean and renewable energy to power the signals and associated equipment. Solar-powered systems can significantly reduce their reliance on the electrical grid, decreasing both energy consumption and greenhouse gas emissions. When coupled with energy storage technologies, such as batteries, these signals can operate even during periods of low solar energy generation or power outages, ensuring uninterrupted functionality.

Energy-Efficient Transportation Infrastructure

Energy-efficient transportation infrastructure refers to the design, construction, and maintenance of transportation systems that minimize energy consumption and decrease environmental impact. It encompasses various modes of transportation, including roads, railways, airports, seaports, and public transit systems.

The goal of energy-efficient transportation infrastructure is to reduce the reliance on fossil fuels and promote the use of renewable energy sources. This can be achieved through several strategies, such as optimizing traffic flow, implementing intelligent transportation systems, improving vehicle efficiency, and encouraging the use of alternative fuels and propulsion technologies.

When planning and designing energy-efficient transportation infrastructure, consideration is given to factors such as route optimization, vehicle electrification, modal shift towards more sustainable modes of transport (e.g., shifting from individual cars to public transport or cycling), and the development of infrastructure to support non-motorized transportation, such as walking and cycling paths.

By adopting energy-efficient transportation infrastructure, cities and regions can reduce greenhouse gas emissions, improve air quality, and enhance overall sustainability. It promotes a shift towards more sustainable transportation modes, which in turn reduces traffic congestion, enhances mobility, and improves the quality of life for residents.

Energy-Efficient Transportation Networks

Energy-efficient transportation networks refer to the design, implementation, and management of infrastructure and systems that minimize energy consumption and environmental impacts associated with transportation. This concept aims to promote sustainable mobility by efficiently utilizing energy resources, reducing greenhouse gas emissions, and mitigating the negative effects of transportation on climate change.

These networks involve various strategies and technologies that optimize the use of energy, emphasizing the importance of renewable and low-carbon energy sources. For instance, the integration of electric vehicles (EVs) and charging stations into the network encourages the transition from fossil fuel-powered vehicles to cleaner alternatives. Additionally, the adoption of advanced traffic management systems, such as smart traffic lights and intelligent transportation systems, helps to streamline traffic flow and minimize idling, reducing energy waste.

Energy-efficient transportation networks also prioritize the development of sustainable infrastructure, including the construction of bike lanes, pedestrian-friendly walkways, and public transportation systems. By promoting active transportation and encouraging the use of public transit, these networks aim to reduce the reliance on private vehicles, which contribute to congestion and pollution. Moreover, the establishment of efficient logistics and freight systems minimizes energy consumption in the transportation of goods, optimizing routes and modes of transport to achieve maximum fuel efficiency.

In conclusion, energy-efficient transportation networks play a crucial role in promoting sustainable mobility and combatting climate change. By prioritizing energy conservation, utilizing renewable energy sources, and optimizing infrastructure and systems, these networks aim to minimize the environmental impact of transportation while ensuring efficient and accessible mobility for individuals and goods.

Energy-Efficient Transportation Solutions

Energy-efficient transportation solutions refer to modes of transportation that minimize the use of energy resources while maximizing the movement of people or goods. These solutions aim to reduce the environmental impact of transportation, particularly in terms of greenhouse gas emissions and fossil fuel consumption.

Energy-efficient transportation encompasses various strategies and technologies that promote sustainable mobility. One such solution is the development and use of electric vehicles (EVs), which rely on electricity rather than fossil fuels for operation. EVs can significantly reduce greenhouse gas emissions, particularly if the electricity used is generated from renewable sources.

Energy-Efficient Transportation

Energy-efficient transportation refers to the use of vehicles and transportation systems that minimize the consumption of energy resources while maximizing the distance traveled or the volume of goods transported. This concept is crucial in the context of sustainability as the transportation sector is one of the largest contributors to greenhouse gas emissions and environmental degradation.

Energy-efficient transportation can be achieved through various means, including technological advancements, fuel choices, and adopting sustainable transportation practices. One approach is improving the fuel efficiency of vehicles by utilizing advanced powertrain technologies, such as hybrid or electric engines, which consume less energy compared to conventional internal combustion engines.

Additionally, optimizing transportation systems and infrastructure can contribute to energy efficiency. This involves improving traffic flow, reducing congestion, and promoting the use of public transportation, cycling, and walking. By providing convenient and sustainable alternatives to personal vehicle usage, energy-efficient transportation can decrease fuel consumption and emissions.

Another aspect of energy-efficient transportation is the integration of renewable energy sources into transportation systems. This can include the use of biofuels, hydrogen, and electricity generated from renewable sources to power vehicles. By utilizing renewable energy, the transportation sector can reduce its dependency on fossil fuels and significantly reduce greenhouse gas emissions.

In conclusion, energy-efficient transportation plays a vital role in achieving sustainability goals by reducing energy consumption, minimizing emissions, and promoting sustainable practices in the transportation sector. By adopting energy-efficient transportation systems, countries and communities can contribute to mitigating climate change, improving air quality, and ensuring the long-term well-being of our planet.

Energy-Efficient Urban Design

Energy-efficient urban design refers to the intentional planning and organization of urban spaces in order to minimize energy consumption and reduce negative environmental impacts. This approach incorporates a combination of sustainable practices, technologies, and design principles to create more efficient and resilient cities.

The main objective of energy-efficient urban design is to optimize resource use and promote a sustainable urban lifestyle. This is achieved by considering various factors such as energy consumption, greenhouse gas emissions, renewable energy generation, transportation systems, building design, and urban infrastructure. By integrating these considerations into the planning and development process, cities can create environments that are not only environmentally friendly, but also economically viable and socially inclusive.

Energy-Efficient Urban Development

Energy-efficient urban development refers to the design and implementation of urban areas that prioritize the efficient use of energy resources, with the goal of reducing energy consumption and minimizing negative environmental impacts. This approach takes into account various aspects of urban planning, architecture, infrastructure, and lifestyles to create sustainable cities and communities.

Energy efficiency in urban development involves the integration of innovative technologies, policies, and practices that promote the optimal use of energy throughout the urban environment. This includes, but is not limited to, energy-efficient buildings, transportation systems, public spaces, and industrial and commercial activities. The aim is to minimize energy waste, emissions, and the overall carbon footprint of the urban area.

166

This concept requires a holistic approach that considers the entire urban ecosystem, taking into account factors such as building design, insulation, efficient heating, ventilation, and air conditioning systems, as well as the use of renewable energy sources. It also focuses on sustainable transportation options, such as public transit, cycling infrastructure, and pedestrian-friendly neighborhoods, which reduce the reliance on private vehicles and promote active mobility.

Furthermore, energy-efficient urban development emphasizes the importance of smart grid infrastructure, energy management systems, and energy monitoring tools to optimize energy consumption and enhance overall energy resilience. By adopting these measures, cities can achieve significant energy savings, reduce greenhouse gas emissions, improve air quality, and enhance the overall quality of life for both current and future urban dwellers.

Energy-Efficient Urban Planning

Energy-efficient urban planning refers to the strategic and sustainable design, development, and management of urban areas with the goal of reducing energy consumption, minimizing greenhouse gas emissions, and preserving natural resources. It involves the integration of various principles, practices, and technologies to create sustainable built environments that promote energy efficiency at both the individual building and citywide levels.

This approach takes into account the entire urban ecosystem, including buildings, transportation systems, public spaces, and infrastructure, to ensure optimal energy performance and resource utilization. It emphasizes the importance of energy-efficient buildings, the use of renewable energy sources, efficient transportation systems, green spaces, and water and waste management strategies. By incorporating these elements in urban planning, cities can mitigate the environmental impact of urbanization, enhance resilience to climate change, and improve the quality of life for residents.

Energy-Efficient Water Heaters

Energy-efficient water heaters are devices that are designed to minimize the amount of energy consumed during the heating process, while still providing hot water for domestic and commercial uses. The main objective of energy-efficient water heaters is to reduce energy consumption and greenhouse gas emissions, as well as to lower utility bills for consumers.

These water heaters typically employ advanced technologies, such as improved insulation, better heat transfer systems, and energy-saving control mechanisms. By utilizing these technologies, energy-efficient water heaters are able to heat water more efficiently and effectively, resulting in reduced energy wastage and lower energy costs.

Energy-Efficient Windows And Doors

Energy-efficient windows and doors are a sustainable solution for reducing energy consumption in residential and commercial buildings. These windows and doors are designed to minimize heat loss or gain, thereby improving the insulation of a building and reducing the need for heating or cooling systems. Energy-efficient windows and doors typically have features such as low-emissivity coatings, multiple panes, insulating gas fills, and thermal breaks.

The low-emissivity (Low-E) coatings on energy-efficient windows and doors help to reflect radiant heat back into the building during the cold months and prevent excessive heat gain in the warmer months. The multiple panes, often double or triple-glazed, provide an extra layer of insulation by trapping air or inert gas between the glass layers. This helps to prevent heat transfer through the glass and reduces the escape of conditioned air, resulting in energy savings.

In addition, energy-efficient windows and doors often have insulating frames with thermal breaks. These breaks are barriers between the interior and exterior frame materials that reduce thermal bridging, which is the transfer of heat through the frame. This further improves the insulation properties of the windows and doors.

By choosing energy-efficient windows and doors, building owners can significantly reduce their

167

energy consumption, lower their utility bills, and decrease their carbon footprint. The improved insulation provided by these windows and doors also enhances indoor comfort by reducing drafts, condensation, and noise transmission. Furthermore, the energy savings achieved through the use of energy-efficient windows and doors contribute to the overall sustainability of a building, helping to conserve natural resources and reduce greenhouse gas emissions.

Energy-Efficient Windows And Insulation

Energy-efficient windows and insulation play an integral role in sustainable practices by reducing energy consumption, promoting thermal comfort, and minimizing environmental impact.

Energy-efficient windows are designed to minimize heat transfer between the interior and exterior of a building, reducing the need for heating or cooling systems. These windows typically incorporate advanced glazing technologies, such as low-emissivity coatings and multiple panes, to improve insulation and solar heat gain. They are strategically designed to allow natural light to enter while reducing the transfer of heat, thereby reducing the reliance on artificial lighting and air conditioning systems. By minimizing energy consumption, energy-efficient windows contribute to lower carbon emissions and a more sustainable built environment.

Insulation is another crucial component of sustainable buildings. It involves the use of materials with high thermal resistance properties to prevent heat loss or gain through walls, roofs, and floors. Proper insulation minimizes the need for artificial heating or cooling, creating a comfortable indoor environment while reducing energy demand. It also helps in mitigating greenhouse gas emissions and enables energy conservation, which aligns with sustainable practices and goals.

Overall, energy-efficient windows and insulation are essential elements in achieving sustainable buildings. They contribute to energy conservation, reduced carbon emissions, improved indoor comfort, and decreased reliance on non-renewable energy sources. By integrating these energy-saving measures, we can move towards a more sustainable and environmentally friendly future.

>

Energy-Efficient Windows

Energy-efficient windows refer to windows that are designed and constructed to minimize the amount of heat transfer between the interior and exterior of a building, thereby reducing the need for heating or cooling energy. These windows are a crucial component of sustainable building design and contribute to increased energy efficiency, reduced carbon emissions, and improved indoor comfort.

The energy efficiency of windows is determined by several key factors. Firstly, the window frame material plays a significant role in reducing heat loss or gain. Materials such as wood, vinyl, or fiberglass are commonly used due to their insulating properties. Additionally, the design and installation of the window frame, including its size and the number of panes, impact its thermal performance. Multi-pane windows, such as double or triple glazing, utilize layers of glass with an insulating gas in between to enhance energy efficiency.

Low-emissivity (low-E) coatings are another feature of energy-efficient windows. These coatings help to reflect infrared heat and ultraviolet rays from the sun, reducing heat gain during the summer months and heat loss during winter. Furthermore, the presence of argon or krypton gas between the panes improves insulation by minimizing convective heat transfer.

Environmental Defense Fund (EDF)

The Environmental Defense Fund (EDF) is a non-profit organization that focuses on finding practical solutions to the most urgent environmental issues, with the ultimate goal of creating a sustainable future for all living beings on Earth.

EDF works with businesses, governments, and communities to address complex sustainability challenges such as climate change, pollution, biodiversity loss, and sustainable agriculture.

Through scientific research, policy advocacy, and market-based approaches, EDF seeks to drive transformative change and achieve long-lasting environmental impact.

Environmental Working Group (EWG)

The Environmental Working Group (EWG) is a non-profit organization that focuses on research and advocacy in the field of environmental sustainability. Their primary goal is to empower consumers and provide them with information on the potential health and environmental impacts of various products and practices.

Through their research, EWG works to identify and raise awareness about the potential dangers of certain chemicals, pollutants, and practices that may harm human health and the environment. They aim to promote sustainable alternatives and advocate for policies that protect public health and the planet.

Environmental Compliance Tracking Software

Environmental compliance tracking software is a technology-based solution that enables organizations to monitor and manage their compliance with environmental regulations and standards. It is specifically designed to support sustainability initiatives by automating the tracking, reporting, and analysis of environmental data.

With this software, organizations can collect and consolidate data from various sources such as sensors, meters, and manual inputs. The software then performs complex calculations and analyses to assess the organization's compliance with environmental regulations, identify areas of improvement, and generate reports for internal and external stakeholders.

Environmental Impact Assessment Software

An environmental impact assessment (EIA) software refers to a computer-based tool designed to assess and evaluate the potential environmental consequences or impacts of a proposed project, policy, or development. The software aids in the prediction, analysis, and monitoring of these impacts to support decision-making processes that promote sustainable development.

EIA software integrates various components and data sources to provide a comprehensive assessment of the environmental implications of a project. It helps identify potential risks and impacts on ecosystems, natural resources, biodiversity, air and water quality, and human well-being. By quantifying and analyzing these impacts, the software enables stakeholders to understand the broader implications of their actions and make informed choices that align with sustainability objectives.

The software typically includes features such as data management, impact modeling, scenario analysis, and reporting capabilities. It allows users to input project information, such as location, scope, and activities, to generate an assessment of potential environmental impacts. The software also provides tools to analyze different scenarios, assess mitigation measures, and compare alternative options. This allows decision-makers to evaluate the feasibility and sustainability of various project alternatives before implementation.

EIA software plays a crucial role in promoting sustainable development by facilitating early identification and consideration of environmental concerns. It supports the integration of environmental considerations into project planning and design, enabling the identification of potential impacts and the development of strategies to minimize or mitigate adverse effects. Additionally, the software enhances transparency and stakeholder engagement by providing a platform for sharing information and involving affected communities in the decision-making process.

Environmental Impact Modeling Tools

Environmental impact modeling tools are computational tools used to assess and analyze the potential environmental effects of various activities, projects, policies, or decisions. These tools enable decision-makers to understand and evaluate the potential consequences of their actions on the environment, helping to inform sustainable decision-making.

These modeling tools use mathematical algorithms, data inputs, and scientific principles to simulate and predict how different environmental factors may be affected by specific interventions or scenarios. The models can take into account a wide range of variables, such as air and water quality, biodiversity, land-use changes, greenhouse gas emissions, and energy consumption.

By using environmental impact modeling tools, stakeholders can quantitatively evaluate the potential outcomes of their actions, helping to identify potential risks and trade-offs. These tools can support the development of sustainable policies and plans by providing decision-makers with insights into the environmental consequences of their choices.

Furthermore, these tools can contribute to improving the environmental performance of projects and initiatives by identifying areas for improvement or mitigation measures. They can be particularly useful in the planning and design phases, offering the opportunity to test different scenarios and optimize strategies to minimize negative environmental impacts.

In conclusion, environmental impact modeling tools are important instruments in sustainability analysis and decision-making. By providing quantitative assessments of potential environmental impacts, these tools support informed and sustainable choices, contributing to a more environmentally conscious and resilient future.

Environmental Sustainability Consulting Services

Environmental sustainability consulting services refer to professional assistance and advice provided to organizations and businesses in order to help them improve their environmental performance, reduce their ecological footprint, and achieve sustainable practices.

These services encompass a range of activities, including conducting environmental audits and assessments, developing and implementing environmental management systems, designing sustainability strategies, providing guidance on regulatory compliance, and offering training and education on sustainable practices. The goal of environmental sustainability consulting is to assist organizations in adopting environmentally responsible practices that align with social and economic objectives.

Consultants in this field work closely with their clients to identify and evaluate their environmental impacts, measure their carbon emissions, identify areas for improvement, and develop practical solutions. They may conduct site visits, collect data, analyze information, and prepare reports that outline recommendations and action plans for achieving sustainability goals.

Environmental sustainability consulting services can be beneficial for a wide range of industries and sectors, including manufacturing, construction, energy, transportation, hospitality, and agriculture. By engaging with these services, organizations can enhance their environmental performance, reduce costs, improve their reputation, comply with regulations, and contribute to the overall well-being of the planet.

Extended Producer Responsibility (EPR)

Extended producer responsibility (EPR) is a sustainability principle that shifts the onus of managing the environmental impacts of a product throughout its lifecycle from the consumer to the producer. It is a policy approach that requires manufacturers and importers to take responsibility for the environmental implications of their products, including their packaging and post-consumer waste disposal.

Under EPR, producers are responsible for the entire product lifecycle, from design and production to disposal, including end-of-life management. This means they must minimize the negative environmental impacts of their products by adopting sustainable production processes, using eco-friendly materials, and implementing efficient waste management systems.

By extending the responsibilities of producers beyond the point of sale, EPR aims to incentivize manufacturers to incorporate environmental considerations into their product design, encouraging the development of more sustainable products. It also promotes the adoption of recycling and waste management strategies, as producers are typically required to establish and finance collection and recycling systems for their products.

EPR is often implemented through legislation or voluntary agreements, and the specific requirements can vary among jurisdictions and product categories. However, the underlying principle remains the same - holding producers accountable for the environmental impacts of their products, with the ultimate goal of reducing waste, promoting recycling, and advancing sustainability.

Floating Solar Arrays

Floating solar arrays are an innovative form of renewable energy technology that involves installing solar panels on water bodies such as lakes, reservoirs, and even offshore locations. These arrays are designed to float on the surface of the water while harnessing sunlight to generate electricity.

By harnessing solar energy on water surfaces, floating solar arrays offer several sustainability benefits. Firstly, they enable dual land use, allowing the utilization of large bodies of water that may otherwise not be used for any productive activities. This promotes efficient land use and minimizes the pressure on terrestrial ecosystems for solar panel installations.

Secondly, the water bodies where floating solar arrays are installed experience reduced evaporation rates. This helps conserve water resources, especially in areas prone to water scarcity. Additionally, the shade provided by the solar panels can help reduce algae growth, maintaining water quality and biodiversity in the ecosystem.

Furthermore, floating solar arrays have the advantage of natural cooling due to the proximity of the panels to the water surface. This improves the overall efficiency of the solar panels, as cooler temperatures enhance their electricity generation capacity. Additionally, the co-location of solar panels and water bodies can potentially reduce transmission losses by locating renewable energy generation close to demand centers.

In conclusion, floating solar arrays offer a sustainable solution for generating clean and renewable energy. Their ability to optimize land use, conserve water resources, and enhance overall energy efficiency make them a promising technology in the transition towards a more sustainable energy future.

Floating Solar Farms

Floating solar farms are a form of renewable energy infrastructure that harnesses solar energy by installing photovoltaic (PV) panels on bodies of water such as lakes, reservoirs, and coastal areas. This innovative approach to solar power generation offers several advantages in terms of sustainability.

Firstly, floating solar farms make efficient use of space by utilizing existing bodies of water that may not be otherwise suitable for traditional land-based solar farms. This helps to minimize the need for additional land usage and reduces potential conflicts with other land purposes such as agriculture or conservation. By repurposing water surfaces, floating solar farms contribute to the preservation of terrestrial ecosystems and biodiversity.

Secondly, these solar farms have the advantage of utilizing the cooling effect of the water beneath them, leading to increased energy efficiency. The cooler surface temperature of the water enhances the performance of the PV panels, resulting in higher electricity yields compared to conventional solar farms. This improved efficiency optimizes the use of resources and reduces the carbon footprint associated with energy production.

Furthermore, the installation of floating solar farms helps to reduce water evaporation from reservoirs and other bodies of water. By shielding the surface area from direct sunlight, these solar installations lessen water loss, particularly in arid regions, and contribute to water conservation efforts. Additionally, by reducing evaporation, floating solar farms support the maintenance of water quality and ecosystem integrity.

Floating Solar Panel Technology

171

Floating solar panel technology refers to the practice of installing photovoltaic (PV) panels on bodies of water, such as lakes, ponds, reservoirs, and oceans. Unlike traditional solar panels that are installed on land or rooftops, floating solar panels float on water surfaces.

This sustainable technology offers numerous environmental benefits. Firstly, the presence of water helps to cool down the solar panels, making them more efficient at generating electricity. Additionally, the water reduces the accumulation of dust and dirt on the panels, resulting in less maintenance and cleaning requirements. Moreover, by utilizing bodies of water, floating solar panels make efficient use of underutilized spaces, preventing land degradation and the destruction of natural habitats.

Furthermore, floating solar panels contribute to water sustainability. When installed on reservoirs or other bodies of water, they help to reduce evaporation by providing shade and minimizing water exposure to direct sunlight, thereby reducing water loss. This is especially important in regions with water scarcity or drought conditions.

Floating solar panel technology also benefits from the proximity to water infrastructure. By utilizing existing water resources, it can leverage pre-existing connections to the electric grid, reducing the need for extensive infrastructure development and associated costs.

In conclusion, floating solar panel technology offers a sustainable solution for generating electricity by utilizing water surfaces. Its cooling effects, prevention of land degradation, conservation of water, and utilization of existing infrastructure make it an environmentally friendly and economically viable option for renewable energy production.

Floating Solar Panels

Floating solar panels are a sustainable technology that involves the installation of photovoltaic panels on the surface of bodies of water, such as lakes, reservoirs, and ponds. These panels are designed to float on the water's surface while harnessing solar energy to generate electricity.

By utilizing water bodies for the installation of solar panels, floating solar technologies offer several sustainability advantages. Firstly, they make use of unutilized space, allowing for the efficient use of land and reducing competition with other land-intensive activities. This is particularly beneficial in densely populated areas where land availability is limited.

Additionally, floating solar panels can help reduce water evaporation from lakes and reservoirs by providing shade and minimizing direct exposure to sunlight. By preventing excessive evaporation, this technology contributes positively to water conservation efforts, particularly in regions facing water scarcity or drought conditions.

Moreover, the cooling effect of the water on which the panels float can enhance the efficiency of the solar panels, as it helps to dissipate excess heat and maintain optimal operating temperatures. This increases the overall energy generation capacity of the panels and improves their performance, making floating solar a more sustainable option compared to land-based solar installations.

Furthermore, floating solar panels have the potential to reduce algae growth in water bodies, as the shade they create limits sunlight penetration and prevents excessive nutrient enrichment. This benefit can help maintain water quality and biodiversity in aquatic ecosystems.

In summary, floating solar panels offer a sustainable solution for harnessing solar energy by utilizing water bodies effectively, conserving water resources, improving solar panel efficiency, and promoting ecological stability in aquatic environments.

Floating Wetland Ecosystems

Floating wetland ecosystems are habitats composed of a matrix of floating vegetation and organic material that support a wide range of diverse species. These ecosystems are crucial for maintaining ecological balance and promoting sustainability.

One key feature of floating wetland ecosystems is their ability to improve water quality. The floating vegetation, such as reeds and grasses, absorb excess nutrients, pollutants, and sediment from the water, acting as natural filters. This process helps to reduce the levels of harmful substances in the water, benefiting both aquatic organisms and humans who rely on the water for various purposes.

In addition to water purification, floating wetland ecosystems provide various other ecosystem services. They serve as crucial habitats for a wide array of plants and animals, including fish, birds, and amphibians. These ecosystems offer abundant food sources, nesting grounds, and shelter, contributing to the overall biodiversity of a region. The presence of diverse species within these ecosystems also helps to control pest populations, regulate nutrient cycling, and support aquatic food webs.

Furthermore, floating wetland ecosystems play a role in climate regulation and carbon sequestration. The dense vegetation in these habitats absorbs carbon dioxide from the atmosphere, thereby mitigating climate change. Additionally, they act as natural buffers against floods and storms, preventing erosion and protecting shorelines.

Overall, the conservation and restoration of floating wetland ecosystems are essential for achieving sustainability. By preserving these habitats, we can enhance water quality, support biodiversity, mitigate climate change, and ensure the long-term health and well-being of both ecosystems and human communities.

Floating Wetlands

Floating wetlands are man-made structures designed to mimic natural wetland ecosystems in order to enhance and restore the ecological functions of degraded water bodies, such as ponds, lakes, and stormwater retention basins. These wetlands consist of floating mats or rafts made from synthetic materials or natural materials like coconut fiber or jute, which are then planted with a variety of wetland plants.

As a sustainable solution, floating wetlands offer several benefits. Firstly, they improve water quality by acting as biofilters, removing excess nutrients, heavy metals, and other pollutants from the water. The plants on the floating mats absorb these substances, while the roots provide an ideal substrate for the growth of beneficial microbes that further break down pollutants.

Furthermore, floating wetlands provide habitat for a diverse range of plant and animal species. The plants support aquatic insects and other invertebrates, which in turn attract birds and small mammals. This additional habitat can help to support biodiversity and contribute to the conservation of local flora and fauna.

In terms of climate change mitigation, floating wetlands play a crucial role. Wetland plants are efficient at sequestering carbon dioxide from the atmosphere. Additionally, the dense vegetation cover helps to reduce water temperature and evaporation rates, contributing to the overall cooling of the surrounding environment and combating the urban heat island effect.

In conclusion, floating wetlands are innovative and sustainable solutions that offer multiple environmental benefits. Through their ability to improve water quality, provide habitat, sequester carbon, and mitigate the impacts of climate change, they contribute to the restoration and long-term sustainability of degraded aquatic ecosystems.

Floating Wind Energy Platforms

Floating wind energy platforms are a sustainable solution for harnessing wind power in deep offshore locations. These platforms consist of floating structures equipped with wind turbines that generate clean and renewable electricity.

Unlike traditional offshore wind farms, which are fixed to the seabed, floating wind energy platforms can be deployed in areas with deeper waters, expanding the potential for offshore wind energy production. By using floating structures, these platforms can be placed far away from the coast, minimizing their visual impact and reducing potential conflicts with other maritime activities.

Floating Wind Turbines

Floating wind turbines are a type of renewable energy technology that harnesses wind power to generate electricity. These turbines are mounted on floating structures that are anchored to the seabed, allowing them to be deployed in deep waters where fixed-bottom wind turbines are not feasible.

One of the main advantages of floating wind turbines is their ability to access stronger and more consistent winds found further offshore. This results in higher electricity production and a more reliable energy source compared to onshore wind turbines. By capitalizing on offshore wind resources, floating wind turbines contribute to the diversification and decentralization of the energy grid.

Additionally, these turbines have minimal environmental impact as they do not require any land usage. They can be located away from coastal areas, preserving valuable ecosystems and minimizing visual impact. Floating wind farms can coexist with other economic activities such as fishing and shipping, further promoting sustainable development.

Moreover, floating wind turbines have the potential to complement other renewable energy sources, providing a reliable power supply that is less dependent on weather conditions. As a clean and renewable energy technology, floating wind turbines contribute to reducing greenhouse gas emissions, mitigating climate change, and achieving sustainability targets.

Food Waste Tracking And Reduction Apps

Food waste tracking and reduction apps are digital tools designed to help individuals or businesses measure, monitor, and minimize the amount of food they waste. These apps aim to promote sustainable practices by providing users with the means to understand and change their behavior towards food consumption and disposal.

These apps typically offer features such as inventory management, shopping list creation, meal planning, and recipe suggestions based on available ingredients. By inputting information about the food items they have and how they plan to use them, users can get a clear picture of their food inventory and avoid purchasing unnecessary items. This reduces the likelihood of food spoiling or going unused, ultimately minimizing waste.

Furthermore, food waste tracking and reduction apps often include tools for tracking wasted food. Users can record and categorize the food items they discard, including details such as the quantity, reasons for disposal, and when it occurred. This data provides valuable insights into patterns and trends, helping users identify areas for improvement and adjust their habits for more sustainable practices.

Many of these apps also provide educational resources and tips to raise awareness about the environmental, economic, and social impacts of food waste. By understanding the consequences of wasting food, users are encouraged to take action to reduce their waste and contribute to a more sustainable future.

Forest Stewardship Council (FSC)

The Forest Stewardship Council (FSC) is an international organization that promotes responsible management of forests worldwide.

FSC sets standards for forest products, certifies companies that adhere to these standards, and provides a label to identify products from responsibly managed forests.

Geopolymer Construction Materials

Geopolymer construction materials are a sustainable alternative to conventional construction materials such as cement and concrete. They are made using a combination of industrial by-products and natural materials, reducing the environmental impact associated with the extraction and production of traditional construction materials.

Geopolymer materials are typically composed of a binder and aggregates. The binder is formed by the chemical reaction of an alkali-activated source material, such as fly ash or slag, with an alkaline activator. This reaction eliminates the need for traditional cement, which is responsible for a significant amount of carbon dioxide emissions during its production. By using industrial by-products as a binder, geopolymer materials help to reduce waste and promote a circular economy.

In addition to their environmental benefits, geopolymer materials also offer superior mechanical properties compared to traditional construction materials. They exhibit high strength and durability, making them suitable for various applications, including structural elements and infrastructure development.

Furthermore, geopolymer materials have a lower embodied energy compared to conventional materials, meaning that less energy is required in their production and transportation. This contributes to the overall reduction of greenhouse gas emissions and energy consumption in the construction industry.

Overall, geopolymer construction materials offer a sustainable and viable alternative for the construction industry. By utilizing industrial by-products and reducing the reliance on traditional cement, they play a crucial role in reducing carbon emissions, minimizing waste, and promoting a more sustainable built environment.

Geospatial Technology For Conservation

Geospatial technology for conservation refers to the use of specialized tools and techniques that integrate geographic information systems (GIS), remote sensing, and global positioning systems (GPS) for the purpose of preserving and managing natural resources in a sustainable manner.

GIS is a software-based mapping technology that allows conservationists to analyze and visualize spatial data, such as habitat maps, land cover classifications, and species distributions. It enables them to identify priority areas for biodiversity conservation, assess the impact of human activities on ecosystems, and monitor changes in land use over time. By overlaying different layers of information, GIS helps in making informed decisions about resource allocation and conservation planning.

Remote sensing, on the other hand, involves the collection of data from satellites, aircraft, or drones to obtain information about the Earth's surface. It provides valuable data on vegetation health, deforestation, water quality, and other environmental indicators. By analyzing these remote sensing images, conservationists can gain insights into the state of ecosystems and identify areas that require immediate attention for conservation efforts.

GPS technology plays a crucial role in geospatial conservation by providing accurate positioning and navigation capabilities. It allows conservationists to precisely determine the location of important ecological features, track the movement of wildlife, and create accurate maps for land management activities. This information helps in developing effective conservation strategies, minimizing human-wildlife conflicts, and promoting sustainable resource use.

Geothermal Heat Pumps

Geothermal heat pumps, also known as ground source heat pumps, are an innovative and sustainable heating and cooling technology that harnesses the natural heat stored in the earth's surface. They utilize a network of pipes buried underground to exchange heat with the ground and provide a highly efficient method of heating or cooling buildings.

These heat pumps work by transferring heat from the earth to a building during the winter and vice versa during the summer. The system consists of a heat pump unit and underground loop system. The heat pump extracts the heat from the ground or transfers it to the ground using a refrigerant fluid that circulates through the underground loop.

Compared to traditional heating and cooling systems, geothermal heat pumps offer several sustainability benefits. Firstly, they significantly reduce greenhouse gas emissions due to their high energy efficiency. By utilizing the earth's natural heat, they require less electricity to operate, resulting in lower carbon emissions. Additionally, they do not burn fossil fuels on-site, further reducing their environmental impact.

Furthermore, geothermal heat pumps have a longer lifespan compared to conventional systems, leading to reduced waste generation. They also have fewer moving parts, requiring less maintenance and fewer replacement parts, which contributes to resource conservation and sustainability.

Geothermal Heating And Cooling

Geothermal heating and cooling is a sustainable energy solution that utilizes the constant temperature of the earth's subsurface to provide efficient and environmentally-friendly heating and cooling for buildings. It taps into the earth's natural heat by utilizing a geothermal heat pump system, which circulates a fluid through underground pipes to transfer heat to or from the ground.

This process takes advantage of the fact that the temperature below the surface remains relatively constant year-round, regardless of the weather conditions above ground. In colder climates, the ground temperature is warmer than the air temperature, allowing the heat pump to extract heat from the ground to warm the building. Conversely, in warmer climates, the ground temperature is cooler than the air temperature, enabling the heat pump to remove heat from the building and transfer it into the cooler ground.

Geothermal heating and cooling systems have several advantages from a sustainability standpoint. Firstly, they have a significantly lower environmental impact compared to traditional heating and cooling methods. They do not burn fossil fuels to generate heat or cool air, resulting in reduced greenhouse gas emissions and air pollution. Additionally, geothermal systems are highly efficient, using approximately 25% to 50% less electricity than conventional heating and cooling systems.

The use of geothermal energy also helps to conserve natural resources. By harnessing the earth's heat, it reduces reliance on finite fossil fuel reserves, which are non-renewable and contribute to climate change when burned. Furthermore, geothermal systems have a long lifespan, typically lasting over 20 years, which can further reduce waste and resource consumption associated with frequent replacements.

Geothermal Power Generation

Geothermal power generation is a sustainable method of producing electricity by harnessing the natural heat energy stored within the Earth's crust. It involves extracting heat from the Earth's interior, usually by drilling deep wells to access hot water or steam reservoirs. This heat is then used to rotate turbines, which generate electricity.

Geothermal power generation is a renewable and environmentally friendly form of energy production. The heat extracted from the Earth is constantly replenished by natural processes, ensuring an ongoing and reliable source of energy. Unlike fossil fuels, such as coal or natural gas, geothermal energy does not produce harmful greenhouse gas emissions or air pollutants during the generation process. It also requires a relatively small land footprint, reducing its impact on natural habitats and ecosystems.

Geothermal Power Plants

Geothermal power plants are sustainable energy facilities that utilize the heat generated from the Earth's core to produce electricity. They harness the naturally occurring thermal energy stored beneath the Earth's surface and convert it into a usable form, reducing the reliance on non-renewable sources such as fossil fuels.

These geothermal power plants typically tap into hot water and steam reservoirs located deep within the Earth. To harness this energy, wells are drilled into the ground, allowing the heated fluid to rise to the surface. The steam is then used to drive turbines, which in turn generate electricity. In some cases, the hot water can also be used directly for heating purposes, further increasing the efficiency of the system.

176

One of the key advantages of geothermal power plants is their low emission profile. Unlike fossil fuel-based power plants, geothermal facilities produce minimal greenhouse gases, contributing significantly to carbon footprint reduction. Additionally, the availability of this renewable energy source is not dependent on weather conditions, making it a reliable and consistent energy option.

Furthermore, geothermal power plants have a long lifespan and require minimal land usage compared to other renewable energy sources like solar or wind. Once the infrastructure is set up, the ongoing operational costs are relatively low, making geothermal energy an economically viable option.

Geothermal Well Drilling

Geothermal well drilling is a sustainable technique used to extract renewable energy from the Earth's subsurface. It involves drilling a well into the ground to access the geothermal reservoirs, which contain heat and steam trapped in rock formations or underground water. The primary objective of geothermal well drilling is to harness this natural heat and convert it into usable energy for heating, cooling, and electricity generation. The process begins with site selection, where geological studies are conducted to identify areas with geothermal potential. Once a suitable site is found, drilling operations commence to reach the reservoir. It typically involves the use of specialized drilling rigs and drill bits capable of penetrating the subsurface layers. Excess heat is generated during drilling, which is captured and utilized as much as possible to minimize energy wastage. After the well has been drilled, various technologies are employed to extract the geothermal energy. In a closed-loop system, a heat exchanger is used to transfer the heat from the fluid circulating inside the well to a separate system that can distribute it for different purposes. In an open-loop system, the geothermal fluid itself is directly utilized for heating or electricity generation, without the need for a heat exchanger. Geothermal well drilling has numerous sustainability benefits. Firstly, it is a renewable energy source as the Earth's heat is continuously replenished by natural processes. Consequently, geothermal energy has a minimal carbon footprint and helps mitigate greenhouse gas emissions. Additionally, the technology has a long lifespan, with wells capable of operating for several decades. It also has a small land footprint compared to other energy sources, making it ideal for urban areas where space is limited. Overall, geothermal well drilling is a sustainable method of harnessing clean and reliable energy from the Earth's natural heat. It offers a promising solution to reduce dependence on fossil fuels while contributing to a greener, more sustainable future.>

Global Energy Interconnection Development And Cooperation Organization (GEIDCO)

The Global Energy Interconnection Development and Cooperation Organization (GEIDCO) is an international organization committed to promoting the development of clean and sustainable energy systems across the globe. Recognizing the urgent need to address climate change and ensure energy security, GEIDCO aims to establish a global energy interconnection system that facilitates the efficient transmission and integration of renewable energy resources.

Through its initiatives and partnerships, GEIDCO works towards the creation of a reliable, affordable, and sustainable energy infrastructure that can support the transition to a low-carbon economy. The organization emphasizes the importance of international cooperation and collaboration to overcome the challenges associated with energy transition.

Global Energy Internet Development Cooperation Organization (GEIDCO)

The Global Energy Internet Development Cooperation Organization (GEIDCO) is an international organization that works towards the development of a sustainable global energy system. It aims to promote the efficient utilization of clean and renewable energy resources worldwide, in order to address the urgent challenges posed by climate change and ensure the long-term sustainability of the planet.

GEIDCO focuses on the concept of an "energy internet," which envisions a highly interconnected and integrated energy infrastructure that enables the seamless transmission and distribution of clean energy across regions and countries. This concept aims to overcome the limitations of traditional energy systems, such as the reliance on fossil fuels and the lack of global connectivity, by utilizing advanced technologies, smart grids, and a diverse mix of energy sources.

As a cooperative platform, GEIDCO actively encourages collaboration and cooperation among governments, organizations, and stakeholders from different nations and sectors. It facilitates the exchange of knowledge, expertise, and best practices in areas such as energy planning, policy development, financing, and technical standards. By promoting international cooperation, GEIDCO aims to foster innovation, enhance energy security, and accelerate the transition towards sustainable energy systems globally.

Global Environment Facility (GEF)

The Global Environment Facility (GEF) is an international financial institution that provides grants to support projects and programs aimed at promoting sustainability and addressing global environmental challenges.

Established in 1991, the GEF operates as a partnership between the United Nations Environment Programme (UNEP), the United Nations Development Programme (UNDP), and the World Bank. It collaborates with other organizations, governments, and stakeholders to fund projects in areas such as biodiversity conservation, climate change mitigation and adaptation, land degradation, sustainable forest management, and the elimination of harmful chemicals and pollutants.

The GEF follows a unique funding model, leveraging financial resources from developed countries and channeling them towards developing countries and economies in transition. It provides grants to these countries to support projects that have the potential to generate global environmental benefits. In addition to financial support, the GEF also offers technical expertise and knowledge sharing to ensure the effective implementation of projects and programs.

The goals of the GEF align with the principles of sustainability by promoting environmental protection, social equity, and economic development. It recognizes the interconnectedness between natural ecosystems, human well-being, and economic growth, and seeks to catalyze transformative change towards more sustainable pathways.

Overall, the GEF plays a crucial role in supporting global sustainability efforts by financing and facilitating projects and programs that address pressing environmental challenges and promote a more sustainable future for all.

Global Footprint Network

The Global Footprint Network is an international research organization that focuses on promoting sustainable development and environmental conservation. The organization measures and tracks the ecological footprint of various countries and individuals to assess their impact on the planet.

The ecological footprint is a measure of the amount of resources consumed and waste generated by an individual, population, or country. It takes into account factors such as energy consumption, food production, transportation, and waste disposal. By calculating the ecological footprint, the Global Footprint Network aims to raise awareness about the global impact of human activities and the need for sustainable practices.

Global Green Growth Institute (GGGI)

The Global Green Growth Institute (GGGI) is an international organization dedicated to promoting sustainable and inclusive green growth. It works with governments and stakeholders to help countries transition to a low-carbon, resilient, and sustainable economy.

GGGI supports its member countries in developing and implementing green growth strategies and policies that address environmental challenges while promoting economic growth and social development. It provides technical expertise, capacity-building, and policy advice to help countries integrate sustainability into their national agendas.

Global Reporting Initiative (GRI)

The Global Reporting Initiative (GRI) is a non-profit organization that has developed a comprehensive framework for sustainability reporting. Sustainability reporting refers to the practice of disclosing the economic, environmental, and social impacts of an organization's activities. The GRI framework is widely used by organizations of all types and sizes to communicate their sustainability performance to stakeholders, including investors, customers, employees, and communities.

The GRI framework is based on the principles of stakeholder inclusiveness, materiality, sustainability context, and completeness. It provides guidance on what should be included in a sustainability report, such as governance structure, strategy, management approach, performance indicators, and targets. The framework also encourages organizations to report on their impacts across a range of sustainability issues, including climate change, human rights, labor practices, biodiversity, and corruption.

By using the GRI framework, organizations are able to provide stakeholders with a transparent and standardized view of their sustainability performance. This enables stakeholders to make informed decisions and hold organizations accountable for their impacts. The GRI framework also helps organizations identify areas where they can improve their sustainability performance and set targets to drive progress over time.

In conclusion, the Global Reporting Initiative (GRI) is an essential tool for organizations to report their sustainability performance in a transparent and standardized manner. By using the GRI framework, organizations can enhance their credibility and demonstrate their commitment to sustainable development.

Global Shea Alliance

The Global Shea Alliance (GSA) is an international non-profit organization dedicated to promoting sustainable shea production and trade. Shea is a valuable resource found within the African savanna, providing rural communities with income and livelihood opportunities. The GSA works towards ensuring the sustainability of shea resources and improving the livelihoods of shea collectors, primarily women.

Through its robust network of stakeholders, including government agencies, NGOs, and private sector entities, the GSA fosters cooperation, knowledge-sharing, and capacity-building initiatives. By coordinating efforts, the GSA aims to address the numerous challenges facing the shea sector, such as deforestation, unsustainable harvesting practices, and limited market access.

Global Sustainable Tourism Council (GSTC)

The Global Sustainable Tourism Council (GSTC) is an international organization that sets the globally recognized criteria and standards for sustainable tourism. Its mission is to promote sustainable tourism practices around the world, aiming to minimize the negative impacts of tourism on the environment, culture, and local communities, while maximizing the positive socio-economic benefits.

The GSTC criteria provide a framework for businesses and destinations to assess their sustainability performance and guide them towards more responsible and sustainable practices. These criteria cover four key areas: Sustainable Management, Socioeconomic Impacts, Cultural Heritage, and Environmental Impacts. By addressing each of these areas, the GSTC criteria encourage tourism stakeholders to adhere to principles of sustainable development and make informed decisions that contribute to the long-term preservation and well-being of destinations.

Global Water Challenge

The Global Water Challenge is a collective effort aimed at addressing the critical issue of water sustainability on a global scale. It brings together individuals, organizations, and governments from across the world to collaborate and find sustainable solutions to water-related challenges.

Water sustainability refers to the responsible management and use of water resources to ensure their availability for present and future generations. It focuses on balancing the needs of humans, the environment, and the economy, while preserving the natural water cycle and reducing negative impacts on ecosystems.

Global Water Partnership (GWP)

The Global Water Partnership (GWP) is a multi-stakeholder network organization that promotes integrated water resource management for sustainable development. Established in 1996, GWP works towards addressing the world's water challenges by fostering collaboration between various stakeholders, including governments, international organizations, civil society, and the private sector.

GWP's overarching goal is to ensure the sustainable management of our planet's water resources to support human well-being, economic development, and the preservation of ecosystems. By promoting the integrated water resource management approach, GWP recognizes that water is intricately linked to other sectors such as energy, agriculture, and climate change mitigation and adaptation. Therefore, ensuring water security requires a holistic and inclusive approach that considers the multiple dimensions of sustainability.

GWP's activities revolve around building partnerships and facilitating dialogue and knowledge sharing. They work at multiple levels, from global to local, to promote the adoption of best practices, policy development, capacity building, and the implementation of sustainable water management solutions. Through their regional and country-level networks, GWP aims to empower local stakeholders and facilitate the mobilization of resources, both financial and technical, to support effective water governance and decision-making processes.

In summary, the Global Water Partnership is a collaborative network that promotes the sustainable management of water resources by fostering partnerships, knowledge sharing, and capacity building. By advocating for integrated water resource management, GWP aims to address the world's water challenges and contribute to sustainable development.

Global Wind Energy Council (GWEC)

The Global Wind Energy Council (GWEC) is an international organization that promotes the sustainable development of wind energy worldwide. It represents the wind power sector, working with governments, businesses, and other stakeholders to accelerate the adoption of wind power as a clean and renewable energy source.

GWEC plays a crucial role in driving the global transition to a more sustainable energy future. It provides a platform for knowledge sharing, collaboration, and advocacy, facilitating the exchange of best practices and promoting the implementation of supportive policy frameworks.

Green Blockchain Solutions

Green blockchain solutions refer to the application of blockchain technology in promoting sustainability and reducing environmental impact. Blockchain is a decentralized and transparent digital ledger that securely records transactions and activities across multiple computers or nodes. It has gained prominence in various industries for its potential to disrupt traditional systems and enhance transparency, traceability, and efficiency.

When applied to sustainability challenges, green blockchain solutions aim to address issues such as carbon emissions, resource utilization, and waste management. By enabling secure and immutable data storage and transactions, blockchain can increase accountability, trust, and collaboration among stakeholders in sustainability initiatives.

For example, in the energy sector, green blockchain solutions can facilitate the development of peer-to-peer energy trading platforms, enabling individuals and businesses to directly transact energy from renewable sources. This decentralized approach empowers consumers and encourages the use of clean energy while minimizing reliance on traditional power grids.

Furthermore, green blockchain solutions can support supply chain transparency and traceability,

180

helping organizations monitor and verify their environmental and social impact. By recording every step of the supply chain on the blockchain, companies can ensure that products are sourced sustainably and produced using environmentally friendly practices.

In summary, green blockchain solutions leverage the inherent characteristics of blockchain technology to foster sustainable practices, encourage renewable energy adoption, and enhance transparency and accountability in various sectors. By harnessing the power of decentralization, transparency, and trust, blockchain has the potential to revolutionize sustainability efforts and contribute to a greener and more sustainable future.

Green Building Certification Tools

Green building certification tools are frameworks or systems used to evaluate and measure the sustainability performance of buildings. These tools are designed to assess various aspects of a building's environmental impact and promote sustainable practices in the construction and operation of the built environment.

The main purpose of green building certification tools is to provide a standardized way of assessing and recognizing buildings that have achieved a high level of sustainability. These tools typically assess factors such as energy efficiency, water conservation, waste management, indoor environmental quality, and materials selection. By evaluating these factors, green building certification tools can help guide decision-making and encourage the adoption of sustainable design and construction practices.

Green Building Certification

A green building certification is a formal recognition given to a building that has been designed, constructed, and operated in a sustainable way. It indicates that the building meets specific criteria and standards set forth by a recognized certification program or organization, demonstrating its commitment to minimizing its environmental impact and promoting resource efficiency.

Such certification programs assess a wide range of factors including the building's energy efficiency, water conservation, use of renewable materials, waste management practices, indoor air quality, and overall environmental performance. They encourage the adoption of sustainable design strategies, innovative technologies, and green building practices to achieve a more sustainable built environment.

Green Building Certifications

Green building certifications refer to official certifications and rating systems that evaluate and recognize the sustainable features and practices of a building. These certifications are awarded by independent organizations and are based on a set of established criteria and standards.

Green building certifications play a crucial role in promoting sustainability in the construction and operation of buildings. They provide a means of assessing the environmental impact and performance of a building throughout its life cycle, including its design, construction, operation, and maintenance. These certifications encourage and incentivize the use of sustainable materials, energy-efficient technologies, water conservation measures, and environmentally responsible practices.

Green Building Codes

Green building codes refer to a set of regulations and standards that are implemented by local governments or building authorities to promote sustainable practices in construction and design. These codes aim to reduce the environmental impact of buildings throughout their lifecycle, including their construction, operation, and eventual demolition.

The primary objective of green building codes is to ensure that buildings are designed and constructed in a manner that conserves resources, improves energy efficiency, minimizes waste, and protects the natural environment. These codes typically address various aspects of building design and performance, such as energy efficiency, water conservation, indoor air

181

quality, use of sustainable materials, and waste management.

By incorporating green building codes into their regulations, governments seek to promote sustainable development, mitigate greenhouse gas emissions, improve the health and well-being of occupants, and reduce the strain on natural resources. Compliance with these codes is often required for obtaining building permits and certifications, such as LEED (Leadership in Energy and Environmental Design) or BREEAM (Building Research Establishment Environmental Assessment Method).

Green building codes play a crucial role in shaping the construction industry towards more sustainable practices. They encourage the adoption of innovative technologies, materials, and designs that minimize environmental impact and contribute to the resilience and long-term sustainability of buildings and communities. These codes also serve as a valuable resource for architects, engineers, and developers, providing guidance on best practices and standards for sustainable building construction.

Green Building Materials Production

Green building materials production refers to the manufacturing of construction materials that are environmentally friendly and sustainable. These materials are produced using processes that minimize resource consumption and environmental impacts.

Green building materials are designed to reduce the negative impacts on the environment throughout their lifecycle – from extraction and production to use and disposal. The production of these materials involves the use of renewable resources, recycled materials, and low-energy manufacturing techniques.

The focus of green building materials production is to create products that conserve resources, emit less pollution, and minimize waste generation. This includes sourcing raw materials from sustainable sources, such as responsibly managed forests and recycling facilities. The manufacturing process also aims to reduce energy consumption by using innovative technologies, improving efficiency, and implementing recycling and waste reduction measures.

Green building materials are commonly used in various construction applications, including residential, commercial, and industrial projects. These materials can include eco-friendly alternatives to traditional building components such as sustainable insulation, energy-efficient windows, and low-emission paints. They can also include structural materials like sustainably sourced wood, recycled steel, and concrete made with fly ash or slag.

Green Building Materials Testing

Green building materials testing refers to the evaluation and analysis of construction materials to determine their environmental sustainability. It involves conducting rigorous assessments to measure the performance, durability, and impact of these materials on the environment throughout their lifecycle.

The testing process aims to assess various attributes, such as energy efficiency, resource conservation, and ecological impact, to ensure that the materials meet specific sustainability standards. This evaluation helps architects, builders, and developers make informed decisions when selecting materials for construction projects, promoting the use of environmentally friendly and energy-efficient products.

During the testing, different parameters are evaluated, including the material's composition, source, production process, and potential for recycling or reuse. The environmental impact of the materials is assessed by measuring factors like carbon footprint, water usage, and waste generation. Additionally, the materials' performance is analyzed in terms of energy efficiency, durability, and indoor air quality.

The use of green building materials in construction helps reduce the negative impact on the environment, conserve resources, and enhance the sustainability of buildings. By conducting thorough testing and analysis, stakeholders can identify materials that minimize energy consumption, reduce greenhouse gas emissions, and promote a healthier indoor environment.

Overall, green building materials testing plays a crucial role in ensuring that construction projects align with sustainability goals and contribute to the long-term well-being of the planet.

Green Building Regulations

Green building regulations are policies and guidelines set by governments and organizations to promote the construction and design of sustainable buildings. These regulations aim to minimize the negative environmental impact of buildings throughout their lifecycle, from the planning and construction phases to their operation and eventual demolition.

The main objective of green building regulations is to encourage the adoption of energy-efficient and resource-efficient practices in the construction industry. This includes reducing greenhouse gas emissions, conserving natural resources, and improving indoor air quality. These regulations typically cover various aspects of building design, such as energy performance, water conservation, waste management, and materials used.

One of the key areas addressed by green building regulations is energy efficiency. Buildings are responsible for a significant amount of global energy consumption, and reducing their energy use can have a positive impact on climate change. Regulations often require the use of energy-efficient technologies, such as insulation, high-performance windows, and energy-efficient lighting systems, to reduce the overall energy demand of buildings.

Water conservation is another important aspect of green building regulations. Buildings consume a substantial amount of freshwater for various purposes, including domestic use, landscaping, and cooling systems. Regulations may enforce the implementation of water-efficient fixtures, rainwater harvesting systems, and graywater recycling to reduce water consumption and minimize strain on local water sources.

Green Building Technologies

Green building technologies refer to the innovative practices and systems that are employed in the construction, design, and operation of buildings with the primary goal of reducing their environmental impact and promoting sustainability. These technologies encompass a wide range of strategies that focus on conserving energy, water, and other vital resources, while also minimizing waste and harmful emissions.

One key aspect of green building technologies is energy efficiency, which involves employing various measures to reduce the overall energy consumption of a building. This can include using energy-efficient lighting and appliances, improving insulation, optimizing heating and cooling systems, and integrating renewable energy sources such as solar panels or wind turbines. By reducing the energy demand, green buildings not only contribute to a significant decrease in greenhouse gas emissions but also result in substantial cost savings for the occupants.

Water conservation is another crucial element of green building technologies. This encompasses strategies such as installing water-saving fixtures, implementing efficient irrigation systems, and incorporating rainwater harvesting methods. By using water more efficiently and responsibly, green buildings help conserve this precious resource, particularly in regions prone to water scarcity. Additionally, green building technologies prioritize the treatment and recycling of wastewater, reducing the strain on municipal water supply systems.

Beyond energy and water considerations, green building technologies also address waste management. By utilizing materials that are locally sourced, sustainable, and recyclable, and by implementing effective waste reduction and recycling programs during construction and operation, green buildings aim to minimize their environmental footprint and contribute to a circular economy.

In conclusion, green building technologies play a pivotal role in promoting sustainable development by integrating innovative strategies that reduce energy consumption, conserve water, minimize waste, and mitigate environmental impact. By incorporating these technologies into the construction and operation of buildings, we can create healthier, more efficient, and environmentally responsible built environments.

Green Business Certifications

A green business certification is an official recognition or verification given to a business or organization that has demonstrated its commitment to sustainability and environmentally responsible practices. This certification is typically awarded by a third-party organization or accrediting body that assesses and evaluates the business's sustainability performance.

The purpose of a green business certification is to encourage and incentivize businesses to adopt sustainable practices, reduce their environmental impact, and promote social and economic responsibility. It serves as a way for businesses to differentiate themselves from their competitors and gain recognition for their efforts in sustainability.

To achieve green business certification, companies are typically required to meet certain criteria and standards, which may include energy efficiency, waste reduction, water conservation, pollution prevention, use of renewable resources, and social responsibility practices. The certification process often involves an assessment of the business's operations, policies, and practices, as well as onsite inspections and audits.

By obtaining a green business certification, companies can demonstrate their commitment to sustainable development and showcase their efforts in reducing their carbon footprint and environmental impact. This certification can also provide businesses with marketing advantages, as consumers and stakeholders increasingly value and support environmentally conscious companies. Additionally, green business certifications contribute to the overall sustainability goals of communities and help promote a more environmentally friendly economy.

Green Cafe Interiors

A green cafe interior refers to the design and setup of a cafe that incorporates sustainable practices and materials in order to minimize its environmental impact. This includes the use of energy-efficient appliances, eco-friendly building materials, and natural lighting options to reduce energy consumption. Green cafes also prioritize waste reduction and recycling by implementing composting systems and encouraging customers to bring their own reusable containers.

In addition to the physical elements, green cafe interiors also focus on promoting sustainable food practices. This involves sourcing locally produced ingredients to reduce carbon emissions from transportation, supporting organic and fair-trade products, and offering vegetarian and vegan options to reduce the impact of meat production on the environment.

The overall aim of green cafe interiors is to create a sustainable and eco-friendly dining experience for customers. By implementing these practices, cafes can contribute to the preservation of natural resources, reduce waste generation, and support local communities and businesses.

Furthermore, green cafes often prioritize the use of renewable energy sources, such as solar panels, to power their operations. They also incorporate water-saving fixtures and systems to minimize water consumption. By utilizing these sustainable strategies, green cafes work towards creating a more environmentally conscious and responsible food industry.

Green Chemistry For Sustainable Materials

Green chemistry for sustainable materials refers to the application of environmentally friendly principles and practices in the design, synthesis, production, and use of materials. It aims to minimize the environmental impact while maximizing the efficiency and sustainability of material production and consumption.

Green chemistry approaches strive to develop materials that are safe, non-toxic, renewable, and energy-efficient. These materials are designed to meet functional requirements while minimizing the use of hazardous or non-renewable resources. By adopting green chemistry principles, the negative impacts associated with traditional materials, such as pollution, waste generation, and depletion of natural resources, are significantly reduced.

Green Chemistry Research Tools

Green chemistry research tools can be defined as scientific methods, techniques, and instruments that are used to study and develop sustainable solutions for chemical processes and products. These tools are designed to minimize the negative impact of chemical reactions on human health and the environment, while also maximizing the efficiency and effectiveness of these processes.

The main objective of green chemistry research tools is to replace or reduce the use of hazardous substances, such as toxic solvents, heavy metals, and harmful byproducts, with more environmentally friendly alternatives. These tools encompass a wide range of approaches, including but not limited to:

1. Designing and synthesizing chemicals that are less hazardous and have lower toxicity profiles.

2. Developing catalysts that promote efficient and selective chemical reactions, reducing the need for high temperatures and energy-intensive processes.

3. Utilizing renewable and sustainable feedstocks, such as biomass, in place of fossil fuels and petrochemicals.

4. Implementing processes that minimize waste generation and maximize atom economy, ensuring that the majority of the starting materials end up in the desired end products.

5. Employing analytical techniques that can monitor and quantify the environmental impact of chemical processes, enabling researchers to evaluate the sustainability of their innovations.

By employing these green chemistry research tools, scientists and researchers aim to develop safer, more efficient, and more sustainable chemical processes that can meet the needs of society without compromising the well-being of future generations or the health of the planet.

Green Cities Initiatives

Green cities initiatives refer to a collective effort aimed at creating sustainable and environmentally friendly urban areas. These initiatives focus on implementing practices and policies that promote the efficient use of resources, reduce pollution and waste, and enhance the overall quality of life for residents.

A green city embraces principles of sustainability, seeking to minimize its ecological footprint and optimize its use of natural resources. This involves various measures and strategies, including the development of green spaces, promotion of renewable energy sources, adoption of eco-friendly transportation systems, and implementation of effective waste management practices.

One critical aspect of green cities initiatives is urban planning that emphasizes the preservation and protection of green infrastructure. This includes the creation and maintenance of parks, forests, and other natural areas within the city limits. These green spaces not only enhance the aesthetic appeal of the urban environment but also provide crucial ecosystem services, such as air purification, temperature regulation, and habitat preservation.

Furthermore, green cities initiatives prioritize sustainable transportation options, such as public transit systems, cycling infrastructure, and pedestrian-friendly streets. By promoting and investing in these alternatives, cities can reduce carbon emissions, alleviate traffic congestion, and improve air quality, ultimately contributing to a healthier and more livable urban environment.

Green Cleaning And Maintenance Products

Green cleaning and maintenance products refer to cleaning and maintenance solutions that are formulated using environmentally friendly ingredients and processes, with the aim of reducing their impact on the environment and promoting sustainability. These products are designed to be less harmful to human health and the planet, offering a safer alternative to traditional cleaning and maintenance products that often contain toxic chemicals and pollutants.

Green cleaning products are typically made from renewable resources, such as plant-based or biodegradable ingredients, and are free from harmful chemicals like chlorine, phosphates, and artificial fragrances. They are often packaged in recyclable or biodegradable containers to further minimize their environmental footprint.

In addition to being safer for the environment, green cleaning and maintenance products are also beneficial for indoor air quality. Traditional cleaning products can release volatile organic compounds (VOCs) that contribute to indoor air pollution and can cause respiratory issues and other health problems. Green products, on the other hand, are formulated to have minimal VOC content, ensuring a healthier indoor environment for occupants.

By opting for green cleaning and maintenance products, individuals and businesses can contribute to sustainable living practices by reducing water and air pollution, conserving energy and resources, and minimizing waste generation. These products not only provide effective cleaning and maintenance solutions but also help create a healthier and more sustainable future for everyone.

Green Construction Materials

Green construction materials refer to products used in the construction or renovation of buildings that are designed to minimize their impact on the environment throughout their lifecycle. These materials are sourced, manufactured, and used in a way that promotes sustainability, reduces waste, and conserves natural resources.

One key aspect of green construction materials is their use of renewable resources. These materials are often made from renewable resources such as sustainably harvested wood, bamboo, or recycled materials. By using these resources, the demand for non-renewable materials, such as virgin timber or newly manufactured plastics, is reduced, helping to conserve natural resources.

Additionally, green construction materials prioritize energy efficiency. They are designed to maximize insulation and reduce heat transfer, minimizing the need for excessive heating or cooling. By reducing energy consumption, these materials help to lower greenhouse gas emissions and reduce reliance on non-renewable energy sources.

Another important characteristic of green construction materials is their minimal impact on indoor air quality. These materials are often low in harmful volatile organic compounds (VOCs), which can contribute to health issues. By using low-VOC or VOC-free materials, the indoor air quality of buildings is improved, creating healthier and more comfortable living or working environments.

Green Data Centers And Cloud Services

Green data centers are facilities that utilize energy-efficient technologies and practices to minimize their environmental impact. These centers are designed to reduce the consumption of electricity, water, and other resources, as well as decrease carbon emissions and waste generation. By implementing sustainable strategies, green data centers strive to achieve a balance between technological advancements and ecological conservation.

One of the key components of a green data center is the use of renewable energy sources, such as solar or wind power, to meet its electricity needs. These centers employ energy-efficient hardware, such as servers, storage devices, and networking equipment, which are designed to consume less power while maintaining optimal performance. Additionally, advanced cooling systems and data center infrastructure management (DCIM) tools are employed to improve energy efficiency and reduce the carbon footprint.

Cloud services, on the other hand, refer to the virtualization and delivery of computing resources, such as servers, storage, and applications, over the internet. Green cloud services aim to minimize the environmental impact of these services by utilizing energy-efficient data centers and promoting resource optimization. By sharing computing resources among multiple users, cloud services can improve overall energy efficiency and reduce the need for individual organizations to maintain their own data centers.

In conclusion, green data centers and cloud services are critical components of sustainable IT infrastructure. By adopting energy-efficient practices and deploying renewable energy sources, these facilities strive to reduce their environmental impact while delivering reliable and scalable computing resources to users.

Green Energy Incentives

Green energy incentives refer to various policies, programs, or financial measures implemented by governments or organizations to promote the adoption and usage of renewable energy sources, with the aim of reducing the environmental impact of energy production and consumption while fostering sustainable development. These incentives are designed to encourage individuals, businesses, and communities to shift from traditional fossil fuel-based energy sources to cleaner and more sustainable alternatives, such as solar, wind, hydro, biomass, and geothermal power.

Common green energy incentives include financial incentives, tax breaks, grants, subsidies, and feed-in tariffs. Financial incentives may involve discounted loans, low-interest financing, or cash rebates provided by the government or utilities to help offset the higher initial costs of installing and using renewable energy systems. Tax breaks, on the other hand, offer individuals and businesses a reduction in their tax liability when they invest in renewable energy technologies or make energy-efficient improvements. Grants and subsidies are typically provided as direct payments or reimbursements to support renewable energy projects or promote research and development in the field. Feed-in tariffs, often utilized for solar and wind energy, guarantee a fixed payment rate for electricity generated from renewable sources and ensure a return on investment over a specific period.

Green Energy Investments

Green energy investments refer to financial allocations made towards renewable energy sources and technologies that have minimal negative impacts on the environment and contribute to sustainable development. These investments aim to reduce greenhouse gas emissions, mitigate climate change, and promote a transition to a low-carbon economy.

Investing in green energy encompasses various sectors such as solar power, wind energy, hydroelectricity, bioenergy, geothermal energy, and energy efficiency. These investments can take various forms, including funding research and development of innovative technologies, supporting the manufacturing and installation of renewable energy systems, and financing infrastructure projects that facilitate the generation and distribution of clean energy.

Green energy investments are driven by the understanding of the urgent need to shift away from fossil fuels and their harmful effects on both the environment and human health. By investing in green energy, individuals, organizations, and governments can promote sustainable energy solutions, reduce dependency on fossil fuels, and create a more resilient and diversified energy system. Furthermore, these investments can stimulate economic growth, create job opportunities, and improve energy access in remote areas.

In order to ensure the effectiveness of green energy investments, it is essential to prioritize technologies and projects that have high efficiency, low environmental impact, and long-term sustainability. This requires careful evaluation of the social, economic, and environmental benefits and risks associated with each investment. Ultimately, green energy investments play a vital role in transitioning towards a sustainable energy future and combatting the challenges posed by climate change.

Green Energy Procurement Platforms

A green energy procurement platform is a digital marketplace that facilitates the purchase and sale of renewable energy resources, such as solar, wind, and hydropower, for commercial and industrial entities. These platforms play a crucial role in promoting sustainability by connecting renewable energy project developers with potential buyers, enabling organizations to procure clean energy to satisfy their electricity needs.

Through green energy procurement platforms, companies can browse and compare different renewable energy projects, assess their environmental impacts, and negotiate deals directly with project developers. These platforms provide transparent and efficient processes, ensuring that renewable energy transactions occur in a secure and standardized manner.

Green Event Catering And Food Services

Green event catering and food services refer to the provision of sustainable food options and environmentally-friendly catering for events. It involves the use of locally sourced, organic, and seasonal ingredients to create menus that prioritize sustainability and reduce the carbon footprint.

Green event catering and food services aim to minimize negative environmental impacts by implementing sustainable practices throughout the entire catering process. This includes reducing food waste by carefully planning portions, utilizing composting and recycling systems, and offering vegetarian or vegan options to minimize the use of animal products, which have a higher carbon footprint. These services also strive to minimize energy consumption and greenhouse gas emissions by using energy-efficient equipment, implementing waste management practices, and promoting the use of renewable energy sources for food production and transportation.

Green Hydrogen Infrastructure

Green hydrogen infrastructure refers to a system of facilities, equipment, and processes that support the production, distribution, and utilization of green hydrogen as a sustainable energy source. Green hydrogen, also known as renewable hydrogen, is produced through the electrolysis of water using renewable energy sources such as solar or wind power, resulting in zero greenhouse gas emissions.

The infrastructure for green hydrogen includes various components, such as electrolyzers, renewable energy generation systems, storage facilities, pipelines or other means of transportation, and end-use applications. Electrolyzers are crucial in the production of green hydrogen, as they split water molecules into hydrogen and oxygen using an electrical current. These devices are typically powered by renewable energy sources, ensuring that the hydrogen produced is truly sustainable.

The distribution and storage of green hydrogen require a well-developed infrastructure, similar to existing systems for natural gas or liquid fuels. Pipelines, tanker trucks, or storage tanks can be used to transport and store green hydrogen, depending on the scale and distance of the operation. To promote the adoption of green hydrogen, collaboration between governments, industries, and stakeholders is essential to facilitate the development of this infrastructure.

The utilization of green hydrogen can be diverse, ranging from power generation to industrial processes, transportation, and even residential heating. Fuel cells that convert hydrogen into electricity are often used in applications where clean and efficient power generation is required, while hydrogen can also be used as a feedstock in industrial processes, replacing fossil fuels.

Overall, an efficient and robust green hydrogen infrastructure is vital for achieving a sustainable energy future. By supporting the production and utilization of green hydrogen, this infrastructure can contribute to reducing greenhouse gas emissions and dependence on fossil fuels, thus enabling a transition towards a greener and more sustainable energy system.

Green Hydrogen Production Plants

Green hydrogen production plants are facilities that use renewable energy sources to produce hydrogen gas through electrolysis, a process that splits water molecules (H_2O) into hydrogen (H_2) and oxygen (O_2) using electricity. These plants specifically employ sustainable energy sources like wind, solar, or hydropower to power the electrolysis process, ensuring that the hydrogen produced is carbon-free and environmentally friendly.

The main objective of green hydrogen production plants is to provide a sustainable alternative to traditional hydrogen production methods, which primarily rely on fossil fuels such as natural gas or coal. By utilizing renewable energy sources, these plants contribute to reducing greenhouse gas emissions and mitigating climate change, as hydrogen produced through electrolysis emits no carbon dioxide when used as an energy source.

Green Hydrogen Production

Green hydrogen production refers to the process of producing hydrogen gas (H_2) using renewable energy sources, such as wind, solar, or hydroelectric power. It is an essential component of sustainable energy systems as it provides a clean and efficient means of storing and transporting energy.

Unlike conventional hydrogen production methods, which primarily rely on fossil fuels such as natural gas or coal, green hydrogen production enables a significant reduction in greenhouse gas emissions. By utilizing renewable energy sources to power the electrolysis process, water is split into hydrogen and oxygen, with hydrogen being the desired end product.

This sustainable approach to hydrogen production holds the potential to address several environmental challenges. Firstly, it contributes to the decarbonization of industries and sectors heavily reliant on hydrogen, such as transportation and industrial manufacturing. By replacing fossil fuel-derived hydrogen with green hydrogen, these sectors can significantly reduce their carbon footprint.

Secondly, green hydrogen production can help overcome the intermittency of renewable energy sources. As excess renewable energy generated during periods of low demand can be used to produce hydrogen, it acts as a form of energy storage. This stored hydrogen can be converted back into electricity when demand exceeds supply, thus providing a consistent and reliable renewable energy solution.

In conclusion, green hydrogen production plays a crucial role in achieving sustainability goals by utilizing renewable energy sources to produce a clean and efficient energy carrier. It enables the decarbonization of various sectors and provides a means of energy storage and transfer, helping to address the intermittent nature of renewable energy sources.

Green Hydrogen Storage Solutions

Green hydrogen storage solutions refer to sustainable methods and technologies used to store hydrogen that is produced from renewable energy sources, such as solar or wind power. As a clean and versatile energy carrier, hydrogen has the potential to play a crucial role in decarbonizing various sectors, including transportation, industry, and power generation.

The storage of green hydrogen is vital to ensure its availability as a reliable and consistent energy source. There are several storage options currently being explored and developed:

1. Compressed hydrogen storage: This method involves compressing hydrogen gas to high pressures and storing it in tanks. The compressed hydrogen can be stored at various scales, including large-scale storage for industrial applications or smaller-scale storage for fuel cell vehicles.

2. Liquid hydrogen storage: In this approach, hydrogen is cooled to very low temperatures (-253 degrees Celsius) to convert it into a liquid state. Liquid hydrogen has a high energy density and can be stored in cryogenic tanks. It is commonly used for aerospace applications and potential future use in large-scale energy storage.

3. Hydrogen carriers: Hydrogen can also be stored in a chemically bound form, such as in ammonia or hydrocarbons. These hydrogen carriers provide a means to transport and store hydrogen more effectively, especially for long-distance transportation or bulk storage.

Investing in and utilizing effective green hydrogen storage solutions is essential to enable the deployment of a hydrogen-based economy. By providing dependable and efficient storage, these solutions support the integration of renewable energies, reducing greenhouse gas emissions and promoting a sustainable energy future.

Green Infrastructure Development

Green infrastructure development refers to the planning, implementation, and maintenance of natural and engineered systems that provide environmental, economic, and social benefits in a sustainable manner.

It involves the use of natural elements, such as vegetation, soil, and water, along with engineered solutions, such as permeable pavements and rain gardens, to manage stormwater, promote biodiversity, enhance air quality, mitigate urban heat island effects, and provide recreational opportunities.

Green infrastructure development aims to mimic natural systems and processes to create resilient and sustainable communities. It prioritizes the conservation and restoration of natural resources, while also considering the needs and preferences of local communities.

This approach recognizes the interconnectedness of human and natural systems and seeks to integrate them harmoniously. It emphasizes the use of nature-based solutions to address environmental challenges, rather than solely relying on more traditional, gray infrastructure approaches.

By incorporating green infrastructure into urban and rural landscapes, communities can reduce their ecological footprint, improve the quality of life for residents, and mitigate the impacts of climate change. It can also provide economic benefits, such as increased property values and job creation.

In summary, green infrastructure development involves the strategic use of natural and engineered systems to create sustainable and resilient communities that prioritize environmental, economic, and social well-being.

Green Infrastructure Planning

Green infrastructure planning is a sustainable approach that aims to integrate natural ecological systems into urban planning and development. It involves the strategic design and management of open spaces, water resources, vegetation, and other natural elements to create a resilient and environmentally-friendly urban environment.

The main objective of green infrastructure planning is to enhance urban sustainability by promoting the conservation and restoration of natural ecosystems within an urban context. This approach recognizes the crucial role that nature plays in mitigating the impacts of climate change, improving air and water quality, reducing urban heat island effects, enhancing biodiversity, and fostering human health and well-being.

Green infrastructure planning involves a comprehensive analysis of the existing natural assets and their functions within the urban ecosystem. It identifies opportunities for the integration of green spaces, such as parks, green roofs, and urban forests, with built infrastructure, such as roads, buildings, and stormwater management systems. It also considers the connectivity between green spaces to create ecological corridors and enhance wildlife habitat.

Through green infrastructure planning, cities can achieve multiple benefits. These include the reduction of stormwater runoff and the improvement of water quality through the use of green infrastructure elements, such as rain gardens and bioswales. Green infrastructure planning also helps to decrease energy consumption by providing shade and cooling effects, as well as reducing the need for artificial lighting and air conditioning. Additionally, it enhances public health by providing recreational opportunities, promoting physical activity, and reducing the prevalence of heat-related illnesses.

Green Infrastructure Projects

Green infrastructure projects are initiatives aimed at incorporating natural systems and processes into built environments to promote sustainability. These projects involve the use of vegetation, soil, and other natural elements to enhance ecological functioning, provide benefits to communities, and mitigate environmental risks.

190

The main objective of green infrastructure projects is to mimic natural ecosystems and their functions within urban areas, improving the overall quality of life for both humans and the environment. These projects can take various forms, such as the creation of urban parks, green roofs, rain gardens, and bioswales. They can also include the preservation and restoration of existing natural areas, such as wetlands and forests.

By integrating green infrastructure into urban design, cities can address a range of sustainability challenges. Green roofs, for example, help reduce the urban heat island effect by providing a cooling effect, decreasing the energy consumption of buildings, and improving air quality. Rain gardens and bioswales help manage stormwater runoff, reducing the risk of flooding and improving water quality by retaining and filtering pollutants before they reach natural water bodies.

Moreover, green infrastructure projects contribute to biodiversity conservation by creating habitats for native plants and animals within urban areas. They also provide opportunities for recreational activities, contribute to mental and physical well-being, and enhance the aesthetics of the built environment.

In summary, green infrastructure projects aim to incorporate natural elements into urban areas to promote sustainability by improving ecological functioning, mitigating environmental risks, and enhancing the well-being of communities and the environment.

Green Infrastructure

Green infrastructure refers to a sustainable approach to design and manage natural and built environments, integrating the principles of environmental protection, resource conservation, and climate resilience. It encompasses a network of natural and semi-natural spaces, such as parks, wetlands, green roofs, green walls, and permeable surfaces, that support ecological functions and provide multiple benefits to communities.

The concept of green infrastructure recognizes the importance of preserving and enhancing natural systems and their services to create liveable, resilient, and healthy urban environments. It includes strategies to address environmental challenges, such as stormwater management, heat island effect mitigation, air pollution reduction, and biodiversity conservation. Green infrastructure aims to improve water quality, regulate temperature, enhance urban biodiversity, and promote human well-being by creating accessible and attractive green spaces.

Green Insulation Materials

Green insulation materials refer to sustainable building materials that are used to reduce energy consumption, improve indoor air quality, and minimize environmental impact. These materials are designed to provide effective insulation while being eco-friendly and energy-efficient.

Common types of green insulation materials include natural fibers, recycled materials, and renewable resources. Natural fibers, such as cotton, wool, and hemp, are widely used due to their effective insulation properties and low environmental impact. These fibers are often harvested from renewable sources and can be recycled or composted at the end of their lifespan.

Recycled materials, such as recycled cellulose, fiberglass, and denim, contribute to sustainability by reducing waste and utilizing existing resources. These materials are typically made from post-consumer or post-industrial waste, diverting it from landfills and reducing the need for virgin materials.

In addition to natural fibers and recycled materials, green insulation options also include renewable resources like cork and straw. Cork insulation is derived from the bark of cork oak trees, which can be harvested without harming the trees. Straw insulation, usually made from agricultural byproducts, provides a sustainable alternative that helps reduce waste.

Using green insulation materials in construction and renovation projects offers various benefits. Firstly, they enhance energy efficiency by reducing heat transfer and improving temperature regulation, resulting in lower heating and cooling costs. Secondly, these materials contribute to better indoor air quality by being free from harmful chemicals and off-gassing. Finally, green insulation materials help reduce the overall carbon footprint of buildings by conserving energy and minimizing environmental impact.

Green Interior Decor

Green interior decor refers to the design and arrangement of indoor spaces using sustainable materials and practices that have minimal impact on the environment. It involves incorporating eco-friendly elements into the overall design, furniture, fixtures, and accessories to create a healthy and sustainable living or working environment.

The concept of green interior decor promotes the use of renewable and recycled materials, such as reclaimed wood, bamboo, cork, and recycled metal. These materials are sourced sustainably, reducing the demand for new resources and minimizing environmental degradation. Additionally, non-toxic and low VOC (Volatile Organic Compounds) paints, adhesives, and finishes are selected, ensuring better indoor air quality and reducing harmful emissions.

Green interior decor also emphasizes energy efficiency by incorporating natural lighting, energy-saving appliances, and smart home technologies. By maximizing natural light, the need for artificial lighting is minimized, reducing energy consumption. Energy-efficient appliances and smart home systems help optimize energy usage, further reducing the carbon footprint of the space.

Incorporating indoor plants and biophilic design is another key element of green interior decor. Plants not only improve air quality by absorbing toxins and releasing oxygen but also add a touch of nature to the space, enhancing the overall well-being of occupants. Biophilic design aims to connect people with nature, creating spaces that stimulate and soothe, improving mood, concentration, and productivity.

Overall, green interior decor embraces sustainable principles and practices to create spaces that are environmentally responsible, energy-efficient, and conducive to the well-being of inhabitants. It promotes a more holistic approach to interior design, considering the environmental, social, and economic impacts of our living spaces.

Green Interior Design

Green interior design refers to the practice of creating interior spaces that are environmentally sustainable and have a minimal impact on natural resources. It involves using strategies and materials that conserve energy, reduce waste, and promote a healthier living environment.

The goal of green interior design is to integrate sustainable practices throughout the entire design process, from concept development and material selection to construction and operation. This approach considers the lifecycle of products, from their extraction and production to their eventual disposal or recycling.

Key principles of green interior design include energy efficiency, use of renewable resources, waste reduction, and improving indoor air quality. Designers aim to reduce energy consumption by utilizing natural light, optimizing insulation, and installing energy-efficient appliances and systems. They also select materials that are eco-friendly, such as recycled or reclaimed materials, organic fabrics, and low VOC (volatile organic compounds) paints and finishes.

Green interior design also focuses on creating healthy indoor environments by minimizing exposure to toxic substances and improving air quality. This includes incorporating proper ventilation, using non-toxic cleaning products, and considering the impact of furniture and finishes on indoor air quality.

In addition to environmental benefits, green interior design can also provide economic advantages by reducing energy and water consumption, minimizing waste, and optimizing the use of space. It can enhance the well-being and productivity of occupants, create a connection to nature, and contribute to a more sustainable future.

Green Logistics And Transportation

Green logistics and transportation refers to the practices and methods that are employed to minimize the environmental impact of moving goods and people from one place to another. It aims to reduce greenhouse gas emissions, minimize energy consumption, and optimize the use of resources while ensuring the efficient delivery of goods and services.

Green logistics and transportation encompasses a wide range of sustainable practices. These include the use of eco-friendly fuels, such as electric or hybrid vehicles, to reduce carbon emissions. It also involves the optimization of transportation routes to minimize fuel consumption and reduce congestion. Additionally, green logistics emphasizes the use of sustainable packaging materials and the implementation of logistics strategies that minimize waste generation.

Green Office Space Design Solutions

Green office space design refers to the practice of creating work environments that prioritize sustainability and the well-being of both employees and the environment. It involves incorporating eco-friendly materials, energy-efficient systems, and mindful design principles to minimize negative impacts on the earth.

The goal of green office space design is to create a healthy and efficient workspace that reduces the ecological footprint of the business. This can be achieved through various strategies, such as utilizing natural light to reduce the need for artificial lighting, implementing effective waste management systems, and using energy-efficient appliances and equipment.

In addition to reducing environmental impact, green office space design aims to improve the well-being and productivity of employees. This can be achieved by incorporating elements that promote physical and mental health, such as ergonomic furniture, indoor plants for improved air quality, and spaces for relaxation, collaboration, and social interaction.

By adopting green office space design solutions, businesses can not only contribute to a more sustainable future but also benefit financially. Energy-efficient systems and sustainable practices can lead to significant cost savings in the long run, as well as enhance the company's reputation and attract environmentally conscious clients and employees.

To sum up, green office space design involves creating sustainable and employee-friendly work environments that prioritize environmental responsibility and the well-being of individuals. It encompasses the implementation of eco-friendly materials, energy-efficient systems, and thoughtful design strategies to minimize negative impacts on the planet while improving the productivity and satisfaction of employees.

Green Product Innovation

Green product innovation refers to the creation of goods or services that have a reduced impact on the environment throughout their life cycle. It involves the development and implementation of new ideas, technologies, and processes that promote sustainability and minimize negative environmental effects.

This type of innovation embraces the concept of the circular economy, which aims to eliminate waste and create a regenerative system. Green products are designed to be more energy-efficient, use fewer resources, and generate less pollution compared to conventional alternatives.

The innovation process starts with the identification of environmental challenges and opportunities. This could include the reduction of greenhouse gas emissions, the conservation of natural resources, or the elimination of toxic substances. Companies then work to develop innovative solutions through research, design, and collaboration with various stakeholders.

Green product innovation often involves the use of sustainable materials, such as recycled or renewable resources, and the adoption of eco-friendly manufacturing techniques. It also takes into consideration the product's entire life cycle, including its production, distribution, use, and disposal stages.

By focusing on green product innovation, businesses can not only minimize their environmental footprint but also gain a competitive advantage by meeting the growing demand for sustainable products. Consumers are increasingly conscious of their purchasing choices and are willing to support brands that prioritize sustainability.

Green Product Labeling

Green product labeling refers to the practice of labeling products with accurate and credible information regarding their environmental impact and sustainable qualities. This labeling system aims to inform consumers about the sustainability attributes of products, allowing them to make informed choices and support more eco-friendly options.

The purpose of green product labeling is to address the increasing consumer demand for sustainable and environmentally responsible goods. By providing clear and standardized information about a product's environmental characteristics, such labels empower consumers to consider the environmental consequences of their purchases. Green labels typically display information about key sustainability aspects such as energy efficiency, emissions, recyclability, and material sourcing.

Green Product Packaging

Green product packaging refers to the use of sustainable materials and practices in the design, production, and disposal of packaging for products, with the aim of reducing its environmental impact. It involves considering the entire lifecycle of packaging, from sourcing and manufacturing to end-of-life disposal, in order to minimize resource consumption, waste generation, and greenhouse gas emissions.

The goal of green product packaging is to achieve a balance between meeting the functional requirements of packaging (such as protection, containment, and convenience) and reducing its environmental footprint. This is achieved through various strategies, including:

1. Material selection: Choosing renewable, recyclable, biodegradable, or compostable materials for packaging instead of traditional, non-renewable, and non-recyclable options.

2. Lightweighting: Designing packaging to be as lightweight as possible without compromising its integrity, thereby reducing the amount of material required and the energy needed for transportation.

3. Minimizing waste: Implementing efficient manufacturing processes to minimize material waste during production and considering ways to reduce packaging waste generated by consumers.

4. Renewable energy use: Incorporating renewable energy sources, such as solar or wind power, into manufacturing facilities to reduce the carbon footprint of packaging production.

5. Design for recyclability: Considering the end-of-life disposal of packaging and designing it in a way that facilitates recycling, such as using mono-materials or incorporating easily separable components.

By adopting these sustainable practices, green product packaging can help conserve resources, reduce pollution, and contribute to a circular economy by promoting recycling and reuse. It also provides consumers with environmentally friendly choices and can enhance the overall sustainability of the products they purchase.

Green Restaurant Interior Design

A green restaurant interior design refers to the sustainable and eco-friendly design elements and practices implemented in the layout and aesthetics of a restaurant.

This approach prioritizes the use of environmentally friendly materials, energy-efficient systems, and sustainable techniques to minimize the negative impact on the environment and promote a healthier and more sustainable dining experience.

Green Retrofitting

Green retrofitting refers to the process of making improvements to existing buildings or infrastructure with the goal of reducing their environmental impact and increasing sustainability. This approach involves upgrading various systems, technologies, and materials to enhance energy efficiency, reduce water consumption, improve indoor air quality, and minimize waste generation.

The purpose of green retrofitting is to transform outdated or inefficient structures into greener, more sustainable spaces. This can be achieved through a range of measures, such as installing energy-efficient lighting systems, implementing renewable energy sources, improving insulation, upgrading HVAC systems, optimizing water usage through low-flow fixtures, and utilizing eco-friendly materials in construction and renovation projects.

The benefits of green retrofitting are manifold. By reducing energy consumption and greenhouse gas emissions, it helps mitigate climate change and contributes towards achieving sustainability targets. It also leads to lower energy costs and operational expenses for the building owner or occupants. Additionally, green retrofitting can enhance the indoor environmental quality, creating healthier and more comfortable living or working environments.

Moreover, green retrofitting plays a crucial role in the transition towards a circular economy by reducing resource consumption and waste production. It promotes the reuse and recycling of materials, thereby minimizing the burden on landfills and preserving natural resources.

In conclusion, green retrofitting is an essential strategy in the pursuit of sustainable development. By improving the environmental performance of existing buildings and infrastructure, it contributes towards a greener, more energy-efficient, and resource-responsible future.

Green Roof Technology

Green roof technology refers to the practice of installing vegetation, such as plants or grass, on the roofs of buildings to provide a range of environmental and sustainability benefits. Also known as living roofs, green roofs have gained popularity due to their ability to help mitigate the negative effects of urbanization and climate change.

By incorporating green spaces into buildings, green roof technology promotes biodiversity by creating habitats for birds, insects, and other wildlife. This helps to counter the loss of green spaces in urban areas and supports a healthier ecosystem. Additionally, green roofs can improve air quality by acting as filters, absorbing pollutants and releasing oxygen into the atmosphere. They also reduce the urban heat island effect by providing natural insulation, cooling buildings, and reducing energy consumption for cooling purposes.

One of the significant benefits of green roof technology is its ability to manage stormwater. Green roofs can absorb and retain rainwater, which helps to reduce runoff and relieve pressure on stormwater infrastructure. This, in turn, helps to prevent urban flooding and alleviate strain on local water treatment facilities.

Furthermore, green roofs contribute to energy efficiency by providing additional insulation for buildings, reducing the need for heating and cooling. This can result in lower energy consumption and reduced carbon emissions, contributing to the overall goal of creating more sustainable and eco-friendly cities.

Green Roofing Design

A green roofing design refers to the practice of incorporating vegetation and sustainable materials into the construction and maintenance of a roof. This approach aims to maximize the environmental benefits of a roof, minimize its negative impacts, and contribute to overall sustainability efforts.

Green roofing designs typically involve the use of various elements, such as green roofs, cool roofs, and vegetative roofs. Green roofs utilize a layer of living vegetation, which can include grass, herbs, or shrubs, planted on top of a waterproofing membrane. These roofs provide numerous environmental benefits, such as reducing stormwater runoff, improving air quality by absorbing pollutants, and reducing the urban heat island effect.

Cool roofs, on the other hand, are designed with materials that reflect more sunlight and absorb less heat than traditional roofs. This helps to reduce the energy consumption required for cooling buildings and mitigates the urban heat island effect. Vegetative roofs combine the benefits of both green roofs and cool roofs, incorporating plantings that provide insulation, shade, and cooling effects.

In addition to the environmental advantages, green roofing designs also offer economic benefits. They can extend the lifespan of a roof by protecting it from weathering and UV radiation, thus reducing the need for frequent repairs or replacements. Moreover, green roofs can improve energy efficiency by providing natural insulation and reducing the need for artificial cooling or heating.

In conclusion, a green roofing design is a sustainable approach that integrates vegetation and sustainable materials into the construction and maintenance of a roof. This design aims to enhance environmental performance, reduce energy consumption, and promote long-term economic savings.

Green Roofing Materials

Green roofing materials refer to sustainable materials that are used in the construction of roofs to minimize the environmental impacts and make the building more eco-friendly. These materials are carefully chosen to provide numerous benefits in terms of energy conservation, stormwater management, and reduction of urban heat island effect.

One commonly used green roofing material is green or vegetative roofs, which involve the installation of plants and green spaces on the roof surface. These roofs provide natural insulation, reduce stormwater runoff by absorbing rainwater, and contribute to air quality improvement by filtering pollutants. Green roofs also reduce the heat island effect by cooling the surrounding air and reducing the energy demand for air conditioning.

Green Roofs

A green roof is a sustainable roofing system that is designed to support vegetation on top of a building structure. It consists of a waterproof membrane, drainage layer, growing medium, and a variety of plants that are specifically selected and cultivated to thrive in an elevated and exposed environment.

Green roofs provide multiple environmental benefits, making them an integral part of sustainable urban planning and design. Firstly, they help to reduce the overall heat island effect in cities by absorbing and evaporating solar radiation instead of reflecting it back into the surrounding environment. This helps to mitigate the urban heat island effect and can lead to reduced energy consumption for cooling buildings.

Additionally, green roofs improve air quality by absorbing pollutants and CO_2 emissions from the atmosphere, as well as releasing oxygen through photosynthesis. They act as natural filters, helping to purify rainwater and reduce stormwater runoff, which can alleviate pressure on stormwater management systems and prevent water pollution.

Furthermore, green roofs enhance biodiversity in urban areas, providing habitat and food for a wide range of insects, birds, and other wildlife. They contribute to urban greening efforts, creating pockets of green space that can improve the overall aesthetics and mental well-being of city residents.

In conclusion, green roofs offer a sustainable solution for urban environments by providing numerous environmental benefits such as heat reduction, improved air quality, water management, and biodiversity support. Their incorporation in urban planning and design can contribute to creating more resilient and livable cities.

196

Green Tech Innovation

Green tech innovation refers to the development and implementation of environmentally friendly technologies that have a positive impact on sustainability. These innovations aim to address pressing global challenges such as climate change, resource depletion, and pollution, by reducing greenhouse gas emissions, conserving natural resources, and promoting cleaner and more efficient energy alternatives.

Green tech innovations encompass a wide range of sectors, including renewable energy, waste management, transportation, agriculture, and construction. Examples of green tech innovations include solar and wind power technologies, energy-efficient vehicles, smart grid systems, sustainable building materials, and waste-to-energy conversion technologies.

These technologies incorporate principles of sustainability by minimizing carbon footprints, reducing waste production, and promoting the efficient use of resources. They often utilize clean and renewable energy sources, such as solar and wind power, as alternatives to fossil fuels. Additionally, green tech innovations focus on improving energy efficiency through optimized processes and the use of advanced materials.

By embracing green tech innovation, societies can transition towards a more sustainable future. These innovations not only mitigate the negative impacts of human activities on the environment but also create economic opportunities and contribute to job creation. Furthermore, green tech innovation fosters a culture of environmental responsibility and promotes the conscious consumption and production of goods and services.

Green Tech Product Design

A green tech product design refers to the process of creating and developing a product that incorporates sustainable principles and practices. It entails considering the environmental impact at every stage of the product's life cycle, from raw material extraction to manufacturing, use, and disposal.

The goal of green tech product design is to minimize the negative ecological footprint while maximizing resource efficiency and promoting a circular economy. This involves utilizing renewable materials, optimizing energy efficiency, reducing waste generation, and implementing recycling and disposal strategies that minimize harm to the environment.

Green Technology Solutions

Green technology solutions refer to the innovations and practices that are designed to create a more sustainable and environmentally friendly society. It involves the development and utilization of technologies, products, and systems that minimize the negative impact on the environment while also promoting economic growth and social well-being.

Green technology solutions encompass a wide range of sectors, including energy, transportation, waste management, and construction. In the energy sector, for example, the focus is on renewable energy sources such as solar power, wind power, and hydroelectric power, which are cleaner and less harmful to the environment compared to fossil fuels. In transportation, green technology solutions involve the development of electric and hybrid vehicles, as well as the implementation of efficient public transportation systems that reduce congestion and emissions.

In waste management, green technology solutions emphasize recycling, composting, and waste-to-energy conversion methods to minimize the amount of waste that ends up in landfills. In construction, sustainable materials and practices are used to reduce the carbon footprint and enhance energy efficiency in buildings.

The goal of green technology solutions is to promote sustainability by reducing greenhouse gas emissions, conserving natural resources, and mitigating pollution. By adopting these solutions, societies can transition to more sustainable and resilient economies, while also improving the quality of life for current and future generations.

Green Urban Infrastructure

Green urban infrastructure refers to the physical and natural elements within a city that are designed and utilized in a sustainable manner to promote environmental health, social well-being, and economic prosperity. It encompasses a range of features, including parks, green spaces, and natural habitats, as well as green buildings, renewable energy systems, and efficient transportation networks.

The main objective of green urban infrastructure is to create resilient and livable cities that minimize their ecological footprint and enhance the quality of life for residents. By incorporating nature-based solutions and sustainable technologies, it aims to address key urban challenges such as climate change, air and water pollution, and the depletion of natural resources.

Green urban infrastructure offers numerous environmental benefits. It helps to mitigate the urban heat island effect by providing shade and cooling through vegetation, reducing energy demand for air conditioning. It also enhances biodiversity and supports ecological processes, contributing to the preservation of local ecosystems and the protection of native species.

In addition to its environmental advantages, green urban infrastructure has significant social benefits. Access to green spaces and natural environments has been shown to improve mental health, reduce stress, and promote physical activity and social interactions. Green buildings with energy-efficient designs not only reduce carbon emissions but also create healthier indoor environments for occupants.

Economically, green urban infrastructure can generate jobs and stimulate economic growth. The development and maintenance of green spaces, green roofs, and renewable energy systems can create employment opportunities in sectors such as landscaping, construction, and renewable energy production. Additionally, energy-efficient buildings and transportation systems can result in cost savings for residents and businesses, enhancing the economic competitiveness of cities.

Green Urban Landscapes

Green urban landscapes refer to environmentally friendly and sustainable developments within urban areas that incorporate the use of green spaces, vegetation, and ecological systems. These landscapes aim to optimize the environmental benefits of cities while improving the quality of life and well-being of their inhabitants.

By integrating green spaces into urban environments, these landscapes provide numerous sustainability benefits. They contribute to improving air quality by absorbing pollutants and greenhouse gases, which helps combat climate change. Additionally, green urban landscapes help mitigate the urban heat island effect by providing shade and cooling through evapotranspiration, reducing the reliance on energy-consuming air conditioning. They also play a crucial role in stormwater management by reducing runoff and improving water quality through natural filtration processes.

In terms of biodiversity, green urban landscapes support and enhance urban ecosystems by providing habitats for various plants, animals, and microorganisms, promoting biodiversity within cities. They offer opportunities for recreational activities, creating a sense of community and fostering social connections among residents. Moreover, these landscapes have been shown to have positive impacts on mental health and overall well-being, providing spaces for relaxation, stress reduction, and physical activity.

In summary, green urban landscapes are an integral part of sustainable urban development. They contribute to mitigating climate change, improving air and water quality, promoting biodiversity, and enhancing the overall well-being of urban residents. By creating harmonious and eco-friendly environments, these landscapes help cities transition towards a more sustainable future.

Green Urban Planning And Design

Green urban planning and design refers to the practice of creating and managing cities and

198

communities in a way that prioritizes sustainability and minimizes negative environmental impacts. It involves integrating sustainable solutions and strategies into the planning and design processes of urban areas to ensure a more environmentally friendly and livable future.

Green urban planning and design encompasses various aspects, including land use, transportation, energy efficiency, water management, waste management, and green spaces. It aims to create compact and walkable cities that promote active transportation and reduce reliance on private vehicles. This can be achieved through the development of mixed-use neighborhoods, pedestrian-friendly streets, and well-connected public transportation systems.

In addition to transportation, green urban planning focuses on energy efficiency and renewable energy sources. This includes incorporating green building practices, such as utilizing sustainable materials, improving insulation, and implementing energy-efficient technologies. It also involves integrating renewable energy sources, such as solar panels and wind turbines, into the urban infrastructure.

Water management is another key aspect of green urban planning and design. This involves implementing measures to conserve water, such as rainwater harvesting systems, greywater recycling, and efficient irrigation techniques. It also includes creating green spaces, such as parks and gardens, to promote biodiversity, enhance air quality, and provide recreational areas for residents.

Overall, green urban planning and design is crucial for creating sustainable cities that are resilient to environmental challenges and provide a high quality of life for their residents. By prioritizing sustainability in urban development, we can mitigate climate change, reduce pollution, and promote a healthier and more sustainable future for all.

Green Vehicle Aerodynamics

Green vehicle aerodynamics refers to the study and implementation of design principles aimed at reducing the air resistance and energy consumption of vehicles, with the objective of promoting sustainability.

Aerodynamic improvements are essential in creating green vehicles as they contribute to enhancing fuel efficiency, reducing greenhouse gas emissions, and minimizing the environmental impact of transportation. By reducing air drag, green vehicle aerodynamics can help decrease the amount of energy required to propel a vehicle, resulting in lower fuel consumption and improved overall performance.

Green Vehicle Design Principles

Green vehicle design principles refer to the set of guidelines and strategies utilized in the development of environmentally-friendly vehicles with the objective of reducing negative impacts on the environment and promoting sustainability. These principles encompass various aspects of vehicle design, including the use of alternative and renewable energy sources, optimization of fuel efficiency, reduction of greenhouse gas emissions, and minimization of material waste during production and operation.

The adoption of green vehicle design principles is vital in addressing the environmental challenges posed by conventional vehicles, such as air pollution, climate change, and resource depletion. By incorporating sustainable practices into their design, green vehicles aim to mitigate these challenges and contribute to a more sustainable transportation system.

Greenhouse Gas Accounting Software

Greenhouse gas accounting software refers to a computer program designed to track, calculate, and report on greenhouse gas emissions produced by an organization or entity. This software plays a crucial role in the field of sustainability and assists companies in understanding and managing their environmental footprint.

The software typically collects and aggregates data from various sources within an organization, including energy consumption, transportation, waste management, and production processes. It then applies standardized calculation methodologies and emission factors to quantify greenhouse gas emissions. By providing accurate and comprehensive data, the software enables organizations to gain insights into their emission sources, identify areas for improvement, and develop strategies to reduce their carbon footprint.

Moreover, greenhouse gas accounting software facilitates compliance with sustainability reporting frameworks and regulatory requirements, such as the Greenhouse Gas Protocol and carbon disclosure initiatives. It helps organizations generate detailed reports and disclosures that provide transparency and accountability to stakeholders, including investors, customers, and regulatory bodies.

In summary, greenhouse gas accounting software plays a crucial role in promoting sustainability by assisting organizations in measuring and managing their greenhouse gas emissions. By accurately tracking and reporting emission data, this software enables organizations to make informed decisions, reduce their environmental impact, and contribute to a more sustainable future.

Greenpeace

Greenpeace is an international non-governmental organization (NGO) that focuses on environmental issues and sustainability. It was founded in 1971 and has since become one of the largest and most recognized environmental organizations in the world.

Greenpeace works to promote and protect the planet's biodiversity and sustainability through direct action, lobbying, research, and education. The organization's activities include advocating for clean energy, fighting against deforestation, protecting marine life, and raising awareness about the impacts of climate change.

Hybrid And Electric Vehicle Fleets

Hybrid and electric vehicle fleets are a crucial component of sustainability efforts in transportation. These fleets primarily consist of vehicles that utilize alternative sources of energy, such as electricity or a combination of electricity and internal combustion engines. The adoption of such fleets is driven by the need to reduce greenhouse gas emissions, minimize air pollution, and promote energy conservation.

Hybrid vehicles integrate both an internal combustion engine and an electric motor, combining the benefits of both systems. They feature regenerative braking, which converts kinetic energy into electricity, and the capability to seamlessly switch between the combustion engine and electric power. By utilizing these technologies, hybrid vehicle fleets reduce fuel consumption and emissions, thereby promoting sustainability and reducing dependence on fossil fuels.

Hybrid Electric Heating Systems

Hybrid electric heating systems refer to a sustainable approach to residential and commercial heating that combines the use of electric heat pumps with traditional heating systems. These systems utilize electricity as their primary energy source and are designed to be highly efficient, minimizing the environmental impact and energy consumption associated with heating buildings.

The fundamental principle of a hybrid electric heating system involves integrating an electric heat pump with an existing heating system, such as a boiler or furnace. The heat pump efficiently captures heat from the ambient air or ground and transfers it to the building, providing heating during colder months. During periods of extreme cold or high heating demand, the traditional heating system is activated to supplement the heat provided by the heat pump.

One of the key advantages of hybrid electric heating systems in terms of sustainability is their ability to significantly reduce greenhouse gas emissions. By relying on electricity as the primary energy source, these systems can take advantage of the increasing share of renewable energy in the electricity grid. This helps to minimize the reliance on fossil fuels and decrease overall carbon emissions associated with heating buildings.

In addition, hybrid electric heating systems are highly energy efficient. Electric heat pumps have a higher coefficient of performance (COP) compared to traditional heating systems, meaning they produce more heat for every unit of electricity consumed. By using a heat pump as the primary heat source and a traditional heating system as a backup, these systems optimize energy usage and reduce energy wastage.

Hybrid Electric Vehicles (HEVs)

A hybrid electric vehicle (HEV) is an automobile that combines an internal combustion engine (ICE) with an electric motor and battery to propel the vehicle. The ICE and electric motor work together to maximize efficiency and reduce fuel consumption, making HEVs an important sustainable transportation option.

HEVs function by using the electric motor for certain driving conditions, such as at low speeds or when idling, where the electric motor provides a smooth, quiet, and emission-free driving experience. The ICE, on the other hand, kicks in at higher speeds or when more power is needed, allowing for a longer driving range and reliable performance.

The integration of the electric motor and battery pack in HEVs presents several environmental benefits. Firstly, the use of electricity reduces the reliance on fossil fuels, which helps to reduce greenhouse gas emissions, air pollution, and overall carbon footprint. Secondly, regenerative braking technology in HEVs allows the electric motor to capture and store energy that would typically be lost during braking, further improving energy efficiency.

HEVs also contribute to sustainability by promoting energy diversification. By utilizing both an ICE and an electric motor, HEVs provide an alternative to conventional gasoline-powered vehicles, ultimately reducing dependence on petroleum resources.

Hybrid Renewable Energy Grids

A hybrid renewable energy grid refers to a sustainable energy system that combines multiple sources of renewable energy to meet the electricity needs of a region or community. This grid integrates different technologies and energy sources such as solar, wind, hydro, geothermal, and biomass, with the aim of maximizing the utilization of clean and renewable energy resources.

The key objective of a hybrid renewable energy grid is to create a reliable and efficient energy system that reduces dependence on fossil fuels and minimizes environmental impact. By diversifying the energy sources, these grids can ensure a consistent and stable power supply, mitigating the intermittent nature of some renewable sources like solar and wind. Additionally, a hybrid renewable energy grid can optimize energy production by leveraging the strengths and capabilities of each technology, improving overall system reliability and performance.

Hybrid Renewable Energy Systems

A hybrid renewable energy system refers to a sustainable power generation system that combines two or more renewable energy sources to provide electricity and meet the energy demands of a community or facility. It is designed to maximize the benefits and overcome the limitations of each individual energy source, ultimately reducing reliance on traditional fossil fuels and minimizing environmental impact.

By integrating multiple renewable energy sources such as solar, wind, biomass, hydro, or geothermal, a hybrid renewable energy system ensures enhanced reliability and stability in power supply. The system utilizes the strengths of different technologies to compensate for intermittent or unpredictable output from individual sources. For example, solar panels may generate electricity during daylight hours, while wind turbines may harness wind energy during night-time and low-solar periods.

This combination of renewable energy sources also enables a hybrid system to cater to varying energy demands, making it more adaptable and suitable for different locations and climates. It balances the availability of renewable resources and ensures a continuous power supply, reducing the need for backup systems or reliance on non-renewable energy sources.

Hybrid renewable energy systems contribute to sustainability by promoting the utilization of clean and renewable energy sources, which significantly reduces greenhouse gas emissions and air pollution. They play a crucial role in mitigating climate change and addressing energy security concerns.

Hybrid Solar Panels

Hybrid solar panels, also known as hybrid PV/T (photovoltaic/thermal) panels, are innovative renewable energy systems that integrate the functionality of both solar photovoltaic panels and solar thermal collectors. These panels aim to maximize the efficient use of solar energy by producing both electricity and heat simultaneously, making them a sustainable and cost-effective solution for meeting energy needs.

By combining photovoltaic cells, which convert sunlight into electricity, with a thermal absorption unit, which captures and utilizes the excess heat generated by the solar cells, hybrid solar panels offer a dual-purpose design that significantly enhances overall energy generation and utilization. The photovoltaic cells capture sunlight and generate electricity, while the thermal absorption unit extracts and utilizes the waste heat from the cells for various applications such as space heating, water heating, or even powering cooling systems.

The integration of photovoltaic and thermal technologies in hybrid solar panels offers several advantages in terms of sustainability. Firstly, these panels make efficient use of valuable land space by combining two technologies into a single system. Additionally, they reduce the overall environmental impact by maximizing the conversion of solar energy into usable forms, thereby minimizing the reliance on traditional fossil fuel-based energy sources.

Furthermore, the dual-purpose functionality of hybrid solar panels enhances energy efficiency, as the waste heat generated by the solar cells is effectively harnessed rather than being wasted. This feature allows for a higher overall energy conversion rate compared to separate solar photovoltaic and thermal systems. The ability to simultaneously produce electricity and heat from the same panel also contributes to energy cost savings and increased energy autonomy.

Hybrid Wind-Solar Systems

A hybrid wind-solar system is a sustainable energy solution that combines the use of both wind and solar power technologies to generate electricity. This innovative system harnesses the abundant and renewable energy sources of wind and sunlight to produce clean and environmentally friendly power.

By integrating wind turbines and solar panels, a hybrid wind-solar system optimizes energy production efficiency and enhances power generation capacity. These systems are designed to take advantage of the complementary nature of wind and solar resources, especially when implemented in regions where both resources are plentiful.

During times when there is ample sunlight but low wind speeds, solar panels can efficiently convert solar radiation into electricity. Conversely, when there is strong wind but low sunlight, wind turbines can capture the kinetic energy from the moving air and convert it into usable electricity. By combining these two sources, a hybrid system can maintain a reliable power supply throughout the day and throughout different weather conditions.

The hybrid wind-solar system greatly contributes to the goal of sustainability by reducing reliance on fossil fuels and mitigating the negative impacts of greenhouse gas emissions. It provides a renewable and clean energy alternative that helps combat climate change and preserve the environment.

Hydrogen Fuel Cells

Hydrogen fuel cells are devices that produce electricity by combining hydrogen fuel with oxygen from the air, generating only water vapor as a byproduct. They are a sustainable energy technology that holds promise in reducing greenhouse gas emissions and addressing climate change.

Fuel cells operate through an electrochemical reaction, where hydrogen atoms are split into protons and electrons at an anode, while oxygen molecules from the air accept these electrons at a cathode. The protons pass through a membrane and combine with oxygen and electrons on the other side, producing water and releasing energy in the form of electricity.

As a sustainable energy source, hydrogen fuel cells offer several advantages. Firstly, hydrogen can be produced from renewable sources such as solar, wind, and hydroelectric power, ensuring a carbon-neutral fuel production process. Additionally, fuel cells have high energy conversion efficiency, converting hydrogen fuel directly into electricity without the need for combustion, resulting in lower greenhouse gas emissions compared to fossil fuel combustion.

The use of hydrogen fuel cells also contributes to a more sustainable transportation sector. Compared to internal combustion engines, fuel cell vehicles produce zero tailpipe emissions, improving local air quality and reducing health impacts. Furthermore, hydrogen fuel cells can provide longer driving ranges and faster refueling times compared to battery electric vehicles, overcoming some of the limitations of current battery technologies.

Hydrogen-Powered Trains

Hydrogen-powered trains are a sustainable transportation solution that use hydrogen fuel cells to generate electricity, providing an alternative to traditional diesel-powered trains. These trains offer a promising solution to reduce greenhouse gas emissions and combat climate change.

Using hydrogen as a fuel source presents several environmental benefits. When hydrogen is combined with oxygen in a fuel cell, the only byproduct is water, making it a clean and emission-free energy source. By replacing diesel engines with hydrogen fuel cells, hydrogen-powered trains can significantly decrease carbon dioxide and air pollutant emissions, improving air quality in urban areas and reducing the transportation sector's contribution to global warming. Moreover, hydrogen can be produced from renewable energy sources, such as wind or solar power, further enhancing the environmental sustainability of these trains.

Hydroponic Farming Systems

Hydroponic farming systems are a sustainable method of growing plants without the use of soil. Instead, plants are grown in water-based nutrient-rich solutions that provide all the necessary elements for their growth.

The key to sustainability in hydroponic farming systems lies in their efficient use of resources. Firstly, water usage is significantly reduced compared to traditional soil-based farming. The hydroponic systems recirculate water, minimizing evaporation and eliminating the need for excessive irrigation. This not only conserves a precious resource but also reduces the strain on local water supplies.

Secondly, hydroponic farming systems require fewer pesticides and fertilizers compared to conventional farming methods. The controlled environment allows for precise monitoring and regulation of nutrients, eliminating the need for chemical treatments. This not only reduces the environmental impact of farming but also ensures safer and healthier produce for consumers.

Furthermore, hydroponic farming systems can be implemented in a variety of locations, including urban areas with limited space. By utilizing vertical farming techniques, these systems can maximize output while minimizing land usage. This is particularly valuable in urban settings where land availability is limited and expensive.

Overall, hydroponic farming systems offer a sustainable alternative to traditional agriculture by conserving water, reducing chemical usage, and optimizing land utilization. With the world facing growing concerns over water scarcity, environmental degradation, and food security, hydroponic farming systems have the potential to play a crucial role in building a more sustainable future for agriculture.

Hydroponic Farming Technology

Hydroponic farming technology refers to an innovative and sustainable method of growing plants without the use of soil. Instead, plants are grown in a controlled environment where essential nutrients are delivered directly to the root system through a nutrient-rich water solution.

This sustainable farming technique offers several advantages in terms of resource efficiency, environmental impact, and overall food production. By eliminating the need for soil, hydroponics significantly reduces water consumption as it allows for precise control and recycling of water. Furthermore, the absence of soil also minimizes the risks of soil erosion and contamination, preventing the release of harmful chemicals into the environment.

In addition to conserving water and reducing environmental harm, hydroponic farming technology also maximizes land use efficiency. Plants can be grown vertically, utilizing multilayered systems, enabling higher crop yields per square meter compared to traditional soil-based farming. This increased productivity, along with the ability to grow crops year-round regardless of seasonal constraints, helps to alleviate food scarcity and promote food security.

Moreover, hydroponic farming ensures optimal nutrient uptake for plants, resulting in faster growth rates and higher nutritional content. The controlled environment also minimizes the need for pesticides and herbicides, making hydroponics a sustainable and chemical-free farming solution. Additionally, this technique eliminates the dependence on arable land, making it suitable for urban areas where space is limited.

In conclusion, hydroponic farming technology is a sustainable and innovative method that provides numerous benefits including efficient resource utilization, minimized environmental impact, higher crop yields, year-round production, improved nutritional content, and adaptable location possibilities. By revolutionizing traditional farming practices, hydroponics offers a promising solution for addressing global food challenges while reducing the ecological footprint associated with agriculture.

Hydroponic Greenhouse Systems

A hydroponic greenhouse system is a sustainable agricultural method that combines hydroponics and greenhouse technology to grow plants in a soilless environment. It optimizes resources such as water, nutrients, and energy, making it an environmentally-friendly and efficient way of cultivating crops.

In a hydroponic greenhouse system, plants are grown in nutrient-rich water solutions instead of traditional soil. This method eliminates the need for large-scale land use and minimizes the risk of soil erosion. By directly delivering nutrients to the plant roots, it promotes faster growth and higher yields, requiring less water compared to conventional farming practices.

The greenhouse component of this system provides control over environmental factors such as temperature, humidity, and light. This allows for year-round production and protection of crops from pests and diseases, reducing the reliance on harmful chemical pesticides and herbicides. Additionally, greenhouse structures can be equipped with renewable energy sources, such as solar panels, further reducing the carbon footprint of the system.

Overall, hydroponic greenhouse systems contribute to sustainability by conserving resources, increasing productivity, and minimizing environmental impacts. By utilizing space more efficiently, minimizing water usage, and reducing chemical inputs, they offer a solution to the challenges of conventional agriculture, such as land degradation, water scarcity, and pollution. Furthermore, the controlled environment provided by the greenhouse allows for optimized growth conditions, leading to better crop quality and higher profitability for farmers.

Hydroponic Nutrient Management

Hydroponic nutrient management refers to the sustainable practice of supplying essential nutrients to plants grown in a hydroponic system. Hydroponics is a method of growing plants in a soil-less environment, where water-based nutrient solutions are used to provide the necessary minerals and elements for plant growth.

In the context of sustainability, hydroponic nutrient management focuses on optimizing resource use, minimizing waste, and reducing environmental impacts. By carefully monitoring and adjusting the nutrient solutions, hydroponic growers can ensure that plants receive exactly what they need, resulting in improved plant health, growth, and productivity.

This approach offers several sustainability benefits. Firstly, hydroponic nutrient management minimizes the use of water compared to traditional soil-based agriculture. The nutrient solutions used in hydroponics are recirculated, reducing water consumption and minimizing the strain on local water resources.

Additionally, by providing plants with precise nutrient levels, hydroponic nutrient management minimizes the need for synthetic fertilizers and pesticides. This reduces the potential for water and soil pollution, improving overall environmental quality. Moreover, the controlled environment of hydroponics reduces the risk of nutrient runoff, as excess nutrients can be easily captured and recycled.

Furthermore, hydroponic systems can be implemented in urban areas, reducing the reliance on long-distance transportation of fresh produce and promoting local food production. This contributes to lower greenhouse gas emissions associated with transportation and supports food security.

Hydroponic Nutrient Solutions

Hydroponic nutrient solutions are sustainable solutions designed to provide essential nutrients to plants grown in hydroponic systems.

Hydroponics is an innovative method of cultivating plants without the use of soil, allowing crops to be grown in controlled environments. Nutrient solutions play a crucial role in this system by providing plants with the required elements for healthy growth, including nitrogen, phosphorus, and potassium, as well as essential micronutrients such as iron, manganese, and zinc.

Compared to traditional soil-based agriculture, hydroponic systems have several sustainability advantages. Firstly, they require less water as the nutrient solutions can be recirculated, minimizing water waste and reducing the strain on freshwater resources. Additionally, hydroponics significantly reduces the need for chemical pesticides and fertilizers, as the controlled environment helps prevent pest infestations and nutrient leaching. This results in lower environmental pollution and healthier produce.

Furthermore, hydroponics enables year-round cultivation, eliminating the limitations of seasonal changes and reducing the need for long-distance transportation of perishable goods. This reduces greenhouse gas emissions associated with transportation, contributing to a more sustainable food production system.

By utilizing hydroponic nutrient solutions, farmers can maximize crop yields in a resource-efficient manner, while minimizing environmental impacts. These solutions offer an sustainable option for meeting the increasing demand for food production in a world with limited arable land and dwindling natural resources.

Hydroponic Vertical Farming

Hydroponic vertical farming is a sustainable agricultural method that involves growing plants in vertically stacked layers or columns in controlled environments, using nutrient-rich water solutions instead of soil. This method optimizes space utilization by growing plants vertically, allowing for higher crop yield in smaller areas compared to traditional farming.

This sustainable farming approach addresses critical sustainability concerns such as land use, water conservation, and pesticide reduction. By eliminating the need for soil, hydroponic vertical farming minimizes the demand for arable land, reducing deforestation and preserving natural habitats. Additionally, this method requires significantly less water compared to conventional agriculture, as water is recirculated within the system, minimizing water loss through evaporation and runoff. The controlled environments of vertical farms also reduce the need for pesticides, as pests and diseases are easier to manage in enclosed spaces.

Hydrothermal Carbonization

Hydrothermal carbonization (HTC) is a sustainable process that converts biomass waste materials into a valuable carbon-rich end product. This innovative technology mimics the natural process of coal formation, utilizing high temperatures and pressure in a liquid water environment to transform organic matter into hydrochar.

HTC offers numerous environmental benefits, making it an attractive solution for managing biomass waste and promoting sustainability. Firstly, it enables the diversion of organic waste from landfills, reducing methane emissions and preventing soil and water contamination. By converting biomass waste into hydrochar, which is a stable and carbon-rich solid, HTC helps sequester carbon and mitigate climate change by preventing the release of greenhouse gases during waste decomposition.

Furthermore, hydrochar produced from HTC has various applications that contribute to sustainable practices. It can be used as a renewable energy source, replacing fossil fuels in power generation and reducing reliance on non-renewable resources. Additionally, hydrochar is a valuable soil amendment, enriching agricultural lands with organic carbon and nutrients while improving soil structure and water-holding capacity. This leads to enhanced crop productivity and reduces the need for synthetic fertilizers, thus minimizing negative environmental impacts associated with their production and use.

In summary, hydrothermal carbonization is an environmentally friendly process that addresses both waste management challenges and sustainability goals. By converting biomass waste into hydrochar, HTC not only reduces greenhouse gas emissions but also provides renewable energy and improves soil health. Its potential in mitigating climate change and promoting sustainable practices makes it a valuable tool for a more sustainable future.

In-Vessel Composting

In-vessel composting is a sustainable waste management technique that involves the controlled decomposition of organic materials in a contained and enclosed environment. It is designed to efficiently convert organic waste, such as food scraps, yard trimmings, and wood chips, into nutrient-rich compost. This process helps divert organic waste from landfills, reducing greenhouse gas emissions and minimizing the environmental impacts associated with waste disposal.

In this method, organic waste is placed inside a closed container or a vessel, often made of concrete, steel, or plastic. The container provides optimal conditions for composting, such as temperature control, moisture retention, and odor management. It also helps facilitate the breakdown of organic materials by creating an ideal environment for beneficial microorganisms to thrive.

Composting in a controlled vessel offers several advantages in terms of sustainability. Firstly, it allows for year-round composting, overcoming seasonal limitations that may exist in outdoor composting methods. Additionally, the enclosed system minimizes odors, prevents the release of pollutants into the air and water, and reduces the risk of attracting pests or rodents.

The end product of in-vessel composting is a valuable resource known as compost, which can be used to enrich soil in various applications. Compost improves soil structure, water retention, and nutrient content, promoting healthier plant growth and reducing the need for synthetic fertilizers. By incorporating compost into agricultural practices, landscape management, and gardening, the reliance on chemical inputs can be reduced, leading to more sustainable and environmentally friendly practices.

Industrial Symbiosis

Industrial symbiosis is a sustainable approach that aims to foster the efficient use of resources and reduce environmental impact within a network of interconnected industries. It involves the exchange of by-products, waste materials, energy, and expertise among different industrial processes, leading to mutual benefits and a more circular economy.

This concept is based on the principle that one industry's waste or by-product can become another industry's input or raw material. By collaborating and sharing resources, industries can minimize their waste generation, reduce pollution, and improve their overall environmental performance. This approach also promotes the conservation of natural resources and the preservation of ecosystems by decreasing the need for extracting and processing virgin materials.

Industrial symbiosis initiatives often involve the establishment of industrial parks or clusters where different companies co-locate to facilitate the exchange of resources and knowledge. These partnerships can result in various synergies, including the optimization of energy use, the reuse of materials, the development of new products, and the creation of economic opportunities.

Implementing industrial symbiosis requires effective collaboration, trust, and communication among participating industries. It also necessitates the identification of compatible businesses and the development of supportive policies and infrastructure. Governments, NGOs, and business associations play vital roles in encouraging and supporting the adoption of industrial symbiosis practices to achieve sustainable development goals.

Institute For Sustainable Communities

The Institute for Sustainable Communities (ISC) is a non-profit organization dedicated to creating sustainable communities and fostering leadership for sustainable development. The organization works with partners around the world to address the complex challenges of sustainability, including climate change, social equity, and economic viability.

ISC believes that sustainable communities are built on three key pillars: environmental responsibility, social equity, and economic prosperity. Through its programs and initiatives, ISC seeks to create lasting change by empowering local leaders, supporting innovative solutions, and promoting collaboration between different sectors and stakeholders.

ISC's approach to sustainability is based on the understanding that environmental issues cannot be solved independently from social and economic challenges. By integrating these three dimensions, ISC aims to create holistic and inclusive solutions that meet the needs of people and the planet.

ISC's work spans across various sectors, including energy, transportation, waste management, and urban planning. The organization provides technical assistance, training, and capacity building to help communities implement sustainable practices and policies. ISC also conducts research and knowledge sharing activities to inform decision-making and promote best practices.

Through its efforts, ISC strives to inspire and empower individuals and communities to take action for a sustainable future. By working together, ISC believes that we can create a world where all people have access to clean air, water, and a healthy environment, while also enjoying social equity and economic well-being.

International Centre For Sustainable Development (ICSD)

The International Centre for Sustainable Development (ICSD) is an organization dedicated to promoting and facilitating sustainable development on a global scale.

ICSD works towards achieving a harmonious balance between economic growth, social well-being, and environmental stewardship. It aims to address the pressing challenges faced by the world today, including poverty, inequality, climate change, and resource depletion.

ICSD conducts research, fosters partnerships, and provides policy recommendations to governments, businesses, and civil society organizations. Through its work, ICSD seeks to foster sustainable development practices that can ensure a better future for present and future generations.

The organization focuses on a multidisciplinary approach, recognizing that sustainability requires the integration of various fields and perspectives. By combining expertise in areas such as economics, environmental science, social sciences, and governance, ICSD aims to develop holistic solutions that are both practical and effective.

Furthermore, ICSD places a strong emphasis on international cooperation and collaboration. It recognizes that sustainable development challenges are global in nature and require collective action. ICSD actively facilitates knowledge-sharing, capacity-building, and networking among stakeholders to foster collaboration and the exchange of best practices.

Ultimately, the International Centre for Sustainable Development strives to be a catalyst for change. It seeks to empower individuals, communities, and organizations to take action towards a more sustainable future, one that ensures social well-being, economic prosperity, and environmental integrity.

International Renewable Energy Agency (IRENA)

The International Renewable Energy Agency (IRENA) is an intergovernmental organization dedicated to promoting and advancing the use of renewable energy sources worldwide. IRENA was established in 2009 with the objective of accelerating the global transition to a sustainable energy future.

IRENA's main focus is to provide countries with the necessary knowledge, technical assistance, and financial support to develop and implement effective renewable energy policies and strategies. The agency serves as a platform for international cooperation and collaboration, bringing together governments, industry leaders, and other stakeholders to facilitate the exchange of knowledge, best practices, and innovative solutions.

By advocating for renewable energy, IRENA aims to address the challenges posed by climate change, energy security, and sustainable development. The agency recognizes the urgent need to reduce greenhouse gas emissions and mitigate the environmental impact of fossil fuel-based energy systems. Through its research, analysis, and advisory services, IRENA promotes the widespread adoption of renewable energy technologies, such as solar, wind, hydro, geothermal, and bioenergy.

IRENA plays a crucial role in supporting countries in their efforts to achieve the United Nations Sustainable Development Goals, particularly Goal 7 (Ensure access to affordable, reliable, sustainable and modern energy for all) and Goal 13 (Take urgent action to combat climate change and its impacts). By facilitating knowledge sharing, capacity building, and project development, IRENA contributes to the global transition towards a more sustainable and secure energy future.

International Union For Conservation Of Nature (IUCN)

The International Union for Conservation of Nature (IUCN) is an international organization dedicated to the conservation and sustainable use of the world's natural resources. It operates as a global authority on the status of the natural world and the measures needed to safeguard it.

IUCN's main objective is to promote the conservation and sustainable use of biodiversity, as well as the equitable and ecologically sustainable development of natural resources. It brings together governments, non-governmental organizations, scientists, and indigenous peoples to advance nature conservation and sustainable development goals.

Low-Impact Architecture

Low-impact architecture is a sustainable approach to building design that minimizes the negative environmental impacts associated with construction and operation. It prioritizes the use of environmentally friendly materials, energy efficiency, and reducing waste and carbon emissions throughout the building's lifecycle.

This architectural philosophy aims to create structures that have a minimal ecological footprint. It emphasizes the integration of natural elements and passive design strategies to decrease reliance on artificial energy sources. By harnessing the power of sunlight, wind, and water, low-impact architecture seeks to achieve a reduced demand for non-renewable resources.

In terms of materials, low-impact architecture promotes the use of sustainable and locally sourced resources. It favors renewable and recyclable materials, such as timber, bamboo, straw, and earth, to minimize the depletion of natural resources. Additionally, the design focuses on reducing waste generation during construction and selecting materials with low embodied energy.

Energy efficiency plays a crucial role in low-impact architecture. It employs strategies like proper insulation, efficient heating and cooling systems, and the integration of renewable energy technologies like solar panels and wind turbines. By maximizing energy efficiency, buildings can decrease their reliance on fossil fuels and reduce greenhouse gas emissions.

Overall, low-impact architecture aims to create environmentally responsible and sustainable structures. It considers the long-term impact on the ecosystem, resource conservation, and the well-being of occupants. By embracing low-impact architecture, we can foster a more sustainable built environment and contribute to the preservation of our planet for future generations.

Low-Impact Development (LID)

Low-impact development (LID) refers to an approach to land development and urban design that aims to minimize the negative environmental impacts associated with conventional development practices. LID emphasizes sustainable and regenerative planning strategies to protect and enhance the natural environment while supporting human needs and activities.

LID takes into account the interconnectedness of natural systems, recognizing that a healthy environment is essential for the well-being of communities and future generations. It promotes the conservation and restoration of ecosystems, water resources, and biodiversity by incorporating green infrastructure, efficient stormwater management techniques, and sustainable landscaping practices.

In LID, site planning and design focus on managing stormwater runoff close to its source. This is typically achieved through the use of decentralized stormwater management practices, such as rain gardens, bioswales, permeable pavements, and green roofs. These strategies help to mimic natural hydrological processes, reducing the volume and velocity of stormwater runoff while promoting groundwater recharge and pollutant filtration.

LID also encourages compact and walkable development patterns that minimize the need for long-distance travel and car dependence. By integrating mixed-use developments, pedestrian-friendly infrastructure, and public transportation options, LID promotes sustainable and efficient land use, reducing greenhouse gas emissions and promoting community cohesion.

Overall, low-impact development seeks to create vibrant, resilient, and sustainable communities that harmonize with the natural environment. By implementing a holistic approach to development, LID aims to minimize ecological disruptions, conserve resources, mitigate climate impacts, and foster social well-being, contributing to a more sustainable and environmentally-conscious future.

Low-Impact Landscaping

Low-impact landscaping, in the context of sustainability, refers to the practice of designing, creating, and maintaining outdoor spaces with minimal negative environmental impact. It involves utilizing sustainable materials, conserving natural resources, and reducing pollution and waste. This approach aims to harmonize the built environment with the natural surroundings, promoting biodiversity and ecological resilience.

Low-impact landscaping involves several key principles. First, it focuses on the preservation and enhancement of the existing ecosystem. This includes protecting and promoting native plants, which are adapted to the local climate and require less water, fertilizer, and pesticides. By using native plants, the need for irrigation and chemical inputs is minimized, reducing water usage and preventing the pollution of soil and water bodies.

Second, low-impact landscaping incorporates water conservation strategies. This includes implementing efficient irrigation systems, such as drip irrigation, and capturing rainwater for reuse. By minimizing water waste and runoff, low-impact landscaping helps conserve this precious resource while reducing the strain on municipal water supplies.

Furthermore, low-impact landscaping aims to minimize the reliance on chemical inputs, such as fertilizers and pesticides. Instead, it emphasizes natural and organic approaches to maintaining healthy plants and controlling pests. This reduces the exposure of humans and wildlife to harmful chemicals, promotes soil health, and maintains a balanced ecosystem.

Overall, low-impact landscaping is a sustainable approach to creating and managing outdoor spaces that considers the ecological, social, and economic impact. By embracing this practice, individuals and communities can contribute to mitigating climate change, preserving biodiversity, and creating harmonious environments that support human and ecological well-being.

Low-Waste Product Packaging

Low-waste product packaging refers to a sustainable approach to designing and implementing packaging techniques that minimize the environmental impact associated with packaging materials. It aims at reducing waste generation, conserving resources, and minimizing pollution throughout the lifecycle of a product's packaging.

By employing a low-waste packaging strategy, companies strive to address the growing concerns surrounding excessive waste generation and its detrimental consequences on the environment. This approach entails various measures such as using recyclable or biodegradable materials, reducing the overall packaging volume, and optimizing packaging designs to maximize space efficiency.

Low-waste product packaging recognizes that traditional packaging practices often result in significant waste accumulation, contributing to issues such as overflowing landfills, air and water pollution, and depletion of natural resources. To counteract these issues, sustainable packaging solutions prioritize the use of renewable materials, such as plant-based or recycled materials, to reduce the reliance on fossil fuels and minimize carbon emissions.

Additionally, low-waste packaging aims to promote circular economy principles by designing packaging that can be easily recycled or repurposed, prolonging the lifecycle of materials. This mitigates the need for single-use packaging and encourages consumers to participate in recycling programs, ultimately reducing waste sent to landfills.

In summary, low-waste product packaging is a sustainable approach that seeks to minimize the environmental impact of packaging by reducing waste generation, conserving resources, and promoting circular economy principles. By adopting these practices, businesses can contribute to a healthier and more sustainable future for the planet.

Marine Energy Technology

Marine energy technology refers to the renewable energy derived from the ocean's various resources, such as tides, waves, currents, and temperature gradients. It involves the harnessing of these natural elements to generate electricity or provide other forms of energy, while simultaneously addressing sustainability concerns.

This technology holds significant potential in contributing to a sustainable future due to several reasons. First, marine energy is a clean and carbon-neutral form of power generation, making it environmentally friendly and reducing greenhouse gas emissions. Unlike traditional fossil fuel-based energy sources, marine energy does not contribute to air pollution or climate change. This aspect aligns with the objectives of sustainable development, as outlined in the United Nations' Sustainable Development Goals (SDGs).

Second, the abundance and predictability of ocean resources make marine energy technology a reliable and consistent energy source. Tides and waves, for example, are highly predictable and occur regularly, providing a consistent supply of renewable energy. This stability helps reduce reliance on non-renewable energy sources and provides greater energy security.

Third, marine energy projects can promote biodiversity and enhance local ecosystems. While the installation and operation of these technologies require careful planning and consideration to minimize potential impacts, they can also act as artificial reefs, providing habitats for marine species and contributing to the restoration of marine ecosystems. This potential co-benefit aligns with the principles of sustainability and conservation of natural resources.

Material Flow Analysis

Material flow analysis is a method used in sustainability assessment to analyze the movement of materials through a system or economy. It provides a quantitative understanding of the inputs, outputs, and transformations of materials, enabling the assessment of resource efficiency, waste generation, and potential environmental impacts.

The process of material flow analysis involves tracking the physical flow of materials across different stages of production, consumption, and disposal. It considers both the direct flows of materials within a system and the indirect flows associated with the extraction and transportation of raw materials, as well as the waste generated along the way.

By quantifying material flows, material flow analysis aims to identify inefficiencies, losses, and opportunities for improvement within systems. It can help identify hotspots of resource consumption, identify potential areas for material recycling or reusing, and assess the environmental impacts associated with material flows, such as greenhouse gas emissions or water pollution.

Material flow analysis is a valuable tool for policymakers, businesses, and researchers to make informed decisions on resource management and design more sustainable systems. It provides a comprehensive and quantitative assessment of material use, which can guide strategies and policies for reducing waste generation, improving resource efficiency, and transitioning to a circular economy.

Materials Passport

A materials passport is a formal documentation that provides a comprehensive overview of the materials used in the construction and operation of a building or infrastructure throughout its entire lifecycle. It serves as a tool to facilitate sustainable practices and promote the circular economy.

The materials passport aims to address the environmental and social impacts associated with the extraction, production, use, and disposal of materials. It provides detailed information about the origin, composition, characteristics, and potential reuse or recycling options of each material used in a project. By documenting this information, the materials passport enables informed decision-making regarding the selection, use, and end-of-life management of materials.

With a materials passport, architects, designers, builders, and other stakeholders can make more sustainable choices by prioritizing materials with lower environmental impacts and higher recyclability. It encourages the use of materials with lower carbon footprint, renewable resources, and non-toxic components. Additionally, the passport can help identify opportunities for material recovery and reuse, ultimately reducing waste and conserving natural resources.

The implementation of materials passports also supports the transition towards a circular economy, where resources are kept in use for as long as possible, and waste is minimized. By promoting the reuse and recycling of materials, the materials passport contributes to the reduction of greenhouse gas emissions, energy consumption, and landfill waste. It encourages the shift from a linear "take-make-dispose" model to a more sustainable and regenerative approach.

Micro-Hydro Power Systems

Micro-hydro power systems, also known as small-scale hydroelectric plants, are sustainable energy solutions that harness the power of flowing or falling water to generate electricity on a small scale. These systems utilize the natural energy potential of water to produce clean, renewable energy, contributing to the overall goal of achieving a sustainable future.

Micro-hydro power systems are designed to be environmentally friendly and have a minimal impact on ecosystems. They typically consist of a water source, such as a river or stream, a turbine, a generator, and a transmission system. The turbine is placed in the flowing water, and as the water moves through it, the kinetic energy of the water is converted into mechanical energy. The generator then converts this mechanical energy into electrical energy, which can be used to power homes, businesses, or communities.

These power systems are considered sustainable for several reasons. Firstly, they rely on a renewable resource - water. Unlike fossil fuels, water is a continuously replenished resource, ensuring long-term production of clean energy. Additionally, micro-hydro power systems produce minimal greenhouse gas emissions, helping to combat climate change and reduce air pollution. The installation of these systems does not require the construction of large dams, which can have negative environmental impacts, but rather utilizes the existing natural flow of water.

Furthermore, micro-hydro power systems provide numerous social and economic benefits. They can be implemented in remote areas, providing electricity to communities that may not have access to the grid. This improves the quality of life, promotes economic development, and reduces dependency on fossil fuels. These systems also contribute to job creation, as they require maintenance and operation, fostering local employment opportunities.

Micro-Wind Turbines

Micro-wind turbines, also known as small wind turbines or residential wind turbines, are sustainable technologies that harness the power of wind to generate electricity on a small scale. These small wind energy systems are designed to produce electricity for individual homes, farms, or small businesses, offering a reliable and renewable energy alternative to traditional electricity sources.

The primary purpose of micro-wind turbines is to reduce reliance on fossil fuels and decrease carbon emissions by utilizing the wind's natural energy. With proper installation in locations where wind resources are sufficient, micro-wind turbines can significantly contribute to a sustainable energy mix while promoting energy independence and reducing energy costs for individual users.

Microalgae Cultivation For Biofuels

Microalgae cultivation for biofuels is a sustainable practice that involves the growth and harvesting of tiny aquatic organisms, known as microalgae, for the purpose of producing renewable biofuels.

Microalgae are photosynthetic organisms that can convert sunlight and carbon dioxide into biomass through the process of photosynthesis. They are rich in oils and carbohydrates, making them a promising feedstock for the production of biofuels such as biodiesel, bioethanol, and biogas. Compared to traditional fossil fuels, biofuels derived from microalgae are considered more sustainable and environmentally friendly as they have a lower carbon footprint and do not contribute to climate change.

The cultivation of microalgae for biofuels offers several advantages in terms of sustainability. First, microalgae can be grown in various types of water, including freshwater, seawater, and even wastewater, reducing the strain on freshwater resources. They also have a high photosynthetic efficiency, meaning they can produce biomass and capture carbon dioxide more effectively compared to other crops used for biofuel production. Additionally, microalgae can be cultivated on non-arable land, minimizing competition with food crops and preserving agricultural land for food production.

Moreover, microalgae cultivation can help mitigate the negative impacts of several environmental issues. By capturing carbon dioxide during photosynthesis, microalgae can act as a carbon sink, reducing greenhouse gas emissions. They can also absorb and remove nutrients from wastewater, mitigating eutrophication in aquatic ecosystems. Additionally, the cultivation of microalgae can contribute to the remediation of polluted water bodies through the absorption of heavy metals and other contaminants.

Microbiome-Based Agriculture

Microbiome-based agriculture refers to the practice of utilizing beneficial microorganisms to enhance the ecological and sustainable aspects of agricultural systems. It involves harnessing the natural interactions between plants, soil, and microorganisms to optimize plant growth, increase nutrient availability, and improve overall plant health. In this approach, the microbiome, which consists of the diverse community of microorganisms living in and around plants, is recognized as a crucial component of the agricultural ecosystem. These microorganisms, such as bacteria, fungi, and viruses, play vital roles in nutrient cycling, disease suppression, and plant defense against pests and pathogens. By promoting a diverse and balanced microbiome, microbiome-based agriculture aims to reduce the reliance on synthetic fertilizers, pesticides, and other agrochemicals. This, in turn, helps to minimize the negative environmental impacts associated with conventional farming practices, such as water pollution, soil degradation, and loss of biodiversity. Moreover, microbiome-based agriculture holds promise for increasing the resilience and productivity of crops in the face of climate change and unpredictable weather patterns. The microbial communities associated with plants can help enhance their tolerance to abiotic stresses, such as drought, heat, and salinity. Overall, microbiome-based agriculture offers a sustainable and holistic approach to crop production by leveraging the power of beneficial microorganisms. By working in harmony with nature, it has the potential to enhance agricultural sustainability, protect ecosystems, and promote food security for future generations.

Microgrid Management Systems

A microgrid management system is a sustainable solution for decentralized and localized energy generation, distribution, and consumption. It efficiently integrates various sources of renewable energy, energy storage systems, and loads within a specific geographical area to optimize energy usage and ensure grid resilience.

Designed to operate independently or in coordination with the main power grid, a microgrid management system enables the effective management of energy supply and demand, reducing reliance on fossil fuels and promoting environmental sustainability. It empowers communities, institutions, and businesses to transition towards a cleaner and more resilient energy future.

Microgrid Technology

Microgrid technology refers to a small-scale localized power system that operates independently or in conjunction with the main power grid. It incorporates various energy sources, such as solar panels, wind turbines, and batteries, to generate electricity and meet the energy needs of a specific area or community. Unlike traditional centralized power grids that rely solely on fossil fuels and are prone to blackouts and inefficiencies, microgrids are designed to enhance sustainability and resilience. Microgrids play a crucial role in promoting sustainability by optimizing the use of renewable energy sources. By integrating solar and wind power generation, they reduce reliance on fossil fuels and help mitigate greenhouse gas emissions. Moreover, microgrids facilitate energy independence and reduce transmission losses, making them more energy-efficient compared to conventional grids. Another key aspect of microgrid technology is its ability to promote local energy generation and consumption. By enabling decentralized energy production, microgrids empower communities to become self-reliant in meeting their energy needs. This localized approach not only enhances energy security but also fosters community resilience during natural disasters or grid outages. Furthermore, microgrids are flexible and scalable, allowing for seamless integration into existing infrastructure or the establishment of new grids in remote areas. They can be customized based on local resources, demand patterns, and climate conditions. Additionally, microgrids are equipped with advanced monitoring and control systems that optimize energy distribution and grid stability. In summary, microgrid technology focuses on creating sustainable and resilient power systems. By harnessing renewable energy sources, promoting local energy production, and enhancing grid efficiency, microgrids contribute to a more sustainable and decentralized energy future.

Microplastic Filtration Systems

Microplastic filtration systems are sustainable technologies designed to remove microplastic particles from water sources. Microplastics are tiny plastic fragments measuring less than 5mm in size that are commonly found in the environment, including oceans, rivers, and lakes.

These filtration systems work by employing various methods to efficiently capture and separate microplastic particles from water. They typically consist of multiple stages, each using different mechanisms to target different sizes of microplastics. Some common filtration methods include sieve filtration, membrane filtration, and adsorption.

Sieve filtration involves using a physical barrier, such as a mesh or screen, with specifically sized openings to prevent larger microplastics from passing through while allowing water to flow freely. Membrane filtration utilizes thin membranes with microscopic pores that can selectively trap microplastics based on their size. Adsorption, on the other hand, involves using materials like activated carbon that have a high affinity for microplastic particles, causing them to stick to the surface of the material and be removed from the water.

By implementing microplastic filtration systems, the negative environmental impacts of microplastics can be mitigated. These systems ensure that water sources remain free from harmful microplastic pollution, protecting aquatic life and preserving overall ecosystem health. Additionally, the removal of microplastics from water sources helps safeguard human health by preventing the potential ingestion of these particles through drinking water and the consumption of aquatic organisms.

Microplastic Filtration Technology

Microplastic filtration technology is a sustainable solution aimed at reducing the impact of microplastic pollution on the environment. It involves the development and implementation of filtration systems that effectively capture and remove microplastic particles from various sources such as water bodies, air, and wastewater.

This technology is designed to address the growing concern surrounding microplastic pollution, which poses significant risks to ecosystems, marine life, and human health. Microplastics, which are tiny plastic particles measuring less than 5mm in size, can enter the environment through various means such as the breakdown of larger plastic items, the shedding of microfibers from textiles, or the fragmentation of plastic waste.

Microplastic filtration technology utilizes specialized filters or membranes that have the ability to selectively trap and remove microplastic particles from the targeted medium. These filters are designed to have small pore sizes, enabling them to effectively retain microplastics while allowing the passage of clean water or air. They are usually made from materials that are resistant to degradation and have high filtration efficiency.

Once the microplastic particles are captured, they can be properly disposed of or processed for recycling. By implementing microplastic filtration technology, the release of microplastics into the environment can be significantly reduced, thereby preserving the ecological balance and safeguarding human health.

Overall, microplastic filtration technology plays a crucial role in promoting sustainability by mitigating the adverse effects of microplastic pollution and contributing to the conservation of natural resources.

Microplastic Monitoring Technology

Microplastic monitoring technology is a scientific approach aimed at identifying and quantifying the presence of microplastics in various environmental matrices. Microplastics, defined as plastic particles smaller than 5 millimeters in size, have emerged as a significant environmental concern due to their widespread presence in the oceans, freshwater bodies, and even terrestrial ecosystems. These tiny plastic particles can originate from multiple sources, such as the fragmentation of larger plastic items, direct release of microbeads found in personal care products, and the degradation of synthetic fibers.

To understand the extent and impact of microplastic pollution, monitoring technology utilizes sampling techniques that collect environmental samples, ranging from water, sediment, soil, and even biota. These samples are then subjected to laboratory analysis, employing various techniques such as microscopy, spectroscopy, and chromatography, to identify and quantify microplastic particles. Additionally, specialized software algorithms are employed to distinguish microplastics from other particles present in the samples and to analyze the size, shape, and composition of the identified microplastics.

Microplastic Pollution Solutions

Microplastic pollution solutions refer to strategies and actions aimed at mitigating, managing, and ultimately reducing the presence and impact of microplastics in the environment. Microplastics are tiny particles of plastic less than 5 millimeters in size that originate from various sources, such as the breakdown of larger plastic items, directly released microbeads, or fibers shed from synthetic textiles. They have become a ubiquitous pollutant in terrestrial and aquatic ecosystems, posing a significant threat to biodiversity and ecosystem health.

Addressing microplastic pollution requires a multi-faceted approach that encompasses prevention, removal, and policy interventions. Prevention strategies focus on reducing the production and consumption of single-use plastics as well as promoting environmentally friendly alternatives. This can include measures such as banning microbeads, implementing extended producer responsibility schemes, and encouraging the use of biodegradable or compostable materials.

Removal methods involve the physical extraction of microplastics from various environmental compartments, including water bodies and soil. These methods can range from manual clean-up efforts, filtration systems, and the deployment of specially designed nets or skimmers. Additionally, innovative technologies such as electrostatic precipitation, ultrasonic cleaning, and bioremediation techniques are being explored to enhance microplastic removal efficiency.

Policy interventions play a crucial role in microplastic pollution solutions by establishing regulations and standards to encourage responsible waste management, recycling, and the circular economy. Governments can impose stricter controls on plastic production and disposal, promote sustainable consumption practices, and support research and development of alternative materials.

Microplastic Research Initiatives

A microplastic research initiative refers to a scientific project or program that focuses on investigating and studying the presence, effects, and mitigation strategies of microplastics in the environment from a sustainability standpoint. It involves conducting systematic and thorough research to understand the sources, distribution, abundance, and potential ecological and human health impacts of these tiny plastic particles.

Typically, microplastic research initiatives aim to contribute to sustainable development by addressing the growing concern surrounding microplastic pollution. These initiatives include interdisciplinary collaborations between scientists, researchers, policymakers, and various stakeholders to gather robust scientific evidence and develop effective solutions to combat the issue.

The objectives of microplastic research initiatives usually encompass several key aspects:

1. Detection and characterization: These initiatives employ advanced analytical techniques to detect, identify, and quantify microplastic particles in different environmental compartments, such as soil, water, air, and biota. Through comprehensive characterization, researchers can understand the composition, morphology, and potential sources of microplastics.

2. Ecological and human health impacts: Research initiatives investigate the ecological consequences of microplastic contamination, including impacts on wildlife, marine ecosystems, and terrestrial habitats. They also explore the potential pathways and consequences of microplastic exposure on human health. By assessing the risks, researchers can provide evidence-based recommendations for sustainable management strategies.

215

3. Source identification and mitigation: Microplastic research initiatives strive to identify the primary sources of microplastic pollution, such as plastic debris, microbeads, synthetic clothing fibers, and tire wear. Understanding these sources is crucial for developing effective mitigation measures aimed at reducing the release of microplastics into the environment.

In summary, microplastic research initiatives play a vital role in advancing knowledge on microplastic pollution to support sustainable practices and policies. They provide scientific insights necessary for developing effective measures to minimize the ecological and health risks associated with microplastics and promote a more sustainable future.

Microplastic Research

Microplastic research is the scientific investigation of tiny plastic particles that are less than 5mm in size and have accumulated in various environmental systems, including oceans, rivers, and landfills. These minuscule plastic fragments have become a growing concern for sustainability as they present significant risks to ecosystems and human health.

This research primarily focuses on understanding the sources, distribution, and impacts of microplastics, as well as developing effective strategies for their detection, prevention, and mitigation. By studying microplastics, scientists aim to determine how these particles are generated, how they enter the environment, and how they interact with living organisms.

The examination of microplastics encompasses the investigation of both primary and secondary microplastics. Primary microplastics directly enter the environment in their small size, such as microbeads used in personal care products or resin pellets used in industrial processes. Secondary microplastics are formed through the degradation and fragmentation of larger plastic items over time.

Researchers employ various methods to study microplastics, including microscope analysis, spectroscopy, thermal analysis, and chemical techniques. These techniques enable the identification, quantification, and characterization of microplastics in different environmental matrices.

The findings of microplastic research contribute to the development of policies and practices aimed at reducing plastic pollution. This research plays a crucial role in promoting sustainable waste management strategies, raising awareness among industries and consumers, and supporting the implementation of regulation to limit the release of microplastics into the environment.

Microplastic Sampling Devices

A microplastic sampling device is a specialized tool used to collect and analyze microplastic particles in various environmental samples, such as water, soil, sediment, and even air. Microplastics are tiny plastic particles measuring less than 5 millimeters in size, either resulting from the breakdown of larger plastic waste or manufactured intentionally for certain products.

These sampling devices are crucial in the field of sustainability as they enable researchers, scientists, and environmentalists to understand the extent and impact of microplastic pollution on ecosystems and human health. By collecting samples from different sources, these devices help in quantifying the presence and concentration of microplastics, identifying the types of microplastics present, and studying their distribution patterns.

Microplastic Source Tracking

Microplastic source tracking refers to the process of identifying and determining the origin or sources of microplastic pollution in the environment. Microplastics are tiny plastic particles less than 5mm in size that are derived from various sources, including the fragmentation of larger plastic products, microbeads, and the breakdown of synthetic fibers. They pose a significant threat to ecosystems and human health, as they can be ingested by marine organisms and enter the food chain.

In the context of sustainability, understanding the sources of microplastics is crucial for developing effective mitigation strategies and policies. Microplastic source tracking involves analyzing the characteristics of microplastics, such as their size, shape, and chemical composition, to determine their likely sources. This can be done through various techniques, including microscopy, spectroscopy, and molecular analysis.

Additionally, source tracking involves monitoring and analyzing environmental samples, such as water and sediment, to identify the presence and concentration of microplastics. By comparing the data from these samples with known sources, researchers can identify potential pathways and transport mechanisms that contribute to microplastic pollution.

The information obtained from microplastic source tracking can help inform policy decisions, guide waste management strategies, and identify priority areas for intervention. By targeting the specific sources of microplastics, it is possible to implement sustainable practices, reduce pollution, and prevent further contamination of the environment.

Microplastic Waste Reduction

Microplastic waste reduction refers to the collective efforts aimed at minimizing the amount of microplastic waste released into the environment. Microplastics are tiny plastic particles measuring less than 5 millimeters in size that originate from various sources such as plastic products, cosmetics, and the breakdown of larger plastic debris. These particles are pervasive in our environment and have become a significant environmental concern due to their widespread distribution and potential harm to ecosystems and organisms.

Sustainability strategies focused on microplastic waste reduction involve implementing measures to prevent the generation of microplastics, as well as reducing their release and promoting their proper management. Firstly, efforts are made to minimize the use of single-use plastics and promote the use of alternative materials that are less likely to break down into microplastics. This can be achieved through policy interventions, industry commitments, and consumer awareness campaigns. Secondly, there is a need to improve waste management practices to prevent plastic waste from entering water bodies and ecosystems. This includes the development of effective recycling systems, waste collection infrastructure, and the proper disposal of plastic products. Additionally, the development of innovative technologies for the removal and treatment of microplastics from wastewater and aquatic environments is crucial.

Microplastic Water Filtration

The concept of microplastic water filtration refers to the use of specialized filtration systems to remove microplastics from water sources, with the aim of minimizing their negative impact on the environment and human health. Microplastics are tiny particles of plastic (less than 5mm in size) that have become widespread pollutants in aquatic ecosystems. They can enter water bodies through various sources, including the fragmentation of larger plastic items, the shedding of microfibers from synthetic textiles, and the release of plastic particles from personal care products.

The presence of microplastics in water has become a growing concern due to their potential long-term consequences for ecosystems and human well-being. These particles can be ingested by aquatic organisms, leading to bioaccumulation and potential toxicity throughout the food chain. Furthermore, microplastics have been found in drinking water sources, raising concerns about the potential health risks associated with their consumption.

Microplastic Water Monitoring

Microplastic water monitoring is a systematic process of assessing and tracking the presence and concentration of microplastics in bodies of water, such as lakes, rivers, and oceans, with the aim of promoting sustainability. Microplastics are tiny plastic particles measuring less than 5mm in size, resulting from the fragmentation and degradation of larger plastic items or being purposefully manufactured at a microscopic scale. These particles pose significant threats to aquatic ecosystems and human health due to their persistence, potential for bioaccumulation, and ability to absorb and transport harmful chemicals.

The objective of microplastic water monitoring is to generate data and insights that inform decision-making processes for the sake of reducing microplastic pollution and its associated environmental and health risks. By understanding the sources, transport patterns, accumulation areas, and potential impacts of microplastics in water bodies, policymakers, researchers, and environmental organizations can develop effective mitigation strategies, policies, and guidelines to combat this global issue.

Minimalist Interior Design

Minimalist interior design is a sustainable approach to creating living spaces that prioritize simplicity, functionality, and environmental consciousness. It involves eliminating unnecessary clutter, opting for clean lines and neutral colors, and utilizing natural and eco-friendly materials.

This design philosophy aims to minimize waste and the use of non-renewable resources by focusing on essential elements and eliminating excess. By reducing the number of items in a space, minimalist interior design promotes a more sustainable lifestyle by discouraging excessive consumption and promoting mindful living.

Minimalist Sustainable Product Concepts

A minimalist sustainable product concept refers to a design or idea that promotes simplicity, durability, and environmental responsibility. It focuses on creating products that are functional, long-lasting, and have a reduced impact on the environment throughout their lifecycle, from production to disposal.

Minimalist sustainable product concepts prioritize the use of fewer materials and resources, avoiding unnecessary features or complexities. They aim to minimize waste and energy consumption during both the manufacturing process and the product's use. This includes selecting eco-friendly materials, incorporating renewable resources, and reducing carbon emissions.

Minimalist sustainable products are designed with a long-term perspective, considering their durability and ability to be repaired or recycled. They encourage conscious consumption, discouraging disposable or short-lived products that contribute to a throwaway culture. Additionally, these concepts often prioritize fair trade practices, social responsibility, and ethical sourcing of raw materials.

By adopting a minimalist approach to design and sustainability, product creators can reduce their ecological footprint while still providing functional and aesthetically pleasing solutions. These concepts align with the principles of a circular economy, where resources are used efficiently and waste is minimized. Ultimately, minimalist sustainable product concepts strive to create a more sustainable and responsible consumer culture.

Minimalist Sustainable Product Design

Sustainable product design is the practice of creating products that have minimal negative impact on the environment, while also meeting the needs of consumers. Minimalist sustainable product design specifically focuses on simplicity, efficiency, and durability.

Minimalist design eliminates unnecessary features, reducing resource consumption in the manufacturing process and minimizing waste. By streamlining the design, fewer materials are required, resulting in decreased energy usage and reduced emissions during production. Additionally, minimalist design often extends the lifespan of products by avoiding excessive ornamentation and focusing on essential functions, reducing the need for replacement and contributing to the overall reduction of waste.

Modular Eco-Home Design

A modular eco-home design refers to a sustainable housing concept that emphasizes the use of prefabricated modular components and eco-friendly materials to create environmentally conscious homes. It combines the principles of modularity and sustainability to provide flexible, efficient, and low-impact housing solutions.

A modular eco-home design takes into account several key aspects of sustainability. Firstly, it focuses on minimizing the environmental footprint of the construction process by using off-site manufacturing of modular components. This approach reduces waste generation, optimizes resource utilization, and decreases energy consumption during construction.

Secondly, modular eco-home designs prioritize energy efficiency and environmental performance after construction. They incorporate features such as efficient insulation, passive solar design, and energy-efficient appliances to reduce energy consumption and reliance on non-renewable resources. Additionally, sustainable materials like recycled and locally sourced materials are used, promoting a smaller carbon footprint and supporting local economies.

Furthermore, modular eco-homes often integrate rainwater harvesting systems, greywater recycling systems, and renewable energy technologies, such as solar panels or wind turbines. These systems help reduce water consumption and reliance on traditional energy grids, leading to increased self-sufficiency and reduced environmental impact.

The modular nature of eco-home designs allows for customization, scalability, and adaptability. Homeowners can easily add or remove modules as their needs change, reducing the requirement for new construction and minimizing waste generation. This aspect also facilitates the relocation and reuse of modular components, extending their lifespan and further reducing environmental impact.

Modular Product Design

Modular product design refers to a sustainable approach in which a product is designed and manufactured in separate modules or components that can be easily assembled or disassembled. Each module serves a specific function and can be replaced or upgraded individually, without having to replace the entire product. This design philosophy promotes resource efficiency, waste reduction, and longevity of products, all of which are essential elements of sustainability.

By using modular product design, manufacturers can reduce the environmental impact associated with the production and disposal of products. It allows for the use of more durable and higher-quality materials since individual modules can be replaced instead of discarding the whole product. This reduces the demand for raw materials, reduces energy consumption, and minimizes waste generation. Additionally, modular design facilitates easy repair, maintenance, and upgrades, extending the lifespan of products and reducing the need for new purchases.

Modular Sustainable Furniture

Modular sustainable furniture refers to furniture designs and systems that embrace principles of sustainability and modularity. Sustainability is a holistic approach that takes into consideration the environmental, social, and economic impacts of a product or system throughout its entire lifecycle. In the context of furniture, sustainable practices involve responsibly sourcing materials, minimizing waste, reducing carbon emissions, and promoting durability and recyclability.

Modularity, on the other hand, refers to the design concept of creating furniture pieces that can be easily disassembled, reconfigured, or added to, allowing for flexibility and adaptability. This allows users to customize their furniture according to their needs and preferences, promoting a longer lifespan for the pieces and reducing the need for frequent replacements.

Molten Salt Energy Storage

is a sustainable energy storage technology that utilizes high-temperature molten salt as a medium to store and release energy. It involves heating the salt to a high temperature using excess electricity generated from renewable sources such as solar or wind power. This stored thermal energy can be later converted into electricity when the demand for energy is high or when renewable energy generation is low. The process of molten salt energy storage consists of three main components: the thermal energy input, the energy storage system, and the thermal energy output. The thermal energy input phase involves using excess electricity to heat the molten salt to its melting point, which can reach temperatures as high as 600 degrees Celsius. This thermal energy is stored in insulated tanks or underground reservoirs, which helps to retain

219

the heat energy for longer durations. During the energy storage phase, the excess thermal energy is stored within the molten salt at a high temperature. The heat transfer fluid within the storage system absorbs this thermal energy, which is then circulated through heat exchangers and converted into electricity by a steam turbine. This process allows for the stored energy to be effectively converted back into electricity when needed. The thermal energy output phase occurs when the stored energy is required. The heated molten salt is then circulated back into the heat exchangers, where the thermal energy is transferred to the heat transfer fluid, which in turn converts it into electricity. This electricity can be supplied to the grid or used directly in various applications. Molten salt energy storage offers numerous sustainability benefits. It allows for the integration of intermittent renewable energy sources into the grid, addressing the issue of renewable energy variability. It helps to stabilize the grid by providing a reliable and dispatchable energy source. Additionally, it reduces the reliance on fossil fuel-based power plants, leading to a significant reduction in greenhouse gas emissions and promoting a cleaner and greener energy system. In conclusion, molten salt energy storage is a sustainable solution that enables the efficient storage and utilization of renewable energy. Its ability to store energy at high temperatures and release it when needed contributes to the stability and reliability of the grid while reducing carbon emissions and promoting a more sustainable energy future.

Multi-Functional Eco-Furniture

A multi-functional eco-furniture refers to a versatile and sustainable piece of furniture that serves multiple purposes while minimizing its impact on the environment. This type of furniture is designed with a focus on reducing waste, conserving resources, and promoting a circular economy.

When we say multi-functional, we mean that the furniture is capable of fulfilling different functions or adapting to various needs. For example, a couch that can transform into a bed or a coffee table that doubles as a storage unit. By combining multiple functions into one piece, this furniture promotes space efficiency, making it ideal for compact living spaces.

However, the key element that sets multi-functional eco-furniture apart is its emphasis on sustainability. These pieces are created using environmentally-friendly materials and manufacturing processes. For instance, they may be made from recycled or upcycled materials, reducing the demand for new resources. Additionally, the production techniques employed prioritize energy efficiency and minimal waste generation.

The durability of multi-functional eco-furniture is another important aspect of sustainability. By ensuring that the furniture is built to last, it reduces the need for frequent replacements, resulting in less waste generation and a longer product lifespan.

In summary, multi-functional eco-furniture is a versatile and sustainable solution for modern living. It combines multiple functions into a single piece of furniture while minimizing its environmental impact through the use of recycled or upcycled materials and energy-efficient production techniques.

Nanotechnology For Sustainability

Nanotechnology for sustainability refers to the application of nanoscale materials and devices to address and resolve environmental challenges, promote efficient use of resources, and enhance the overall sustainability of various industries and systems.

This field focuses on harnessing the unique properties and capabilities of nanomaterials, which exhibit size-dependent properties and behaviors, to develop innovative and sustainable solutions. Nanotechnology enables precise control and manipulation of matter at the nanoscale, typically ranging from 1 to 100 nanometers, allowing for the design and production of materials with desired properties and functionalities.

Nanotechnology offers numerous potential benefits for sustainability. It allows for the development of more energy-efficient products and processes, reducing energy consumption and associated carbon emissions. Nanomaterials can enhance the performance and lifespan of various products, leading to resource conservation and waste reduction. Moreover, nanotechnology enables the creation of purification and filtration systems that remove contaminants from air, water, and soil, contributing to improved environmental quality.

In the field of renewable energy, nanotechnology plays a critical role in the development of efficient solar cells, energy storage devices, and catalysts for clean energy production. It also enables advancements in fuel cells and hydrogen technologies, which have the potential to replace fossil fuels and significantly reduce greenhouse gas emissions.

Overall, nanotechnology for sustainability offers a promising avenue for addressing various environmental challenges and creating a more sustainable future by leveraging the unique properties of nanomaterials and devices to enhance resource efficiency, promote renewable energy technologies, and mitigate environmental impacts.

National Audubon Society

The National Audubon Society is a non-profit organization that works to protect birds and their habitats through advocacy, science-based conservation efforts, and education. Founded in 1905, the organization is dedicated to promoting sustainable practices that benefit both birds and the environment.

The Audubon Society's approach to sustainability involves several key principles. First, the organization emphasizes the importance of protecting and restoring natural habitats that are essential for bird populations to thrive. This includes advocating for the preservation of important bird areas, promoting responsible land management practices, and supporting habitat restoration projects.

In addition to habitat conservation, the Audubon Society also focuses on addressing other threats to bird populations, such as climate change and pollution. The organization conducts scientific research to better understand how these factors impact birds and works to develop strategies for mitigating their effects. This includes advocating for policies and actions that reduce greenhouse gas emissions, supporting renewable energy development, and promoting sustainable agriculture practices.

Furthermore, the Audubon Society places a strong emphasis on education and community engagement. They believe that fostering a connection to nature and inspiring a love for birds is instrumental in promoting sustainable behaviors and conservation efforts. Through their network of local chapters and educational programs, the organization works to empower individuals and communities to take action in support of birds and the environment.

In summary, the National Audubon Society is a leading organization in the field of bird conservation and sustainability. Their work encompasses habitat conservation, addressing threats such as climate change and pollution, and fostering education and community engagement. Through their efforts, they strive to create a sustainable future for birds and the environments they rely on.

National Council For Science And The Environment (NCSE)

The National Council for Science and the Environment (NCSE) is an organization focused on promoting the integration of scientific knowledge and sustainability practices for the betterment of society and the environment.

NCSE serves as a platform for scientists, educators, policymakers, and other stakeholders to collaborate and exchange ideas, research findings, and best practices related to sustainability. By facilitating these exchanges, NCSE aims to bridge the gap between science and policy, with the ultimate goal of informing decision-making processes that promote sustainable development.

National Geographic Society

The National Geographic Society is a renowned organization that is dedicated to the exploration, conservation, and promotion of the world's natural and cultural heritage. With a strong commitment to sustainability, the National Geographic Society strives to protect and preserve the planet for future generations.

Sustainability, as promoted by the National Geographic Society, refers to the responsible use and management of natural resources to ensure their availability for current and future generations. It involves a balanced approach that takes into account the social, economic, and environmental aspects of human activities.

The National Geographic Society aims to raise awareness about sustainability issues through its extensive research, education, and media programs. By highlighting the importance of sustainable practices, the Society encourages individuals, communities, and governments to take action to protect the Earth's ecosystems.

The Society's initiatives focus on various aspects of sustainability, including biodiversity conservation, climate change mitigation, and sustainable development. Through partnerships and collaborations with scientists, explorers, and local communities, the National Geographic Society works towards finding innovative solutions to environmental challenges.

Overall, the National Geographic Society plays a vital role in promoting sustainability through its efforts to understand, protect, and celebrate the planet's natural wonders. By inspiring people to appreciate and care for the Earth, the Society strives to create a more sustainable future for all.

National Wildlife Federation

The National Wildlife Federation (NWF) is a conservation organization working towards sustainability in the United States. It aims to protect and restore the country's wildlife and their habitats, while also addressing the environmental challenges of the present and future.

The NWF believes that sustainability is essential for the long-term well-being of both humans and nature. It recognizes that ecosystems provide a range of services necessary for life, such as clean air and water, food, and climate regulation. By promoting sustainable practices and policies, the NWF aims to ensure these services are available to future generations.

Natural Resources Defense Council (NRDC)

Natural Ventilation Systems

Natural ventilation systems are designed to utilize the natural airflow and temperature differences between the indoor and outdoor environments to create a comfortable and healthy living or working space. These systems rely on passive design principles to reduce the reliance on mechanical ventilation, which often consumes a significant amount of energy. By harnessing natural forces such as wind, stack effect, and buoyancy, natural ventilation systems promote fresh air exchange and provide thermal comfort without the need for artificial cooling or heating. In this way, they contribute to greater energy efficiency and lessen the environmental impact associated with HVAC (Heating, Ventilation, and Air Conditioning) systems. The main components of a natural ventilation system typically include openings such as windows, doors, vents, and louvers that are strategically placed to facilitate air movement. These openings allow fresh air to enter the space while facilitating the removal of stale air. Additionally, natural ventilation systems often incorporate features like windcatchers, atriums, or clerestory windows to enhance airflow and create a natural cooling effect. One of the significant advantages of natural ventilation systems is their ability to improve indoor air quality. By enabling the regular exchange of air, these systems reduce the concentration of pollutants, moisture, and odors, creating a healthier environment for occupants. Furthermore, natural ventilation systems can contribute to the overall sustainability of a building by reducing energy consumption, enhancing thermal comfort, and minimizing reliance on mechanical equipment. In summary, natural ventilation systems make use of natural airflow and temperature differences to create a comfortable and healthy indoor environment. By reducing the need for mechanical ventilation, they contribute to energy efficiency and help to create sustainable buildings.>

Net-Zero Carbon Footprint Communities

A net-zero carbon footprint community refers to a sustainable community that strives to balance the carbon dioxide emissions it produces with the amount of carbon dioxide it removes from the atmosphere through carbon offsetting and renewable energy sources. This means that over time, the community's overall contribution to greenhouse gas emissions is effectively neutralized, thus mitigating the negative impacts of climate change.

Such communities are designed and operated with a strong focus on energy efficiency, waste reduction, and the utilization of clean and renewable energy sources, such as solar and wind power. By minimizing energy consumption and adopting alternative energy solutions, these communities aim to limit their carbon emissions to a bare minimum. Additionally, net-zero carbon footprint communities often utilize advanced technologies and sustainable practices to optimize resource management, reduce water consumption, improve air quality, and promote sustainable transportation options.

Net-Zero Carbon Footprint Homes

A net-zero carbon footprint home is a sustainable residential structure that produces zero net greenhouse gas emissions during its operation. It is designed and built to minimize its environmental impact by utilizing renewable energy sources, reducing energy consumption, and implementing efficient waste management and water conservation practices.

Net-zero carbon footprint homes achieve a balance between the energy they consume and the renewable energy they generate. This is accomplished through the installation of renewable energy systems such as solar panels, wind turbines, or geothermal heat pumps. These systems harness clean and renewable sources of energy to power the home's electricity, heating, cooling, and other energy requirements.

In addition to incorporating renewable energy technologies, these homes are highly energy efficient. They utilize advanced insulation, efficient HVAC systems, energy-saving appliances, and smart meters to minimize energy consumption. This not only reduces greenhouse gas emissions but also results in lower energy bills for the homeowners.

Furthermore, net-zero carbon footprint homes focus on sustainable water management. They implement rainwater harvesting, greywater recycling, and efficient water fixtures to reduce water consumption and promote water conservation.

Overall, net-zero carbon footprint homes are designed to minimize their ecological footprint and contribute to the long-term sustainability of the planet. By generating clean energy and reducing energy consumption, they play a crucial role in mitigating climate change and reducing dependency on fossil fuels.

Net-Zero Energy Buildings

A net-zero energy building, also known as a zero-energy building or ZEB, is a sustainable structure that produces as much energy as it consumes over the course of a year. This type of building aims to achieve a balance between energy consumption and energy production, resulting in a net-zero energy usage.

Net-zero energy buildings are designed to minimize energy consumption through various strategies, including high levels of insulation, energy-efficient lighting and appliances, and advanced HVAC systems. These buildings also integrate renewable energy systems, such as solar panels or wind turbines, to generate clean and renewable energy on-site.

Net-Zero Energy Museums

A net-zero energy museum is a type of museum that is designed and operated to produce as much energy as it consumes on an annual basis, resulting in a net-zero energy balance. This means that the total amount of energy generated by the museum's renewable energy sources, such as solar panels or wind turbines, is equal to or greater than the total amount of energy used by the museum for its operations, including lighting, HVAC systems, and other electrical equipment.

Net-zero energy museums are a sustainable solution for the cultural sector, as they significantly reduce their carbon footprint and dependence on traditional energy sources. By harnessing renewable energy, these museums contribute to the mitigation of climate change and the preservation of natural resources. They serve as innovative and educational spaces that promote environmental awareness and sustainable practices, inspiring visitors to adopt similar energy-efficient strategies in their own lives.

Net-Zero Energy School Buildings

A net-zero energy school building is a sustainable and energy-efficient facility that produces as much energy as it consumes on an annual basis. This type of building is designed to reduce its environmental impact and reliance on fossil fuels by utilizing renewable energy sources and implementing energy-efficient technologies and practices.

Net-zero energy school buildings are characterized by their ability to generate energy on-site through the use of renewable energy systems such as solar panels, wind turbines, or geothermal heat pumps. These systems capture and convert energy from the natural environment into electricity or thermal energy, providing power and heating/cooling for the building.

In addition to energy generation, net-zero energy school buildings also focus on energy conservation. They incorporate various design strategies and technologies to minimize energy consumption, including proper insulation, high-performance windows, efficient lighting systems, and advanced HVAC systems. Furthermore, these buildings often employ smart energy management systems to monitor and optimize energy usage in real-time.

The net-zero energy concept goes beyond energy performance and extends to other sustainability aspects as well. These buildings frequently incorporate sustainable materials, such as recycled or locally sourced materials, and prioritize efficient water usage through features like rainwater harvesting and water-efficient fixtures.

By achieving a net-zero energy balance, these school buildings play a crucial role in reducing greenhouse gas emissions and combatting climate change, while also serving as educational tools to promote sustainability and environmental stewardship among students and educators.

Net-Zero Energy Schools

Net-zero energy schools are educational institutions that are designed and operated to produce as much energy as they consume on an annual basis, resulting in a neutral impact on the grid. These schools prioritize energy efficiency and renewable energy generation in order to minimize their carbon footprint and promote sustainability. The concept of net-zero energy schools aligns with the broader goal of achieving net-zero energy buildings, which aim to reduce energy consumption through efficient design, insulation, lighting, and HVAC systems. To accomplish this, net-zero energy schools typically integrate advanced technologies such as solar panels, wind turbines, geothermal systems, and energy storage solutions. In addition to minimizing their environmental impact, net-zero energy schools provide a number of benefits. These schools serve as educational tools, allowing students to learn about energy conservation, renewable energy, and sustainable practices. By incorporating renewable energy systems into the curriculum, students gain a practical understanding of energy consumption, production, and the potential for positive change. Net-zero energy schools also contribute to cost savings by reducing energy bills and the reliance on non-renewable sources of energy. Over time, the initial investment in energy-efficient infrastructure can be recouped through reduced energy expenses. These schools serve as examples of sustainable practices for the community, inspiring others to adopt environmentally friendly measures. In conclusion, net-zero energy schools are educational institutions that prioritize energy efficiency and renewable energy generation, seeking to produce as much energy as they consume. By implementing sustainable practices, these schools reduce their environmental impact, provide hands-on learning experiences for students, and inspire the broader community to embrace sustainable living.>

Ocean Conservancy

The Ocean Conservancy is a non-profit organization that works towards achieving sustainable use and conservation of the world's oceans. With a focus on addressing environmental threats and promoting ocean health, the organization engages in various initiatives and campaigns to protect marine ecosystems and support the communities that rely on them.

Through research, advocacy, and partnerships, the Ocean Conservancy aims to address critical challenges such as marine pollution, overfishing, and habitat destruction. The organization advocates for the implementation of science-based policies and collaborates with governments, businesses, and individuals to promote sustainable practices and drive positive change.

Ocean Cleanup Technology

Ocean cleanup technology refers to the methods and techniques aimed at removing and reducing marine debris and pollution from the Earth's oceans. It involves the development and implementation of various tools, systems, and strategies designed to address the growing issue of ocean pollution caused by human activities.

This technology focuses on the removal of different types of marine debris, including plastics, discarded fishing gear, chemical pollutants, and oil spills, among others. It aims to prevent the detrimental effects of this pollution on marine ecosystems and biodiversity, as well as on human health and well-being.

Ocean cleanup technology typically encompasses a range of approaches, including the use of specialized vessels and machinery to collect and remove debris from the water, the development of innovative waste management systems to properly dispose of the collected materials, and the implementation of educational and awareness programs to promote behavior change and prevent further pollution.

The sustainability aspect of ocean cleanup technology lies in its ability to mitigate the negative impacts of marine pollution, preserve the integrity of delicate marine ecosystems, and contribute to the sustainable use and conservation of ocean resources. By removing pollutants from the oceans, this technology helps protect marine life, maintain biodiversity, and support the long-term viability of industries that depend on clean and healthy oceans, such as fisheries and tourism.

Ocean Pollution Tracking Systems

Ocean pollution tracking systems are sustainability tools designed to monitor and analyze the presence and spread of pollutants in oceanic ecosystems. These systems incorporate various technologies and methodologies to collect, process, and interpret data related to different types of pollutants, including plastic waste, chemical spills, oil leaks, and sewage discharge. By tracking and mapping the locations and movements of pollution sources, these systems enable policymakers, scientists, and environmental organizations to assess the extent of contamination, identify areas of high risk, and make informed decisions on mitigation and remediation strategies.

Ocean pollution tracking systems utilize a combination of remote sensing technologies, such as satellites and airborne sensors, as well as in-situ monitoring devices, such as buoys, floats, and autonomous underwater vehicles. These technologies enable the collection of real-time or near-real-time data on water quality parameters, pollutant concentrations, and waste accumulation patterns. The collected data is then processed and analyzed using advanced algorithms and modeling techniques to derive meaningful insights and actionable information.

The main objectives of ocean pollution tracking systems are to understand the sources and pathways of pollutants, assess their impacts on marine ecosystems and human health, and facilitate effective management and conservation strategies. By identifying pollution hotspots, these systems can assist in the enforcement of environmental regulations and the prioritization of cleanup efforts. Furthermore, the data generated by these systems can contribute to scientific research, helping to advance our understanding of the long-term effects of pollution on marine biodiversity and ecosystem resilience.

In summary, ocean pollution tracking systems play a crucial role in promoting sustainability by providing essential data and insights for informed decision-making, pollution control, and the protection of marine ecosystems.>

Ocean Thermal Energy Conversion

Ocean thermal energy conversion (OTEC) is a sustainable method of generating electricity by harnessing the temperature difference between warm surface seawater and cold deep seawater. This renewable energy technology taps into the vast thermal energy stored in the world's oceans to produce clean and reliable power.

In an OTEC system, warm surface water is used to vaporize a working fluid with a low boiling point, such as ammonia or refrigerants. The resulting vapor drives a turbine and generates electricity. The now-cooled working fluid is then condensed using cold deep seawater, which absorbs the heat and returns to the surface to repeat the cycle.

OTEC has several sustainability benefits. Firstly, it eliminates the need for fossil fuels, reducing greenhouse gas emissions and air pollution associated with traditional power generation methods. Secondly, the energy source, the temperature difference in the ocean, is renewable and virtually limitless. The Earth's oceans retain an enormous amount of thermal energy that can be continuously utilized without depletion. Thirdly, OTEC has the potential to provide electricity to coastal areas with high energy demand, reducing dependence on distant power grids and increasing energy independence.

Despite its potential, OTEC is still in the early stages of development and faces technical and economic challenges. The construction and maintenance of OTEC plants can be costly, and the technology requires specific ocean conditions to be efficient. However, ongoing research and advancements in OTEC systems hold promise for its future deployment as a sustainable and clean energy solution.

Off-Grid Home Design

An off-grid home design refers to a sustainable residential building that is completely independent of a centralized power grid and other public utilities. It is designed to generate its own energy, manage its own waste, and conserve resources.

Off-grid homes usually incorporate renewable energy sources such as solar panels, wind turbines, or geothermal systems to create clean, green, and reliable power. These systems typically store excess energy in batteries for use during periods of low or no energy production. This allows the home to remain powered even when there is no access to conventional electricity sources.

In addition to energy production, off-grid home designs focus on minimizing energy consumption through various architectural and technological solutions. These include efficient insulation, passive solar design, energy-efficient appliances, LED lighting, and smart energy management systems. By reducing energy demand, off-grid homes can meet their energy needs with smaller renewable energy systems, making them more cost-effective and environmentally friendly.

Off-grid homes also prioritize water conservation and management. This may involve implementing rainwater harvesting systems, greywater recycling, and water-efficient fixtures. Some designs even incorporate wastewater treatment systems to minimize the environmental impact of waste disposal.

Overall, off-grid home designs aim to create self-sufficient and sustainable living spaces that minimize reliance on centralized utilities, reduce carbon footprint, and promote environmental stewardship.

Off-Grid Renewable Energy Systems

Off-grid renewable energy systems refer to sustainable energy solutions that are not connected to a centralized power grid. These systems utilize renewable energy sources such as solar, wind, hydro, or biomass to generate electricity and meet the energy needs of a specific location or community.

Unlike traditional energy systems that rely on fossil fuels and are often associated with environmental degradation and finite resources, off-grid renewable energy systems offer a sustainable alternative. They harness the natural energy provided by the sun, wind, or water, which are replenished naturally and indefinitely. By using renewable sources, these systems contribute to reducing greenhouse gas emissions, mitigating climate change, and promoting a more sustainable future.

Off-Grid Sustainable Housing

Off-grid sustainable housing refers to a type of residential dwelling that functions independently from the utility grid, relying on self-produced energy sources and sustainable practices to meet its inhabitants' needs. This housing model aims to minimize its ecological footprint, prioritize energy efficiency, and promote self-sufficiency.

Off-grid sustainable housing typically incorporates renewable energy systems such as solar panels, wind turbines, or hydropower to generate electricity. These energy sources allow the dwelling to meet its power demands without relying on fossil fuel-based energy. Additionally, sustainable housing often integrates features like passive solar design, enhanced insulation, and energy-efficient appliances to minimize energy consumption.

Water conservation and self-sufficiency are also integral aspects of off-grid sustainable housing. These dwellings may employ rainwater harvesting techniques, greywater recycling systems, or innovative wastewater treatment solutions to reduce water consumption and promote responsible water management. Waste reduction and recycling practices are often emphasized as well.

Furthermore, off-grid sustainable housing strives to blend harmoniously with the natural environment. It may utilize eco-friendly construction materials, like reclaimed wood or recycled materials, and design principles that minimize habitat disruption and promote biodiversity. Additionally, sustainable landscaping practices, such as native plantings and water-wise irrigation systems, are often employed to create a symbiotic relationship with the surrounding ecosystems.

The ultimate goal of off-grid sustainable housing is to create living spaces that are self-sufficient, environmentally friendly, and in balance with nature. By reducing reliance on non-renewable resources, minimizing waste, and embracing sustainable practices, this housing model contributes to the long-term well-being of both individuals and the planet as a whole.

Off-Grid Waste Management

Off-grid waste management refers to the sustainable and environmentally-friendly practices and technologies used to handle and dispose of waste in areas that are not connected to the traditional power grid or municipal waste management systems.

In off-grid settings, such as remote communities, rural areas, or off-grid homes, waste management becomes a crucial aspect of maintaining a clean and healthy environment. Without access to the centralized waste management infrastructure, off-grid waste management focuses on minimizing waste generation, utilizing renewable energy sources, and employing innovative methods to treat, reuse, recycle, or dispose of waste materials.

One of the key principles of off-grid waste management is to reduce waste generation at the source. This involves promoting the use of reusable products, encouraging composting of organic waste for nutrient-rich soil, and raising awareness about sustainable consumption patterns. Additionally, off-grid waste management often incorporates decentralized waste treatment technologies, such as anaerobic digesters, which convert organic waste into biogas and fertilizers. This not only reduces the amount of waste sent to landfills but also produces renewable energy for heating or cooking purposes.

Furthermore, off-grid waste management aims to promote recycling and reuse practices to minimize the extraction of raw materials and reduce the environmental impact of waste disposal. This includes establishing recycling programs, supporting local artisans who create products from recycled materials, and encouraging the repair and repurposing of items.

By implementing off-grid waste management strategies, communities and households can significantly reduce their ecological footprint, conserve resources, protect ecosystems, and promote sustainable development. These practices contribute to a cleaner and healthier environment, while also fostering resilience and self-sufficiency in communities that are disconnected from traditional waste management systems.

Off-Grid Wastewater Treatment Solutions

Off-grid wastewater treatment solutions refer to sustainable methods of treating and recycling wastewater in areas that are not connected to a central sewer system. These solutions are designed to minimize environmental impact, conserve resources, and provide safe and sanitary disposal of wastewater without relying on external infrastructure.

Off-grid wastewater treatment solutions typically involve the use of decentralized systems that can be implemented in various settings, including rural areas, remote communities, and off-grid facilities such as campsites or eco-resorts. These systems aim to remove contaminants and pollutants from wastewater, making it safe for reuse or release back into the environment.

There are several technologies and approaches used in off-grid wastewater treatment, depending on factors such as available space, water usage, and local regulations. Common methods include septic systems, constructed wetlands, and advanced treatment systems such as membrane bioreactors or aerobic digestion.

These solutions are sustainable as they address multiple aspects of environmental and social responsibility. By treating wastewater locally, off-grid systems reduce the need for long-distance transportation of waste and minimize the energy and resources required for centralized treatment plants. They also promote water conservation by reusing treated water for non-potable purposes, such as irrigation or toilet flushing.

Off-Grid Wastewater Treatment

Off-grid wastewater treatment refers to a sustainable method of managing and purifying wastewater in areas that are not connected to a centralized sewer system or where conventional treatment options are limited. This approach is essential for promoting environmental sustainability by reducing water pollution and conserving precious freshwater resources.

Off-grid wastewater treatment systems typically utilize a combination of physical, biological, and chemical processes to remove contaminants, pathogens, and pollutants from wastewater, making it safe for reuse or discharge into the environment. These systems may involve various components, such as septic tanks, anaerobic digesters, constructed wetlands, sand filters, and disinfection units, depending on the specific requirements and the desired level of treatment.

The main objective of off-grid wastewater treatment is to minimize the ecological footprint associated with wastewater disposal and protect the local ecosystem and public health. By treating wastewater on-site, this approach eliminates the need for long-distance transport of wastewater and reduces the energy consumption and greenhouse gas emissions associated with conventional centralized treatment methods. It also reduces the dependency on freshwater sources for flushing toilets or irrigating gardens, as purified wastewater can be reused for non-potable purposes like irrigation, industrial processes, and toilet flushing.

Off-grid wastewater treatment plays a crucial role in promoting sustainable development, particularly in rural and remote areas, eco-friendly resorts, disaster-stricken regions, and off-grid communities. By implementing these decentralized systems, we can ensure responsible wastewater management, minimize pollution, and support the long-term well-being of both human populations and the environment.

Off-Grid Water Purification Design

An off-grid water purification design refers to a system that enables sustainable and independent water treatment and purification without relying on external sources of energy or infrastructure. This design aims to address the need for clean and safe drinking water, especially in remote locations or areas with limited access to utilities. It promotes self-sufficiency and minimizes reliance on traditional water purification methods that may be costly, energy-intensive, or environmentally harmful.

Off-grid water purification designs typically involve the use of renewable energy sources, such as solar power or wind power, to generate the necessary electricity for the purification process. These designs often incorporate innovative technologies and treatment processes that are energy-efficient and environmentally friendly. Advanced filtration systems, such as activated carbon filters or membrane filtration, are commonly employed to remove contaminants and impurities from water sources.

Off-Grid Water Purification Systems

Off-grid water purification systems are sustainable technologies that provide communities or individuals with access to clean drinking water without reliance on traditional water sources or infrastructure. These systems are designed to operate independently from the power grid and are typically self-sustaining, making them ideal for remote or underserved areas where access to clean water is limited.

Off-grid water purification systems utilize various methods to treat and purify water from natural sources such as rivers, lakes, or wells. These methods often include filtration, disinfection, and desalination processes, depending on the water source and its specific contaminants. These systems are designed for long-term use and can withstand harsh environmental conditions, ensuring continuous access to safe and clean drinking water.

Organic Farming Certification

Organic farming certification is a formal recognition given to agricultural practices that meet specific sustainability criteria outlined by authoritative bodies. It serves as an assurance to consumers that the food and other agricultural products they purchase are produced in an environmentally responsible manner, with minimal harm to ecosystems and human health.

Organic farming certification ensures that farmers adhere to strict guidelines that prohibit the use of synthetic fertilizers, pesticides, antibiotics, and genetically modified organisms (GMOs) in their farming operations. Instead, organic farmers employ practices that aim to foster soil health, conserve water resources, protect biodiversity, and promote animal welfare. These practices include crop rotation, composting, natural pest control, and humane animal treatment.

Organic Food Cooperatives

An organic food cooperative is a sustainable agricultural system that promotes and supports the production and distribution of organic food. It is a collaborative organization where consumers and producers work together to create a more environmentally friendly and socially responsible food system.

Organic food cooperatives prioritize the use of natural resources, minimize environmental impact, and prioritize the health and well-being of consumers. They encourage the use of organic farming practices that promote biodiversity, limit the use of synthetic pesticides and fertilizers, and enhance soil health. By supporting local and regional food systems, organic food cooperatives reduce the carbon footprint associated with long-distance transportation and contribute to the economic vitality of their communities.

Organic Photovoltaic Cells (OPVs)

Organic photovoltaic cells (OPVs) are sustainable devices that convert sunlight into electricity using organic molecules. Unlike traditional solar cells made from inorganic materials, OPVs are lightweight, flexible, and can be manufactured at a lower cost.

OPVs consist of thin layers of organic semiconductors, which absorb photons from sunlight and generate free electrons and positive charges. These charges are then separated and collected at different electrodes to create an electric current. The organic materials used in OPVs are typically carbon-based polymers or small molecules that have specific optical and electronic properties.

The sustainability aspect of OPVs lies in their production, usage, and disposal. Firstly, the manufacturing process of OPVs requires fewer resources and less energy compared to

229

traditional solar cell production. The use of organic materials also reduces the reliance on scarce and environmentally harmful elements, such as silicon or rare earth metals.

Secondly, OPVs offer advantages in terms of versatility and flexibility. They can be easily integrated into various objects and surfaces, enabling the generation of electricity from unconventional sources, such as windows, clothing, or even smartphone screens. This flexibility opens up new opportunities for renewable energy generation in urban environments and reduces the need for dedicated solar panel installations.

Lastly, OPVs are potentially recyclable due to their organic components. Unlike inorganic solar cells, which often involve complex and energy-intensive recycling processes, OPVs can be broken down and repurposed with relative ease. This promotes a circular economy approach to renewable energy technologies.

Organic Waste-To-Compost Technology

Organic waste-to-compost technology refers to the process of converting organic waste materials, such as food scraps, yard trimmings, and agricultural residues, into compost through a sustainable and environmentally friendly approach. This technology aims to divert organic waste from landfills and incinerators, reducing methane emissions and conserving natural resources.

The process typically involves collecting and sorting organic waste materials, which are then transported to a composting facility. At the facility, the waste undergoes a series of controlled decomposition processes, facilitated by microorganisms, heat, and oxygen. These processes break down the organic materials, resulting in the formation of compost.

Composting is a natural process that mimics the decomposition of organic matter in nature. By utilizing organic waste-to-compost technology, valuable nutrients from the organic waste are retained in the compost and can be used to enrich soil quality, enhance plant growth, and reduce the need for synthetic fertilizers.

This technology aligns with the principles of sustainability by addressing several environmental concerns. Firstly, it helps reduce greenhouse gas emissions, particularly methane, which is a potent contributor to climate change. By diverting organic waste from landfills, where it would decompose anaerobically and release methane, the technology significantly reduces the carbon footprint associated with waste management.

Secondly, the use of compost produced through organic waste-to-compost technology contributes to sustainable agriculture and landscaping. Compost improves soil structure and water retention, reduces erosion, and promotes the growth of healthy plants, ultimately reducing the need for chemical pesticides and fertilizers. This reduces the risk of water contamination and the negative effects on biodiversity normally associated with chemical usage.

In summary, organic waste-to-compost technology represents a sustainable solution for managing organic waste by converting it into a valuable resource. By reducing greenhouse gas emissions and promoting sustainable agriculture, this technology plays a crucial role in the transition towards a more resilient and ecologically responsible society.

Passive Cooling Techniques

Passive cooling techniques refer to sustainable methods used to cool a building or space without the need for mechanical systems or active energy consumption. These techniques take advantage of natural resources and environmental conditions to maintain a comfortable indoor temperature, reducing the reliance on artificial cooling systems and consequently lowering energy consumption and greenhouse gas emissions.

Passive cooling techniques employ various strategies to minimize heat gain and maximize heat dissipation. This includes the use of building orientation and design, natural ventilation, shading elements, thermal insulation, and thermal mass. Building orientation ensures that the structure is aligned properly to optimize the use of natural air movements and solar radiation. Natural ventilation is achieved through carefully placed windows, vents, and openings, allowing fresh air to circulate and remove stale air, thus reducing the need for air conditioning.

Shading elements, such as awnings, canopies, and vegetation, provide protection from direct sunlight and reduce heat gain. Thermal insulation materials are used to prevent heat transfer between the indoor and outdoor environment, thereby maintaining a more stable and comfortable temperature inside the building. Thermal mass materials possess the ability to absorb, store, and release heat, helping to regulate temperature fluctuations.

The adoption of passive cooling techniques contributes to sustainability by reducing the energy demand associated with mechanical cooling systems, conserving natural resources, and minimizing carbon emissions. It also promotes a healthier indoor environment by enhancing natural ventilation, reducing humidity, and preventing the accumulation of pollutants. By incorporating these techniques into building designs, both residential and commercial spaces can achieve significant energy savings, enhance occupant comfort, and contribute to a more environmentally friendly future.

Passive House Design

A passive house is a design approach that aims to significantly reduce the energy consumption of a building, while providing a comfortable and healthy living environment for its occupants. It is a sustainable building design strategy that focuses on energy efficiency, thermal insulation, and airtightness to achieve its goals.

In a passive house design, various strategies are implemented to minimize energy loss and maximize energy gains. These strategies include a highly insulated building envelope, airtight construction, energy-efficient windows and doors, and controlled ventilation systems. The goal is to create a building that requires very little energy for heating, cooling, and overall operation.

Passive house designs rely on passive solar design principles, taking advantage of natural sources of heat and light. This includes optimizing the building's orientation and utilizing appropriately sized and positioned windows to allow for solar heat gain during the winter months, while minimizing overheating during the summer.

Furthermore, passive house designs prioritize high indoor air quality by incorporating mechanical ventilation systems with efficient heat recovery. This ensures a constant supply of fresh air and removes pollutants from the indoor environment.

By incorporating these sustainable design strategies, passive houses reduce the reliance on fossil fuels and decrease greenhouse gas emissions associated with traditional buildings. They contribute to a more sustainable built environment by reducing energy consumption, promoting natural resource conservation, and improving the overall quality of living spaces.

Passive Solar Building Layouts

Passive solar building layouts refer to the design and arrangement of a building to maximize the use of sunlight for heating and lighting purposes, while minimizing the need for artificial energy sources. This sustainable approach takes into account the orientation, placement, and layout of a building in relation to the sun's path throughout the day and the changing seasons.

Passive solar building layouts typically involve specific architectural features and design strategies. South-facing windows are positioned to capture the most sunlight, allowing the building to benefit from natural light and passive solar heat gain. Thermal mass, such as dense materials like concrete or stone, is strategically placed to absorb and store heat from the sun during the day and release it slowly during the cooler periods, helping to maintain a comfortable indoor temperature.

Passive Solar Building Materials

Passive solar building materials refer to construction materials and design elements that harness and maximize the use of solar energy for heating, cooling, and lighting a building, without the need for active mechanical systems. These materials are an essential component of sustainable building practices as they allow for reduced dependence on non-renewable energy sources, minimizing the building's environmental impact and improving energy efficiency.

Passive solar building materials are carefully selected based on their ability to absorb, store, and distribute heat efficiently. They utilize the principles of solar gain, thermal mass, and natural ventilation to regulate indoor temperatures. Materials such as concrete, stone, and water feature high thermal mass, allowing them to absorb and retain solar heat during the day before releasing it gradually when temperatures drop. This natural heat regulation reduces the need for artificial heating systems, thereby decreasing energy consumption and reliance on fossil fuels.

In addition to thermal mass, passive solar building materials commonly include high-performance windows with insulated glazing to optimize natural light while minimizing heat loss or gain. These windows are strategically positioned to capture maximum sunlight during the colder months while providing shading during the summer, further enhancing energy efficiency. Thicker insulation materials, such as straw bales or recycled cellulose, are often incorporated into walls and roofs to reduce heat transfer and improve insulation value.

In conclusion, passive solar building materials play a vital role in sustainable construction by harnessing and optimizing the power of natural sunlight for heating, cooling, and lighting. By reducing reliance on non-renewable energy sources and minimizing energy consumption, these materials contribute to a more eco-friendly and energy-efficient built environment.

Passive Solar Building Orientation

Passive solar building orientation refers to the strategic positioning of a building in relation to the sun's path in order to optimize energy efficiency and reduce dependence on artificial heating and cooling systems. It is a sustainable design approach that takes advantage of the sun's natural energy to provide thermal comfort and minimize the building's environmental impact.

The orientation of a passive solar building is based on the principles of solar gain and shading. By aligning the building's windows and walls to face the sun's path, it allows for maximum solar gain during the winter months when the sun is low in the sky. This direct exposure to sunlight helps to heat the building, reducing the need for mechanical heating systems and lowering energy consumption. South-facing windows are particularly important in capturing the most sunlight throughout the day.

On the other hand, passive solar building orientation also considers the need for shading during the hot summer months. By incorporating elements such as overhangs, awnings, or trees, the building can block the direct sunlight and prevent overheating. This shading technique helps to maintain a comfortable indoor temperature and reduces reliance on air conditioning systems, decreasing energy demand and greenhouse gas emissions.

Overall, passive solar building orientation is a sustainable design practice that maximizes energy efficiency, reduces reliance on artificial heating and cooling systems, and minimizes the ecological footprint of buildings. By designing and positioning buildings in a way that optimizes solar gain and shading, we can create environmentally friendly structures that promote a more sustainable future.

Passive Solar Design

Passive solar design is a sustainable architectural approach that harnesses the energy from the sun to minimize the need for artificial heating, cooling, and lighting in buildings. It utilizes the natural elements of sunlight, air, and thermal mass to create a comfortable living environment while minimizing the reliance on non-renewable energy sources.

This design strategy focuses on orienting and designing buildings in a way that maximizes solar gain during the winter months and reduces solar heat gain during the summer months. Important factors in passive solar design include the building's orientation, window placement and size, insulation, and the use of thermal mass materials.

Passive Solar Heating

Passive solar heating is a sustainable approach that utilizes the energy from sunlight to heat

232

homes and buildings without the need for mechanical systems or external power sources. It is a passive technique that takes advantage of the natural properties of materials to capture, store, and distribute solar heat effectively.

This method harnesses the sun's energy through the strategic design and orientation of the structure, as well as the use of materials with specific thermal properties. The building's design aims to optimize the intake of solar radiation during the winter months while minimizing heat gain during the summer. This approach helps maintain a comfortable indoor temperature, reducing the need for heating or cooling appliances, resulting in energy and cost savings.

The primary components of passive solar heating include the placement and size of windows, thermal mass materials, insulation, and ventilation systems. South-facing windows are typically larger to allow more sunlight into the building, while north-facing windows are smaller to minimize heat loss. Thermal mass materials, such as concrete or brick, absorb and store solar heat during the day, then release it slowly at night, stabilizing indoor temperatures.

Proper insulation and airtightness are crucial to prevent heat loss and maintain a consistent indoor climate. Ventilation systems, such as vents and fans, facilitate air movement to distribute heat evenly throughout the building. Additionally, shading devices like overhangs or awnings can be employed to block excessive sunlight during summertime.

Passive solar heating plays a vital role in achieving sustainability goals by reducing greenhouse gas emissions and dependence on fossil fuel-based heating systems. It is a passive and renewable energy solution that minimizes environmental impact while maximizing comfort and energy efficiency.

Permaculture Garden Design

Permaculture garden design is a sustainable approach to gardening that integrates natural ecosystems and regenerative practices to create a self-sufficient and resilient system. It is an ecological design framework that aims to mimic the patterns and processes found in nature to create productive and harmonious gardens.

At its core, permaculture garden design focuses on maximizing the use of resources, minimizing waste, and promoting biodiversity. It follows the principles of sustainability by using renewable resources, reducing reliance on external inputs, and enhancing the overall health of the ecosystem.

Permaculture Garden Layouts

A permaculture garden layout refers to the design and arrangement of plants, structures, and systems within a garden, following the principles of permaculture. Permaculture is an approach to sustainable agriculture and land use that aims to create ecosystems that are self-sustaining and have minimal impact on the environment.

In a permaculture garden layout, the design takes into account various factors such as climate, soil conditions, and available resources. The layout is planned in a way that maximizes the use of space and promotes beneficial relationships between different elements of the garden.

The key principles of permaculture, such as observing and interacting with nature, using renewable resources, and valuing diversity, are applied in the design process. The layout often incorporates different types of gardens, including vegetable beds, fruit trees, and herb gardens, as well as areas for composting, water harvesting, and wildlife habitats.

By carefully considering the elements and interactions within the garden, a permaculture layout aims to create a productive and resilient ecosystem. It seeks to minimize the need for external inputs such as fertilizers and pesticides, and to create a closed-loop system where waste is turned into resources. The goal is to create a sustainable and regenerative environment that can provide for the needs of humans while supporting biodiversity and conserving natural resources.

Permaculture Practices

Permaculture practices are sustainable farming and gardening methods that aim to create productive, self-sufficient, and resilient systems by imitating natural ecosystems. It is an integrated design approach that emphasizes the interconnections between plants, animals, people, and the environment.

In permaculture, the design and management of the system are based on three core ethics: Earth Care, People Care, and Fair Share. These ethics guide the implementation of various permaculture principles, such as observation, diversity, and integration, to create regenerative and sustainable systems.

The key principles of permaculture include:

1. Observation and Interaction: Careful observation of natural patterns and processes to inform design decisions and interactions within the system.

2. Catch and Store Energy: Efficiently capture and store energy from natural resources, such as sunlight, water, and wind, to meet the system's needs and reduce external inputs.

3. Obtain a Yield: Achieve productive outputs from the system while ensuring long-term sustainability and resilience.

4. Apply Self-Regulation and Accept Feedback: Continuously monitor and adapt the system based on feedback to maintain balance and sustainability.

5. Use and Value Renewable Resources and Services: Prioritize the use of renewable resources and ecosystem services to minimize environmental impact.

Permaculture practices include techniques such as organic gardening, agroforestry, companion planting, water harvesting, soil regeneration, and natural pest management. By applying these practices, permaculturists aim to create ecosystems that are abundant, diverse, and self-sustaining, while contributing to the overall health of the planet and the well-being of its inhabitants.

Permeable Concrete

Permeable concrete is an innovative and sustainable paving material that allows water to pass through its surface and infiltrate the soil beneath. Unlike traditional concrete, which is impermeable and causes rainwater to runoff, permeable concrete helps to manage stormwater runoff and mitigate flooding.

This eco-friendly alternative is designed with a network of interconnected voids or pores, which enable water to rapidly drain through the pavement and be naturally filtered as it percolates through the ground. The porous structure of permeable concrete promotes groundwater recharge, reduces the burden on stormwater systems, and improves water quality by removing pollutants and sediments.

Permeable Pavement Design

Permeable pavement design is a sustainable solution for paving surfaces that allows water to naturally infiltrate and recharge the underlying soil. It is a technique that promotes stormwater management, reduces runoff and pollutants, and helps combat issues related to urbanization and climate change.

By using permeable materials, such as pervious concrete, porous asphalt, or interlocking pavers, permeable pavement design allows water to gradually seep through the surface and into the ground. This minimizes the amount of stormwater runoff that would otherwise flow into storm drains, causing flooding and overwhelming the existing infrastructure.

Permeable Pavement Layouts

Permeable pavement layouts refer to the design and arrangement of pavement surfaces that are specifically designed to allow the movement of water through their surface and into the underlying soil or drainage system. This type of paving system is chosen for its sustainability benefits as it helps mitigate stormwater runoff, reduce the strain on conventional stormwater infrastructure, and promote groundwater recharge.

Permeable pavement layouts typically consist of a combination of porous and permeable materials such as pervious concrete, porous asphalt, or interlocking pavers. These materials are specifically chosen for their ability to allow water to pass through, either through the surface itself or through gaps between the pavers. The layout of these materials is planned in such a way that it maximizes water infiltration, ensuring that it is absorbed by the soil and replenishes the groundwater instead of being directed to storm drains.

Permeable Pavement Systems

Permeable pavement systems are sustainable infrastructure solutions designed to manage stormwater runoff while minimizing the negative impacts of urban development on the environment. These systems are specifically engineered to allow water to infiltrate into the ground rather than being carried away by traditional stormwater drainage systems.

The main objective of permeable pavement systems is to reduce the volume and velocity of stormwater runoff, thus decreasing the risk of flooding, erosion, and pollution in urban areas. By allowing water to permeate through the pavement surface, these systems promote groundwater recharge, improve water quality, and alleviate strain on stormwater management infrastructure.

Perovskite Solar Cells

Perovskite solar cells are a type of photovoltaic device that have gained significant attention in the field of sustainable energy due to their potential to revolutionize solar power generation. These cells are constructed using a crystalline structure inspired by the mineral perovskite, which enables them to efficiently convert sunlight into electricity.

One of the key advantages of perovskite solar cells is their low production cost and ease of manufacturing. Unlike traditional solar cells, which require expensive and complex processes, perovskite solar cells can be produced using relatively simple and inexpensive methods such as solution processing or vapor deposition. This makes them highly attractive from a sustainability standpoint, as it reduces the environmental impact associated with the production of solar panels.

In addition to their lower production cost, perovskite solar cells also exhibit excellent power conversion efficiency. Recent advancements have pushed the efficiency of these cells to over 25%, surpassing the performance of some commercially available solar technologies. Higher efficiency means that perovskite solar cells can generate more electricity from the same amount of sunlight, making them more suitable for large-scale solar power installations and further contributing to the goal of sustainability.

However, perovskite solar cells do face some challenges to overcome before widespread commercialization. They are highly sensitive to moisture and tend to degrade over time. Researchers are actively working on developing protective coatings and encapsulation techniques to enhance their stability and make them more durable.

In conclusion, perovskite solar cells have the potential to play a significant role in the transition to renewable energy sources. Their low production cost, high efficiency, and ongoing research efforts to improve their stability make them an attractive option for a sustainable and clean energy future.

Personal Electric Aircraft

A personal electric aircraft is an environmentally-friendly aerial vehicle that operates on electric propulsion systems and is designed to transport a small number of passengers or cargo.

With a focus on sustainability, personal electric aircrafts aim to reduce carbon emissions and noise pollution compared to traditional aircrafts that rely on fossil fuels. By utilizing electric motors, these aircrafts eliminate the need for traditional combustion engines, resulting in significantly reduced emissions of greenhouse gases and other pollutants.

Phytoremediation

Phytoremediation is a sustainable approach to addressing environmental pollution by using plants to remove, degrade, or immobilize contaminants in soil, water, and air. It is a cost-effective and eco-friendly method that takes advantage of the natural abilities of certain plants to absorb and break down pollutants.

Through phytoremediation, plants can remove heavy metals, organic compounds, and other harmful substances from contaminated sites, reducing the risk of human exposure and improving the overall health of ecosystems. This process involves various mechanisms, including phytoextraction, phytodegradation, phytostabilization, and rhizofiltration.

Phytoextraction involves plants absorbing contaminants from the soil or water into their roots, which are then transported to the above-ground parts of the plant. Plants with high metal uptake abilities, such as hyperaccumulators, are commonly used for this purpose. Phytodegradation is the breakdown of pollutants through enzymatic or microbial processes within the plant's tissues. Phytostabilization aims to immobilize contaminants, preventing their movement and spread. Rhizofiltration utilizes plants with extensive root systems to filter pollutants from water, effectively purifying it.

Phytoremediation offers numerous advantages over traditional remediation methods, such as excavation and chemical treatments. It is less invasive, requires less energy, and has lower maintenance costs. Additionally, it can be applied in various settings, including industrial sites, landfills, and agricultural areas. Furthermore, phytoremediation promotes the restoration and reclamation of contaminated land, making it suitable for future use or development.

In conclusion, phytoremediation is a sustainable technique that utilizes the natural abilities of plants to remediate environmental pollution. By harnessing the power of nature, phytoremediation offers a viable solution for the cleanup and restoration of contaminated sites, contributing to long-term sustainability and environmental protection.

Product Leasing Models

Product leasing models refer to sustainable business practices where customers have the option to lease products instead of buying them outright. This approach promotes the circular economy, reducing waste and conserving resources by extending the lifespan of products.

Leasing models offer a range of benefits in terms of sustainability. Firstly, they encourage the reuse and repurposing of products, minimizing the need for new production and its associated environmental impact. By leasing instead of purchasing, customers can access high-quality products without contributing to the excessive consumption and disposal of goods.

Product Life Cycle Analysis

A product life cycle analysis refers to a comprehensive examination of the environmental impact of a product throughout its entire lifespan, from raw material extraction to disposal. It is a tool used to assess the sustainability of a product and identify opportunities for improvement in terms of resource efficiency, waste reduction, and overall environmental performance.

The analysis typically consists of four stages: extraction and processing of raw materials, manufacturing and production, distribution and use, and end-of-life disposal. In each stage, the environmental impact is evaluated, including energy consumption, emissions, waste generation, and resource depletion. This analysis helps in understanding the product's ecological footprint and identifying environmental hotspots where improvements can be made.

During the extraction and processing stage, the analysis examines the impact of resource extraction, such as deforestation or mining, and the associated environmental damage. In the manufacturing and production stage, the focus is on energy consumption, emissions, and waste generated during the manufacturing process. The distribution and use stage considers transportation-related emissions and energy consumption by the product during its use phase.

Lastly, the end-of-life stage assesses the disposal and recycling options, as well as potential hazardous waste generation.

Understanding the product life cycle allows companies to make informed decisions regarding the design, production, and disposal of products. It provides insights into where sustainability efforts should be concentrated, such as using renewable materials, optimizing production processes, or implementing recycling programs. By conducting a comprehensive life cycle analysis, businesses can minimize the environmental impact of their products and contribute to a more sustainable future.

Product Life Cycle Assessment

A product life cycle assessment is a method used to evaluate the environmental impacts of a product throughout its entire lifespan, from extraction of raw materials to disposal. It is a tool commonly employed in the field of sustainability to measure the sustainability performance of a product.

The life cycle of a product is typically divided into four stages: extraction of raw materials, production, use, and end-of-life. The assessment takes into account the energy consumption, resource usage, emissions, and waste generation associated with each stage.

In the extraction stage, the assessment looks at the environmental impacts of obtaining the raw materials needed to produce the product, such as mining or agricultural practices. The production stage evaluates the energy and resources utilized in manufacturing the product, as well as the emissions and waste generated during this process.

During the use stage, the assessment assesses the energy consumption and environmental impacts associated with the product's operation or usage. This includes factors such as energy efficiency and emissions during use.

Finally, the end-of-life stage considers the disposal or recycling of the product and examines the environmental impacts of these processes. This stage aims to identify opportunities for waste reduction or recycling to minimize environmental harm.

By conducting a product life cycle assessment, companies and organizations can identify areas for improvement and make informed decisions to reduce the environmental impact of their products. It helps promote sustainable practices and support the development of more eco-friendly products and processes.

Product Life Cycle Optimization

The product life cycle optimization refers to the strategic approach used to enhance the sustainability of a product throughout its entire life cycle. This includes the design, manufacturing, use, and disposal stages of the product. The goal is to minimize environmental impacts, conserve resources, and promote social responsibility.

In the design stage, sustainable materials and technologies are used to reduce energy consumption, waste generation, and emissions. The manufacturing stage focuses on optimizing production processes to minimize resource use, pollution, and the release of hazardous substances. This may involve implementing eco-friendly manufacturing techniques, such as lean manufacturing or clean production methods.

The use phase aims to maximize the energy efficiency of the product, encourage responsible consumption, and extend its lifespan. This can be achieved through energy-efficient designs, user education, and promoting maintenance and repair services. Additionally, the use of renewable energy sources to power the product can contribute to its sustainability.

The end-of-life stage focuses on the proper disposal or recycling of the product. Efforts are made to design products that are easily recyclable or biodegradable to reduce waste and prevent environmental pollution. Implementing take-back programs and encouraging responsible disposal practices are also part of product life cycle optimization.

Overall, product life cycle optimization in the context of sustainability involves a holistic and proactive approach to minimize the environmental, social, and economic impacts of a product throughout its life cycle. It promotes the concept of a circular economy where resources are kept in use for as long as possible, and waste is minimized through recycling and responsible disposal practices.

Product Life Extension

Product life extension refers to the practice of prolonging the lifespan of a product by implementing strategies and actions that reduce its environmental impact and maximize its usefulness and value. This concept is a key component of sustainability, as it aims to minimize resource consumption, waste generation, and pollution throughout a product's lifecycle.

The goal of product life extension is to shift away from the traditional linear model of production and consumption, where products are constantly discarded and replaced, and instead embrace a circular economy approach. This involves implementing various techniques and measures to extend the useful life of products, repair and refurbish them, and enable their reuse. By doing so, the need for manufacturing new products is reduced, and the environmental and social burdens associated with extraction, production, and disposal are diminished.

Product Reconditioning

Product reconditioning is a sustainable process that involves repairing and refurbishing used or damaged products to extend their lifecycle and minimize waste. It is an important aspect of the circular economy, where resources are maximized and waste is minimized.

By reconditioning products, we can reduce the need for new production, which in turn conserves natural resources and reduces the environmental impact associated with manufacturing. This process helps to decrease the demand for raw materials, energy, water, and other resources required for new production. It also reduces the amount of waste generated by disposing of used or damaged products.

Reconditioning involves various steps, including thorough inspection, repair, cleaning, and restoration of products to their original or near-original condition. This process not only extends the lifespan of products but also enhances their value and functionality. Reconditioned products are often sold at a lower price compared to new ones, making them an affordable and sustainable option for consumers.

Moreover, product reconditioning contributes to the creation of job opportunities and stimulates economic growth. It encourages the development of specialized repair and refurbishment industries, requiring skilled technicians and workers. By supporting these industries, we can promote local businesses and contribute to the overall well-being of communities.

In summary, product reconditioning plays a vital role in achieving sustainability goals by reducing waste, conserving resources, and promoting a circular economy. It demonstrates the principle of "reduce, reuse, recycle" and encourages a shift towards more sustainable consumption and production patterns.

Product Recycling Centers

Product recycling centers are facilities that focus on the collection, processing, and disposal of various products with the aim of minimizing waste, conserving resources, and promoting sustainability. These centers play a crucial role in managing the end-of-life phase of products and ensuring that valuable materials are properly recycled or reused instead of being discarded in landfills or incinerated. They serve as centralized locations where individuals and businesses can responsibly dispose of products that have reached the end of their useful life.

At product recycling centers, items such as electronics, batteries, plastics, paper, glass, and metals are accepted and processed through various recycling technologies. These facilities employ state-of-the-art equipment and techniques to sort, separate, and recover valuable materials from the discarded products. The collected materials are then transformed into raw materials or used in the manufacturing of new products, reducing the need for extracting and processing virgin resources.

Product Recycling Facilities

A product recycling facility refers to a specialized establishment that receives, processes, and manages the disposal of different types of products or materials in an environmentally responsible manner. These facilities play a crucial role in promoting sustainability and reducing the negative environmental impacts associated with product waste.

Product recycling facilities typically follow a systematic process to ensure the effective recycling and disposal of products. They may accept various items such as electronics, plastics, glass, paper, metal, and organic waste. Upon arrival, these products are sorted and categorized based on their material composition. The facility employs specialized machinery and manual labor to disassemble and separate different components or materials within each product.

After the initial sorting and separation, the recyclable materials undergo further processing. They are cleaned, shredded, melted, or converted into raw materials that can be used in the manufacturing of new products. For example, plastic bottles may be melted down and transformed into pellets, which can then be used to produce new plastic items. Metals are often melted and purified to be used in various industries, reducing the need for virgin resource extraction.

Aside from recycling, product recycling facilities also handle the disposal of non-recyclable or hazardous materials. These materials are carefully managed to prevent their release into the environment and minimize potential harm. Various methods such as incineration, neutralization, or landfilling may be employed in accordance with regulations and best practices.

In conclusion, product recycling facilities serve as essential infrastructures for promoting sustainability by facilitating the proper recycling and disposal of various products. Through their operations, these facilities contribute to reducing resource consumption, minimizing waste generation, and mitigating environmental impacts, ultimately supporting the transition towards a more sustainable and circular economy.

Product Recycling Incentives

Product recycling incentives refer to the various incentives and rewards provided to individuals, businesses, and communities to encourage them to engage in sustainable recycling practices. These incentives aim to promote the recycling of products as a means to reduce waste, conserve resources, and protect the environment.

Recycling incentives can take various forms, including financial incentives, such as cash rewards, tax credits, or reduced waste management fees for recycling activities. These economic incentives provide individuals and businesses with a tangible benefit for their recycling efforts, motivating them to participate in recycling programs. Additionally, product manufacturers may offer incentives to consumers for recycling their products, such as discounts on future purchases or loyalty rewards.

In addition to economic incentives, recycling programs can also offer educational incentives to raise awareness and promote sustainable behaviors. These may include workshops, training programs, or educational materials that provide information on the importance of recycling and the positive environmental impact it can have.

Furthermore, some communities and organizations may implement recognition incentives, such as awards or certificates, to acknowledge and celebrate the efforts of individuals or businesses that prioritize recycling. These recognition incentives not only encourage participation but also inspire others to adopt sustainable practices.

In conclusion, product recycling incentives aim to motivate individuals, businesses, and communities to engage in sustainable recycling practices by providing them with economic, educational, and recognition-based rewards. By encouraging recycling and reducing waste, these incentives contribute to the broader goal of achieving a more sustainable and environmentally conscious society.

Product Recycling Infrastructure

Product recycling infrastructure refers to the physical facilities, systems, and networks that are put in place to support and enable the proper recycling and disposal of products at the end of their life cycle. This infrastructure is crucial for promoting sustainability by encouraging the reuse, recovery, and recycling of valuable materials from products, thus reducing the demand for virgin resources, conserving energy, and minimizing waste generation.

The product recycling infrastructure includes a range of components and activities. At the core, it involves collection systems that allow consumers and businesses to conveniently and responsibly discard their used products. These collection systems may include designated recycling bins, drop-off points, or even specific programs like take-back initiatives by manufacturers or retailers. Efficient transportation networks are also essential to facilitate the movement of collected products to recycling facilities.

Once collected, the products are processed in recycling facilities, where they are sorted, separated, and prepared for recycling. These facilities employ various technologies and techniques to extract recyclable materials from the products, such as metals, plastics, paper, and glass. The recovered materials are then transformed into new products or used as raw materials in other manufacturing processes. The recycling infrastructure also extends to the market for recycled products, ensuring that there is demand for and utilization of the recycled materials.

A robust product recycling infrastructure is vital for achieving a circular economy, where products are designed, produced, used, and recycled in a closed-loop system. It promotes the principles of reduce, reuse, and recycle by extending the lifespan of products, reducing resource consumption, and minimizing the environmental impact of production and disposal. By investing in and continuously improving this infrastructure, we can enhance the effectiveness and efficiency of recycling systems, contributing to a more sustainable future.

Product Recycling Initiatives

Product recycling initiatives refer to sustainable practices aimed at reducing waste and environmental impact by collecting and repurposing products at the end of their life cycle. These initiatives are designed to divert materials from the waste stream and promote the reuse and recycling of valuable resources.

Through product recycling initiatives, companies and organizations create systems and processes to enable the responsible disposal and recovery of products, preventing them from ending up in landfills or being incinerated. These initiatives often involve the establishment of collection points or programs where consumers can return used products, such as electronic devices, packaging materials, or household items, for proper recycling or refurbishment.

Product recycling initiatives contribute to sustainability by closing the loop in the product life cycle, minimizing resource extraction, and reducing the need for manufacturing new materials. They help conserve energy, reduce greenhouse gas emissions, and preserve natural resources by reusing materials and preventing pollution associated with resource extraction and production.

Furthermore, these initiatives can stimulate the development of a circular economy by promoting the use of recycled materials in the manufacturing process. By incorporating recycled content into new products, companies can reduce their dependence on virgin resources, conserve energy, and lower their carbon footprint.

Product Recycling Technologies

Product recycling technologies refer to the methods and processes used to recover valuable materials from discarded products, with the aim of reducing waste, conserving resources, and promoting sustainability. These technologies play a crucial role in the circular economy, which aims to minimize the linear 'take-make-waste' model of production and consumption.

There are various product recycling technologies available, each suited to different types of products and materials. Mechanical recycling, for instance, involves the physical treatment and sorting of waste materials to produce secondary raw materials that can be used to manufacture new products. This is commonly used for materials like plastics, metals, and paper.

Chemical recycling technologies, on the other hand, involve breaking down complex materials into their basic chemical components, which can then be used to create new products. This method is particularly useful for materials that are difficult or costly to recycle through mechanical means, such as certain plastics.

Additionally, energy recovery technologies can be used to convert non-recyclable waste into energy. This involves processes like incineration or gasification, where the energy content of the waste is harnessed and used for heat or power generation.

Implementing effective product recycling technologies is essential for achieving sustainability goals, as it helps conserve resources, reduce landfill waste, and minimize the carbon footprint associated with resource extraction and production. By recovering valuable materials from discarded products, these technologies contribute to the creation of a more sustainable and circular economy.

Product Redesign

A product redesign in the context of sustainability refers to the process of modifying an existing product in order to improve its environmental performance throughout its lifecycle. This involves evaluating the product's design, materials, manufacturing processes, packaging, use phase, and end-of-life options with the goal of minimizing resource consumption, waste generation, and negative environmental impacts.

The primary objective of a product redesign for sustainability is to enhance the product's overall sustainability profile. This includes reducing its carbon footprint, conserving natural resources, minimizing pollution, and promoting circularity. The redesign may involve incorporating eco-friendly materials, implementing energy-efficient manufacturing processes, optimizing packaging to reduce materials and improve recyclability, and enabling reuse or recycling of the product at its end-of-life.

Additionally, a sustainable product redesign may also consider social and economic aspects. It can aim to enhance user experience, promote fair labor practices, support local communities, and foster affordability and accessibility.

The process of product redesign for sustainability often involves collaboration between designers, engineers, materials specialists, sustainability experts, and other stakeholders. It requires a holistic approach, considering the entire product lifecycle and considering the trade-offs between various environmental, social, and economic considerations.

By implementing a sustainable product redesign, companies can contribute to the transition towards a more sustainable and circular economy, reduce their environmental footprint, align with customer expectations for eco-friendly products, and enhance their brand reputation.

Product Reengineering

Product reengineering in the context of sustainability refers to the process of redesigning and reformulating products with the goal of improving their environmental performance throughout their lifecycle. This approach takes into account the entire product lifecycle, from raw material extraction to disposal, and aims to minimize the negative impact on the environment.

The objective of product reengineering is to create products that are more sustainable by reducing their carbon footprint, minimizing resource consumption, and promoting a circular economy. This involves using materials that are renewable, recyclable, or biodegradable, as well as optimizing energy efficiency and reducing waste generation during manufacturing, distribution, use, and disposal.

Product Reevaluation

A product reevaluation in the context of sustainability refers to a comprehensive assessment of a product's environmental impact and social responsibility throughout its lifecycle. This process involves examining the entire supply chain, from raw material extraction to disposal, with the aim of identifying and implementing measures to minimize negative effects on the environment and society.

During a product reevaluation, key aspects such as resource consumption, greenhouse gas emissions, pollutants released, waste generation, and social implications are considered. The evaluation may also take into account factors such as energy efficiency, recyclability, ethical sourcing, fair trade, and worker welfare.

Product Refurbishing

Product refurbishing refers to the process of restoring or repairing used or damaged products to a like-new condition, with the aim of extending their lifespan and reducing waste. This sustainable practice involves identifying and addressing any defects or malfunctions in the product, as well as cleaning, repainting, and replacing any worn-out components.

By refurbishing products, valuable resources and energy are conserved, as the need for producing new products is reduced. This process aligns with the principles of sustainability by minimizing waste, reducing the consumption of raw materials, and lowering greenhouse gas emissions associated with manufacturing. Additionally, product refurbishing promotes the concept of a circular economy, where products are kept in circulation for as long as possible before being recycled or disposed of.

Product Regeneration

A product regeneration is a sustainable process of restoring or renewing a product to its original state or function, with the aim of extending its lifespan and reducing waste. This approach focuses on reducing the environmental impact associated with the production and disposal of products.

Product regeneration involves various activities such as repairing, refurbishing, remanufacturing, and upgrading products. These activities help to effectively utilize the resources, energy, and materials invested in the initial production, while reducing the need for new materials and minimizing waste generation.

By choosing product regeneration over traditional manufacturing processes, companies can contribute to a circular economy model and promote sustainability. This approach helps to conserve natural resources and reduce greenhouse gas emissions, pollution, and landfill waste. It also supports the development of new business models, such as leasing or subscription services, where products are maintained and continuously regenerated by the company.

Product regeneration requires collaboration among stakeholders, including manufacturers, designers, consumers, and policymakers. It involves the implementation of sustainable design principles, the use of eco-friendly materials, and the adoption of efficient production and regeneration processes. Additionally, product regeneration promotes consumer awareness, encouraging individuals to choose regenerated products and participate in end-of-life recycling programs to ensure the responsible disposal of products that cannot be effectively regenerated.

Overall, product regeneration is a fundamental aspect of sustainable development, as it contributes to resource conservation, waste reduction, and the creation of a more circular and efficient economy.

Product Reintegration

Product reintegration refers to the process of reintroducing a product or its components back into the value chain after its useful life or when it becomes obsolete. It is an essential aspect of sustainable practices as it aims to minimize waste, conserve resources, and reduce environmental impacts.

The process of product reintegration involves various steps, including collection, sorting, disassembly, and refurbishment. These activities ensure that valuable materials and components are recovered from the product and can be reused or recycled, extending their life cycle and reducing the need for new resource extraction.

By reintegrating products, companies can reduce the demand for virgin materials, save energy, and decrease greenhouse gas emissions associated with manufacturing new products. This contributes to the concept of a circular economy, where resources are used more efficiently and continuously, reducing the overall environmental footprint.

Product reintegration also offers economic benefits by creating opportunities for businesses involved in the collection, refurbishment, and resale of used products. It can lead to the development of new markets and job opportunities, particularly in industries related to recycling and remanufacturing.

In conclusion, product reintegration is a key strategy for achieving sustainability goals. It not only helps in waste reduction but also supports resource conservation and the transition towards a more circular economy. By implementing effective reintegration practices, businesses can contribute to a more sustainable and environmentally friendly future.

Product Remanufacturing

Product remanufacturing is a sustainable process that involves restoring used products to their original specifications and performance levels. It is a form of recycling that allows for the extension of a product's lifespan, reducing the demand for new products and minimizing waste generated from the disposal of old ones.

Remanufacturing begins with the collection of used products, often referred to as "cores." These cores undergo a thorough inspection, disassembly, and cleaning process to identify any faulty or worn-out components. The damaged parts are then replaced or repaired, ensuring that the remanufactured product meets or exceeds its original functionality.

One of the key advantages of product remanufacturing is its positive impact on the environment. By reusing materials and components, remanufacturing reduces the need for raw materials extraction and energy-intensive manufacturing processes associated with producing new products. This helps to conserve natural resources, reduce greenhouse gas emissions, and lessen the overall environmental footprint.

Remanufacturing also offers economic benefits. It creates job opportunities in the refurbishment and restoration industry while providing consumers with affordable options for high-quality products. Additionally, remanufacturing encourages a circular economy by fostering a system where products are not solely disposed of after use but instead reentered into the market as new, fully functional items.

In conclusion, product remanufacturing plays a crucial role in sustainable development by promoting resource efficiency, reducing waste, and providing economic opportunities. By extending the life of products, this process contributes to the preservation of the environment and the creation of a more sustainable society.

Product Repackaging

Product repackaging refers to the process of redesigning the packaging of a product to minimize its environmental impact and improve its sustainability. It involves the replacement or modification of the existing packaging materials, design, or structure, with the aim of reducing waste generation, promoting recycling, and conserving resources.

The goal of product repackaging is to create packaging that is eco-friendly throughout its lifecycle, from production to disposal. This includes using materials that are renewable, biodegradable, or recyclable, as well as reducing the overall amount of packaging used. By using less material, repackaging can help conserve resources, reduce energy consumption, and lower greenhouse gas emissions associated with transportation and production.

Product Repairability

Product repairability refers to the ease, ability, and cost-effectiveness of repairing a product rather than replacing it when it becomes faulty or damaged. It is a crucial aspect of sustainability as it promotes the conservation of resources, reduces waste generation, and minimizes the environmental impact of manufacturing and disposal.

When a product is repairable, it means that its design, construction, and availability of spare parts enable technicians or end-users to mend or replace faulty components, extending the product's lifespan and functionality. Repairability often involves considerations such as the accessibility of internal components, the availability of repair manuals or guides, and the standardization of parts across different models.

Promoting product repairability is essential for achieving a more sustainable and circular economy. By encouraging repairs instead of replacement, valuable materials and resources are conserved, reducing the need for extracting, processing, and manufacturing new resources. Repairing products also minimizes the amount of waste going to landfills or incinerators, preventing pollution and associated environmental harms.

Furthermore, repairability contributes to economic sustainability by creating job opportunities in repair and maintenance sectors. It encourages local repair businesses and supports a more resilient and diverse economy. Repairable products also provide consumers with greater control and ownership over their possessions, fostering a sense of empowerment, self-sufficiency, and responsible consumption.

Product Reprocessing

Product reprocessing, in the context of sustainability, refers to the practice of collecting, treating, and transforming waste materials or used products into new products or raw materials, with the aim of reducing the consumption of natural resources and minimizing environmental impacts.

This process is part of the circular economy approach, which aims to create a closed-loop system where products and materials are reused, repurposed, or recycled instead of ending up as waste in landfills or incinerators. Instead of simply disposing of products after use, product reprocessing enables the recovery of valuable materials and resources from these products, extending their lifespan and reducing the need for virgin resources.

Product reprocessing plays a significant role in sustainable development by reducing the extraction of raw materials, conserving energy, and reducing pollution and greenhouse gas emissions associated with traditional manufacturing processes. By diverting waste from landfills and incinerators, it also helps to conserve valuable landfill space and reduce the environmental and social impacts of waste disposal.

Additionally, product reprocessing contributes to the creation of a more circular and sustainable economy by promoting resource efficiency, reducing waste generation, creating job opportunities in the recycling and reprocessing industries, and fostering innovation in product design and manufacturing.

Product Repurposing

Product repurposing refers to the practice of transforming or adapting a product for a different purpose or use than its original intended function. It involves finding new and innovative ways to utilize existing products, extending their lifespan, and reducing waste in the process.

By repurposing products, businesses and individuals can contribute to the principles of sustainability by minimizing resource consumption, reducing the need for new production, and diverting items from the waste stream. This practice aligns with the concept of the circular economy, where products are kept in use for as long as possible, rather than being discarded and replaced.

Product Reusability

Product reusability refers to the ability of a product to be used multiple times, either by the same user or by different users, without significantly losing its functionality or performance. It is a key concept in sustainability as it promotes the efficient use of resources and reduces waste and environmental impact.

A reusable product is designed and manufactured in a way that allows for its repeated use over an extended period of time. This can be achieved through durable materials, modular design, and the incorporation of repairable and replaceable parts. By extending the lifespan of products, reusability helps to minimize the need for new resource extraction, manufacturing, and disposal, leading to a reduction in energy consumption, greenhouse gas emissions, and waste generation.

Additionally, product reusability encourages a shift from a linear economy to a more circular economy model. In a linear economy, products are typically produced, used, and then discarded after a relatively short period of time. In contrast, a circular economy aims to close the loop by designing products that can be reused, repaired, or recycled, thereby reducing the demand for new resources and minimizing waste.

Companies and individuals can promote product reusability by adopting practices such as implementing take-back programs, designing for durability and repairability, and encouraging the sharing or renting of products. This approach not only benefits the environment but also offers economic opportunities, as reusable products can lead to cost savings for consumers and create new business models focused on product lifespan extension and resource efficiency.

Product Reuse Programs

Product reuse programs refer to initiatives or strategies implemented by organizations or governments to promote the reuse of products instead of disposing them after their initial use. These programs aim to minimize waste and reduce the environmental impact associated with the production, transportation, and disposal of goods.

Product reuse programs can take various forms, including the implementation of product take-back schemes, where manufacturers take back used products and refurbish or repair them for resale or reuse. These programs may also involve the development of rental or leasing systems, where consumers have access to products without needing to own them outright. Another approach is the establishment of second-hand markets or online platforms that facilitate the exchange or sale of used products.

Product Reutilization

Product reutilization is a key concept in sustainability, which refers to the practice of extending the lifespan or usefulness of a product by finding alternative ways to use it, rather than disposing of it as waste. It involves identifying potential secondary uses or repurposing opportunities for products that would otherwise be discarded, thereby reducing the need for new production and minimizing the environmental impact associated with resource extraction, manufacturing, and waste generation.

The process of product reutilization involves various strategies such as refurbishing, remanufacturing, and recycling. Refurbishing entails repairing or restoring a product to its original condition, allowing it to serve its intended purpose once again. Remanufacturing involves disassembling a product and replacing worn-out or damaged components to bring it back to its original specifications. Recycling, on the other hand, involves breaking down a product into its basic materials to create new products or raw materials.

By promoting reutilization, sustainability endeavors to minimize the consumption of finite resources and reduce the negative environmental impacts associated with production and waste disposal. Reutilization not only conserves energy and natural resources but also helps to prevent pollution and greenhouse gas emissions that result from the extraction and processing of raw materials. Moreover, product reutilization can contribute to the reduction of waste sent to landfills, alleviating the burden on waste management infrastructure and promoting a circular economy.

Overall, product reutilization plays a vital role in the transition towards a sustainable society by extending the lifespan of products, conserving resources, and reducing environmental harm. By embracing reutilization practices, individuals, businesses, and communities can contribute to a more sustainable and resource-efficient future.

Product Revaluation

Product revaluation is a process that involves assessing the impact of a product on the environment and society throughout its lifecycle, with the aim of identifying ways to make the product more sustainable. This revaluation takes into account various factors, including the extraction of raw materials, production processes, transportation, use, and disposal of the product.

The goal of product revaluation is to minimize the negative environmental and social impacts associated with a product and maximize its positive contributions. This process involves evaluating the product's design, materials, manufacturing methods, and packaging to identify opportunities for improvement. It also considers the product's energy efficiency, resource use, and waste generation, as well as its social implications, such as worker welfare and community impact.

By revaluing products, companies can make informed decisions about how to reduce their environmental footprint and enhance their social responsibility. This may involve finding alternative materials or production methods that have lower environmental impacts, improving energy efficiency, implementing recycling programs, or working towards a circular economy model where products are designed to be reused or recycled.

Product revaluation is an essential part of sustainable development as it promotes the development and adoption of more environmentally and socially responsible products. It allows companies to align their business practices with the principles of sustainability, thereby reducing their ecological footprint and contributing to a more sustainable future.

Product Take-Back Incentives

Product take-back incentives refer to the strategies and policies implemented by businesses or governments to encourage and reward consumers for returning their used products for recycling or proper disposal. These incentives aim to promote sustainability by reducing waste, conserving resources, and minimizing the environmental impacts associated with product disposal.

One common form of product take-back incentives is the offering of financial rewards or rebates to consumers who return their products at the end of their useful life. This can include monetary compensation or discounts on future purchases. By providing these incentives, businesses not only encourage consumers to recycle their products instead of throwing them away but also create a sense of value and responsibility towards the environment.

Another approach to product take-back incentives involves partnering with third-party recycling organizations or establishing drop-off points to make the return process convenient for consumers. Businesses may also offer additional services such as free shipping or collection services to encourage participation. These initiatives not only make it easier for consumers to participate in take-back programs but also demonstrate the company's commitment to sustainability.

Furthermore, product take-back incentives can also be integrated into extended producer responsibility (EPR) regulations. EPR requires manufacturers to take responsibility for the entire life cycle of their products, including their disposal. By implementing take-back programs and providing incentives, manufacturers can meet their EPR obligations while also encouraging consumer participation.

Product Take-Back Programs

Product take-back programs are initiatives implemented by companies or organizations to promote sustainability by facilitating the return and recycling of used products. These programs aim to reduce waste and minimize the environmental impact of discarded items, preventing them from ending up in landfills or polluting natural resources.

Through product take-back programs, customers are encouraged to return their used products to the manufacturer or designated collection points. The returned items are then recycled or responsibly disposed of, ensuring that valuable resources are recovered and kept in circulation for as long as possible. By taking part in these programs, customers actively contribute to the reduction of waste and the conservation of raw materials.

Product Upcycling

Product upcycling is a sustainable practice that involves transforming existing products or materials into new, higher-value items, often extending their lifespan and reducing waste. Unlike recycling, which involves breaking down materials for reuse, upcycling focuses on repurposing items without degradation.

By upcycling, manufacturers and consumers contribute to the reduction of resource consumption and waste generation, promoting a circular economy. This approach minimizes the need for virgin materials and avoids the energy-intensive processes required for recycling. Instead of discarding products at the end of their useful life, upcycling allows them to be creatively transformed into new, functional products.

Product-As-A-Service (PaaS)

Product-as-a-Service (PaaS) is a business model and approach that offers products to customers as a service, rather than through traditional ownership. It involves providing customers with access to products and their associated functionalities on a pay-per-use basis, instead of selling products outright. This model aims to promote sustainability by reducing resource consumption, minimizing waste, and encouraging circular economy principles.

PaaS enables companies to retain ownership of their products and take responsibility for their entire lifecycle, including production, maintenance, and disposal. This approach encourages the development and implementation of sustainable practices throughout the product's life. It incentivizes manufacturers to design products with durability, recyclability, and reusability in mind, as they bear the responsibility for the product's performance and longevity.

Product-To-Product Recycling

Product-to-product recycling, also known as closed-loop recycling, is a sustainability practice that involves the transformation of discarded products or materials into new products of equal or higher value. This process aims to reduce waste and conserve resources by diverting materials from the traditional linear economy model of extraction, production, consumption, and disposal.

In product-to-product recycling, the materials from a product that has reached the end of its useful life are collected and sorted to remove any contaminants. These materials are then processed and converted into raw materials that can be used to manufacture new products. This approach promotes a circular economy by closing the loop between the production and consumption stages, minimizing the need for virgin resources and the consequent environmental impacts associated with their extraction and processing.

Rainforest Foundation

The Rainforest Foundation is a non-profit organization committed to the preservation and sustainable management of tropical rainforests. Their mission is to support indigenous peoples and local communities in their efforts to protect these vital ecosystems and maintain their cultural and biological diversity.

Through various initiatives, the Rainforest Foundation aims to address the complex issues facing rainforests, including deforestation, land rights, and climate change. They work closely with indigenous and forest-dependent communities, helping them gain legal recognition of their traditional territories and supporting their efforts to secure sustainable livelihoods.

Rainwater Harvesting System Architecture

Rainwater harvesting system architecture refers to the design and arrangement of components and processes involved in collecting, storing, and utilizing rainwater for various purposes. This sustainable practice aims to minimize water scarcity and reduce reliance on traditional water sources, such as underground aquifers and freshwater bodies.

A rainwater harvesting system typically includes several key components. The catchment area consists of rooftops, pavements, or other surfaces that collect rainwater. Gutters and downspouts are used to channel the collected rainwater into storage tanks or reservoirs.

The storage component of the system may consist of aboveground or underground tanks, depending on the available space and water demand. These tanks are designed to withstand the weight of water and prevent contamination. Filtration systems are incorporated to remove debris, sediments, and pollutants from the collected rainwater before storage or use.

The distribution network allows the harvested rainwater to be used for various purposes. It may include pumps, pipes, and valves to transport the water to different areas of a building or landscape. Utilization of rainwater can range from non-potable applications, such as toilet flushing, gardening, and car washing, to potable uses with additional treatment processes.

Rainwater harvesting system architecture promotes sustainability by reducing the demand for mains water supply, alleviating pressure on traditional water sources, and mitigating the risk of water scarcity. By utilizing free and abundant rainwater resources, this practice can contribute to the conservation of freshwater, reduction of stormwater runoff, and overall water management efficiency. It also helps to reduce energy consumption associated with water treatment and distribution, thus reducing carbon emissions and supporting environmental sustainability.

Rainwater Harvesting System Design

A rainwater harvesting system is a sustainable solution that collects and stores rainwater for various purposes, reducing the dependency on freshwater sources and promoting efficient use of available resources. This system comprises of various components designed to efficiently collect, filter, and store rainwater for future use.

The design of a rainwater harvesting system involves several key considerations, including the size of the catchment area, the type of storage facility, and the filtration methods employed. The catchment area refers to the surface area that collects rainwater, typically the roof of a building. The design must account for factors such as the rainfall pattern in the region, the surface area available for collection, and the estimated water demand.

The collected rainwater is generally channeled through gutters and pipes into a storage facility, such as a tank or cistern, which can be located above or below ground. It is important to ensure that the storage facility is properly sealed and designed to prevent contamination and evaporation losses. In addition, the design should include an overflow mechanism to prevent flooding during heavy rainfall events.

Filtration is a crucial component of a rainwater harvesting system to remove impurities and ensure the water is safe for various uses. This can involve using filters, screens, or even simple techniques such as allowing sedimentation to occur in the storage tank. The design should also consider regular maintenance and cleaning of these filtration mechanisms to maintain water quality.

Rainwater Harvesting Systems

Rainwater harvesting systems are sustainable approaches used to collect, store, and utilize rainwater for various purposes such as irrigation, domestic use, or groundwater replenishment.

These systems aim to address water scarcity and promote sustainable water management by capturing rainwater that would otherwise run off and be wasted. Rainwater is collected from rooftops, surfaces, or catchment areas and directed through gutters and pipes into storage tanks or reservoirs.

Rainwater Harvesting

Rainwater harvesting is a sustainable practice that involves the collection, storage, and use of rainwater for various purposes, such as irrigation, drinking water, or groundwater recharge. It is an effective method of using a valuable natural resource and reducing the demand for freshwater sources, thus contributing to sustainable water management.

This practice is particularly important in regions with limited water resources or facing water scarcity issues, as it allows for the utilization of rainwater as an alternative water source. By capturing rainwater, it prevents water from running off and being lost as surface runoff, which is especially crucial in urban areas where a significant portion of rainwater is wasted due to impermeable surfaces like roads and buildings.

Rainwater harvesting systems typically involve the collection of rainwater from rooftops or other elevated surfaces, which is then channeled to storage facilities such as tanks, cisterns, or underground reservoirs. The collected rainwater can undergo basic filtration or treatment to ensure its quality meets the intended use, such as removing debris or contaminants.

Implementing rainwater harvesting can have numerous environmental and economic benefits. It helps to reduce the strain on freshwater sources, such as rivers and groundwater, by providing an additional water supply. This, in turn, mitigates the risk of depletion or contamination of such sources. Additionally, rainwater harvesting can contribute to water conservation, energy savings, and reduced costs for water utilities, as well as reducing flood risks by managing stormwater runoff.

Reclaimed Wood Furniture

Reclaimed wood furniture refers to furniture made from old or discarded wood that has been salvaged and repurposed for a new use. This practice aligns with sustainability principles as it reduces the demand for new timber extraction, minimizes waste, and alleviates pressure on natural resources.

The process of producing reclaimed wood furniture involves sourcing wood from a variety of reclaimed sources such as old buildings, barns, warehouses, and fences. This reclaimed wood is carefully dismantled, cleaned, and prepared for use in furniture production. The wood is typically re-milled to remove any old finishes or imperfections, revealing the natural beauty and character of the salvaged material.

By using reclaimed wood, the furniture industry helps to reduce deforestation and habitat destruction, as no additional trees are felled for production. Furthermore, the reuse of reclaimed wood extends its lifespan and preserves the embodied energy and carbon that would have been lost if the wood were discarded. Reclaimed wood furniture also offers distinct aesthetic appeal, as it often features unique patterns, textures, and colors that cannot be replicated by new wood.

The use of reclaimed wood furniture contributes to a circular economy, where materials are reused and repurposed rather than disposed of. It supports the principles of reduce, reuse, and recycle by giving new life to discarded wood, reducing the need for virgin resources, and minimizing waste generation. By choosing reclaimed wood furniture, consumers can be confident in their contribution to sustainable practices and the preservation of our planet's natural resources.

Reclaimed Wood Interior Design

Reclaimed wood interior design refers to the practice of using salvaged or recycled wood materials in the construction and decoration of indoor spaces. It embraces sustainability principles by reducing the demand for new timber and minimizing waste.

Reclaimed wood is sourced from various places, including old barns, factories, houses, and even sunken logs from rivers and lakes. The wood is carefully collected, processed, and prepared for use in interior design applications such as flooring, wall paneling, furniture, and decorative accents.

The use of reclaimed wood contributes to environmental protection in multiple ways. Firstly, it lessens the need for harvesting virgin timber, which helps to conserve forests and wildlife habitats. Additionally, by repurposing existing wood, it reduces the amount of waste generated by demolition and construction activities.

Reclaimed wood also possesses unique aesthetic qualities that make it a popular choice for interior design. Each piece of reclaimed wood carries a history and character that cannot be replicated by new materials. Its natural imperfections, such as knots, nail marks, and weathering, lend a rustic charm and sense of authenticity to spaces.

From a sustainability perspective, reclaimed wood interior design aligns with the principles of reduce, reuse, and recycle. By incorporating reclaimed wood into their projects, designers and homeowners can contribute to a more sustainable and eco-friendly built environment while creating distinctive and visually appealing spaces.

Recyclable Product Design

A recyclable product design refers to the creation of products that can be recovered and processed into new materials or products after their original use. This design approach aims to minimize waste generation, conserve resources, and reduce environmental impacts.

In the context of sustainability, recyclable product design plays a crucial role in the circular economy model. It involves incorporating materials and components that have the potential to be recycled at the end of their life cycle, rather than being disposed of in landfills or incinerated. By designing products with recyclability in mind, manufacturers contribute to the overall goal of reducing waste and promoting a more sustainable future.

Recyclable product design involves considering the entire life cycle of a product, from sourcing raw materials to end-of-life disposal. It entails selecting materials that are compatible with existing recycling systems and processes, as well as designing products that can easily be disassembled and separated into recyclable components.

The design process may also involve minimizing or eliminating the use of hazardous materials that can impede the recycling process or pose risks to human health and the environment. Additionally, factors such as product durability, functionality, and market demand play a role in determining the viability and effectiveness of recyclable product designs.

Overall, recyclable product design is a sustainable approach that aims to extend the lifespan of materials, conserve resources, and minimize waste generation. By considering recyclability in the design stage, manufacturers and designers contribute to a more circular economy and help address the environmental challenges associated with excessive resource consumption and waste disposal.

Recycled And Upcycled Fashion Marketplaces

A recycled fashion marketplace is an online platform that connects buyers and sellers of second-hand clothing and accessories. These marketplaces play a crucial role in promoting sustainability by extending the lifecycle of clothing items and reducing waste in the fashion industry.

Upcycled fashion marketplaces, on the other hand, offer a unique twist on second-hand shopping by featuring products that have been creatively transformed from their original form into new and improved items. This process involves repurposing or redesigning used garments and materials to give them a new lease on life.

Both recycled and upcycled fashion marketplaces contribute to sustainable fashion practices in several ways. By providing a platform for buying and selling pre-loved and upcycled items, they help divert clothing from landfills and reduce the need for new production. This not only saves valuable resources like water and energy but also minimizes the environmental impact associated with the manufacturing, transportation, and disposal of clothing.

Moreover, these marketplaces support the circular economy by encouraging a culture of reuse and extending the lifespan of garments and accessories. They give consumers the opportunity to shop consciously, embracing the concept of "slow fashion" and reducing their contribution to the throwaway culture that dominates the fast fashion industry.

By promoting the sale of recycled and upcycled fashion items, these marketplaces also contribute to reducing the overall demand for new clothing, which in turn helps decrease the harmful environmental and social impacts associated with large-scale garment production.

Recycled Building Materials

Recycled building materials refer to materials that have been salvaged or recovered from construction sites, demolition projects, or other sources, and then processed and reconditioned for future use in construction or renovation projects.

The use of recycled building materials promotes sustainable practices by reducing the demand for new raw materials and minimizing the environmental impact associated with extraction, manufacturing, and disposal. These materials can include a wide range of products such as reclaimed wood, recycled concrete, salvaged metal, and repurposed glass.

Recycled building materials offer several advantages in terms of sustainability. Firstly, they help to conserve natural resources by reducing the need for virgin materials. By using recycled materials, we can minimize the extraction of finite resources like timber, minerals, and fossil fuels, thereby preserving ecosystems and habitats. Secondly, utilizing recycled building materials reduces the amount of waste that ends up in landfills. Construction and demolition waste are major contributors to landfill waste, creating environmental concerns and depleting valuable land resources. By reusing materials that would otherwise be discarded, we can minimize waste generation and conserve landfill space. Furthermore, incorporating recycled materials into building projects can lower the associated energy consumption and greenhouse gas emissions. The production of new building materials typically requires significant energy inputs and releases carbon dioxide into the atmosphere. In contrast, using recycled materials generally requires less energy and results in fewer emissions, helping to mitigate climate change impacts. In conclusion, recycling building materials plays a vital role in sustainable construction practices. By minimizing resource consumption, reducing waste generation, and mitigating greenhouse gas emissions, the use of recycled materials contributes to a more environmentally friendly and economically viable built environment.

Recycled Furniture Design

Recycled furniture design refers to the process of creating furniture using materials that have been repurposed and diverted from the waste stream, thereby reducing the consumption of virgin resources and minimizing environmental impact. It is a sustainable approach to furniture manufacturing that promotes the principles of circular economy and waste reduction.

The design process of recycled furniture involves collecting discarded or unused materials such as wood, metal, plastics, and textiles, and transforming them into functional and aesthetically pleasing furniture pieces. These materials can come from various sources, including old furniture, construction and demolition waste, industrial byproducts, and even ocean plastic.

Recycled furniture design not only helps to conserve natural resources and reduce waste sent to landfills, but it also promotes creativity and innovation in the design industry. Designers who specialize in recycled furniture need to think outside the box and find new ways to give materials a second life, often incorporating unique textures, colors, and patterns into their creations.

By using recycled materials, furniture designers can contribute to a more sustainable and circular economy by closing the loop of resource consumption. They can also inspire consumers to make more environmentally conscious choices by demonstrating the potential beauty and functionality of furniture made from recycled materials.

In conclusion, recycled furniture design is a sustainable approach to furniture manufacturing that repurposes materials to reduce waste and environmental impact. It offers a creative and innovative way to create functional and aesthetically pleasing furniture while promoting the principles of a circular economy.

Recycled Paper And Packaging

251

Recycled paper and packaging refer to materials that have been processed and transformed from waste paper and packaging objects into new products. The aim of recycling paper and packaging is to reduce the consumption of natural resources, decrease energy and water usage, minimize pollution, and contribute to sustainable development.

Recycled paper is made from fibers derived from used paper products, such as newspapers, cardboard, magazines, and office paper. These materials undergo a recycling process that includes sorting, de-inking, pulping, filtering, and papermaking. The resulting recycled paper can be used for various purposes, including printing, writing, packaging, and tissue production.

Recycled packaging involves reusing or remanufacturing materials that were previously used for packaging purposes. This can include cardboard boxes, plastic containers, glass bottles, and metal cans. The recycling process for packaging typically involves sorting, cleaning, shredding, melting, and reshaping the materials into new packaging products.

By utilizing recycled paper and packaging, businesses and consumers contribute to sustainability by reducing the demand for virgin materials, conserving natural resources, and minimizing waste sent to landfills or incinerators. The production of recycled paper and packaging also generally requires less water, energy, and chemicals compared to manufacturing products from raw materials. Additionally, recycling paper and packaging helps to decrease air and water pollution associated with the extraction and processing of virgin materials.

In conclusion, recycled paper and packaging are essential components of sustainable practices. They help to conserve resources, reduce environmental impacts, and promote a circular economy by transforming waste materials into new usable products.

Recycled Paper Product Design

Recycled paper product design refers to the process of creating sustainable and eco-friendly paper products by utilizing recycled paper materials. This design approach aims to reduce the environmental impact of conventional paper production by conserving resources and minimizing waste.

The design process involves selecting and sourcing recycled paper materials, such as post-consumer waste or pre-consumer waste from manufacturing processes. These paper materials are then processed and transformed into various paper products, including packaging, stationery, and household items.

Recycled paper product design prioritizes sustainability by using materials that would otherwise end up in landfills. By recycling paper, the demand for virgin pulp, which requires the cutting down of trees, is reduced. This helps to conserve forests, protect wildlife habitats, and support biodiversity.

In addition to minimizing the use of natural resources, recycled paper product design also reduces energy consumption and greenhouse gas emissions. The production of recycled paper requires less energy compared to traditional paper production methods, leading to a lower carbon footprint.

The sustainable design principles are applied throughout the entire lifecycle of the paper products. This includes considering factors such as durability, recyclability, and biodegradability. Designers strive to create products that can be easily recycled or composted after use, ensuring that they do not contribute to the accumulation of waste in landfills.

Overall, recycled paper product design plays a crucial role in promoting sustainable consumption and production patterns. By embracing this design approach, we can contribute to the preservation of natural resources, reduction of waste, and mitigation of climate change.

Recycled Paper Product Lines

Recycled paper product lines refer to a range of products that are manufactured using recycled paper as the primary raw material. Sustainability is at the core of these product lines, as they are designed to reduce the demand for virgin paper and minimize the environmental impact associated with traditional paper production.

The production of recycled paper products begins with the collection and sorting of used paper materials, such as newspapers, magazines, and office paper. This process helps divert these materials from ending up in landfills, reducing the need for additional waste disposal space.

Once collected, the paper is carefully processed to remove any contaminants, such as inks or coatings. This purified paper is then mixed with water to create a pulp, which can be used to manufacture a wide variety of products, including paper towels, tissue paper, cardboard, packaging materials, and more.

In addition to reducing waste, recycled paper product lines contribute to the conservation of natural resources. The production of recycled paper requires significantly less water and energy compared to the production of paper from virgin fibers. It also helps preserve forests, as fewer trees need to be cut down for paper production.

Furthermore, the use of recycled paper products helps to close the recycling loop. By purchasing and supporting these product lines, individuals and businesses promote a circular economy, where waste materials are continually reused and repurposed instead of being discarded. This contributes to the overall sustainability of the paper industry and helps mitigate the environmental impacts associated with deforestation and greenhouse gas emissions.

Recycled Plastic Art Installations

Recycled plastic art installations are artistic creations made from discarded plastic materials that have been repurposed and transformed into visually captivating and thought-provoking works of art. These installations not only provide aesthetic value but also serve as a powerful medium to raise awareness about sustainability and the environmental impact of plastic waste.

By utilizing recycled plastic materials, these art installations promote the concept of circular economy, where waste is seen as a valuable resource that can be reused and repurposed. They symbolize the potential of transforming waste into something beautiful and meaningful, challenging the traditional notion of what constitutes as art. Through their sheer size and striking designs, they capture the attention of viewers and ignite conversations about the urgent need to reduce, reuse, and recycle plastic waste to protect our planet.

Recycled Plastic Art

Recycled plastic art refers to the creative and innovative use of discarded plastic materials to create aesthetic and functional artwork. It involves collecting plastic waste, such as bottles, containers, and packaging, and transforming them into unique and visually appealing sculptures, installations, and other artistic forms.

This form of art holds significant importance in the context of sustainability. By repurposing plastic waste, recycled plastic art helps to mitigate the environmental impact of plastic pollution. It addresses the growing concern of plastic waste accumulation, particularly in landfills and oceans, by giving these materials a second life. Through artistic expression, recycled plastic art raises awareness about the urgent need to reduce, reuse, and recycle plastic, urging individuals and communities to adopt more sustainable habits and waste management practices.

Recycled Plastic Furniture

Recycled plastic furniture refers to furniture that is made from post-consumer or post-industrial plastic waste materials, which have been processed and transformed into usable products. This sustainable form of furniture is designed to reduce the demand for new plastic materials and minimize environmental impacts.

The production process of recycled plastic furniture involves collecting plastic waste such as bottles, containers, and packaging materials, and then sorting and cleaning them to remove any contaminants. The plastic waste is then shredded into small pieces or melted down into a liquid form before being shaped into various furniture items such as chairs, tables, benches, and outdoor play equipment.

By using recycled plastic materials, this type of furniture contributes to the circular economy by diverting plastic waste from landfills and reducing the need for virgin plastic production. It helps conserve natural resources, reduce energy consumption, and minimize greenhouse gas emissions associated with the production of new plastic products.

Recycled plastic furniture is also highly durable and resistant to rot, decay, and pests, making it suitable for both indoor and outdoor use. It requires minimal maintenance and is weather-resistant, which prolongs its lifespan and reduces the need for frequent replacements.

In addition to its sustainability benefits, recycled plastic furniture offers a wide range of design options, styles, and colors, making it a versatile choice for different settings such as homes, gardens, parks, and public spaces. It provides a practical solution to reduce plastic waste while offering functional and aesthetically pleasing furniture options.

Recycled Shipping Container Architecture

Recycled shipping container architecture is an innovative approach to sustainable construction that repurposes decommissioned shipping containers into functional and habitable structures.

By utilizing these used containers, which would otherwise go to waste, architects and designers are able to create affordable and environmentally-friendly buildings, such as houses, offices, schools, and even shopping complexes. These structures offer numerous benefits in terms of sustainability.

The use of recycled shipping containers helps to reduce the demand for new construction materials, such as bricks, cement, and timber. This reduces the need for resource extraction, minimizes landfill waste, and conserves energy that would be required in the production of new materials. Furthermore, repurposing shipping containers also extends their lifespan, preventing them from becoming additional waste in landfills.

Shipping containers are inherently durable and weather-resistant due to their original purpose of withstanding long sea journeys. This inherent strength makes them suitable for withstanding natural disasters, such as earthquakes and hurricanes, and reduces the need for additional structural reinforcements. As a result, the construction process is streamlined, saving time, energy, and money.

In addition to their sustainability benefits, recycled shipping container architecture is also highly customizable and adaptable. These containers can be easily modified to create unique and tailored designs, allowing for creative and flexible architectural solutions. They can be stacked, joined together, or arranged in various configurations to meet specific spatial requirements.

Overall, recycled shipping container architecture presents an innovative and sustainable solution to the increasing demand for affordable and environmentally-friendly construction. It not only repurposes waste materials but also reduces resource consumption, minimizes carbon emissions, and offers adaptable design options.

Recycled Shipping Container Structures

Recycled shipping container structures are architectural constructions created by repurposing discarded shipping containers, typically made of steel or aluminum, into habitable spaces or functional structures. These structures are designed with sustainability in mind, offering an environmentally-friendly approach to construction by reducing waste and utilizing existing resources.

By repurposing shipping containers, this innovative approach to architecture helps to decrease the demand for new materials and the energy required for their production. Rather than contributing to the depletion of resources and the generation of excessive waste, recycled shipping container structures focus on reusing existing materials, reducing the carbon footprint associated with traditional construction methods.

Recycled Textile Fashion Lines

Recycled textile fashion lines refer to clothing collections that are created using discarded or post-consumer textiles, with the aim of reducing waste and promoting sustainability in the fashion industry. These lines typically include a range of garments and accessories made from materials that have been recovered from landfill or recycling facilities.

The process of creating recycled textile fashion lines involves collecting used textiles, such as old clothes, fabric scraps, or discarded household textiles, and sorting them based on their composition and condition. The textiles are then cleaned, sorted, and processed to remove any impurities or contaminants. Once the materials are prepared, they are transformed into new fabrics or yarns through various techniques, such as shredding, melting, or spinning.

The recycled textiles are then used to design and produce fashionable and sustainable garments and accessories. These fashion lines may include items such as dresses, tops, pants, jackets, bags, and shoes. Designers often use innovative techniques and creative approaches to transform the recycled textiles into stylish and desirable products, showcasing the potential of reusing materials and reducing the environmental impact of the fashion industry.

By choosing recycled textile fashion lines, consumers can contribute to the circular economy and minimize the use of virgin resources. These collections promote the principles of reduce, reuse, and recycle, highlighting the importance of sustainability and conscious consumption in the fashion industry. Additionally, recycled textile fashion lines help to raise awareness about the environmental impact of textile waste and encourage individuals and businesses to embrace more sustainable practices in their wardrobe choices.

Recycled Textile Fashion

Recycled textile fashion refers to the practice of utilizing discarded or waste fabrics to create new and innovative clothing items and accessories. This sustainable approach to fashion design aims to reduce the environmental impact of the textile industry by minimizing the use of virgin resources.

By repurposing existing textiles, such as old garments, scraps, or industrial waste, and transforming them into new fashion pieces, recycled textile fashion promotes circularity and extends the lifespan of materials. This process helps alleviate the strain on natural resources, reduce energy consumption, and divert textile waste from landfills.

Recycled Textile Materials

Recycled textile materials refer to fabrics and textiles that have been processed and transformed from pre-consumer or post-consumer waste into new and usable textiles. These materials are part of a sustainable approach in the fashion and textile industry, aimed at reducing the environmental impact of textile production and waste generation.

Recycling textile materials involves various processes, such as sorting, shredding, and reprocessing, to convert discarded textiles into new raw materials or products. Pre-consumer waste includes fabric scraps, trimmings, and off-cuts generated during the manufacturing process, while post-consumer waste includes discarded clothing, household textiles, and other textiles that have been used and thrown away.

The recycling of textile materials helps to conserve natural resources and reduce energy consumption, water usage, and greenhouse gas emissions. By diverting textiles from landfills and incineration, recycling also addresses the waste management challenges associated with textile disposal. Additionally, the recycling process can help to reduce the need for virgin materials, such as cotton or polyester, which require substantial resources for production.

Recycled textile materials can be used in various applications, including apparel, home furnishings, and industrial products. The quality and properties of the recycled materials may vary depending on the recycling processes and technologies employed. To ensure the sustainability and transparency of recycled textile materials, certifications and standards, such as Global Recycled Standard (GRS) or Recycled Claim Standard (RCS), have been established to verify the recycled content and traceability of these materials.

In conclusion, recycled textile materials are a vital component of a circular and sustainable textile industry. Through recycling, these materials contribute to reducing waste, conserving resources, and minimizing the environmental impact of textile production and disposal.

Recycled Tire Playground Designs

A recycled tire playground is a sustainable playground design that utilizes old and discarded tires to create a safe and attractive play area for children. These playgrounds are built with the aim of reducing waste and promoting environmental responsibility by repurposing tires that would otherwise end up in landfills or contribute to pollution.

The design of a recycled tire playground typically involves using tires in various ways, such as constructing climbing structures, swings, and even creating soft ground surfaces. The tires are cleaned, painted, and modified to ensure they are safe for children to play on. By reusing the tires, these playgrounds help to conserve natural resources and reduce the need for new materials, contributing to a more sustainable future.

Recycled Tire Playgrounds

Recycled tire playgrounds are sustainable play spaces that are created using discarded tires. These playgrounds are designed with the goal of reducing waste and promoting environmental responsibility. By repurposing old tires that would otherwise end up in landfills, these playgrounds provide a practical solution for recycling and reducing the impact of tire waste on the environment.

Recycled tire playgrounds offer several environmental benefits. Firstly, they help to conserve natural resources by using existing materials instead of creating new ones. This reduces the demand for raw materials such as rubber and reduces the energy required for production. Secondly, these playgrounds help to minimize waste and landfill use. Tires take a long time to break down naturally, and by repurposing them into playground materials, their lifespan is extended, diverting them from the waste stream. Additionally, the playgrounds themselves can be recycled or repurposed at the end of their lifespan, further reducing waste.

Recycled Tire Products

Recycled tire products refer to items that are made from discarded or used tires and have undergone a process of recycling or repurposing. These products are created with the aim of reducing waste, conserving resources, and promoting sustainability.

The process of recycling tires involves collecting and sorting used tires, removing any metal or fabric components, and then shredding or grinding them into smaller pieces. These smaller pieces are then used as raw material for various products.

One common type of recycled tire product is rubberized asphalt, which is a pavement material made by blending ground tire rubber with asphalt. This helps to improve road durability and reduce noise pollution. Another example is rubber mulch, which is made from shredded tires and used as a landscaping material. It helps to prevent weed growth, retain moisture, and protect plant roots.

Recycled tire products also include rubber mats, tiles, and flooring, which are commonly used in gyms, playgrounds, and other high-impact areas. These products provide a cushioning and non-slip surface while reducing the need for virgin materials.

In addition, recycled tire products are used in the manufacturing of various consumer goods, such as footwear, bags, and mats. By utilizing recycled materials, these products help to conserve resources and reduce the environmental impact associated with producing new materials from scratch.

Recycled-Content Materials

Recycled-content materials, in the context of sustainability, refer to products that are made from materials that have been recovered or diverted from the waste stream. These materials are processed and transformed into new products, reducing the demand for virgin materials and conserving natural resources.

Recycled-content materials play a significant role in promoting sustainability as they help reduce the environmental impact associated with the extraction, processing, and transportation of raw materials. By using recycled materials, less energy is required and fewer greenhouse gas emissions are produced compared to the production of new products from virgin materials.

Recycling Bin Placement Strategies

Recycling bin placement strategies refer to the deliberate and strategic positioning of recycling bins in diverse locations to encourage and facilitate the proper disposal of recyclable materials. This sustainability-driven approach aims to optimize recycling rates, minimize contamination, and ultimately reduce the environmental footprint associated with waste generation.

Effective recycling bin placement strategies take into account several factors, such as population density, usage patterns, and accessibility. Placing recycling bins in high traffic areas, such as public parks, shopping centers, or office buildings, increases their visibility and encourages individuals to participate in recycling activities. By placing bins near trash receptacles, individuals are prompted to make a conscious choice between discarding waste or recycling it appropriately.

Moreover, placing recycling bins in strategic locations can help address specific recycling challenges. For instance, placing separate bins for specific materials, such as plastic, glass, or paper, helps facilitate proper sorting and minimizes contamination. Additionally, in large facilities or multi-story buildings, strategically placing recycling bins on each floor or in communal areas ensures convenience and accessibility for all occupants, promoting recycling behavior.

To further enhance the effectiveness of recycling bin placement strategies, clear signage and educational materials can be incorporated. Informative signs outlining the types of materials that can be recycled and providing simple instructions on proper disposal can help individuals make informed choices. Additionally, educational campaigns and awareness programs can be implemented to promote the importance of recycling and highlight the positive environmental impacts of participating in recycling efforts.

In conclusion, recycling bin placement strategies involve the intentional placement of bins in various locations to promote sustainable waste management practices. By strategically positioning recycling bins and providing clear guidance, these strategies aim to inspire individuals to make environmentally responsible choices, ultimately contributing to the preservation of natural resources and the reduction of waste sent to landfills.

Recycling Education Programs

A recycling education program refers to a structured initiative aimed at educating individuals and communities on the importance of recycling and promoting sustainable practices related to waste management. The program provides information, resources, and practical tools to raise awareness and encourage the adoption of recycling habits and behaviors.

Sustainability lies at the core of recycling education programs, which are designed to address the pressing environmental challenges posed by increasing waste generation and limited natural resources. These programs emphasize the three pillars of sustainability: social, economic, and environmental. By imparting knowledge and fostering understanding, they aim to empower individuals to make informed choices that contribute to a more sustainable future.

Recycling Incentive Programs

Recycling incentive programs refer to initiatives and measures implemented by governments, organizations, and communities to encourage individuals and businesses to participate in recycling activities. These programs aim to promote sustainability by diverting waste from landfills, reducing resource consumption, and minimizing environmental impacts.

Typically, recycling incentive programs involve offering rewards, incentives, or economic benefits to individuals or businesses that engage in recycling practices. These rewards can come in various forms, such as cash incentives, discounts on goods and services, tax deductions, or credits. By providing tangible benefits, these programs motivate individuals and businesses to actively participate in recycling efforts.

Recycling Infrastructure Development

Recycling infrastructure development refers to the systematic planning, establishment, and improvement of the physical and logistical components necessary to support the efficient and effective recycling of waste materials. It encompasses the creation and maintenance of facilities, such as recycling centers, material recovery facilities, composting sites, and collection points, as well as the implementation of supporting systems, such as waste collection and sorting mechanisms, transportation networks, and technology integration.

The development of recycling infrastructure is an essential aspect of sustainability as it plays a crucial role in minimizing the negative environmental impacts associated with the production, consumption, and disposal of materials. By providing accessible and conveniently located recycling facilities, individuals and communities are encouraged to properly manage and divert waste from landfills, promoting resource conservation and reducing greenhouse gas emissions.

Recycling Innovations

Recycling innovations refer to the development and implementation of new and improved methods, technologies, and processes that enhance the sustainability of recycling practices. These innovations aim to address the environmental challenges associated with waste disposal and resource depletion by promoting effective and efficient waste management.

Such innovations encompass various aspects of the recycling cycle, including collection, sorting, processing, and reuse. For example, advancements in recycling technologies have led to the creation of more sophisticated sorting systems that can accurately separate different types of recyclable materials with greater precision. This enhances the efficiency of recycling facilities, allows for better resource recovery, and reduces the amount of waste that ends up in landfills or incinerators.

Additionally, recycling innovations also involve the development of new materials or products that utilize recycled content. For instance, the use of recycled plastic in the production of durable goods reduces the demand for virgin materials and helps to close the loop in the product lifecycle. Furthermore, innovative approaches to recycling, such as chemical or biological processes, enable the transformation of waste materials into valuable resources, further optimizing the recycling process.

In conclusion, recycling innovations play a crucial role in advancing sustainability by improving the effectiveness and efficiency of recycling practices. By continuously exploring and implementing new ideas and technologies, we can maximize the benefits of recycling, minimize environmental impacts, and contribute to a more circular and resource-efficient economy.

Recycling Mobile Apps

A recycling mobile app is a smartphone application that provides information and resources to promote and facilitate the recycling of various materials in order to reduce waste and promote sustainability. These apps are designed to educate and engage users by providing them with information on recycling centers, collection schedules, and proper disposal methods for different types of waste.

By using a recycling mobile app, individuals can easily find nearby recycling facilities and drop-off locations, making it convenient for them to properly dispose of items such as plastics, paper, glass, and electronics. These apps often include search functions and GPS capabilities to help users locate the most convenient recycling options in their area.

In addition to providing information, recycling mobile apps often offer features that incentivize and encourage users to recycle. These features may include recycling challenges, rewards programs, and informative articles or tips on sustainable living. By offering these interactive elements, the apps aim to motivate and inspire individuals to adopt environmentally-friendly habits and actively participate in recycling efforts.

Overall, recycling mobile apps play a crucial role in promoting sustainability by making recycling more accessible and engaging for individuals. By providing easy access to information on recycling options and offering incentives for participation, these apps contribute to the overall effort of reducing waste and conserving resources, ultimately helping to create a more sustainable future.

Recycling Rewards Programs

Recycling rewards programs are initiatives designed to incentivize individuals and communities to engage in recycling activities by offering rewards or benefits in return. These programs aim to promote sustainable practices, reduce waste, and conserve resources by motivating people to participate in recycling efforts.

Through recycling rewards programs, participants are typically encouraged to deposit their recyclable materials, such as plastic bottles, glass, paper, or aluminum cans, at designated collection points. Upon doing so, they can accumulate points, credits, or incentives that can be redeemed for various rewards or benefits. These rewards often include discounts on purchases, vouchers for goods or services, or even cash incentives.

The implementation of recycling rewards programs serves multiple purposes in the context of sustainability. Firstly, they encourage individuals to adopt environmentally friendly behaviors by diverting waste from landfills and promoting recycling as a routine practice. This reduces the need for raw materials extraction, energy consumption, and greenhouse gas emissions associated with the production of new goods.

Secondly, recycling rewards programs foster a sense of community engagement and collective responsibility towards environmental protection. By participating in these programs, individuals become active contributors to the broader goal of waste reduction and resource conservation. This collective effort can lead to increased awareness and education about the importance of recycling, ultimately fostering a more sustainable and environmentally conscious society.

Recycling Robotics

Recycling robotics refers to the application of advanced technology and automation in the recycling process, aiming to improve efficiency, accuracy, and sustainability. It involves the use of robotic systems and artificial intelligence to automate various stages of recycling, including sorting, dismantling, and processing of recyclable materials.

These recycling robots are designed to identify and separate different types of materials, such as plastics, metals, and paper, from the waste stream. They use advanced sensors, cameras, and machine learning algorithms to analyze and categorize items based on their composition, size, and shape. By automating the sorting process, recycling robots help to reduce reliance on manual labor, increase throughput, and minimize human error.

In addition to sorting, recycling robotics also play a crucial role in the dismantling and processing of electronic waste (e-waste). These robots are capable of disassembling electronic devices, such as smartphones, laptops, and televisions, in a safe and efficient manner. They can extract valuable components and materials, such as circuit boards, batteries, and precious metals, which can be recycled and reused in the manufacturing of new products.

By integrating recycling robotics into the waste management infrastructure, we can significantly enhance the sustainability of recycling operations. These robots can help optimize the utilization of resources, reduce environmental impact, and conserve energy and raw materials. Moreover, by improving the efficiency of recycling processes, they contribute to the circular economy by closing the loop and promoting the reuse and recycling of materials instead of their disposal.

Recycling Sorting Robots

Recycling sorting robots are automated machines designed to streamline the process of sorting and separating recyclable materials. These robots use advanced technology, such as artificial intelligence and computer vision, to identify and categorize different types of recyclables, including plastic, metal, paper, and glass.

By implementing recycling sorting robots, waste management facilities can significantly improve the efficiency and accuracy of their recycling operations. Traditional manual sorting methods are often time-consuming and labor-intensive, leading to potential errors and inconsistencies in the sorting process. In contrast, recycling sorting robots can work continuously and tirelessly, ensuring a consistent and high-quality sorting outcome.

Furthermore, recycling sorting robots contribute to sustainability by promoting waste diversion and reducing contamination in recycling streams. By accurately sorting different materials, these robots enable the recycling industry to maximize the value and potential of recyclables, minimizing the need for new raw materials extraction and reducing greenhouse gas emissions associated with manufacturing processes.

In addition to their environmental benefits, recycling sorting robots also offer economic advantages. The enhanced efficiency provided by these machines can lead to cost savings in waste management operations, including reduced labor costs and increased recycling facility throughput. Moreover, recycling sorting robots can help stimulate the development and growth of the recycling industry, creating new job opportunities and driving economic growth in the sustainable sector.

In summary, recycling sorting robots are technological innovations that play a crucial role in improving the sustainability and efficiency of recycling operations. By automating the sorting process, these robots contribute to waste diversion, minimize contamination, and facilitate the transition towards a circular economy.

Regenerative Materials

Regenerative materials refer to natural resources that can be replenished, restored, and reused over time, without depleting or damaging the environment. These materials play a crucial role in promoting sustainability and reducing the negative impact of human activity on the planet.

Unlike non-renewable resources like fossil fuels and minerals, regenerative materials are derived from renewable sources such as plants and animals, and their utilization does not exceed the rate of their natural replenishment. This ensures the preservation and conservation of ecosystems and biodiversity, as well as the sustainable management of resources for future generations.

Regenerative materials are essential for addressing key environmental challenges, such as climate change and resource scarcity. By utilizing these materials instead of non-renewable alternatives, we can significantly reduce carbon emissions and minimize waste. Additionally, regenerative materials are often biodegradable, meaning they can naturally break down without causing harm to the environment.

Furthermore, regenerative materials can contribute to the circular economy by being reused, repurposed, or recycled. Through careful design and innovation, these materials can be transformed into new products or integrated back into natural systems, thus closing the loop and minimizing waste generation.

Incorporating regenerative materials into various industries and sectors, such as construction, packaging, and manufacturing, is crucial for achieving long-term sustainability goals. With their ability to support ecological balance, conserve resources, and promote a healthier planet, regenerative materials are a cornerstone of a more sustainable and resilient future.

Remanufacturing Processes

Remanufacturing processes refer to the systematic and controlled processes that transform used products and components into new or like-new condition, ensuring that they meet original performance specifications and quality standards. These processes involve disassembling, cleaning, inspecting, repairing, and reassembling the products or components, while also incorporating any necessary design changes and updates.

Remanufacturing is a sustainable approach that seeks to extend the life cycle of products, minimizing waste and resource consumption. By reusing existing materials and components, remanufacturing reduces the need for extracting and processing raw materials, which helps to conserve energy, reduce pollution, and protect natural resources.

One of the key benefits of remanufacturing is its contribution to a circular economy, where products are kept in use for as long as possible. This is in contrast to a linear economy, where products are manufactured, used, and then disposed of. By remanufacturing products, valuable resources are preserved and the environmental impacts associated with manufacturing new products are minimized.

Moreover, remanufacturing processes often incorporate technological advancements and innovations, resulting in products that are more energy-efficient, durable, and environmentally friendly. The quality assurance and testing procedures during remanufacturing ensure that the end products meet the same performance and safety standards as brand-new products.

Overall, remanufacturing processes play a crucial role in promoting sustainability by reducing waste, conserving resources, and enabling the transition to a circular economy. They contribute to a more environmentally responsible and economically viable approach to manufacturing and consumption.

Renewable Energy Policy Network For The 21st Century (REN21)

The Renewable Energy Policy Network for the 21st Century (REN21) is a global multi-stakeholder network that promotes the transition to a sustainable energy future. REN21 serves as a platform for collaboration, knowledge sharing, and the exchange of best practices between governments, international organizations, research institutions, industry associations, and civil society.

REN21's main focus is on renewable energy, which includes sources such as solar, wind, hydro, and biomass. The network works towards accelerating the deployment of renewable energy technologies and increasing their share in the global energy mix. REN21 aims to provide policy-relevant information, facilitate dialogue, and foster international cooperation to advance the understanding and implementation of renewable energy policies and measures.

As sustainability is a key aspect of REN21's mandate, the network emphasizes the importance of transitioning to renewable energy sources to mitigate climate change, reduce greenhouse gas emissions, and improve energy access and security. REN21 recognizes that the sustainable development of renewable energy requires not only technological advancements but also supportive policies, financing mechanisms, and capacity building.

By bringing together diverse stakeholders and fostering collaboration, REN21 seeks to promote the adoption of renewable energy solutions worldwide, contributing to sustainable development, environmental protection, and the achievement of global climate and energy targets. The network plays a crucial role in facilitating the exchange of knowledge and experiences, enabling countries and organizations to learn from each other and accelerate the transition towards a more sustainable and renewable energy future.

Renewable Energy And Energy Efficiency Partnership (REEEP)

The Renewable Energy and Energy Efficiency Partnership (REEEP) is an international organization that promotes sustainable solutions for energy generation and consumption. Its primary goal is to accelerate the global transition towards a low-carbon and climate-resilient future.

REEEP focuses on two key areas: renewable energy and energy efficiency. Renewable energy refers to energy sources that are naturally replenished, such as solar, wind, and hydro power. Energy efficiency, on the other hand, refers to using less energy to achieve the same or better outcomes. By promoting both of these approaches, REEEP aims to reduce greenhouse gas emissions, enhance energy security, and foster sustainable economic development.

Renewable Energy Adoption

Renewable energy adoption refers to the utilization and integration of energy sources that do not deplete natural resources and have a significantly lower impact on the environment compared to traditional energy sources. This process aims to transition from non-renewable, finite resources such as fossil fuels to renewable energy sources that replenish naturally and can be used indefinitely without harming the planet's ecosystem.

Sustainability is the overarching principle guiding renewable energy adoption, as it seeks to meet the present energy needs without compromising the ability of future generations to fulfill their own needs. The adoption of renewable energy technologies and practices addresses the dual challenges of mitigating climate change by reducing greenhouse gas emissions and minimizing the depletion of finite natural resources.

Renewable energy sources encompass various forms, including solar power, wind power, hydropower, biomass, and geothermal energy. These sources provide an abundant supply of clean energy while significantly reducing or eliminating harmful emissions associated with fossil fuel combustion. By strategically deploying and scaling up renewable energy technologies, communities, governments, and industries can reduce their carbon footprint, improve air quality, and enhance energy security.

The successful adoption of renewable energy requires comprehensive planning, policy support, and investment in research and development. It encompasses a range of activities, such as the installation of solar panels, wind turbines, or hydropower plants, the development of bioenergy crops and infrastructure, and the implementation of energy efficiency measures to optimize energy consumption.

Ultimately, renewable energy adoption is a crucial component of a sustainable future, fostering economic growth, creating green jobs, and promoting social and environmental well-being. By embracing renewable energy sources, societies can transition to a more resilient and equitable energy system that supports long-term prosperity while safeguarding the planet for future generations.

Renewable Energy Alternatives

Renewable energy alternatives refer to sustainable sources of energy that can be naturally replenished and do not harm the environment or deplete natural resources. These sources are considered renewable because their availability is not limited and they have the potential to provide a continuous supply of energy without relying on finite resources, such as fossil fuels.

Examples of renewable energy alternatives include solar power, wind power, hydropower, biomass, and geothermal energy. Solar power harnesses the energy from sunlight through the use of photovoltaic cells or solar thermal systems, converting it into electricity or heat. Wind power utilizes the kinetic energy from wind to generate electricity through wind turbines. Hydropower uses the gravitational force of flowing or falling water to produce electricity, often through the use of dams or water turbines.

Biomass energy is derived from organic materials, such as crop residues, wood waste, or dedicated energy crops. It can be converted into heat, electricity, or liquid fuels. Geothermal energy, on the other hand, utilizes heat from the Earth's core to generate electricity or provide heating and cooling for buildings.

Renewable energy alternatives play a crucial role in sustainability efforts as they emit fewer greenhouse gases compared to conventional energy sources. By reducing reliance on fossil fuels, which contribute to climate change and air pollution, these alternatives help mitigate environmental degradation and promote a cleaner, more sustainable future. Additionally, investing in renewable energy can stimulate economic growth through the creation of jobs in manufacturing, installation, and maintenance of renewable energy systems.

Renewable Energy Asset Evaluation Agencies

Renewable energy asset evaluation agencies play a crucial role in assessing and evaluating the viability and sustainability of renewable energy projects and assets. These agencies provide objective and independent analysis to investors, policymakers, and other stakeholders in the renewable energy sector.

The primary goal of these agencies is to measure the economic, social, and environmental impact of renewable energy projects, helping to guide decision-making processes. They employ standardized evaluation methodologies and metrics to assess the performance, cost-effectiveness, and environmental benefits of renewable energy assets.

Through their evaluations, these agencies provide valuable information and insights into the long-term sustainability and feasibility of different renewable energy technologies and projects. This helps investors make informed investment decisions, ensuring that resources are allocated efficiently and effectively. Decision-makers, such as policymakers, can also benefit from these evaluations as they inform the development of policies and regulations that encourage the growth and integration of renewable energy sources within the energy mix.

Furthermore, these agencies play a key role in ensuring transparency and trust in the renewable energy market. Their evaluations provide a reliable and standardized benchmark for comparing different projects, technologies, and companies. This allows for more accurate risk assessments and performance evaluations, which are essential for building trust and attracting investment in the sector.

Renewable Energy Asset Evaluation Services

Renewable energy asset evaluation services provide comprehensive assessment and valuation of sustainable energy infrastructure and projects. This process involves the analysis and estimation of the economic and environmental potential of renewable energy assets, such as solar farms, wind turbines, hydroelectric plants, and biomass facilities.

These evaluation services play a critical role in the sustainability sector by assisting stakeholders in making informed decisions regarding renewable energy investments. By assessing the value of renewable energy assets, these services aid in determining their financial viability, feasibility, and potential returns on investment.

The evaluation process typically includes a thorough examination of several factors, including the project's location, resource availability, technology employed, regulatory environment, operational risks, and market conditions. By considering these aspects, renewable energy asset evaluation services provide valuable insights into the long-term profitability and sustainability of renewable energy projects.

Furthermore, these services also evaluate the environmental impact of renewable energy assets. They analyze the greenhouse gas emissions reduction potential, land use requirements, and water consumption associated with each project. By quantifying the environmental benefits, renewable energy asset evaluation services support the sustainability agenda by promoting green energy development and contributing to the reduction of carbon emissions.

In summary, renewable energy asset evaluation services assist in the assessment and valuation of sustainable energy infrastructure and projects. By considering economic, environmental, and operational factors, these services facilitate informed decision-making, support investment planning, and contribute to the promotion of renewable energy and sustainability.

Renewable Energy Asset Management Software

Renewable energy asset management software is a technological solution designed to efficiently manage and optimize the operation and maintenance of renewable energy assets. This software plays a crucial role in promoting sustainability by enabling organizations to monitor, control, and maximize the performance of renewable energy systems such as solar, wind, and hydroelectric power plants.

The primary goal of renewable energy asset management software is to facilitate the seamless integration of renewable energy sources into the existing energy infrastructure. It provides real-time data analysis and reporting capabilities, allowing asset managers to monitor the performance, availability, and health of renewable energy assets. By constantly collecting and analyzing data, this software identifies potential issues and alerts operators to take proactive measures, minimizing downtime and maximizing energy production.

Furthermore, renewable energy asset management software helps streamline the maintenance processes by automating tasks such as scheduling inspections, tracking maintenance activities, and managing spare parts inventory. By optimizing maintenance activities, organizations can reduce costs and extend the lifespan of renewable energy assets, thereby maximizing the return on investment and reducing the environmental impact associated with their deployment.

In summary, renewable energy asset management software is an essential tool in ensuring the long-term viability and sustainability of renewable energy projects. By enabling effective monitoring, control, and maintenance of renewable energy assets, this software empowers organizations to harness the full potential of clean energy sources and contribute to the transition towards a more sustainable energy future.

Renewable Energy Certificate Trading

A renewable energy certificate (REC) trading refers to the process of buying and selling certificates that represent the environmental benefits produced by generating electricity from renewable sources. These certificates are used to track and verify renewable energy generation and consumption in order to support sustainability goals and promote the adoption of clean energy.

The trading of RECs plays a crucial role in incentivizing and promoting renewable energy development. It allows renewable energy generators to monetize the environmental attributes of their electricity generation, while also providing a means for industries and individuals to meet their sustainability targets. By purchasing RECs, businesses can claim that a portion or all of their electricity consumption comes from renewable sources, even if they are physically connected to a conventional grid.

The process typically involves the creation and issuance of RECs by a regulatory authority or an independent third-party certification agency. These certificates represent a certain amount of renewable energy production and are tracked in a central registry. Both renewable energy generators and purchasers of RECs must be registered in the registry to participate in the trading market.

Trading platforms or brokers facilitate the buying and selling of RECs. Generators can sell their certificates to interested buyers, while buyers, such as businesses, can purchase RECs to offset their conventional energy consumption. The trading process ensures transparency, credibility, and accountability by providing clear records of renewable energy generation and consumption.

Renewable Energy Community Cooperatives

Renewable energy community cooperatives are collaborative and grassroots organizations that aim to promote sustainable development by harnessing and generating renewable energy resources. These cooperatives are formed and owned by community members who pool their resources to collectively invest in, operate, and maintain renewable energy projects.

These cooperatives typically focus on the development of renewable energy sources such as solar, wind, hydro, biomass, and geothermal power. By leveraging the collective power of their community, they seek to reduce dependence on fossil fuels, mitigate climate change impacts, and create a more sustainable future.

Renewable Energy Community Education Initiatives

Renewable energy community education initiatives refer to programs, activities, and campaigns aimed at increasing public awareness and understanding of sustainable and clean energy sources, such as solar, wind, hydropower, and geothermal energy. These initiatives are designed to engage and educate individuals, communities, and organizations about the benefits and importance of transitioning from fossil fuels to renewable energy for a more sustainable and environmentally friendly future.

Through renewable energy community education initiatives, various educational resources, tools, and platforms are utilized to disseminate information about the potential of renewable energy, its role in reducing greenhouse gas emissions, mitigating climate change, and ensuring energy security. These initiatives often involve partnerships among government agencies, non-profit organizations, educational institutions, and industry stakeholders to collectively promote renewable energy education to a wider audience.

Renewable Energy Community Education Programs

A renewable energy community education program refers to a structured initiative aimed at promoting awareness and understanding of renewable energy sources, technologies, and practices within a community. The program focuses on educating community members about the benefits, opportunities, and challenges associated with renewable energy, with the ultimate goal of encouraging sustainable energy consumption and reducing dependence on fossil fuels.

Through a range of educational activities, such as workshops, seminars, webinars, and informational materials, the program aims to engage community members of all ages and backgrounds. The curriculum covers various aspects of renewable energy, including solar, wind, hydropower, geothermal, and bioenergy. Participants learn about the principles, application, and potential of each renewable energy source, as well as the environmental, social, and economic impacts of renewable energy adoption.

The program also emphasizes the importance of energy conservation and efficiency, showcasing ways to reduce energy consumption through behavioral changes and technological advancements. Additionally, community education programs may provide information on available financial incentives, government policies, and community-based initiatives to support and encourage renewable energy adoption.

By fostering greater understanding and knowledge of renewable energy, these programs empower community members to make informed decisions and take actions towards a more sustainable future. Through increased awareness and participation, communities can collectively contribute to mitigating climate change, reducing greenhouse gas emissions, and creating a more resilient and self-sufficient energy system.

Renewable Energy Credits (RECs)

Renewable Energy Credits (RECs), also known as Green Certificates or Renewable Energy Certificates, are a financial and accounting instrument that supports the development of renewable energy sources and encourages their use over conventional fossil fuels. RECs function as a way to track and verify the generation, sale, and use of renewable energy.

RECs are created when a renewable energy facility, such as a wind farm or solar power plant, produces one megawatt-hour (MWh) of electricity. Each REC represents the environmental attributes and benefits associated with the generation of that MWh of renewable energy. These attributes include the reduction of greenhouse gas emissions, decreased dependence on finite fossil fuel resources, and the promotion of sustainable energy practices.

RECs are transferable and can be bought and sold in the marketplace, providing a way for individuals, organizations, and utilities to support renewable energy even if they don't directly use it. By purchasing RECs, businesses can offset their carbon footprints, meet sustainability goals, and demonstrate their commitment to reducing greenhouse gas emissions. Similarly, utilities can fulfill their renewable energy requirements by purchasing RECs to meet their renewable portfolio standards.

RECs are an essential tool for promoting the growth of renewable energy sources, as they provide a way to monetize and incentivize the generation of clean, sustainable energy. They play a crucial role in stimulating investment in renewable energy projects, driving innovation, and transitioning towards a low-carbon economy.

Renewable Energy Crowdfunding Platforms

Renewable energy crowdfunding platforms are online platforms that bring together individuals, businesses, and organizations to collectively fund renewable energy projects. These platforms provide a way for people to contribute financially to the development and implementation of sustainable energy solutions, with the aim of reducing dependency on fossil fuels and mitigating the environmental impacts of traditional energy sources.

Through renewable energy crowdfunding platforms, investors can browse and select from a range of renewable energy projects, such as solar farms, wind turbines, biomass facilities, and hydropower installations. Each project typically has a dedicated funding target, and contributors can invest any amount towards that target, often receiving returns or incentives based on the project's success. This allows individuals and organizations to directly support and benefit from the growth of renewable energy infrastructure.

These platforms serve as a crucial link between renewable energy project developers and potential investors, providing a transparent and accessible avenue for funding. By connecting investors with projects and offering secure payment mechanisms, renewable energy crowdfunding platforms help accelerate the development and deployment of sustainable energy technologies.

Moreover, these platforms enable individuals to become active participants in the transition towards a more sustainable future, empowering them to make a positive impact on climate change, energy security, and environmental sustainability. Through their financial contributions, participants can drive the adoption of renewable energy sources and help combat global challenges associated with greenhouse gas emissions, resource depletion, and pollution.

Renewable Energy Cybersecurity Solutions

Renewable energy cybersecurity solutions refer to the strategic measures and practices implemented to protect the digital infrastructure, systems, and operations of renewable energy sources from various cyber threats. It involves developing and implementing robust security measures to safeguard renewable energy technologies, such as solar, wind, geothermal, and hydroelectric power plants, against unauthorized access, data breaches, and malicious activities.

In the context of sustainability, renewable energy cybersecurity solutions play a critical role in ensuring the uninterrupted and secure functioning of renewable energy systems. These solutions aim to mitigate the risks associated with cyberattacks, which have the potential to disrupt the generation, transmission, and distribution of clean energy. By safeguarding renewable energy infrastructures, cybersecurity solutions contribute to the sustainability efforts by reducing the vulnerability of the energy sector to cyber threats.

As the world increasingly relies on renewable energy sources to address environmental concerns and reduce dependence on fossil fuels, the importance of protecting these systems from cyber threats becomes paramount. Renewable energy cybersecurity solutions encompass a range of strategies, including network monitoring, incident response planning, access controls, encryption, regular vulnerability assessments, and employee training.

By implementing these solutions, the renewable energy sector can enhance the security and reliability of clean energy sources, minimizing the risks of disruptions and ensuring a sustainable energy future. Furthermore, as renewable energy systems often rely on interconnected networks and smart technologies, effective cybersecurity measures are essential to prevent unauthorized access or manipulation of data, ultimately safeguarding the integrity and efficiency of renewable energy generation and distribution.

Renewable Energy Data Analytics Tools

Renewable energy data analytics tools refer to a set of software applications and technologies that are specifically designed to collect, process, analyze, and interpret data related to renewable energy sources. These tools enable organizations and policymakers to make informed decisions and take appropriate actions to promote sustainability and accelerate the transition towards renewable energy.

By utilizing various data sources, such as weather data, power plant performance data, and energy consumption data, renewable energy data analytics tools can generate valuable insights and predictions. These insights can help identify patterns, optimize energy generation, detect anomalies and inefficiencies, and forecast future energy production. By understanding these trends and patterns, organizations can develop strategies to increase energy efficiency, reduce emissions, and better plan for future renewable energy deployment.

These tools often incorporate advanced analytics techniques, including machine learning and artificial intelligence, to process large amounts of data and uncover hidden patterns and correlations. They provide users with user-friendly interfaces and visualizations, enabling non-experts to understand complex energy data and make evidence-based decisions. Additionally, these tools can support monitoring and evaluation of renewable energy projects, enabling stakeholders to track progress, identify bottlenecks, and improve the performance of renewable energy systems.

In summary, renewable energy data analytics tools play a crucial role in promoting sustainability by enabling organizations and policymakers to analyze and interpret renewable energy data, identify trends, optimize energy generation, reduce emissions, and facilitate evidence-based decision-making for a greener future.

Renewable Energy Financing Platforms

A renewable energy financing platform refers to a specialized financial system that facilitates the funding and investment of projects related to renewable energy sources, such as solar, wind, hydro, and geothermal power. The primary objective of these platforms is to support the transition towards sustainable energy solutions by connecting project developers, investors, and lenders.

These platforms typically operate as online marketplaces, bringing together various stakeholders interested in renewable energy projects. Project developers can showcase their proposals and seek financial support, while investors and lenders can assess the project's potential and provide funding. Through these platforms, renewable energy projects gain access to the necessary capital to initiate, develop, and operate their initiatives.

Renewable Energy Forecasting Software

Renewable energy forecasting software refers to a technological tool designed to predict and estimate the production and usage of renewable energy sources over a specific time period. This software leverages advanced data analytics, algorithms, and statistical models to provide accurate insights regarding the expected generation and consumption levels of renewable energy.

With the global shift towards sustainable energy sources, the demand for renewable energy forecasting software has grown significantly. One of the main reasons for this surge in popularity is the intermittent nature of renewable energy generation, which makes it crucial to forecast and plan energy distribution effectively.

This software aids in optimizing the integration of renewable energy resources into the existing power grid by predicting the availability and output of renewable sources such as solar, wind, hydro, and biomass. By forecasting these variables, energy system operators can make informed decisions and develop efficient strategies for grid balancing, storage management, and demand response.

The accurate prediction of renewable energy generation and consumption helps improve the overall reliability and stability of the power system, reducing dependence on conventional energy sources and enhancing sustainability. It allows for better planning and utilization of renewable energy, maximizing its potential and minimizing the need for backup fossil fuel-based power generation.

Renewable Energy Grid Forecasting Tools

A renewable energy grid forecasting tool refers to a software or system that utilizes data analysis techniques to accurately predict and forecast the generation and consumption of renewable energy sources within a power grid. This tool plays a crucial role in supporting the efficient and sustainable integration and management of renewable energy into the existing power infrastructure.

By analyzing historical data, weather patterns, and other relevant factors, the forecasting tool can provide valuable insights into the future availability and output of renewable energy sources such as solar, wind, or hydroelectric power. It enables grid operators, energy providers, and policymakers to make informed decisions regarding capacity planning, grid stability, and energy trading.

Renewable Energy Grid Infrastructure

Renewable energy grid infrastructure refers to the physical system designed to distribute and transmit electricity generated from renewable sources to consumers, ensuring a sustainable energy supply.

This infrastructure plays a critical role in the adoption and integration of renewable energy technologies into the existing power grid. It includes a network of power lines, transformers, substations, and distribution systems that enable the transfer of electricity from renewable energy generation facilities, such as solar, wind, hydro, and geothermal power plants, to homes, businesses, and industries.

Renewable energy grid infrastructure is designed with the principles of sustainability in mind. It aims to reduce dependence on fossil fuels, decrease greenhouse gas emissions, and mitigate the environmental impacts of conventional energy sources. By integrating renewable energy sources into the grid, this infrastructure helps to promote a cleaner, more sustainable energy mix.

In addition to facilitating the distribution of renewable energy, the infrastructure also enables the efficient management and optimization of the power grid. Advanced technologies, such as smart grids and energy storage systems, can be integrated into the infrastructure to improve grid stability, reliability, and flexibility.

Overall, renewable energy grid infrastructure is a vital component of building a sustainable energy future. It supports the transition to a low-carbon economy, enhances energy security, and fosters the development of local, decentralized energy systems. By investing in and expanding this infrastructure, societies can reduce their environmental footprint and achieve long-term energy sustainability.

Renewable Energy Grid Integration Solutions

Renewable energy grid integration solutions refer to the various methods and strategies used to incorporate and optimize the integration of renewable energy sources into existing power grids in a sustainable manner.

As the demand for clean and sustainable energy continues to increase, the integration of renewable energy sources, such as wind, solar, hydro, and geothermal power, into existing power grids has become a key focus for ensuring a reliable and sustainable energy supply. Renewable energy grid integration solutions aim to address the challenges associated with the intermittent nature of renewable energy sources and their variability in generation output.

These solutions involve the use of advanced technologies and systems to manage the variability and unpredictability of renewable energy generation, as well as the effective transmission and distribution of renewable energy across the grid. Key components of renewable energy grid integration solutions include energy storage systems, smart grid technologies, demand response programs, and enhanced forecasting tools.

By implementing renewable energy grid integration solutions, we can maximize the utilization of renewable energy sources, reduce greenhouse gas emissions, and minimize the reliance on fossil fuels for electricity generation. This not only contributes to the reduction of carbon footprints but also enhances the resilience and sustainability of the power grid.

Renewable Energy Grid Integration

Renewable energy grid integration refers to the process of incorporating renewable energy sources into an existing power grid system in order to meet energy demands sustainably. It involves the efficient and seamless integration of renewable energy technologies such as solar, wind, hydro, and biomass with the traditional grid infrastructure.

This integration is crucial for achieving a sustainable energy system as it allows for the reduction of greenhouse gas emissions and dependence on fossil fuels. By integrating renewable energy sources, we can harness clean, abundant, and inexhaustible sources of energy, reducing our reliance on finite resources and mitigating the adverse effects of climate change. Moreover, renewable energy grid integration promotes energy diversification, enhancing energy security and reducing geopolitical risks associated with fossil fuel dependence.

Renewable Energy Grid Maintenance Services

Renewable energy grid maintenance services refer to the activities conducted to ensure the efficient and reliable operation of the infrastructure supporting the generation, transmission, and distribution of renewable energy. These services are essential to sustainably harness the power of renewable sources like solar, wind, hydro, and geothermal, and ensure their integration into the electrical grid.

The maintenance services for renewable energy grids encompass various tasks aimed at maximizing the system's performance, longevity, and environmental sustainability. These tasks include regular inspections, preventive maintenance, repairs, and upgrades of equipment and components involved in the generation, transmission, and distribution processes. The goal is to minimize downtime, optimize energy generation, and enhance the overall grid efficiency.

Additionally, renewable energy grid maintenance services include monitoring and managing the grid's performance, including the collection and analysis of data to identify potential issues, mitigate risks, and improve operations. This proactive approach helps in predicting and preventing failures, optimizing equipment usage, and reducing unplanned outages.

By ensuring the proper functioning of renewable energy grids, maintenance services support the continuous availability of clean and sustainable power sources. This contributes to the reduction of greenhouse gas emissions, dependence on fossil fuels, and the overall environmental impact of the energy sector. Furthermore, through regular maintenance and upgrades, these services enable the integration of new technologies and advancements in renewable energy generation, storage, and distribution, fostering the growth of a more resilient and sustainable energy infrastructure.

Renewable Energy Grid Maintenance Tools

Renewable energy grid maintenance tools are resources and equipment used to ensure the efficient and reliable operation of sustainable energy systems.

These tools are vital in supporting the sustainability of renewable energy grids, which aim to reduce the environmental impact of electricity generation by utilizing sources such as solar, wind, hydro, and geothermal power. The maintenance tools help monitor, diagnose, and rectify issues to minimize downtime, maximize energy production, and optimize grid performance.

One example of a renewable energy grid maintenance tool is a monitoring system. This tool continuously collects data on energy generation, transmission, and distribution parameters. It enables operators to identify underperforming components or irregularities in the grid, allowing for timely repairs or adjustments to prevent system failures or energy losses. Monitoring systems can also help identify opportunities for improvement, such as optimizing the placement of solar panels or wind turbines.

Another essential maintenance tool is diagnostic equipment, which aids in identifying faults or malfunctions in renewable energy systems. These tools help technicians pinpoint the root causes of issues, enabling swift and accurate repairs. Diagnostic equipment includes specialized instruments like thermal cameras, power analyzers, and vibration sensors that provide valuable insights into system health.

In conclusion, renewable energy grid maintenance tools are key to sustaining the functionality and performance of sustainable energy systems. By utilizing monitoring systems and diagnostic equipment, operators can identify and address issues promptly, minimizing downtime and optimizing energy production. These tools play a critical role in ensuring the long-term viability and reliability of renewable energy grids.

Renewable Energy Grid Maintenance

Renewable energy grid maintenance refers to the ongoing efforts and activities undertaken to ensure the efficient and sustainable operation of a grid that relies on renewable energy sources for electricity generation.

It involves the regular inspection, repair, and replacement of components and equipment within the grid, such as wind turbines, solar panels, biomass generators, and hydroelectric facilities. These maintenance tasks are crucial for maximizing the performance and lifespan of renewable energy assets, reducing downtime, and minimizing environmental impacts.

The maintenance of a renewable energy grid also includes monitoring and managing the transmission and distribution systems that deliver electricity to consumers. This entails detecting and addressing any issues that may arise, such as line faults, voltage fluctuations, or grid instability, to ensure a reliable supply of renewable energy to homes, businesses, and other users.

Furthermore, preventive maintenance measures are implemented to identify potential problems before they escalate, which helps to prevent costly breakdowns and system failures. This may involve regular inspections, scheduled component replacements, and the use of advanced monitoring technologies to detect any abnormalities or performance deviations.

Overall, renewable energy grid maintenance plays a vital role in supporting the transition towards a sustainable energy future. By ensuring the reliable and efficient operation of renewable energy infrastructure, it helps to reduce greenhouse gas emissions, decrease reliance on fossil fuels, and promote the long-term viability of renewable energy as a clean and renewable power source for generations to come.

Renewable Energy Grid Management Systems

A renewable energy grid management system is a sustainable solution designed to efficiently manage and regulate the flow of electricity generated from renewable sources such as solar, wind, hydro, and geothermal power. It encompasses various software, hardware, and communication technologies that integrate renewable energy generation, distribution, and consumption.

In the context of sustainability, renewable energy grid management systems play a crucial role in optimizing the utilization of renewable resources, minimizing greenhouse gas emissions, and promoting a cleaner and greener energy sector. These systems enable real-time monitoring, forecasting, and decision-making, ensuring the reliable and stable operation of renewable energy grids.

Renewable Energy Grid Optimization Software

The renewable energy grid optimization software is a specialized tool that aids in the efficient management and utilization of renewable energy sources in a sustainable manner. It encompasses a range of algorithms, models, and data analytics techniques to optimize the functioning and performance of the renewable energy grid.

This software plays a crucial role in supporting the transition towards a sustainable energy system by addressing challenges such as intermittency, fluctuating supply, and demand patterns. It helps balance the renewable energy supply and demand, ensuring a reliable and stable power supply while minimizing environmental impacts.

Through advanced forecasting, the software facilitates accurate predictions of renewable energy generation, considering factors such as weather conditions, solar radiation, and wind speed. These forecasts enable grid operators to plan and manage the distribution of renewable energy effectively, maximizing its utilization and minimizing curtailment.

Moreover, the software also optimizes energy storage and dispatch strategies, helping to integrate and manage various energy storage technologies like batteries, pumped hydro, and compressed air. It assists in determining the optimal storage capacity, charging, and discharging schedules to ensure a cost-effective and efficient use of stored energy.

Overall, the renewable energy grid optimization software acts as a critical tool for achieving sustainability goals by enabling the seamless integration of renewable energy into the grid infrastructure, enhancing grid reliability and stability, and reducing greenhouse gas emissions.

Renewable Energy Grid Optimization

Renewable energy grid optimization refers to the process of improving the efficiency and reliability of a sustainable energy distribution system. It involves the use of advanced technologies and the implementation of strategies to maximize the utilization of renewable energy sources while minimizing environmental impact.

The goal of renewable energy grid optimization is to create a well-balanced and resilient energy grid that can effectively meet the increasing demand for clean and sustainable power. This is achieved through various measures such as the integration of different types of renewable energy sources, the use of energy storage systems, and the implementation of smart grid technologies.

By optimizing the renewable energy grid, it becomes possible to better match the supply and demand of electricity, ensuring a stable and reliable power supply. This helps reduce the dependency on fossil fuels and mitigates the environmental impact associated with their combustion.

Renewable energy grid optimization also offers economic benefits by reducing energy costs and creating new job opportunities in the renewable energy sector. Additionally, it contributes to the overall resilience of the energy infrastructure, making it more resistant to disruptions and enabling faster recovery in the event of natural disasters or other emergencies.

Renewable Energy Insurance Providers

A renewable energy insurance provider is an entity that offers insurance coverage specifically tailored for renewable energy projects. These projects generate energy from renewable sources such as wind, solar, hydro, geothermal, or biomass, which are all sustainable and environmentally friendly ways to produce power.

Insurance coverage provided by these providers is designed to protect renewable energy project owners and investors against various risks associated with these types of projects. This can include risks such as physical damage to the project infrastructure, business interruption, liability, and loss of revenue.

Renewable Energy Integration

Renewable energy integration refers to the process of incorporating sustainable energy sources into the existing energy infrastructure and systems to maximize their utilization and reduce dependence on fossil fuels. It involves the seamless integration of renewable energy technologies, such as solar, wind, hydro, and geothermal, into the traditional power grid and energy networks.

This integration promotes the shift towards a more sustainable and environmentally friendly energy system by harnessing the abundant and freely available renewable resources. It aims at increasing the share of renewable energy in the overall energy mix to ensure long-term energy security, reduce greenhouse gas emissions, mitigate climate change impacts, and promote sustainable development.

Renewable energy integration involves several key aspects, including grid modernization, storage solutions, and demand-side management. Grid modernization entails upgrading the existing transmission and distribution infrastructure to accommodate the intermittent nature of renewable energy sources. Storage solutions, such as batteries and pumped hydro storage, are crucial in enabling the effective use of renewable energy by providing a means to store excess energy for times when the renewable sources are not generating sufficient power. Demand-side management involves optimizing energy consumption and adjusting electricity demand to align with the availability of renewable energy, thereby reducing the need for conventional energy sources.

Overall, renewable energy integration plays a vital role in promoting sustainability by facilitating the transition towards a cleaner, more resilient, and diversified energy system that minimizes environmental impact and maximizes energy efficiency.

Renewable Energy Investment Platforms

A renewable energy investment platform is a digital platform that enables individuals, organizations, and institutions to invest in projects and companies focused on sustainable and clean energy sources. These platforms facilitate the financing of renewable energy projects, allowing investors to contribute to the global transition towards a more sustainable and low-carbon future.

Through these platforms, investors can browse and select from a wide range of renewable energy investment opportunities, including solar, wind, hydro, geothermal, and biomass projects. The platforms typically provide detailed information about each investment opportunity, including project description, financial projections, and expected returns.

Investors can participate in these opportunities by contributing funds, either as equity or debt, depending on the structure of the investment. Some platforms may also offer crowdinvesting options, allowing smaller investors to pool their resources together to invest in larger-scale projects.

By investing in renewable energy projects through these platforms, individuals and organizations can directly support the development and expansion of clean energy infrastructure. This contributes to the reduction of greenhouse gas emissions, mitigates climate change, and promotes energy independence and security.

Renewable energy investment platforms play a crucial role in accelerating the transition to a sustainable energy system by connecting investors with promising projects that align with their sustainability goals and financial objectives.

Renewable Energy Legal Advisory Services

Renewable energy legal advisory services refer to the provision of guidance and support in legal matters related to sustainable energy sources. This includes assistance with regulatory compliance, contract negotiation, risk assessment, and dispute resolution in the renewable energy sector.

The transition to renewable energy sources is a crucial aspect of achieving sustainability and combating climate change. Renewable energy legal advisory services play a vital role in facilitating this transition by ensuring that projects and initiatives align with relevant laws and regulations, and by addressing any legal challenges that may arise.

These services can help renewable energy developers and investors navigate the complex legal landscape surrounding renewable energy projects. They provide expertise in various areas, such as renewable energy incentives, permits and licenses, land agreements, environmental impact assessments, and power purchase agreements. By understanding the legal implications and requirements, clients can make informed decisions and effectively manage legal risks in their renewable energy ventures.

Renewable energy legal advisors also assist in negotiating contracts with stakeholders, such as suppliers, contractors, and off-takers. They help structure agreements that protect the interests

272

of their clients while promoting the growth of renewable energy markets.

In addition, these services address legal issues that may arise during the operation of renewable energy projects, including environmental compliance, project financing, and dispute resolution. By offering specialized legal expertise, renewable energy legal advisory services contribute to the sustainability and long-term success of renewable energy ventures.

Renewable Energy Legal Consulting

Renewable energy legal consulting refers to the practice of providing legal advice and guidance in matters related to the development, deployment, and regulation of renewable energy resources. This field of legal consulting focuses on helping individuals, businesses, and governments navigate the complex legal and regulatory landscape surrounding sustainable energy projects.

As the world increasingly prioritizes sustainability and the transition to cleaner sources of energy, renewable energy legal consulting plays a crucial role in ensuring that renewable energy projects are developed and implemented in compliance with relevant laws and regulations. This may involve assisting clients in obtaining the necessary permits and licenses, negotiating agreements with stakeholders and investors, and navigating the legal framework for renewable energy incentives and subsidies.

Renewable Energy Market Analysis Software

A renewable energy market analysis software is a tool that provides a comprehensive assessment and evaluation of the renewable energy sector. It enables users to gather, analyze, and interpret data related to the market trends, opportunities, and challenges in the renewable energy industry.

This software helps organizations and stakeholders in the sustainability field make informed decisions and formulate effective strategies. It allows users to examine critical factors such as renewable energy technologies, policy frameworks, regulatory landscape, energy prices, and market demand. By analyzing these factors, the software helps identify potential growth areas, investment opportunities, and potential risks in the renewable energy market.

Renewable Energy Market Intelligence

Renewable energy market intelligence refers to the systematic collection, analysis, and dissemination of relevant information and insights about the market for renewable energy sources and technologies, with the primary objective of promoting sustainable development. It involves monitoring and tracking the latest trends, regulatory frameworks, technological advancements, and investment opportunities in the renewable energy sector.

This form of market intelligence aims to empower policymakers, investors, energy companies, and other stakeholders with reliable and up-to-date information to make informed decisions in advancing sustainable energy solutions. It provides a holistic understanding of the market dynamics, including supply and demand patterns, market growth potential, competitive landscape, and market barriers and opportunities.

Renewable Energy Market Research Firms

A renewable energy market research firm is an organization that conducts systematic investigations and analysis to gather information and insights on various aspects of the renewable energy market. Their primary focus is to study and understand the trends, dynamics, and potential growth opportunities within the sustainable energy sector.

These firms gather data from multiple sources such as surveys, interviews, market reports, and government records to provide accurate and comprehensive assessments. They analyze this information using various research methodologies to identify patterns, forecast future market developments, and evaluate the impact of policy changes on the renewable energy industry.

Their research findings help businesses, investors, policymakers, and other stakeholders make

273

informed decisions regarding renewable energy investments, market positioning, and policy development. These firms often publish reports, white papers, and industry analyses that provide valuable insights into the latest market trends, emerging technologies, and factors driving the growth of the renewable energy sector.

In addition to market research, these firms may also offer consulting services, helping clients develop sustainable energy strategies, conduct feasibility studies for renewable projects, and evaluate the potential risks and returns associated with such initiatives. They play a crucial role in fostering the development and adoption of renewable energy by facilitating the flow of reliable market information and supporting evidence-based decision-making processes.

Renewable Energy Materials Research

Renewable energy materials research is a critical field of study that aims to develop sustainable solutions for meeting our energy needs. It involves the investigation and exploration of materials that can be utilized in the production of renewable energy sources, such as solar, wind, hydro, and geothermal power.

The main objective of renewable energy materials research is to identify and develop materials that are abundant, affordable, and environmentally friendly. These materials should possess properties that enhance the efficiency, durability, and performance of renewable energy technologies, enabling a more sustainable and cleaner energy future.

Renewable Energy Microgrid Systems

A renewable energy microgrid system refers to a localized power grid that incorporates various renewable energy sources to generate electricity and provide reliable and sustainable energy to a specific area or community. It is designed to operate independently or in conjunction with the main grid, ensuring energy independence and stability, especially during power outages or disruptions.

Microgrids consist of multiple energy generation sources, such as solar panels, wind turbines, biomass, or hydroelectric power, which harness and convert renewable resources into electricity. These sources are often complemented by energy storage systems, such as batteries, to store excess energy and distribute it when needed.

The deployment of renewable energy microgrid systems promotes sustainability by reducing greenhouse gas emissions, dependence on fossil fuels, and reliance on centralized power plants. It enables the integration of intermittent renewable energy sources into the grid, ensuring a continuous and reliable power supply even in remote or rural areas.

Microgrids offer several advantages in terms of environmental impact, energy efficiency, and resilience. They facilitate the utilization of clean energy sources, mitigating the harmful effects of climate change and promoting a transition towards a low-carbon economy. Moreover, these systems enhance energy efficiency since they prioritize local energy generation and consumption, reducing transmission and distribution losses.

Furthermore, renewable energy microgrid systems enhance the resilience of communities by providing a decentralized energy infrastructure. In the event of natural disasters or grid failures, these systems can continue to supply power, ensuring essential services like hospitals, schools, and emergency response centers remain functional.

Renewable Energy Microgrids

A renewable energy microgrid is a localized energy system that utilizes renewable energy sources to generate electricity and provide power to a specific geographic area, such as a building, neighborhood, or community. These microgrids are designed to enhance sustainability by reducing reliance on traditional fossil fuel-based power grids and promoting the use of clean and renewable energy sources.

By integrating various renewable energy technologies, such as solar panels, wind turbines, hydroelectric generators, and battery storage systems, microgrids can generate electricity from abundant and eco-friendly sources. The energy generated can be used to meet the local demand for electricity, reducing the need to transmit power over long distances and minimizing transmission losses.

Renewable energy microgrids offer several key advantages in terms of sustainability. Firstly, they contribute to the reduction of greenhouse gas emissions by replacing the use of fossil fuels with clean energy sources. This helps combat climate change and air pollution, leading to a healthier and more sustainable environment.

Secondly, these microgrids enhance energy resilience and reliability. By decentralizing energy generation and incorporating energy storage systems, such as batteries, microgrids can continue supplying electricity even during grid outages or natural disasters. This improves the overall reliability and stability of the energy system.

Renewable Energy Peer-To-Peer Networks

A renewable energy peer-to-peer network refers to a decentralized system that allows individuals or entities to share and trade renewable energy resources directly with each other. This network enables the generation, consumption, and distribution of renewable energy in a sustainable manner.

Unlike traditional energy systems that are centralized and rely on fossil fuels, renewable energy peer-to-peer networks emphasize the use of clean and sustainable sources such as solar, wind, hydro, and geothermal energy. Participants in these networks can connect their renewable energy generation systems, such as solar panels or wind turbines, to the network and contribute excess energy to the grid. Other participants can then access this energy when needed.

These networks promote sustainability by minimizing transmission losses and reducing the reliance on traditional energy providers. By directly exchanging energy between peers, the need for extensive energy transportation infrastructure is reduced, leading to lower energy losses during transmission. Additionally, renewable energy peer-to-peer networks encourage the use of locally produced renewable energy, reducing the carbon footprint associated with long-distance energy transportation and promoting community-level sustainability.

In summary, renewable energy peer-to-peer networks foster the sustainable generation, distribution, and consumption of renewable energy by enabling direct exchanges between individuals or entities. These networks contribute to a more decentralized, environmentally friendly energy system, reducing greenhouse gas emissions, promoting local energy production, and minimizing transmission losses.

Renewable Energy Policy Advocacy Groups

Renewable energy policy advocacy groups are organizations that aim to promote and advance the use of renewable energy sources as a sustainable alternative to fossil fuels. These groups work towards the development and implementation of policies that support the growth and adoption of renewable energy technologies.

Renewable energy policy advocacy groups advocate for the transition to renewable energy sources due to their numerous environmental, economic, and social benefits. They typically engage with policymakers, legislators, and other stakeholders to influence the creation and implementation of regulations, incentives, and investment frameworks that support renewable energy development.

Renewable Energy Policy Consulting Firms

A renewable energy policy consulting firm is a specialized consultancy that provides expert advice and guidance to governments, organizations, and businesses on the development, implementation, and evaluation of renewable energy policies. These policies aim to promote and facilitate the transition to a sustainable energy system that relies on renewable sources such as solar, wind, hydro, geothermal, and biomass.

Renewable energy policy consulting firms assist their clients in various ways. They conduct thorough analyses of the existing energy landscape and assess the potential for renewable energy development. Based on these assessments, they help formulate policies and strategies that align with sustainable development goals and national priorities. This may involve designing feed-in tariffs, renewable portfolio standards, tax incentives, and other mechanisms that encourage renewable energy investment and deployment.

In addition, renewable energy policy consulting firms provide support in the implementation phase, assisting in the establishment of regulatory frameworks, institutional capacity building, and stakeholder engagement. They monitor and evaluate policy effectiveness, making recommendations for adjustments and improvements as needed. These firms also play a crucial role in knowledge dissemination, organizing workshops, conferences, and training programs to transfer expertise and best practices to government officials, policymakers, and industry stakeholders.

The services offered by renewable energy policy consulting firms contribute to the advancement of sustainability by facilitating the adoption of renewable energy technologies, reducing greenhouse gas emissions, enhancing energy security, and promoting economic growth through the development of a green energy sector.

Renewable Energy Project Consulting Firms

A renewable energy project consulting firm is a company that specializes in providing expert advice and guidance on sustainable energy initiatives. These firms work with clients who are looking to develop, implement, or improve renewable energy projects, such as solar, wind, geothermal, or hydroelectric power systems.

The primary goal of a renewable energy project consulting firm is to help their clients achieve sustainability by transitioning from traditional fossil fuel-based energy sources to renewable sources. They analyze the feasibility of renewable energy projects, provide technical expertise, and assist in the development of comprehensive strategies to maximize the efficiency and effectiveness of these projects.

These consulting firms typically offer a range of services, including project planning, feasibility studies, financial analysis, environmental impact assessments, and regulatory compliance. They help clients navigate the complex landscape of renewable energy regulations, policies, and incentives, ensuring that projects meet all required standards and guidelines.

In addition, renewable energy project consulting firms may assist with project management, procurement of equipment, technology selection, and vendor evaluation. They work collaboratively with their clients to identify the most suitable renewable energy solutions and offer tailored recommendations to optimize project performance and mitigate risks.

Overall, a renewable energy project consulting firm plays a crucial role in promoting and advancing sustainable energy practices. By offering specialized knowledge and expertise, these firms contribute to the growth of renewable energy industries and support the transition to a more sustainable and environmentally friendly energy future.

Renewable Energy Project Development Services

Renewable energy project development services refer to the specialized range of activities that aim to foster the growth and establishment of sustainable energy infrastructure. These services encompass the entire lifecycle of renewable energy projects, from initial conception and planning to implementation, operation, and continuous improvement. The primary goal of renewable energy project development services is to accelerate the deployment of renewable energy technologies while ensuring their long-term viability and sustainability.

These services typically involve conducting comprehensive feasibility studies and site assessments to identify suitable locations for renewable energy projects. This includes evaluating factors such as solar radiation, wind patterns, geothermal resources, and available land or water bodies. Once a viable site is identified, renewable energy project development services involve securing the necessary permits, licenses, and regulatory approvals required for project implementation.

Furthermore, these services assist in securing financing options and facilitating partnerships with relevant stakeholders, including investors, technology providers, government agencies, and local communities. They play a crucial role in coordinating and managing the various aspects of project development, such as engineering design, equipment procurement, construction supervision, and grid integration.

In addition, renewable energy project development services also encompass monitoring and evaluation activities to ensure the effective operation and performance of renewable energy systems. This may involve undertaking regular performance assessments, maintenance activities, and implementing strategies to optimize energy generation and reduce environmental impacts.

Overall, renewable energy project development services form an essential component of sustainable development strategies, seeking to address the pressing concerns of climate change, energy security, and resource depletion. By fostering the growth of renewable energy infrastructure, these services contribute to reducing greenhouse gas emissions, diversifying energy sources, promoting local economic development, and creating a more sustainable and resilient energy future.

Renewable Energy Project Development Software

A renewable energy project development software refers to a digital tool or platform designed specifically for the planning, management, and implementation of sustainable energy projects. It is a comprehensive software solution that aids in the effective coordination and facilitation of all stages involved in renewable energy project development.

This software serves as a centralized hub where project managers, engineers, and stakeholders can collaboratively work towards the successful realization of sustainable energy initiatives. It integrates various functionalities and features that streamline processes and optimize project outcomes, ultimately contributing to the overarching goal of sustainability.

The main objective of renewable energy project development software is to support the transition to cleaner and more sustainable energy sources. It enables users to assess the feasibility of potential projects, conduct site analyses, and evaluate the environmental impact of proposed developments. Through advanced modeling capabilities, the software helps in optimizing the design and configuration of renewable energy systems, ensuring maximum efficiency and cost-effectiveness.

Furthermore, this software assists in financial analysis and risk assessment, providing valuable insights into the economic viability and potential profitability of renewable energy projects. It aids in project planning and scheduling, resource management, and the tracking of progress, enabling efficient and transparent project execution.

In conclusion, renewable energy project development software plays a crucial role in facilitating the planning, implementation, and management of sustainable energy projects. By streamlining processes, optimizing designs, and supporting effective decision-making, this software contributes to the advancement of renewable energy technologies, ultimately helping to combat climate change and ensure a more sustainable future.

Renewable Energy Project Finance Platforms

A renewable energy project finance platform is a system or platform that enables the funding, investment, and development of sustainable energy projects. It serves as a medium for connecting project developers, investors, and lenders, facilitating the creation and implementation of renewable energy initiatives.

These platforms aim to address the financial challenges faced by renewable energy projects, which often require significant upfront investments. By providing a centralized marketplace, they allow project developers to showcase their proposals and attract potential investors. Simultaneously, they offer investors access to a diverse range of renewable energy projects, allowing them to allocate their funds toward initiatives that align with their sustainability goals.

One of the key features of renewable energy project finance platforms is their ability to provide transparency and efficiency in the investment process. They streamline the due diligence procedures, risk assessment, and financial analysis, enabling all stakeholders to make informed decisions. Additionally, these platforms offer tools for financial modeling and forecasting, helping project developers assess the economic viability of their initiatives and demonstrate value to potential investors.

Furthermore, renewable energy project finance platforms often incorporate sustainability criteria in their selection process. They assess the social, environmental, and governance aspects of the projects, ensuring that investments contribute positively to global sustainability goals. By facilitating the flow of capital towards renewable energy projects, these platforms play a crucial role in accelerating the transition to a low-carbon economy and promoting a more sustainable future.

Renewable Energy Research And Development

Renewable energy research and development refers to the scientific investigation and innovation aimed at advancing sustainable energy sources that can be replenished naturally in a relatively short period of time. It is a key component of efforts to transition from fossil fuels to renewable sources of energy in order to mitigate the adverse effects of climate change and ensure long-term environmental sustainability.

Renewable energy research involves the exploration of various technologies and methods for harnessing energy from sources such as sunlight, wind, water, and biomass. It includes the study of their efficiency, scalability, and environmental impact. Development further entails the improvement and deployment of these technologies to create practical solutions for energy generation, transmission, and storage.

The objectives of renewable energy research and development are multifold. Firstly, it aims to enhance the efficiency and cost-effectiveness of renewable energy systems, making them more competitive with traditional energy sources. Additionally, it seeks to address challenges associated with intermittency, storage, and grid integration of renewable energy, enabling their reliable and widespread deployment. Furthermore, research and development efforts focus on reducing the environmental footprint of renewable energy technologies, such as minimizing land use, water consumption, and emissions.

By advancing renewable energy research and development, societies can foster a sustainable energy future that promotes economic growth, energy security, and environmental protection. It offers the potential to lessen dependence on fossil fuels, decrease greenhouse gas emissions, and mitigate the impacts of climate change. Through ongoing research and development, new technological breakthroughs and innovations can be achieved, propelling the world towards a cleaner and more sustainable energy landscape.

Renewable Energy Storage Solutions

Renewable energy storage solutions, in the context of sustainability, refer to technologies and strategies that allow for the capture, storage, and efficient utilization of renewable energy sources. These solutions aim to address the intermittent nature of renewable energy generation, ensuring continuous power supply and maximizing the utilization of clean energy.

As the dependence on renewable energy sources like solar and wind power continues to grow, the development of effective storage solutions is vital to overcome the challenges of intermittent power generation. These solutions enable the storage of excess energy produced during periods of high renewable energy generation and its subsequent use during times of low generation or high demand. By storing energy, these solutions ensure a consistent and reliable power supply, reducing the reliance on fossil fuels and minimizing greenhouse gas emissions.

Renewable energy storage solutions encompass a range of technologies, including batteries, pumped hydroelectric storage, compressed air energy storage, flywheels, and thermal storage systems. These technologies store energy in various forms such as chemical, gravitational potential, compressed air, kinetic, or thermal energy, allowing for its conversion and release when needed.

Furthermore, these solutions play a crucial role in enabling the integration of renewable energy into existing power grids, facilitating grid stability and resilience. By maintaining a balanced supply-demand ratio, energy storage solutions contribute to a sustainable energy future by reducing reliance on non-renewable resources, enhancing energy efficiency, and mitigating the environmental impacts associated with traditional energy generation.

Renewable Energy Trade Associations

A renewable energy trade association is an organization that represents the interests of companies, organizations, and individuals involved in the production, distribution, and promotion of renewable energy sources. These associations play a crucial role in advocating for the adoption and implementation of sustainable energy practices to support the transition towards a low-carbon and environmentally friendly energy sector.

Renewable energy trade associations provide a platform for stakeholders to collaborate, exchange knowledge, and address common challenges related to renewable energy policies, technologies, and market dynamics. They engage in activities such as policy advocacy, research and development, networking events, educational programs, and industry standards development.

These trade associations work closely with governments, regulatory bodies, and other relevant institutions to influence policy decisions that support the growth and development of renewable energy markets. They often provide expert advice, conduct analysis, and participate in public consultations to ensure that the interests of the renewable energy sector are effectively represented in policy-making processes.

Furthermore, renewable energy trade associations facilitate the sharing of best practices, technical expertise, and industry insights among their members. Through conferences, seminars, workshops, and publications, they contribute to the dissemination of knowledge and advancements in renewable energy technologies, fostering innovation and collaboration within the sector.

In summary, renewable energy trade associations are instrumental in promoting the sustainability and advancement of renewable energy sources by fostering collaboration, advocacy, and knowledge-sharing among stakeholders in the industry.

Renewable Energy Transmission Infrastructure

The renewable energy transmission infrastructure refers to the network of physical structures and systems that facilitate the generation, transmission, and distribution of renewable energy sources. It is an essential component of a sustainable energy system, as it enables the efficient and reliable delivery of clean, renewable energy from the point of generation to end users.

This infrastructure encompasses various elements, including power plants, transmission lines, substations, transformers, and distribution networks. Power plants, such as solar farms or wind turbines, convert renewable sources such as sunlight or wind into electricity. Transmission lines carry the electricity over long distances, typically at high voltages, while substations facilitate the transformation of voltage levels for efficient transmission. Finally, distribution networks deliver the electricity to homes, businesses, and other consumers.

Renewable Energy Workforce Development Programs

Renewable energy workforce development programs are initiatives aimed at cultivating a skilled and diverse labor force to support the growth and sustainability of renewable energy industries. These programs focus on providing individuals with the knowledge, skills, and training necessary to participate in the design, installation, operation, and maintenance of renewable energy systems.

The purpose of these programs is to address the increasing global demand for renewable energy and the need for qualified workers in this rapidly evolving sector. They aim to bridge the gap between the growing job opportunities in renewable energy and the lack of trained professionals in the field. These workforce development programs offer a range of training and education opportunities, including vocational and technical courses, apprenticeships, and certification programs. They cover various aspects of renewable energy, such as solar, wind, hydro, geothermal, and bioenergy. Participants learn about the principles, technologies, and best practices associated with each of these renewable energy sources. Additionally, these programs often emphasize the importance of sustainability and environmental stewardship, promoting a holistic approach to renewable energy development. They highlight the potential of renewable energy to reduce greenhouse gas emissions, mitigate climate change, and promote a more sustainable and resilient energy infrastructure. Overall, renewable energy workforce development programs play a critical role in equipping individuals with the skills and knowledge needed to contribute to the transition to clean and renewable energy sources. By training a diverse workforce, these programs contribute to the long-term sustainability of renewable energy industries and support a more sustainable future for our planet.

Renewable Energy Workforce Training Programs

Renewable energy workforce training programs refer to educational initiatives aimed at equipping individuals with the knowledge and skills needed to work in the field of renewable energy. These programs typically focus on teaching the technical, operational, and maintenance aspects of renewable energy technologies such as solar power, wind power, hydropower, geothermal energy, and bioenergy.

The main objective of renewable energy workforce training programs is to address the growing demand for skilled workers in the renewable energy sector, as well as to support the transition to a more sustainable and clean energy system. By training individuals in the various aspects of renewable energy technologies, these programs help to develop a competent and capable workforce that can contribute to the development, installation, operation, and maintenance of renewable energy projects.

Renewable energy workforce training programs typically cover a wide range of topics, including renewable energy principles, energy efficiency, electrical systems, safety procedures, project management, and environmental considerations. The training may be delivered through various formats, such as classroom lectures, hands-on practical exercises, virtual simulations, and on-the-job training.

These programs can be offered by universities, colleges, vocational schools, technical institutes, government agencies, industry associations, and private training providers. They may lead to the attainment of certificates, diplomas, or degrees, depending on the level and duration of the program.

Renewable Natural Gas (RNG)

Renewable natural gas (RNG) is a sustainable energy source produced from organic materials that would otherwise be considered waste. It is derived from the decomposition of organic matter, such as food scraps, agricultural waste, and wastewater, through a process called anaerobic digestion. During this process, microorganisms break down the organic matter in the absence of oxygen, releasing biogas.

The biogas produced from anaerobic digestion consists primarily of methane, which is a potent greenhouse gas. By capturing and treating this biogas, RNG is created. RNG is similar to conventional natural gas and can be used interchangeably in existing natural gas infrastructure and vehicles. However, RNG is distinct because it is a carbon-neutral fuel, meaning that the emissions released when it is burned are offset by the carbon dioxide absorbed during the growth of the organic materials used to produce it. This makes RNG an attractive solution for reducing greenhouse gas emissions and mitigating climate change.

In addition to its environmental benefits, RNG also has economic and social advantages. It helps to diversify the energy supply, reduces reliance on fossil fuels, and creates job opportunities in the renewable energy sector. Furthermore, RNG production can divert organic waste from landfills, reducing methane emissions from decomposition and minimizing the release of harmful pollutants into the environment.

Overall, RNG is a sustainable energy source that promotes a circular economy by utilizing organic waste to generate renewable fuel. Its production and use contribute to achieving climate goals, improving air quality, and fostering a more sustainable and resilient energy system.

Renewable Natural Gas

Renewable natural gas is a sustainable energy source derived from organic waste materials, such as agriculture, landfills, and wastewater treatment plants. It is a renewable form of natural gas that can be produced through various processes, including anaerobic digestion and thermal conversion.

By capturing methane emissions from organic waste and converting them into renewable natural gas, this energy source helps to reduce greenhouse gas emissions and combat climate change. Unlike fossil fuels, renewable natural gas is considered carbon neutral since it releases an equal amount of carbon dioxide when used as a fuel, as the organic waste would release naturally through decomposition.

Repair And Refurbishment

Repair and refurbishment refer to the processes of fixing and refreshing products or goods that have experienced wear, damage, or obsolescence. These practices aim to extend the lifespan and functionality of items, reducing the need for new production and minimizing waste, energy consumption, and resource depletion. Repair involves addressing specific issues or malfunctions in a product to restore it to proper working condition. It often requires diagnosing the problem, replacing or repairing faulty components, and ensuring the product meets safety and performance standards. Refurbishment, on the other hand, entails more extensive renovation and improvement of a product's appearance, features, and performance. This may involve cleaning, repainting, replacing worn-out parts, upgrading technology, or enhancing design. Both these processes contribute to sustainability by enabling the reuse of materials and reducing the overall demand for new products. By repairing and refurbishing goods rather than disposing of them, valuable resources are conserved, and the environmental impacts associated with manufacturing, shipping, and disposing of new products are minimized. Furthermore, repair and refurbishment can also provide economic benefits, such as supporting local repair businesses, creating jobs, and reducing costs for consumers who can opt for more affordable repaired or refurbished items instead of purchasing new ones.

Resource Recovery Strategies

Resource recovery strategies refer to the methods and actions utilized to extract valuable materials and energy from waste and other discarded resources. These strategies emphasize sustainable practices and ensure that valuable resources are not lost or wasted. The ultimate goal of resource recovery strategies is to minimize the environmental impact of waste disposal while maximizing resource utilization, thus promoting a circular economy.

There are several resource recovery strategies employed to achieve these objectives. One such strategy is recycling, which involves collecting and processing materials such as paper, plastics, and metals to create new products. By diverting these materials from landfills, recycling conserves resources, reduces energy consumption, and minimizes greenhouse gas emissions. Another important strategy is composting, wherein organic waste such as food scraps and garden trimmings are decomposed to produce nutrient-rich compost. This compost can then be used as a natural fertilizer, reducing the need for synthetic fertilizers and promoting soil health.

Additionally, technologies like waste-to-energy (WtE) conversion systems play a crucial role in resource recovery. WtE technologies convert non-recyclable waste into usable energy, typically in the form of electricity or heat. This not only reduces the volume of waste going to landfills but also harnesses the energy potential of these materials. Similarly, anaerobic digestion processes can be employed to break down organic waste, releasing methane gas that can be captured and used as a renewable energy source.

Overall, resource recovery strategies are vital components of sustainable waste management. By diverting waste from disposal sites and harnessing its potential, these strategies enable the efficient use of resources, reduce pollution, conserve energy, and contribute to the transition towards a more sustainable and circular economy.

Resource-Efficient Agriculture

Resource-efficient agriculture refers to the effective and sustainable use of natural resources in the agricultural sector. It is an approach that aims to minimize the negative impact of farming practices on the environment while maximizing productivity and economic efficiency.

In resource-efficient agriculture, farmers employ techniques and technologies that reduce resource wastage and promote conservation. This includes implementing precision farming methods, such as variable rate application of inputs like water, fertilizers, and pesticides, based on the specific requirements of different areas within a field. By tailoring inputs to the actual needs of crops, farmers can optimize their use and minimize waste.

Another key aspect of resource-efficient agriculture is the promotion of sustainable farming practices. This involves the adoption of techniques that reduce soil erosion, improve soil health, and promote biodiversity on farms. Conservation tillage methods, such as minimum till or no-till, help to reduce erosion by leaving crop residues on the field to protect the soil from water and wind damage.

Water management is also a critical component of resource-efficient agriculture. Farmers utilize efficient irrigation techniques, such as drip irrigation or precision sprinklers, to minimize water usage and ensure that plants receive water in the most effective manner. Additionally, the adoption of water-saving technologies, such as soil moisture sensors, helps farmers make more informed decisions about irrigation timing and quantities.

Resource-Efficient Circular Economy Awareness Campaigns

A resource-efficient circular economy refers to a sustainable economic model that aims to minimize resource consumption and waste generation through the promotion of circular practices. In this context, awareness campaigns play a crucial role in informing and educating individuals, businesses, and communities about the principles and benefits of a circular economy.

These awareness campaigns are designed to raise public consciousness and understanding of the finite nature of resources and the need for their efficient and responsible use. The main objective is to encourage individuals and organizations to adopt circular economy practices such as recycling, reuse, repair, and sharing, in order to reduce dependence on finite resources, minimize waste, and create a regenerative economic system.

Resource-Efficient Circular Economy Conferences

A resource-efficient circular economy conference is an event that focuses on promoting and advancing sustainable practices in various industries and sectors. The conference brings together experts, practitioners, policymakers, and researchers to explore and discuss strategies, technologies, and solutions to achieve a circular economy.

The concept of a circular economy is based on the principles of reducing waste, minimizing resource consumption, and maximizing the value of products and materials throughout their lifecycle. It aims to shift from the traditional linear "take-make-dispose" model to a regenerative and restorative system that ensures resources are kept in use for as long as possible.

The resource-efficient circular economy conferences cover a wide range of topics including sustainable production and consumption, waste management and recycling, eco-design and innovation, resource efficiency, renewable energy, and sustainable business models. The conferences provide a platform for knowledge exchange, networking, and collaboration to accelerate the transition towards a circular economy.

These conferences feature keynote speeches, panel discussions, interactive workshops, and presentations from industry leaders, policymakers, and researchers. Participants have the opportunity to learn about cutting-edge technologies and best practices, discover innovative solutions, and engage in dialogue to address the challenges and opportunities of the circular economy.

By attending resource-efficient circular economy conferences, individuals and organizations can gain insights and knowledge to improve their own sustainability practices, find partnerships and collaboration opportunities, and contribute to the global efforts in achieving a more sustainable and resource-efficient future.

>

Resource-Efficient Circular Economy Courses

A resource-efficient circular economy course is a type of educational program that aims to provide learners with knowledge and skills to promote sustainability through the effective management of resources. It focuses on the principles of the circular economy, which aims to shift from the current linear "take-make-dispose" model of production and consumption to one that is regenerative, restorative, and circular in nature.

In this course, participants are introduced to various tools and strategies to achieve resource efficiency and to develop a circular mindset. These may include analyzing and reducing waste generation, implementing recycling and upcycling practices, and designing products and systems that prioritize durability, repairability, and reusability. The course also explores methods to minimize resource consumption and identify renewable and alternative resources to reduce dependence on finite resources.

Through case studies, practical exercises, and group discussions, learners gain a deeper understanding of the interconnectedness of social, environmental, and economic aspects of a circular economy. They learn to identify and address the challenges and opportunities associated with transitioning to a circular economy, such as policy and regulatory frameworks, supply chain management, and stakeholder engagement.

By completing a resource-efficient circular economy course, participants are equipped with the knowledge and skills to drive change within their organizations or communities. They can apply the principles and strategies learned in the course to promote sustainable resource management, reduce waste, and contribute to the development of a more resilient and environmentally friendly economy.

Resource-Efficient Circular Economy Educational Programs

A resource-efficient circular economy is an approach to sustainable development that aims to minimize waste and maximize resource use throughout the entire lifecycle of a product or service. It involves the sustainable management of resources, including materials, energy, and water, to ensure their continual reuse and recycling.

Resource-efficient circular economy educational programs are educational initiatives designed to promote awareness and understanding of the principles and practices of a resource-efficient circular economy. These programs provide individuals and organizations with the knowledge and skills needed to adopt sustainable practices, such as reducing consumption, reusing materials, and recycling waste.

Resource-Efficient Circular Economy Entrepreneurship Support

A resource-efficient circular economy entrepreneurship support refers to the assistance and encouragement provided to entrepreneurs and businesses that adopt sustainable practices in their operations, with a focus on minimizing resource use and maximizing resource productivity.

The concept of a circular economy recognizes the limited availability and finite nature of resources on our planet. It aims to move away from the traditional linear economic model of 'take-make-waste' and instead promote a system where resources are used efficiently and kept in circulation for as long as possible, through strategies such as recycling, reusing, and remanufacturing.

Entrepreneurship support in the context of a resource-efficient circular economy involves various activities and initiatives. It includes providing training, mentoring, and financial support to entrepreneurs who develop innovative and sustainable business models that minimize waste, reduce resource consumption, and promote the use of renewable energy sources. This support also encompasses facilitating access to markets, networks, and partnerships that enable entrepreneurs to scale up their sustainable businesses.

The aim of resource-efficient circular economy entrepreneurship support is to create a supportive ecosystem that fosters the growth of sustainable businesses. By assisting entrepreneurs in adopting sustainable practices, optimizing resource use, and minimizing waste generation, such support helps in achieving environmental, social, and economic benefits. It encourages the transition towards a more sustainable and resilient economy, where resources are used efficiently, waste is minimized, and the impact on the planet is reduced.

Resource-Efficient Circular Economy Events

A resource-efficient circular economy event refers to an event or gathering that follows the principles of sustainability and aims to minimize waste, maximize resource efficiency, and promote the circularity of materials and resources.

In a circular economy, the goal is to design out waste and pollution, keep products and materials in use for as long as possible, and regenerate natural systems. Resource-efficient circular economy events emphasize these principles by adopting strategies such as reducing energy consumption, reusing materials, recycling waste, and encouraging sustainable consumption and production patterns.

Resource-Efficient Circular Economy Forums

A resource-efficient circular economy forum is a platform for promoting and discussing sustainable practices and strategies that aim to minimize resource consumption and waste generation in the economy. It provides a space for stakeholders from various sectors such as government, business, academia, and civil society to exchange knowledge, ideas, and experiences on how to transition towards a circular economy model.

In the context of sustainability, a circular economy is an alternative to the traditional linear economy where resources are extracted, used, and disposed of. Instead, a circular economy aims to close the loop by keeping products and materials in use for as long as possible through recycling, reuse, and repair. This approach reduces the dependence on raw material extraction, minimizes environmental impacts, and promotes the efficient use of resources.

A resource-efficient circular economy forum facilitates dialogue and collaboration among different stakeholders to identify barriers, share best practices, and develop innovative solutions that promote resource efficiency and sustainability. It serves as a platform for discussing policies, regulations, and market incentives that can support the transition towards a circular economy. The forum may also host workshops, seminars, and conferences to disseminate knowledge and raise awareness about circular economy principles and practices.

In summary, a resource-efficient circular economy forum plays a crucial role in advancing sustainable development by fostering collaboration, knowledge sharing, and the adoption of resource-efficient practices necessary for a transition towards a circular economy.

Resource-Efficient Circular Economy Incubators

A resource-efficient circular economy incubator, in the context of sustainability, refers to a supportive environment or facility that fosters the development and growth of innovative businesses and start-ups focused on the principles of circular economy and resource efficiency.

Resource efficiency is the concept of using materials, energy, and resources in the most efficient and sustainable way possible, minimizing waste and maximizing value creation. Circular economy, on the other hand, aims to decouple economic growth from resource consumption by promoting the reuse, recycling, and regeneration of materials, ultimately creating a closed-loop system.

An incubator plays a crucial role in nurturing and supporting early-stage companies and entrepreneurs, providing them with the necessary resources, mentorship, and networking opportunities to thrive. In the context of a circular economy, a resource-efficient incubator goes beyond the traditional support provided to start-ups and focuses specifically on businesses that align with the principles of resource efficiency and circularity.

A resource-efficient circular economy incubator may offer services such as access to state-of-the-art facilities and shared resources, research and development support, technical expertise, funding opportunities, and connections to a network of like-minded businesses, investors, and industry experts.

By providing a dedicated space and tailored support for circular economy enterprises, these incubators contribute to the transition towards a more sustainable and regenerative economic model. They help drive innovation, promote collaboration, and enable business ideas that optimize the use of resources, reduce waste, and contribute to the development of a more environmentally and socially responsible economy.

Resource-Efficient Circular Economy Innovation Challenges

The concept of resource-efficient circular economy innovation challenges revolves around the idea of creating sustainable solutions to resource management and economic development. It is an approach that seeks to minimize waste and maximize the value of resources in a closed-loop system.

In a resource-efficient circular economy, the focus is on designing products and services that are durable, repairable, and recyclable, with the aim of reducing both the consumption of raw materials and the generation of waste. This approach promotes the use of renewable energy sources and encourages the adoption of sustainable production and consumption practices.

Resource-Efficient Circular Economy Keynotes

A resource-efficient circular economy, in the context of sustainability, refers to an economic system that aims to minimize waste and maximize the use of resources through the principles of reduce, reuse, and recycle. It involves designing products and processes to be as resource-efficient as possible, and ensuring that materials are kept in use for as long as possible.

Keynotes of a resource-efficient circular economy include:

- Reducing the consumption of finite resources by promoting sustainable production and consumption patterns. This includes minimizing resource extraction and using renewable materials whenever possible.

- Designing products and services to be durable, repairable, and recyclable, ensuring that they have a longer lifespan and can easily be repaired or disassembled for recycling at the end of their life cycle.

- Encouraging the reuse and sharing of products through innovative business models such as rental or leasing, which reduce the need for new production and minimize waste generation.

- Implementing effective waste management systems that prioritize recycling and recovery over disposal. This involves promoting the sorting and separation of waste at the source and investing in infrastructure for recycling and composting.

A resource-efficient circular economy aims to decouple economic growth from resource consumption and environmental degradation, creating a more sustainable and resilient society. By optimizing resource use, minimizing waste generation, and promoting the reuse and recycling of materials, it aims to achieve long-term environmental and economic benefits while preserving natural resources for future generations.

Resource-Efficient Circular Economy Online Resources

A resource-efficient circular economy refers to a system that aims to minimize waste and maximize the use of resources throughout the entire lifecycle of products, including their design, manufacturing, use, and disposal. It is a sustainable approach that promotes the loop of materials and resources, reducing the need for virgin materials and minimizing the generation of waste.

In a resource-efficient circular economy, products and materials are designed to be durable, repairable, and recyclable. The focus is on extending their lifespan and keeping them within the economic and productive cycle for as long as possible. This involves implementing strategies such as product design for longevity, remanufacturing, repair and refurbishment, and recycling.

By adopting a resource-efficient circular economy, businesses and industries can reduce their environmental impact, conserve natural resources, and reduce greenhouse gas emissions. It also presents opportunities for cost savings, innovation, and job creation. Ultimately, it is a shift away from the traditional linear take-make-dispose model towards a more sustainable and regenerative system.

Resource-efficient circular economy practices can be applied in various sectors, including manufacturing, construction, agriculture, and consumer goods. They require collaboration and cooperation among stakeholders, including businesses, governments, and consumers, to ensure the effective implementation of sustainable practices and policies.

Resource-Efficient Circular Economy Practices

A resource-efficient circular economy is a sustainable system that aims to minimize resource consumption, waste generation, and environmental impact by promoting the effective use, recycling, and reuse of resources throughout the entire lifecycle of products. In this system, resources are managed in a way that maximizes their value and lifespan, reducing the need for new resource extraction. Products are designed to be durable, repairable, and easily disassembled so that their components and materials can be recovered and reused. This approach encourages manufacturers to adopt practices such as remanufacturing, refurbishing, and reconditioning to extend the life of products. Furthermore, the circular economy promotes the use of renewable resources and seeks to eliminate the use of harmful substances that can pose risks to human health and the environment. It also emphasizes the importance of eco-design, which involves considering the entire lifecycle of a product and minimizing its environmental impact during production, use, and disposal. By adopting resource-efficient circular economy practices, societies can significantly reduce their reliance on finite resources, minimize waste generation, and mitigate environmental degradation. This approach not only enhances resource security but also fosters economic growth by creating new business opportunities, promoting innovation, and increasing resource productivity. Ultimately, a resource-efficient circular economy offers a promising pathway towards achieving sustainable development, where the needs of the present generation are met without compromising the ability of future generations to meet their own needs.>

Resource-Efficient Circular Economy Publications

A resource-efficient circular economy is a sustainable economic model that aims to minimize resource consumption, waste generation, and environmental impact by maximizing the reuse, recycling, and recovery of materials and products throughout their lifecycles.

Publications on resource-efficient circular economy provide valuable information on strategies, policies, and practices that promote the transition to a more sustainable and circular economy. These publications explore various aspects of the circular economy, including design for circularity, resource efficiency, waste management, and product lifecycle management.

Resource-Efficient Circular Economy Reports

A resource-efficient circular economy is a sustainable approach to economic development that aims to maximize the utilization of resources throughout their entire life cycle. It promotes the transition from a linear, wasteful model of production and consumption to a closed-loop system that focuses on reducing waste, conserving resources, and minimizing environmental impacts.

In a resource-efficient circular economy, materials are kept in use for as long as possible through strategies such as recycling, reusing, and repairing. This reduces the need for extracting new raw materials and decreases the amount of waste generated. The main principles of a circular economy include designing products for longevity and recyclability, implementing sustainable manufacturing processes, and fostering collaboration and cooperation among stakeholders.

This approach is based on the understanding that resources are finite and that the current linear model of production and consumption is not sustainable in the long term. By adopting a circular economy, economies can become more resilient, reduce their reliance on virgin resources, and minimize the negative environmental and social impacts associated with resource extraction and waste generation.

Resource-efficient circular economy reports provide valuable insights, data, and recommendations on how businesses, governments, and individuals can transition to a more sustainable and circular economy. These reports often include information on best practices, innovative technologies, policy frameworks, and case studies that demonstrate the benefits and possibilities of a circular economy. They serve as important resources for driving the adoption of circular economy principles and fostering sustainable development.

Resource-Efficient Circular Economy Seminars

Resource-efficient circular economy seminars are educational events focused on promoting sustainability by providing knowledge and strategies to implement a circular economy. In the context of sustainability, a circular economy aims to minimize waste and maximize the efficient use of resources by closing the loop of the production and consumption cycle.

A circular economy is a system that aims to eliminate the concept of waste by replacing the traditional linear model of production and consumption. Instead of the traditional take-make-waste approach, a circular economy seeks to create a closed-loop system where resources are continuously reused and regenerated. This system requires the collaboration and participation of various stakeholders, including businesses, governments, and consumers.

The resource-efficient circular economy seminars are designed to address the challenges and opportunities associated with transitioning to a circular economy. These seminars provide a platform for experts, practitioners, and policymakers to share their knowledge, experiences, and best practices related to resource efficiency, waste reduction, and sustainable production and consumption. The seminars cover a wide range of topics, including sustainable design, eco-innovation, resource management, and sustainable business models.

Through these seminars, participants gain insights and understanding of the principles and practices of a circular economy. They learn about the importance of resource efficiency and how it contributes to the overall sustainability goals. The seminars also provide networking opportunities, allowing participants to connect with like-minded individuals and organizations that are committed to driving change towards a more sustainable future.

Resource-Efficient Circular Economy Stakeholder Engagement

Resource-efficient circular economy stakeholder engagement refers to the process of actively involving and collaborating with various stakeholders, including businesses, governments, communities, and individuals, to promote and implement a circular economy approach that minimizes resource consumption while maximizing resource efficiency and sustainability.

This form of stakeholder engagement aims to address the challenges of resource scarcity and environmental degradation by shifting from the linear "take-make-dispose" model to a circular system that focuses on reducing, reusing, and recycling resources. It requires the participation and cooperation of all stakeholders throughout the entire value chain, from production and consumption to waste management and recycling.

The goal of resource-efficient circular economy stakeholder engagement is to create a shared understanding of the benefits and opportunities of adopting a circular economy approach. It involves fostering dialogue, collaboration, and knowledge-sharing among stakeholders to identify and develop sustainable solutions. This may include promoting the use of eco-design principles, encouraging the adoption of innovative technologies and business models, and supporting the development of effective policies and regulations.

By engaging stakeholders in the transition towards a resource-efficient circular economy, businesses and governments can gain valuable insights, build trust and credibility, and ensure the successful implementation of sustainable practices. This engagement can lead to the development of new markets and new business opportunities, reduce waste generation, conserve resources, and protect the environment for future generations. It also contributes to social and economic development by creating green jobs, enhancing competitiveness, and promoting a more inclusive and equitable society.

Resource-Efficient Circular Economy Strategies

Resource-efficient circular economy strategies are a set of practices aimed at promoting sustainable development by maximizing the use of resources and minimizing waste generation. It is a holistic approach that seeks to close the loop between production and consumption, emphasizing the importance of reusing, recycling, and remanufacturing materials and products.

These strategies are designed to move away from the traditional linear economy model, which is based on a "take-make-dispose" approach. In a circular economy, resources are seen as valuable assets that should be preserved and utilized efficiently throughout their entire lifecycle. This involves implementing measures such as product design for longevity and durability, encouraging the use of renewable or recyclable materials, and promoting the sharing and leasing of goods.

In addition to reducing the consumption of finite resources, resource-efficient circular economy strategies also aim to minimize the negative environmental impacts associated with production and waste disposal. By closing the loop, these strategies contribute to reducing greenhouse gas emissions, preserving biodiversity, and conserving natural habitats.

Furthermore, adopting resource-efficient circular economy strategies can lead to significant economic benefits. It can foster innovation, create new business opportunities, and generate job growth in sectors such as recycling and remanufacturing. By decoupling economic growth from resource consumption, these strategies promote a more sustainable and resilient economy.

Resource-Efficient Circular Economy Symposiums

A resource-efficient circular economy symposium is an event that aims to promote and explore sustainable solutions for resource management within a circular economy framework. In the context of sustainability, a circular economy refers to an economic system that aims to minimize waste by keeping resources in use for as long as possible and recovering and regenerating products and materials at the end of their life cycle.

These symposiums bring together experts, researchers, policymakers, and industry professionals to discuss and share knowledge on resource-efficient practices that can contribute to the transition towards a circular economy. The focus of these events is on finding innovative ways to reduce the consumption of finite resources, decrease waste generation, and increase resource productivity.

Resource-Efficient Circular Economy Toolkits

A resource-efficient circular economy toolkit refers to a set of guidelines, strategies, and practices designed to promote sustainability and minimize waste in the context of resource management. It aims to support businesses, organizations, and individuals in transitioning from a linear economy, where resources are extracted, used, and disposed of, to a circular economy, where resources are kept in use for as long as possible, through recycling, repurposing, and reusing.

The toolkit provides a comprehensive framework that fosters the efficient utilization of resources,

288

reduces resource extraction, and minimizes waste generation. It includes tools and techniques to assess the environmental impact of resource use, identify areas of improvement, and implement strategies to optimize the use of resources. These may include eco-design principles, material substitution, waste prevention measures, resource recovery systems, and the adoption of renewable energy sources.

Additionally, the toolkit assists in promoting sustainable consumption and production patterns by raising awareness, providing educational resources, and encouraging collaboration among stakeholders. It supports the adoption of sustainable business models, such as product-as-a-service and sharing economy, which emphasize product longevity, durability, repairability, and recycling at the end of service life.

By implementing a resource-efficient circular economy toolkit, organizations and individuals can minimize resource depletion, reduce environmental pollution, and contribute to the attainment of sustainable development goals. The toolkit serves as a comprehensive resource for integrating sustainability principles into various sectors and driving the necessary transition towards a more sustainable and regenerative economy.

Resource-Efficient Circular Economy Training Programs

Resource-efficient circular economy training programs refer to educational initiatives that aim to equip individuals and organizations with the knowledge, skills, and tools necessary to adopt sustainable practices and efficiently utilize resources within the context of a circular economy.

A circular economy is an economic model that seeks to decouple economic growth from resource consumption and environmental degradation. It promotes the transition from a linear "take-make-dispose" approach to a closed-loop system where products, materials, and resources are kept in use for as long as possible through strategies such as recycling, reusing, repairing, and remanufacturing.

Resource-efficient circular economy training programs provide participants with insights into the principles and concepts underlying the circular economy framework. These programs promote a systemic understanding of how different industries and sectors can integrate circular practices into their operations, supply chains, and business models.

These training programs cover a wide range of topics, including sustainable design, eco-innovation, waste prevention, industrial symbiosis, resource management, and sustainable consumption and production patterns. They aim to foster a sustainable mindset by raising awareness about the environmental and social impacts of linear economies, as well as the potential benefits and opportunities of transitioning towards a circular economy.

By equipping individuals and organizations with resource-efficient circular economy training, they can become better equipped to identify opportunities for resource productivity, waste reduction, and environmental stewardship. These programs contribute to the overall goal of achieving a more sustainable and resilient society, where economic activities are conducted within the limits of our planet's resources and support the well-being of present and future generations.

Resource-Efficient Circular Economy Transition Strategies

A resource-efficient circular economy transition strategy refers to a set of approaches and actions aimed at promoting sustainability through the efficient use of resources within a circular economy framework. This strategy is designed to move away from the traditional linear "take-make-dispose" model of production and consumption, and instead foster a regenerative system that minimizes waste, maximizes resource utilization, and promotes the reuse, repair, and recycling of materials.

Key components of a resource-efficient circular economy transition strategy include the promotion of sustainable production and consumption patterns, the adoption of eco-design principles, the development of innovative business models, and the implementation of effective waste management and recycling systems. By prioritizing resource efficiency, this strategy seeks to reduce environmental impact and preserve natural resources, while also fostering economic growth, job creation, and social well-being.

Resource-Efficient Circular Economy Transition

A resource-efficient circular economy transition is a sustainable approach to economic systems that aims to minimize resource consumption and waste generation while promoting the reuse, recycling, and regeneration of materials and resources. This transition involves a shift from the linear "take-make-dispose" model to a circular model, where resources are used more efficiently and continuously circulated within the economy.

In a resource-efficient circular economy, the focus is on reducing the extraction of virgin resources and extending the lifespan of products and materials through strategies such as repair, refurbishment, and remanufacturing. This not only reduces the environmental impact associated with resource extraction and waste disposal but also creates new business opportunities and jobs in the recycling and repair sectors.

Furthermore, a resource-efficient circular economy promotes the design of products and services that are easily disassembled, repaired, and recycled. This requires collaboration between different stakeholders, including businesses, policymakers, and consumers, to ensure that products are designed with circularity in mind.

The transition to a resource-efficient circular economy also involves the adoption of sustainable and low-carbon technologies, such as renewable energy sources and efficient production processes. These technologies help minimize greenhouse gas emissions and further enhance the sustainability of the circular economy.

Resource-Efficient Circular Economy Webinars

A resource-efficient circular economy webinar refers to an online seminar dedicated to promoting and increasing awareness about the principles, strategies, and practices of a circular economy that prioritizes resource efficiency. Derived from the concept of sustainability, a circular economy aims to minimize waste, extend product lifecycles, and optimize resource utilization by adopting a closed-loop system, where materials and products are reused, recycled, or repurposed instead of being disposed of after use.

These webinars serve as a platform for experts, organizations, and individuals to share knowledge, insights, and experiences related to resource efficiency within the context of a circular economy. They typically cover various aspects of sustainability, such as eco-design, waste management, renewable energy, sustainable consumption, and production, as well as the role of technology and innovation in facilitating the transition towards a circular economy.

Resource-Efficient Circular Economy Workshops

Resource-efficient circular economy workshops are a form of educational sessions or training programs that aim to promote and facilitate the transition towards a more sustainable and circular economy. The workshops focus on enhancing knowledge, understanding, and skills related to resource efficiency and circularity among individuals and organizations.

By adopting a resource-efficient circular economy, we aim to move away from the traditional linear model of production and consumption, which follows a "take-make-dispose" approach. Instead, the circular economy emphasizes the concept of reducing, reusing, and recycling materials to create a closed-loop system, where resources are used more efficiently and waste generation is minimized.

Resource-Efficient Circularity Assessments

Resource-efficient circularity assessments refer to the evaluation and measurement of the effectiveness and efficiency of circularity practices in achieving sustainable resource management. These assessments focus on understanding and quantifying the extent to which circular economy principles are integrated into resource management processes.

The aim of resource-efficient circularity assessments is to identify and evaluate the potential for reducing waste generation, optimizing resource use, and minimizing environmental impacts through the adoption of circularity strategies. These assessments provide a framework for assessing the performance of circularity initiatives and identifying areas for improvement.

Resource-efficient circularity assessments typically involve the examination of various aspects related to resource use, including material flows, energy consumption, waste generation, and emissions. This evaluation is done by collecting and analyzing data on resource inputs, outputs, and utilization throughout the entire lifecycle of a product or process.

The results of these assessments can help businesses, policymakers, and stakeholders make informed decisions about resource management strategies. By identifying opportunities for resource efficiency and circularity, organizations can enhance their sustainability performance, reduce costs, and contribute to the conservation of natural resources.

In conclusion, resource-efficient circularity assessments play a crucial role in promoting sustainable resource management. By providing a comprehensive evaluation of circularity practices, these assessments enable organizations to identify opportunities for improvement and optimize resource utilization, ultimately contributing to a more sustainable and resilient future.

Resource-Efficient Circularity Models

Resource-efficient circularity models refer to sustainable economic systems that aim to minimize resource consumption and waste generation by promoting the closed-loop use of materials. These models prioritize the reduction, reuse, and recycling of resources to minimize the extraction of raw materials and minimize the environmental impacts associated with resource extraction, production, and disposal.

In resource-efficient circularity models, the focus is on designing products, processes, and systems that maintain the value of resources for as long as possible. This involves extending the lifespan of products through strategies such as product durability, repairability, and remanufacturing. Additionally, these models emphasize the extraction of maximum value from resources by recovering materials and energy through recycling and waste-to-energy technologies.

Resource-efficient circularity models also encourage the adoption of renewable and sustainable sources of energy and the use of eco-friendly materials. By implementing these models, businesses and industries can reduce their environmental impact, enhance resource productivity, and contribute to the transition to a more sustainable and circular economy.

In summary, resource-efficient circularity models are sustainable approaches that prioritize the efficient use of resources, closing the loop of material flows, and reducing environmental impacts. By adopting these models, societies can promote long-term sustainability, conserve resources, and minimize the negative effects of resource extraction and waste generation.

Resource-Efficient Construction

Resource-efficient construction refers to the use of sustainable practices and techniques in the construction industry to minimize the consumption of natural resources and reduce environmental impacts. It involves the careful planning, design, and implementation of building projects with the aim of optimizing resource use, minimizing waste generation, and promoting long-term environmental, social, and economic sustainability.

This approach to construction takes into consideration various factors such as materials selection, energy efficiency, water conservation, waste reduction, and the use of renewable resources. It seeks to balance the needs of the present generation while ensuring the ability of future generations to meet their own needs. By implementing resource-efficient construction methods, we can significantly reduce the carbon footprint and negative ecological effects associated with traditional construction practices.

Resource-Efficient Distribution

Resource-efficient distribution refers to the implementation of strategies and practices that aim to minimize the consumption of resources while distributing goods and services. It encompasses a range of activities and considerations, including the transportation, packaging, and storage of products, as well as the optimization of related processes and systems.

This approach recognizes the finite nature of resources and seeks to minimize waste, energy usage, and environmental impact throughout the distribution process. It involves the efficient utilization of resources, such as raw materials, water, energy, and fuel, as well as the reduction of emissions and pollution associated with distribution activities. Resource-efficient distribution not only benefits the environment but also contributes to the long-term viability and sustainability of businesses.

Resource-Efficient Energy Production

Resource-efficient energy production refers to the generation of energy in a manner that maximizes the utilization of available resources while minimizing waste and environmental impact. It involves the adoption of sustainable technologies and practices that promote the efficient use of natural resources, reduce greenhouse gas emissions, and conserve energy.

This approach to energy production focuses on improving the efficiency and effectiveness of energy generation processes, such as the extraction of fossil fuels, the harnessing of renewable energy sources, and the management of energy distribution systems. It encompasses a range of strategies and technologies that aim to minimize resource depletion, pollution, and carbon emissions throughout the energy production life cycle.

Resource-Efficient Logistics

Resource-efficient logistics refers to the implementation of sustainable practices and strategies in the transportation and distribution of goods and services. It focuses on optimizing the use of resources, such as energy, water, and materials, throughout the entire logistics value chain to minimize negative environmental impacts and enhance overall operational efficiency.

This approach encompasses various measures and initiatives aimed at reducing resource consumption and waste generation in the logistics processes. One of the key aspects of resource-efficient logistics is the adoption of green transportation systems, which prioritize the use of eco-friendly vehicles, such as electric or hybrid trucks, trains, and ships, to minimize carbon emissions and air pollution. Additionally, it involves the optimization of transport routes to minimize distance and fuel consumption, as well as the consolidation of shipments to reduce empty space and improve load capacity.

Furthermore, resource-efficient logistics entails the implementation of efficient inventory management techniques, such as just-in-time (JIT) inventory systems, to minimize the storage of excess goods and reduce the need for additional resources. It also involves the use of advanced tracking and monitoring technologies to enhance supply chain visibility and enable real-time data analysis for better decision-making and resource allocation.

Overall, resource-efficient logistics plays a crucial role in promoting sustainability within the logistics industry by reducing resource waste, minimizing environmental impacts, and enhancing operational efficiency. It enables companies to not only contribute to environmental preservation but also achieve cost savings and remain competitive in a rapidly changing business landscape.

Resource-Efficient Manufacturing Practices

Resource-efficient manufacturing practices refer to the systematic and strategic management of resources, including raw materials, energy, water, and waste, in order to minimize the environmental impact of manufacturing operations while maintaining or enhancing productivity and economic performance. These practices are rooted in the principles of sustainability, which aim to meet the needs of the present generation without compromising the ability of future generations to meet their own needs.

In resource-efficient manufacturing, a comprehensive approach is adopted to optimize resource utilization across the entire value chain. This involves adopting cleaner production methods and technologies, improving energy and water efficiency, reducing material waste, and implementing recycling and reuse strategies. It also involves rethinking product design and manufacturing processes to minimize resource consumption and eliminate or minimize the use of hazardous substances.

Through the adoption of resource-efficient manufacturing practices, companies can achieve multiple benefits. Firstly, it contributes to the preservation and conservation of natural resources and ecosystems, reducing the overall ecological footprint of manufacturing activities. Secondly, it helps in reducing greenhouse gas emissions and mitigating climate change impacts. Additionally, by minimizing waste generation and implementing circular economy principles, resource-efficient manufacturing can lead to cost savings, improved operational efficiencies, and enhanced competitiveness.

Resource-Efficient Manufacturing Technologies

Resource-efficient manufacturing technologies refer to processes and technologies implemented in manufacturing industries, aiming to optimize the use of resources while minimizing waste generation and environmental impact. These technologies focus on improving the efficiency and effectiveness of production systems, enabling companies to manufacture products with reduced resource consumption, energy usage, and emissions.

Resource-efficient manufacturing technologies encompass a variety of practices, including advanced automation, digitization, robotics, and the adoption of cleaner production methods. These technologies enable manufacturers to streamline their operations, minimize material waste, reduce energy consumption, and enhance overall resource productivity. By implementing these technologies, companies can achieve significant cost savings, improve their competitiveness, and contribute to sustainable development.

One example of a resource-efficient manufacturing technology is the implementation of smart sensors and Internet of Things (IoT) devices in production processes. These technologies collect real-time data, enabling manufacturers to monitor and optimize resource utilization and energy consumption. Additionally, advanced robotics and automation systems can be employed to automate repetitive and energy-intensive tasks, leading to increased efficiency and reduced resource consumption.

Overall, resource-efficient manufacturing technologies play a crucial role in promoting sustainable industrial practices. By implementing these technologies, companies can reduce their environmental footprint, conserve valuable resources, and contribute to the transition towards a more sustainable and circular economy.

Resource-Efficient Manufacturing

Resource-efficient manufacturing refers to the process of producing goods with minimal waste and optimal utilization of resources, in a manner that aligns with the principles of sustainability. It involves designing and implementing manufacturing systems that minimize the consumption of raw materials, energy, and water, while maximizing the use of renewable resources and reducing greenhouse gas emissions.

This approach to manufacturing aims to minimize the environmental impact associated with production activities, while also addressing social and economic concerns. By reducing waste generation and resource consumption, resource-efficient manufacturing helps conserve natural resources, mitigate pollution, and reduce the overall carbon footprint of the manufacturing sector.

Resource-Efficient Packaging Design

Resource-efficient packaging design refers to the development and implementation of packaging materials and structures that minimize the use of natural resources and reduce environmental impacts throughout their lifecycle. This approach aims to optimize the use of materials, energy, and water, while minimizing waste generation and emissions.

The main goal of resource-efficient packaging design is to reduce the environmental burdens associated with packaging, including the extraction of raw materials, manufacturing processes, transportation, and end-of-life disposal. This is achieved through the use of innovative strategies such as lightweighting, material substitution, and design optimization.

Lightweighting involves the reduction of packaging material consumption through the use of thinner materials or alternative materials with lower environmental footprints. Material substitution aims to replace conventional packaging materials with more sustainable alternatives, such as renewable or recycled materials. Design optimization focuses on the development of packaging structures that maximize functionality and minimize material waste.

In addition to reducing resource consumption, resource-efficient packaging design aims to minimize environmental impacts associated with packaging waste. This includes designing packaging that is recyclable, compostable, or reusable. By ensuring that packaging materials can be efficiently recovered and recycled, the overall environmental impact can be significantly reduced.

Overall, resource-efficient packaging design plays a crucial role in promoting sustainability by minimizing resource consumption, reducing waste generation, and lowering greenhouse gas emissions. By optimizing packaging design, businesses can contribute to a more circular economy and help address pressing environmental challenges.

Resource-Efficient Packaging

Resource-efficient packaging refers to the use of materials, design techniques, and processes that minimize the environmental impact of packaging throughout its lifecycle. It encompasses the reduction of resources used, the use of recycled or renewable materials, the optimization of packaging design to reduce waste and improve functionality, and the promotion of recycling and proper disposal.

One of the key principles of resource-efficient packaging is the reduction of the overall amount of packaging material used. This can be achieved through various methods such as lightweighting, which involves designing packaging to be as lightweight as possible without compromising its protective function. Other strategies include downsizing, simplifying, or eliminating unnecessary components of packaging. By reducing the amount of raw materials used, less energy and resources are required in production and transportation, leading to lower carbon emissions and a reduced ecological footprint.

Resource-Efficient Procurement

Resource-efficient procurement refers to the process of acquiring goods, services, and works in a manner that minimizes the consumption and waste of natural resources throughout the entire procurement lifecycle. It involves incorporating sustainability considerations into all stages of the procurement process, from planning and specification development to contract implementation and evaluation.

This approach aims to optimize the use of resources, including energy, water, raw materials, and land, while also minimizing environmental impacts such as greenhouse gas emissions, pollution, and waste generation. Resource-efficient procurement ultimately seeks to achieve sustainable development by balancing economic, social, and environmental factors.

Resource-Efficient Product Distribution

Resource-efficient product distribution refers to the process of distributing products in a sustainable manner, minimizing the use of resources and reducing negative environmental impacts throughout the supply chain. This approach aims to optimize the allocation and utilization of resources, including energy, materials, and transportation, to deliver products to consumers in the most efficient and environmentally-friendly way possible.

The goal of resource-efficient product distribution is to reduce waste, pollution, and the depletion of natural resources associated with the distribution process. This involves designing logistics systems that minimize the distance traveled, the number of delivery vehicles, and the packaging materials used. It also entails optimizing inventory management to avoid overproduction and excess stock, thus reducing unnecessary resource consumption.

One of the key strategies to achieve resource-efficient product distribution is through the use of innovative technologies and approaches. This can include the adoption of alternative fuels and vehicles, such as electric or hybrid trucks, to reduce greenhouse gas emissions. It may also involve the implementation of smart systems and data analytics to improve route planning, load optimization, and real-time monitoring of delivery activities.

Furthermore, resource-efficient product distribution emphasizes the importance of collaboration and cooperation among all stakeholders in the supply chain. This includes manufacturers, distributors, retailers, and consumers, who need to work together to develop and implement sustainable distribution strategies. It requires a holistic and integrated approach that considers the entire life cycle of a product, from raw material extraction to end-of-life disposal or recycling.

Resource-Efficient Production Methods

Resource-efficient production methods refer to practices and techniques implemented in the production process to optimize the use of resources, minimize waste, and reduce environmental impact. These methods aim to achieve sustainable production by maximizing resource efficiency, which involves lowering energy consumption, raw material usage, and waste generation while maintaining or improving productivity and product quality.

In resource-efficient production, various strategies are employed to minimize resource inputs and maximize outputs. This involves adopting technologies that enhance energy efficiency, such as using renewable energy sources, implementing energy-saving measures, and optimizing production processes to reduce energy consumption. Additionally, the selection of raw materials and inputs is carefully considered, favoring those with low environmental impact, recyclable or renewable materials, and reducing the overall material used where possible.

To further improve resource efficiency, waste prevention and recycling measures are implemented. This includes minimizing production waste by optimizing production processes, reusing by-products or waste materials within the production system, and recycling or responsibly disposing of waste materials to avoid their accumulation in landfills. Furthermore, product design is a crucial element in resource-efficient production methods, as it focuses on durability, reparability, recyclability, and eco-friendly materials, contributing to the circular economy approach.

Resource-efficient production methods align with the principles of sustainability by prioritizing the responsible and efficient use of resources, reducing environmental impacts, and promoting long-term viability. By adopting these methods, businesses can enhance their competitiveness, reduce operational costs, and contribute to a more sustainable and resilient economy.

Resource-Efficient Production Systems

Resource-efficient production systems refer to systems that are designed to minimize the use of resources such as raw materials, energy, and water, while maximizing the output of goods and services. These systems aim to achieve a sustainable balance between economic growth, social well-being, and environmental protection.

Such production systems employ various strategies to achieve resource efficiency. This includes adopting cleaner production techniques, implementing recycling and waste reduction measures, optimizing production processes to minimize energy and water consumption, and promoting the use of renewable energy sources. Resource-efficient production systems also take into consideration the entire life cycle of products, from the extraction of raw materials to the disposal or recycling of waste.

Resource-Efficient Recycling Technologies

In the context of sustainability, resource-efficient recycling technologies refer to processes and techniques that effectively convert waste materials into valuable resources while minimizing the consumption of energy, water, and other finite resources. These technologies aim to reduce the environmental impact of waste management and contribute to a circular economy by promoting the reuse and recycling of materials. Resource-efficient recycling technologies involve various methods and systems that aim to improve the efficiency of waste management processes. One example is mechanical recycling, which involves sorting and processing waste materials to produce recycled materials that can be used as raw materials in the production of new products. This process helps reduce the need for extracting virgin resources and reduces the overall energy consumption required for manufacturing. Another example is chemical recycling, which uses chemical processes to convert waste materials into feedstock for the production of new materials or fuels. This technology allows for the recycling of materials that are difficult to mechanically process or that cannot be recycled through traditional methods. Additionally, resource-efficient recycling technologies also encompass technologies that promote the reuse and remanufacturing of products. These processes aim to extend the lifespan of products by repairing, refurbishing, or upgrading them, reducing the need for new production and minimizing waste generation. Implementing resource-efficient recycling technologies requires an integrated approach that considers the entire lifecycle of products, from design and production to consumption and disposal. It involves collaboration among different stakeholders, including governments, industries, and consumers, to ensure the effective implementation and scale-up of these technologies. By adopting resource-efficient recycling technologies, societies can significantly reduce waste generation, conserve natural resources, and mitigate the negative environmental impacts associated with waste disposal. These technologies play a crucial role in transitioning towards a sustainable future where waste is viewed as a valuable resource rather than a burden on the environment. Efforts should be made to further develop and optimize these technologies to enhance their efficiency and effectiveness. Additionally, raising awareness and promoting the adoption of resource-efficient recycling technologies can help drive positive change towards a more sustainable and circular economy.>

Resource-Efficient Retailing

Resource-efficient retailing refers to the practice of optimizing the use of resources in the retail industry to minimize environmental impact and improve sustainability. It involves reducing the consumption of energy, water, raw materials, and other resources throughout the retail supply chain, from sourcing and manufacturing to distribution and operations.

This approach to retailing aims to maximize efficiency by implementing innovative strategies and technologies that minimize waste, minimize greenhouse gas emissions, and reduce overall environmental footprint. For example, retailers can adopt energy-efficient lighting systems, utilize renewable energy sources, implement water-saving technologies, and optimize transportation routes to reduce fuel consumption and emissions.

Resource-efficient retailing also emphasizes the importance of reusing, recycling, and reducing waste. Retailers can promote the use of reusable bags, packaging, and other sustainable materials, as well as implement effective recycling programs for waste, such as paper, plastics, and electronics. By minimizing waste production and maximizing recycling efforts, resource-efficient retailing contributes to a more circular economy.

Furthermore, resource-efficient retailing involves promoting sustainable and ethical sourcing practices. Retailers can work closely with suppliers to ensure the use of responsibly sourced materials, support fair trade initiatives, and promote product traceability. This helps reduce the negative environmental and social impacts associated with the production and extraction of raw materials.

In conclusion, resource-efficient retailing plays a crucial role in promoting sustainability within the retail industry. By optimizing resource usage, reducing waste, and promoting sustainable and ethical practices, retailers can contribute to a more environmentally friendly and socially responsible future.

Resource-Efficient Supply Chains

A resource-efficient supply chain refers to the implementation of sustainable practices and strategies that minimize the use of resources, such as energy, water, materials, and waste, while maximizing economic efficiency. It encompasses the efficient utilization of resources throughout the entire supply chain, from the sourcing of raw materials to the production, distribution, and disposal of products.

In a resource-efficient supply chain, the focus is on reducing the amount of resources consumed while maintaining or improving the quality and performance of the products being delivered. This involves adopting eco-friendly technologies, optimizing production processes, and implementing measures to reduce waste generation and increase recycling and reuse. By improving resource efficiency, supply chains can contribute to environmental protection and sustainability goals.

Resource-Efficient Transportation Systems

Resource-efficient transportation systems refer to the design, implementation, and management of transportation networks that effectively utilize resources while minimizing negative environmental impacts. These systems aim to optimize the use of energy, materials, and natural resources, reducing waste generation and greenhouse gas emissions.

In the context of sustainability, resource efficiency is essential for creating environmentally friendly transportation systems that contribute to long-term economic and social development. By optimizing resource utilization, these systems promote a more sustainable use of finite resources, reduce dependency on fossil fuels, and mitigate climate change.

Resource-Efficient Transportation

Resource-efficient transportation refers to the utilization of transportation systems and technologies that minimize the consumption of natural resources and reduce negative environmental impacts. This concept aims to optimize the efficiency and sustainability of the transportation sector by implementing various strategies and practices.

Resource efficiency in transportation involves reducing the use of energy, materials, and space while maximizing the output and functionality of transportation systems. This can be achieved through the adoption of cleaner and more fuel-efficient technologies, such as electric vehicles, hybrid vehicles, and alternative fuels. Additionally, resource-efficient transportation emphasizes the efficient use of existing infrastructure, promoting public transit, and encouraging modes of transport that require less energy and space, such as walking, cycling, and carpooling.

This approach also encompasses the concept of sustainable mobility, which seeks to provide accessible, safe, and affordable transportation options for all individuals while minimizing the negative impacts on the environment and society. Resource-efficient transportation strategies include the development of integrated transportation systems, the promotion of multi-modal transportation, and the implementation of smart transportation solutions that utilize data and technology to optimize travel routes and reduce congestion.

In conclusion, resource-efficient transportation plays a vital role in promoting sustainability by minimizing the consumption of resources, reducing greenhouse gas emissions, and improving overall environmental performance in the transportation sector.

Resource-Efficient Warehousing

Resource-efficient warehousing refers to the practice of maximizing the utilization of resources and minimizing waste in the storage and management of goods in a warehouse, with the aim of reducing the environmental impact and improving sustainability. This approach involves the efficient use of energy, water, and materials, as well as the implementation of innovative technologies, processes, and practices that optimize resource consumption.

In resource-efficient warehousing, energy-saving measures, such as the use of LED lighting, insulation, and efficient heating and cooling systems, are implemented to reduce energy consumption. Water-efficient practices, such as the installation of water-saving fixtures and the reuse of water for non-potable purposes, help minimize water waste. The use of eco-friendly packaging materials, recycling programs, and the adoption of circular economy principles contribute to the reduction of material consumption and waste generation.

In addition, resource-efficient warehousing focuses on optimizing the use of space within the warehouse through effective inventory management, layout design, and the implementation of intelligent storage systems. This ensures that the available space is maximized, reducing the need for additional warehouse construction and land use.

By adopting resource-efficient warehousing practices, businesses can achieve significant environmental benefits. These include reduced greenhouse gas emissions, energy and water conservation, waste reduction, and preservation of natural resources. Moreover, improved resource efficiency can lead to cost savings through lower utility bills, decreased material costs, and increased operational efficiency.

Overall, resource-efficient warehousing plays a crucial role in promoting sustainability within the logistics and supply chain industry. It enables companies to minimize their environmental footprint, enhance their reputation as socially responsible organizations, and contribute to the long-term well-being of the planet.

Resource-Efficient Waste Management

Resource-efficient waste management refers to the process of managing waste in a way that reduces its impact on the environment and optimizes the use of resources. It involves implementing strategies and practices that minimize the generation of waste, promote the reuse and recycling of materials, and maximize the recovery of value from waste.

By adopting resource-efficient waste management practices, we can minimize the depletion of natural resources, reduce greenhouse gas emissions, and mitigate the negative impacts of waste disposal on ecosystems and human health. This approach prioritizes the prevention of waste generation through measures such as product redesign, waste reduction in manufacturing processes, and the promotion of sustainable consumption patterns.

Resource-efficient waste management also entails the effective collection, separation, and sorting of waste to enable proper treatment and disposal. Recycling and composting are key strategies to divert waste from landfills and incineration facilities, thereby conserving resources and reducing pollution. Additionally, the recovery of energy from waste through technologies like anaerobic digestion and waste-to-energy facilities can help to generate renewable energy and reduce reliance on fossil fuels.

Overall, resource-efficient waste management is an integral component of sustainable development as it contributes to the conservation of resources, minimizes environmental pollution, and supports the transition towards a circular economy. It requires the collaboration and participation of individuals, communities, businesses, and governments to implement and promote sustainable waste management practices.

Resource-Efficient Waste-To-Energy

Resource-efficient waste-to-energy refers to a sustainable approach that aims to convert waste materials into usable energy, while minimizing the negative impact on the environment and maximizing the efficient use of resources. This process involves the conversion of non-recyclable waste, including municipal solid waste, agricultural residues, and industrial waste, into various forms of energy such as electricity, heat, or biofuels.

The key principle behind resource-efficient waste-to-energy is to not only reduce the volume of waste that ends up in landfills but also to harness its potential value as a source of energy. By extracting energy from waste, the method contributes to the reduction of greenhouse gas emissions, decreases dependency on fossil fuels, and conserves natural resources.

Resource-Efficient Water Management

Resource-efficient water management refers to the effective and sustainable use of water resources, with the goal of optimizing water usage while minimizing waste and negative environmental impacts. It involves the implementation of strategies and practices that focus on conserving and managing water in a way that is both efficient and sustainable.

This approach to water management takes into account the finite nature of water resources and the need to protect and preserve them for present and future generations. It recognizes that water is a vital and essential resource for human activities, ecosystems, and climate regulation.

Resource-efficient water management encompasses a range of measures and techniques, including water conservation, water reuse and recycling, rainwater harvesting, and the use of water-efficient technologies and systems. It promotes responsible water use at various levels, including individual, household, community, and industrial levels.

By adopting resource-efficient water management practices, societies and organizations can reduce their water consumption, minimize water losses, and enhance the overall efficiency of water use. This can lead to significant environmental benefits, such as the preservation of aquatic habitats, the prevention of water pollution, and the reduction of greenhouse gas emissions associated with water production and distribution.

In addition to its environmental benefits, resource-efficient water management can also contribute to economic and social sustainability. It can help to ensure reliable access to clean and safe water for all, support livelihoods and economic activities that depend on water resources, and promote resilience in the face of climate change and water scarcity.

Rocky Mountain Institute

The Rocky Mountain Institute (RMI) is an organization dedicated to advancing sustainability practices and solutions worldwide. Founded in 1982 by Amory and Hunter Lovins, RMI operates as an independent, non-profit think tank that drives the global transition to a clean energy future.

Through research, analysis, and collaboration with partners across various sectors, RMI aims to accelerate the adoption of environmentally and socially beneficial technologies, policies, and business models. The organization focuses on transforming key sectors such as electricity, transportation, buildings, and industry to achieve a low-carbon and resilient future that supports both human well-being and planetary health.

Seawater Greenhouse Technology

Seawater greenhouse technology is a sustainable agricultural system that uses desalinated seawater for farming in arid and semi-arid areas. It combines principles of hydroponics, solar power, and greenhouse architecture to create an innovative and eco-friendly solution to food and water scarcity.

The seawater greenhouse operates by evaporating seawater using solar energy to create a cool and humid climate within the greenhouse. This evaporation process not only produces freshwater but also removes salt from the seawater. The cool and humid climate inside the greenhouse creates an ideal environment for growing crops even in arid regions where traditional farming is not viable due to lack of freshwater and high temperatures.

One of the main advantages of seawater greenhouse technology is its sustainability. By utilizing abundant seawater resources and harnessing solar energy, this system significantly reduces water consumption and carbon emissions compared to conventional agriculture. It not only minimizes pressure on limited freshwater sources but also helps combat climate change by reducing reliance on fossil fuels.

In addition to its environmental benefits, seawater greenhouse technology also provides social and economic advantages. It enables local communities in arid regions to have a reliable and consistent food supply, reducing their dependency on imported food. This technology also creates employment opportunities for local populations, contributing to the socio-economic development of the region.

Seaweed Farming

Seaweed farming is a sustainable practice that involves the cultivation of species of seaweed in controlled marine environments. The aim of this method is to provide a renewable source of seaweed, which can be used for various purposes including food, feed, biofuel, bioplastics, and pharmaceuticals, while minimizing negative environmental impacts.

Seaweed is a highly versatile and fast-growing marine plant that does not require freshwater, arable land, or synthetic fertilizers to thrive. As a result, seaweed farming holds promising potential for sustainable food production and mitigating climate change. By absorbing and storing significant amounts of carbon dioxide during its growth, seaweed farming helps to offset greenhouse gas emissions and improve the health of marine ecosystems.

The cultivation of seaweed offers numerous environmental benefits. The plants provide habitat and nursery grounds for a variety of marine organisms, contributing to ecosystem diversity and supporting local fisheries. Seaweed farming also helps to reduce nutrient pollution in coastal waters, as it can efficiently extract nitrogen and phosphorus from the water, preventing harmful algal blooms and enhancing water quality.

In addition to its ecological advantages, seaweed farming also provides socio-economic benefits. The industry creates employment opportunities in coastal communities, particularly in regions where traditional fisheries may be declining. Seaweed farming can also improve food security by providing nutritious food sources, especially in regions vulnerable to climate change and food insecurity.

Overall, seaweed farming is a sustainable practice that not only offers economic opportunities but also helps to protect and restore marine ecosystems, reduce climate change impacts, and improve food security. By harnessing the immense potential of seaweed, we can promote a more sustainable and resilient future for both our oceans and our communities.

Second-Life Products

Second-life products are items that have been reconditioned, repurposed, or recycled to extend their lifespan and reduce overall environmental impact. These products are typically made from materials that have already been used in a previous product, but have been reclaimed and transformed into new, usable items.

The concept of second-life products aligns with the principles of sustainability by reducing the need for raw materials extraction and minimizing waste generation. By giving new life to materials that would otherwise end up in landfills, second-life products contribute to a more circular economy, where resources are kept in use for as long as possible.

Smart Grids For Energy Management

A smart grid is an advanced electrical power system that uses digital communication technology, real-time data analytics, and automation to improve the efficiency, reliability, and sustainability of electricity generation, transmission, distribution, and consumption.

With a focus on sustainability, smart grids aim to optimize energy management by integrating renewable energy sources, such as solar and wind power, as well as energy storage systems. By leveraging advanced sensors, data analytics, and control mechanisms, smart grids enable real-time monitoring and control of the entire electricity supply chain, from generation to consumption.

Smart Irrigation Systems For Agriculture

Smart irrigation systems for agriculture refer to technologically advanced irrigation methods and tools that aim to optimize water usage, increase crop yield, and minimize environmental impact. These systems employ various sensors, controllers, and actuators to collect real-time data about soil moisture, weather conditions, and crop water requirements.

The collected data is then analyzed and processed to determine the optimal timing, duration, and amount of irrigation needed for crops. This information is used to automate and control the irrigation process, reducing water waste and ensuring that crops receive the right amount of water at the right time. By addressing the specific water needs of each crop and adjusting irrigation accordingly, these systems help to prevent over- or under-irrigation, which can lead to water loss, reduced crop productivity, and ecological damage.

Smart irrigation systems also contribute to sustainability by promoting water conservation and resource efficiency. By using real-time data and advanced algorithms, these systems can reduce water usage by up to 50% compared to traditional irrigation methods. This not only conserves water, a finite and valuable resource, but also reduces energy consumption associated with water pumping and delivery. Additionally, by optimizing irrigation practices and minimizing water runoff and evaporation, these systems help to protect water quality and preserve aquatic ecosystems.

In conclusion, smart irrigation systems for agriculture integrate technology and data analysis to optimize irrigation practices, improve crop yield, and conserve water resources. By using real-time information and automation, these systems promote sustainability by minimizing water waste, increasing resource efficiency, and reducing environmental impact.

Smart Water Management Systems

A smart water management system refers to a sophisticated, technology-driven approach to maximizing the efficient use of water resources while minimizing waste and environmental impact. This system involves the integration of various components such as sensors, data analytics, and automation to monitor, control, and optimize water usage in different settings, including residential, commercial, and industrial sectors.

By leveraging advanced technologies, smart water management systems enable real-time monitoring and management of water consumption, allowing for the detection of leaks, accurate measurement of water flow, and identification of areas of excessive water use. These systems also provide valuable insights into water usage patterns, helping users make informed decisions about water conservation and efficiency measures.

One of the main objectives of a smart water management system is to promote sustainability by reducing the overall demand for water and preserving precious water resources. Through proactive management and optimization of water use, these systems can significantly reduce water wastage, prevent water scarcity, and contribute to a healthier and more sustainable environment.

Furthermore, smart water management systems support the integration of renewable energy sources and the use of alternative water sources such as rainwater harvesting and wastewater recycling. This holistic approach further enhances the sustainability of these systems by reducing reliance on traditional water sources and minimizing the energy footprint associated with water management.

Smart Water Metering Systems

Smart water metering systems are advanced technology-based devices that accurately measure and monitor the consumption of water in residential, commercial, and industrial settings. These systems use digital sensors, communication networks, and data analytics to provide real-time information about water usage, enabling better resource management and promoting sustainability.

By installing smart water meters, individuals and organizations can gain a deeper understanding of their water consumption patterns, identify potential leaks or inefficiencies, and implement conservation measures accordingly. The meters track water usage on a continuous basis, generating data that can be accessed remotely and analyzed to optimize water consumption, reduce waste, and save costs in the long run.

Solar Desalination Systems

Solar desalination systems are sustainable technologies that harness solar energy to remove salt and other impurities from seawater or brackish water in order to produce freshwater suitable for consumption or agricultural use. This process helps mitigate water scarcity and promotes sustainable development by offering an alternative source of clean water in regions that are prone to drought or have limited access to freshwater resources.

These systems utilize solar power, typically through photovoltaic panels or solar thermal collectors, to generate electricity or heat. The energy obtained is then used to power the desalination process, which can involve various techniques such as reverse osmosis, multi-stage flash distillation, or solar stills. These methods enable the separation of salt and contaminants from the water, resulting in purified freshwater output.

Solar desalination systems offer several advantages in terms of sustainability. Firstly, they rely on renewable solar energy, reducing the dependence on fossil fuels and minimizing greenhouse gas emissions associated with traditional desalination methods. Additionally, the systems can operate independently of grid power, making them suitable for remote areas without access to electricity. This decentralized approach enhances resilience and provides a reliable source of freshwater even during power outages or natural disasters.

Moreover, solar desalination systems contribute to water conservation by utilizing abundant seawater resources that are otherwise unsuitable for human consumption or irrigation. This reduces the strain on freshwater supplies and helps protect and preserve fragile ecosystems that may be affected by excessive water extraction. By utilizing renewable energy and maximizing water efficiency, solar desalination systems support sustainable water management and promote environmental stewardship.

Solar Water Heating Systems

Solar water heating systems are sustainable technology systems that utilize solar energy to heat water for various domestic, commercial, and industrial purposes. They are designed to reduce the dependence on fossil fuel-based energy sources and minimize the carbon footprint associated with water heating.

These systems typically consist of solar collectors, a heat transfer fluid, storage tanks, and various control mechanisms. The solar collectors, often positioned on rooftops or in open areas, are responsible for capturing and converting sunlight into thermal energy. The heat transfer fluid, such as water or an antifreeze solution, circulates through the collectors to absorb this thermal energy and transfer it to the storage tanks.

By harnessing the power of the sun, solar water heating systems provide a renewable and clean energy alternative to conventional water heaters. They can significantly reduce energy consumption and greenhouse gas emissions, making them an environmentally friendly choice. Furthermore, these systems are highly compatible with sustainable building practices and can contribute to achieving green building certifications and standards.

In addition to their environmental benefits, solar water heating systems offer economic advantages. They can lead to substantial savings in electricity or fuel costs, especially in regions with abundant sunlight. The initial investment required for installing these systems can be recouped within a reasonable period through reduced energy bills.

Overall, solar water heating systems play a crucial role in promoting sustainability by enabling efficient and renewable water heating and reducing the reliance on non-renewable energy sources.

Solar Water Heating

Solar water heating refers to the process of utilizing the energy from the sun to heat water for various purposes. It is a sustainable and environmentally-friendly alternative to conventional water heating methods that rely on fossil fuels or electricity.

The system typically consists of solar collectors, also known as solar panels, which are mounted on the roof or any other suitable location where they can absorb sunlight. These collectors contain pipes or tubes that circulate a heat transfer fluid, such as water or antifreeze, which absorbs the solar radiation and heats up. The heated fluid then transfers its thermal energy to the water storage tank through a heat exchanger or directly, depending on the system design.

Solar water heating offers several advantages from a sustainability perspective. Firstly, it significantly reduces the reliance on non-renewable energy sources, such as coal or natural gas, for water heating purposes. By harnessing the power of the sun, it takes advantage of an abundant and clean energy resource, reducing greenhouse gas emissions and decreasing environmental impact.

Secondly, solar water heating systems can help reduce energy consumption and lower utility bills. As they operate mainly on solar energy, they can significantly reduce the usage of electricity or fossil fuels, leading to financial savings in the long run.

In conclusion, solar water heating is a sustainable technology that harnesses the sun's energy to heat water for various applications. By reducing reliance on non-renewable energy sources and decreasing energy consumption, it offers both environmental and economic benefits.

Solar-Powered Air Conditioning

Solar-powered air conditioning is a sustainable technology that utilizes solar energy to power cooling systems. This innovative approach reduces reliance on fossil fuels and electricity grids, making it an eco-friendly and cost-effective solution for maintaining indoor comfort.

By harnessing the sun's energy through solar panels, solar-powered air conditioning systems convert sunlight into electricity. This electricity is then used to operate the air conditioning unit, which cools the air and circulates it within a building or space. Unlike conventional air conditioning systems that rely on electricity generated from non-renewable sources, solar-powered air conditioning reduces greenhouse gas emissions and decreases the overall carbon footprint.

Solar-powered air conditioning offers several advantages in terms of sustainability and energy efficiency. Firstly, it reduces dependency on non-renewable energy sources such as coal or natural gas, which significantly contribute to climate change. By using clean and renewable solar energy, it helps mitigate the environmental impact associated with traditional air conditioning systems.

In addition to its environmental benefits, solar-powered air conditioning also provides financial advantages. As solar energy is abundant and free, it reduces electricity bills and operating costs. Furthermore, solar-powered air conditioning systems require minimal maintenance compared to conventional systems, resulting in lower maintenance expenses over time.

Solar-Powered Desalination Plants

Solar-powered desalination plants are sustainable solutions for converting sea or brackish water into fresh, potable water using solar energy as the primary power source. These plants harness the renewable and abundant energy of the sun to drive the desalination process without relying on fossil fuels.

Desalination is the process of removing salt and other impurities from water to produce freshwater. Traditional desalination methods, such as thermal distillation or reverse osmosis, require significant amounts of energy, often derived from non-renewable sources. In contrast, solar-powered desalination plants utilize photovoltaic (PV) panels or concentrated solar power (CSP) systems to generate electricity directly from sunlight.

The integration of solar power with desalination technologies offers multiple benefits for sustainability. Firstly, solar energy is clean, renewable, and non-polluting, reducing greenhouse gas emissions and minimizing the ecological footprint of the desalination process. Secondly, solar-powered desalination plants provide a decentralized and independent water supply, especially in remote or arid regions where access to freshwater is limited. This reduces the reliance on long-distance water transportation and helps alleviate water scarcity concerns.

Furthermore, solar-powered desalination plants can operate in a modular and scalable manner, allowing for flexible capacity expansion based on demand. The abundance of sunlight in many coastal areas makes these plants highly suitable for harnessing local resources for water production, contributing to a more self-sufficient and resilient water infrastructure.

In summary, solar-powered desalination plants are sustainable solutions that leverage solar energy to convert saline water into freshwater. By minimizing environmental impacts, promoting decentralized water supply, and utilizing local resources, these plants contribute to a more sustainable and resilient water management system.

Solar-Powered Desalination

Solar-powered desalination is a sustainable method that uses solar energy to convert saltwater into freshwater. It involves the use of solar panels or mirrors to harness sunlight and generate electricity, which is then utilized to power the desalination process. This innovative technology addresses the pressing global water shortage while minimizing negative impacts on the environment.

Traditional desalination methods such as reverse osmosis and distillation are energy-intensive and heavily reliant on fossil fuels, exacerbating climate change and pollution. In contrast, solar-powered desalination offers a cleaner, greener alternative by utilizing renewable solar energy. This reduces greenhouse gas emissions, contributing to the mitigation of climate change and air pollution.

Besides its environmental benefits, solar-powered desalination also provides economic advantages. By harnessing abundant solar energy, the operating costs of desalination plants are significantly reduced. This technology is particularly beneficial for regions with high solar irradiation and limited freshwater resources, such as arid and coastal areas. It not only offers a sustainable water resource but also creates opportunities for job creation in the renewable energy sector, fostering economic growth.

Furthermore, solar-powered desalination promotes water independence and resilience. As it relies on an abundant source of energy, it allows for decentralized and off-grid water production. This reduces vulnerability to power disruptions and enables communities to meet their water needs, especially in remote or underserved areas.

In conclusion, solar-powered desalination is an environmentally-friendly and economically-viable solution to tackle water scarcity. By harnessing solar energy, this sustainable technology provides clean freshwater while minimizing the carbon footprint and dependence on fossil fuels.

Solar-Powered Electric Vehicles

Solar-powered electric vehicles (EVs) are sustainable transportation options that utilize solar energy as their primary source of power. These vehicles combine the advantages of both solar energy and electric propulsion, contributing to reduced dependence on fossil fuels and minimizing harmful emissions.

By harnessing the power of the sun, solar-powered EVs convert sunlight into electricity through photovoltaic (PV) panels integrated into the vehicle's structure. This electricity is then used to charge the vehicle's battery, which in turn powers the electric motor. As a result, these vehicles operate without using any gasoline or diesel fuel, reducing greenhouse gas emissions and minimizing environmental impacts.

Solar-Powered Heating Systems

Solar-powered heating systems are sustainable technologies that use the sun's energy to provide heat for residential and commercial buildings. These systems utilize solar panels to capture the sunlight and convert it into usable heat energy.

By harnessing the power of the sun, solar-powered heating systems help reduce reliance on fossil fuels and contribute to a cleaner and more sustainable future. They offer numerous environmental benefits, including the reduction of greenhouse gas emissions and air pollution.

Solar-Powered Product Design

Solar-powered product design is a sustainable approach to creating products that harness and utilize solar energy as a source of power. It involves the integration of solar panels or photovoltaic cells into the design of various consumer goods, allowing them to convert sunlight into electricity to operate or supplement their functionality.

This design philosophy aims to reduce reliance on traditional energy sources such as fossil fuels, thus minimizing the associated environmental impacts, such as greenhouse gas emissions and air pollution. By harnessing the abundant and renewable energy of the sun, solar-powered products help to mitigate climate change and promote a more sustainable future.

Solar-Powered Transportation

Solar-powered transportation refers to the use of solar energy as the primary source of power for various modes of transportation, such as cars, trains, boats, and aircraft. This sustainable approach aims to reduce reliance on fossil fuels and decrease carbon emissions, contributing to a cleaner and greener environment.

Solar-powered transportation typically involves the installation of solar panels on the vehicles themselves or alongside roads and parking areas. These panels capture sunlight and convert it into electricity, which is then used to power the vehicle's motor or charge its batteries. The energy generated from the sun is clean and renewable, providing an eco-friendly alternative to conventional transportation systems.

By utilizing solar power, transportation systems can reduce their dependency on non-renewable resources and decrease greenhouse gas emissions, thus playing a crucial role in mitigating climate change. Solar energy is abundant and widely available, making it a sustainable solution for powering vehicles without depleting natural resources.

Benefits of solar-powered transportation include decreased air pollution, improved air quality, and reduced noise pollution. It also offers potential cost savings in terms of fuel expenses and maintenance, as solar-powered vehicles typically have fewer mechanical parts and require less regular servicing.

In conclusion, solar-powered transportation is a sustainable approach that harnesses the power of the sun to propel various modes of transportation. By utilizing clean and renewable solar energy, it reduces reliance on fossil fuels, decreases carbon emissions, and contributes to a cleaner and greener environment.

Solar-Powered Vehicles

Solar-powered vehicles are a type of sustainable transportation that utilize solar energy as a primary source of power. These vehicles are designed to convert sunlight into electricity by using photovoltaic (PV) cells, which are typically mounted on the vehicle's roof or other suitable surfaces. The electricity generated from these cells is then stored in a rechargeable battery, which powers the vehicle's electric motor.

Solar-powered vehicles offer several advantages in terms of sustainability. Firstly, they significantly reduce greenhouse gas emissions compared to traditional petrol or diesel-powered vehicles. Since they rely on renewable solar energy, they do not contribute to air pollution or climate change. Secondly, solar-powered vehicles reduce dependency on fossil fuels, which are finite and non-renewable resources. This contributes to energy security and can help mitigate the environmental and geopolitical issues associated with fossil fuel extraction and consumption.

Furthermore, solar-powered vehicles can be considered as a clean and quiet form of transportation. They produce minimal noise pollution, reducing sound disturbances in urban areas. Additionally, the maintenance costs of solar-powered vehicles are often lower compared to traditional vehicles, as they have fewer moving parts and do not require regular refueling with expensive fossil fuels.

In conclusion, solar-powered vehicles play a crucial role in promoting sustainability and reducing the negative environmental impact of transportation. They offer a clean and renewable alternative, minimizing greenhouse gas emissions and reducing dependency on fossil fuels. By utilizing the power of the sun, solar-powered vehicles contribute to a more sustainable and eco-friendly future.

Solar-Powered Water Pumps

A solar-powered water pump is a sustainable technology that utilizes solar energy to pump water from a water source to a desired location without the need for grid electricity or fossil fuels. It consists of solar panels that convert sunlight into electrical energy, which is then used to power a pump that draws water from the source and pushes it to the surface or through a network of pipes.

This sustainable solution addresses several environmental and energy challenges. By harnessing the renewable and abundant energy of the sun, solar-powered water pumps reduce reliance on polluting and finite fossil fuels, reducing greenhouse gas emissions and mitigating climate change impacts. Additionally, they eliminate the need for electrical grids in remote or off-grid areas, providing access to clean water where conventional electricity infrastructure is inaccessible or unreliable.

Solar-powered water pumps offer numerous benefits related to sustainability. They are cost-effective in the long term, as they eliminate the need for recurring fuel costs, ongoing maintenance, and electricity bills. Their low operational costs make them particularly relevant for rural communities and farmers who often face financial constraints. Moreover, these pumps improve water and food security by enabling irrigation for agriculture, livestock watering, and access to safe drinking water, which are essential for livelihoods and well-being.

Furthermore, the design and operation of solar-powered water pumps prioritize efficiency and durability to maximize resource use and lifespan. The technology's modularity allows for easy scalability and adaptability, enabling it to cater to different water demands and supply systems. Overall, solar-powered water pumps play a crucial role in promoting sustainable development, empowering communities, and conserving resources for future generations.

Solar-Powered Water Purification

Solar-powered water purification refers to the process of using solar energy to eliminate impurities and contaminants from water sources, thus making it safe for consumption and other purposes. This sustainable approach to water treatment utilizes the power of the sun to drive various purification methods, ensuring a renewable and environmentally friendly solution to the global water crisis.

The process typically involves the use of solar panels or solar-powered systems to generate electricity or heat, which is then utilized to power water treatment technologies such as solar stills, solar disinfection, or photovoltaic-powered filtration systems. Solar stills use sunlight to evaporate water, leaving behind impurities, and then condense the purified vapor into liquid form. Solar disinfection, on the other hand, involves exposing water to solar radiation, which destroys harmful microorganisms through the combined effect of heat and ultraviolet (UV) radiation.

The advantages of solar-powered water purification are manifold. Firstly, it eliminates the need for traditional energy sources like electricity or fuel, reducing greenhouse gas emissions and dependence on fossil fuels. Additionally, it offers a sustainable solution for remote or off-grid areas where access to clean water and energy supply might be limited or unreliable. Solar-powered water purification systems are often low-maintenance and have long lifespans, making them cost-effective and durable options for sustainable water treatment.

In summary, solar-powered water purification harnesses the power of the sun to treat and purify water, providing a sustainable and renewable solution for clean water access while minimizing environmental impact and promoting resilience in communities worldwide.

SolarAid

SolarAid is a sustainable organization that focuses on providing affordable solar lights to communities in Africa, with the goal of eliminating the use of dangerous and environmentally harmful kerosene lamps.

The use of solar lights not only improves the quality of life for individuals in off-grid areas but also contributes to the long-term sustainability of local economies and environments. By eliminating the need for kerosene lamps, SolarAid helps reduce carbon emissions, deforestation, and indoor air pollution, leading to improved health outcomes and a cleaner environment.

Sustainability Accounting Standards Board (SASB)

The Sustainability Accounting Standards Board (SASB) is an independent, non-profit organization that sets standards for the disclosure of financially material sustainability information by companies to their investors. SASB's mission is to develop and disseminate globally applicable standards that help companies identify, manage, and communicate their sustainability risks and performance. These standards are designed to provide investors with the information needed to evaluate the long-term sustainability of companies and make informed investment decisions.

SASB standards are industry-specific and cover a wide range of sustainability topics such as environmental stewardship, social capital, employee well-being, human rights, and corporate governance. They are developed through a rigorous process that involves extensive research, stakeholder engagement, and public comment. SASB's standards focus on financially material issues, which are those that have a direct or indirect impact on a company's financial performance. By focusing on materiality, SASB ensures that companies provide relevant and useful information to investors, while also avoiding unnecessary reporting burdens.

Sustainability Reporting Software

A sustainability reporting software is a digital tool that enables organizations to collect, organize, analyze, and report data related to their sustainability performance. It is designed to help companies measure, manage, and communicate their environmental, social, and governance (ESG) efforts and impacts.

Sustainability reporting plays a crucial role in a company's overall sustainability strategy, as it provides a standardized framework for disclosing key information about their sustainability practices, goals, and achievements. By using a dedicated software, organizations can streamline the reporting process, ensure data accuracy, and improve stakeholder engagement.

The software typically offers various features and functions, including data collection modules, performance indicators, data visualization tools, and reporting templates. It allows companies to track their ESG data across multiple dimensions, such as energy consumption, waste management, greenhouse gas emissions, employee well-being, diversity and inclusion, community engagement, and ethical sourcing.

Furthermore, sustainability reporting software facilitates the integration and consolidation of data from different sources, such as internal systems, external databases, and third-party assessments. It enables companies to monitor their progress towards sustainability targets, identify areas for improvement, and make data-driven decisions to drive positive environmental and social outcomes.

Overall, sustainability reporting software helps organizations enhance transparency, accountability, and credibility in their sustainability commitments. It enables them to comply with reporting frameworks and standards, such as the Global Reporting Initiative (GRI), the Sustainability Accounting Standards Board (SASB), and the Task Force on Climate-related Financial Disclosures (TCFD).

Sustainable 3D Printing Materials

Sustainable 3D printing materials refer to materials that are environmentally friendly and have a minimal negative impact on the planet throughout their entire lifecycle, from production and usage to disposal. These materials are designed to conserve resources, reduce waste, and minimize emissions, making them a more sustainable option compared to traditional materials used in 3D printing.

In order to be considered sustainable, 3D printing materials must meet certain criteria. Firstly, they should be made from renewable or recycled sources, such as bio-based polymers or post-consumer waste. By using materials that can be replenished or repurposed, the reliance on finite resources is reduced, helping to conserve the earth's natural resources.

Secondly, sustainable 3D printing materials should have a lower carbon footprint compared to traditional materials. This means that the production process for these materials should generate fewer greenhouse gas emissions, helping to mitigate climate change. Additionally, the manufacturing of these materials should consume less energy and water, further reducing their environmental impact.

Lastly, sustainable 3D printing materials should be designed with end-of-life considerations in mind. This means that they should be recyclable or biodegradable, allowing them to be safely disposed of without causing harm to the environment. The ability to recycle or biodegrade these materials ensures that they do not contribute to the growing issue of plastic pollution.

Sustainable Agriculture Network (SAN)

Sustainable Agriculture Network (SAN) encompasses a network of organizations, farmers, and stakeholders committed to promoting sustainable practices in agriculture. It serves as a platform for collaboration and the dissemination of knowledge, tools, and standards that support the implementation of sustainable agriculture.

The SAN aims to address the environmental, social, and economic challenges faced by the agricultural sector. It emphasizes the need to produce food in a way that conserves natural resources, minimizes negative impacts on ecosystems, and maintains the long-term viability of farming systems. The network encourages the adoption of sustainable agricultural practices that enhance soil health, conserve water, reduce greenhouse gas emissions, and protect biodiversity.

SAN's work involves the development and promotion of sustainability criteria and certification systems. These criteria provide guidelines and benchmarks for evaluating and rewarding farmers who adopt sustainable practices. Through certification, farmers can demonstrate their commitment to sustainability and access markets that prioritize sustainably-produced agricultural products.

In addition to certification, SAN offers capacity building and training programs to support farmers in implementing sustainable practices. These programs focus on enhancing farmers' knowledge and skills in areas such as agroecology, integrated pest management, crop rotation, and waste management. By equipping farmers with the necessary tools, SAN aims to facilitate the transition towards more sustainable agricultural systems.

Sustainable Apparel Association (SAA)

The Sustainable Apparel Association (SAA) is an organization that promotes sustainable practices within the apparel industry. It is dedicated to transforming the way garments are produced, consumed, and disposed of in order to minimize their negative impact on the environment and society.

The SAA works with various stakeholders, including apparel brands, manufacturers, retailers, and consumers, to drive positive change in the industry. By advocating for sustainable practices, the association aims to address the social, economic, and environmental challenges associated with apparel production and consumption.

Sustainable Apparel Coalition (SAC)

The Sustainable Apparel Coalition (SAC) is a nonprofit organization established in 2011 that aims to generate a sustainable future for the apparel, footwear, and textile industry. The SAC brings together leading brands, retailers, manufacturers, government agencies, and non-governmental organizations (NGOs) to collaboratively address the environmental and social impacts of the industry.

Through its membership-based platform, the SAC provides tools, resources, and initiatives that enable companies to measure, evaluate, and improve their sustainability performance. One of the key initiatives developed by the SAC is the Higg Index, a suite of standardized assessment tools that enables companies to measure and communicate the sustainability performance of their products, manufacturing facilities, and value chains.

The SAC believes in the power of collaboration and transparency to drive positive change in the apparel industry. By working together, member companies can share best practices, knowledge, and innovations to accelerate the adoption of sustainable practices throughout the industry. The organization also collaborates with external stakeholders, such as governments and NGOs, to advocate for policies and initiatives that promote sustainability.

Overall, the Sustainable Apparel Coalition plays a crucial role in promoting sustainability within the apparel industry. By providing a platform for collaboration, tools for measurement, and resources for improvement, the SAC empowers companies to make informed decisions and drive meaningful change towards a more sustainable future.

Sustainable Brands

Sustainable Brands refers to companies and organizations that prioritize environmental and social responsibility in their business practices. These brands are committed to reducing their negative impact on the environment, while also contributing positively to society and promoting the well-being of all stakeholders involved.

Sustainable Brands aim to create long-term value by incorporating sustainable strategies into their core operations. They recognize the interconnectedness of social, environmental, and economic factors and strive to make decisions that consider the well-being of both current and future generations. This involves adopting sustainable sourcing and production practices, minimizing waste and emissions, and promoting transparency and ethical behavior throughout their supply chains.

Sustainable Brands often engage in innovative approaches to business, implementing circular economy models, renewable energy solutions, and other sustainable technologies. They prioritize customer engagement and communication, seeking to educate and empower consumers to make more sustainable choices. Through these efforts, they seek to create a positive impact on the environment, society, and their own bottom line.

In order to be considered a Sustainable Brand, companies must demonstrate a genuine commitment to sustainability beyond mere greenwashing. They should continuously assess their impact on the environment and society, set ambitious sustainability goals, and regularly report on their progress. By doing so, Sustainable Brands inspire trust and loyalty among consumers, attract top talent, and contribute to a more sustainable and equitable future.

Sustainable Buildings Industry Council (SBIC)

The Sustainable Buildings Industry Council (SBIC) is an organization that focuses on advancing sustainability in the building industry. It serves as a resource and advocate for professionals and organizations involved in the design, construction, and operation of sustainable buildings.

SBIC promotes the use of sustainable practices and technologies to minimize the environmental impact of the building sector. It works towards promoting energy efficiency, reducing waste, conserving natural resources, and improving indoor air quality in buildings.

Sustainable Business Network (SBN)

The Sustainable Business Network (SBN) is an organization that promotes sustainability in business practices. The network brings together businesses of all sizes and sectors, as well as other stakeholders such as government agencies, non-profit organizations, and academia, to collaborate and take action towards a more sustainable and regenerative economy.

SBN serves as a platform for its members to exchange knowledge, ideas, and best practices on sustainable business strategies. Through various events, workshops, and conferences, SBN facilitates learning and networking opportunities, enabling businesses to stay informed about the latest trends and innovations in sustainability.

One of the key focuses of the Sustainable Business Network is to promote the principles of the triple bottom line: people, planet, and profit. This means that businesses should not only strive to generate economic profit but also consider the social and environmental impacts of their operations. SBN encourages its members to adopt sustainable practices that benefit society, protect the environment, and contribute to long-term economic viability.

SBN also supports businesses in their journey towards sustainability by providing resources, tools, and guidance. This includes access to information on sustainable supply chains, energy efficiency, waste management, and other relevant topics. The network helps businesses navigate the transition to more sustainable practices, empowering them to integrate sustainability into their core business strategies.

Overall, the Sustainable Business Network plays a vital role in promoting and advancing sustainability within the business community. By fostering collaboration, knowledge-sharing, and providing support, SBN contributes to the growth of a sustainable economy that ensures a bright future for both businesses and the planet.

Sustainable Energy For All (SEforALL)

Sustainable Energy for All (SEforALL) is an initiative launched by the United Nations in 2011 with the goal of ensuring universal access to sustainable energy by the year 2030. It aims to address the challenges of energy poverty, climate change, and economic development through the promotion and implementation of renewable energy solutions.

SEforALL works towards its objectives by advocating for policy and regulatory frameworks that support the expansion of renewable energy technologies, promoting investment in clean energy projects, and fostering global cooperation and knowledge sharing. By partnering with governments, businesses, and civil society organizations, SEforALL seeks to mobilize resources, expertise, and innovation to accelerate the transition to sustainable energy for all.

Sustainable Food Trade Association (SFTA)

The Sustainable Food Trade Association (SFTA) is an organization that aims to promote and support the sustainable food trade industry. Sustainability in this context refers to the use of environmentally and socially responsible practices throughout the entire food supply chain.

SFTA works towards its mission by providing tools, resources, and guidance to food producers, distributors, retailers, and other stakeholders in the food industry. The association encourages its members to adopt sustainable practices in their operations and helps them navigate the complex landscape of sustainability certifications, regulations, and standards.

By promoting sustainable food trade, SFTA seeks to address various environmental and social challenges associated with conventional food production. This includes reducing greenhouse gas emissions, preserving natural resources, promoting biodiversity, and ensuring the welfare of workers and local communities.

SFTA facilitates collaboration among its members and encourages the exchange of best practices and innovative solutions. The association also engages with policymakers, consumers, and other stakeholders to raise awareness about the benefits of sustainable food trade and advocate for supportive policies and regulations.

Sustainable Forestry Initiative (SFI)

The Sustainable Forestry Initiative (SFI) is a comprehensive system of principles, objectives, and performance measures designed to promote sustainable forest management practices. SFI works to ensure the health and vitality of our forests, while also considering the social, economic, and environmental aspects of forestry.

SFI supports the long-term sustainability of our forests by promoting responsible practices such as reforestation, protection of water quality, and conservation of biodiversity. It sets standards that address a range of forest management issues, including harvesting techniques, wildlife habitat conservation, and community engagement.

Sustainable Packaging Coalition (SPC)

The Sustainable Packaging Coalition (SPC) is an industry association that focuses on promoting and advancing sustainable packaging practices. It is a collaborative organization that brings together stakeholders from across the packaging supply chain, including manufacturers, retailers, government agencies, and nonprofit organizations.

The SPC is committed to driving the development and implementation of more sustainable packaging solutions. It works towards this goal by facilitating knowledge sharing, developing resources and tools, and driving innovation in sustainable packaging design. The Coalition also seeks to engage and educate the public about the importance of sustainable packaging and its role in reducing environmental impact.

Sustainable Purchasing Leadership Council (SPLC)

The Sustainable Purchasing Leadership Council (SPLC) is an organization dedicated to promoting sustainable purchasing practices among businesses and organizations. The SPLC provides leadership, tools, resources, and a platform for collaboration to help businesses integrate sustainability into their supply chain and procurement processes.

Sustainable purchasing refers to the practice of considering the environmental, social, and economic impacts of products and services throughout their entire life cycle, from extraction of raw materials to disposal. It involves making purchasing decisions that prioritize products and services that have a lower impact on the environment, are ethically sourced, and contribute to the well-being of communities and workers.

The SPLC aims to drive change in the marketplace by advocating for sustainable purchasing practices and providing guidance to businesses on how to effectively integrate sustainability into their procurement strategies. The council works with a diverse range of stakeholders, including purchasing professionals, sustainability experts, suppliers, and policymakers, to develop standards, tools, and best practices that support sustainable purchasing.

By joining the SPLC, businesses gain access to a network of like-minded organizations and resources that can help them navigate the complexities of sustainable procurement. Through collaboration and knowledge sharing, the SPLC helps businesses build sustainable supply chains, reduce their environmental footprint, and enhance the social and economic benefits of their purchasing decisions.

Sustainable Shipping Initiative (SSI)

The Sustainable Shipping Initiative (SSI) is a collective and collaborative initiative that aims to transform the shipping industry into a more sustainable and environmentally responsible sector. It brings together key stakeholders from across the maritime value chain, including shipping companies, industry associations, and other relevant organizations, to drive positive change in the industry.

The SSI focuses on addressing the key sustainability challenges in the shipping sector, such as greenhouse gas emissions, marine pollution, and social responsibility. It aims to develop and promote industry-led solutions and best practices that can help reduce the environmental impact of shipping operations while ensuring the industry remains economically viable.

Sustainable Agriculture Certification Services

Sustainable agriculture certification services refer to the process of evaluating and certifying agricultural practices that are in line with sustainable development principles. These services aim to promote agricultural practices that minimize negative environmental impacts, preserve natural resources, and promote social and economic equity.

The certification process typically involves the assessment of various aspects of agriculture such as soil conservation, water management, biodiversity conservation, pest and disease management, and worker welfare. It also incorporates considerations of greenhouse gas emissions, energy use, and waste management.

311

By certifying farms and farming practices as sustainable, these services provide assurance to consumers and other stakeholders that the agricultural products are produced in an environmentally responsible and socially equitable manner. Certification may be granted by independent organizations or government agencies that set specific standards and criteria for sustainable agriculture.

The certification process often involves on-site inspections and audits to verify compliance with the established standards. Documentation, record-keeping, and traceability are important components of the certification process as they help ensure transparency and accountability.

Overall, sustainable agriculture certification services play a crucial role in promoting sustainable farming practices and providing consumers with reliable information about the environmental and social impacts of agricultural products. They contribute to the development of a more sustainable and resilient agriculture sector that addresses the challenges of climate change, biodiversity loss, and resource scarcity.

Sustainable Agriculture Data Analytics

Sustainable agriculture data analytics refers to the practice of collecting, analyzing, and interpreting data related to sustainable agricultural practices, with the goal of improving productivity, reducing environmental impact, and promoting long-term ecological balance.

This field combines the principles of sustainable agriculture with the power of data analytics to make informed decisions and drive positive change in agricultural systems. By examining various data sources, such as weather patterns, soil conditions, crop yields, pest outbreaks, and water consumption, sustainable agriculture data analytics provides valuable insights to farmers, policymakers, researchers, and other stakeholders.

Through data analytics, patterns and trends can be identified, enabling the optimization of resource allocation, crop selection, irrigation techniques, and pest management strategies. This data-driven approach helps in minimizing the use of chemical inputs, reducing waste, and conserving natural resources.

The knowledge obtained through sustainable agriculture data analytics can also support the development of precision agriculture techniques, including the use of sensors, drones, and other technologies to monitor and manage farming operations more efficiently. By integrating data analytics into sustainable agriculture practices, farmers can make smarter decisions, improve crop yields, minimize losses, and enhance overall sustainability.

Sustainable Agriculture Drones

Sustainable agriculture drones are unmanned aerial vehicles (UAVs) that are used in farming practices designed to maintain ecological balance and minimize environmental impact. These drones are equipped with advanced imaging and sensing technologies to gather data and monitor crops, soil conditions, and other indicators of agricultural health.

The primary goal of sustainable agriculture drones is to support sustainable farming practices that promote long-term viability and reduce negative impacts on the environment. These drones enable farmers and agronomists to collect real-time, high-resolution data about their fields, allowing for precise and targeted actions. By providing accurate information about crop health, soil moisture levels, and pest or weed infestations, these drones help farmers optimize resource allocation, minimize the use of chemical inputs, and reduce water and nutrient wastage.

Using sustainable agriculture drones can lead to a number of environmental benefits. First, it helps farmers adopt precision agriculture techniques, leading to improved productivity and reduced resource consumption. Secondly, it enables the identification of early signs of crop stress or diseases, minimizing the need for broad-spectrum pesticide applications. Additionally, sustainable agriculture drones facilitate water management by providing accurate information on soil moisture levels, allowing for precise irrigation schedules and reducing water usage. They also contribute to soil health and conservation efforts by supporting the implementation of sustainable soil management practices.

Sustainable agriculture drones are an innovative tool that aids farmers in implementing sustainable practices, reducing environmental impact, and ensuring the long-term viability of agricultural systems.

Sustainable Agriculture Management Software

Sustainable agriculture management software refers to a computer-based tool designed to assist farmers, agricultural organizations, and policymakers in implementing and promoting sustainable practices in the agricultural sector.

Its primary purpose is to provide a comprehensive system for managing various aspects of agricultural operations while considering the environmental, economic, and social dimensions of sustainability. The software encompasses a range of features and functionalities, including data collection, analysis, monitoring, and decision support.

This software facilitates the collection and management of data related to soil health, crop yield, water usage, fertilizer application, and pest management. It enables farmers to analyze this data and make informed decisions that optimize resource efficiency, minimize environmental impact, and enhance overall sustainability.

Furthermore, sustainable agriculture management software helps farmers adopt practices such as precision farming, organic farming, agroforestry, and integrated pest management. It allows them to create customized plans, track progress, and evaluate performance against sustainability indicators. This enables continuous improvement and encourages the adoption of innovative and regenerative practices.

The software also supports collaboration and knowledge sharing among farmers, researchers, and policymakers interested in sustainable agriculture. It provides a platform for exchanging best practices, conducting research, and developing evidence-based policies that foster sustainable agricultural systems.

In conclusion, sustainable agriculture management software is a valuable tool for promoting and implementing sustainable practices in the agricultural sector. By integrating data management, analysis, and decision support functionalities, it empowers farmers and stakeholders to optimize resource utilization, minimize environmental impact, and ensure the long-term viability of agricultural systems.

Sustainable Agriculture Monitoring Drones

Sustainable agriculture monitoring drones refer to unmanned aerial vehicles (UAVs) equipped with sensors and imaging technology that are used to monitor and assess the health and productivity of agricultural systems in an environmentally friendly and sustainable manner.

These drones play a crucial role in improving sustainability practices in agriculture by providing real-time data and insights to farmers, enabling them to make informed decisions about resource allocation, crop protection, and land management. By monitoring various aspects of crop growth, soil health, and irrigation systems, sustainable agriculture monitoring drones help optimize resource usage, reduce environmental impacts, and increase overall agricultural productivity.

With the help of advanced sensors and imaging technology, these drones can collect and analyze data on crop health and nutrient levels, detect diseases and pests, and assess soil conditions. This information allows farmers to identify and address issues early on, reducing the need for excessive use of fertilizers, pesticides, and water. By minimizing the use of chemical inputs and optimizing resource allocation, sustainable agriculture monitoring drones contribute to the protection of biodiversity, preservation of natural resources, and reduction of pollution.

Furthermore, by providing precise and detailed information about the state of crops and land, these drones enable farmers to implement precision agriculture techniques. This involves using targeted interventions, such as applying fertilizers and pesticides only where and when necessary, leading to reduced costs, increased yields, and minimized environmental impacts. Sustainable agriculture monitoring drones also facilitate the implementation of sustainable land management practices, such as contour farming and precision irrigation, which help conserve soil moisture, prevent erosion, and improve water use efficiency.

Overall, sustainable agriculture monitoring drones are a valuable tool in promoting and achieving sustainable agricultural practices. By providing accurate and timely information, they empower farmers to make informed decisions that optimize resource usage, protect the environment, and ensure long-term food security.

Sustainable Agriculture Precision Technology

Sustainable agriculture precision technology refers to the use of advanced technology and techniques to optimize and improve the efficiency and sustainability of agricultural practices.

This approach involves the integration of various technologies such as remote sensing, Geographic Information System (GIS), Global Positioning System (GPS), and data analytics to gather and analyze precise information about soil, weather, and plant conditions. This information is then used to make data-driven decisions and implement targeted interventions in farming practices.

By using sustainable agriculture precision technology, farmers can enhance their understanding of the ecosystem and make informed choices regarding the application of inputs such as water, fertilizers, and pesticides. This technology enables farmers to minimize waste, reduce the environmental impact of agriculture, and optimize resource utilization.

Furthermore, sustainable agriculture precision technology promotes precision farming techniques such as variable rate application, site-specific management, and crop rotation. These practices help in conserving soil fertility, reducing erosion, and managing pest and weed populations more effectively.

This technology-driven approach also facilitates the adoption of regenerative agricultural practices that focus on building soil health, enhancing biodiversity, and reducing greenhouse gas emissions from agricultural activities.

In conclusion, sustainable agriculture precision technology offers a proactive and data-intensive approach to farming that aims to optimize productivity, minimize the environmental footprint, and ensure long-term sustainability of agricultural systems.

Sustainable Agriculture Research Institutes

Sustainable agriculture research institutes are organizations that focus on studying and promoting agricultural practices that are ecologically sound, socially just, and economically viable. These institutes aim to develop and disseminate knowledge and techniques to support sustainable farming systems that minimize negative environmental impacts while maximizing productivity and profitability.

Through research, education, and outreach activities, sustainable agriculture research institutes seek to address the complex challenges facing modern agriculture, such as soil degradation, water pollution, biodiversity loss, and climate change. They work towards finding innovative solutions that integrate sustainable practices into all aspects of agricultural production, including crop and livestock management, soil conservation, water and energy use, and waste management.

These institutes often collaborate with farmers, scientists, policymakers, and other stakeholders to ensure that their research is practical, relevant, and responsive to the needs of local communities and the broader agricultural sector. They provide training and technical assistance to farmers, extension agents, and agricultural professionals to promote the adoption of sustainable practices and support the transition to more environmentally friendly and socially equitable farming systems.

By conducting research and disseminating knowledge, sustainable agriculture research institutes play a crucial role in advancing the principles of sustainability in agriculture. Their work contributes to improving the long-term resilience, productivity, and profitability of agricultural systems, while also helping to preserve natural resources, protect biodiversity, and enhance the well-being of farmers and rural communities.

Sustainable Agriculture Soil Sensors

Sustainable agriculture soil sensors are devices used to measure and monitor various parameters of the soil in order to optimize agricultural practices while minimizing negative environmental impacts. These sensors are designed to provide real-time data on soil conditions, allowing farmers and agriculturalists to make informed decisions about irrigation, fertilization, and other farming practices.

The use of sustainable agriculture soil sensors is rooted in the principles of sustainability, which aim to harmonize agricultural practices with the natural environment. By accurately measuring soil moisture levels, temperature, nutrient content, and other relevant factors, farmers can target their inputs more efficiently, reducing waste and minimizing the risk of overuse or underuse of resources.

These sensors contribute to the broader goals of sustainable agriculture by promoting resource efficiency, environmental conservation, and soil health. By optimizing water and nutrient use, farmers can reduce their reliance on synthetic inputs, such as chemical fertilizers, which can have detrimental effects on water quality and ecosystem health.

In addition to optimizing resource use, sustainable agriculture soil sensors also help prevent soil erosion and degradation. By monitoring soil moisture levels, farmers can adjust irrigation practices to prevent soil erosion caused by excessive water runoff. By measuring nutrient levels, farmers can prevent the buildup of excess nutrients in the soil, which can lead to pollution of nearby water bodies.

In conclusion, sustainable agriculture soil sensors are important tools in promoting environmentally friendly and efficient farming practices. By providing real-time data on soil conditions, these sensors enable farmers to optimize resource use, minimize environmental impacts, and promote soil health.

Sustainable Agriculture Supply Chain Solutions

Sustainable agriculture supply chain solutions refer to the strategies and practices implemented throughout the entire agricultural supply chain to minimize negative environmental impacts while ensuring the long-term viability of the agricultural system.

These solutions focus on achieving sustainability by promoting ecological balance, conserving natural resources, and enhancing the well-being of farmers, rural communities, and consumers. They aim to address various challenges in the agricultural supply chain, such as soil degradation, water pollution, loss of biodiversity, greenhouse gas emissions, food waste, and unfair labor practices.

Sustainable Agriculture Techniques

Sustainable agriculture techniques refer to practices and methods that promote the long-term viability and productivity of agricultural systems while minimizing negative environmental impacts. These techniques aim to ensure food security for the growing population, protect and enhance natural resources, and maintain the ecological balance.

One of the key aspects of sustainable agriculture is the preservation of soil health. Soil erosion, depletion of nutrients, and loss of organic matter are major concerns in conventional farming. Sustainable agriculture techniques, such as conservation tillage, crop rotation, and cover cropping, are implemented to prevent soil erosion, improve soil fertility, and promote soil biodiversity. These practices not only enhance crop yields but also minimize the need for synthetic fertilizers and pesticides, reducing the harmful impacts on water and air quality.

Water conservation is another critical component of sustainable agriculture. Efficient irrigation methods, such as drip irrigation and precision farming, are utilized to minimize water usage and reduce the strain on limited water resources. Additionally, rainwater harvesting and water recycling systems are implemented to conserve water and maintain its availability for future generations.

Furthermore, sustainable agriculture techniques focus on minimizing energy consumption and greenhouse gas emissions. Integrated pest management, agroforestry, and agroecological approaches are adopted to reduce reliance on fossil fuels and promote natural pest control. The use of renewable energy sources, such as solar and wind power, for on-farm operations and processing facilities further contributes to the sustainability of agricultural systems.

In summary, sustainable agriculture techniques encompass a range of practices that prioritize environmental stewardship, social responsibility, and economic viability. By implementing these techniques, farmers can meet the needs of the present generation without compromising the ability of future generations to meet their own needs.

Sustainable Aquaculture

Sustainable aquaculture refers to the practice of cultivating and harvesting fish, shellfish, and aquatic plants in a manner that ensures the long-term viability and health of both the aquaculture system and the surrounding environment. It involves implementing methods and strategies that minimize negative impacts on natural resources, while promoting the efficient use of energy, water, and feed resources.

This approach to aquaculture prioritizes the preservation and enhancement of biodiversity, water quality, and ecosystem health. It aims to prevent and reduce pollution, minimize the use of antibiotics and chemicals, and avoid the escape of farmed species into the wild. Sustainable aquaculture also embraces responsible and ethical practices, such as humane treatment of farmed animals and adherence to labor laws and standards.

Sustainable Architecture And Design Firms

Sustainable architecture and design firms are companies that specialize in creating and implementing environmentally-friendly building designs and construction practices. These firms focus on reducing the negative impact that buildings have on the environment, while also promoting the health and well-being of the occupants.

Through the use of sustainable materials, energy-efficient technologies, and innovative design strategies, these firms strive to minimize resource consumption, waste production, and greenhouse gas emissions associated with buildings. They also prioritize the use of renewable energy sources and aim to create buildings that are self-sufficient in terms of energy generation.

Additionally, sustainable architecture and design firms often consider the social and economic aspects of sustainability. They aim to create buildings that enhance the quality of life for occupants by providing comfortable and healthy indoor environments. These firms also prioritize the use of local materials and labor, contributing to the development of the local economy and reducing transportation-related emissions.

Furthermore, sustainable architecture and design firms often engage in extensive research and analysis to inform their design decisions. They conduct thorough assessments of site conditions, climate data, and energy performance to optimize building performance and reduce energy consumption. They also collaborate with other professionals, such as engineers and landscape architects, to create integrated and holistic design solutions that maximize environmental, social, and economic benefits.

Sustainable Architecture And Design Services

Sustainable architecture and design services refer to the practice of creating buildings and spaces that are environmentally friendly, energy-efficient, and socially responsible. It involves incorporating sustainable principles and strategies into the planning, design, construction, and operation of buildings, with the goal of minimizing negative impacts on the environment and promoting the well-being of occupants.

These services emphasize the use of renewable and recyclable materials, efficient energy and water systems, and sustainable construction techniques. The design process takes into account factors such as site selection, orientation, daylighting, natural ventilation, and the incorporation of green spaces. By optimizing these elements, sustainable architecture and design services aim to reduce energy consumption, minimize waste generation, and improve indoor air quality.

In addition to the environmental benefits, sustainable architecture and design services also consider the social and cultural aspects of a project. They take into account the needs and preferences of the community, as well as the cultural context and heritage of the area. The design approach prioritizes creating healthy, inclusive, and accessible spaces that promote social interaction and well-being.

Overall, sustainable architecture and design services are focused on creating built environments that harmonize with the natural surroundings, conserve resources, and improve the quality of life for both current and future generations. By integrating sustainability principles into every stage of the design and construction process, these services strive to create buildings that are not only aesthetically pleasing but also environmentally responsible and socially conscious.

Sustainable Architecture Design Tools

Sustainable architecture design tools are resources and techniques utilized in the field of architecture to create environmentally-friendly and socially responsible buildings and structures. These tools aim to minimize the negative impact of construction on the environment and enhance the overall sustainability of the built environment.

Incorporating sustainable design practices into architecture involves considering various factors such as energy efficiency, water conservation, waste management, and the use of non-toxic materials. Sustainable architecture design tools help architects and designers make informed decisions throughout the design process to achieve these goals.

One key tool is the use of advanced modeling and simulation software that allows architects to assess the environmental performance of a building design. This software can predict energy consumption, daylighting levels, and indoor air quality, enabling designers to optimize the building's performance and reduce its carbon footprint.

Another essential tool is life cycle assessment (LCA), which evaluates the environmental impact of a building from its construction to its eventual demolition. LCA takes into account the extraction of raw materials, transportation, energy use during construction, maintenance, and end-of-life disposal. By considering the entire life cycle of a building, architects can make more informed decisions to minimize environmental impact and maximize resource efficiency.

Additionally, sustainable architecture design tools may include passive design strategies that take advantage of natural elements to reduce energy consumption. These strategies can include the optimal orientation of a building to maximize daylight and minimize heat gain, choosing materials with high thermal mass, and incorporating natural ventilation systems.

Sustainable architecture design tools play a crucial role in promoting sustainable development and mitigating the environmental impact of the built environment. By utilizing these tools, architects can create buildings that are not only aesthetically pleasing but also contribute to a healthier and more sustainable future.

Sustainable Architecture Software

Sustainable architecture software refers to computer programs or applications that are designed to aid architects, designers, and other professionals in creating environmentally friendly and sustainable building designs. These software tools help users analyze and evaluate the environmental impact of their designs, as well as propose and implement solutions to minimize negative effects on the environment.

The primary focus of sustainable architecture software is to support the integration of sustainable design principles that aim to reduce energy consumption, minimize waste, and promote the use of renewable resources. These tools often provide features such as simulation and modeling capabilities, allowing users to assess various aspects of a building's performance, including energy efficiency, daylighting, thermal comfort, and water usage. This enables architects to make informed decisions and optimize their designs to achieve sustainable outcomes.

Additionally, sustainable architecture software facilitates collaboration and communication among project stakeholders, such as architects, engineers, contractors, and clients. It enables the sharing of design data and information, supporting the coordination of sustainable design strategies throughout the building lifecycle. Users can also create visualizations and presentations to effectively communicate the sustainability aspects of their designs to clients, government agencies, and other relevant parties.

In summary, sustainable architecture software serves as a valuable tool for professionals in the construction industry, offering innovative solutions to address the environmental challenges associated with building design. By utilizing such software, architects and designers can play a crucial role in creating sustainable, energy-efficient, and environmentally responsible buildings that contribute to a more sustainable future.

Sustainable Architecture

Sustainable architecture is an approach to architectural design and construction that aims to minimize the negative environmental impact of buildings while promoting the efficient use of resources and creating healthy living spaces. It seeks to balance the needs of the present generation without compromising the ability of future generations to meet their own needs.

Sustainable architecture integrates various strategies and techniques to achieve environmentally responsible designs. These strategies include passive design principles, such as optimizing building orientation, natural ventilation, and daylighting, to reduce energy consumption and reliance on mechanical systems. Additionally, sustainable architecture emphasizes the use of renewable energy sources, such as solar and wind power, to further reduce carbon emissions and dependence on fossil fuels.

Materials selection is another crucial aspect of sustainable architecture. The use of environmentally friendly and non-toxic materials, as well as recycled and locally sourced materials, helps to reduce the extraction of natural resources and minimize waste during the construction process. Furthermore, sustainable architecture aims to create long-lasting and adaptable buildings to reduce the need for frequent renovations and demolition waste.

Beyond these technical aspects, sustainable architecture also takes into account the social and cultural aspects of the built environment. It focuses on creating designs that enhance the well-being of occupants, promote community engagement, and contribute to the overall quality of life. By considering the triple bottom line of environmental, social, and economic sustainability, sustainable architecture strives to create buildings that harmonize with their surroundings and positively impact both the present and future generations.

Sustainable Building Codes

Sustainable building codes are regulations and standards that are implemented to promote and ensure environmentally responsible construction practices. These codes are designed to minimize the negative impact of buildings on the environment and to enhance the overall sustainability of the built environment.

The primary objective of sustainable building codes is to promote energy efficiency, conservation of natural resources, and reduction of greenhouse gas emissions. These codes establish requirements and guidelines for various aspects of construction, such as materials selection, energy performance, water efficiency, indoor environmental quality, and waste management.

By adhering to sustainable building codes, designers, builders, and policymakers can contribute to the creation of green and healthy spaces that are economically viable, socially equitable, and environmentally friendly. Some of the key principles addressed by sustainable building codes include the use of renewable energy sources, efficient use of water resources, optimal insulation and ventilation, and the integration of nature and green spaces within the built environment.

Furthermore, sustainable building codes also focus on reducing and managing waste during construction and demolition, promoting recycling and reuse of materials, and encouraging the use of environmentally friendly products and technologies. These codes typically involve a combination of performance-based criteria, mandatory regulations, and voluntary certifications to ensure compliance and to recognize exemplary sustainable practices.

Sustainable Building Energy Modeling

Sustainable building energy modeling is a method used in the field of sustainability to evaluate and optimize the energy performance of buildings. It involves the use of computer models and simulations to analyze various aspects of a building, such as its design, materials, and systems, in order to determine the most efficient and sustainable strategies for energy consumption.

By using sustainable building energy modeling, designers and architects can explore different scenarios and options to reduce energy use and greenhouse gas emissions, while still meeting the functional and aesthetic requirements of the building. The models take into account variables such as the building's location, orientation, and climate, as well as factors like occupancy, lighting, heating and cooling systems, and insulation. This allows for a comprehensive analysis of the energy performance and potential improvements of a building.

Sustainable Building Facades

Sustainable building facades refer to the exterior walls or faces of a building that are designed and constructed in a way that minimizes their negative environmental impact and maximizes their positive contributions to sustainability.

The main goal of sustainable building facades is to create a harmonious integration between the building and its surrounding environment, while ensuring energy efficiency, resource conservation, and occupant comfort. This is achieved through careful selection of materials, innovative design strategies, and the use of advanced technologies.

In terms of material selection, sustainable building facades prioritize the use of environmentally friendly and renewable materials, such as responsibly sourced timber, recycled metals, and low-impact composites. These materials should have a long lifespan, be recyclable or biodegradable, and have a low embodied energy, which refers to the energy consumed during their production and transportation.

Design strategies for sustainable building facades typically aim to improve energy efficiency by optimizing insulation, minimizing air leakage, and maximizing the use of natural daylight. This can be achieved through the use of high-performance insulation materials, efficient glazing systems, and properly sized and positioned windows and openings. Additionally, shading devices, such as overhangs or louvers, can be incorporated to reduce solar heat gain and improve thermal comfort.

The integration of advanced technologies, such as photovoltaic panels or solar thermal systems, can further enhance the sustainability of building facades by generating renewable energy or providing hot water. Rainwater harvesting systems and green walls can also be integrated into the facade design to promote water conservation and improve air quality.

Overall, sustainable building facades play a crucial role in reducing the environmental footprint of buildings, improving energy performance, and creating healthier and more comfortable living or working environments for occupants.

Sustainable Building Materials Testing

Sustainable building materials testing refers to the evaluation and analysis of construction materials, such as wood, concrete, steel, and insulation, to determine their impact on the environment, human health, and overall sustainability.

This testing involves conducting various assessments and measurements to assess the materials' performance in terms of energy efficiency, resource conservation, waste reduction, and carbon emissions. It aims to identify and promote materials that have lower environmental footprints and contribute to the long-term sustainability of the built environment.

Sustainable Building Materials

Sustainable building materials are materials that are sourced, produced, and used in a manner that minimizes negative environmental impacts and promotes long-term environmental, social, and economic sustainability.

These materials are typically renewable, meaning they can be replenished over time, or are made from recycled or reused components. They also have a lower carbon footprint compared to traditional building materials, as they require less energy and resources to produce and transport.

Sustainable building materials prioritize the use of natural resources in a responsible and efficient way. They are often chosen based on their durability, performance, and ability to enhance energy efficiency, water conservation, and indoor air quality. Examples include sustainably harvested wood, bamboo, straw bales, adobe, rammed earth, and recycled metal and glass.

By using sustainable building materials, construction projects can contribute to reducing pollution, conserving natural resources, and minimizing waste. They can also improve the overall environmental performance of buildings, leading to energy savings, improved occupant health, and reduced operating costs in the long run.

Sustainable City Planning Software

Sustainable city planning software is a digital tool that enables urban planners and decision-makers to design and manage cities in an environmentally, socially, and economically sustainable manner. This software integrates various data sources and analytical algorithms to provide valuable insights and support informed decision-making for urban development projects.

The primary goal of sustainable city planning software is to optimize the use of resources, minimize negative environmental impacts, and enhance the quality of life for residents. It facilitates the evaluation and visualization of different planning scenarios, allowing planners to simulate and assess the potential outcomes of various interventions before implementation.

By utilizing this software, planners can analyze and model the impacts of infrastructure development, transportation systems, energy consumption, waste management, and other urban factors. They can identify opportunities for energy efficiency, renewable energy integration, green spaces, public transportation networks, and sustainable building practices.

Additionally, sustainable city planning software enables the identification of potential risks and vulnerabilities cities may face due to climate change, population growth, and resource constraints. It assists in formulating strategies and policies to mitigate these risks and promote resilience. The software fosters collaboration and stakeholder engagement by providing a platform for sharing information, feedback, and participation in the decision-making process.

In summary, sustainable city planning software empowers urban planners to make data-driven, holistic, and sustainable decisions for the development and management of cities. It supports the creation of resilient, inclusive, and environmentally conscious urban environments that enhance the well-being of residents and promote a sustainable future.

Sustainable City Planning

Sustainable city planning refers to the process of designing and developing urban areas in a way that minimizes their impact on the environment and promotes long-term social and economic well-being. It involves considering various factors such as land use, transportation, energy consumption, waste management, and social equity to create cities that are sustainable and resilient.

The concept of sustainability in city planning recognizes the interconnectedness of environmental, social, and economic systems. It aims to achieve a balance between economic development, social inclusion, and environmental preservation. Sustainable city planning seeks to create cities that provide a high quality of life for residents while minimizing resource depletion, pollution, and social inequalities.

Sustainable Cityscapes

A sustainable cityscape refers to the design and management of urban areas in a way that promotes environmental, social, and economic sustainability.

This includes implementing sustainable practices and technologies, such as green building design, renewable energy sources, efficient transportation systems, waste management strategies, and preservation of natural resources. A sustainable cityscape aims to minimize negative impacts on the environment while enhancing the quality of life for its residents.

Sustainable Clothing Materials

Sustainable clothing materials are materials that are sourced, produced, and used in a manner that minimizes their negative environmental and social impacts throughout their lifecycle. These materials are designed to promote sustainability by considering the ecological footprint, human rights, and social responsibility.

There are various characteristics that define sustainable clothing materials. Firstly, they are made from renewable resources, such as organic cotton, hemp, or bamboo. These materials reduce dependence on non-renewable resources like petroleum-based synthetic fibers. Additionally, sustainable materials are sourced and produced in ways that conserve water, reduce energy consumption, and minimize pollution. This includes using eco-friendly production processes, such as organic farming for natural fibers, or recycling plastic bottles to create polyester.

Sustainable clothing materials also prioritize fair trade and ethical practices. This means ensuring safe working conditions, fair wages, and fair trade practices throughout the supply chain. Materials like organic cotton often come with certifications that guarantee their ethical production, such as the Global Organic Textile Standard (GOTS).

Furthermore, sustainable clothing materials aim to reduce waste by promoting durability and recyclability. They are designed to be long-lasting, with considerate attention to quality and craftsmanship. When they reach the end of their life, they can either be biodegradable or easily recycled, reducing the strain on landfill sites.

In conclusion, sustainable clothing materials align with the principles of sustainability by minimizing environmental impact, promoting ethical practices, and reducing waste. By opting for clothing made from sustainable materials, individuals can contribute to a more sustainable and responsible fashion industry.

Sustainable Community Engagement Platforms

A sustainable community engagement platform is a digital tool or platform that facilitates meaningful and ongoing participation, collaboration, and communication between individuals, organizations, and communities towards sustainable development goals.

It provides a space where community members can actively engage in decision-making processes, share ideas, and contribute to the shaping of their community's sustainable future. The platform fosters inclusive participation, enabling diverse voices, perspectives, and expertise to be heard, ensuring that marginalized groups are not excluded.

Through the platform, community members can access information about sustainability initiatives, projects, and events, empowering them to make informed choices and take actions that contribute to a more sustainable community. It serves as a central hub for sharing knowledge, best practices, and resources related to sustainable living, energy conservation, waste management, and other relevant topics.

The platform also facilitates collaboration and coordination among community members, local organizations, businesses, and government agencies. It allows for the formation of partnerships, the pooling of resources, and the implementation of joint initiatives to address sustainability challenges effectively.

Furthermore, the platform promotes transparency and accountability by providing visibility into decision-making processes and outcomes. It ensures that community members have access to information about sustainability goals, targets, and progress, promoting trust and engagement.

In summary, a sustainable community engagement platform is a digital space that enables inclusive participation, collaboration, and communication among community members, fostering sustainable development and empowering individuals to actively contribute to the creation of a more sustainable future.

Sustainable Community Planning

Sustainable community planning refers to the strategic and holistic approach of creating and managing communities that meet the present needs of their residents without compromising the ability of future generations to meet their own needs. It involves considering social, economic, and environmental factors to create resilient and harmonious communities.

At its core, sustainable community planning aims to promote sustainable development by integrating principles of environmental conservation, social equity, and economic prosperity. It involves identifying and addressing the complex interdependencies between urban planning, transportation systems, housing, infrastructure, and natural resources.

Sustainable Construction Materials Recycling

Sustainable construction materials recycling refers to the practice of reusing or repurposing materials from demolished or renovated buildings in order to reduce waste, conserve resources, and minimize the environmental impact of construction projects. This process involves carefully collecting, sorting, and processing construction and demolition waste to extract useful materials that can be reintroduced into the construction industry.

Construction and demolition waste, which includes materials such as concrete, wood, bricks, metals, and plastics, is a significant source of waste and greenhouse gas emissions. By recycling these materials, the demand for new raw materials and the associated energy consumption and pollution from extraction and manufacturing processes can be reduced.

Sustainable construction materials recycling offers several environmental and economic benefits. It helps to conserve natural resources by reducing the need for virgin materials and limits the amount of waste sent to landfill, which in turn reduces methane emissions and the release of harmful substances into the environment. It also has economic benefits, as recycled materials can often be less expensive than newly manufactured ones.

In order to achieve sustainable construction materials recycling, it is important to have effective waste management practices in place. This includes implementing recycling plans and strategies, ensuring proper sorting of materials, and utilizing appropriate processing technologies to extract usable materials from the waste stream.

Sustainable Construction Site Management

Sustainable construction site management refers to the practice of incorporating environmentally-friendly and socially responsible practices throughout the lifecycle of a construction project. It involves integrating sustainable principles into the planning, design, construction, and operation of the site, with the aim of minimizing negative impacts on the environment and maximizing positive social and economic outcomes.

This approach to site management considers a range of factors, including energy efficiency, resource conservation, waste management, water management, and the use of sustainable materials. It involves the implementation of strategies and technologies that promote energy and water efficiency, reduce waste generation, and minimize pollution. It also takes into account the social aspects of construction, such as the health and safety of workers, community engagement, and the creation of local employment opportunities.

Sustainable Consumption Patterns

Sustainable consumption patterns refer to the choices and behaviors of individuals and societies that contribute to the long-term well-being of the environment and future generations.

These patterns involve the adoption of practices and lifestyles that minimize resource use, waste generation, and pollution, while promoting social equity and economic development. Sustainable consumption encompasses a wide range of activities, such as the purchase and use of goods and services, transportation choices, energy consumption, and food consumption.

Key principles that guide sustainable consumption include reducing material and energy inputs, minimizing the generation of waste and emissions, promoting the use of renewable resources, and prioritizing the well-being of people and the planet over short-term economic gains.

By adopting sustainable consumption patterns, individuals and societies can contribute to the global efforts to address pressing environmental challenges, such as climate change, biodiversity loss, and resource depletion. This requires a shift away from a culture of overconsumption towards more mindful and responsible consumption practices.

Sustainable consumption patterns are not only beneficial for the environment but also for human well-being. They can lead to improved health and quality of life, reduced inequality, and enhanced resilience. Moreover, they can create new economic opportunities and promote sustainable business practices.

>

Sustainable Corporate Reporting Software

Sustainable corporate reporting software refers to a digital tool that enables companies to accurately and transparently measure, record, analyze, and report their sustainability performance and impacts. It provides a comprehensive framework for organizations to track and communicate their environmental, social, and governance (ESG) practices, allowing stakeholders to gain insights into their sustainability efforts.

This software typically offers a range of features and functionalities, including data collection, performance monitoring, key performance indicator (KPI) tracking, and report generation. It enables companies to collect data from various sources, such as energy consumption, waste management, carbon emissions, social impact, and diversity metrics, and consolidate them into meaningful reports.

The software facilitates the process of sustainability reporting, which involves the systematic disclosure of information related to a company's environmental and social performance. It ensures that the reported data is accurate, reliable, and in line with recognized reporting frameworks, such as the Global Reporting Initiative (GRI) or the Sustainability Accounting Standards Board (SASB).

By using sustainable corporate reporting software, companies can streamline their sustainability management processes, enhance data integrity, and improve stakeholder engagement. The tool enables them to identify areas for improvement, set sustainability targets, and track progress over time. It also facilitates the communication of sustainability information to stakeholders, including investors, customers, employees, and regulators, fostering trust and transparency.

Sustainable Cosmetics

Sustainable cosmetics refers to beauty and personal care products that are designed and produced using environmentally friendly practices, with the goal of minimizing negative impacts on the planet and its resources. These products are created and packaged in a way that minimizes waste, reduces energy consumption, and utilizes renewable resources whenever possible.

In order to be considered sustainable, cosmetics must adhere to several key principles. Firstly, they should prioritize the use of natural and organic ingredients, derived from renewable sources. This means avoiding the use of synthetic chemicals and potentially harmful substances such as parabens, sulfates, and phthalates. Instead, sustainable cosmetics aim to harness the power of nature, utilizing plant-based ingredients and botanical extracts that are ethically sourced and harvested.

Furthermore, sustainable cosmetics should consider the entire lifecycle of a product, from production to disposal. They should be manufactured using sustainable practices that minimize pollution and waste, such as recycling and reusing materials, implementing energy-efficient processes, and reducing carbon emissions. Packaging should be made from recyclable or biodegradable materials, aiming to minimize plastic waste and promote a circular economy.

Ultimately, the goal of sustainable cosmetics is to provide consumers with high-quality personal care products that not only enhance beauty, but also contribute to a healthier planet. By making conscious choices and supporting brands that prioritize sustainability, individuals can play their part in promoting a more environmentally friendly and socially responsible beauty industry.

Sustainable Data Center Design Tools

A sustainable data center design tool is a software or a set of software solutions that assist in the planning, construction, and operation of data centers with a focus on sustainability. This tool provides the necessary guidance and analysis to ensure that the design and operation of a data center meet specific environmental and energy efficiency goals.

These tools offer a range of features and capabilities to evaluate the environmental impact of data center infrastructure, optimize energy consumption, and reduce carbon footprint. They help in implementing green strategies such as energy-efficient server arrangements, intelligent cooling systems, renewable energy integration, and efficient utilization of resources.

Sustainable Disaster Recovery Planning

Sustainable disaster recovery planning refers to the proactive and systematic approach of preparing for and responding to disasters in a manner that minimizes environmental, social, and economic impacts while promoting long-term resilience and community well-being.

Unlike traditional disaster recovery planning, which focuses primarily on short-term recovery efforts, sustainable disaster recovery planning takes a broader view that considers the interdependencies between ecological systems, social dynamics, and economic activities. It recognizes that disasters not only cause immediate physical damage but also have long-lasting consequences for the environment and human populations.

This approach emphasizes the importance of integrating environmental considerations into all phases of disaster recovery, including mitigation, preparedness, response, and recovery. It seeks to identify and implement strategies that promote ecological sustainability, reduce greenhouse gas emissions, conserve natural resources, and enhance the resilience of communities to future disasters.

Sustainable disaster recovery planning also recognizes the social dimension of disasters and aims to address the needs and vulnerabilities of diverse populations, including marginalized communities and individuals. It promotes inclusive decision-making processes, community engagement, and the equitable distribution of resources, ensuring that recovery efforts do not exacerbate existing social inequalities.

In summary, sustainable disaster recovery planning is a holistic and forward-thinking approach that seeks to minimize the adverse impacts of disasters on the environment, society, and economy while fostering long-term sustainability and resilience.

Sustainable Distilleries

A sustainable distillery refers to a facility that incorporates environmentally conscious and socially responsible practices during the production of distilled spirits. It aims to minimize its impact on the natural environment, conserve resources, and promote the well-being of local communities and workers.

Sustainable distilleries prioritize the use of renewable energy sources, such as solar or wind power, to reduce their carbon footprint. They employ energy-efficient technologies and processes to minimize energy consumption and greenhouse gas emissions. By implementing energy-saving measures, such as insulation and equipment optimization, sustainable distilleries strive to lessen their environmental impact and contribute to the mitigation of climate change.

In addition to energy conservation, sustainable distilleries focus on water conservation and wastewater management. They adopt water-saving practices, such as recycling and reusing water in various stages of the production process. These distilleries also implement proper wastewater treatment systems to minimize water pollution and protect local ecosystems.

Furthermore, sustainable distilleries source their raw materials locally whenever possible, supporting nearby farmers and reducing transportation-related emissions. They prioritize organic and non-genetically modified ingredients to promote healthier and more sustainable agricultural practices. Through partnerships with local farmers and suppliers, sustainable distilleries strive to create a positive economic impact on their communities.

Social responsibility is another key aspect of sustainable distilleries. They provide fair wages and safe working conditions for their employees, fostering a supportive and inclusive work environment. These distilleries engage in community initiatives, such as volunteering, educational programs, and outreach activities, to contribute positively to local societies.

In summary, a sustainable distillery is a production facility that integrates environmentally conscious practices, resource conservation, and social responsibility into its operations. By prioritizing renewable energy, water conservation, local sourcing, and community engagement, sustainable distilleries aim to create a more sustainable and equitable future for all.

Sustainable Eco-Village Design

A sustainable eco-village design refers to the planning and development of a community that is built and operated in an environmentally and socially responsible manner, with a focus on long-term sustainability and minimal ecological impact.

Such a design encompasses various elements, including the use of renewable energy sources like solar and wind power, efficient water management systems, waste reduction and recycling practices, and the preservation of natural resources such as green spaces and biodiversity.

The sustainable eco-village design also emphasizes the creation of a strong sense of community and social cohesion. It promotes the idea of shared resources, cooperative decision-making, and healthy living practices. This may include the incorporation of communal gardens, shared workshops, and common spaces for residents to interact and collaborate.

Additionally, a sustainable eco-village design takes into account the principles of sustainable transportation, aiming to reduce car dependency and encourage the use of alternative modes of transportation like biking and walking. It also promotes the integration of local businesses and services within the village, reducing the need for long-distance travel for essentials.

In summary, a sustainable eco-village design is a holistic approach to community development that considers both environmental and social factors. It strives to create a self-sufficient and harmonious living environment that minimizes its ecological footprint while fostering a strong sense of community and well-being among its residents.

Sustainable Educational Facility Architecture

Sustainable educational facility architecture refers to the design and construction of educational buildings that prioritize ecological balance, resource efficiency, and the well-being of occupants. This approach combines elements of sustainable design, green building principles, and educational pedagogy to create a facility that supports and promotes sustainable practices and education.

At its core, sustainable educational facility architecture seeks to minimize the environmental impact of the building throughout its lifecycle. This includes reducing energy consumption, conserving water, and using renewable materials. The design integrates passive heating and cooling strategies, natural lighting, and efficient insulation to reduce the building's carbon footprint. Renewable energy systems such as solar panels or wind turbines may be incorporated to generate clean energy on-site.

In addition to environmental considerations, sustainable educational facility architecture also prioritizes the health and comfort of occupants. The design incorporates features that enhance indoor air quality, acoustics, and thermal comfort. Natural ventilation systems, low-emission materials, and proper daylighting contribute to a healthy learning environment.

Furthermore, sustainable educational facility architecture recognizes the role of education in fostering sustainability. The design includes spaces and features that facilitate experiential learning and environmental awareness. These may include outdoor classrooms, rooftop gardens, recycling stations, and interactive displays that showcase sustainable practices.

In summary, sustainable educational facility architecture aims to create buildings that are not only environmentally responsible but also provide an inspiring and healthy space for learning. By integrating sustainability principles into the design, these facilities serve as living examples of sustainable practices and help cultivate a more environmentally conscious generation.

Sustainable Educational Facility Design

Sustainable educational facility design refers to the process of creating educational buildings that minimize environmental impact, conserve resources, and promote a healthy and supportive learning environment.

Such designs take into consideration various factors, including energy efficiency, water conservation, use of renewable materials, indoor air quality, and accessibility. The goal is to create learning spaces that are economically, socially, and environmentally sustainable.

Sustainable Energy Storage Technologies

Sustainable energy storage technologies refer to systems or methods that enable the storage of renewable energy in an efficient and environmentally friendly manner. These technologies play a crucial role in the sustainable development and integration of renewable energy sources into our energy systems.

One of the main challenges in transitioning to a renewable energy future is the intermittent nature of renewable energy sources such as solar and wind. Energy storage technologies address this challenge by capturing excess energy during periods of high production and storing it for use during periods of low production or high demand. By leveling out the fluctuations in energy supply, these technologies ensure a more reliable and stable energy system.

There are various sustainable energy storage technologies available, including battery energy storage systems, pumped hydro storage, compressed air energy storage, and thermal energy storage. Battery energy storage systems, such as lithium-ion batteries, are becoming increasingly popular due to their high efficiency, rapid response times, and declining costs. Pumped hydro storage involves using excess energy to pump water to a higher elevation for later release to generate hydroelectric power. Compressed air energy storage compresses air using excess energy and releases it to drive turbines when needed. Thermal energy storage stores heat or cold for later use in heating or cooling applications.

These sustainable energy storage technologies are vital for achieving a renewable energy transition and reducing our dependence on fossil fuels. They enable a higher penetration of renewable energy sources into the grid, contribute to grid stability, and support the overall sustainability and resilience of our energy systems.

Sustainable Energy-Efficient HVAC Systems

Sustainable energy-efficient HVAC systems are heating, ventilation, and air conditioning systems that are designed to prioritize environmental sustainability and energy efficiency. These systems aim to reduce the overall energy consumption and environmental impact of the building by effectively managing the heating, cooling, and ventilation processes.

With a focus on sustainability, these systems are designed to minimize greenhouse gas emissions, reduce reliance on non-renewable energy sources, and optimize energy usage. They incorporate advanced technology and innovative design features to achieve high energy efficiency, such as variable speed compressors, thermal energy storage, and smart controls.

Sustainable Energy-Efficient Building Materials

Sustainable energy-efficient building materials are materials that are designed and used in construction projects with the aim of reducing energy consumption and minimizing environmental impact. These materials are carefully selected and manufactured to promote energy efficiency, reduce waste, and support sustainable building practices.

One key characteristic of sustainable energy-efficient building materials is their ability to effectively insulate buildings. By providing superior thermal insulation, these materials help to reduce the amount of energy required for heating and cooling, thereby lowering greenhouse gas emissions and decreasing dependence on non-renewable energy sources.

In addition to insulation, sustainable energy-efficient building materials often possess properties that enable them to capture and utilize renewable energy sources. For instance, solar panels integrated into roofing materials can generate electricity from sunlight, while passive solar design techniques utilize building materials that maximize the use of natural light and heat from the sun.

Another important aspect of these materials is their resource efficiency. Sustainable energy-efficient building materials are often made from recycled or renewable resources, reducing the demand for virgin materials and minimizing the extraction of natural resources. Furthermore, these materials are designed to be long-lasting and durable, reducing the need for frequent replacement and contributing to the reduction of waste and landfill usage.

In conclusion, sustainable energy-efficient building materials play a crucial role in promoting environmentally conscious construction practices. By reducing energy consumption, utilizing renewable energy, and prioritizing resource efficiency, these materials contribute to the creation of buildings that are environmentally friendly, economically viable, and comfortable for occupants.

Sustainable Event Catering And Food Services

Sustainable event catering and food services refers to the provision of food and beverage options that are environmentally responsible and socially conscious throughout the entire process of planning, preparing, and serving meals for events. Sustainability in event catering aims to minimize negative impacts on the environment and society, while promoting the well-being of individuals and the planet.

This approach involves various key elements that contribute to sustainability. Firstly, sustainable event catering focuses on sourcing local, organic, and seasonal ingredients whenever possible. This reduces the carbon footprint associated with transportation and supports local farmers and producers. Additionally, sustainable caterers prioritize the use of sustainable packaging, such as compostable or reusable materials, to minimize waste generation.

Furthermore, sustainable event catering practices include efficient energy and water usage during food preparation and service, as well as proper waste management, including recycling and composting. By adopting these practices, caterers can reduce their environmental impact and contribute to the overall sustainability of the event.

Sustainability extends beyond the food itself to encompass ethical considerations. Sustainable event caterers strive to provide fair trade and ethically sourced products, ensuring that workers involved in the production and supply chain are treated fairly and receive fair wages.

In conclusion, sustainable event catering and food services integrate environmentally responsible practices, ethical sourcing, and social consciousness to provide food options that align with the principles of sustainability. By choosing sustainable catering options, event organizers can not only satisfy their guests but also support a healthier and more sustainable future.

Sustainable Event Catering Services

A sustainable event catering service refers to a catering service that prioritizes environmental, social, and economic sustainability in its operations and practices. Sustainable event catering aims to minimize negative environmental impacts, promote social responsibility, and support the local economy.

Environmental sustainability is achieved by implementing various practices such as sourcing local and seasonal ingredients to reduce food miles and carbon emissions associated with transportation. It involves using organic and pesticide-free produce to protect ecosystems and reduce chemical contamination. Sustainable caterers also focus on reducing food waste by carefully planning menus, portion sizes, and utilizing food scraps for compost or donation.

Social sustainability entails considering the well-being of all people involved in the catering service, including workers, suppliers, and customers. Ethical labor practices, fair wages, and safe working conditions are essential aspects of sustainable event catering. Additionally, sustainable caterers may engage in community partnerships, donate surplus food to charities, or support local sustainable farming initiatives.

Economic sustainability is vital for the longevity of sustainable event catering services. This involves ensuring profitability while also considering the long-term social and environmental costs and benefits. Sustainable caterers may invest in energy-efficient equipment, manage resources wisely, and explore innovative methods to reduce costs and improve efficiency.

In summary, sustainable event catering services go beyond providing delicious food and excellent service. They strive to minimize their environmental footprint, nurture social well-being, and contribute to the local economy, resulting in a more sustainable and responsible approach to event catering.

Sustainable Event Planning Tools

Sustainable event planning tools are digital resources designed to assist event organizers in ensuring environmentally and socially responsible practices throughout the planning and execution of an event. These tools help to minimize the negative impacts of events on the environment, communities, and resources, while maximizing positive contributions and ensuring long-term sustainability.

Sustainable event planning tools typically include various features and functionalities that support eco-friendly event management. These may include:

- Waste management: Tools that help organizers reduce waste generation, promote recycling and composting, and minimize the use of single-use items.

- Energy management: Tools that enable efficient energy use, encourage the use of renewable energy sources, and track and reduce energy consumption during event setup and operations.

- Transportation management: Tools that assist with promoting sustainable transportation options such as public transit, cycling, and carpooling, and help minimize the carbon footprint associated with attendee transportation.

- Sustainable sourcing: Tools that facilitate the identification and procurement of sustainable and ethically sourced materials for event merchandise, decorations, and food and beverage services.

- Stakeholder engagement: Tools that support effective communication and collaboration with event attendees, sponsors, vendors, and local communities to raise awareness about sustainable practices and enhance social and environmental outcomes.

By utilizing sustainable event planning tools, organizers can align their events with principles of sustainability, reduce environmental impacts, and contribute positively to society. These tools aid in creating memorable and impactful events that respect the planet and its resources, while fostering a culture of conscious consumption and responsible event management.

Sustainable Event Waste Diversion Services

Sustainable event waste diversion services refer to the practice of managing and minimizing waste generated during events in an environmentally responsible manner. This includes strategies and actions aimed at diverting waste from landfills, promoting recycling and composting, and reducing overall waste generation.

These services are implemented to address the significant environmental impacts associated with event waste, such as depletion of natural resources, pollution, and contribution to climate change. By diverting waste from landfills and implementing sustainable waste management practices, event organizers can significantly reduce their ecological footprint and contribute to a more sustainable event industry.

Sustainable Event Waste Diversion

Sustainable event waste diversion refers to the practice of minimizing the amount of waste generated during an event and diverting it away from landfills through various sustainable strategies. This concept focuses on the principles of reduce, reuse, and recycle to ensure that the environmental impact of an event is minimized.

The goal of sustainable event waste diversion is to promote environmentally responsible behavior among event organizers, attendees, and vendors. It involves the implementation of waste management strategies that prioritize waste reduction, resource recovery, and proper disposal. This includes reducing the overall waste generation by using environmentally friendly products and materials, encouraging the reuse of items, and implementing effective recycling programs.

Event waste diversion also involves the proper separation and collection of waste materials during the event. This may include providing clearly labeled recycling and compost bins, as well as educating attendees about the importance of sorting their waste correctly. By effectively diverting waste from landfills, events can reduce their carbon footprint, conserve natural resources, and prevent pollution.

Sustainable event waste diversion is an integral part of overall event sustainability efforts. It helps to create a more eco-friendly and socially responsible event by minimizing the negative environmental impact associated with waste generation. By implementing sustainable waste management practices, events can contribute to a circular economy where materials are reused, recycled, or composted, rather than discarded as waste.

Sustainable Event Waste Management Services

Sustainable event waste management services refer to the practices and procedures implemented to responsibly manage and reduce the waste generated during events, such as conferences, exhibitions, and festivals, with the goal of minimizing the environmental impact and promoting sustainability.

These services typically involve the comprehensive planning, collection, segregation, and proper disposal or recycling of waste generated at events. They aim to divert waste from landfills, conserve resources, and reduce greenhouse gas emissions associated with waste disposal.

Sustainable event waste management services include the use of recycling stations and bins strategically placed throughout event venues to encourage attendees to separate their waste into recyclable materials, such as paper, plastic, and glass. Composting stations may also be provided to facilitate the composting of organic waste, such as food scraps and biodegradable materials.

In addition to waste collection and segregation, sustainable event waste management services often involve partnerships with local recycling facilities or waste management companies to ensure that collected waste is properly processed and recycled. This may include the sorting, cleaning, and transportation of recyclable materials to the appropriate recycling facilities.

Furthermore, education and awareness campaigns are an integral part of sustainable event waste management services. Through signage, announcements, and informational materials, event organizers can promote responsible waste disposal practices to attendees, encouraging them to actively participate in waste reduction efforts.

Sustainable Farming IoT Devices

Sustainable farming IoT devices are technological tools that are used in agricultural practices to promote environmentally friendly and efficient farming methods.

These devices utilize the Internet of Things (IoT) technology to collect and analyze data from various sources, such as soil moisture sensors, weather stations, and crop health monitoring systems. By monitoring and analyzing this data, farmers can make informed decisions about irrigation, fertilization, pest control, and other farming practices, reducing the use of water, energy, and chemicals.

Sustainable farming IoT devices help optimize the use of resources and minimize waste, contributing to the overall sustainability of agricultural systems. They enable farmers to implement precision farming techniques, which involve using data-driven insights to improve crop productivity while minimizing negative environmental impacts.

By using IoT devices, farmers can remotely monitor and control various aspects of their farms, such as irrigation systems and greenhouse conditions. This remote monitoring and control capability reduces the need for unnecessary physical presence on the farm, saving time, labor, and fuel. Additionally, these devices can send real-time alerts and notifications to farmers, allowing them to respond promptly to changing conditions and prevent crop loss.

In conclusion, sustainable farming IoT devices are essential tools for promoting eco-friendly and efficient farming practices. By harnessing the power of IoT technology, these devices enable farmers to make data-driven decisions, optimize resource use, and reduce waste, contributing to a more sustainable agricultural sector.

Sustainable Fashion Accessory Design

Sustainable fashion accessory design refers to the development and production of accessories that are created with a focus on minimizing negative environmental and social impacts throughout their life cycle.

This approach involves conscious decision-making at every stage of the design process, from sourcing materials to manufacturing techniques, and even packaging and distribution methods. The aim is to create accessories that contribute positively to the planet and the communities involved in their production and use.

Sustainable Fashion Accessory Lines

Sustainable fashion accessory lines are product lines that are created and designed in a manner that is environmentally friendly and socially responsible. These accessory lines aim to minimize the negative impacts on the environment and promote sustainable practices throughout the entire supply chain.

When it comes to sustainable fashion accessory lines, the focus is on using materials that are renewable and have a low environmental footprint. This includes materials such as organic cotton, bamboo, recycled plastics, and reclaimed materials. The production processes involved in creating these accessories also prioritize energy efficiency, water conservation, and waste reduction.

In addition to the selection of materials and production processes, sustainable fashion accessory

330

lines also take into consideration the social and ethical aspects of the industry. This means ensuring fair wages and safe working conditions for the workers involved in the manufacturing process. It also involves promoting transparency and accountability within the supply chain, from sourcing the materials to the final product.

The goal of sustainable fashion accessory lines is to create products that are not only stylish and on-trend but also promote a more sustainable and responsible fashion industry. By choosing accessories from these lines, consumers can support ethical practices and contribute to a more sustainable future.

Sustainable Fashion Brand Identity

A sustainable fashion brand identity refers to the unique set of characteristics and values that distinguish a fashion brand committed to sustainability. It encompasses the fundamental principles, goals, and actions taken by the brand to minimize its environmental impact and promote social responsibility throughout its entire value chain.

Sustainable fashion brands prioritize the use of eco-friendly materials, such as organic cotton, recycled polyester, and renewable fibers, in their products. They also take into consideration the entire lifecycle of the garment, striving for sustainable production processes, efficient use of resources, and minimal waste generation. This includes practices such as reducing water usage, implementing renewable energy, and adopting circular business models that encourage reusing, repairing, and recycling clothes.

Furthermore, a sustainable fashion brand identity involves fair treatment of workers and suppliers. These brands ensure fair wages, safe working conditions, and ethical labor practices, actively supporting the rights of the individuals involved in their supply chains. They may also collaborate with local artisans and communities, promoting cultural diversity and preserving traditional craftsmanship.

In terms of transparency, sustainable fashion brands communicate openly about their practices, origins of materials, and manufacturing processes. They may obtain certifications or participate in third-party audits to verify their sustainability claims, providing consumers with the necessary information to make informed choices.

Overall, a sustainable fashion brand identity is built on the principles of environmental stewardship, social responsibility, and transparency. It aims to disrupt the traditional fashion industry by offering conscious alternatives that promote a more sustainable and equitable future for both people and the planet.

Sustainable Fashion Collections

Sustainable fashion collections are clothing lines or ranges that are designed, produced, and marketed with a focus on minimizing the environmental impact and promoting social responsibility throughout the entire lifecycle of the products. These collections prioritize the use of sustainable materials, such as organic or recycled fabrics, and prioritize fair trade practices in the production process.

The concept of sustainability in fashion involves considering the impacts of every step in the supply chain, including design, sourcing, manufacturing, transportation, and end-of-life disposal. By emphasizing sustainable practices, these collections aim to reduce water and energy consumption, minimize waste and pollution, and ensure safe and fair working conditions for garment workers.

Sustainable Fashion Design Software

Sustainable fashion design software refers to computer programs or applications specifically designed for the fashion industry, with a focus on promoting sustainability throughout the design process.

These software tools aim to assist fashion designers in creating environmentally friendly and socially responsible garments by integrating sustainable design principles into their work. They provide designers with various features and functionalities that allow them to make informed decisions and reduce the environmental impact of their designs.

Sustainable fashion design software typically includes features such as material sourcing and selection, waste reduction and optimization, energy-efficient pattern making, and ethical supply chain management. It enables designers to explore sustainable materials and production techniques, calculate the carbon footprint of their designs, and make more sustainable choices by considering factors such as durability, recyclability, and eco-friendly manufacturing processes.

By using sustainable fashion design software, designers can streamline their design process, reduce waste, and create clothing that is more environmentally friendly and socially conscious. These software tools contribute to a more sustainable fashion industry by encouraging designers to consider the entire lifecycle of their products, from sourcing to end-of-life disposal.

Sustainable Fashion E-Commerce Platforms

A sustainable fashion e-commerce platform refers to an online platform that promotes and sells fashion products with a primary focus on sustainability. The platform supports and encourages ethical and eco-friendly fashion practices, including the use of sustainable materials, fair labor practices, and environmentally conscious production processes.

These platforms play a crucial role in transforming the fashion industry into a more sustainable and responsible sector. They offer consumers a wide range of sustainable fashion options, including clothing, accessories, and footwear, that have a reduced impact on the environment and prioritize social responsibility.

Sustainable Fashion Materials Sourcing Platforms

Sustainable fashion materials sourcing platforms are online platforms that connect fashion brands and designers with suppliers and manufacturers that offer sustainable and eco-friendly materials for the production of garments and accessories.

These platforms aim to promote sustainable practices in the fashion industry by providing a wide range of material options that are produced with minimal harm to the environment and social communities. They enable designers and brands to source materials that meet their sustainability goals, such as organic fibers, recycled fabrics, and low-impact dyes.

By facilitating the sourcing process, these platforms help fashion brands and designers easily find and connect with suppliers that prioritize environmentally friendly practices and uphold ethical standards. They provide a transparent and reliable channel for sourcing materials, ensuring that the products created are in line with sustainable values and contribute to a greener fashion industry.

Furthermore, sustainable fashion materials sourcing platforms often provide information and certifications about the materials offered, allowing brands and designers to make informed decisions and educate consumers about the sustainability of their products. This promotes transparency and accountability within the fashion supply chain.

In summary, sustainable fashion materials sourcing platforms play a crucial role in advancing sustainability in the fashion industry by connecting brands and designers with eco-friendly suppliers. They provide a convenient and transparent way to source materials that align with sustainable values, promoting responsible production and consumption in the fashion sector.

Sustainable Fashion Materials Sourcing

Sustainable fashion materials sourcing refers to the process of procuring raw materials for the production of clothing and accessories in a manner that minimizes negative environmental impacts and promotes social and economic responsibility.

In the context of sustainability, the sourcing of materials for fashion production is aimed at reducing the exploitation of natural resources, minimizing pollution, and ensuring ethical labor practices throughout the supply chain. This involves selecting materials that have a lower ecological footprint, such as organic cotton, bamboo, hemp, and recycled fibers. These materials are often grown or produced using methods that do not involve harmful chemicals or excessive water usage, thereby reducing the overall environmental impact.

Sustainable sourcing also emphasizes the importance of transparency and traceability in the supply chain. It involves partnering with suppliers and manufacturers who prioritize ethical practices and provide fair working conditions for their employees. This includes ensuring fair wages, safe working environments, and the absence of child labor.

In addition to environmental and social considerations, sustainable fashion materials sourcing also takes into account the economic viability of the materials. This includes evaluating the availability, cost, and durability of the materials to ensure long-term sustainability and profitability.

Sustainable Fashion Rental Services

Sustainable fashion rental services refer to the practice of renting clothing and accessories for a temporary period, with the aim of minimizing the negative environmental and social impacts associated with the fashion industry.

These services offer a more sustainable alternative to traditional fashion consumption by promoting the reuse and recycling of clothing items. By renting instead of buying, customers can enjoy a variety of trendy and high-quality clothes without the need for constant purchases and wardrobe expansion. This reduces the demand for new products, leading to fewer resources being extracted, less energy being consumed, and fewer greenhouse gas emissions being generated throughout the lifecycle of fashion items.

Sustainable Fashion Store Interiors

Sustainable fashion store interiors refer to the design and layout of retail spaces that prioritize eco-friendly practices and materials, aiming to minimize their negative impact on the environment. These interiors are carefully crafted to align with the principles of sustainability, incorporating various strategies to reduce energy consumption, waste generation, and pollution.

One key aspect of sustainable fashion store interiors is the use of renewable and recycled materials. This includes utilizing reclaimed wood for furniture and fixtures, recycled glass for decorations, and eco-friendly paints and finishes. By opting for these materials, the store minimizes the need for new resources and decreases the amount of waste that ends up in landfills.

In addition, sustainable fashion store interiors emphasize energy efficiency through the use of natural lighting, energy-saving LED bulbs, and motion-controlled lighting systems. This reduces the reliance on artificial lighting and helps to reduce the store's overall carbon footprint. Furthermore, sustainable stores might incorporate skylights, large windows, and light-colored surfaces to maximize natural light and reduce the need for artificial lighting during daytime hours.

Another consideration in sustainable store interiors is water conservation. Stores may implement low-flow plumbing fixtures, such as faucets and toilets, to reduce water consumption. Additionally, water-efficient irrigation systems can be used for any indoor greenery or living walls to minimize water wastage.

Overall, sustainable fashion store interiors strive to create an aesthetically pleasing and functional environment while integrating sustainable design principles. By using renewable and recycled materials, optimizing energy consumption, and conserving water resources, these interiors promote the longevity and well-being of both the store and the environment.

Sustainable Fashion Store Layouts

Sustainable fashion store layouts refer to the arrangement and design of physical spaces in fashion stores that promote environmentally and socially responsible practices in the fashion industry. These layouts aim to minimize the negative impact on the environment and maximize the positive impact on communities and workers.

Sustainable fashion store layouts typically prioritize several key elements. Firstly, they focus on optimizing energy efficiency by using natural lighting, energy-efficient fixtures, and renewable energy sources. This helps to reduce the carbon footprint of the store and minimize energy consumption. Secondly, sustainable layouts emphasize the use of eco-friendly materials, such as recycled or upcycled display fixtures, flooring, and wall coverings. This reduces the demand for virgin materials and decreases waste generation. Thirdly, these layouts incorporate thoughtful space planning and design to maximize flexibility and adaptability. This allows for easy reconfiguration of the store layout as needed, reducing the need for major renovations and minimizing waste. Additionally, sustainable fashion store layouts often prioritize the use of non-toxic and low VOC (volatile organic compounds) materials in paint and finishes to ensure a healthy indoor environment. Lastly, these layouts may integrate green spaces or living walls to create a connection with nature and improve air quality.

Sustainable Fashion Supply Chain Software

A sustainable fashion supply chain software is a digital tool that helps fashion brands and companies streamline and optimize their supply chain processes in a way that minimizes negative environmental and social impacts, while promoting sustainable practices.

By using this software, fashion brands can track and monitor their entire supply chain, from raw material sourcing to production, transportation, distribution, and retail. The software provides real-time data and analytics on various sustainability indicators, such as carbon emissions, water usage, waste generation, and worker conditions. This enables brands to identify areas of improvement and take corrective actions to mitigate their environmental footprint and improve social welfare.

The software also facilitates transparency and traceability in the supply chain by recording and storing information about suppliers, materials, and production processes. This allows brands to verify the sustainability claims of their suppliers and ensure compliance with ethical and environmental standards throughout the supply chain.

Moreover, a sustainable fashion supply chain software enables brands to collaborate and communicate with suppliers, customers, and other stakeholders to foster shared sustainability goals and initiatives. It also supports the implementation of circular economy principles, such as recycling and extending product life, by enabling efficient inventory management and product lifecycle tracking.

In summary, a sustainable fashion supply chain software helps fashion brands integrate sustainability into their supply chain management, by providing tools and insights to drive responsible sourcing, reduce environmental impacts, ensure social welfare, enhance transparency, and promote collaboration towards a more sustainable fashion industry.

Sustainable Fashion Trend Analysis

Sustainable fashion refers to the practice of producing clothing, accessories, and footwear in an environmentally and socially responsible manner. It is a comprehensive approach that takes into account the entire lifecycle of a product, from design to disposal, with the aim of minimizing its negative impact on the environment and society.

In the context of sustainability, sustainable fashion involves various key principles. Firstly, it focuses on reducing the use of finite resources, such as water, energy, and raw materials, by adopting more efficient production processes and materials. This includes sourcing fabrics from sustainable suppliers, utilizing organic or recycled materials, and implementing technologies to minimize waste and pollution.

Secondly, sustainable fashion emphasizes fair and ethical practices throughout the supply chain. This means ensuring the fair treatment of workers, providing safe working conditions, and paying fair wages. It also involves supporting local artisans and craftsmen, promoting cultural diversity, and fostering community development.

Furthermore, sustainable fashion encourages the adoption of circular economy models, which aim to maximize resource efficiency and minimize waste. This includes designing products for durability and longevity, offering repair and recycling services, and promoting secondhand or rental markets.

Overall, sustainable fashion seeks to create a more conscious and responsible fashion industry that not only protects the environment but also respects human rights and social well-being. It is an ongoing process of innovation and collaboration across the fashion value chain, driven by a commitment towards a more sustainable future.

Sustainable Fisheries Management Apps

Sustainable fisheries management apps are digital tools designed to support the sustainability of fishery resources and the ecosystems they depend on. These apps provide valuable information and functionalities to assist fisheries managers, fishers, and other stakeholders in making informed decisions and taking actions towards sustainable fishing practices.

These apps typically offer features such as real-time data on fish stocks, weather conditions, and fishing regulations, enabling users to assess the current state of the fishery and make decisions based on the most up-to-date information. They may also include tools for tracking fishing activities, recording catches, and monitoring compliance with regulations to ensure sustainable fishing practices are being followed.

Additionally, sustainable fisheries management apps often incorporate educational resources and training materials to promote awareness and understanding of sustainable fishing practices. They may provide guidance on best practices for reducing bycatch and avoiding overfishing, as well as tips for minimizing environmental impacts and maximizing the long-term productivity of fishery resources.

By leveraging the power of technology, these apps contribute to the sustainable management of fisheries by facilitating data-driven decision-making, promoting compliance with regulations, and empowering stakeholders with the knowledge and tools needed to engage in responsible fishing practices. They play a crucial role in improving the long-term sustainability of fishery resources and conserving marine ecosystems for future generations.

Sustainable Fisheries Management Software

Sustainable fisheries management software refers to a computer program or system that assists in the effective and responsible management of fisheries resources while ensuring long-term sustainability. This software is designed to support fisheries managers in making informed decisions based on scientific data and analysis, promoting the conservation of fish populations and their habitats.

The primary purpose of sustainable fisheries management software is to monitor and regulate fishing activities, ensuring that they align with sustainable fishing practices and international regulations. The software helps in collecting and analyzing various data sets, such as fish population size, fishing effort, catch quotas, and environmental factors, to assess the health of fish stocks and determine appropriate management strategies.

By utilizing sustainable fisheries management software, fisheries managers can establish and maintain a balance between the economic benefits derived from fisheries activities and the preservation of marine ecosystems. The software aids in implementing measures such as catch limits, fishing season restrictions, and spatial management, contributing to the prevention of overfishing, bycatch, and habitat degradation.

Furthermore, sustainable fisheries management software facilitates data sharing and collaboration between different stakeholders, including scientists, fishermen, government agencies, and non-governmental organizations. This promotes transparency, inclusivity, and participatory decision-making, allowing for the incorporation of diverse perspectives and knowledge in the management process.

In summary, sustainable fisheries management software plays a crucial role in promoting the sustainable use of fisheries resources by supporting data-driven decision-making, fostering compliance with regulations, and fostering collaboration among stakeholders.

Sustainable Fisheries Marketplaces

A sustainable fisheries marketplace refers to a system or platform that promotes the trade and consumption of seafood products that are harvested or farmed in an environmentally and socially responsible manner, with the aim of ensuring the long-term health and viability of global fisheries and marine ecosystems.

Such marketplaces play a crucial role in supporting sustainable fishing practices by connecting consumers, retailers, and seafood suppliers who prioritize sustainability and adhere to specific criteria or certifications. These criteria may include factors such as limiting catch quotas, avoiding overfishing and destructive fishing methods, protecting endangered or vulnerable species, and maintaining the overall health and biodiversity of marine ecosystems. The goal is to establish a transparent and traceable supply chain that enables consumers to make informed choices about the seafood they purchase and consume.

By promoting sustainable fisheries, these marketplaces also contribute to the achievement of various environmental and social objectives. They help to protect marine ecosystems from irreversible damage, safeguard the livelihoods and well-being of fishing communities, and ensure the availability of seafood resources for future generations. Additionally, sustainable fisheries marketplaces can encourage innovation and investment in sustainable fishing practices, driving positive change across the seafood industry as a whole.

In conclusion, sustainable fisheries marketplaces facilitate the responsible trade and consumption of seafood products, aiming to safeguard the health of fisheries and marine ecosystems while meeting the needs of both present and future generations.

Sustainable Fisheries Traceability Solutions

A sustainable fisheries traceability solution is a system or process that enables the tracking and tracing of seafood products from their point of origin to the final consumer, with the goal of promoting sustainability in the fishing industry.

Sustainability in fisheries refers to the responsible management and utilization of fish stocks, ensuring their long-term viability and minimizing negative impacts on the marine ecosystem. Traceability plays a crucial role in achieving this by providing a transparent and accountable supply chain that allows for the identification of the exact source and journey of seafood products.

By implementing a sustainable fisheries traceability solution, companies and consumers can have confidence in the legitimacy and sustainability of the seafood they buy and consume. This helps prevent illegal, unreported, and unregulated (IUU) fishing practices and ensures that seafood products are sourced from well-managed fisheries with minimal environmental impact.

Furthermore, traceability solutions enable the collection and analysis of data throughout the supply chain, allowing for better decision-making and improved management of fisheries. This information can be used to monitor stocks, detect patterns of overfishing, and implement effective conservation measures.

In summary, a sustainable fisheries traceability solution is a tool that fosters sustainability by ensuring the traceability of seafood products, promoting responsible fishing practices, reducing illegal fishing activities, and facilitating data-driven management of fisheries.

Sustainable Fishing Management Software

Sustainable fishing management software refers to a computer-based system developed to support and enhance the sustainable management of fishing activities. It is designed to assist fisheries managers and operators in making informed decisions that promote the long-term viability of fish stocks and the marine ecosystem.

This software provides a range of functionalities aimed at optimizing the utilization of fishery resources while minimizing negative impacts on the environment. It enables the monitoring and assessment of fishing activities, allowing stakeholders to track and evaluate the performance of different fishing operations in relation to sustainability goals.

The software typically includes features such as data collection and analysis tools, reporting capabilities, and simulation models. It allows users to gather and analyze various types of data, including catch information, fishing effort, spatial distribution, and environmental factors. By integrating these data sources, the software enables users to generate comprehensive reports and visualizations, facilitating the interpretation and communication of fisheries-related information.

Furthermore, sustainable fishing management software often incorporates simulation models that can predict the consequences of different management strategies on fish stocks and ecosystem dynamics. These models help decision-makers evaluate the potential outcomes of alternative management scenarios, enabling them to select the most sustainable and effective options.

Sustainable Fishing Practices

Sustainable fishing practices refer to the responsible and balanced harvesting of aquatic resources, ensuring the long-term health and productivity of the marine environment. These practices aim to maintain and restore fish populations, minimize the impact on the ecosystem, and support the livelihoods of those dependent on fishing.

Key elements of sustainable fishing practices include:

1. Conservation of target species: Limiting fishing efforts to sustainable levels that allow fish populations to reproduce and replenish their numbers. This involves setting catch limits, implementing size restrictions, and protecting spawning grounds and breeding areas.

2. Ecosystem-based management: Taking a holistic approach that considers the interactions between different species and their habitats. This includes protecting biodiversity, avoiding damage to essential habitats (such as coral reefs and seagrass beds), and minimizing bycatch and discards.

3. Minimizing environmental impact: Employing fishing methods and gear that have the least impact on the marine ecosystem. This may involve using selective fishing gear that targets specific species, reducing gear entanglement and habitat destruction, and avoiding the use of destructive practices like bottom trawling.

4. Monitoring and enforcement: Regularly assessing the status of fish stocks and the effectiveness of management measures. This includes implementing fishery monitoring programs, improving data collection and analysis, and enforcing regulations to prevent illegal, unreported, and unregulated fishing.

By adopting sustainable fishing practices, we can ensure the long-term viability of fisheries, protect marine biodiversity, and support the livelihoods of fishing communities, while also meeting the growing global demand for seafood.

Sustainable Fishing Technology

Sustainable fishing technology refers to the use of practices, techniques, and tools that ensure the long-term viability and health of marine ecosystems, while also allowing for the continued harvesting of fish and other aquatic species. It involves incorporating strategies that minimize the environmental impact of fishing activities, promote conservation, and protect biodiversity.

There are several key principles that underpin sustainable fishing technology. First and foremost, it focuses on maintaining fish populations at levels that can support their reproduction and natural growth rates. This involves employing methods that prevent overfishing and promote the recovery of depleted species. It also requires the implementation of science-based fisheries management systems to ensure that fishing is conducted within sustainable limits.

Sustainable fishing technology also prioritizes the reduction of bycatch, which refers to the unintentional capture of non-target species, including marine mammals, seabirds, and turtles. By using selective fishing gear and implementing measures to minimize the capture and mortality of non-target species, it helps minimize the ecological impact of fishing activities.

Furthermore, sustainable fishing technology aims to minimize habitat destruction and the alteration of marine ecosystems. This involves avoiding fishing practices that damage vulnerable habitats, such as coral reefs, seagrass beds, and breeding or nursery grounds. It also includes adopting responsible fishing techniques that minimize bottom trawling and other destructive fishing practices that can disrupt marine ecosystems.

In summary, sustainable fishing technology encompasses a range of strategies and approaches that are geared towards ensuring the long-term sustainability of fisheries and the preservation of marine ecosystems. By adopting these practices, fishing activities can be conducted in a manner that minimizes their environmental impact, protects marine biodiversity, and promotes the resilience and health of marine ecosystems for future generations.

Sustainable Fishing Traceability

Sustainable fishing traceability refers to the ability to track and record the entire journey of a fish from the point of capture to the point of consumption, ensuring that it is sourced in a manner that supports the long-term health and viability of fish populations and the marine ecosystem.

It involves the use of technologies, such as electronic tagging, barcoding, and blockchain, to collect and store data about each fish, including its species, size, location of capture, and the fishing method used. This data is then used to create a transparent and verifiable record that can be accessed by various stakeholders, including fishermen, seafood processors, retailers, and consumers.

Sustainable fishing traceability plays a crucial role in promoting responsible fisheries management and combating illegal, unreported, and unregulated (IUU) fishing. By accurately identifying the source of each fish, it helps to ensure that only legally caught and properly managed fish enter the market.

Moreover, it enables consumers to make informed choices about the seafood they buy, empowering them to support sustainable fishing practices and avoid purchasing products that contribute to overfishing or environmental degradation. By promoting transparency and accountability in the seafood supply chain, sustainable fishing traceability promotes the conservation of fish stocks, protects marine habitats, and supports the livelihoods of fishermen and coastal communities.

Sustainable Fishing Vessels

Sustainable fishing vessels can be defined as fishing boats or ships that are designed, operated, and managed in a manner that ensures the long-term viability of fish stocks, minimizes negative impacts on the environment, and promotes social and economic benefits for local communities.

These vessels prioritize sustainability by adopting various practices and technologies that aim to reduce their ecological footprint. For example, sustainable fishing vessels may employ selective fishing gear such as hooks or traps that target specific species, allowing non-target species to be released unharmed. They may also utilize onboard technology, such as fish finders and satellite systems, to enhance precision and reduce bycatch.

In addition to these technological advancements, sustainable fishing vessels adhere to sustainable fishing practices. This involves following regulations and guidelines set forth by governing bodies to ensure that fishing activities are conducted within sustainable limits. It may also involve participating in fisheries management programs that monitor and assess fish stocks, set quotas, and implement conservation measures.

Furthermore, sustainable fishing vessels consider the social and economic aspects of fishing. They strive to maintain the well-being of fishing communities by promoting fair labor practices, supporting small-scale fishers, and contributing to local economies. These vessels may be involved in initiatives that involve community engagement, partnering with local organizations or implementing certification schemes that recognize and reward sustainable fishing practices.

Sustainable Food Delivery And Meal Kits

A sustainable food delivery and meal kit refers to a service that provides customers with pre-portioned ingredients and recipes, as well as the delivery of ready-to-eat meals, all of which align with sustainable practices.

Sustainability in the context of food delivery and meal kits encompasses various aspects, including the sourcing of ingredients, packaging materials, transportation methods, and waste management.

Firstly, sustainable meal kits prioritize the use of locally sourced, organic, and seasonal ingredients. This sourcing approach reduces environmental impact by minimizing transportation distance, supporting local farmers, and avoiding the use of harmful pesticides and fertilizers. Additionally, it promotes the consumption of fresh and nutritious food, which is beneficial to both the consumers and the environment.

Secondly, sustainable meal kit providers employ eco-conscious packaging materials. They strive to reduce the use of plastic and opt for biodegradable or compostable alternatives. By minimizing packaging waste, these services help mitigate the environmental burden associated with single-use plastics.

Further, sustainable food delivery and meal kits prioritize efficient transportation practices. They aim to optimize delivery routes, reduce emissions, and partner with eco-friendly delivery providers. This approach reduces carbon footprints and contributes to mitigating climate change.

Lastly, successful sustainability-focused meal kit providers implement comprehensive waste management strategies. They minimize food waste by providing precise ingredient portions and offer solutions for composting or recycling packaging materials. By doing so, these services prevent excess resource consumption and reduce the amount of waste that ends up in landfills.

In summary, a sustainable food delivery and meal kit is a service that considers the entire lifecycle of food, from sourcing to waste management, with the aim of minimizing environmental impact and promoting sustainable practices.

Sustainable Food Delivery

Sustainable food delivery refers to the practice of delivering food from a source to a destination in an environmentally and socially responsible manner. It involves considering the entire supply chain involved in the delivery process, including the sourcing of ingredients, packaging, transportation, and end-of-life disposal.

In terms of environmental sustainability, sustainable food delivery aims to minimize the carbon footprint by utilizing efficient transportation methods and reducing energy consumption. This can be achieved through the use of electric vehicles, bicycles, or even walking for short-distance deliveries. Additionally, sustainable food delivery promotes the use of eco-friendly packaging materials and encourages customers to opt for minimal packaging or reusable containers.

Social sustainability is also an important aspect of sustainable food delivery. It focuses on fair labor practices, ensuring that workers involved in the delivery process are treated ethically and receive fair wages. This may involve partnering with delivery companies that provide fair working conditions and prioritize worker well-being.

Furthermore, sustainable food delivery promotes the support of local and organic food sources. By sourcing ingredients from local farmers and producers, it reduces the environmental impact associated with long-distance transportation and supports the local economy. Additionally, prioritizing organic and sustainable farming practices helps to protect the environment, conserve natural resources, and promote biodiversity.

Sustainable Food Distribution

Sustainable food distribution refers to the practice of transporting and delivering food in an environmentally, economically, and socially responsible manner, with the goal of minimizing negative impacts on the environment and promoting long-term well-being.

This approach involves various strategies and principles aimed at reducing greenhouse gas emissions, conserving natural resources, and supporting local economies. Sustainable food distribution seeks to address the environmental and social pitfalls of traditional distribution systems, such as excessive use of fossil fuels, excessive packaging waste, and limited access to fresh and healthy food options in underserved communities.

Key components of sustainable food distribution include:

- Efficient transportation: Utilizing fuel-efficient vehicles, optimizing logistics, and promoting alternative modes of transportation such as rail and waterways to minimize carbon footprint and reduce traffic congestion.

- Local sourcing: Prioritizing locally produced and seasonal foods to support small-scale farmers and reduce the energy and emissions associated with long-distance transportation.

- Waste reduction: Implementing strategies to minimize food waste throughout the supply chain, including improved inventory management, proper handling and storage, and redirecting surplus food to food banks or composting facilities.

- Access and equity: Ensuring that all communities, especially those in food deserts or low-income areas, have access to affordable and nutritious food by establishing farmers markets, community gardens, or mobile markets.

Overall, sustainable food distribution aims to create a more resilient and equitable food system that can meet the needs of present and future generations while minimizing environmental degradation and promoting social well-being.

Sustainable Food Packaging Materials

Sustainable food packaging materials refer to materials used for packaging food products that are environmentally friendly, socially responsible, and economically viable throughout their life cycle.

These materials are designed to minimize negative impacts on the environment, conserve resources, and reduce waste generation. They are derived from renewable or recycled sources, and they can be recycled or composted at the end of their useful life.

Sustainable Food Production Analytics

Sustainable food production analytics refers to the systematic process of collecting, analyzing, and interpreting data related to the production of food in a manner that is environmentally, socially, and economically sustainable.

It involves the use of various analytical techniques to monitor and evaluate the impact of food production on natural resources, biodiversity, climate change, and social welfare. By analyzing this data, sustainable food production analytics helps identify and implement strategies to minimize negative environmental and social effects while maximizing the efficiency and productivity of food production systems.

Sustainable Food Production Certification Bodies

Sustainable food production certification bodies are organizations that assess and certify agricultural practices to ensure they meet specific environmental, social, and economic criteria. These criteria are designed to promote sustainable and responsible approaches to food production that minimize negative impacts on the planet, support local communities, and prioritize long-term viability.

Certification bodies conduct audits and inspections to verify that food producers adhere to sustainable practices, such as minimizing the use of synthetic chemicals and antibiotics, conserving water and energy, protecting biodiversity, and promoting fair and ethical labor standards. They also assess the overall ecological footprint of the production process, considering factors like carbon emissions, waste management, and soil conservation.

Sustainable Food Production Certifications

Sustainable food production certifications are formal recognitions granted to food producers who demonstrate their commitment to sustainability in their operations. These certifications serve as proof that a food producer meets specific criteria and standards set for sustainable farming, processing, and distribution practices.

To obtain a sustainable food production certification, food producers must meet certain guidelines and criteria that address various aspects of sustainability. These criteria typically include considerations such as environmental impact, social responsibility, and economic viability. Food producers must demonstrate that their operations minimize environmental harm by implementing practices such as reducing water and energy consumption, minimizing waste and pollution, and protecting biodiversity. They must also ensure the fair treatment of workers, promote community engagement, and contribute to the economic development of the local area.

Obtaining a sustainable food production certification requires food producers to undergo a thorough assessment and regular audits conducted by independent certification bodies. These bodies evaluate the producer's adherence to the established sustainability standards and verify compliance with the specified criteria. Once a food producer successfully meets all the requirements, they are granted the certification, which they can display on their products or marketing materials.

Sustainable food production certifications play a crucial role in promoting sustainable practices throughout the food industry. They provide transparency and assurance to consumers, allowing them to make informed choices about the food they purchase. These certifications also incentivize food producers to adopt and maintain sustainable practices, fostering a more environmentally friendly and socially responsible food system.

Sustainable Food Sourcing

Sustainable food sourcing refers to the practice of obtaining food in a manner that supports the long-term health and well-being of both the environment and communities. It involves minimizing the negative impacts of food production, distribution, and consumption on the planet and promoting fair trade and social equity.

Sustainable food sourcing focuses on various aspects of the food supply chain, including agriculture, fishing, livestock farming, and food processing. It emphasizes the use of environmentally friendly and socially responsible practices to ensure the availability of nutritious food for future generations.

In sustainable agriculture, farmers use organic and regenerative farming techniques to minimize the use of synthetic pesticides and fertilizers, reduce soil erosion, and preserve biodiversity. They also prioritize the welfare of farm animals, providing them with adequate space, natural diets, and humane treatment.

Sustainable fishing involves implementing measures to prevent overfishing, protect marine ecosystems, and support the livelihoods of fishers and coastal communities. This includes adhering to fishing quotas, using selective fishing gear, and promoting responsible aquaculture practices.

Furthermore, sustainable food sourcing prioritizes local and seasonal produce, reducing the carbon footprint associated with long-distance transportation and supporting local economies. It also encourages the reduction of food waste through proper storage, distribution, and consumer education.

Overall, sustainable food sourcing recognizes the interdependence between the health of the environment, society, and economy. By adopting sustainable practices, individuals,

341

organizations, and governments can contribute to a more resilient and equitable food system for present and future generations.

Sustainable Food Systems

Sustainable food systems can be defined as the production, distribution, and consumption of food in a manner that promotes long-term environmental, social, and economic well-being. These systems aim to minimize negative impacts on the environment, conserve natural resources, support fair and equitable access to food, and enhance the overall resilience of the food system.

At the core of sustainable food systems is the integration of sustainable agricultural practices, which involve utilizing farming methods that reduce greenhouse gas emissions, maintain soil health, preserve water quality, and protect biodiversity. These practices prioritize organic and regenerative farming techniques, such as composting, crop rotation, and agroforestry, to minimize the use of synthetic fertilizers and pesticides.

In addition to sustainable production methods, sustainable food systems also focus on improving the efficiency and equity of food distribution networks. This includes reducing food waste throughout the supply chain, implementing local and regional food systems to minimize transportation emissions, and ensuring access to nutritious and affordable food for all members of society. Encouraging short food supply chains, promoting farmers markets, and supporting community-supported agriculture are some strategies employed to enhance the accessibility of sustainably produced food.

Furthermore, sustainable food systems prioritize the promotion of healthy and sustainable diets. This involves educating consumers about the environmental and health impacts of their food choices and encouraging the consumption of plant-based foods, sustainably sourced seafood, and locally produced foods. By shifting towards more sustainable dietary patterns, such as reducing meat consumption and increasing the intake of fruits, vegetables, and whole grains, individuals can contribute to the overall sustainability of the food system.

Sustainable Food Traceability Solutions

Sustainable food traceability solutions refer to the systems and technologies that enable tracking and monitoring of food products from their origin throughout the supply chain to ensure sustainability. These solutions aim to provide transparent and reliable information about the production, processing, and distribution of the food, allowing consumers, retailers, and regulators to make informed decisions that promote sustainability.

Implementing sustainable food traceability solutions involves the use of various tools and practices, such as barcodes, QR codes, RFID tags, and blockchain technology. These technologies enable the collection and storage of detailed data about the food products, including the farm or facility where they were produced, the methods and inputs used in production, and the transportation routes taken. By capturing such information, traceability solutions enable the identification of potential sustainability issues, such as unethical labor practices, excessive resource use, or environmental harm, and facilitate the implementation of necessary improvements.

By providing transparency and accountability, sustainable food traceability solutions can help promote sustainable practices throughout the food supply chain. They enable consumers to make conscious choices by providing information on the environmental and social impacts associated with different products. Retailers and food manufacturers can use traceability data to ensure compliance with sustainable sourcing standards and address any potential risks. Regulators can rely on traceability systems to enforce sustainability regulations and verify claims made by food producers and suppliers.

Sustainable Food Traceability Systems

A sustainable food traceability system is a system that allows for the tracking and recording of information about food products throughout the entire supply chain in a way that promotes environmental, social, and economic sustainability.

Such a system is designed to ensure that food products can be traced back to their origin, providing transparency and accountability in the production and distribution process. It enables consumers, retailers, and regulators to have access to reliable and accurate information about the sources, methods of production, and transportation of the food they consume or handle.

By implementing a sustainable food traceability system, potential risks and inefficiencies in the supply chain can be identified and mitigated. This includes reducing the environmental impact of food production and distribution, such as minimizing food waste, optimizing transportation routes, and promoting sustainable farming practices.

In addition to its environmental benefits, a sustainable food traceability system also addresses social and economic sustainability. It helps to ensure fair trade practices, by allowing for the tracking of fair labor and ethical sourcing efforts. It also supports local economies by enabling consumers to make informed choices about supporting local food producers.

In conclusion, a sustainable food traceability system is a crucial tool for achieving sustainability goals in the food industry. It provides transparency, accountability, and promotes environmentally, socially, and economically responsible practices throughout the food supply chain.

Sustainable Forest Management Apps

Sustainable forest management apps refer to mobile applications that are designed to assist in the planning, monitoring, and decision-making processes related to the sustainable management of forests. These apps typically provide a range of tools and features that facilitate the collection, analysis, and interpretation of data pertaining to forest ecosystems and resources.

One of the primary objectives of sustainable forest management is to ensure the long-term viability of forests and their ability to provide a wide range of ecological, social, and economic benefits. Sustainable forest management apps contribute to this objective by enhancing the efficiency and effectiveness of forest management practices through the use of digital technology.

Sustainable Forest Management Software

Sustainable forest management software refers to computer-based tools and applications that provide support in managing forests in a sustainable manner. This software assists in the planning, monitoring, and decision-making processes related to forest management, with the goal of promoting environmental, social, and economic sustainability.

This type of software typically integrates various functionalities and data sources to facilitate comprehensive and holistic forest management practices. It allows users to gather, analyze, and interpret information related to forest ecosystems, including data on tree species, forest structure, biodiversity, and ecosystem services.

Key features of sustainable forest management software often include:

1. Spatial analysis capabilities: This enables users to assess and visualize different aspects of forest ecosystems, such as forest cover, deforestation rates, and habitat connectivity. It supports the identification of priority areas for conservation and restoration efforts.

2. Planning and decision support tools: The software aids in the development of sustainable forest management plans, taking into account multiple objectives, stakeholder interests, and resource constraints. It assists in optimizing land use, timber harvesting, and reforestation activities.

3. Monitoring and reporting functionalities: The software allows for the collection and analysis of data on forest condition, carbon sequestration, and other indicators of ecosystem health. It supports the assessment of management effectiveness and the reporting of sustainability outcomes.

Sustainable forest management software plays a crucial role in promoting responsible and sustainable forest practices. By harnessing the power of technology, it enables forest managers, policymakers, and other stakeholders to make informed decisions, enhance transparency, and ensure the long-term viability of forest resources.

Sustainable Forest Restoration Projects

Sustainable forest restoration projects refer to initiatives aimed at rehabilitating and revitalizing degraded or deforested areas of land, with a focus on long-term environmental, social, and economic sustainability.

These projects involve a range of activities, including tree planting, invasive species removal, soil erosion control, and the promotion of sustainable land management practices. The primary goal of sustainable forest restoration projects is to restore the ecological integrity of the forest ecosystem, enhance biodiversity, and mitigate the impacts of climate change.

Key principles that guide sustainable forest restoration projects include the use of native tree species, the involvement of local communities and stakeholders, and the consideration of ecological and social factors. By employing these principles, these projects aim to create resilient forests that can provide a wide range of ecosystem services, such as clean air and water, wildlife habitat, and timber resources, while also ensuring the well-being and livelihoods of local communities.

Furthermore, sustainable forest restoration projects contribute to the achievement of several sustainable development goals, including combating climate change, promoting sustainable forestry, and conserving terrestrial ecosystems. They also have the potential to support rural development, poverty alleviation, and the enhancement of biodiversity and natural capital.

Sustainable Forestry Certification Services

Sustainable forestry certification services refer to the process of evaluating and verifying the sustainability practices employed in forestry operations. These services assess whether a forest is managed in an environmentally responsible, socially beneficial, and economically viable manner.

Sustainable forestry certification services involve an independent assessment by a third-party organization to ensure compliance with rigorous international standards. These standards address various aspects of forest management, including biodiversity conservation, ecosystem services, and the rights and welfare of local communities. The assessment process evaluates factors such as forest planning, harvesting practices, reforestation efforts, and stakeholder engagement.

The primary objective of sustainable forestry certification services is to promote sustainable forest management and reward operators who demonstrate their commitment to environmental stewardship. By certifying a forest as sustainable, these services provide assurance to consumers and businesses that the forest products they purchase are derived from responsibly managed forests.

Furthermore, sustainable forestry certification services play a crucial role in driving continuous improvement in forest management practices. Forest operators are encouraged to adopt best practices and implement measures to address any identified shortcomings during the certification process. This helps to protect and enhance forest ecosystems, conserve biodiversity, mitigate climate change, and support the socio-economic well-being of forest-dependent communities.

Sustainable Forestry Management Platforms

Sustainable forestry management platforms refer to digital tools and systems that facilitate the planning, monitoring, and implementation of sustainable practices in forest management. These platforms enable stakeholders to optimize forest resources while ensuring long-term ecological, economic, and social benefits.

At its core, sustainable forestry management involves the responsible use and conservation of forests to meet the needs of present and future generations. It aims to balance the extraction of forest resources with the preservation of ecosystem integrity, biodiversity, and the livelihoods of local communities. Sustainable forestry management platforms play a crucial role in achieving these objectives by providing comprehensive solutions for forest planning, monitoring, and reporting.

These platforms offer features such as geo-spatial mapping, inventory management, and real-time data collection, allowing forest managers to assess forest cover, track tree growth, and monitor wildlife populations. By analyzing this data, stakeholders can make informed decisions about timber harvesting, habitat conservation, and habitat restoration.

Sustainable forestry management platforms also support the integration of socio-economic factors into decision-making processes. They help stakeholders consider the economic viability of forestry activities, community involvement, and the equitable distribution of benefits. Additionally, these platforms enable the monitoring of illegal logging and other unsustainable practices, contributing to the preservation of forests as carbon sinks and the prevention of biodiversity loss.

Sustainable Forestry Practices

Sustainable forestry practices refer to the management and conservation of forests in a way that ensures their long-term ecological, economic, and social viability. These practices aim to meet the current and future needs of society while maintaining the health and biodiversity of forest ecosystems.

Sustainable forestry involves a holistic approach that takes into account the principles of sustainable development. It recognizes that forests provide a wide range of valuable resources and services, including timber, non-timber forest products, carbon sequestration, water regulation, and habitat for biodiversity. Therefore, sustainable forestry practices strive to achieve a balance between the extraction of forest products and the maintenance of forest ecosystem integrity.

Key elements of sustainable forestry practices include:

1. Responsible harvesting: Forests are managed in a way that ensures the long-term productivity and regeneration of timber resources. This involves carefully planning and executing logging operations to minimize ecosystem disturbance and protect vulnerable habitats. It also includes reforestation efforts to restore harvested areas.

2. Biodiversity conservation: Sustainable forestry practices prioritize the conservation of biodiversity by protecting and preserving the habitats of endangered species and maintaining forest connectivity. This includes leaving buffer zones around sensitive areas and adopting selective logging techniques that minimize collateral damage.

3. Stakeholder engagement: Sustainable forestry engages local communities, indigenous peoples, and other stakeholders in decision-making processes regarding forest management. This ensures that their needs and perspectives are considered, and promotes equitable sharing of benefits from forest resources.

By following sustainable forestry practices, we can ensure the long-term sustainability of forests, promote biodiversity conservation, mitigate climate change, and support the livelihoods and well-being of communities that depend on forests.

Sustainable Gardening And Farming Apps

Sustainable gardening and farming apps refer to mobile applications that promote and support environmentally friendly practices in the cultivation of plants and the raising of animals for food. These apps provide users with tools, resources, and information to adopt sustainable methods and make informed decisions about their gardening and farming practices.

The apps often offer features such as:

345

- Crop and plant selection: Users can access databases and guides to identify and choose crops and plants that are suitable for their local climate, soil conditions, and ecological context. This helps minimize water and energy consumption, reduce the use of chemical inputs, and promote biodiversity.

- Pest and disease management: Sustainable gardening and farming apps provide information on natural and organic pest and disease control methods, such as companion planting, biological control, and crop rotation. This reduces the dependence on chemical pesticides and promotes the overall health of the ecosystem.

- Water and resource conservation: These apps offer guidance on efficient irrigation techniques, rainwater harvesting, and water-saving methods. They also promote composting and recycling to reduce waste and enhance soil fertility.

- Sustainable practices: The apps educate users about the principles of sustainable agriculture, including soil health management, agroforestry, and integrated farming systems. They encourage the use of renewable energy sources, such as solar power, and advocate for responsible land management to prevent soil erosion and degradation.

In summary, sustainable gardening and farming apps empower individuals and communities to engage in sustainable food production by providing them with knowledge, tools, and resources to adopt environmentally friendly practices. These apps play a crucial role in promoting sustainable agriculture and contributing to the global efforts towards a more sustainable and resilient food system.

Sustainable Gardening Tools

Sustainable gardening tools refer to gardening tools that are designed and manufactured with environmentally friendly materials and practices, with the goal of reducing negative impacts on the environment and promoting long-term sustainability.

These tools are typically made from materials that can be easily recycled or biodegraded, such as bamboo, wood, or recycled plastic. They are also designed to be durable and long-lasting, reducing the need for frequent replacement and minimizing waste. In addition, sustainable gardening tools often prioritize ergonomic design and user comfort, promoting healthier and more enjoyable gardening experiences.

Furthermore, sustainable gardening tools may incorporate energy-efficient features or technologies, such as solar-powered lights or electric motors. This helps to reduce the use of fossil fuels or electricity, leading to lower carbon emissions and a smaller ecological footprint.

Another important aspect of sustainable gardening tools is their contribution to biodiversity and ecosystem health. These tools are designed to minimize the disturbance or destruction of natural habitats, allowing plants and animals to thrive. For example, gardening tools with sharp and precise cutting edges can minimize damage to plants, while tools with ergonomic handles and grips can provide better control and reduce accidental harm.

In summary, sustainable gardening tools prioritize environmental responsibility, durability, ergonomic design, energy efficiency, and biodiversity preservation. By choosing and using these tools, gardeners can engage in sustainable practices that promote the health of both their gardens and the planet as a whole.

Sustainable Home Energy Management

Sustainable home energy management refers to the practice of optimizing and controlling the energy consumption and production within a residential building in a manner that is environmentally friendly, economically viable, and socially responsible. It involves the integration of various technologies, strategies, and behavioral changes to reduce energy waste, minimize greenhouse gas emissions, and promote renewable energy sources.

The primary goal of sustainable home energy management is to achieve energy efficiency by maximizing the utilization of available resources and minimizing energy wastage. This is typically done through the implementation of smart grid systems, energy monitoring devices, and advanced energy management software. These tools enable homeowners to monitor and control their energy consumption, identify areas of inefficiency, and make informed decisions to optimize their energy usage.

Furthermore, sustainable home energy management also emphasizes the use of renewable energy sources such as solar panels, wind turbines, and geothermal systems to generate clean energy on-site. This reduces the reliance on fossil fuels and lowers the carbon footprint of the household. Additionally, energy storage systems, such as batteries, can be utilized to store excess energy generated by renewable sources for later use, further enhancing the sustainability of the system.

In order to achieve long-term sustainability, it is crucial to educate homeowners about energy-efficient practices and encourage behavioral changes that promote energy conservation. This may involve providing energy-saving tips, offering incentives for energy-saving behaviors, and fostering a culture of sustainability within communities.

Sustainable Industrial Design

Sustainable industrial design refers to the practice of creating products and systems that minimize environmental impact, conserve resources, and support social responsibility. It involves incorporating sustainable principles throughout the entire design process, from concept development to product disposal.

The primary goal of sustainable industrial design is to reduce the negative environmental and social impacts associated with industrial production. This is achieved by considering the entire life cycle of a product, including its extraction, manufacturing, use, and eventual disposal or recycling. By adopting a holistic approach, designers can identify opportunities to optimize materials, energy, and water usage, as well as minimize waste and emissions.

Sustainable industrial design also emphasizes the use of renewable and non-toxic materials, as well as the incorporation of energy-efficient technologies. It encourages the adoption of circular economy principles, where products are designed for durability, reuse, and recycling. Additionally, sustainable industrial design promotes social equity by ensuring safe and fair working conditions throughout the supply chain, as well as considering the needs and preferences of diverse communities and users.

Overall, sustainable industrial design aims to create products that not only fulfill their intended purpose but also contribute to a more sustainable and regenerative future. It recognizes the interconnectedness of economic, environmental, and social aspects and strives to strike a balance that meets the needs of present and future generations.

Sustainable Industrial Waste Management

Sustainable industrial waste management refers to the efficient and responsible handling, treatment, and disposal of waste generated by industrial activities in a manner that minimizes negative impacts on the environment, human health, and natural resources, while promoting economic growth and social well-being.

This approach to waste management recognizes the interconnectedness of environmental, economic, and social factors, and strives to find a balance between them. It aims to prevent or reduce waste generation at the source, maximize recycling and resource recovery, and ensure the safe and proper treatment and disposal of remaining waste. By doing so, sustainable industrial waste management helps to conserve resources, reduce pollution and greenhouse gas emissions, and protect human health and ecosystems.

Sustainable Infrastructure Development

Sustainable infrastructure development refers to the design, construction, and maintenance of infrastructure systems that minimize their environmental impact, prioritize social equity, and promote long-term economic viability. It involves the integration of sustainable practices and principles into every phase of infrastructure development, from planning and design to implementation and operation.

At its core, sustainable infrastructure development aims to meet the current needs of society without compromising the ability of future generations to meet their own needs. It recognizes that infrastructure plays a crucial role in supporting economic development, improving quality of life, and minimizing resource depletion and pollution.

In practice, sustainable infrastructure development involves the use of renewable energy sources, efficient resource management, waste reduction and recycling, and the protection and restoration of natural ecosystems. It also emphasizes the importance of community engagement, stakeholder collaboration, and inclusive decision-making processes.

By adopting sustainable infrastructure practices, societies can mitigate the negative impacts of infrastructure development, such as greenhouse gas emissions, habitat destruction, and social inequalities. It helps to create resilient, adaptable, and environmentally friendly infrastructure systems that can withstand the challenges posed by climate change, population growth, and resource scarcity.

In summary, sustainable infrastructure development is a holistic approach to designing, building, and maintaining infrastructure systems that prioritize environmental, social, and economic sustainability. It seeks to ensure that infrastructure meets the needs of the present while safeguarding the well-being of future generations.

Sustainable Infrastructure

Sustainable infrastructure refers to the design, construction, and management of infrastructure systems that prioritize long-term environmental, social, and economic sustainability. It involves the integration of sustainable principles and practices into the planning, development, and maintenance of infrastructure projects.

Sustainability in infrastructure focuses on minimizing the negative environmental impacts associated with the development and operation of infrastructure while maximizing positive social and economic outcomes. This involves considering the life cycle of infrastructure projects, from the extraction of raw materials to the end of the project's useful life.

Key aspects of sustainable infrastructure include:

- Environmental sustainability: Sustainable infrastructure aims to reduce resource consumption, decrease greenhouse gas emissions, protect natural ecosystems, and promote the use of renewable energy sources. It involves incorporating green technologies, such as energy-efficient systems and sustainable materials, into the design and operation of infrastructure projects.

- Social sustainability: Sustainable infrastructure considers the needs and well-being of the communities affected by the project. It involves engaging with stakeholders, including local communities, to ensure their voices are heard and their interests are considered. It also focuses on enhancing accessibility, promoting social equity, and improving the quality of life for all individuals.

- Economic sustainability: Sustainable infrastructure seeks to optimize investment returns while minimizing costs. It aims to create long-term value by considering potential economic risks and benefits associated with the project. This includes factors such as life cycle cost analysis, economic feasibility, and promoting innovation to drive economic growth.

In summary, sustainable infrastructure strives to meet the present needs of society without compromising the ability of future generations to meet their own needs. It represents a holistic approach to infrastructure development that takes into account environmental, social, and economic factors to create resilient, inclusive, and environmentally-friendly infrastructure systems.

Sustainable Land Use And Zoning

Sustainable land use refers to the practice of utilizing land resources in a manner that supports long-term environmental, economic, and social viability. It involves the planning, development, and management of land in a way that minimizes negative impacts on the natural environment and maximizes the benefits for present and future generations.

Zoning, on the other hand, is a regulatory framework that divides land into different zones or areas with specific designated uses, such as residential, commercial, industrial, or agricultural. Sustainable land use and zoning work in conjunction to guide and regulate the development and use of land in a manner that is consistent with sustainable development goals.

Sustainable Landscape Design

Sustainable landscape design refers to the practice of creating outdoor spaces that are environmentally friendly, socially responsible, and economically viable. It aims to minimize the negative impacts on natural resources, maximize the benefits for local communities, and ensure long-term ecological balance.

This type of design takes into account various factors such as water conservation, energy efficiency, waste reduction, and habitat preservation. Water conservation techniques may include the use of native plants that require less irrigation, installation of rainwater harvesting systems, and the incorporation of permeable surfaces to reduce runoff. Energy efficiency measures can involve the strategic placement of trees and shrubs to provide shade and reduce the need for air conditioning, as well as the use of solar-powered lighting and irrigation systems. Waste reduction efforts may include composting, recycling, and the utilization of organic materials for mulching and fertilizing.

Moreover, sustainable landscape design also emphasizes the preservation and creation of habitats for local wildlife. This can involve the incorporation of native plants that attract and support local fauna, the creation of water features like ponds or birdbaths, and the installation of nesting boxes or insect hotels.

By implementing sustainable landscape design principles, we can create outdoor spaces that not only enhance the beauty and functionality of our surroundings but also contribute to the overall well-being of the environment, society, and economy.

Sustainable Landscaping Design Software

Sustainable landscaping design software refers to a digital tool that enables the creation and implementation of environmentally friendly and resource-efficient landscape designs. It is a technology-driven solution aimed at promoting sustainable practices in the field of landscaping.

This software incorporates various features and functionalities that facilitate the integration of sustainable elements into the landscape design process. It allows landscape designers, architects, and planners to conceptualize, visualize, and analyze landscapes that minimize negative environmental impacts and maximize ecological benefits.

With sustainable landscaping design software, users can access a wide range of tools for creating environmentally responsible designs. These tools include options for selecting native plants, drought-tolerant species, and low-maintenance vegetation, as well as features for managing water usage, minimizing chemical inputs, and reducing energy consumption.

The software typically incorporates databases with extensive information on sustainable landscaping practices, enabling users to make informed decisions based on local climate, soil conditions, and available resources. It provides users with the ability to evaluate the ecological performance of their designs, assess potential environmental risks, and identify opportunities for improvement.

Ultimately, the goal of sustainable landscaping design software is to support the implementation of landscape designs that promote biodiversity, conserve natural resources, enhance ecosystem services, and create aesthetically pleasing and functional outdoor spaces. By harnessing the power of digital technology, this software contributes to a more sustainable and resilient built environment.

Sustainable Materials Innovation

Sustainable materials innovation refers to the development and utilization of materials that are environmentally friendly, socially responsible, and economically viable throughout their lifecycle.

It involves the exploration and implementation of new materials, manufacturing processes, and design techniques that minimize the negative impact on the environment and human health, while also addressing social and economic considerations. This includes reducing resource consumption, minimizing waste generation, and promoting the use of renewable resources.

By focusing on sustainability, materials innovation aims to find innovative solutions to the challenges posed by traditional materials and their production methods. This can involve the development of biodegradable and compostable materials that can be safely returned to the environment, the incorporation of recycled or upcycled materials into new products, and the adoption of efficient manufacturing processes that require less energy and produce less emissions.

Sustainable materials innovation is crucial in the transition towards a more sustainable and circular economy. Through the development and adoption of eco-friendly materials, industries can reduce their dependence on finite resources, minimize pollution, and contribute to the creation of a more resilient and equitable society.

Sustainable Materials Sourcing

Sustainable materials sourcing is the practice of identifying, procuring, and utilizing materials in a manner that minimizes negative environmental impacts and promotes long-term ecological balance. It involves a comprehensive approach that considers the entire life cycle of materials, from extraction or production to disposal or recycling.

At its core, sustainable materials sourcing aims to reduce the environmental footprint associated with the sourcing and use of materials. This includes minimizing the depletion of natural resources, reducing greenhouse gas emissions, and minimizing the generation of waste and pollution. It also considers the social and economic impacts of material sourcing, including issues such as worker welfare and fair trade practices.

To achieve sustainable materials sourcing, organizations must carefully evaluate the environmental and social impacts of different materials and make informed decisions based on this assessment. This may involve sourcing materials from renewable or recycled sources, choosing materials with low embodied energy, or selecting materials that can be easily repaired, reused, or recycled.

Additionally, sustainable materials sourcing often involves optimizing the supply chain to reduce transportation energy and emissions, promoting sustainable and responsible extraction or production practices, and prioritizing local sourcing to support local economies and reduce transportation distances.

Overall, sustainable materials sourcing is an essential component of sustainable development, as it plays a crucial role in addressing environmental challenges and promoting a more sustainable and resilient future.

Sustainable Mining And Minerals Tracking

Sustainable mining refers to the responsible extraction and utilization of mineral resources that minimizes environmental damage, ensures workers' safety and well-being, and supports the long-term social and economic development of the communities affected by mining activities.

Minerals tracking, on the other hand, involves the systematic and transparent tracing of mineral resources from their extraction sites through various stages of processing, refining, and distribution, to ensure that they are sourced and traded ethically, without contributing to conflicts, human rights abuses, or environmental degradation.

Sustainable Mining Equipment

Sustainable mining equipment refers to the machinery and tools used in the mining industry that are designed and operated in a manner that minimizes the environmental impact, conserves natural resources, and promotes the well-being of communities and workers involved in the mining activities.

These types of mining equipment are designed with a focus on reducing carbon emissions, energy consumption, and waste generation. They also prioritize the use of renewable energy sources and incorporate technologies that improve energy efficiency, such as advanced motors and control systems. Additionally, sustainable mining equipment includes features that minimize the release of pollutants into the air, water, and soil, as well as strategies for mitigating the effects of mining operations on biodiversity and ecosystems.

Moreover, sustainable mining equipment takes into account the social aspects of mining by ensuring the safety and well-being of workers, as well as promoting fair labor practices and community engagement. This includes providing adequate training and protective gear for miners, implementing measures to prevent occupational hazards, and supporting local economies through job creation and responsible procurement practices.

Overall, sustainable mining equipment plays a significant role in achieving sustainable development goals by reducing the negative impacts of mining activities on the environment, society, and economy. It is a crucial component of responsible mining practices that contribute to the long-term viability and resilience of the mining industry while ensuring the protection and welfare of both current and future generations.

Sustainable Mining Practices Software

A sustainable mining practices software is a digital tool that aids in promoting environmentally friendly and responsible mining operations. It is designed to assist mining companies in managing their activities in a way that minimizes negative impacts on the environment and surrounding communities while maximizing the efficient use of resources.

By utilizing a sustainable mining practices software, mining companies can track and analyze various aspects of their operations, such as energy consumption, water usage, waste management, and emissions. The software provides data-driven insights and recommendations that enable companies to identify areas for improvement and implement strategies to reduce their environmental footprint.

Furthermore, a sustainable mining practices software facilitates compliance with regulatory requirements and industry standards, ensuring that mining operations adhere to sustainable practices. It enables companies to monitor and report on their sustainability performance, enabling transparency and accountability.

In addition to environmental benefits, the software also helps improve social and economic sustainability. It can assist in monitoring and managing the social impacts of mining, including community relations, health and safety, and labor practices. By promoting responsible mining practices, the software contributes to the overall well-being of local communities and the sustainable development of mining regions.

Sustainable Mobility Solutions

Sustainable mobility solutions refer to methods and systems of transportation that prioritize the efficient use of resources, minimize environmental impacts, and promote social and economic equity. These solutions aim to meet the mobility needs of individuals and communities while reducing the negative consequences associated with traditional modes of transportation.

One key aspect of sustainable mobility is reducing greenhouse gas emissions and air pollution. This can be achieved through the adoption of cleaner technology in vehicles, such as electric or hybrid cars, or the promotion of alternative modes of transportation, such as cycling or walking. By reducing reliance on fossil fuels and promoting zero-emission alternatives, sustainable mobility solutions contribute to mitigating climate change and improving air quality.

In addition to environmental benefits, sustainable mobility solutions also prioritize social equity.

351

This means ensuring that transportation options are accessible and affordable for all individuals, regardless of their income, ability, or location. Strategies like investing in public transit, implementing bike-sharing programs, and creating pedestrian-friendly infrastructure help reduce transportation costs, improve access to essential services, and enhance the overall quality of life for communities.

Economic sustainability is another essential element of sustainable mobility. By supporting the development and use of innovative transportation technologies and services, sustainable mobility solutions can drive economic growth and create job opportunities. This includes the manufacturing and maintenance of electric vehicles, the construction of new cycling and pedestrian infrastructure, and the provision of sustainable transportation services.

Sustainable Mobility

Sustainable mobility refers to the development and implementation of transportation systems and practices that minimize negative impacts on the environment, society, and economy, while optimizing the efficient use of resources. It aims to address the challenges posed by traditional modes of transportation, such as high energy consumption, emissions of greenhouse gases and air pollutants, congestion, and unequal access to transportation services.

Sustainable mobility encompasses various strategies and approaches, including the promotion of public transportation systems, the development of alternative fuel vehicles, the improvement of infrastructure for walking and cycling, and the adoption of intelligent transportation systems. These measures aim to reduce reliance on fossil fuels, decrease emissions, enhance the accessibility and affordability of transportation options, and promote more sustainable patterns of mobility.

One key aspect of sustainable mobility is the concept of multimodality, which encourages the use of multiple modes of transportation for different purposes. This can involve combining walking and cycling with public transportation, carpooling or car-sharing, and the integration of different modes within a single trip. By providing individuals with a range of transportation options, sustainable mobility enables more efficient and environmentally friendly travel, while also reducing congestion and promoting a healthier and more active lifestyle.

In summary, sustainable mobility seeks to transform transportation systems to minimize their environmental impact, enhance social equity, and support economic prosperity. By prioritizing the principles of sustainability, it aims to create a more inclusive, efficient, and environmentally conscious mobility system for present and future generations.

Sustainable Packaging Design Software

Sustainable packaging design software refers to a computer program or application that enables designers and manufacturers to create packaging solutions that are environmentally friendly and socially responsible throughout their lifecycle. This software facilitates the development and optimization of packaging materials, structures, and designs that minimize negative impacts on the environment, conserve resources, and promote sustainable practices.

In the context of sustainability, this software aids in the reduction of packaging waste, energy consumption, and carbon emissions by allowing designers to assess and improve the efficiency and effectiveness of packaging designs. It enables users to explore various packaging options, materials, and configurations, considering factors such as recyclability, reusability, biodegradability, and compostability.

By integrating life cycle assessment (LCA) techniques, sustainable packaging design software assists in evaluating the environmental impacts of different packaging choices throughout their entire lifespan. It helps identify opportunities for improvement and innovation, optimizing packaging designs to align with sustainability goals.

The software may also incorporate features that enable collaboration and communication between designers, manufacturers, suppliers, and other stakeholders involved in the packaging design process. This fosters a holistic and integrated approach to sustainable packaging design, considering factors like material sourcing, manufacturing processes, transportation, and end-of-life considerations.

Overall, sustainable packaging design software supports the creation of packaging solutions that reduce resource consumption, minimize waste generation, and contribute to a more sustainable and circular economy.

Sustainable Packaging Labeling Systems

Sustainable packaging labeling systems are standardized methods used to communicate the environmental attributes and sustainability credentials of packaging materials and products. These systems are designed to provide transparent and reliable information to consumers, businesses, and other stakeholders about the environmental impacts associated with a particular packaging choice.

Typically, sustainable packaging labeling systems take into consideration a range of factors, including the material composition of the packaging, the energy and water requirements for its production, the potential for recycling or reuse, and the overall carbon footprint of the packaging throughout its lifecycle. These systems may also consider other environmental impacts, such as the use of renewable resources, the reduction of waste and pollution, and the protection of biodiversity.

The goal of sustainable packaging labeling systems is to help consumers make informed choices by providing clear and consistent information about the environmental performance of different packaging options. By labeling packaging with standardized symbols or logos, these systems allow consumers to quickly and easily identify packaging that meets certain sustainability criteria. This can help drive demand for more sustainable packaging materials and encourage businesses to adopt more environmentally friendly practices.

In addition to informing consumers, sustainable packaging labeling systems also play a role in promoting transparency and accountability within the packaging industry. By providing a common set of criteria and standards, these systems enable businesses to benchmark and compare the sustainability performance of their packaging against industry norms and best practices.

Sustainable Packaging Production Equipment

Sustainable packaging production equipment refers to machinery and tools used in the manufacturing process of packaging materials that are environmentally friendly, economically feasible, and socially responsible.

These equipment are designed and built with the objective of minimizing the negative impact on the environment throughout their lifecycle. They are specifically engineered to reduce energy consumption, water usage, and waste generation, while also ensuring the safety and well-being of workers.

Sustainable Packaging Testing Services

Sustainable packaging testing services refer to the evaluation and analysis of packaging materials and designs to ensure they meet environmentally conscious and socially responsible criteria. These services focus on assessing the sustainability aspects of packaging, including its impact on the environment, carbon footprint, recyclability, and use of renewable resources.

The goal of sustainable packaging testing services is to provide accurate and reliable information about the environmental performance of packaging options. This allows businesses to make informed decisions when selecting materials and designs for their products' packaging. By examining various factors such as material sourcing, energy consumption, waste generation, and end-of-life disposal, these services help identify the most sustainable packaging choices.

Sustainable Pest Control Solutions

Sustainable pest control solutions refer to methods and practices that effectively manage pests while minimizing negative impacts on the environment, human health, and non-target organisms. These solutions prioritize long-term sustainability by incorporating principles of ecological balance, resource conservation, and reduced chemical usage.

One key aspect of sustainable pest control is the use of integrated pest management (IPM) techniques. IPM involves the strategic combination of various pest control methods, such as biological control, cultural practices, and targeted chemical treatments, to minimize pest populations while minimizing harm to beneficial organisms and the environment. It emphasizes the use of non-chemical approaches as the first line of defense and the judicious use of pesticides only when necessary.

Sustainable Pest Management Apps

A sustainable pest management app refers to a digital tool or application developed with the objective of promoting environmentally-friendly and long-term solutions for controlling pests while minimizing harm to the ecosystem and human health. These apps integrate sustainable pest management practices by providing information, guidance, and resources to individuals, homeowners, farmers, and pest control professionals.

These apps typically offer a range of features that facilitate sustainable pest management. They may include identification guides, allowing users to accurately identify pest species and differentiate between harmful pests and beneficial insects. This knowledge enables users to implement targeted and effective control measures while minimizing the use of potentially harmful chemicals.

Sustainable pest management apps also provide access to educational resources such as articles, videos, or tutorials that promote the understanding of pest behavior, ecology, and biology. By enhancing knowledge and awareness, these apps empower users to make informed decisions about pest control methods that are both effective and sustainable.

In addition, sustainable pest management apps often incorporate integrated pest management (IPM) principles. IPM aims to manage pests in a manner that minimizes economic, environmental, and health risks. Apps may include IPM planning tools, pest monitoring features, and recommendations for non-chemical control methods such as biological controls, cultural practices, and physical barriers.

By promoting sustainable pest management practices, these apps contribute to reducing the reliance on conventional pesticides and minimizing the negative impacts associated with their use, such as pollution, harm to beneficial organisms, and health risks. They support the transition towards more ecologically balanced and resilient pest management strategies.

Sustainable Product Certifications

Sustainable product certifications are formal recognitions given to products that meet certain criteria of sustainability. These certifications validate that the product has been produced, manufactured, and distributed in an environmentally responsible and socially conscious manner.

Typically, sustainable product certifications are awarded by independent third-party organizations that have established rigorous standards for sustainability in various industries. These organizations assess a range of factors such as the product's lifecycle, resource consumption, waste generation, carbon emissions, and social impact to determine whether it meets their sustainability criteria.

By obtaining a sustainable product certification, manufacturers and businesses can provide consumers with an assurance that their product has undergone a thorough evaluation against sustainable benchmarks. This allows consumers to make informed choices by selecting products that align with their own values and sustainability goals.

In addition to benefiting consumers, sustainable product certifications also incentivize businesses to adopt sustainable practices throughout their supply chains. Manufacturers are compelled to minimize their environmental footprint, reduce waste, conserve resources, and ensure fair labor practices in order to obtain and retain the certification.

Moreover, sustainable product certifications help promote transparency and accountability in the marketplace. They encourage businesses to disclose information about their sustainability efforts, allowing consumers, investors, and other stakeholders to evaluate and compare products based on their environmental and social performance. This transparency drives competition and innovation toward more sustainable practices within industries.

Sustainable Product Innovations

Sustainable product innovations refer to the development and implementation of new products that prioritize environmental, economic, and social sustainability. These innovations seek to create products that minimize negative impacts on the environment, promote resource efficiency, and improve overall quality of life.

Within the context of sustainability, sustainable product innovations consider the entire product lifecycle. This includes the sourcing of raw materials, the manufacturing process, distribution and transportation, usage, and end-of-life disposal. The goal is to create products that have a reduced carbon footprint, minimize waste, and are made with renewable and recyclable materials.

Furthermore, sustainable product innovations also encompass social aspects such as fair trade, ethical sourcing, and providing safe and healthy working conditions. Companies focusing on sustainable product innovations aim to create products that not only benefit the environment but also contribute to the well-being of communities and workers involved in the production process.

These innovations can take various forms, including the development of new materials, improvement in production processes, and the design of products that are energy-efficient and promote sustainable consumption habits. Sustainable product innovations often involve collaboration and knowledge sharing between different stakeholders, including businesses, government agencies, non-profit organizations, and consumers.

Sustainable Product Labeling Services

Sustainable product labeling services refer to the process of evaluating and certifying products based on their environmental, social, and economic sustainability attributes. The goal of these services is to provide accurate and reliable information to consumers, allowing them to make informed choices that align with their values and contribute to a more sustainable future.

Through sustainable product labeling services, products are assessed using a set of predefined criteria that consider various aspects of sustainability. These criteria may include factors such as resource efficiency, greenhouse gas emissions, renewable energy use, social welfare, and ethical sourcing. The evaluation process often involves life cycle assessments, supply chain analysis, and third-party verification to ensure the credibility and transparency of the labeling.

By labeling products with their sustainability credentials, these services empower consumers to support companies that prioritize sustainability in their practices. This labeling system provides a clear and standardized way to compare products based on their environmental and social impact. It enables consumers to make decisions that align with their values, encouraging market demand for more sustainable products.

Moreover, sustainable product labeling services also drive positive changes within industries by incentivizing companies to improve their sustainability performance. As consumers become more conscious of the environmental and social impact of their purchases, businesses are motivated to adopt more sustainable practices, innovate greener technologies, and reduce their carbon footprint.

Sustainable Product Labeling

Sustainable product labeling is a system that involves the identification and communication of environmental and social attributes of a product throughout its entire lifecycle. It aims to provide consumers with transparent and reliable information about the sustainability performance of a product, enabling them to make more informed purchasing decisions.

Through sustainable product labeling, relevant data and indicators are provided, highlighting factors such as the product's energy and water efficiency, use of environmentally-friendly materials, carbon emissions, and social impact. The labeling also takes into account the product's manufacturing processes, transportation, and disposal methods, ensuring a holistic assessment of its sustainability.

By implementing sustainable product labeling, organizations can showcase their commitment to sustainability and differentiate their products in the market. It also provides a platform for businesses to understand and improve their environmental and social impact, driving innovation towards more sustainable practices.

Sustainable product labeling contributes to the broader goals of promoting sustainable consumption and production. It empowers consumers to consider sustainability factors when making purchases, encouraging them to choose products that align with their values and contribute to a more sustainable future.

Sustainable Product Lifecycle Analysis

A sustainable product lifecycle analysis refers to the systematic evaluation of the environmental, economic, and social impacts associated with the production, use, and disposal of a product. This analysis aims to identify and quantify the potential negative effects a product can have on the environment and society throughout its entire life cycle, from the extraction of raw materials to the final disposal.

The key objective of a sustainable product lifecycle analysis is to provide decision-makers and stakeholders with crucial information about the sustainability performance of a product. By assessing its impacts on various aspects of sustainability, including carbon emissions, resource use, biodiversity loss, and social equity, this analysis enables informed decision-making towards more sustainable practices in product design, manufacturing, and consumption.

Sustainable Product Packaging

Sustainable product packaging refers to the use of materials and design strategies that minimize the environmental impact of packaging throughout its lifecycle. It involves adopting practices that prioritize the principles of reduce, reuse, and recycle, while also considering the social and economic aspects of packaging.

In the context of sustainability, sustainable product packaging aims to minimize the use of non-renewable resources, reduce greenhouse gas emissions, and minimize waste generation. This can be achieved through various means:

Firstly, sustainable packaging focuses on reducing the overall amount of packaging material used. This includes using thinner and lighter materials without compromising product protection and ensuring appropriate packaging dimensions to optimize space utilization.

Secondly, it encourages the use of renewable and recyclable materials. Sustainable packaging materials can include bioplastics made from plant-based sources, recycled paper and cardboard, and compostable materials that can safely return to the environment after use.

Thirdly, sustainable product packaging promotes the concept of reuse. This can be achieved through the design of packaging that can be easily repurposed or transformed into a different functional item, encouraging consumers to reuse it rather than disposing of it after a single use.

Finally, the end-of-life stage of packaging is also considered in sustainability efforts. Packaging should be designed for easy recycling or composting to minimize waste sent to landfills. Additionally, packaging should be labeled clearly to inform consumers about correct disposal methods and to assist in the recycling process.

Sustainable Public Transportation

Sustainable public transportation refers to the use of environmentally friendly and energy-efficient modes of transportation that serve the needs of the general population. It aims to reduce the negative impacts of transportation systems on the environment, promote social equity, and enhance the overall quality of life.

This form of transportation emphasizes the use of renewable energy sources, such as electricity, biofuels, and hydrogen, which produce lower greenhouse gas emissions compared to traditional fossil fuel-based vehicles. By incorporating sustainable technologies, such as hybrid or electric buses and trains, public transportation can significantly reduce air pollution and dependence on finite resources.

Sustainable Seafood Certification

Sustainable seafood certification refers to the process by which seafood products are evaluated and certified as being harvested or farmed in a manner that supports the long-term health and viability of the species and the marine environment. It is a way for consumers, businesses, and governments to ensure that the seafood they are buying or promoting is sourced responsibly and is not contributing to overfishing, habitat destruction, or other harmful impacts on the marine ecosystem.

The certification process typically involves a third-party organization or certification body that sets and verifies the criteria for sustainable seafood. This may include factors such as the health and abundance of the target species, the impact of the fishing or farming method on the surrounding ecosystem, and the effectiveness of the management and governance systems in place. Certified seafood products are often labeled with a logo or seal to indicate their sustainability, making it easier for consumers to make informed choices.

Sustainable Seafood Traceability Tools

Sustainable seafood traceability tools refer to a set of practices and technologies used to track and monitor the journey of seafood from its origin to the market, with the ultimate goal of promoting sustainability in the seafood industry.

These tools play a crucial role in ensuring that seafood products are harvested, processed, and traded in a manner that minimizes negative environmental impacts, protects marine ecosystems, and supports the livelihoods of fishing communities.

Sustainable seafood traceability tools typically involve the use of various technologies such as barcodes, RFID tags, and electronic systems to collect and store information about the identity, location, and timing of seafood products at each stage of the supply chain. This information includes details such as the species, catch method, and fishing location, as well as information about the vessel, crew, and fishing practices employed.

By providing transparent and verifiable information about the provenance and sustainability of seafood products, these traceability tools enable consumers, retailers, and regulators to make informed choices and support responsible seafood consumption. They also help to detect and deter illegal, unreported, and unregulated fishing practices, which contribute to overfishing and the depletion of marine resources.

Overall, sustainable seafood traceability tools play a vital role in promoting sustainable fishing practices, enhancing seafood supply chain integrity, and fostering increased transparency and accountability in the seafood industry.

Sustainable Stormwater Management

Sustainable stormwater management refers to the practice of effectively managing stormwater runoff in a way that minimizes negative impacts on the environment, promotes water conservation, and enhances overall sustainability. It involves implementing strategies and techniques that help mitigate the adverse effects of stormwater, such as pollution, flooding, erosion, and depletion of natural water resources.

One key aspect of sustainable stormwater management is the use of green infrastructure. This includes the implementation of natural systems, such as rain gardens, bioswales, and permeable pavement, that mimic the natural hydrologic cycle and help capture and treat stormwater runoff at its source. By incorporating these practices, stormwater can be effectively managed on-site, reducing the strain on traditional stormwater infrastructure and minimizing the need for costly expansion or upgrades.

Another important component of sustainable stormwater management is the promotion of water conservation and reuse. This can be achieved through the use of rainwater harvesting systems, which capture rainwater for non-potable uses such as irrigation or toilet flushing. By reducing the demand for potable water, these systems not only help conserve valuable water resources but also alleviate the burden on wastewater treatment facilities.

Overall, sustainable stormwater management plays a crucial role in achieving a more sustainable and resilient water infrastructure. By implementing practices that reduce stormwater pollution, mitigate flooding risks, and promote water conservation, communities can effectively manage stormwater in an environmentally-friendly manner, contributing to the overall sustainability and resilience of their water resources.

Sustainable Supply Chain Analytics

A sustainable supply chain is the implementation of environmentally and socially responsible practices across the entire supply chain, from sourcing of raw materials to the delivery of final products or services. It involves optimizing processes and minimizing negative impacts on the environment, while also considering the well-being of workers and communities involved.

Sustainable supply chain analytics refers to the use of data and analytical tools to track, measure, and assess the sustainability performance of a supply chain. It involves collecting and analyzing various types of data, such as energy consumption, greenhouse gas emissions, waste generation, labor conditions, and supplier certifications, to identify areas of improvement and make informed decisions.

Sustainable Supply Chain Management Software

Sustainable supply chain management software refers to a digital solution that enables organizations to manage their supply chain processes in a sustainable manner. It is specifically designed to address sustainability issues, such as reducing carbon emissions, minimizing waste generation, and promoting ethical sourcing practices.

This software typically includes a wide range of features and functionalities that facilitate sustainability management throughout the entire supply chain. It allows businesses to track and analyze their environmental performance, identify areas for improvement, and implement effective sustainability initiatives.

Sustainable Tourism Booking Platforms

Sustainable tourism booking platforms are online platforms that facilitate the booking of travel services, accommodations, and activities while prioritizing environmental, social, and economic sustainability.

These platforms aim to promote sustainable practices in the tourism industry by offering a wide range of options that meet certain criteria for sustainability. This may include partnering with eco-friendly accommodations, promoting local and traditional experiences, supporting conservation initiatives, and encouraging responsible travel behavior.

Sustainable Tourism Destination Certification

Sustainable tourism destination certification is a formal recognition process that evaluates and validates the sustainability performance of a tourism destination. It serves as a tool to assess the environmental, social, and economic practices and impacts of a destination, ensuring that it meets certain criteria and standards set by an independent certification body or organization.

The certification process involves a thorough assessment and audit of various aspects of the destination, including its management and governance structures, tourism policies, environmental conservation measures, cultural preservation efforts, community engagement and empowerment, and economic benefits distribution. The evaluation criteria are based on internationally recognized sustainability principles, such as those outlined in the Global Sustainable Tourism Council (GSTC) criteria.

By obtaining a sustainable tourism destination certification, destinations can showcase their commitment to sustainability and responsible tourism practices. It provides a credible and transparent way to communicate to travelers, stakeholders, and the wider public that the destination is actively working towards reducing its environmental footprint, preserving its natural and cultural heritage, and enhancing the well-being of its local communities.

Moreover, sustainable tourism destination certification can contribute to capacity-building and knowledge sharing among destinations, foster collaboration and networking opportunities, and promote best practices in sustainable tourism. It can also attract environmentally conscious and socially responsible travelers, who are increasingly seeking destinations that align with their values and contribute positively to the planet and local communities.

Sustainable Tourism Destinations

Sustainable tourism destinations are places that aim to minimize their negative impact on the environment, preserve and protect their cultural heritage, and contribute to the local communities' economic development. These destinations prioritize the principles of sustainability, which include conserving natural resources, promoting social and cultural diversity, and supporting the well-being of both locals and tourists.

In sustainable tourism destinations, there is a focus on responsible travel practices that minimize pollution, waste, and carbon emissions. Efforts are made to protect and restore natural habitats, conserve energy and water, and implement waste management strategies. These destinations often promote eco-friendly modes of transportation and encourage visitors to participate in activities that have a low environmental impact.

Preserving and promoting the local culture is also a key aspect of sustainable tourism destinations. These destinations value the traditions, customs, and heritage of the local communities, and seek to educate and engage tourists in respectful and authentic cultural experiences. This not only helps to foster a sense of pride and ownership among the local residents but also enriches the overall travel experience for visitors.

Furthermore, sustainable tourism destinations strive to benefit the local economy by supporting local businesses, artisans, and service providers. They encourage tourists to purchase locally made products and services, which helps to create jobs and support small-scale enterprises. By involving the local community in tourism initiatives, these destinations aim to enhance economic opportunities while maintaining a sustainable balance between tourism activities and the well-being of the residents.

Sustainable Tourism Management Platforms

Sustainable tourism management platforms are online systems designed to support and promote sustainable practices in the tourism industry. These platforms provide a comprehensive set of tools and resources that enable tourism businesses and destinations to effectively manage their environmental, social, and economic impacts.

With a focus on sustainability, these platforms offer features such as:

- Environmental monitoring and reporting: Allows businesses and destinations to track and measure their resource consumption, waste generation, and greenhouse gas emissions. This data is crucial for identifying areas for improvement and setting targets for reducing environmental impacts.
- Stakeholder engagement: Facilitates communication and collaboration between tourism stakeholders, including businesses, local communities, and governments. Effective stakeholder engagement ensures that decision-making processes consider the perspectives and interests of all parties, leading to more inclusive and sustainable tourism development.

- Education and training: Provides access to educational content and training programs on sustainable tourism practices. This helps tourism professionals and organizations gain knowledge and skills necessary to adopt and implement sustainable measures in their operations.
- Certification and accreditation: Supports the certification and accreditation of tourism businesses and destinations that meet specific sustainability criteria. These certifications serve as a reliable indicator of a business or destination's commitment to sustainable practices and can help attract environmentally and socially conscious tourists.
- Data analysis and reporting: Enables businesses and destinations to analyze their sustainability performance through data visualization and reporting features. This allows for the identification of trends, patterns, and areas of improvement, leading to informed decision-making and continuous improvement in sustainability performance.

Sustainable tourism management platforms play a crucial role in driving the transition towards more sustainable tourism practices. By providing the necessary tools and resources, these platforms help businesses and destinations minimize their negative environmental and social impacts while maximizing the positive benefits of tourism, such as economic development and cultural preservation.

Sustainable Tourism Marketing Platforms

Sustainable tourism marketing platforms are online platforms that promote and advertise tourism activities and destinations while emphasizing and supporting sustainable practices.

These platforms aim to increase awareness and understanding of sustainable tourism among travelers and provide them with information on sustainable travel options. They play a vital role in promoting responsible travel choices and encouraging tourists to minimize their negative impacts on the environment, culture, and communities.

Sustainable tourism marketing platforms often feature eco-friendly accommodations, tour operators, and attractions that adhere to sustainability principles. They highlight establishments that prioritize conservation, minimize resource consumption, promote community engagement, and contribute positively to local economies. These platforms enable tourists to make informed decisions when planning their trips and support businesses that prioritize sustainability.

Through sustainable tourism marketing platforms, travelers can find information on eco-certifications, sustainable tourism labels, and best practices for minimizing their ecological footprint. They may also include tips and guidelines on responsible behavior during travel, such as reducing waste, supporting local businesses, and respecting cultural norms.

By promoting sustainable tourism practices, these platforms contribute to the preservation of natural and cultural heritage, the protection of biodiversity, and the well-being of local communities. They also foster a greater appreciation for sustainable tourism among travelers, encouraging them to make more conscious choices that benefit the environment and society.

Sustainable Transportation Apps

A sustainable transportation app is a mobile application designed to promote and facilitate eco-friendly transportation methods, such as walking, cycling, public transit, and carpooling. These apps provide users with real-time information, tools, and resources to make informed decisions about their transportation choices.

By leveraging technology and data, sustainable transportation apps aim to reduce the environmental impact of transportation by encouraging and enabling more sustainable modes of travel. They typically offer features such as:

- Trip planning: Users can input their desired destination and receive multiple route options, including information about public transit schedules, bike lanes, and walking paths.

- Real-time transit updates: These apps often integrate with public transit systems and provide users with live updates on bus or train arrival times, delays, and service disruptions.

- Bike sharing and rental information: Sustainable transportation apps may include details about nearby bike-sharing stations or bike rental services, allowing users to easily access and use bicycles for short-distance travel.

- Carpool matching: Some apps also include features to connect users with potential carpool partners, reducing the number of vehicles on the road and promoting resource sharing.

Overall, sustainable transportation apps aim to empower individuals to make greener transportation choices, reduce dependence on private vehicles, and contribute to a more sustainable and environmentally friendly future.

Sustainable Transportation Development

Sustainable transportation development refers to the planning, construction, and operation of transportation systems that minimize negative social, economic, and environmental impacts, while maximizing benefits for current and future generations.

It involves the design and implementation of transportation infrastructure, modes of transport, and policies that promote efficient, equitable, and environmentally-friendly mobility options.

Sustainable Transportation Fleet Management

Sustainable transportation fleet management refers to the practice of strategically planning, organizing, and controlling a fleet of vehicles to minimize environmental impact and promote long-term sustainability. It involves implementing various measures and adopting eco-friendly practices to optimize the performance and efficiency of transportation fleets while reducing their carbon footprint.

The goal of sustainable transportation fleet management is to achieve a balance between meeting transportation demands and mitigating the negative effects of vehicle usage on the environment. This includes reducing greenhouse gas emissions, minimizing energy consumption, reducing air and noise pollution, and conserving natural resources.

Sustainable Transportation Infrastructure

Sustainable transportation infrastructure refers to the development and maintenance of transportation systems that have minimal negative impacts on the environment, while promoting economic growth and social equity. It involves the creation of an integrated network of transportation modes and facilities that prioritize the use of renewable energy, reduce greenhouse gas emissions, conserve natural resources, and enhance the quality of life for communities.

Sustainable transportation infrastructure aims to reduce reliance on fossil fuels and decrease air pollution by promoting the use of public transportation, walking, cycling, and other forms of active transportation. It also emphasizes the efficient use of existing infrastructure through smart planning and design, optimizing travel routes, and improving traffic management systems. In addition, sustainable transportation infrastructure takes into account the needs of disadvantaged communities, ensuring equitable access to transportation options and affordable services.

Sustainable Transportation Initiatives

Sustainable transportation initiatives refer to actions and strategies aimed at promoting environmentally friendly transportation systems that minimize negative impacts on the planet and create a more sustainable future.

These initiatives focus on reducing greenhouse gas emissions, preserving natural resources, improving air quality, and enhancing public health. They include various measures such as the promotion of public transportation, the development of cycling and walking infrastructure, the implementation of carpooling and ridesharing programs, and the adoption of electric vehicles.

Sustainable Transportation Management Tools

Sustainable transportation management tools refer to a range of strategies, technologies, and practices employed to improve the efficiency and environmental performance of transportation systems while minimizing their negative impacts on natural resources and human health. These tools are designed to promote sustainable mobility options, reduce greenhouse gas emissions, enhance energy efficiency, and encourage the use of renewable energy sources in transportation.

These tools encompass various approaches to transportation planning, operation, and monitoring. They include but are not limited to:

1. Intelligent Transportation Systems (ITS): ITS leverage advanced communication and information technologies to optimize the use of existing transportation infrastructure, manage traffic flow, reduce congestion, and minimize fuel consumption and emissions. These systems integrate real-time data from sensors and other sources to enhance transportation efficiency and safety.

2. Alternative Fuels and Vehicles: This tool promotes the adoption of low-carbon and zero-emission vehicles, such as electric cars, hybrid vehicles, and those powered by biofuels or hydrogen fuel cells. It also encourages the development of infrastructure for alternative fuel distribution, including charging stations and hydrogen refueling stations.

3. Public Transportation and Active Mobility: The promotion of convenient, reliable, and affordable public transportation systems, such as buses, light rail, and commuter trains, is another important tool for sustainable transportation management. It also includes supporting infrastructure for cycling and walking to create a more pedestrian-friendly and bike-friendly urban environment.

4. Transportation Demand Management (TDM): TDM strategies aim to reduce private vehicle use by promoting carpooling, ridesharing, telecommuting, flexible work hours, and other measures that help decrease traffic congestion, energy consumption, and air pollution associated with daily commuting.

Overall, sustainable transportation management tools seek to transform transportation systems into more sustainable, efficient, and equitable networks that meet the mobility needs of societies while minimizing their environmental footprint.

Sustainable Transportation Networks

A sustainable transportation network refers to a system of transportation that supports the principles of sustainability, which ensures the efficient movement of people and goods while minimizing negative environmental, social, and economic impacts.

Such a network aims to meet the current transportation needs without compromising the ability of future generations to meet their own needs. It emphasizes the use of renewable energy sources, encourages the reduction of greenhouse gas emissions, minimizes air and noise pollution, and promotes the conservation of resources.

Sustainable Transportation Planning Strategies

Sustainable transportation planning strategies refer to the development and implementation of methods and actions aimed at creating a transportation system that minimizes negative impacts on the environment, promotes social equity, and enhances economic viability. These strategies involve comprehensive planning, design, and management approaches that prioritize the use of alternative and clean modes of transportation, such as walking, cycling, mass transit, and electric vehicles, while reducing reliance on fossil fuel-based transportation modes.

The goal of sustainable transportation planning is to achieve a balance between meeting the mobility needs of individuals and communities and reducing environmental degradation, congestion, and health risks associated with traditional transportation systems. This requires integrating land use planning and transportation planning to optimize infrastructure, maximize accessibility, and minimize travel distances. Additionally, sustainable transportation planning emphasizes the efficient use of limited resources, the promotion of healthy lifestyles through active transportation, and the reduction of greenhouse gas emissions and other pollutants.

Sustainable Transportation Planning

Sustainable transportation planning refers to the process of developing and implementing strategies and initiatives that promote environmentally friendly and socially responsible transportation systems. It involves considering the long-term impacts of transportation on the environment, economy, and quality of life, while addressing the needs of present and future generations.

At its core, sustainable transportation planning aims to reduce the negative environmental and social impacts of transportation, such as greenhouse gas emissions, air pollution, congestion, and inequitable access to transportation options. It promotes the use of clean and efficient modes of transport, such as walking, cycling, public transit, and electric vehicles.

This planning approach considers various factors, including land use patterns, transportation infrastructure, technology, policy frameworks, and community engagement. It seeks to create a transportation system that is accessible, affordable, safe, and reliable for all individuals, regardless of their socioeconomic status or physical abilities.

Key components of sustainable transportation planning include the integration of land use and transportation planning, the promotion of compact and mixed-use development, the provision of safe and comfortable infrastructure for pedestrians and cyclists, the enhancement of public transit systems, the adoption of alternative fuel technologies, and the implementation of demand management strategies.

By adopting sustainable transportation planning practices, communities can reduce their reliance on fossil fuels, mitigate climate change, improve air quality, enhance public health, promote social equity, and create vibrant and livable neighborhoods. It requires collaboration among various stakeholders, including government agencies, transportation planners, urban designers, policymakers, community organizations, and the general public.

Sustainable Transportation Policies

Sustainable transportation policies refer to the strategies and actions implemented by governments, organizations, and individuals to promote environmentally responsible and socially equitable transportation systems.

These policies aim to reduce the negative impacts of transportation on the environment, such as greenhouse gas emissions, air pollution, and habitat destruction, while also addressing social and economic issues, such as accessibility, affordability, and public health.

Examples of sustainable transportation policies include the promotion of public transit systems, cycling infrastructure, and walking-friendly cities to encourage the use of alternative modes of transportation. Additionally, the development of electric or hybrid vehicles, as well as the implementation of vehicle emission standards, contributes to the sustainable transportation goals.

Furthermore, sustainable transportation policies prioritize efficient resource use, such as improving fuel economy, reducing traffic congestion through smart transportation systems, and integrating land-use planning with transportation planning to create compact and mixed-use communities.

By implementing sustainable transportation policies, societies can strive towards reducing dependence on fossil fuels, mitigating climate change impacts, improving air quality, enhancing public health, and increasing social inclusivity and equity in transportation systems. These policies play a vital role in creating a sustainable future by promoting the overall well-being of communities and minimizing the adverse effects of transportation on the environment and society.

Sustainable Transportation Projects

Sustainable transportation projects refer to initiatives and strategies designed to promote environmentally-friendly and socially-responsible modes of transportation that reduce greenhouse gas emissions, improve air quality, and enhance overall quality of life.

These projects aim to address the negative impacts of transportation, such as pollution, congestion, and dependence on fossil fuels, by emphasizing the use of sustainable alternatives. This may include the development and expansion of public transportation systems, the promotion of walking and cycling infrastructure, the adoption of cleaner and more fuel-efficient vehicles, and the implementation of smart transportation technologies.

By prioritizing sustainability, these projects contribute to the achievement of several important objectives. They help mitigate climate change by reducing the carbon footprint associated with transportation. They also help improve air quality by reducing the emissions of pollutants that pose health risks to humans and harm ecosystems. Additionally, they promote social equity by providing affordable and accessible transportation options to all members of society, including those in underserved communities.

Ultimately, sustainable transportation projects play a crucial role in creating more livable and resilient cities and communities. They support the transition towards a low-carbon, energy-efficient future while prioritizing the well-being and quality of life for current and future generations.

Sustainable Transportation Solutions

Sustainable transportation solutions are approaches and strategies that prioritize environmental, social, and economic sustainability in the movement of people and goods. They aim to reduce the negative impact of transportation on the natural environment, promote social equity and accessibility, and ensure long-term economic viability.

These solutions typically involve shifting away from traditional single-occupancy vehicles powered by fossil fuels towards more sustainable modes of transportation such as public transit, cycling, walking, and shared mobility options. By encouraging the use of these modes, sustainable transportation solutions seek to minimize greenhouse gas emissions, improve air quality, and reduce noise pollution.

In addition to promoting cleaner modes of transportation, sustainable transportation solutions also involve designing and planning transportation infrastructure in a way that supports sustainable development. This includes creating efficient public transit systems, building pedestrian and cycling infrastructure, integrating land use and transportation planning, and adopting smart transportation technologies.

Furthermore, sustainable transportation solutions prioritize social equity by ensuring that transportation options are accessible and affordable for all members of society, regardless of their socioeconomic status or physical ability. This involves improving public transit services in underserved areas, implementing fare policies that are fair and inclusive, and designing transportation systems that are accessible to people with disabilities.

In summary, sustainable transportation solutions aim to address the negative environmental, social, and economic impacts of transportation by promoting cleaner modes of transportation, planning and designing sustainable transportation infrastructure, and prioritizing social equity and accessibility.

Sustainable Transportation Systems

A sustainable transportation system refers to a network of infrastructure, modes of transport, and policies that prioritize the long-term well-being of society, the environment, and the economy. It aims to minimize negative impacts such as pollution, energy consumption, congestion, and dependence on fossil fuels, while promoting efficiency, accessibility, and social equity.

Such a system focuses on reducing greenhouse gas emissions by promoting alternatives to private car usage, such as walking, cycling, and public transportation. It supports the development of clean and renewable energy sources and encourages the use of electric vehicles or other low-emission modes of transport. Additionally, sustainable transportation systems prioritize compact and mixed-use urban planning to minimize travel distances and promote active mobility.

Sustainable Transportation

Sustainable transportation refers to the movement of goods and people in a manner that minimizes negative impacts on the environment, society, and the economy. It is an approach that seeks to meet current transportation needs without compromising the ability of future generations to meet their own needs.

This type of transportation aims to reduce greenhouse gas emissions, air pollution, and other environmental pollutants associated with traditional modes of transportation. It promotes the use of cleaner and more efficient fuels, such as renewable energy sources or electric power, and encourages the development and use of sustainable modes of transportation, such as walking, cycling, and public transit.

Sustainable transportation also considers the social and economic aspects of transportation. It focuses on creating accessible and affordable transport options for all members of society, regardless of income or ability. This includes improving infrastructure, such as bike lanes and sidewalks, to enhance safety and mobility for pedestrians and cyclists.

In addition, sustainable transportation aims to reduce reliance on fossil fuels and promote energy efficiency in the transport sector. It involves strategies like promoting carpooling, ridesharing, and the use of shared mobility services to decrease the number of single-occupancy vehicles on the road. It also encourages the integration of transportation systems with land use planning and urban design to create more sustainable and livable communities.

In summary, sustainable transportation entails adopting measures and practices that minimize the negative environmental, social, and economic impacts associated with transportation. It emphasizes the conservation of resources, reduction of emissions, and promotion of equitable and efficient mobility options to ensure a sustainable future for generations to come.

Sustainable Urban Development Projects

A sustainable urban development project refers to an initiative or scheme that aims to promote long-term environmental, social, and economic well-being within a city or urban area.

Such projects typically focus on implementing strategies and practices that minimize negative impacts on the environment while maximizing the efficient use of resources. This includes incorporating renewable energy sources, improving energy efficiency, reducing greenhouse gas emissions, and mitigating pollution. Additionally, sustainable urban development projects often prioritize the conservation of biodiversity, water resources, and natural habitats.

Furthermore, these projects aim to create a socially inclusive and economically vibrant urban environment. This involves enhancing public transportation systems, promoting affordable housing options, improving access to healthcare and education, and fostering community engagement and participation. The goal is to create resilient and equitable cities that provide a high quality of life for all residents, regardless of socioeconomic status.

In order to achieve these objectives, sustainable urban development projects often require collaboration between various stakeholders, including government agencies, non-profit organizations, businesses, and community members. They rely on comprehensive planning, effective governance, and innovative design and technology solutions to address the complex challenges of urbanization and ensure a sustainable future for cities.

Sustainable Urban Development

Sustainable urban development refers to the planning, design, and management of cities and communities that strive to meet the needs of present and future generations while minimizing negative impacts on the environment and promoting social and economic wellbeing.

It involves creating urban spaces that are environmentally friendly, socially inclusive, and economically viable. This includes considerations such as efficient use of resources, reduction of greenhouse gas emissions, preservation of natural habitats, promotion of renewable energy, provision of affordable housing, access to quality healthcare and education, and promotion of sustainable transportation options.

Sustainable Urban Mobility Apps

Sustainable urban mobility apps refer to digital applications that aim to promote and enable sustainable transportation options within urban areas. These apps leverage technology to provide innovative solutions to the challenges associated with transportation in cities, including traffic congestion, air pollution, and limited access to public transportation.

These apps typically offer a range of features and functionalities that encourage and facilitate sustainable modes of transportation, such as walking, cycling, and the use of public transit. They utilize real-time data and advanced algorithms to provide users with information on the availability, routes, and schedules of various transportation options, allowing them to make informed decisions based on their specific needs and preferences.

Furthermore, sustainable urban mobility apps often incorporate elements of gamification and social networking, aiming to incentivize and motivate individuals to choose sustainable transportation options. They may include features such as rewards, challenges, and community-based initiatives to encourage active participation and engagement among users.

By promoting sustainable transportation alternatives, these apps contribute to reducing greenhouse gas emissions, improving air quality, and alleviating traffic congestion in urban areas. They also have the potential to enhance accessibility and inclusivity, making transportation more equitable and convenient for all individuals, regardless of their socioeconomic background or physical abilities.

In summary, sustainable urban mobility apps harness the power of technology to promote sustainable transportation options and address the environmental, social, and economic challenges associated with urban mobility. Through their innovative features and functionalities, they encourage individuals to make informed choices and actively participate in creating more sustainable and livable cities.

Sustainable Urban Mobility Design

Sustainable urban mobility design refers to the planning, development, and implementation of transportation systems in urban areas that prioritize efficiency, equity, and environmental sustainability. It aims to improve the accessibility, safety, and convenience of urban transportation while minimizing negative impacts on the environment and public health.

This approach to urban mobility design takes into consideration the long-term social, economic, and environmental effects of transportation systems. It seeks to reduce greenhouse gas emissions, air pollution, noise pollution, and congestion by promoting alternative modes of transportation such as walking, cycling, public transit, and carpooling.

Key principles of sustainable urban mobility design include:

1. Integration and connectivity: Designing transportation systems that seamlessly connect different modes of transportation, such as integrating bike lanes with public transit routes or creating pedestrian-friendly streets with easy access to shops, parks, and public amenities.

2. Accessibility and inclusivity: Ensuring that transportation infrastructure is accessible to all individuals, regardless of their socioeconomic background, age, or physical abilities. This may involve implementing universal design principles, providing affordable transportation options, and prioritizing the needs of marginalized communities.

366

3. Land use and urban planning: Coordinating transportation planning with land use planning to reduce the need for long-distance commuting, promote mixed-use development, and encourage compact, walkable neighborhoods.

4. Sustainable technologies and practices: Embracing innovative technologies and practices that reduce fuel consumption, promote energy efficiency, and utilize renewable energy sources. This may include the adoption of electric vehicles, intelligent transportation systems, and smart city initiatives.

... (remaining answer)>

Sustainable Urban Mobility Planning Software

A sustainable urban mobility planning software is a technological tool designed to assist cities and urban areas in creating and implementing strategies that promote sustainable transportation choices and reduce the negative impacts of urban mobility on the environment, society, and the economy.

This software incorporates various features and functionalities that enable urban planners and decision-makers to collect and analyze data related to mobility patterns, traffic volumes, emissions, and other relevant factors. It helps them assess the current state of mobility within their cities and identify areas for improvement.

Moreover, this software allows for the simulation and evaluation of different scenarios and measures, such as the introduction of public transportation systems, pedestrian zones, cycling infrastructure, or car-free zones. It assists in analyzing the potential effects of these interventions on traffic flow, air quality, energy consumption, and social equity.

Furthermore, the sustainable urban mobility planning software facilitates the creation of comprehensive and integrated mobility plans that address the diverse needs and challenges of urban areas. It supports the development of strategies that not only prioritize the use of sustainable modes of transport but also consider factors such as land use, urban design, and social inclusion.

In summary, a sustainable urban mobility planning software is a powerful tool that empowers cities to design and implement sustainable transportation strategies. By harnessing the capabilities of this software, cities can create more livable, resilient, and environmentally friendly urban environments.

Sustainable Urban Mobility Solutions

Sustainable urban mobility solutions refer to transportation strategies and systems that prioritize the long-term well-being of people, the environment, and the economy in urban areas. These solutions aim to reduce the negative impacts of transportation, such as air pollution, congestion, and noise, while promoting accessibility, equity, and efficiency.

Urban mobility plays a crucial role in shaping the sustainability of cities. It determines how people move around, access essential services, and interact with their surroundings. Sustainable urban mobility solutions seek to address the challenges posed by traditional modes of transportation, such as private cars, and advocate for more sustainable alternatives.

One key aspect of sustainable urban mobility solutions is the promotion of active transportation modes, such as walking and cycling. Encouraging and improving infrastructure for these modes not only reduces traffic congestion but also promotes physical activity and improves public health. Additionally, these solutions often prioritize the use of public transit, such as buses and trains, which can significantly reduce greenhouse gas emissions and energy consumption compared to individual car use.

Furthermore, sustainable urban mobility solutions emphasize the integration of different transportation modes through smart and innovative technologies. This includes the implementation of intelligent transport systems, ride-sharing platforms, and electric mobility options. By leveraging these technologies, cities can enhance connectivity, optimize routes, and reduce overall energy consumption.

In summary, sustainable urban mobility solutions envision a future where cities prioritize accessible, affordable, and environmentally-friendly transportation options. By implementing these solutions, cities can reduce their carbon footprint, improve the quality of life for their residents, and enhance overall urban sustainability.

Sustainable Urban Planning And Development

Sustainable urban planning and development refers to a set of practices and strategies aimed at designing and managing cities in a way that promotes environmental, social, and economic sustainability. It involves incorporating principles of sustainability into urban planning processes to create livable, healthy, and vibrant cities.

This approach focuses on balancing the needs of the present generation with the needs of future generations, taking into account the finite resources of the planet. It aims to minimize the negative impact of urbanization on the environment and maximize the benefits for both current and future residents.

Sustainable urban planning and development involves various aspects, including land use planning, transportation systems, energy efficiency, green infrastructure, waste management, and social equity. Key principles include compact, mixed-use development to reduce the need for car travel and promote walkability and access to public transportation. It also emphasizes the preservation and enhancement of natural systems and open spaces to improve air and water quality, support biodiversity, and provide recreational opportunities for residents.

By adopting sustainable practices, cities can reduce greenhouse gas emissions, conserve natural resources, promote social equity, and improve the quality of life for their residents. Sustainable urban planning and development requires collaboration among government agencies, private sector stakeholders, and local communities to ensure a holistic and inclusive approach to city planning.

Sustainable Urban Planning Software

Sustainable urban planning software refers to specialized computer programs or applications that aid in the design and analysis of urban environments with a focus on promoting sustainability. This software assists urban planners and architects in making informed decisions to create more environmentally friendly and socially equitable cities.

The primary objective of sustainable urban planning software is to develop urban areas that balance economic growth, social development, and environmental protection. It utilizes various data sources, including demographic information, land use patterns, transportation systems, energy consumption, and environmental factors, to model and evaluate different scenarios for urban development.

By simulating the impacts of different design choices, such as building density, transportation networks, green spaces, and renewable energy sources, sustainable urban planning software enables planners to assess the environmental, social, and economic implications of their decisions. This allows for better understanding and mitigation of the potential negative consequences associated with urbanization, such as increased pollution, resource depletion, traffic congestion, and social inequality.

In addition to supporting decision-making processes, sustainable urban planning software often includes visualization tools to generate 3D models, maps, and simulations. These visual representations help communicate and engage stakeholders, such as policymakers, community members, and developers, fostering collaboration and enhancing the understanding of sustainable development concepts.

Overall, sustainable urban planning software plays a vital role in shaping cities that are environmentally resilient, socially inclusive, and economically viable. By providing planners with reliable data and analysis capabilities, it promotes evidence-based decision-making and enables the implementation of sustainable practices in urban design and development.

Sustainable Urban Planning Strategies

Sustainable urban planning strategies refer to the planning and development approaches aimed at creating cities and communities that are environmentally, socially, and economically sustainable. These strategies take into account the long-term impacts of urban growth and seek to minimize negative environmental effects, promote social equity, and optimize economic prosperity.

One key aspect of sustainable urban planning is the promotion of compact and mixed land use. This entails designing cities in a way that reduces sprawl and encourages the efficient use of land and resources. By locating residential, commercial, and recreational areas in close proximity, sustainable urban planning strategies aim to minimize the need for long commutes and promote active modes of transportation such as walking, cycling, and public transit.

Another important element of sustainable urban planning is the integration of green infrastructure. This involves incorporating natural features like parks, green roofs, urban forests, and stormwater management systems into the urban fabric. By doing so, sustainable urban planning strategies can enhance biodiversity, improve air and water quality, reduce the urban heat island effect, and mitigate the impacts of climate change.

In addition to physical design considerations, sustainable urban planning also considers social equity and community engagement. This means ensuring that urban development benefits all residents, regardless of income or social status. Sustainable urban planning strategies aim to create inclusive neighborhoods by providing affordable housing options, access to quality education and healthcare, and opportunities for community participation in decision-making processes.

Sustainable Urban Planning

Sustainable Urban Regeneration Initiatives

Sustainable urban regeneration initiatives refer to the efforts and strategies implemented by governments, organizations, and communities to revitalize and improve urban areas in a way that promotes long-term environmental, social, and economic sustainability.

These initiatives aim to address the challenges faced by cities, such as population growth, aging infrastructure, pollution, inequality, and climate change. Through a holistic approach, sustainable urban regeneration initiatives seek to create more livable, resilient, and inclusive cities.

Key elements of sustainable urban regeneration include: - Environmental sustainability: Initiatives focus on reducing greenhouse gas emissions, improving energy efficiency, promoting renewable energy sources, preserving green spaces, and enhancing biodiversity. - Social sustainability: Initiatives strive to enhance social cohesion, equity, and inclusivity by providing affordable housing, improving public transportation systems, increasing access to healthcare and education, and fostering community engagement and participation. - Economic sustainability: Initiatives aim to stimulate economic growth, attract investments, create job opportunities, and ensure the efficient use of resources. - Cultural sustainability: Initiatives value heritage preservation, promote cultural diversity, support local businesses, and encourage the revitalization of historical sites. - Governance and collaboration: Initiatives require strong governance structures, effective policies, and collaboration between different stakeholders, including government agencies, private entities, academia, and local communities.

Overall, sustainable urban regeneration initiatives play a crucial role in transforming cities into more sustainable, equitable, and resilient environments, with the well-being of both current and future generations in mind.

Sustainable Urban Regeneration

Sustainable urban regeneration refers to the process of revitalizing and transforming urban areas in a way that promotes long-term environmental, social, and economic sustainability. It aims to address the challenges and issues faced by cities, such as population growth, climate change, and limited resources, while improving quality of life for the community and preserving

369

cultural heritage.

This approach involves the implementation of integrated and holistic strategies that consider various aspects of sustainable development. It encompasses different dimensions, including land use planning, transportation, energy efficiency, waste management, and social inclusion.

Sustainable urban regeneration seeks to create vibrant, inclusive, and resilient cities by promoting environmentally friendly practices and reducing the environmental footprint. This can be achieved through the revitalization of brownfield sites, the redevelopment of deteriorated infrastructure, the promotion of green spaces, and the implementation of sustainable building designs and technologies.

In addition, social and cultural considerations play a crucial role in sustainable urban regeneration. The involvement and active participation of local communities, stakeholders, and organizations are essential in shaping the development process and ensuring that it meets the needs and aspirations of the people.

Overall, sustainable urban regeneration aims to transform cities into sustainable, livable, and prosperous environments that benefit current and future generations. It requires a collaborative and interdisciplinary approach, as well as long-term commitment and investment, to achieve its goals.

Sustainable Urban Renewal Projects

Sustainable urban renewal projects refer to initiatives that aim to revitalize and improve urban areas in an environmentally, socially, and economically sustainable manner. These projects prioritize the long-term well-being of both the natural environment and human communities, seeking to create vibrant, resilient, and inclusive cities.

Such projects typically involve the redevelopment and transformation of existing urban areas, with a focus on maximizing the efficient use of resources, reducing environmental impact, and enhancing quality of life. They often address challenges related to outdated infrastructure, deteriorating buildings, pollution, social inequality, and lack of green spaces.

Sustainable Urban Renewal

Sustainable urban renewal refers to the process of revitalizing and transforming urban areas in a way that promotes long-term environmental, social, and economic sustainability. It involves the thoughtful planning and implementation of strategies to improve the quality of life for residents, while minimizing negative impacts on the environment and ensuring the efficient use of resources.

This approach to urban renewal aims to create vibrant, inclusive, and resilient communities by addressing key sustainability challenges such as climate change, resource depletion, social inequality, and economic instability. It recognizes that traditional approaches to urban development have often resulted in social and environmental dislocation, urban sprawl, and unsustainable resource consumption.

Sustainable urban renewal seeks to reverse these trends by promoting compact, mixed-use development, enhancing public transportation infrastructure, and fostering the preservation and regeneration of green spaces. It encourages the adoption of renewable energy sources, energy-efficient buildings, and sustainable waste management practices to reduce carbon emissions and minimize waste generation.

Furthermore, sustainable urban renewal emphasizes community engagement and participatory decision-making processes to ensure that the diverse needs and interests of residents are taken into account. It promotes social cohesion, inclusiveness, and affordable housing options, aiming to create a balanced and equitable urban environment.

In summary, sustainable urban renewal is a comprehensive and integrated approach to urban development that prioritizes the well-being of residents, the preservation of natural resources, and the mitigation of climate change. It seeks to create sustainable, livable, and resilient cities for present and future generations.

Sustainable Urban Revitalization Efforts

Sustainable urban revitalization efforts refer to the ongoing actions and initiatives taken to improve the environmental, social, and economic sustainability of urban areas that have experienced decline or decay. These efforts aim to restore, revive, and transform deteriorated urban neighborhoods, districts, or regions into more vibrant, resilient, and equitable places.

Sustainable urban revitalization involves a holistic approach that considers various dimensions of sustainability. It takes into account the environmental impacts of urban development and seeks to mitigate them through practices such as green infrastructure, energy-efficient buildings, waste reduction, and green transportation options. Additionally, it addresses social issues by promoting affordable housing, community engagement, access to essential services, and cultural preservation. Economic sustainability is also a crucial aspect, with efforts focused on attracting investments, creating job opportunities, supporting local businesses, and generating sustainable economic growth.

These revitalization efforts often require collaboration and participation from various stakeholders, including local government, community organizations, private sector entities, and residents. They integrate long-term planning, strategic investments, and policy interventions to ensure a balanced and inclusive urban development. The ultimate goal is to create urban environments that are environmentally responsible, socially just, and economically prosperous.

In summary, sustainable urban revitalization efforts refer to comprehensive and proactive measures undertaken to enhance the sustainability of urban areas by addressing environmental, social, and economic challenges. These initiatives aim to rejuvenate and transform declining neighborhoods into thriving and resilient communities that promote a high quality of life for residents while minimizing negative impacts on the environment.

Sustainable Urban Revitalization

Sustainable urban revitalization refers to the process of improving and redeveloping urban areas in a way that is environmentally, socially, and economically sustainable.

This involves a holistic approach that takes into account various aspects, such as energy efficiency, transportation, waste management, green spaces, and social equity, to create thriving and livable communities. The goal is to transform existing urban areas into sustainable neighborhoods that meet the needs of current and future generations.

In terms of environmental sustainability, sustainable urban revitalization focuses on reducing the ecological footprint of cities by promoting energy-efficient buildings, renewable energy sources, and sustainable transportation options. It also emphasizes the preservation and restoration of natural habitats and the integration of green infrastructure, such as parks, gardens, and urban forests, to enhance biodiversity and mitigate climate change effects.

From a social perspective, sustainable urban revitalization aims to create inclusive communities where everyone has access to affordable housing, healthcare, education, and recreational facilities. It seeks to foster a sense of community and promote social cohesion, while also addressing issues of social inequality and exclusion.

Economically, sustainable urban revitalization recognizes the importance of creating jobs, attracting investment, and supporting local businesses. It encourages the development of a diverse and resilient economy that is not solely reliant on one industry or sector.

Overall, sustainable urban revitalization aims to balance the environmental, social, and economic aspects of urban development to create vibrant, livable, and resilient cities for present and future generations.

Sustainable Urban Waste Management

Sustainable urban waste management refers to the practice of efficiently and responsibly managing the waste generated in urban areas, with the objective of promoting environmental preservation and social well-being while minimizing the negative impacts on natural resources and public health. It involves a holistic approach that encompasses waste reduction, recycling, reuse, energy recovery, and proper disposal.

By adopting sustainable waste management practices, cities aim to achieve a closed-loop system that minimizes the extraction of virgin resources, reduces greenhouse gas emissions, and prevents pollution and contamination of water, soil, and air. The principles of sustainability guide decision-making processes, ensuring that waste management strategies are aligned with long-term environmental, economic, and social goals.

Sustainable urban waste management involves several key components, including waste segregation at the source, effective collection and transportation systems, advanced recycling facilities, sustainable treatment technologies, and public education and awareness programs. It also involves the engagement and cooperation of various stakeholders, including government authorities, waste management companies, industries, communities, and individuals.

Implementing sustainable waste management practices can yield numerous benefits. It contributes to the preservation of natural resources, reduces the reliance on landfilling, conserves energy, and mitigates climate change. Additionally, it creates employment opportunities, encourages innovation and technology development, and promotes a cleaner and healthier environment for urban residents. Ultimately, sustainable urban waste management plays a crucial role in building sustainable cities and achieving the broader goals of sustainable development.

Sustainable Urbanization

Sustainable urbanization refers to the process of planning, developing, and managing cities in a way that ensures the economic, social, and environmental well-being of current and future generations. It involves designing and constructing cities in a manner that promotes resource efficiency, environmental protection, and social inclusivity.

A sustainable urbanization approach takes into consideration various aspects of sustainability, including reducing greenhouse gas emissions, improving air and water quality, conserving natural resources, promoting renewable energy sources, and enhancing community resilience. This approach prioritizes the use of green building materials, sustainable transportation systems, and smart technologies to create cities that are livable, healthy, and economically vibrant.

Sustainable urbanization aims to achieve a balance between urban development and environmental conservation by minimizing the ecological footprint of cities. It involves creating compact, mixed-use urban environments that encourage walking, cycling, and the use of public transportation, thus reducing reliance on private cars and alleviating traffic congestion. It also emphasizes the preservation of green spaces, the protection of biodiversity, and the promotion of sustainable waste management practices.

Furthermore, sustainable urbanization seeks to ensure social equity and inclusivity by providing affordable housing, quality education, healthcare services, and recreational facilities for all residents. It aims to foster a sense of community and cultural diversity, promoting social cohesion and harmony.

In summary, sustainable urbanization entails integrating environmental, economic, and social considerations into the planning and development of cities, with the ultimate goal of creating livable, resilient, and inclusive urban spaces that can thrive for generations to come.

Sustainable Waste Diversion Programs

Sustainable waste diversion programs refer to initiatives and strategies implemented to reduce the amount of waste sent to landfills, while promoting environmentally-friendly practices and resource conservation. These programs aim to divert waste through various means, such as recycling, composting, reusing, and repurposing.

The goal of sustainable waste diversion programs is to minimize the negative impact of waste on the environment and human health by encouraging responsible waste management practices. By diverting waste from landfills, these programs help conserve natural resources, reduce pollution, and minimize greenhouse gas emissions associated with waste decomposition.

Sustainable Waste Management

Sustainable waste management refers to the process of minimizing the generation and disposal of waste through environmentally friendly practices that promote long-term sustainability. It involves various methods and strategies aimed at reducing, reusing, and recycling waste materials to conserve resources, minimize pollution, and protect the environment.

The concept of sustainable waste management recognizes that waste is a valuable resource that can be utilized and managed efficiently to achieve economic, social, and environmental benefits. It aims to move away from the traditional linear model of waste disposal, where materials are used once and then discarded, towards a circular economy approach that supports the concept of "reduce, reuse, recycle."

Key components of sustainable waste management include waste prevention, source separation, recycling, composting, and proper disposal of non-recyclable waste. Waste prevention involves the implementation of practices that reduce the generation of waste, such as promoting the use of reusable products, encouraging responsible consumption, and implementing packaging reduction measures.

Source separation refers to the process of sorting and separating different types of waste at the point of generation to facilitate recycling and composting. Recycling involves collecting and processing various materials to produce new products, reducing the demand for virgin resources and minimizing the environmental impacts associated with extraction and production.

Composting involves the decomposition of organic waste materials, such as food scraps and yard waste, into nutrient-rich soil amendments that can be used in agriculture and landscaping. Proper disposal of non-recyclable waste encompasses the safe and responsible management of waste that cannot be recycled or composted, such as hazardous materials.

Sustainable Waste Sorting And Disposal

Sustainable waste sorting and disposal refers to the practice of categorizing and managing waste materials in an environmentally responsible manner, with the aim of minimizing the negative impacts on the planet and promoting long-term sustainability. It involves the systematic separation and treatment of different types of waste to facilitate recycling, reuse, and proper disposal.

The process of sustainable waste sorting begins with the segregation of waste into various categories such as recyclables, organic waste, and hazardous materials. This categorization is crucial as it enables the implementation of specific waste management strategies for each type of waste.

Recyclable materials, such as paper, plastic, glass, and metal, are separated and sent to recycling facilities where they undergo processes to transform them into new products. This reduces the demand for virgin resources and decreases energy consumption and greenhouse gas emissions associated with the production of new materials.

Organic waste, including food scraps and yard trimmings, can be composted to create nutrient-rich soil additives. Composting not only diverts waste from landfills but also helps improve soil structure, water retention, and plant growth, thereby supporting sustainable agricultural practices.

Hazardous waste, such as chemicals, batteries, and electronic waste, requires special handling and disposal to prevent environmental contamination. These materials are typically sent to specialized centers where they undergo safe treatment or disposal methods that minimize the release of harmful substances into the environment.

By implementing sustainable waste sorting and disposal practices, communities and industries

373

can contribute to the conservation of natural resources, reduction in landfill space, prevention of pollution, and the creation of a circular economy where waste is reused and recycled for future generations.

Sustainable Waste-To-Energy Solutions

Sustainable waste-to-energy solutions refer to methods and technologies that convert waste materials into usable forms of energy while minimizing environmental impacts and promoting long-term sustainability.

These solutions focus on the efficient and responsible management of waste materials, such as solid waste, agricultural waste, or biomass, to generate clean and renewable energy sources like electricity, heat, or biofuels. This approach helps to reduce the reliance on fossil fuels and reduce greenhouse gas emissions, contributing to climate change mitigation efforts.

One common method is incineration, where waste is burned at high temperatures in specially designed facilities called waste-to-energy plants. The heat generated from the combustion process is then used to produce steam, which drives turbines to generate electricity. Advanced technologies like flue gas treatment systems are employed to minimize air pollution and capture harmful emissions.

Another approach is anaerobic digestion, which involves the decomposition of organic waste in the absence of oxygen. This biological process produces biogas, primarily composed of methane, which can be used as a fuel for heating, electricity generation, or transportation. The remaining byproduct, called digestate, can be used as a nutrient-rich fertilizer for agricultural purposes.

These waste-to-energy solutions not only provide a sustainable source of energy but also help reduce landfill waste, preventing the release of harmful methane gases. Additionally, they contribute to the circular economy by recovering valuable materials from the waste stream and reducing the need for virgin resources. However, it is essential to ensure proper waste management practices, including waste reduction, recycling, and sorting, to minimize the environmental impact and maximize the efficiency of these solutions.

Sustainable Waste-To-Energy Systems

Sustainable waste-to-energy systems refer to integrated systems that convert waste materials into energy while minimizing negative environmental impacts and promoting resource conservation. These systems aim to address the dual challenges of waste management and energy generation, aligning with the principles of sustainability.

By harnessing the potential energy stored in various waste streams, such as municipal solid waste, agricultural residues, or biomass, these systems generate heat, electricity, or biofuels. This energy production not only reduces the reliance on fossil fuels but also diverts waste from landfills, mitigating greenhouse gas emissions and potential land and water pollution.

Key considerations for a sustainable waste-to-energy system include efficient waste sorting and segregation practices to maximize resource recovery and minimize the release of harmful pollutants during the conversion process. Additionally, emissions control technologies are employed to minimize the release of air pollutants and ensure compliance with environmental regulations.

Integrated waste management approaches, such as the use of anaerobic digestion or thermal technologies like incineration or gasification, can be employed in these systems based on the characteristics of the waste stream and the desired energy output. The end products of these processes, such as digestate or ash, can also be utilized for further resource recovery or land application.

Overall, sustainable waste-to-energy systems offer a holistic approach to waste management and energy production, addressing environmental and social challenges while contributing to a circular economy. By converting waste into valuable energy resources, these systems promote resource efficiency, reduce environmental pollution, and contribute to a more sustainable and resilient future.

Sustainable Waste-To-Energy Technologies

Sustainable waste-to-energy technologies are processes that convert waste materials into usable forms of energy, while minimizing negative impacts on the environment and promoting the efficient use of resources. These technologies aim to address the challenges of waste management and energy production, by turning waste into a valuable resource.

The concept of sustainable waste-to-energy encompasses various technologies and methods, each with its own unique processes and benefits. Some common examples include anaerobic digestion, incineration, and gasification.

Anaerobic digestion involves the decomposition of organic matter in the absence of oxygen, producing biogas that can be used to generate electricity or heat. This process not only reduces the volume of waste but also produces a renewable energy source, decreasing dependency on fossil fuels.

Incineration, on the other hand, involves the combustion of waste materials at high temperatures, converting them into ash and flue gases. The heat generated during this process can be recovered to produce steam or electricity, contributing to the overall energy production.

Gasification is another waste-to-energy technology that converts biomass or non-recyclable waste into a gas called syngas. Syngas can be used as a fuel for electricity generation or as a raw material for the production of chemicals and fuels, reducing the reliance on traditional fossil fuels.

Overall, sustainable waste-to-energy technologies offer an environmentally friendly solution to waste management, by reducing landfill waste and greenhouse gas emissions, while simultaneously producing clean and renewable energy.

Sustainable Waste-To-Energy Technology

Sustainable waste-to-energy technology refers to the process of converting waste materials into usable forms of energy, while minimizing negative environmental impacts and promoting long-term ecological balance. It involves the conversion of various waste materials, such as organic waste, agricultural waste, and municipal solid waste, into valuable energy sources, such as electricity, heat, and fuel.

This technology supports the principles of sustainability by addressing two major challenges: waste management and energy generation. Firstly, it tackles the ever-increasing issue of waste disposal by reducing the volume of waste that ends up in landfills. Instead of allowing waste to decompose and release harmful greenhouse gases, sustainable waste-to-energy technology harnesses its energy potential. This not only alleviates the strain on landfill space but also helps to reduce air and water pollution caused by waste decomposition.

Secondly, sustainable waste-to-energy technology contributes to the diversification of energy sources, reducing dependency on non-renewable fossil fuels. By harnessing the energy content of waste materials, it helps to offset the need for traditional energy production methods, such as burning fossil fuels. This leads to a reduction in greenhouse gas emissions and helps mitigate climate change effects.

In addition to waste reduction and renewable energy production, sustainable waste-to-energy technology often incorporates measures to minimize environmental impacts. These may include emission control systems to reduce air pollutants, proper ash disposal, and the capture and utilization of byproducts like biogas. Moreover, this technology promotes a circular economy approach by recycling valuable materials from waste streams.

Sustainable Wastewater Treatment Systems

Sustainable wastewater treatment systems are environmentally-friendly and resource-efficient mechanisms that effectively and safely remove pollutants from wastewater. These systems aim to minimize adverse impacts on the ecosystem while conserving energy and water resources.

These systems employ a combination of physical, chemical, and biological processes to treat wastewater and transform it into a form that is safe for discharge or reuse. The primary objective is to remove organic matter, nutrients, and harmful substances from the wastewater, preventing contamination of surface water bodies, groundwater, and soil.

In sustainable wastewater treatment systems, emphasis is placed on reducing energy consumption and carbon footprint. This can be achieved through various energy-efficient practices such as the use of renewable energy sources, optimization of treatment processes, and heat recovery techniques. Additionally, minimizing water consumption and maximizing water reuse are key aspects of sustainability in these systems.

Moreover, sustainable wastewater treatment systems consider the long-term viability of the treated effluent. The effluent should meet applicable regulatory standards for discharge, but there is also growing interest in exploring opportunities for its beneficial use. This can include irrigation of crops, replenishment of groundwater, or even indirect potable reuse.

In conclusion, sustainable wastewater treatment systems are designed to efficiently and effectively treat wastewater while minimizing environmental impact and resource usage. By implementing these systems, communities can contribute to the preservation of ecosystems, conserve energy and water resources, and promote a more sustainable future.

Sustainable Water Conservation Technologies

Sustainable water conservation technologies refer to innovative methods, practices, and technologies that promote the efficient use and preservation of water resources while minimizing adverse environmental impacts. These technologies aim to address the increasing water scarcity and environmental concerns associated with water usage in various sectors.

One example of a sustainable water conservation technology is the use of smart irrigation systems. These systems employ advanced sensors, weather data, and artificial intelligence algorithms to optimize irrigation schedules and water usage. By continuously monitoring soil moisture levels and weather conditions, smart irrigation systems ensure that plants receive just the right amount of water, reducing water waste and promoting plant health.

Another example is the implementation of water-efficient fixtures and appliances in buildings. Low-flow toilets, faucets, and showerheads, as well as water-efficient washing machines and dishwashers, help reduce water consumption without compromising performance. These technologies often incorporate aerators, pressure regulators, or other mechanisms that limit water flow while maintaining usability.

Furthermore, greywater recycling systems are gaining popularity as a sustainable water conservation technology. These systems collect and treat wastewater from sources such as sinks, showers, and laundry machines, making it suitable for purposes like irrigation or toilet flushing. By reducing the reliance on fresh water for non-potable uses, greywater recycling systems help conserve water resources and reduce the strain on wastewater treatment plants.

Overall, sustainable water conservation technologies play a crucial role in promoting responsible and efficient water usage. By implementing these innovative methods and technologies, individuals, communities, and industries can contribute to the long-term sustainability of water resources while minimizing their environmental footprint.

Sustainable Water Filtration Systems

Sustainable water filtration systems refer to technologies and processes that are designed to remove impurities and contaminants from water in an environmentally friendly and socially responsible manner, while also ensuring the long-term availability and accessibility of clean water for current and future generations.

These systems are characterized by their ability to minimize the negative impacts on the environment and human health throughout their entire life cycle, from production and operation

376

to disposal. They aim to conserve natural resources, minimize energy consumption, reduce waste generation, and prevent pollution.

Sustainable Water Quality Monitoring

Sustainable water quality monitoring refers to the ongoing assessment and analysis of water resources with the goal of ensuring the long-term health and viability of these resources. It involves the collection, measurement, and evaluation of various physical, chemical, and biological parameters to determine the quality of water and identify any potential risks or contaminants.

This monitoring process is designed to support sustainable water management practices by providing reliable and up-to-date information on the condition of water sources. By tracking key indicators, such as pH levels, dissolved oxygen content, nutrient concentrations, and the presence of pollutants or pathogens, sustainable water quality monitoring helps identify potential threats to human health, aquatic ecosystems, and overall water quality.

One of the key principles of sustainable water quality monitoring is the use of environmentally friendly and low-impact monitoring techniques. This includes minimizing the use of harmful chemicals and reducing the negative impact on aquatic environments during sampling activities.

Furthermore, sustainable water quality monitoring involves the collaboration and engagement of various stakeholders, including government agencies, local communities, and scientific experts. Effective communication and sharing of monitoring data are essential for making informed decisions and taking appropriate measures to protect and restore the quality of water resources.

Sustainable Water Treatment Solutions

Sustainable water treatment solutions refer to methods, technologies, and practices that are designed to effectively and efficiently treat water while minimizing their impact on the environment, conserving resources, and ensuring long-term availability of clean and safe water for current and future generations.

These solutions aim to address the increasing water scarcity and pollution challenges faced by communities and industries around the world. They promote the use of renewable energy sources, such as solar or wind power, to reduce the carbon footprint associated with water treatment processes. Additionally, sustainable water treatment solutions focus on minimizing waste generation and maximizing resource recovery through the implementation of innovative and eco-friendly technologies.

Examples of sustainable water treatment solutions include the use of natural and biological treatment processes, such as constructed wetlands, which rely on natural vegetation and microorganisms to remove contaminants from water. Another example is the application of decentralized and modular treatment systems, which allow for flexible and scalable solutions that can be tailored to the specific needs of a community or industry.

By adopting sustainable water treatment solutions, communities and industries can reduce their dependence on finite resources, protect ecosystems, and contribute to the overall conservation of water resources. These solutions play a crucial role in ensuring the availability of clean water for drinking, irrigation, and industrial purposes, thus promoting a more sustainable and resilient future.

Sustainable Water-Efficient Landscaping

Sustainable water-efficient landscaping refers to the practice of designing, installing, and maintaining landscapes that minimize water consumption while promoting environmental sustainability.

This approach involves the use of various techniques and strategies to maximize the efficient use of water resources in landscaping. It aims to reduce the reliance on irrigation water and minimize water waste, especially in regions facing water scarcity or drought conditions.

Sustainable water-efficient landscaping incorporates principles of water conservation, biodiversity, and ecological balance. It involves careful selection of plants, soil management, proper irrigation systems, and other measures that enhance water efficiency.

The selection of plant species is crucial for sustainable water-efficient landscaping. Drought-tolerant and native plants are preferred as they require less water and are better adapted to local climate conditions. These plants have developed natural mechanisms to withstand periods of drought, reducing the need for excessive watering.

Soil management techniques, such as incorporating organic matter and mulching, play a vital role in water efficiency. Organic matter improves soil structure, enabling better water retention and reducing runoff. Mulching helps conserve soil moisture by reducing evaporation and preventing weed growth, which competes for water resources.

Efficient irrigation systems, such as drip irrigation or smart controllers, are essential components of sustainable water-efficient landscaping. These systems deliver water directly to plant roots, minimizing losses due to evaporation or runoff. Smart controllers use sensors and weather data to adjust watering schedules based on actual plant needs, further optimizing water usage.

In summary, sustainable water-efficient landscaping aims to create and maintain beautiful, functional landscapes while minimizing water consumption and environmental impact. It involves implementing water conservation practices, selecting appropriate plant species, and utilizing efficient irrigation systems to promote a sustainable and water-wise approach to landscaping.

Sustainable Wildlife Conservation Technology

Sustainable wildlife conservation technology refers to the implementation of technological solutions that contribute to the long-term protection and preservation of wildlife species and their habitats, while considering the principles of sustainability. This approach aims to find a balance between conservation efforts and the needs of local communities, while minimizing negative impacts on the environment.

The use of sustainable wildlife conservation technology involves the application of various tools and techniques, such as advanced monitoring systems, remote sensing technologies, data analysis, and innovative management strategies. These technologies assist in gathering accurate data about wildlife populations, tracking their movements, identifying threats, and implementing effective conservation measures.

Textile-To-Textile Recycling

Textile-to-textile recycling is a sustainable process that involves recovering and reprocessing textiles to create new textile products. This method aims to minimize waste generation, conserve resources, reduce energy consumption, and mitigate the environmental impact associated with the textile industry.

The process of textile-to-textile recycling begins by collecting discarded textiles, including garments, household textiles, and industrial fabrics. These items are sorted based on their quality and composition, as different types of textiles require different recycling techniques. The sorted textiles are then cleaned to remove any impurities, such as buttons or zippers, and are shredded into small fibers.

The next step involves transforming the shredded fibers into a reusable form. This is typically done through mechanical or chemical processes. In mechanical recycling, the fibers are mixed and carded to create a new textile material that can be spun into yarn and woven or knitted into new fabric. Chemical recycling, on the other hand, breaks down the fibers into their chemical components, which can be used to produce new fibers or textiles.

Once the recycled fibers or textiles are created, they can be used in the production of various textile products, such as clothing, home furnishings, and industrial textiles. By utilizing recycled materials, textile-to-textile recycling reduces the demand for virgin resources, minimizes water and energy consumption, and prevents the accumulation of textile waste in landfills or incineration facilities.

The Climate Group

The Climate Group is an international non-profit organization that works towards advancing sustainability and combating climate change. It brings together influential leaders from business, government, and civil society to drive climate action and accelerate the transition towards a low-carbon economy.

With a vision to create a prosperous, net-zero carbon future, The Climate Group advocates for ambitious climate policies and encourages businesses to adopt sustainable practices. The organization plays a crucial role in helping to shape and implement global frameworks, such as the Paris Agreement, by mobilizing its influential network of members and partners.

The Climate Group operates through various initiatives, such as RE100, EV100, and Under2 Coalition, that focus on different aspects of sustainability. RE100 aims to accelerate the transition to 100% renewable electricity among businesses, while EV100 focuses on the adoption of electric vehicles. The Under2 Coalition brings together regional governments committed to keeping the global temperature rise below 2 degrees Celsius.

By promoting sustainable solutions, fostering collaboration, and facilitating knowledge sharing, The Climate Group drives positive change and supports the global effort to address climate change. Through its initiatives and advocacy work, the organization aims to inspire and empower both businesses and governments to take bold climate action, demonstrating that a sustainable and prosperous future is achievable.

The Conservation Fund

The Conservation Fund is a non-profit organization working towards achieving sustainability by conserving and protecting natural resources and land in the United States.

The organization aims to balance environmental, economic, and community benefits through their conservation efforts. They work with various stakeholders including individuals, businesses, and governments to develop innovative and lasting solutions for natural resource management.

The Earthworm Foundation

The Earthworm Foundation is an organization that focuses on promoting sustainability in various sectors such as agriculture, forestry, and apparel. They work collaboratively with companies, governments, and communities to implement sustainable practices that conserve natural resources, protect ecosystems, and improve livelihoods.

The Earthworm Foundation's approach involves conducting thorough research and data analysis to assess the environmental and social impacts of different industries. By understanding the challenges and opportunities, they develop strategies and solutions to address these issues effectively.

One key aspect of the Earthworm Foundation's work is their commitment to transparency and traceability. They believe in building strong partnerships and engaging in open dialogues with stakeholders to ensure that sustainability goals are met. This includes working closely with suppliers, farmers, and local communities to implement responsible sourcing practices and create positive change throughout the supply chain.

The Earthworm Foundation also plays a vital role in advocating for policy changes and promoting best practices in sustainability. Through their research, they generate evidence-based recommendations and share knowledge with governments and industry leaders to influence decision-making processes.

Overall, the Earthworm Foundation serves as a catalyst for positive change in sustainability by fostering collaboration, supporting innovation, and driving impactful initiatives that benefit both the planet and people.

The Nature Conservancy

The Nature Conservancy is a non-profit organization that works towards the protection and preservation of the environment and natural resources. It focuses on implementing sustainable solutions to address environmental challenges and promote long-term sustainability. One of the main goals of The Nature Conservancy is to conserve biodiversity and protect critical habitats. They work to identify and protect important ecological areas, such as forests, wetlands, and marine ecosystems, which are vital for maintaining the Earth's biodiversity and overall health. Through their conservation efforts, they aim to ensure the survival of numerous species and maintain the balance of ecosystems. Another key aspect of their work is promoting sustainable land and water use. The Nature Conservancy partners with governments, local communities, and other stakeholders to develop and implement sustainable practices that ensure the responsible use of land and water resources. This includes initiatives such as sustainable agriculture, forestry, and fisheries, which help reduce the negative impact on the environment while supporting local livelihoods. In addition, The Nature Conservancy actively engages in climate change mitigation and adaptation. They work to reduce greenhouse gas emissions through various initiatives, such as reforestation and the promotion of renewable energy sources. They also focus on adapting to the impacts of climate change, such as sea-level rise and extreme weather events, by implementing nature-based solutions that help communities and ecosystems become more resilient. Overall, The Nature Conservancy plays a crucial role in advancing sustainability by promoting the wise and responsible use of natural resources, conserving biodiversity, and addressing the challenges posed by climate change. Through their collaborative efforts, they strive towards a more sustainable future for both people and nature.>

The Ocean Cleanup

The Ocean Cleanup is a sustainable initiative that aims to tackle the problem of plastic pollution in our oceans. It was founded by Boyan Slat in 2013 and is committed to developing advanced technologies to remove plastic waste from ocean waters.

Plastic pollution is a significant threat to marine ecosystems and the global environment. It affects more than 600 marine species and leads to the release of harmful toxins into the water. The Ocean Cleanup's main objective is to design and deploy systems that are efficient, scalable, and environmentally friendly in order to address this issue.

The initiative primarily focuses on the Great Pacific Garbage Patch, a massive accumulation of plastic waste located between California and Hawaii. They have developed a system known as "System 001" or "Wilson," which consists of floating barriers that harness the natural oceanic currents to gather and concentrate plastic debris. The collected waste is then extracted and transported to land for proper disposal and recycling.

The Ocean Cleanup's approach to sustainability involves utilizing the natural forces of the ocean to clean up the pollution caused by human activities. By implementing advanced technologies and innovative solutions, they aim to reduce the impact of plastic waste on marine ecosystems and promote a more sustainable future for our oceans.

The Sierra Club

The Sierra Club is a prominent environmental organization that focuses on advancing sustainability and protecting natural resources. Founded in 1892, the Sierra Club has become one of the largest and most influential grassroots environmental organizations in the United States.

The Sierra Club's mission is to promote the responsible use and protection of the Earth's ecosystems and resources, with a particular emphasis on addressing climate change, conserving clean air and water, and preserving wildlife habitats. The organization strives to build a sustainable future by advocating for policies and practices that prioritize renewable energy, conservation, and environmental justice.

The Sustainability Consortium

The Sustainability Consortium (TSC) is an organization focused on driving sustainability in consumer goods supply chains. It was established in 2009 as a global non-profit organization, with the aim of creating tools and solutions to improve the environmental and social performance of products and supply chains.

TSC works collaboratively with companies, academics, nonprofits, and government organizations to develop science-based tools and metrics that enable businesses to measure, manage, and improve their sustainability performance. By providing a common framework and language for sustainability, TSC helps companies drive transparency, accountability, and positive change throughout their supply chains.

One of the key initiatives of TSC is the development of the Sustainability Measurement and Reporting System (SMRS). This tool enables companies to collect and report consistent and comparable data on the environmental and social impacts of their products. SMRS covers a wide range of areas including greenhouse gas emissions, water use, waste management, labor practices, and community engagement.

Through the use of SMRS, companies can identify areas of improvement, set targets, and track progress over time. By measuring and reporting their sustainability performance, companies can gain insights into their environmental and social risks and opportunities, and work towards more sustainable practices.

Union Of Concerned Scientists

The Union of Concerned Scientists (UCS) is a non-profit organization that strives for a sustainable future by promoting scientifically-based solutions to environmental and social challenges. Founded in 1969, the UCS brings together experts in various fields, including science, economics, and policy, to identify and address the greatest threats to global sustainability.

The UCS focuses on a range of issues related to sustainability, such as climate change, clean energy, and sustainable agriculture. Through research, advocacy, and outreach, the organization aims to inform and empower individuals, communities, and policymakers to make evidence-based decisions that protect the planet and promote social equity.

United Nations Environment Programme (UNEP)

The United Nations Environment Programme (UNEP) is an international organization dedicated to promoting environmental sustainability and coordinating global efforts to address environmental challenges.

UNEP carries out its mandate by providing leadership and guidance on environmental issues, promoting environmental awareness, advocating for sustainable development, and mobilizing resources to implement effective environmental policies and programs. The organization works with governments, non-governmental organizations, and other stakeholders to develop and implement sustainable practices and policies in various sectors, including climate change, biodiversity, sustainable energy, and waste management. UNEP also supports countries in implementing international environmental agreements, such as the Paris Agreement on climate change and the Convention on Biological Diversity.

Upcycled Fashion Brands

An upcycled fashion brand is a clothing company that specializes in creating new garments or accessories from old or used materials. Unlike recycling, which breaks down materials into their original components to create new products, upcycling involves taking discarded or unwanted items and transforming them into something of higher value and quality.

With a strong focus on sustainability, upcycled fashion brands help reduce waste by repurposing materials that would otherwise end up in landfills. They breathe new life into discarded fabrics, garments, and accessories by incorporating creative design techniques and craftsmanship.

Upcycled fashion brands often source their materials from a variety of sources, including vintage clothing, second-hand stores, textile waste from factories, and even household items such as curtains or bedsheets. Through careful selection, sorting, and cleaning, these materials are transformed into unique and one-of-a-kind fashion pieces.

By upcycling materials, these brands minimize the environmental impact associated with the production of new materials, such as water and energy consumption, greenhouse gas emissions, and chemical usage. In addition, upcycled fashion brands typically prioritize ethical manufacturing practices, ensuring fair wages and safe working conditions for their workers.

Overall, upcycled fashion brands play a vital role in promoting sustainability within the fashion industry. They offer an alternative to fast fashion by creating garments that are not only eco-friendly but also possess a sense of individuality and character. By choosing to support upcycled fashion brands, consumers can actively participate in reducing waste and making more conscious shopping choices.

Upcycled Home Decor

Upcycled home decor refers to the process of transforming or repurposing materials or products that would otherwise be discarded as waste, into new and valuable items for decorating a home. This practice promotes sustainability by reducing the amount of waste that goes into landfills and minimizing the consumption of new resources.

Unlike recycling, which involves breaking down materials to create new ones, upcycling focuses on reusing and enhancing the existing form and structure of materials. It embraces the concept of "waste not, want not" by finding creative ways to give new life to old or unused objects. This can include anything from furniture made from reclaimed wood or repurposed pallets, to decorative items crafted from upcycled glass bottles or tin cans.

By choosing upcycled home decor, individuals contribute to the preservation of the environment in multiple ways. Firstly, upcycling reduces the demand for new raw materials, including timber and metals, which require energy-intensive extraction processes and contribute to deforestation and pollution. It also minimizes the energy consumption and carbon emissions associated with the manufacturing and transportation of new products.

Additionally, upcycling helps to decrease the amount of waste that ends up in landfills, reducing the release of harmful greenhouse gases and leachate into the environment. This is particularly important given the growing concern over the limited availability of landfill space and the negative impacts of waste disposal on ecosystems and human health.

Upcycling Innovations

Upcycling innovations refers to the practice of transforming waste materials or unwanted products into new and higher-value items, thereby reducing waste and promoting sustainability. Unlike recycling, which typically involves breaking down materials to create new products, upcycling involves repurposing existing materials in creative and innovative ways.

The concept of upcycling is rooted in the principles of the circular economy, which seeks to minimize resource consumption, waste generation, and environmental impact. By upcycling, materials that would have otherwise been discarded or sent to landfill can be given a second life, extending their lifespan and reducing the need for new production processes and virgin resources.

The practice of upcycling can take many forms, including repurposing old clothing to create unique fashion pieces, turning discarded pallets into furniture, or transforming glass bottles into decorative objects. Upcycling encourages individuals and businesses to think creatively and find new uses for items that are no longer in their original form or function.

One of the key benefits of upcycling is that it reduces the demand for new raw materials and the energy required to extract, refine, and process them. This, in turn, helps to conserve natural resources, reduce greenhouse gas emissions, and mitigate the environmental impacts associated with resource extraction, including deforestation, water pollution, and habitat destruction.

In addition to its environmental benefits, upcycling also offers economic and social advantages.

It can create new business opportunities and jobs, particularly in the creative and artisanal sectors. Moreover, upcycled products often have unique qualities, adding value to consumers and attracting those who appreciate personalized, one-of-a-kind items that stand out from mass-produced goods.

Upcycling Of Waste Materials

Upcycling is a sustainable approach to waste management that involves transforming discarded materials into new products of higher quality or value. It is a form of creative reuse that aims to reduce waste, conserve resources, and minimize environmental impact.

Unlike recycling, which involves breaking down materials into their raw form to create new products, upcycling focuses on repurposing waste materials without significantly altering their basic structure. This process encourages innovation and promotes the development of alternative solutions to conventional manufacturing and consumerism.

Through upcycling, items that would otherwise end up in landfills or incinerators can be given a new lease on life. These materials are often reimagined and transformed into unique and functional pieces, such as furniture, accessories, or works of art. Upcycling not only extends the lifespan of discarded items but also reduces the need for extracting new resources, conserves energy, and minimizes the emission of greenhouse gases associated with traditional manufacturing processes.

Upcycling also fosters a shift in mindset, encouraging individuals and businesses to rethink the value and potential of discarded materials. It promotes creativity, resourcefulness, and a more sustainable approach to consumption. By upcycling waste materials, we can contribute to a circular economy, where resources are continuously reused and waste is minimized.

Urban Agriculture Planning

Urban agriculture planning refers to the deliberate and systematic approach of integrating agricultural practices into the urban landscape, with the aim of promoting sustainability and improving the quality of life for urban dwellers. It entails the strategic allocation of available urban spaces for food production, such as community gardens, rooftop gardens, and vertical farming, among others.

The concept of urban agriculture planning embodies the principles of sustainability, as it seeks to address various challenges faced by urban areas, including food insecurity, environmental degradation, and health issues. By incorporating agricultural practices within urban areas, cities can reduce their dependence on external food sources, minimize the carbon footprint associated with long-distance transportation of food, and create a resilient and self-sustaining food system.

Furthermore, urban agriculture planning contributes to the social and economic well-being of urban communities. It provides opportunities for local residents to actively participate in food production, fostering community engagement, and empowerment. Access to fresh, locally grown produce improves food security and nutrition, promoting healthier lifestyles and reducing the prevalence of diet-related diseases.

In conclusion, urban agriculture planning offers a multifaceted approach to addressing the challenges of urbanization and advancing sustainability. By integrating agricultural practices into the urban fabric, cities can achieve a more sustainable, resilient, and equitable food system, while enhancing community welfare and preserving the environment.

Urban Biodiversity Conservation

Urban biodiversity conservation refers to the preservation and management of biological diversity within urban areas, with the aim of promoting sustainable development and creating healthier, more resilient cities.

As urbanization continues to accelerate globally, it is crucial to address the impact of human activities on the natural environment and to recognize the value of biodiversity in urban settings. Urban biodiversity encompasses the variety of plants, animals, and microorganisms, as well as the ecological processes they support, that exist within cities.

Conserving urban biodiversity involves various strategies and actions. These include protecting and restoring natural habitats such as green spaces, parks, wetlands, and urban forests, as well as creating artificial habitats such as green roofs and faunal bridges. It also involves promoting the use of native plant species, enhancing urban connectivity for wildlife movement, and implementing sustainable land-use planning and design.

Urban biodiversity conservation is essential for sustaining ecosystems, improving air and water quality, mitigating climate change, and enhancing overall urban resilience. Biodiversity in cities plays a vital role in providing ecological services, such as pollination, pest control, and water purification, which are beneficial for human well-being and the functioning of urban ecosystems.

Incorporating biodiversity conservation into urban planning and development requires collaboration between various stakeholders including government authorities, urban planners, developers, and local communities. It requires the integration of ecological considerations into urban policies, regulations, and practices, as well as raising awareness and engaging citizens in conservation efforts.

By prioritizing urban biodiversity conservation, cities can foster a more sustainable and livable environment for both humans and wildlife, promoting harmony between urban areas and the natural world.

Urban Farming Technology

Urban farming technology refers to the implementation of various innovative techniques, tools, and systems to cultivate plants and produce food in urban areas. This sustainable practice aims to address the growing demand for fresh and locally sourced food, while also mitigating the environmental impact of traditional agriculture.

Urban farming technology encompasses a range of practices, including vertical farming, rooftop gardening, hydroponics, and aquaponics. Vertical farming involves cultivating crops in vertically stacked layers or towers, using artificial lighting and a controlled environment. Rooftop gardening utilizes rooftop spaces to grow plants and vegetables, making efficient use of available land in urban areas. Hydroponics is a soil-less cultivation method that uses nutrient-rich water solutions to grow plants, reducing water usage and allowing for year-round production. Aquaponics combines aquaculture (raising fish) and hydroponics, creating a symbiotic system where fish waste provides nutrients for plants.

By utilizing urban farming technology, communities can reduce their reliance on long-distance food transportation, which contributes to greenhouse gas emissions. Furthermore, these techniques often require less land and water compared to traditional agriculture, making urban farming a more sustainable solution for food production. Urban farming technology also promotes the use of organic fertilizers and natural pest control methods, reducing the need for synthetic chemicals and minimizing environmental pollution.

Urban Green Infrastructure

Urban green infrastructure refers to the interconnected network of natural and semi-natural elements, such as parks, gardens, trees, green roofs, wetlands, and green walls, within an urban environment. It encompasses both the physical elements, such as vegetation and water bodies, and the ecological processes and functions they provide.

The main purpose of urban green infrastructure is to enhance the sustainability and resilience of urban areas, addressing various environmental, social, and economic challenges. From an environmental perspective, it helps to mitigate climate change by sequestering carbon dioxide, reducing the urban heat island effect, and managing stormwater runoff. It also promotes biodiversity by providing habitat for various plant and animal species.

Socially, urban green infrastructure contributes to the well-being and quality of life of city dwellers by providing spaces for recreation, relaxation, and physical exercise. It improves air quality by filtering pollutants and noise reduction through the absorption of sound. Moreover, it

384

has been proven to have positive impacts on mental health, reducing stress levels and improving cognitive function.

Economically, urban green infrastructure can increase property values, attract investment, and promote tourism. It also offers cost-effective solutions for managing stormwater and reducing the need for energy consumption by providing shade and reducing heat stress.

Overall, urban green infrastructure plays a crucial role in creating more sustainable and livable cities. By integrating nature into the urban fabric, it helps to create healthier and more resilient communities, enhancing the well-being of both humans and the environment.

Urban Greening Projects

Urban greening projects refer to initiatives and actions taken to enhance the presence and quality of green spaces in urban areas, with the aim of promoting sustainability and improving the overall well-being of city dwellers.

These projects typically involve the development and maintenance of parks, gardens, and other natural areas within urban environments. They focus on increasing the amount of vegetation, creating habitats for wildlife, and enhancing the aesthetic appeal of cities. Urban greening projects also encompass measures such as tree planting, green roofs, and vertical gardens, which help to improve air quality, mitigate the heat island effect, and reduce energy consumption.

Urban Reforestation Design

Urban reforestation design refers to the intentional planning and implementation of green spaces within urban areas with the aim of restoring and enhancing the natural environment. It involves the strategic planting of trees, shrubs, and other vegetation to create a more sustainable and resilient urban ecosystem.

The primary goal of urban reforestation design is to mitigate the negative impacts of urbanization on the environment, society, and economy. By incorporating green spaces into urban landscapes, cities can counteract the heat island effect, reduce air and water pollution, conserve energy, and improve the overall quality of life for residents.

This sustainable approach to urban planning recognizes the importance of preserving and restoring natural systems within built environments. It emphasizes the use of native and drought-tolerant plant species, as well as the incorporation of green infrastructure features such as rain gardens and bioswales to manage stormwater runoff and promote water conservation.

Urban reforestation design also plays a crucial role in biodiversity conservation by providing habitat for wildlife and supporting ecological processes. Green spaces can act as corridors for wildlife movement, enabling the dispersal of plants and animals across fragmented urban landscapes.

In conclusion, urban reforestation design is an essential strategy for promoting sustainability in cities. By integrating nature into urban environments, it helps create healthier, more livable communities and contributes to the overall well-being of both humans and the natural world.

Urban Reforestation Initiatives

Urban reforestation initiatives refer to planned efforts aimed at increasing the green cover in urban areas through the planting and maintenance of trees and other vegetation. These initiatives are implemented in order to improve the environmental, social, and economic sustainability of cities.

The primary objective of urban reforestation initiatives is to address the negative impacts of urbanization, including air and water pollution, heat island effect, and loss of biodiversity. By strategically planting trees and other vegetation, these initiatives promote numerous benefits for both humans and the environment.

From an environmental standpoint, urban reforestation initiatives help mitigate the effects of climate change by reducing carbon dioxide levels through the process of photosynthesis. Trees act as carbon sinks, absorbing carbon dioxide and releasing oxygen. Furthermore, they help reduce air pollution by capturing particulate matter and harmful gases, such as nitrogen dioxide and sulfur dioxide.

On a social level, urban reforestation initiatives enhance the quality of life for urban dwellers. Trees provide shade, reducing the urban heat island effect and improving thermal comfort. They also contribute to mental health and well-being by creating aesthetically pleasing green spaces for relaxation and recreation.

Finally, urban reforestation initiatives offer economic benefits by increasing property values and attracting businesses and tourists. The presence of well-maintained green spaces contributes to a city's image and attractiveness, bolstering the local economy.

Overall, urban reforestation initiatives play a crucial role in creating sustainable and resilient cities. Through the careful planning and implementation of these initiatives, urban areas can become greener, healthier, and more livable environments for current and future generations.

Urban Resilience Planning

Urban resilience planning refers to the process of developing and implementing strategies to enhance the capacity of cities and urban areas to adapt, respond, and recover from various social, economic, and environmental shocks and stresses. It encompasses a range of approaches and measures that aim to build more resilient and sustainable communities in the face of challenges such as climate change, natural disasters, population growth, and resource scarcity.

This planning process involves the identification and analysis of vulnerabilities and risks faced by urban areas, as well as the assessment of their adaptive capacity and preparedness to cope with these challenges. It requires the collaboration and engagement of multiple stakeholders, including government authorities, urban planners, community organizations, businesses, and residents.

The goal of urban resilience planning is to foster sustainable development and ensure that cities and urban areas are equipped to withstand and recover from shocks and stresses, while also addressing underlying social, economic, and environmental issues. It involves integrating resilience considerations into urban policies, infrastructure development, land-use planning, and resource management.

Urban resilience planning encompasses a wide range of strategies and actions, such as enhancing the resilience of critical infrastructure, promoting sustainable and inclusive urban development, improving disaster preparedness and response capabilities, fostering social cohesion and community engagement, and adopting nature-based solutions for climate change adaptation.

In conclusion, urban resilience planning is an essential component of sustainable development, as it seeks to create cities and urban areas that are better equipped to face future challenges and ensure the well-being and resilience of their communities.

Urban Rooftop Garden Planning

An urban rooftop garden is a sustainable practice of transforming the otherwise underutilized space on rooftops of buildings into green gardens. It involves the design, construction, and maintenance of plantings, including trees, shrubs, flowers, and vegetables, on the roof of a building.

This practice is a result of the increasing concern for environmental sustainability in urban areas, where green spaces are often limited. Urban rooftop gardens contribute to the overall sustainability of cities in several ways.

Firstly, they provide numerous environmental benefits. The vegetation on rooftops helps to reduce the urban heat island effect by absorbing and deflecting sunlight, which in turn decreases energy consumption for cooling buildings. Moreover, rooftop gardens act as natural insulators, reducing the need for heating during winter months. The plants also capture and filter rainwater, reducing stormwater runoff and alleviating pressure on urban drainage systems.

Secondly, rooftop gardens enhance biodiversity in urban environments. They provide habitat for plants, insects, birds, and other wildlife, particularly in areas where green spaces are limited or fragmented. This biodiversity contributes to the overall ecological health of the city and promotes a sense of connection with nature for urban dwellers.

Additionally, urban rooftop gardens can improve air quality by absorbing carbon dioxide and releasing oxygen through photosynthesis, mitigating the negative impacts of air pollution. The vegetation also helps to reduce noise pollution by absorbing and reflecting sound waves, creating a more peaceful and pleasant environment for nearby residents.

In conclusion, urban rooftop gardens are a sustainable solution that maximizes unused space in cities and offers a range of environmental benefits. By promoting biodiversity, reducing the urban heat island effect, improving air and water quality, and creating a greener landscape, rooftop gardens contribute to the overall sustainability and livability of urban areas.

Urban Rooftop Gardens

Urban rooftop gardens are environmentally-friendly and sustainable spaces created on the rooftops of buildings, typically in urban areas. These gardens serve as green spaces, providing a range of benefits to the environment, local communities, and building occupants.

Rooftop gardens contribute to sustainability by mitigating the heat island effect in cities, reducing energy consumption, and improving air quality. The plants and vegetation on rooftops help absorb solar radiation, lowering the temperature of the building and its surrounds. By reducing the heat island effect, rooftop gardens help conserve energy by minimizing the need for air conditioning during hot periods.

In addition to temperature regulation, rooftop gardens also sequester carbon dioxide, helping to combat climate change. The vegetation acts as a carbon sink, absorbing greenhouse gases and reducing the overall carbon footprint of the building and the city.

Beyond their environmental benefits, these gardens improve the overall livability of urban areas. They provide opportunities for residents and communities to engage with nature, fostering a sense of well-being and mental rejuvenation. Furthermore, rooftop gardens can support biodiversity by providing habitats for native plants and animals that may be displaced by urban development.

Overall, urban rooftop gardens offer an innovative approach to sustainable urban development. By utilizing underutilized rooftop spaces, they provide multiple environmental, social, and economic benefits. Through improving energy efficiency, enhancing biodiversity, and promoting well-being, rooftop gardens contribute to creating more sustainable and resilient cities.

Urban Stormwater Management

Urban stormwater management refers to the implementation of strategies and practices aimed at effectively and sustainably managing stormwater runoff in urban areas. Stormwater runoff is water from rainfall or snowmelt that does not infiltrate into the ground, but instead flows over land surfaces and is directed into stormwater drainage systems.

The management of urban stormwater is crucial for environmental sustainability as it helps to mitigate the negative impacts of stormwater runoff, such as flooding, erosion, and water pollution. Sustainable stormwater management practices focus on reducing the volume and velocity of stormwater runoff, promoting natural infiltration, and treating runoff to remove pollutants.

Key components of sustainable urban stormwater management include the use of green infrastructure, such as rain gardens and bioswales, which help to capture and absorb stormwater, allowing it to infiltrate into the ground and recharge aquifers. This approach mimics natural hydrological processes and helps to replenish groundwater supplies.

In addition, stormwater management strategies may include the use of detention and retention ponds to temporarily store stormwater and control its release, as well as the incorporation of permeable pavement in urban surfaces to promote infiltration. These practices help to recharge groundwater, reduce peak flows, and minimize the transport of pollutants into water bodies.

Overall, sustainable urban stormwater management aims to balance the needs of urban development with the protection and preservation of natural hydrological systems. By implementing effective stormwater management strategies, cities can reduce flooding risks, improve water quality, and enhance the overall environmental sustainability of urban areas.

Urban Sustainable Mobility

Urban sustainable mobility refers to the efficient and environmentally friendly movement of people and goods within urban areas, with a focus on reducing the negative impact on the environment and improving the overall quality of life for urban residents.

It involves the implementation of policies, strategies, and infrastructure that promote the use of sustainable modes of transportation such as walking, cycling, public transportation, and electric vehicles, while minimizing the reliance on private cars and reducing greenhouse gas emissions.

Urban sustainable mobility aims to create a transportation system that is accessible, affordable, safe, and reliable for all urban dwellers, regardless of their socioeconomic status or physical abilities. It seeks to reduce congestion, noise pollution, and air pollution, thereby improving the health and well-being of urban residents.

The development of sustainable transport options in urban areas also contributes to the sustainable development goals, as it enhances social inclusion, economic growth, and environmental sustainability. It promotes more compact and connected urban development, encourages the use of renewable energy sources, and supports the transition towards a low-carbon economy.

Urban sustainable mobility requires the collaboration and coordination of various stakeholders, including governments, transport planners, urban designers, businesses, and citizens. It calls for the implementation of integrated and innovative solutions that prioritize people over cars and prioritize the long-term sustainability of cities.

In summary, urban sustainable mobility is a holistic approach to transportation planning and management that prioritizes the needs of people, minimizes environmental impacts, and contributes to the overall sustainability of urban areas.

Urban Tree Canopy Design

Urban tree canopy design refers to the intentional planning, implementation, and management of trees within urban environments to enhance sustainability.

The concept of urban tree canopy design recognizes the crucial role that trees play in urban ecosystems and their contribution to environmental, social, and economic sustainability. It involves a proactive approach to strategically selecting, planting, and maintaining trees in urban areas to maximize their benefits and minimize potential adverse effects.

By carefully considering factors such as species selection, placement, and maintenance practices, urban tree canopy design aims to create functional and resilient tree cover in cities. This includes promoting biodiversity by diversifying the species composition of urban forests, enhancing air quality through the capture and filtration of pollutants, mitigating the urban heat island effect through shading and evapotranspiration, conserving energy by providing natural cooling and reducing the need for air conditioning, managing stormwater runoff through interception and infiltration, and creating aesthetically pleasing landscapes that improve overall well-being and quality of life.

Furthermore, urban tree canopy design is an essential component of sustainable urban planning and development strategies. It facilitates the integration of trees into urban infrastructure, such as streetscapes, parks, and green spaces, to enhance urban resilience, promote social cohesion, and mitigate the impacts of climate change.

Urban Tree Planting Programs

An urban tree planting program is a sustainability initiative aimed at promoting the growth and maintenance of trees in urban areas. It involves the deliberate planting of trees in urban spaces such as parks, streets, and public areas, with the goal of improving the overall quality of life for city residents.

Urban tree planting programs play a crucial role in promoting sustainability by addressing several environmental and social challenges faced by urban areas. The strategic placement of trees helps to mitigate the effects of climate change by reducing the urban heat island effect and improving air quality through carbon dioxide absorption and oxygen production. Trees also act as natural filters, reducing noise pollution and providing shade, thereby contributing to energy conservation by reducing the need for air conditioning.

Furthermore, these programs contribute to the overall well-being of urban communities by creating green spaces for recreational activities and enhancing the aesthetics of the cityscape. The presence of trees has been linked to increased physical and mental health benefits, as well as improved social cohesion among residents.

Successful urban tree planting programs rely on collaboration between various stakeholders, including government bodies, non-profit organizations, and community members. These initiatives typically involve careful planning, species selection, and ongoing maintenance to ensure the long-term survival and effectiveness of the planted trees.

In conclusion, urban tree planting programs are integral to sustainable urban development. By prioritizing the growth and preservation of urban trees, these initiatives contribute to environmental resilience, public health, and the overall livability of cities.

Urban Waste Recycling

Urban waste recycling is a sustainable practice that aims to divert waste materials generated in urban areas away from disposal in landfills and towards their potential reuse or recovery. It involves the collection, sorting, processing, and transformation of waste materials into new products or energy sources.

The primary goal of urban waste recycling is to minimize the negative environmental impacts associated with waste disposal while conserving natural resources and reducing energy consumption. By recycling, valuable materials such as paper, plastics, glass, and metals can be extracted and reintegrated into the manufacturing process, reducing the need for virgin resources extraction. This contributes to the preservation of finite resources, such as trees, oil, and ores.

Additionally, urban waste recycling can help mitigate pollution and greenhouse gas emissions. When waste decomposes in landfills, it releases methane, a potent greenhouse gas. By diverting waste from landfills and recycling it, greenhouse gas emissions can be significantly reduced. Furthermore, recycling conserves energy as it often requires less energy to produce goods from recycled materials compared to virgin resources.

Moreover, urban waste recycling promotes sustainable waste management practices, including waste reduction and reuse. By reducing the amount of waste generated in urban areas and encouraging the reuse of products, the overall impact on the environment and the need for raw materials can be minimized. Additionally, recycling creates employment opportunities in the recycling industry, contributing to the local economy and social well-being.

In summary, urban waste recycling plays a vital role in achieving sustainability by minimizing waste generation, conserving resources, reducing pollution and energy consumption, and promoting a circular economy. It is an essential practice for managing urban waste in an environmentally and socially responsible manner.

Urban Waste Reduction Initiatives

Urban waste reduction initiatives are sustainable actions implemented in urban areas to minimize the generation of waste and promote recycling, reuse, and proper disposal practices. These initiatives aim to address the environmental, social, and economic impacts of waste generation and manage waste in a more sustainable and responsible manner.

Urban areas face significant challenges in waste management due to the high population density and consumption rates, leading to increased waste generation and associated environmental issues. Urban waste reduction initiatives focus on various aspects of waste management, including waste prevention, waste separation, recycling, and promoting a circular economy.

Waste prevention strategies aim to minimize the generation of waste by encouraging behavior change, such as reducing packaging, promoting reusable products, and implementing effective waste management systems. Waste separation initiatives involve educating and encouraging residents to separate different types of waste at source for efficient recycling and better resource recovery.

Recycling initiatives are crucial in urban waste reduction, as they divert recyclable materials from landfills and promote their transformation into new products. These initiatives involve implementing recycling programs, establishing collection systems, and promoting awareness and education on recycling practices.

Promoting a circular economy is an essential aspect of urban waste reduction initiatives. It involves creating a system where waste is seen as a valuable resource, and materials are continuously used, recycled, and reprocessed instead of being discarded. This approach reduces the need for extracting virgin resources and reduces environmental impacts associated with resource extraction and waste disposal.

Urban Waste Reduction Programs

Urban waste reduction programs refer to initiatives and strategies implemented in urban areas to minimize the amount of waste generated, promote recycling and composting, and stimulate sustainable waste management practices. These programs aim to address the significant environmental, social, and economic challenges associated with increasing waste generation and limited landfill space in cities.

Urban waste reduction programs typically involve various components, including public awareness campaigns, waste segregation and recycling schemes, waste-to-energy projects, and policies promoting the use of sustainable materials and packaging. These programs often engage multiple stakeholders, including local governments, community groups, waste management companies, and residents, to collectively work towards achieving waste reduction goals.

The primary objectives of urban waste reduction programs are to minimize the environmental impacts of waste disposal, conserve resources, and reduce greenhouse gas emissions associated with waste management. By diverting waste from landfills and promoting recycling, these programs help conserve raw materials, reduce energy consumption, and minimize pollution caused by waste decomposition. They also contribute to the circular economy by promoting the reuse and recycling of materials, thereby reducing the reliance on virgin resources.

Furthermore, urban waste reduction programs often have positive social and economic benefits. By promoting waste segregation and recycling, they create employment opportunities in the recycling industry and contribute to the local economy. These programs also foster a sense of community engagement and responsibility towards waste management practices, leading to improved neighborhood aesthetics and quality of life. Additionally, the reduction of waste disposal costs can free up financial resources for other urban development projects.

Urban Waste-To-Energy Solutions

Urban waste-to-energy solutions refer to the various methods and technologies that are utilized to convert urban waste, such as municipal solid waste, into usable energy while prioritizing environmental sustainability.

These solutions aim to address the challenge of managing and disposing of the ever-increasing amounts of waste generated by urban areas, while also seeking to reduce greenhouse gas emissions and promote a circular economy. By converting waste into energy, these systems help to reduce the dependency on fossil fuels and contribute to the transition towards renewable energy sources.

One common method of waste-to-energy conversion is through the process of incineration, where waste is burned at high temperatures to produce heat and electricity. Advanced technologies and strict emission control measures ensure that the combustion process is environmentally sound and minimize the release of harmful pollutants into the atmosphere.

Another approach to urban waste-to-energy solutions is through anaerobic digestion, a biological process where organic waste is broken down by microorganisms to produce biogas, which can be used as a renewable energy source. This method not only generates energy but also helps to divert organic waste from landfills, thereby reducing methane emissions, which is a potent greenhouse gas.

In addition to energy generation, waste-to-energy solutions often incorporate other sustainable practices, such as material recovery and recycling, to maximize resource efficiency and minimize environmental impact. These systems can play a vital role in achieving sustainable waste management goals, reducing landfill usage, and promoting the transition to a more circular economy.

Urban Water Conservation

Urban water conservation refers to the sustainable management and responsible use of water resources in urban areas to ensure long-term availability and environmental balance. It involves various strategies and measures to reduce water consumption, promote efficient water use, and minimize wastage in urban settings.

The goal of urban water conservation is to mitigate water scarcity, preserve natural ecosystems, and support the overall sustainability of cities and towns. By implementing effective water management practices, such as efficient irrigation systems, water-efficient appliances and fixtures, and water reuse and recycling programs, urban areas can reduce their reliance on freshwater sources and alleviate strain on water supplies.

Furthermore, urban water conservation encompasses public awareness campaigns and educational initiatives to promote water-saving behaviors among residents, businesses, and institutions. These efforts aim to foster a culture of water conservation, where individuals understand the value of water resources and actively contribute to their preservation.

In line with sustainable development principles, urban water conservation also considers the social, economic, and environmental aspects of water management. It seeks to find a balance between meeting the water needs of urban populations while minimizing negative impacts on ecosystems, ensuring equitable access to water, and fostering economic growth.

Overall, urban water conservation plays a crucial role in securing a sustainable future for cities by managing water resources efficiently, reducing water waste, and promoting responsible water use.

Urban Water Purification

Urban water purification is a sustainable process that involves treating and purifying water to make it safe for consumption and use in urban areas. It is an essential aspect of water management in cities, as it ensures the provision of clean and safe water to meet the growing needs of the urban population while minimizing the negative impact on the environment.

The process of urban water purification typically involves several stages, including coagulation, sedimentation, filtration, disinfection, and sometimes advanced treatment technologies. Coagulation is the initial step where chemicals are added to the water to help particles clump together and form larger, easier-to-remove particles. Sedimentation follows, allowing the particles to settle at the bottom of a tank. Filtration comes next, where the water passes through different layers of materials like sand, gravel, or activated carbon to remove any remaining impurities.

Following filtration, disinfection takes place to kill or neutralize any pathogens present in the water. Common disinfection methods include the use of chlorine, ozone, or UV light. In some cases, advanced treatment technologies like reverse osmosis or activated carbon may be employed to remove additional contaminants or improve the taste and odor of the water.

By implementing urban water purification systems, cities can ensure a sustainable supply of clean and safe water for their residents. This not only protects public health but also helps reduce the strain on natural water sources, such as rivers and lakes, by minimizing the need for excessive extraction. Moreover, by treating and reusing wastewater, urban water purification can contribute to water conservation efforts and promote a circular economy approach to water management.

Urban Waterway Revitalization

Urban waterway revitalization refers to the process of restoring and enhancing the environmental, social, and economic functions of a waterway in an urban setting, with a focus on promoting sustainability. It involves implementing various measures and strategies to improve water quality, increase biodiversity, and create recreational and cultural opportunities.

One of the key goals of urban waterway revitalization is to improve the overall health and resilience of the waterway ecosystem. This may include reducing pollution from stormwater runoff, restoring natural habitats, and enhancing water flow and circulation. By improving water quality and increasing biodiversity, urban waterway revitalization contributes to the overall sustainability of the urban environment.

Urban Wildlife Habitat Design

Urban wildlife habitat design refers to the intentional creation or modification of urban spaces in a sustainable manner to support and enhance biodiversity and ecological functions. It involves designing and managing urban landscapes to provide suitable and diverse habitats for a range of wildlife species, including plants, animals, and insects.

The goal of urban wildlife habitat design is to create harmony between human activities and the natural environment, fostering connectivity between urban areas and surrounding natural ecosystems. By incorporating elements such as native vegetation, water features, and sheltering structures, urban habitats can be transformed into thriving ecosystems that support the survival and reproduction of local flora and fauna.

This design approach considers the principles of sustainability, ensuring that habitat modifications are ecologically sound, socially responsible, and economically viable. It takes into account the unique challenges and opportunities of urban environments, such as limited space, fragmented habitats, and potential conflicts with human populations. The use of sustainable materials, efficient resource management, and minimization of pollutants are crucial aspects of urban wildlife habitat design to mitigate negative impacts on the environment.

Through urban wildlife habitat design, cities can play a vital role in conservation efforts by providing refuge and resources for native species, promoting genetic diversity, and contributing to the overall health and resilience of ecosystems. Additionally, these habitats offer numerous benefits to humans, such as improved air and water quality, increased recreational opportunities, and enhanced overall well-being.

Urban Wildlife Habitat Planning

Urban wildlife habitat planning is a sustainable approach that aims to create and maintain suitable environments for wildlife within urban areas. It involves the identification, design, and implementation of strategies to support and enhance biodiversity in cities.

This planning process acknowledges the importance of preserving and restoring ecological balance in urban landscapes, recognizing that urban areas can provide valuable habitats for diverse wildlife species. By incorporating green spaces, such as parks, gardens, and green roofs, into the urban fabric, wildlife habitat planning seeks to create interconnected networks of habitats that facilitate the movement and survival of wildlife.

Key elements of urban wildlife habitat planning include the protection of existing natural areas, the creation of new habitats, the selection of appropriate native plant species, and the implementation of wildlife-friendly practices in urban development. This planning approach also promotes the conservation of natural resources, such as water and energy, by integrating sustainable design features that benefit both wildlife and human residents.

Furthermore, urban wildlife habitat planning addresses the potential conflicts between humans and wildlife by considering ways to minimize negative interactions and maximize coexistence. It may involve the development of educational programs to raise awareness about the importance of urban wildlife and the implementation of measures to mitigate human-wildlife conflicts.

In summary, urban wildlife habitat planning is a sustainable strategy that aims to create and maintain biodiverse habitats within urban areas. It seeks to strike a balance between urban development and the preservation of wildlife, ultimately contributing to the overall sustainability and resilience of cities.

Vertical Farming Automation

Vertical farming automation refers to the use of technology and machinery to automate and control various processes in vertical farming systems. Vertical farming is a sustainable agricultural practice that involves growing crops in vertically stacked layers or on vertically inclined surfaces, using artificial lighting and climate control systems.

The automation of vertical farming operations is driven by the goal of maximizing efficiency, productivity, and sustainability while minimizing resource consumption and negative environmental impacts. It involves the integration of sensors, robotics, artificial intelligence, and data analytics to monitor and optimize various aspects of plant growth, such as temperature, humidity, nutrient levels, and light intensity.

By automating tasks such as seeding, transplanting, watering, fertilizing, and harvesting, vertical farming systems can operate more efficiently and with reduced labor requirements. Automation also enables precise control over environmental conditions, resulting in consistent crop quality and yields throughout the year.

Furthermore, vertical farming automation enables the use of resource-efficient techniques, such as hydroponics or aeroponics, which require less water and space compared to traditional field farming. It also reduces reliance on synthetic pesticides and fertilizers by enabling integrated pest management and nutrient recycling systems.

Overall, vertical farming automation plays a crucial role in achieving sustainable and resilient food production systems. It offers the potential to produce fresh and nutritious crops locally, reduce food transportation distances, minimize water usage, decrease reliance on chemical inputs, and mitigate the effects of climate change on traditional agriculture.

Vertical Farming System Designs

Vertical farming system designs refer to innovative and sustainable methods of cultivating crops indoors, in multi-level structures, with minimal use of land and resources. This farming practice aims to address the challenges posed by traditional agriculture, such as limited arable land, water scarcity, and environmental degradation, while ensuring a reliable and efficient food production system.

These designs typically feature several key elements that contribute to their sustainability. One crucial aspect is the use of vertical space, where crops are grown in stacked layers or vertically inclined structures. This vertical layout maximizes land efficiency, allowing for higher crop yields in a smaller footprint. Additionally, the controlled indoor environment provides optimal conditions for plant growth, including precise control over temperature, humidity, light intensity, and nutrient distribution.

Another significant feature of vertical farming system designs is their integration of advanced technologies, such as hydroponics or aeroponics. These soil-less cultivation methods enable the efficient use of water and nutrients by delivering them directly to the plant roots. By minimizing water consumption and nutrient waste, vertical farming systems contribute to water conservation and nutrient stewardship, promoting sustainable agricultural practices.

The reliance on artificial lighting is another characteristic of vertical farming system designs. Energy-efficient LED lights are used to provide the necessary spectrum and intensity needed for optimal plant growth. While electricity consumption can be a consideration for sustainability, vertical farming systems often incorporate renewable energy sources, minimizing their carbon footprint and overall environmental impact.

Vertical Farming System Planning

A vertical farming system is a sustainable method of growing plants in a vertically stacked arrangement, typically within a controlled environment, such as a skyscraper, warehouse, or shipping container, using hydroponic or aeroponic techniques. This innovative system allows for the highly efficient use of land, water, and energy resources, making it a promising solution to address food security and environmental challenges.

By utilizing vertical space, vertical farming maximizes the productivity per square meter of land. Tall structures enable multiple layers or racks of plants, extending the growing capacity compared to traditional flat field farming. This vertical arrangement also optimizes sunlight exposure, ensuring that plants receive adequate light throughout the day, regardless of their position within the structure.

Additionally, vertical farming employs soilless cultivation methods such as hydroponics or aeroponics, which eliminate the need for traditional soil-based agriculture. Instead, plants are grown in nutrient-rich water solutions, enabling precise control over nutrient levels and minimizing water usage. This approach significantly reduces the environmental impact associated with soil degradation, water pollution, and excessive water consumption.

Furthermore, vertical farming systems often incorporate advanced technologies, such as artificial lighting, climate control systems, and automation, to create optimal conditions for plant growth. These technologies enable year-round cultivation, independent of seasonal and weather constraints, resulting in consistent and reliable crop production. Moreover, the controlled environment reduces the reliance on harmful pesticides, herbicides, and fertilizers, promoting sustainable and organic farming practices.

Overall, vertical farming systems offer a sustainable solution to meet the increasing demand for food production while minimizing land use, conserving water resources, and reducing reliance on harmful substances. This innovative approach has the potential to revolutionize agriculture by providing a more efficient, climate-resilient, and environmentally-friendly means of cultivating crops.

Vertical Farming Systems

Vertical farming systems are sustainable agricultural systems that involve cultivating plants in vertically stacked layers or structures. Instead of using traditional methods of growing crops on sprawling horizontal fields, vertical farming utilizes specialized indoor environments to maximize productivity and minimize negative environmental impacts.

These systems typically employ advanced technologies such as hydroponics, aeroponics, and aquaponics to provide plants with the necessary nutrients, water, and light to thrive. By growing crops in vertical layers, vertical farming systems save space and reduce the need for expansive land areas, making them suitable for urban areas with limited available land.

A key advantage of vertical farming systems is their ability to significantly reduce water usage compared to traditional farming methods. The closed-loop systems used in vertical farming minimize water loss through evaporation and runoff, resulting in up to 90% less water usage. Additionally, by optimizing the usage of water and nutrients, vertical farming systems contribute to the conservation of these valuable resources.

Moreover, vertical farming systems are designed to be highly energy-efficient, utilizing technologies such as LED lighting and efficient climate control systems. By carefully controlling the indoor environment, these systems reduce the reliance on natural resources and minimize energy waste. This sustainable approach to agricultural production helps mitigate the negative impacts of conventional farming practices, such as deforestation, soil erosion, and pollution from pesticide and fertilizer use.

In conclusion, vertical farming systems offer a sustainable solution to the challenges of modern agriculture by maximizing productivity in limited spaces, conserving water and energy, and reducing the ecological footprint of food production. Through their innovative design and advanced technologies, these systems contribute to a more environmentally friendly and efficient approach to farming.

Vertical Farming Tower Design

A vertical farming tower design refers to a sustainable agricultural approach that involves the cultivation of crops in vertically stacked layers. This innovative farming method utilizes limited space to maximize agricultural output, making it an environmentally-friendly and resource-efficient solution to the challenges of traditional farming.

By utilizing vertical space, these tower designs can grow crops in urban areas and other locations where land is scarce. The vertical farming tower design optimizes natural resources such as sunlight, water, and nutrients, reducing waste and minimizing the need for artificial inputs. This sustainable design harnesses advanced technologies, including artificial lighting systems, hydroponics, and automated environmental controls, to create ideal growing conditions for various plant species.

The vertical farming tower design has numerous sustainability advantages. Firstly, it reduces the dependence on traditional agricultural practices that often deplete soil nutrients and contribute to deforestation. Instead, the vertical farming tower design promotes soilless cultivation techniques such as hydroponics or aeroponics, minimizing the need for pesticides and fertilizers. This leads to improved water quality and reduces the risk of pesticide contamination in water bodies.

Moreover, vertical farming towers are energy-efficient due to their localized production and reduced transportation needs. These self-contained systems reduce carbon emissions associated with long-distance crop transportation and provide fresh produce to local communities. Additionally, this design promotes food security by enabling year-round production and minimizing the risk of crop failures due to climate change or natural disasters.

Vertical Farming Tower Layouts

Vertical farming is a sustainable agricultural practice that involves growing crops in vertically stacked layers or towers. This innovative approach maximizes the use of limited space, reduces the need for traditional land, and minimizes environmental impact while meeting the demands of a growing population.

The layout of vertical farming towers is carefully designed to optimize resource efficiency and promote sustainability. Each tower consists of multiple levels or shelves that are equipped with hydroponic or aeroponic systems to nourish the plants. These systems provide the necessary nutrients and water to the crops, eliminating the need for soil. Additionally, advanced LED lighting is used to simulate natural sunlight and promote photosynthesis, ensuring optimal growth throughout the vertical structure.

One key advantage of vertical farming tower layouts is their ability to significantly reduce water consumption compared to conventional farming methods. The closed-loop irrigation systems used in these towers recycle and reuse water, minimizing waste and conserving this precious resource. Furthermore, vertical farming also eliminates the need for harmful pesticides and herbicides, as crops are grown in a controlled indoor environment, reducing soil erosion and contamination.

Another important aspect of sustainability in vertical farming is energy efficiency. By utilizing LED lighting and efficient climate control systems, these towers can minimize energy consumption while providing the ideal conditions for plant growth. Moreover, the proximity of vertical farms to urban areas reduces the need for long-distance transportation, decreasing carbon emissions associated with food delivery.

Overall, vertical farming tower layouts present a sustainable solution to the challenges of traditional agriculture, allowing for year-round crop production, reduced land use, minimized water consumption, and improved energy efficiency. With the potential to revolutionize food production, vertical farming contributes to a more sustainable future by addressing key environmental concerns and enhancing food security.

Waste Management And Recycling Software

Waste management and recycling software is an innovative tool that aids in the sustainable management and optimization of waste and recycling processes. It is designed to enhance efficiency, transparency, and accountability, ultimately reducing the environmental footprint and promoting circular economy principles.

This software provides a comprehensive platform to track, monitor, and manage the entire waste management cycle – from waste collection and sorting to processing and disposal. It enables organizations to streamline their operations, make data-driven decisions, and minimize waste generation.

The software facilitates the digitization of waste management processes, eliminating the need for manual record-keeping and paperwork. This not only saves time and resources but also ensures accuracy and accessibility of data. It allows for real-time monitoring and analysis of waste streams, enabling organizations to identify inefficiencies, set targets, and measure performance towards sustainability goals.

Furthermore, waste management and recycling software enables effective communication and collaboration among stakeholders, including waste generators, recyclers, and government agencies. It provides a platform to exchange information, track compliance with regulations, and promote best practices, fostering a coordinated approach towards sustainable waste management.

In conclusion, waste management and recycling software is a vital tool in the pursuit of sustainable waste management. By digitizing and optimizing waste processes, it empowers organizations to reduce waste generation, improve resource efficiency, and contribute to the long-term sustainability of our planet.

Waste Plastic Upcycling

Waste plastic upcycling refers to the process of converting discarded or non-recyclable plastic materials into new products or materials of higher value and quality, thereby extending their lifespan and reducing the environmental impact associated with plastic waste. This practice aligns with the principles of sustainability by promoting resource efficiency, reducing the consumption of virgin materials, and diverting plastic waste from landfills or incineration.

In upcycling, the waste plastic undergoes various treatments, such as sorting, cleaning, shredding, and transforming it through different processes like melting, extrusion, or molding. Through these processes, the waste plastic can be transformed into new products with improved functionality and durability, such as building materials, furniture, household items, and even fashion accessories.

By upcycling plastic waste, several environmental benefits can be achieved. Firstly, it helps reduce the pollution and energy consumption associated with the production of new plastic materials. Upcycling also reduces the demand for fossil fuel feedstocks, such as oil and natural gas, which are primary sources for plastic production. Additionally, by diverting plastic waste from landfills or incineration, it helps alleviate the burden on waste management systems and reduces the release of harmful greenhouse gases and other pollutants.

Furthermore, waste plastic upcycling contributes to the circular economy, as it allows plastic materials to remain in use for longer periods and prevents them from becoming waste prematurely. It promotes the concept of "reduce, reuse, recycle" by actively seeking alternatives to single-use plastics and generating value from materials that would otherwise be considered waste.

Waste Prevention Measures

Waste Reduction In Agriculture

The term waste reduction in agriculture refers to the practice of minimizing and managing waste generated in the agricultural sector in order to promote sustainability. This involves adopting strategies and implementing measures that aim to reduce the amount of agricultural waste produced and its negative environmental impacts.

Waste in agriculture can take various forms, including crop residues, animal manure, packaging materials, and chemical containers. These wastes can contribute to pollution, soil degradation, and greenhouse gas emissions, which can have detrimental effects on the environment and human health. To address these issues, waste reduction in agriculture aims to minimize waste generation, as well as properly manage and dispose of any waste produced.

There are several approaches to achieve waste reduction in agriculture. These include implementing efficient farming practices, such as precision agriculture, which optimizes the use of fertilizers and pesticides to reduce waste. Additionally, promoting sustainable crop rotation and diversification can help minimize crop residues and soil erosion. Proper waste management techniques, including composting and proper disposal of waste, are also essential in reducing the overall environmental impact.

By reducing waste in agriculture, the industry can move towards a more sustainable and environmentally friendly model. This not only benefits the environment but also helps to ensure the long-term viability of agricultural systems. Waste reduction in agriculture is an integral part of promoting sustainability and achieving a more sustainable and resilient food system.

Waste Reduction In Construction

Waste reduction in construction refers to the implementation of sustainable practices aimed at minimizing the generation of waste throughout the construction process. This approach focuses on reducing, reusing, and recycling materials and resources in order to minimize the environmental impact of construction activities.

By adopting waste reduction strategies, construction projects strive to minimize the amount of waste sent to landfill and to conserve natural resources. To achieve this, sustainable construction practices focus on several key areas:

1. Design: Sustainable design principles prioritize the use of low-impact, durable, and recyclable materials. Architects and engineers aim to optimize building layouts and dimensions to minimize waste during construction and future renovations.

2. Material selection: Construction projects that prioritize waste reduction carefully select materials based on their sustainability characteristics. This includes choosing materials with a high recycling potential, utilizing recycled content, and sourcing locally when possible to reduce carbon emissions associated with transportation.

3. Waste management: Effective waste management systems are implemented on construction sites to separate and properly dispose of different types of waste. Recycling programs, on-site sorting, and the use of efficient waste disposal methods help reduce the amount of waste sent to

landfill and promote the recycling of construction and demolition debris.

In conclusion, waste reduction in construction is a vital component of sustainable development. By implementing these practices, construction projects can minimize their environmental impact by reducing the amount of waste generated and conserving valuable resources for future generations.

Waste Reduction In Fashion

Waste reduction in fashion refers to the practice of minimizing the negative environmental and social impacts associated with the production, consumption, and disposal of clothing and accessories. It involves the implementation of strategies to decrease the amount of waste generated and promote more sustainable practices throughout the entire fashion supply chain.

This sustainability-focused approach aims to address the excessive volume of waste produced by the fashion industry, which is known for its fast pace of production and disposal. Waste reduction in fashion encompasses various measures such as reducing the amount of discarded textiles, adopting sustainable materials, promoting circularity through recycling and upcycling, and implementing efficient manufacturing processes.

By prioritizing waste reduction, the fashion industry can mitigate the adverse consequences of its unsustainable practices. It helps conserve dwindling natural resources, such as water, energy, and raw materials, by minimizing their use and promoting more resource-efficient production methods. Additionally, waste reduction in fashion contributes to the reduction of greenhouse gas emissions, as the production and disposal of clothing are significant contributors to global carbon emissions.

Beyond the environmental benefits, waste reduction in fashion also has social implications. It prioritizes fair and safe working conditions for garment workers and promotes better labor practices throughout the supply chain. Furthermore, it encourages conscious consumer behavior by fostering awareness about the environmental and social impacts of fashion consumption.

Waste Reduction In Forestry

Waste reduction in forestry refers to the implementation of measures and strategies aimed at minimizing the generation and disposal of waste throughout the various stages of forest management and timber production. It is an integral component of sustainable forestry practices, focusing on minimizing environmental impact, preserving natural resources, and promoting long-term ecological balance.

This process involves the adoption of sustainable harvesting techniques that optimize the use of forest resources while minimizing waste generation. This includes carefully planning and executing logging operations to prevent unnecessary damage to trees and ensuring efficient utilization of harvested timber. By implementing selective logging methods, landowners and forestry professionals can minimize the amount of non-productive wood and biomass left behind during extraction.

Furthermore, waste reduction in forestry also encompasses strategies for minimizing waste during processing and manufacturing operations. This includes optimizing the utilization of harvested timber through the reduction of processing waste, such as bark, wood residuals, and sawdust. Efforts are made to repurpose these by-products for other uses, such as energy generation, wood-based products, or as inputs for other industrial processes.

The overarching goal of waste reduction in forestry is to achieve a more sustainable and efficient use of forest resources, while mitigating the negative impacts on the environment. Through the implementation of waste reduction measures, the forestry sector can contribute to the conservation of forests, the preservation of biodiversity, and the reduction of greenhouse gas emissions associated with waste disposal and inefficient resource utilization.

Waste Reduction In Healthcare

Waste reduction in healthcare refers to the implementation of strategies and practices aimed at minimizing the generation and disposal of waste materials within the healthcare industry. It involves the conscious effort to reduce, reuse, and recycle waste to minimize its environmental impact and promote sustainability.

The healthcare sector generates a significant amount of waste, including medical supplies, packaging materials, pharmaceuticals, and biological waste. This waste can have adverse effects on the environment if not managed properly, as it can contribute to pollution, resource depletion, and greenhouse gas emissions.

By implementing waste reduction measures, healthcare facilities can minimize their environmental footprint while also realizing cost savings. These measures can include:

- Source reduction: This involves reducing the amount of waste generated at the source by implementing practices such as purchasing in bulk, using reusable instruments and supplies, and reducing packaging waste.

- Recycling: Healthcare facilities can implement recycling programs for materials such as paper, plastics, metal, and glass. This can involve segregating waste at the source and partnering with recycling companies for proper disposal and recycling.

- Energy recovery: Waste materials that cannot be recycled can still be used for energy recovery through processes such as incineration or anaerobic digestion. This allows for the generation of renewable energy while diverting waste from landfills.

Overall, waste reduction in healthcare is an essential component of sustainability efforts within the industry. By minimizing waste generation and adopting environmentally-friendly practices, healthcare facilities can contribute to a more sustainable future while also promoting the well-being of their patients and communities.

Waste Reduction In Manufacturing

Waste reduction in manufacturing is a crucial aspect of sustainability, aimed at minimizing the production of waste materials and optimizing resource utilization throughout the manufacturing process. It involves the implementation of strategies and techniques that reduce the generation of waste and promote the efficient use of raw materials, energy, and other resources.

This approach focuses on minimizing waste at each stage of the manufacturing lifecycle, including raw material extraction, processing, production, distribution, and end-of-life disposal. By implementing waste reduction practices, manufacturers can not only minimize their environmental impact but also achieve economic benefits through increased resource efficiency and cost savings.

Waste Reduction In Marine Conservation

Waste reduction in marine conservation is a fundamental component of sustainability efforts aimed at preserving and protecting the world's oceans and their ecosystems. It entails the implementation of strategies and practices to minimize, mitigate, and eliminate waste generated by human activities that poses a threat to marine life and habitats.

The objective of waste reduction in marine conservation is to prevent and minimize the release of harmful pollutants, debris, and materials into the marine environment. This includes reducing the amount of plastic, chemical pollutants, oil spills, sewage, and other waste that enters the oceans, which can cause severe harm to marine organisms, ecosystems, and biodiversity.

Efforts to achieve waste reduction in marine conservation focus on various key areas. These include promoting the use of sustainable and eco-friendly materials, implementing effective waste management systems both on land and at sea, raising awareness about the negative impacts of marine pollution, and advocating for policy changes and regulations to enforce responsible waste management practices.

By reducing waste, particularly single-use plastics, the risk of entanglement and ingestion by marine animals can be mitigated. Additionally, waste reduction efforts contribute to the preservation of marine ecosystems, including coral reefs, seagrass beds, and coastal habitats, which are vital for biodiversity, shoreline protection, and carbon sequestration.

In conclusion, waste reduction in marine conservation plays a crucial role in ensuring the long-term sustainability and health of our oceans. By adopting sustainable practices and finding innovative solutions to minimize waste generation and disposal, we can protect marine ecosystems and the countless species that depend on them.

Waste Reduction In Retail

Waste reduction in retail refers to the implementation of strategies and practices aimed at minimizing the amount of waste generated within the retail industry, while promoting environmental sustainability. It encompasses efforts to reduce waste at every stage of the retail process, from manufacturing and distribution to consumption and disposal.

In the retail sector, waste reduction is essential for mitigating the negative impacts of excessive waste production on the environment. By implementing effective waste management strategies, retailers can minimize their carbon footprint, conserve natural resources, and contribute to a more sustainable future.

Waste Reduction In Technology

Waste reduction in technology refers to the application of strategies and measures aimed at minimizing the negative environmental impact associated with the manufacturing, use, and disposal of technological devices and systems. It involves the implementation of sustainable practices throughout the life cycle of technology, from the extraction of raw materials to the end-of-life management.

The primary objective of waste reduction in technology is to minimize the generation of waste and the consumption of natural resources, contributing to the overall goal of sustainability. This encompasses various aspects, including the reduction of energy and resource intensity in production processes, the implementation of circular economy principles, and the promotion of eco-design and responsible consumption.

Efforts to reduce waste in technology involve optimizing the design, production, and use of technological products to minimize material and energy consumption, as well as extending product lifecycles through repair, refurbishment, and recycling. This can be achieved through the adoption of eco-friendly manufacturing processes, the use of recyclable and non-toxic materials, and the development of products that are repairable and upgradable.

Furthermore, waste reduction in technology also entails proper end-of-life management, including the responsible disposal and recycling of electronic waste. This involves the establishment of collection systems, the separation and treatment of hazardous components, and the extraction of valuable materials for reuse.

Waste Reduction In Transportation

Waste reduction in transportation refers to the implementation of measures and strategies aimed at minimizing resource consumption, energy usage, and environmental impact associated with transportation activities. It involves the reduction of waste generated throughout the entire transportation lifecycle, including the production, operation, and disposal stages.

This concept is rooted in the principles of sustainability, which emphasizes the need to achieve a balance between economic growth, social development, and environmental protection. Waste reduction in transportation is essential for sustainable development as it contributes to the conservation of natural resources, reduction of greenhouse gas emissions, and improvement of air and water quality.

Waste Reduction In Urban Planning

Waste reduction in urban planning refers to the process of integrating sustainable practices and strategies into the design, development, and management of cities and other urban areas, with the ultimate goal of minimizing the generation of waste and promoting long-term environmental sustainability.

This concept recognizes the significant role that urban areas play in contributing to waste generation and environmental degradation. By incorporating waste reduction measures into urban planning, cities can strive to minimize the amount of waste produced, as well as implement effective waste management systems to handle the remaining waste in an environmentally responsible manner.

Waste Reduction In Waste Management

Waste reduction in waste management refers to the systematic effort to minimize the amount of waste generated by businesses, households, and industries, with the aim of preserving natural resources, reducing environmental pollution, and promoting sustainability. It involves implementing strategies and practices that prioritize the reduction of waste at its source, rather than solely focusing on its disposal or treatment.

The goal of waste reduction is to prevent waste generation in the first place, or when this is not feasible, to reduce the overall quantity of waste produced. This is achieved through various approaches such as waste prevention, recycling, reuse, and composting. Waste prevention aims to minimize the generation of waste by implementing measures that eliminate or reduce the use of materials that are not necessary or can be replaced with more sustainable alternatives. Recycling involves the processing of waste materials into new products, thus reducing the need for raw materials extraction and decreasing energy consumption. Reuse entails extending the lifespan of products or materials through repair, refurbishment, or redistribution, reducing the need for new resource extraction. Composting focuses on the decomposition of organic waste into nutrient-rich compost, which can be used as a natural fertilizer in various applications.

Waste Reduction In Water Management

Waste reduction in water management is a key aspect of achieving sustainability in the management of water resources. It refers to the implementation of strategies and practices that minimize the generation, release, and disposal of waste materials in the water sector.

Efficient and responsible water management is crucial to maintain the balance between water availability and sustainable development. Waste reduction plays a pivotal role in achieving this balance by minimizing the negative impacts of waste on the environment, human health, and the overall sustainability of water resources.

Various approaches can be adopted to reduce waste in water management. These include the implementation of advanced technologies to treat and recycle wastewater, the promotion of water conservation practices, the enforcement of regulations and policies to control pollution, and the adoption of best practices in industrial and agricultural water use.

By reducing waste in water management, multiple benefits can be achieved. Firstly, it helps to protect and preserve water resources for future generations by minimizing the depletion of freshwater sources and preventing the contamination of water bodies. Secondly, waste reduction promotes sustainable ecosystems by preventing the release of harmful substances into aquatic environments. Thirdly, it contributes to the efficient use of resources by recovering valuable materials and energy from waste streams, thus promoting a circular economy.

In conclusion, waste reduction in water management is a critical aspect of achieving sustainability by minimizing waste generation, optimizing resource use, and protecting water resources and ecosystems for future generations.

Waste Reduction In Wildlife Conservation

Waste reduction in wildlife conservation refers to the active effort to minimize the production of waste and its negative impact on wildlife and their habitats, in order to promote long-term sustainability.

It involves adopting strategies and practices that aim to reduce, reuse, and recycle waste materials, while also avoiding pollution and the depletion of natural resources. This includes minimizing the use of single-use plastics, promoting responsible tourism and eco-friendly practices, and implementing proper waste management systems.

By reducing waste in wildlife conservation, we can minimize the risk of pollution and its harmful effects on ecosystems. Many wildlife species are particularly vulnerable to the negative impacts of waste, such as entanglement in plastic debris, ingestion of toxic substances, and habitat destruction caused by landfill sites. Waste reduction efforts not only protect the biodiversity and natural beauty of wildlife areas but also contribute to the overall health and balance of ecosystems.

Furthermore, waste reduction in wildlife conservation aligns with the principles of sustainability. It helps to preserve natural resources, reduce greenhouse gas emissions, and promote the responsible use of resources. By adopting waste reduction strategies, we can minimize the need for landfills and incineration facilities, and instead prioritize practices such as composting and recycling.

Waste Reduction Strategies

Waste reduction strategies refer to actions and measures implemented to minimize the amount of waste generated and improve sustainability. In the context of sustainability, waste reduction strategies aim to reduce the use of resources, promote recycling and reuse, and minimize waste disposal.

These strategies involve a variety of approaches, including waste prevention, recycling, composting, and resource recovery. Waste prevention focuses on reducing the generation of waste at its source. This can be achieved through practices such as designing products with less packaging, encouraging the use of eco-friendly materials, and promoting responsible consumption habits.

Recycling plays a crucial role in waste reduction strategies by diverting waste from landfills and conserving resources. It involves collecting and processing materials such as paper, plastic, glass, and metal to create new products. Recycling helps to reduce the demand for virgin materials, conserve energy, and decrease pollution associated with extracting and processing raw materials.

Composting is another essential waste reduction strategy that involves the decomposition of organic waste, such as food scraps and yard trimmings, into nutrient-rich compost. This process not only reduces the amount of waste sent to landfills but also provides a valuable resource for enhancing soil health and promoting sustainable agriculture.

Resource recovery strategies aim to extract valuable materials from waste streams that would otherwise end up in landfills. Technologies such as waste-to-energy plants can convert non-recyclable waste into heat or electricity, reducing the reliance on fossil fuels and minimizing greenhouse gas emissions.

In summary, waste reduction strategies encompass a range of actions and approaches aimed at minimizing waste generation, promoting recycling and composting, and recovering valuable resources. By implementing these strategies, communities and industries can contribute to the preservation of natural resources, reduction of pollution, and overall sustainability.

Waste-Reducing Packaging Design

Waste-reducing packaging design refers to a sustainable approach in the development and implementation of packaging materials and structures with the aim of minimizing environmental impact and reducing waste generation across the product's life cycle.

This design strategy focuses on several key principles that contribute to waste reduction and sustainability. Firstly, it aims to optimize the use of materials, ensuring that only the necessary amount of packaging is used to protect and deliver the product. This involves employing innovative techniques such as lightweighting and using materials with higher strength-to-weight ratios.

Another important aspect of waste-reducing packaging design is the promotion of recyclability and the use of recycled or renewable materials. Packaging materials and components are chosen or developed to be easily recyclable, ensuring that they can be efficiently recovered and reintroduced into the production cycle.

Additionally, waste-reducing packaging design focuses on minimizing the use of potentially harmful substances in packaging materials, such as toxic additives or chemicals that hamper the recycling process. This helps to reduce both the environmental and health risks associated with packaging waste.

Furthermore, this design approach emphasizes the use of packaging designs that facilitate easy disassembly and separation of different materials, making it easier for consumers to recycle or compost packaging components properly.

Overall, waste-reducing packaging design plays a crucial role in advancing sustainability goals by minimizing waste generation, promoting material efficiency, and fostering a circular economy where packaging materials are reused, recycled, or composted, thus reducing the need for virgin resources and minimizing environmental impacts.

Waste-To-Biogas Conversion

Waste-to-biogas conversion refers to the process of transforming organic waste materials, such as food waste, agricultural waste, and sewage sludge, into biogas through anaerobic digestion. This method is a sustainable solution that addresses both waste management and energy production.

Through anaerobic digestion, microorganisms break down the organic waste materials in the absence of oxygen, resulting in the production of biogas. Biogas is a mixture of methane, carbon dioxide, and small amounts of other gases. It can be utilized as a renewable energy source for various applications, including electricity generation, heating, and transportation fuel.

This conversion process offers several sustainability benefits. Firstly, it helps reduce the amount of organic waste that would otherwise end up in landfills, where it would contribute to greenhouse gas emissions. By converting this waste into biogas, the greenhouse gas emissions are significantly reduced. Furthermore, the leftover digestate from the process can be used as a fertilizer, reducing the need for synthetic fertilizers and promoting agricultural sustainability.

Additionally, waste-to-biogas conversion plays a role in the transition to a circular economy, as it enables the recycling and reuse of organic materials. This process not only reduces waste but also provides a reliable and locally sourced energy supply. Biogas can be produced from various waste streams, making it a versatile and accessible renewable energy option.

Waste-To-Energy Conversion

Waste-to-energy conversion is an essential process that contributes to sustainability by transforming waste materials into a usable form of energy. It is a method of generating electricity or heat by incinerating or gasifying waste materials such as municipal solid waste, agricultural residues, or industrial waste.

This process helps to reduce the reliance on fossil fuels and minimize the environmental impact of waste disposal. By converting waste into energy, waste-to-energy conversion facilities not only provide a renewable source of energy but also help to reduce greenhouse gas emissions and alleviate the strain on landfills.

Waste-To-Energy Facilities

Waste-to-energy facilities, also known as waste incineration plants, are sustainable infrastructure that convert non-recyclable waste materials into valuable resources such as heat, electricity, and other forms of useful energy. These facilities play a crucial role in the management of solid waste while simultaneously promoting sustainable development.

The process involves the controlled combustion of municipal solid waste (MSW) or other organic materials in specially designed incinerators. Through this thermal treatment, waste materials are transformed into energy-rich gases, steam, or ash. The energy generated can be harnessed and utilized for various purposes. Heat recovered during the incineration process can be used for district heating or converted into electricity through steam turbines, thereby reducing dependence on fossil fuels and conventional energy sources. Furthermore, the ash leftover from the incineration process can be used as a construction material, reducing the need for quarried aggregates.

By diverting waste from landfill sites, waste-to-energy facilities contribute to the reduction of greenhouse gas emissions and prevent the release of harmful pollutants into the environment. These facilities also help alleviate the strain on finite natural resources by harnessing energy from waste that would otherwise be discarded. In addition to its energy benefits, waste-to-energy technology reduces the volume of waste, thereby conserving valuable landfill space and mitigating health and environmental hazards associated with open dumping.

Overall, waste-to-energy facilities serve as a sustainable solution for managing non-recyclable waste while generating clean energy. By enabling the recovery and utilization of valuable resources, these facilities contribute to the circular economy model, reduce reliance on fossil fuels, and minimize environmental impacts associated with waste disposal.

Waste-To-Energy Technologies

Waste-to-energy technologies refer to a range of processes that convert various forms of waste into energy sources, while simultaneously mitigating the environmental impacts associated with waste disposal. These technologies are an important component of sustainable development, as they contribute to the efficient utilization of resources, reduction of greenhouse gas emissions, and promotion of circular economy principles.

One commonly used waste-to-energy technology is incineration, which involves the combustion of waste materials to produce electricity or heat. Incineration not only reduces the volume of waste that needs to be disposed of in landfills but also generates energy that can be utilized for various purposes. However, the process must be carefully managed to minimize air pollution and the release of harmful substances.

An alternative approach is anaerobic digestion, which involves the decomposition of organic waste in the absence of oxygen. This process produces biogas, a mixture of methane and carbon dioxide, which can be used as a renewable energy source. Anaerobic digestion not only reduces the release of methane, a potent greenhouse gas, but also produces nutrient-rich digestate that can be used as a fertilizer.

Pyrolysis and gasification are other waste-to-energy technologies that involve the thermal decomposition of waste materials in oxygen-limited environments. These processes produce syngas, a mixture of carbon monoxide and hydrogen, which can be used to generate electricity or produce biofuels. Additionally, the residual ash from pyrolysis and gasification can be used as a construction material or as a raw material for other industries.

In conclusion, waste-to-energy technologies play a vital role in promoting sustainability by transforming waste into valuable energy resources, reducing environmental pollution, and minimizing the reliance on finite fossil fuel sources.

Waste-To-Fuel Conversion

Waste-to-fuel conversion refers to the process of transforming various types of waste materials into usable fuel sources, thereby promoting sustainability by reducing waste and dependence on fossil fuels. This innovative method involves the conversion of organic and inorganic waste, such as food waste, agricultural residues, plastics, and paper, into valuable forms of energy.

The waste-to-fuel conversion process generally involves several steps, including collection, sorting, preprocessing, and conversion. Firstly, the waste materials are gathered from various sources and sorted to separate recyclable materials from non-recyclables. Next, the non-recyclable waste is preprocessed to remove any contaminants and prepare it for conversion.

This involves shredding, grinding, or compacting the waste to achieve a homogeneous composition.

After preprocessing, the waste undergoes conversion through different methods such as thermal, chemical, or biological processes. Thermal processes involve incineration or pyrolysis, which use high temperatures to break down the waste and produce fuel gases, liquids, or solids. Chemical processes, on the other hand, utilize various chemical reactions to convert waste into fuels like ethanol or biodiesel. Biological processes employ microorganisms to decompose organic waste and produce biogas or biofuels.

The benefits of waste-to-fuel conversion are manifold. Firstly, it reduces the amount of waste going to landfills, minimizing environmental pollution and conserving valuable landfill space. Secondly, generating fuel from waste reduces the reliance on fossil fuels and helps mitigate climate change by reducing greenhouse gas emissions. Moreover, waste-to-fuel conversion promotes circular economy principles, as it transforms waste into a valuable resource, contributing to a more sustainable and resource-efficient society.

Waste-To-Hydrogen Technology

Waste-to-hydrogen technology refers to the process of converting various types of waste materials into hydrogen gas through a sustainable and environmentally friendly method. It is considered a crucial aspect of sustainability as it addresses the challenges of waste management and contributes to the production of a clean and renewable energy source.

This technology involves several steps, starting with the collection and sorting of waste materials such as biomass, organic waste, and municipal solid waste. These waste materials are then treated through different processes such as gasification, pyrolysis, or anaerobic digestion, depending on the specific waste type. These processes break down the waste into a mixture of gases, primarily consisting of carbon monoxide, carbon dioxide, and hydrogen.

The hydrogen gas produced through waste-to-hydrogen technology can be further purified and used as a valuable energy source in various applications. It can be utilized in fuel cells to generate electricity, providing a cleaner alternative to traditional fossil fuel-based power generation. Additionally, hydrogen can be used as a feedstock for the production of chemicals and transportation fuels, further reducing dependence on non-renewable resources.

This technology contributes to sustainability by addressing two significant environmental concerns: waste management and the transition to cleaner energy sources. By diverting waste materials from landfills and incineration, it helps reduce greenhouse gas emissions and minimizes the environmental impact of waste disposal. Moreover, producing hydrogen from waste materials promotes a circular economy by transforming waste into a valuable resource, reducing resource depletion and promoting resource efficiency.

Waste-To-Material Conversion Technologies

Waste-to-material conversion technologies refer to processes that transform waste materials into usable and valuable resources, with the aim of promoting sustainability. These technologies support the circular economy concept by diverting waste from landfill and reducing the consumption of raw materials.

The underlying principle of waste-to-material conversion technologies is to extract and recover valuable materials or energy from waste streams. This is accomplished through various methods such as recycling, composting, anaerobic digestion, and thermal processes. Each of these techniques targets different types of waste and employs specific mechanisms to convert them into new products or energy sources.

Recycling is one of the most widely known waste-to-material conversion technologies. It involves the collection and processing of materials like plastics, glass, paper, and metals, which are then transformed into new products. Composting, on the other hand, focuses on converting organic waste into nutrient-rich compost that can be used as fertilizer in agriculture or horticulture.

Furthermore, anaerobic digestion utilizes microorganisms to break down organic waste in the

405

absence of oxygen, producing biogas as a byproduct. This biogas can be used for heat, electricity generation, or converted into biomethane for transport fuel. Lastly, thermal processes such as incineration or gasification involve the controlled combustion of waste to generate heat or electricity while minimizing environmental impacts.

By employing waste-to-material conversion technologies, societies can reduce the environmental burden associated with waste disposal and resource extraction. These technologies promote sustainability by conserving natural resources, decreasing greenhouse gas emissions, and preventing pollution. Additionally, they contribute to the creation of a circular economy, where waste materials are viewed as valuable resources that can be continuously reused and repurposed.

Waste-To-Material Conversion

Waste-to-material conversion is a sustainable process that involves transforming waste materials into reusable or valuable resources. It is an essential component of the circular economy, where materials are considered to have continuous value throughout their lifecycle.

The process of waste-to-material conversion aims to prevent the disposal of waste in landfills or its release into the environment, reducing the environmental impact of waste generation. Instead of treating waste as a burden, this approach recognizes the potential value and opportunities within waste streams. By applying various technologies and methods, waste materials can be converted into new products, raw materials, or energy sources.

Waste-to-material conversion can involve different techniques such as recycling, upcycling, composting, and bioconversion. Recycling involves breaking down waste materials into their constituent parts and using them to produce new products. Upcycling refers to transforming waste materials into higher-value products. Composting involves the decomposition of organic waste materials, producing nutrient-rich compost for use in agriculture or horticulture. Bioconversion utilizes biological processes to convert organic waste into biofuels or chemicals.

This conversion process can help to conserve natural resources, reduce energy consumption, and minimize pollution associated with the extraction and manufacturing of virgin materials. It also promotes a more sustainable and circular economy by reducing the reliance on finite resources and promoting the reuse and regeneration of materials. Waste-to-material conversion is a crucial strategy in achieving a more sustainable future by turning waste into a valuable resource.

Waste-To-Material Innovations

Waste-to-material innovations refer to the development and implementation of technologies, processes, and practices that convert waste materials into valuable resources. These innovations are part of a broader effort to promote sustainability by reducing waste, conserving resources, and minimizing environmental impacts.

Waste materials, including industrial waste, municipal solid waste, agricultural waste, and other forms of discarded materials, are often treated as a problem to be disposed of. However, waste-to-material innovations recognize that these materials still possess inherent value and can be transformed into useful products, thereby reducing the need for virgin resources and the associated environmental burdens.

The goal of waste-to-material innovations is to extract the maximum value from waste materials through various techniques such as recycling, upcycling, and conversion processes. Recycling involves breaking down waste materials into their constituent parts and reusing them in manufacturing processes. Upcycling, on the other hand, involves transforming waste materials into higher-value products with improved functionality or aesthetics. Conversion processes include technologies like pyrolysis and anaerobic digestion, which convert organic waste into biofuels, biogas, or other forms of energy.

By employing waste-to-material innovations, businesses, industries, and communities can mitigate the impacts of waste generation, conserve resources, and reduce reliance on finite raw materials. These innovations also contribute to the circular economy, where materials are kept in productive use for as long as possible. Ultimately, waste-to-material innovations play a crucial role in achieving a more sustainable and resource-efficient society.

Waste-To-Material Reclamation

Waste-to-material reclamation refers to the process of converting waste materials into usable materials, with the aim of reducing waste generation and promoting sustainability. It involves various techniques and technologies to recover and transform waste into valuable resources, contributing to the circular economy.

This process involves the sorting, separation, and treatment of waste materials to extract their reusable components. It includes activities such as recycling, composting, and transforming waste into energy sources. The goal is to minimize the dependence on virgin resources, conserve energy, and reduce the environmental impact associated with waste disposal.

Waste-to-material reclamation plays a significant role in achieving sustainability targets by reducing greenhouse gas emissions, conserving natural resources, and minimizing the use of landfills. By recovering materials from waste, it brings economic benefits by creating new revenue streams and job opportunities in the recycling and reclamation industry.

Moreover, waste-to-material reclamation helps in mitigating pollution and preventing the release of harmful substances into the environment. It also promotes the concept of waste reduction and encourages a shift towards a more circular and resource-efficient society.

Overall, waste-to-material reclamation is a crucial approach in sustainable waste management, as it focuses on transforming waste into valuable resources while reducing the negative environmental impact associated with waste generation and disposal.

Waste-To-Material Recycling

Waste-to-material recycling is a sustainable approach to managing waste by converting discarded materials into useful resources, contributing to the circular economy. It involves the transformation of waste materials, such as plastic, paper, and metal, through a series of processes that enable their incorporation back into the production cycle.

This recycling method aims to reduce the reliance on virgin materials and mitigate the negative environmental impacts associated with their extraction and production. By redirecting waste from landfills, waste-to-material recycling helps to conserve natural resources, minimize energy consumption, and reduce greenhouse gas emissions.

Waste-To-Material Reformation

Waste-to-material reformation is a sustainable process that aims to transform waste materials into new products or raw materials, reducing the demand for virgin resources and minimizing the environmental impact associated with waste disposal.

This process involves the conversion of waste materials, such as plastics, organic matter, and metals, into valuable resources through various methods like recycling, composting, and upcycling. Recycling, for instance, involves the collection, sorting, and processing of waste materials to create new products with similar or different properties. Composting, on the other hand, breaks down organic waste into nutrient-rich compost that can be used as a soil amendment, promoting healthy plant growth and reducing the need for chemical fertilizers.

Waste-to-material reformation plays a vital role in achieving a circular economy, where resources are continually used and waste is minimized. By diverting waste from landfills and incineration, this approach not only reduces greenhouse gas emissions but also conserves energy and reduces pollution associated with the extraction and production of virgin materials. Additionally, it helps to conserve natural resources, as recycled and reclaimed materials can substitute for primary resources in manufacturing processes.

Furthermore, waste-to-material reformation contributes to the creation of new job opportunities in the recycling and waste management sectors. It also promotes innovation in waste management technologies and encourages the development of eco-friendly products and packaging. By implementing waste-to-material reformation strategies, societies can move towards a more sustainable and resource-efficient future, where waste is viewed as a valuable resource rather than a burden on the environment.

Waste-To-Material Regeneration

Waste-to-material regeneration refers to the process of transforming waste materials into new, usable materials with the aim of promoting sustainability. It involves diverting waste from disposal sites and landfills by collecting, sorting, and treating it through various techniques to recover valuable resources. This practice aligns with the principles of the circular economy, where waste is considered a potential resource that can be reintroduced into the production cycle.

The waste-to-material regeneration process typically involves several stages. First, waste is collected and sorted to separate recyclable and non-recyclable materials. Recyclable items are then treated using appropriate technologies such as mechanical sorting, composting, or chemical processes to extract valuable components. These components may include metals, plastics, organic matter, or energy-rich substances.

Once the valuable materials are recovered, they go through a regeneration process to convert them into secondary raw materials or energy sources. This can involve processes such as recycling, upcycling, composting, or converting waste into biofuels. The resulting regenerated materials can then be used to manufacture new products, reducing the reliance on virgin raw materials and minimizing the environmental impact associated with their extraction and production.

Waste-to-material regeneration plays a crucial role in promoting sustainability by reducing waste generation, conserving natural resources, and minimizing greenhouse gas emissions. By transforming waste into valuable resources, this approach contributes to the efficient use of materials, energy, and water. It also helps reduce the burden on landfills and prevents pollution of air, water, and soil. Furthermore, waste-to-material regeneration supports the development of a green economy and creates new job opportunities in industries related to waste management, recycling, and resource recovery. Overall, this practice allows for a more sustainable and circular approach to waste management, integrating social, economic, and environmental considerations.

Waste-To-Material Renewal

Waste-to-material renewal refers to the process of converting waste materials into new materials that can be used for various purposes, thus minimizing the need for virgin resources and reducing overall waste generation. It is an integral part of sustainability efforts as it helps in achieving a circular economy, where resources are continuously reused and recycled to minimize environmental impact.

This process involves the collection and segregation of waste materials, followed by treatment or processing to transform them into new materials or products. The waste materials can be categorized into different streams, such as organic waste, plastics, metals, or paper, each requiring specific treatment methods for recycling or conversion into new materials.

Waste-to-material renewal aims to divert waste from landfills and incineration, which contribute to pollution and greenhouse gas emissions. By transforming waste into valuable materials, it reduces the extraction of raw materials from the earth, conserves energy, and reduces pollution associated with resource extraction and manufacturing.

The benefits of waste-to-material renewal are manifold. It conserves natural resources, reduces the need for landfill space, saves energy, and decreases greenhouse gas emissions. Additionally, it creates new job opportunities by establishing recycling facilities and promoting a sustainable and circular economy.

In conclusion, waste-to-material renewal is a critical component of sustainability efforts, promoting the efficient use of resources and minimizing environmental impact. By transforming waste into new materials, we can reduce our dependency on virgin resources and move towards a more sustainable future.

Waste-To-Material Repurposing

Waste-to-material repurposing, also known as waste-to-resource or waste valorization, is a sustainable approach to managing waste by transforming it into valuable materials or products. This process aims to reduce the reliance on virgin resources and minimize the negative environmental impacts associated with waste disposal.

In this context, waste refers to any unwanted or discarded material that would otherwise be sent to landfill or incineration. Instead of treating waste as a burden, waste-to-material repurposing involves identifying potential resource value in the waste stream and finding innovative ways to extract or convert this value.

The repurposing of waste materials can take various forms, depending on the nature of the waste and the desired end product. It may involve mechanical processes such as sorting, shredding, or grinding to break down waste into smaller components. Chemical or biological processes can also be utilized to transform waste into new materials through decomposition, fermentation, or conversion. Additionally, technologies such as recycling, upcycling, and reusing can be employed to give waste materials a second life.

By repurposing waste materials, this approach contributes to a more circular economy, where resources are kept in use for longer periods. It helps to conserve natural resources, reduce energy consumption, and decrease greenhouse gas emissions. Furthermore, waste-to-material repurposing fosters innovation and promotes the development of new industries and job opportunities in the sustainable waste management sector.

Waste-To-Material Transformation

The waste-to-material transformation is a sustainable process that aims to convert waste materials into valuable resources, reducing the consumption of virgin resources, minimizing waste generation, and promoting circularity. It is a crucial component of the waste management hierarchy, prioritizing waste prevention, reuse, and recycling over disposal.

This transformation involves various techniques such as physical, chemical, and biological processes to convert waste into useful materials. Physical processes include sorting, shredding, and grinding to separate different types of waste and reduce their size for further processing. Chemical processes involve transforming waste through techniques like pyrolysis and gasification, which convert organic waste into fuels, chemicals, or other valuable products. Biological processes, such as composting and anaerobic digestion, decompose organic waste into nutrient-rich compost or biogas.

Waste-to-material transformation contributes to sustainable development by addressing several environmental, social, and economic challenges. Firstly, it helps conserve natural resources by reducing the extraction and consumption of raw materials. Secondly, it mitigates environmental pollution by diverting waste from landfills and reducing greenhouse gas emissions. Moreover, it creates economic opportunities by generating employment in the waste management sector and promoting the growth of the circular economy.

Overall, waste-to-material transformation plays a vital role in achieving sustainable waste management practices and fostering a more resource-efficient society. By converting waste into valuable materials, it supports the principles of sustainability, circular economy, and environmental stewardship.

Waste-To-Methane Conversion

Waste-to-methane conversion is a sustainable process aimed at converting organic waste materials into methane gas, a valuable source of renewable energy. It involves the decomposition of organic matter through various biochemical reactions, such as anaerobic digestion or fermentation, in the absence of oxygen.

This process plays a significant role in sustainable waste management and energy production. By diverting organic waste from landfills, waste-to-methane conversion helps reduce greenhouse gas emissions, minimize environmental pollution, and alleviate the strain on limited landfill capacity. Organic waste, including food scraps, agricultural residues, and animal manure, is transformed into methane gas, which can be used as a clean, renewable fuel for heating, electricity generation, or transportation.

Waste-To-Product Reclamation Programs

Waste-to-product reclamation programs, in the context of sustainability, pertain to initiatives and processes that aim to convert waste materials into valuable and usable products. These programs align with the principles of the circular economy, which promotes the efficient use and reuse of resources in order to minimize waste generation and maximize resource recovery.

Waste-to-product reclamation programs involve various strategies and techniques, such as recycling, upcycling, composting, and energy recovery. By diverting waste from landfills and incinerators, these programs contribute to reducing environmental pollution, conserving natural resources, and mitigating the negative impacts of waste on ecosystems and human health.

In recycling, waste materials, such as paper, plastic, glass, and metal, undergo a series of sorting, processing, and transforming steps to produce new products or raw materials. Upcycling goes beyond recycling by creatively repurposing waste items into higher-value products or materials, thereby extending their lifecycle. Composting involves the decomposition of organic waste, such as food scraps and yard trimmings, to produce nutrient-rich soil amendments. Energy recovery methods, including waste-to-energy processes, convert non-recyclable waste into electricity, heat, or fuel.

Waste-to-product reclamation programs not only address the growing waste problem but also offer economic opportunities and job creation. They reduce the need for virgin resources, lower energy consumption, and decrease greenhouse gas emissions associated with the extraction, production, and transportation of new materials.

In conclusion, waste-to-product reclamation programs play a crucial role in promoting sustainability by transforming waste materials into valuable resources, reducing environmental impacts, and fostering a circular and more resource-efficient economy.

Waste-To-Product Reconversion

Waste-to-product reconversion is a sustainable process that involves transforming waste materials into valuable products, thereby reducing the ecological impact of waste disposal and promoting resource conservation. This concept embodies the principles of the circular economy, where waste materials are seen as valuable resources that can be reintroduced into the production cycle.

The aim of waste-to-product reconversion is to minimize the amount of waste that ends up in landfills or incinerators, as these methods often result in environmental pollution and the loss of potentially useful materials. Instead, this process focuses on reusing, recycling, or repurposing waste to create new products or generate energy.

There are various methods employed in waste-to-product reconversion, depending on the type of waste and the desired product. Examples include composting organic waste to produce nutrient-rich soil amendments, recycling plastic waste to create new plastic products, and converting biomass into biofuels.

This approach to waste management offers several benefits for sustainability. Firstly, it helps to reduce the consumption of virgin resources by utilizing waste as a secondary resource. This reduces the extraction of raw materials, minimizing environmental degradation associated with resource extraction. Secondly, waste-to-product reconversion reduces the amount of waste that is sent to landfills, reducing the release of greenhouse gases and the risk of pollution. Finally, by creating valuable products from waste, this process encourages economic growth and job

410

creation within the recycling and reprocessing industries.

Waste-To-Product Recycling Programs

Waste-to-product recycling programs are sustainable initiatives that aim to convert waste materials into new products. These programs contribute to reducing waste accumulation in landfills, conserving resources, and minimizing environmental pollution.

Waste-to-product recycling involves several steps, including waste sorting, processing, and transformation. Initially, waste materials are collected and separated based on their composition. This sorting process ensures that recyclable items, such as paper, plastic, glass, and metals, are separated from non-recyclable materials.

Once sorted, the recyclable waste is processed through various methods, such as shredding, melting, or cleaning, depending on the material type. These processes break down the waste into raw materials or components that can be used for the production of new products. For example, recycled paper can be turned into new paper products, recycled plastic can be transformed into new plastic items, and recycled metal can be used in the manufacturing of new metal goods.

By transforming waste into new products, waste-to-product recycling programs help conserve resources by reducing the need for virgin materials. This, in turn, reduces energy consumption and greenhouse gas emissions associated with the extraction and production of raw materials. Additionally, these programs decrease the amount of waste sent to landfills, which not only helps preserve limited landfill space but also minimizes the release of harmful pollutants and toxins into the environment.

Furthermore, waste-to-product recycling programs contribute to the circular economy by promoting the concept of "reduce, reuse, and recycle." They encourage individuals, businesses, and industries to adopt sustainable practices and embrace a more environmentally friendly approach to waste management.

Waste-To-Product Recycling

Waste-to-product recycling is a sustainable approach that involves transforming waste materials into new products, thereby reducing the need for raw materials and minimizing the environmental impacts of waste disposal. This process aims to close the loop in the product lifecycle by diverting waste from the traditional linear economy model, where materials are extracted, used, and then discarded, and instead creates a circular economy that promotes resource efficiency and waste reduction.

By implementing waste-to-product recycling, various types of waste, such as plastic, paper, metal, and organic matter, can be converted into usable materials or energy sources. The waste materials undergo specific treatment processes, such as sorting, cleaning, and refining, to extract or convert them into valuable resources. These resources can be further used to manufacture new products, reducing the demand for virgin materials and the associated energy and water consumption, as well as greenhouse gas emissions.

Waste-To-Product Reformation

Waste-to-product reformation refers to the process of converting waste materials into valuable and useful products, thereby reducing the negative impacts of waste on the environment and enhancing sustainable practices. This concept aims to minimize the amount of waste generated and maximize resource efficiency by transforming waste into new raw materials or energy sources. Through waste-to-product reformation, waste is seen as a valuable resource that can be recovered and repurposed instead of being disposed of in landfills or incinerated. This approach aligns with the principles of the circular economy, where materials are kept in a continuous loop of use and reuse, minimizing the need for virgin resources and reducing environmental degradation. There are various ways to implement waste-to-product reformation, including recycling, composting, and anaerobic digestion. Recycling involves the collection and processing of waste materials such as plastics, paper, glass, and metals, which are then transformed into new products or materials. Composting refers to the decomposition of organic

411

waste, such as food scraps and yard trimmings, to produce nutrient-rich compost that can be used in agriculture and landscaping. Anaerobic digestion involves the breakdown of biodegradable waste in the absence of oxygen, producing biogas that can be used for energy generation. By implementing waste-to-product reformation strategies, societies can reduce the demand for raw materials, conserve energy, decrease pollution, and mitigate climate change. It also creates economic opportunities by fostering innovation, job creation, and the development of sustainable industries. Overall, waste-to-product reformation plays a crucial role in achieving a more sustainable future by transforming waste into valuable resources and promoting a circular economy.>

Waste-To-Product Regeneration Processes

Waste-to-product regeneration processes refer to sustainable practices that aim to convert waste materials into valuable products, thereby minimizing the environmental impact of waste disposal and promoting resource efficiency. These processes involve technological advancements and innovative approaches to transform waste materials into new materials, energy sources, or other usable products.

By adopting waste-to-product regeneration processes, societies can reduce the generation of waste, conserve natural resources, and minimize greenhouse gas emissions. These practices contribute to the circular economy concept, where waste is viewed as a valuable resource that can be utilized to create new products instead of simply being discarded.

Waste-To-Product Regeneration

Waste-to-product regeneration, in the context of sustainability, refers to the process of transforming waste materials into usable products or resources, thereby minimizing the negative environmental impact of waste generation and promoting circular economy principles. This approach aims to divert waste from landfills, reduce the consumption of virgin resources, and mitigate the release of greenhouse gases.

Through waste-to-product regeneration, various waste streams such as organic waste, plastics, paper, and metal can be transformed into valuable resources through recycling, upcycling, or conversion technologies. Recycling involves breaking down waste materials and reprocessing them into new products, reducing the need for virgin resources and saving energy. Upcycling, on the other hand, entails creatively repurposing waste materials to give them a new life and value, thereby extending their lifespan and minimizing waste generation.

Additionally, waste-to-product regeneration can also involve advanced conversion technologies such as anaerobic digestion and pyrolysis, which can convert organic waste into renewable energy sources like biogas or biofuels. These technologies not only reduce waste volume but also provide sustainable alternatives to fossil fuels, contributing to the reduction of greenhouse gas emissions and the promotion of a more sustainable energy system.

In conclusion, waste-to-product regeneration is a crucial aspect of sustainable waste management and resource utilization. By effectively converting waste materials into valuable products or resources, this approach helps minimize environmental pollution, conserve natural resources, and contribute to the establishment of a more circular and sustainable economy.

Waste-To-Product Rejuvenation Programs

Waste-to-product rejuvenation programs are initiatives that aim to promote sustainability by transforming waste materials into useful and valuable products. These programs address the pressing issue of waste generation and its detrimental impacts on the environment, while also offering economic and social benefits.

By implementing waste-to-product rejuvenation programs, organizations and governments can minimize the amount of waste that ends up in landfills or the natural environment, reducing pollution and resource depletion. These programs promote the principles of the circular economy, which focus on recycling, reusing, and repurposing materials to create a closed-loop system.

Waste-to-product rejuvenation programs typically involve various processes such as sorting, cleaning, and transforming waste materials into new products through innovative techniques. These techniques can include composting organic waste to create nutrient-rich soil, recycling plastics and metals to produce new materials, and converting biomass into biofuels for energy production.

Not only do waste-to-product rejuvenation programs mitigate environmental harm, but they also present economic opportunities. By recovering and repurposing waste materials, these programs can support the growth of green industries and create jobs in waste management, recycling, and renewable energy sectors.

In addition, waste-to-product rejuvenation programs contribute to social sustainability by raising awareness about the importance of waste reduction and promoting responsible consumption. These programs encourage individuals and communities to adopt more sustainable behaviors and participate in recycling and waste management initiatives.

Waste-To-Product Rejuvenation

Waste-to-product rejuvenation is a sustainable process that aims to transform waste materials into new products, thereby reducing the negative environmental impacts associated with waste disposal and resource extraction. This process involves the application of innovative technologies and creative thinking to identify value in what would otherwise be considered as waste. By converting waste into useful products, waste-to-product rejuvenation promotes the principles of the circular economy, where materials and resources are kept in circulation for as long as possible.

This approach to waste management not only helps to conserve natural resources but also reduces the amount of waste that ends up in landfills or incinerators. By repurposing waste materials, waste-to-product rejuvenation minimizes the need for extraction of virgin resources, such as minerals and fossil fuels, which contributes to the depletion of natural resources and the release of greenhouse gases.

Waste-To-Product Remanufacturing

Waste-to-product remanufacturing is a sustainable process that involves transforming discarded materials into new, fully functional products through advanced technology and efficient resource management. This approach aims to minimize waste generation, conserve resources, and reduce environmental impact.

In this process, potential waste materials, such as end-of-life products or industrial by-products, are carefully collected, sorted, and disassembled. The components and materials are then carefully inspected and evaluated for suitability for reuse or reprocessing. Any viable components are refurbished or repaired, while recyclable materials are extracted for further processing.

The remaining materials that cannot be reused or recycled are subjected to advanced treatment methods, such as chemical or thermal processes, to extract valuable resources or convert them into useful input materials for other industries. This ensures that the maximum value is extracted from every waste material, diverting them from landfills and reducing the need for virgin resources.

Waste-to-product remanufacturing offers numerous environmental benefits. By diverting waste materials from disposal sites, it reduces the pressure on existing landfill capacities and mitigates the environmental risks associated with landfilling, including soil and water pollution. Additionally, it helps decrease greenhouse gas emissions that would otherwise be produced in the manufacturing of new products from virgin materials.

Furthermore, waste-to-product remanufacturing conserves natural resources by minimizing the demand for raw materials. By reusing and repurposing components and materials, it reduces the consumption of energy, water, and other resources required in the extraction, processing, and transportation of virgin resources. This contributes to the preservation of biodiversity, reduces

413

habitat destruction, and minimizes ecological disturbance associated with resource extraction.

Waste-To-Product Renewal

Waste-to-product renewal refers to the process of transforming waste materials into new products or resources, thereby minimizing the amount of waste that ends up in landfills or is released into the environment. This sustainable approach aims to create a closed-loop system where waste is seen as a valuable resource rather than something to be disposed of.

The process of waste-to-product renewal typically involves sorting and separating different types of waste materials, such as plastics, metals, and organic matter. These materials are then treated through various methods, such as recycling, composting, or converting them into energy sources like biogas or biofuels.

By implementing waste-to-product renewal strategies, societies can achieve several environmental and economic benefits. Firstly, it helps conserve natural resources by reducing the need for extracting raw materials from the earth. This reduces the environmental impact associated with mining, deforestation, and other extraction activities.

Secondly, waste-to-product renewal reduces the amount of waste that accumulates in landfills. Landfills pose several environmental risks, including the release of greenhouse gases, water pollution, and the destruction of habitats. By diverting waste materials from landfills, waste-to-product renewal mitigates these risks and helps protect ecosystems.

Furthermore, waste-to-product renewal can contribute to the creation of a circular economy, where materials are continuously reused or repurposed. This not only reduces the consumption of new resources but also provides opportunities for job creation and economic growth in the recycling and renewable energy sectors.

Waste-To-Product Renovation

Waste-to-product renovation is a sustainable approach that involves transforming waste materials into new products, thereby reducing the environmental impact of waste disposal and conserving resources. It is a key strategy in the circular economy, where the aim is to minimize waste generation and maximize resource efficiency.

This renovation process typically involves identifying waste materials that can be repurposed or recycled and implementing innovative techniques to transform them into usable products. It may involve physical, chemical, or biological processes depending on the nature of the waste and the desired end product. Examples of waste-to-product renovation include converting food waste into compost or biogas, recycling plastics into new plastic products, and repurposing construction waste materials for building renovation or new construction.

Waste-To-Product Reprocessing

Waste-to-product reprocessing refers to the process of converting waste materials into useful and valuable products, with the aim of reducing waste generation and promoting sustainability. This approach addresses the challenges associated with traditional waste management practices, such as landfilling or incineration, by extracting value from what would otherwise be considered as waste.

The waste-to-product reprocessing concept is grounded in the principles of the circular economy, where waste is seen as a resource that can go through multiple life cycles. It involves the transformation of various types of waste, including organic waste, plastic waste, industrial byproducts, and post-consumer materials, into new materials or products through different techniques such as recycling, composting, or upcycling.

By redirecting waste streams towards productive uses, waste-to-product reprocessing offers several environmental and economic benefits. Firstly, it reduces the amount of waste sent to landfills, alleviating the pressure on limited disposal space and reducing greenhouse gas emissions associated with waste decomposition. Secondly, it helps conserve natural resources by minimizing the need for raw materials extraction. Additionally, waste-to-product reprocessing can contribute to the creation of jobs and the development of new industries centered around recycling and resource recovery.

In conclusion, waste-to-product reprocessing plays a crucial role in transitioning towards a more sustainable and circular economy. By transforming waste into valuable resources, it minimizes environmental impacts, conserves resources, and promotes economic growth. Embracing waste-to-product reprocessing as a fundamental component of waste management strategies is essential in moving towards a more sustainable future.>

Waste-To-Product Repurposing Initiatives

Waste-to-product repurposing initiatives refer to sustainable practices aimed at transforming waste materials into new, useful products or resources, thereby minimizing waste generation and promoting a circular economy. These initiatives involve identifying waste streams, assessing their potential for repurposing, and utilizing innovative techniques to convert them into valuable resources.

By implementing waste-to-product repurposing initiatives, organizations and communities can reduce the environmental impact of waste disposal, conserve natural resources, and create economic opportunities. This approach aligns with the principles of sustainability, as it addresses both the social and environmental aspects of waste management.

Waste-To-Product Repurposing

Waste-to-product repurposing refers to the practice of converting waste materials into useful products or resources, with the aim of reducing waste generation and promoting sustainability. In an era where the production and consumption of goods continue to rise, waste management has become a critical issue, with overflowing landfills and environmental degradation being the consequences of inefficient waste disposal. Waste-to-product repurposing offers an innovative and sustainable solution to this problem by diverting waste from landfills and utilizing it as raw materials for the production of new goods. This concept involves a series of processes, including the collection and sorting of waste materials, followed by treatment and transformation into viable products. The waste materials can range from organic waste, such as food scraps and agricultural residues, to non-biodegradable waste, such as plastics and metals. Through various techniques like recycling, composting, and upcycling, these waste materials are given a new lease of life and turned into valuable resources. The benefits of waste-to-product repurposing are multifold, both for the environment and the economy. Firstly, it helps in reducing the demand for virgin materials, thereby conserving natural resources and minimizing the associated environmental impacts of resource extraction and manufacturing. Additionally, it decreases the volume of waste sent to landfills, reducing pollution and greenhouse gas emissions produced during waste decomposition. Moreover, waste-to-product repurposing can create new business opportunities and generate economic value by turning waste into marketable products. Overall, waste-to-product repurposing represents a sustainable approach to waste management. By transforming waste materials into useful resources, it helps to mitigate the environmental impact of waste generation while promoting a more circular and resource-efficient economy.>

Waste-To-Product Technologies

Waste-to-product technologies refer to sustainable methods and processes that aim to convert various forms of waste materials into valuable, usable products. These technologies play a crucial role in promoting sustainability by minimizing waste generation, reducing environmental pollution, and conserving natural resources.

These innovative technologies involve transforming waste materials into new products through different processes such as recycling, upcycling, and advanced conversion technologies. Recycling involves breaking down waste materials to their original components and then using them to manufacture new products. Upcycling, on the other hand, involves transforming waste materials into products of higher value or usefulness. Advanced conversion technologies include methods like waste-to-energy, bioconversion, and chemical conversion, which utilize organic waste to produce electricity, heat, biofuels, or other valuable resources.

415

By utilizing waste-to-product technologies, a significant reduction in waste sent to landfills is achieved, thereby minimizing the release of harmful pollutants and greenhouse gases into the environment. These technologies also contribute to the conservation of natural resources by reducing the need for extracting new raw materials. Additionally, waste-to-product technologies promote the circular economy concept by extending the lifespan of materials and reducing the reliance on the traditional linear model of production and disposal.

In conclusion, waste-to-product technologies are essential components of sustainable practices as they provide a means to transform waste materials into valuable resources. These technologies contribute to waste reduction, environmental protection, and resource conservation, making them crucial in achieving a more sustainable future.

Waste-To-Product Upcycling

Waste-to-product upcycling refers to the process of transforming waste materials into new products or materials of higher value and quality. It is a key principle of sustainability as it reduces the amount of waste sent to landfills, conserves resources, and minimizes negative environmental impacts.

Upcycling differs from recycling in that it involves creatively reusing waste materials without breaking them down completely. Instead of downgrading or degrading materials through recycling, upcycling focuses on enhancing their value and extending their lifespan.

The process of waste-to-product upcycling involves identifying and selecting suitable waste materials, and then applying innovative design and manufacturing techniques to transform them into new, functional, and aesthetically pleasing products. This can include repurposing materials, combining different waste materials to create new composite materials, or refurbishing and repairing damaged items to give them a second life. By upcycling, the consumption of new raw materials is reduced, as waste materials are used as a valuable resource.

Waste-to-product upcycling offers various benefits for sustainability. It helps to reduce the extraction and depletion of natural resources, decrease energy consumption, and minimize greenhouse gas emissions associated with raw material production and waste management. Additionally, upcycling reduces landfill waste, which can have harmful effects on ecosystems and human health. It also promotes creativity, innovation, and circular economy principles, where waste is seen as a valuable resource, rather than a disposable item.

Wastewater Nutrient Recovery

Wastewater nutrient recovery refers to the process of extracting and repurposing valuable nutrients, such as phosphorus and nitrogen, from wastewater for use in agricultural, industrial, or environmental applications. This sustainable approach aims to minimize the release of nutrients into the environment while simultaneously creating a valuable resource that can be used to promote sustainable practices and reduce the reliance on traditional fertilizers.

During the wastewater treatment process, nutrients present in the wastewater, which are typically derived from human and animal waste, are concentrated and separated from the treated water. These nutrients, which are essential for plant growth and development, can be recovered and turned into a nutrient-rich product known as biosolids or struvite.

The recovered nutrients can be used in a variety of ways. In agriculture, they can be applied as organic fertilizers, providing crops with the necessary nutrients for optimal growth while reducing the reliance on synthetic fertilizers. The use of recovered nutrients in agriculture also helps to close the nutrient cycle, preventing nutrient runoff and eutrophication of water bodies. In addition, recovered nutrients can be used in industrial processes, such as the production of biofuels or bioplastics, contributing to the development of a circular economy.

Overall, wastewater nutrient recovery plays a crucial role in promoting sustainable practices by reducing nutrient pollution, minimizing the use of non-renewable resources, and creating a valuable resource from an otherwise waste stream. By utilizing recovered nutrients, we can simultaneously address environmental concerns, enhance the efficiency of wastewater treatment processes, and promote sustainable agriculture and industrial practices.

Wastewater Nutrient Removal

Wastewater nutrient removal is a sustainable process that aims to reduce the level of nutrients, such as nitrogen and phosphorus, in wastewater before it is discharged into the environment. Nutrients, particularly nitrogen and phosphorus, are essential for plant growth and are often found in domestic and industrial wastewater streams. However, high levels of nutrients in wastewater can have negative impacts on water bodies, leading to eutrophication and harmful algal blooms.

Wastewater nutrient removal processes typically involve various treatment methods, including biological, chemical, and physical processes, to effectively remove or transform nutrients in wastewater. These processes aim to break down or convert nitrogen and phosphorus compounds into less harmful forms, such as nitrogen gas or precipitated phosphorus, which can be safely discharged or used as a beneficial resource.

This sustainable practice helps to protect and preserve water quality in surface water bodies, such as rivers, lakes, and oceans. By reducing the level of nutrients in wastewater, it minimizes the potential harm to aquatic ecosystems and supports the long-term sustainability of these environments. Moreover, wastewater nutrient removal also contributes to the sustainable management of water resources, as it reduces the need for additional water treatment downstream and helps maintain a healthy balance in the natural nutrient cycles.

Wastewater Treatment Innovation

Wastewater treatment innovation refers to the development and implementation of new and improved technologies, processes, and approaches aimed at efficiently and effectively treating wastewater in a manner that promotes sustainability.

This innovation stems from the recognition of the urgent need to address the environmental, social, and economic challenges associated with inadequate wastewater treatment. As the global population continues to grow and urbanize, the volume of wastewater generated also increases, posing significant risks to both human and ecological health if left untreated.

Sustainability lies at the core of wastewater treatment innovation, encompassing various dimensions such as environmental protection, resource conservation, and social equity. In terms of environmental protection, innovative wastewater treatment techniques strive to minimize or eliminate the release of harmful pollutants into water bodies, thereby preserving water quality and biodiversity. Furthermore, sustainable wastewater treatment aims to optimize energy efficiency, reduce carbon emissions, and minimize the consumption of natural resources to mitigate the impact on climate change and promote resource conservation.

In addition to mitigating environmental impacts, wastewater treatment innovation also addresses social equity by enhancing public health and improving access to clean water. By efficiently removing pathogens and contaminants from wastewater, these innovations help prevent the spread of waterborne diseases and ensure a safe water supply for communities. Moreover, they contribute to reducing water scarcity by enabling the safe reuse of treated wastewater for various non-potable purposes, such as irrigation or industrial processes.

Overall, wastewater treatment innovation is a critical component of sustainable development, providing solutions to the pressing challenges associated with wastewater management. Through the continuous improvement and adoption of innovative technologies and practices, the ultimate goal of achieving sustainable wastewater treatment can be realized, benefiting both present and future generations.

Wastewater Treatment Innovations

Wastewater treatment innovations refer to the development and implementation of new technologies, processes, and practices aimed at improving the sustainability of wastewater treatment systems. These innovations strive to address the environmental, social, and economic challenges associated with treating and disposing of wastewater.

Sustainability, in the context of wastewater treatment, refers to the ability to meet the present needs of wastewater treatment without compromising the ability of future generations to meet their own needs. It involves minimizing the negative impacts of wastewater treatment on the environment, conserving resources, and maximizing the efficiency of the treatment process.

Wastewater Treatment Technologies

Wastewater treatment technologies encompass various processes and techniques applied to treat and purify wastewater for its safe discharge or reuse, with a focus on sustainable practices. These technologies aim to efficiently remove contaminants and pollutants from wastewater, ensuring the protection of ecosystems and human health, while minimizing negative impacts on the environment.

The implementation of sustainable wastewater treatment technologies involves the integration of resource-efficient and environmentally friendly approaches throughout the entire treatment process. This includes practices such as energy conservation, utilization of renewable energy sources, reduction of greenhouse gas emissions, and the application of advanced treatment methods that minimize the use of chemicals and energy-intensive processes.

Key sustainable wastewater treatment technologies focus on the utilization of natural processes for purification, including the use of constructed wetlands, sand filters, and biological treatment systems such as activated sludge, rotating biological contactors, and moving bed biofilm reactors. These systems promote the natural treatment of wastewater through the degradation of organic matter and the removal of nutrients by microorganisms.

Additionally, advanced technologies such as membrane filtration, ultraviolet disinfection, and ozonation are employed to further improve the treatment efficiency and ensure the removal of pathogens, pharmaceuticals, and other emerging contaminants from wastewater. These technologies contribute to the preservation of water resources and protect against the potential risks associated with the discharge of untreated or inadequately treated wastewater into the environment.

Water Management And Conservation Software

A water management and conservation software refers to a digital tool that aids in monitoring, analyzing, and optimizing water usage in order to promote sustainability. This software is designed to assist individuals, organizations, and communities in efficiently managing their water resources by providing data-driven insights and facilitating informed decision-making.

Through its various features and functionalities, a water management and conservation software enables users to track their water consumption, identify areas of inefficiency or waste, and implement strategies to minimize water usage. It typically includes tools for collecting and analyzing data, generating reports, and implementing water-saving measures. Additionally, some software may offer integrations with IoT devices or sensors to provide real-time monitoring and alerts regarding water usage.

By utilizing a water management and conservation software, users can gain a comprehensive understanding of their water usage patterns and identify potential areas of improvement. This software can help identify leaks or inefficiencies in water systems, leading to prompt repairs and reduced water loss. It can also assist in optimizing irrigation systems, implementing water-saving practices, and managing water resources more sustainably.

In summary, a water management and conservation software serves as a digital solution to enhance water management practices by promoting efficient water usage, minimizing waste, and conserving this valuable resource for present and future generations.

Water-Efficient Fixtures

Water-efficient fixtures are sustainable plumbing devices designed to reduce water consumption without compromising functionality or user experience. These fixtures aim to minimize water waste and promote conservation by maximizing water efficiency in households, commercial buildings, and public spaces.

By incorporating advanced technologies and innovative designs, water-efficient fixtures help conserve one of the earth's most precious resources. They are engineered to use less water while still providing adequate flow rates and performance. Examples of water-efficient fixtures include low-flow faucets, showerheads, toilets, and urinals.

Water-Efficient Irrigation

Water-efficient irrigation refers to the use of techniques and technologies that minimize water consumption and reduce waste in agricultural and landscape irrigation practices. It is an important aspect of sustainable water management, aiming to optimize water use and conserve this valuable resource.

The implementation of water-efficient irrigation strategies involves various methods, such as improving irrigation systems, using advanced technologies, and adopting best management practices. These approaches aim to ensure that water is efficiently applied to crops, gardens, or landscapes, minimizing losses due to evaporation, runoff, or overwatering.

One common method of water-efficient irrigation is the use of drip irrigation systems, where water is delivered directly to the plant's root zone through a network of tubes or pipes with emitters. This technique reduces water loss through evaporation and ensures that the water reaches the plants' roots efficiently. Another approach is the use of precision irrigation systems, which apply water based on the specific needs of the crop and soil conditions, avoiding over- or under-watering.

Water-efficient irrigation not only helps conserve water resources but also contributes to other sustainability goals. By reducing water consumption, it can alleviate pressure on water supplies, especially in areas facing water scarcity. Additionally, it can minimize the energy required for water pumping and treatment, contributing to reduced greenhouse gas emissions.

Water-Efficient Landscaping Solutions

Water-efficient landscaping solutions refer to the design and management of outdoor spaces that minimize water usage and promote sustainability. It involves the implementation of strategies and techniques that conserve water, reduce runoff, and support biodiversity.

Water-efficient landscaping focuses on selecting plants, trees, and grasses that are native to the region and have low water requirements. These species are adapted to the local climate and soil conditions, allowing them to thrive with minimal irrigation. Additionally, incorporating drought-tolerant plants helps reduce the need for excessive watering and ensures long-term sustainability in water usage.

In order to maximize water efficiency, it is essential to consider soil health and moisture retention. The use of organic matter, mulch, and compost improves soil quality, enhances water absorption, and reduces evaporation. Proper irrigation techniques such as drip irrigation or micro-sprinklers deliver water directly to the plants' roots, minimizing water loss through evaporation or overspray.

Furthermore, the design of water-efficient landscapes takes into account the layout and slope of the terrain to prevent water runoff. Implementing features like rain gardens, swales, or permeable paving allows rainwater to infiltrate the soil, replenishing groundwater and minimizing stormwater runoff into local water bodies.

Overall, water-efficient landscaping solutions aim to preserve water resources, reduce reliance on irrigation systems, and create sustainable outdoor environments that require minimal maintenance and inputs. By employing these strategies, individuals, communities, and organizations can contribute to water conservation efforts and promote a more sustainable future.

Water-Efficient Landscaping

Water-efficient landscaping refers to the practice of designing and maintaining outdoor areas in a way that minimizes water consumption while promoting environmental sustainability. It

419

involves the use of various techniques and strategies to ensure that the landscaping design and plants are able to thrive with minimal water resources.

This approach to landscaping is crucial in promoting sustainable water usage, especially in regions facing water scarcity or drought conditions. By implementing water-efficient landscaping, individuals and communities can significantly reduce their water footprint and contribute to water conservation efforts.

Water-Efficient Technologies

Water-efficient technologies refer to systems or devices that are designed to minimize the consumption of water while maintaining or improving the efficiency and effectiveness of various processes or activities. In the context of sustainability, water-efficient technologies play a crucial role in conserving and preserving water resources, mitigating water scarcity, and reducing the overall environmental impact associated with water usage.

These technologies encompass a wide range of approaches and applications across different sectors such as agriculture, industry, and households. For instance, in agriculture, water-efficient technologies may include precision irrigation systems, such as drip irrigation or micro-sprinklers, which deliver water directly to the plant roots, minimizing evaporation and reducing water waste. Similarly, in industrial settings, water-efficient technologies can involve the use of closed-loop systems, water recycling and reclamation processes, or the implementation of water-saving equipment like low-flow fixtures or automated controls.

By implementing water-efficient technologies, significant reductions in water consumption can be achieved. This not only helps mitigate the strain on freshwater sources but also contributes to the overall sustainability goals by minimizing energy demands, reducing carbon emissions, and preventing the contamination and depletion of water bodies.

Furthermore, the adoption of water-efficient technologies can also generate economic benefits. The reduced water consumption leads to lower water bills and operational costs in both commercial and residential settings. Additionally, the implementation of these technologies can create new job opportunities in industries related to water management, technology development, and installation and maintenance services.

Wave Energy Converters

Wave energy converters (WECs) are devices that harness the kinetic energy from ocean waves and convert it into usable electricity. They are a sustainable solution for generating renewable energy as they rely on the natural motion of waves, which are a consistent and abundant resource.

WECs work by capturing the energy of waves and converting it into mechanical or electrical power. There are several types of WECs, including oscillating water columns, point absorbers, and attenuators. Each design utilizes different mechanisms to harness wave energy, but all aim to capture the wave's motion and convert it into usable power.

One of the key advantages of wave energy converters is their potential for long-term sustainability. Unlike fossil fuels, which are finite and contribute to greenhouse gas emissions, waves are a renewable resource that will continue to exist as long as the Earth's oceans exist. By harnessing wave energy, WECs offer a clean and environmentally friendly alternative to traditional forms of energy generation.

Furthermore, wave energy converters have a relatively low carbon footprint compared to other renewable energy technologies. While their initial manufacturing and installation may require some carbon emissions, the operation of WECs produces no greenhouse gas emissions. This makes them a viable option for reducing carbon dioxide and mitigating climate change.

Wave Energy Technology

Wave energy technology, also known as ocean wave power, harnesses the energy produced by the movement of ocean waves and converts it into usable electricity. This renewable energy

420

source holds promise for sustainable development and contributes to reducing our dependence on fossil fuels.

By utilizing the power of waves, this technology offers several environmental benefits. Firstly, it produces clean electricity without emitting greenhouse gases or other harmful pollutants into the atmosphere, leading to reduced air pollution and mitigating climate change. Furthermore, as wave energy is derived from a renewable resource - the ocean - it can help decrease our reliance on finite fossil fuel reserves, promoting energy security and reducing the risks associated with traditional energy generation and extraction.

From a sustainability perspective, wave energy technology also has the potential to support marine ecosystems. Unlike other renewable energy sources, such as wind or solar power, wave energy installations have a relatively low visual and auditory impact. This makes them more suitable for coexisting with marine wildlife and minimizes disturbance to their habitats. Additionally, wave energy devices can serve as artificial reefs, providing habitats for various marine species and potentially enhancing biodiversity.

Furthermore, wave energy technology offers the advantage of predictability, as the movement of waves is a consistent and reliable energy source. This predictability allows for better integration with existing power grids, contributing to a stable and efficient energy supply.

In conclusion, wave energy technology presents a sustainable solution for electricity generation, offering clean energy, reducing environmental impact, supporting marine ecosystems, and providing a reliable source of power. It holds significant potential for contributing to a more sustainable and resilient energy future.

Wildlife Tracking And Conservation Technology

Wildlife tracking and conservation technology refers to the use of technological advancements to monitor, study, and protect wildlife species and their habitats, with the ultimate goal of achieving sustainable practices. This field integrates various tools and methods such as GPS tracking, remote sensing, camera traps, acoustic monitoring, and genetic analysis to collect data and gain valuable insights into wildlife populations, behavior, and spatial distribution.

By employing wildlife tracking and conservation technology, researchers and conservationists can track animal movements, migration patterns, and habitat use, which in turn helps in understanding their ecological interactions, identifying key conservation areas, and addressing potential threats to their survival. This technology enables the collection of accurate and reliable data over large spatial and temporal scales, allowing for evidence-based decision-making that is crucial for effective biodiversity management and conservation.

Wind Turbine Recycling

Wind turbine recycling refers to the process of dismantling and reusing materials from wind turbines, with the aim of minimizing waste and maximizing resource efficiency. As a crucial aspect of the broader sustainability framework, wind turbine recycling plays a vital role in reducing the environmental impact associated with the lifecycle of wind energy systems.

At the end of their operational life, wind turbines are decommissioned and taken apart through various recycling methods. These methods involve separating different components, such as the tower, blades, nacelle, and generator, to ensure that each can be appropriately recycled or disposed of. The recycling process aims to recover valuable and reusable materials, such as steel, copper, aluminum, and fiberglass, while minimizing the amount of waste sent to landfills.

In addition to reducing the demand for raw materials, wind turbine recycling offers several environmental benefits. By recycling the materials used in wind turbines, the energy and carbon emissions required for manufacturing new components are significantly reduced. Furthermore, recycling helps prevent pollution caused by the release of hazardous substances, such as rare earth metals, which are commonly used in wind turbine magnets.

Overall, wind turbine recycling is an essential practice in sustainable energy production and circular economy initiatives. By extending the lifespan of wind energy systems and minimizing waste generation, it contributes to the long-term viability of renewable energy and supports the transition to a more sustainable and environmentally conscious society.

Wind Turbine Technology

Wind turbine technology refers to the use of mechanical devices, called wind turbines, to harness the power of wind and convert it into clean and sustainable energy. These turbines consist of large rotor blades that are mounted on a tall tower and are designed to capture the kinetic energy of the wind. When the wind blows, it causes the blades to rotate, which in turn activates a generator to produce electricity.

Wind turbines are crucial in the context of sustainability as they offer numerous benefits. First and foremost, they generate electricity without burning fossil fuels, thus reducing greenhouse gas emissions and combating climate change. This enables us to move away from the reliance on non-renewable energy sources and towards a more sustainable energy future.

Furthermore, wind turbine technology is highly versatile and can be deployed in various settings, from onshore wind farms to offshore installations. This flexibility allows for the utilization of wind resources in different regions, increasing diversity in energy production and reducing dependency on a single energy source.

In addition to mitigating climate change and promoting energy diversity, wind turbines also have minimal environmental impact. They do not produce harmful pollutants or waste during operation, and with proper planning and consideration, their impact on wildlife and ecosystems can be minimized.

Overall, wind turbine technology plays a crucial role in sustainability by providing a clean, renewable, and abundant source of energy. By harnessing the power of wind, we can reduce our carbon footprint, enhance energy security, and pave the way towards a more sustainable and environmentally friendly future.

Wind-Solar Hybrid Power Plants

Wind-solar hybrid power plants are sustainable energy generation facilities that combine wind and solar power technologies to produce electricity. These power plants harness the renewable energy from the sun and wind, utilizing their complimentary nature to optimize energy output and overall efficiency.

By integrating wind and solar resources, hybrid power plants offer several advantages in terms of sustainability. Firstly, they provide a more reliable and consistent energy supply compared to standalone wind or solar power projects. This is due to the fact that wind and solar power generation have complementary production patterns – wind power tends to be more prominent during the night or in inclement weather, while solar power is at its peak during daytime. By combining these two sources, hybrid power plants can ensure continuous electricity production throughout the day and night, irrespective of environmental conditions.

Wind-Solar-Battery Systems

Wind-solar-battery systems are sustainable energy systems that combine the power of wind, solar, and batteries to generate renewable electricity. These systems harness the power of the wind and sunlight to generate clean energy, which is then stored in batteries for later use. By integrating all three components, wind-solar-battery systems offer a reliable and efficient way to produce electricity while minimizing environmental impact and promoting sustainability.

In wind-solar-battery systems, wind turbines and solar panels are used to capture renewable energy from the environment. Wind turbines convert the kinetic energy of the wind into electrical energy, while solar panels harness the energy from sunlight and convert it into electricity. The electricity generated from these sources is then stored in batteries, which act as energy storage devices for periods when wind and solar resources are low or unavailable.

The integration of wind, solar, and batteries in these systems allows for a more consistent and reliable power supply compared to relying solely on wind or solar energy. By combining the two renewable sources and utilizing energy storage, wind-solar-battery systems can provide electricity even during periods of low wind or solar resource availability. This reduces dependency on fossil fuels and helps to mitigate the negative environmental impacts associated with traditional energy generation methods.

Furthermore, wind-solar-battery systems contribute to the overall sustainability goals by reducing greenhouse gas emissions, air pollution, and reliance on finite energy resources. They offer a sustainable solution for meeting energy demands while minimizing environmental degradation and promoting a cleaner and healthier future.

World Business Academy

The World Business Academy is an organization focused on fostering a sustainable and equitable world through innovative business practices and systems thinking.

Sustainability, in the context of the World Business Academy, refers to the concept of meeting the needs of the present generation without compromising the ability of future generations to meet their own needs. It involves the responsible management of resources, ecosystems, and social systems for long-term viability and resilience.

World Business Council For Sustainable Development (WBCSD)

The World Business Council for Sustainable Development (WBCSD) is a global, CEO-led organization that was established in 1995 with the aim of promoting sustainable development in the business sector.

WBCSD is comprised of more than 200 member companies from various industries across the world. These companies are committed to driving the transition to a sustainable future by integrating sustainability into their business strategies and practices.

World Council On Renewable Energy (WCRE)

The World Council on Renewable Energy (WCRE) is an international organization dedicated to promoting and advancing the use of renewable energy sources in a sustainable manner. The council works towards achieving a global transition from fossil fuel dependency to renewable energy systems, with the goal of mitigating climate change, reducing environmental impact, and ensuring socio-economic development.

Acting as a platform for collaboration and knowledge sharing, WCRE brings together governments, businesses, academic institutions, non-governmental organizations, and other stakeholders from around the world. Through various initiatives, programs, and events, the council facilitates dialogue and cooperation to accelerate the adoption and implementation of renewable energy technologies, policies, and best practices.

WCRE plays a vital role in promoting the understanding and awareness of the environmental, economic, and social benefits of renewable energy. By advocating for renewable energy integration in national and international energy strategies, the council aims to create a sustainable and resilient energy system that can meet the current and future energy needs of the global population.

Additionally, WCRE promotes research, innovation, and capacity building in the renewable energy sector. By fostering collaboration between researchers, engineers, and industry experts, the council helps drive advancements in renewable energy technologies and fosters the development of sustainable energy solutions.

Overall, the World Council on Renewable Energy plays a crucial role in advancing the sustainability agenda by promoting the greater use of renewable energy sources worldwide. Through its efforts, the council contributes to the development of a more environmentally friendly, economically viable, and socially equitable energy system.

World Ocean Council

The World Ocean Council (WOC) is an international, industry-led organization that aims to advance sustainable ocean stewardship. It serves as a platform for collaboration and dialogue among various sectors of the ocean economy, including shipping, fishing, energy, tourism, and technology.

With its primary focus on business and industry engagement, the WOC facilitates partnerships and initiatives that promote the responsible use and conservation of the world's oceans. By bringing together stakeholders from both developed and developing countries, the WOC aims to address the complex challenges facing marine ecosystems and coastal communities.

World Resources Institute (WRI)

The World Resources Institute (WRI) is an international research organization that focuses on addressing urgent sustainability challenges. Established in 1982, WRI works towards creating a sustainable future by analyzing global issues and developing practical solutions.

WRI collaborates with governments, businesses, and civil society organizations to ensure a healthy and thriving planet. The organization's research and analysis serve as a foundation for designing sustainable policies and practices, with the goal of balancing economic development with environmental and social well-being. WRI's work spans a wide range of areas, including climate change, energy, water, forests, cities, and the ocean.

World Wildlife Fund (WWF)

The World Wildlife Fund (WWF) is an international organization focused on promoting environmental conservation and sustainability. Founded in 1961, WWF works to protect the planet's natural resources and wildlife, while also addressing the negative impacts of human activities on the environment.

Through various initiatives, programs, and projects, WWF aims to create a world where humans and nature can coexist in harmony. The organization's primary areas of focus include conservation of forests, oceans, freshwaters, and wildlife, as well as the reduction of pollution and the mitigation of climate change.

WWF operates on a global scale, collaborating with governments, businesses, communities, and individuals to implement sustainable practices and raise awareness about environmental issues. By partnering with local communities, WWF strives to empower them to become active participants in the conservation of their natural resources.

One of WWF's key approaches is the establishment and management of protected areas, such as national parks and wildlife reserves, to preserve biodiversity and provide habitat for endangered species. Additionally, WWF supports sustainable development practices, advocating for the responsible use of natural resources to ensure their longevity for future generations.

Through its conservation efforts, research, and policy work, WWF plays a crucial role in promoting sustainability and addressing the urgent challenges facing our planet. By engaging and inspiring individuals, businesses, and governments, WWF aims to create a future where humanity lives in harmony with nature.

Worldwatch Institute

The Worldwatch Institute is a globally recognized research organization that focuses on sustainability. Its mission is to provide information and insights to help create a sustainable future for humanity.

The Institute conducts research, analyzes data, and publishes reports and articles on various topics related to sustainability. Its work covers a wide range of issues, including climate change, energy, food security, population growth, and water resources.

Through its research and publications, the Worldwatch Institute aims to raise awareness about the challenges facing our planet and to promote sustainable solutions. It seeks to inform policymakers, businesses, and the general public about the need for action and the potential pathways to a more sustainable future.

The Institute also plays a key role in promoting international cooperation and collaboration on sustainability issues. It provides a platform for experts, policymakers, and stakeholders from around the world to exchange ideas and share best practices.

Overall, the Worldwatch Institute is a respected authority on sustainability and serves as a valuable resource for anyone interested in understanding and addressing the environmental, social, and economic challenges of our time.

X-Ray Fluorescence (XRF) Analysis

X-ray fluorescence (XRF) analysis refers to a method used in sustainability research and practice to determine the elemental composition of various materials. It involves the use of X-ray radiation to excite the atoms in a sample, causing them to emit characteristic X-ray fluorescence radiation. By measuring the energy and intensity of these emitted X-rays, researchers can identify and quantify the elements present in the sample.

In the context of sustainability, XRF analysis plays a key role in various areas of research and decision-making. It can be used to assess the composition of waste materials, allowing for efficient recycling and resource recovery. By identifying the elements in a waste stream, XRF analysis enables the identification of valuable metals that can be extracted and reused, reducing the need for mining and preserving natural resources.

X-Ray Photoelectron Spectroscopy

X-ray photoelectron spectroscopy (XPS) is a surface analysis technique used to investigate the elemental composition, chemical bonding states, and electronic properties of materials. It plays a crucial role in various aspects of sustainability, including environmental monitoring, energy research, and the development of green technologies.

In the context of sustainability, XPS helps in understanding and improving the performance of materials used in renewable energy technologies such as solar cells, fuel cells, and batteries. By analyzing the chemical composition and electronic structure of these materials, researchers can identify ways to enhance efficiency, durability, and recyclability, thereby contributing to the development of sustainable energy sources.

Moreover, XPS is valuable in environmental monitoring and pollution control. It can identify and quantify contaminants on surfaces, enabling efficient analysis of air and water quality. By understanding the composition and behavior of pollutants, researchers can develop effective remediation strategies and implement sustainable practices to minimize environmental impact.

Furthermore, XPS aids in the development of sustainable materials and manufacturing processes. It enables the characterization of nanomaterials, coatings, and catalysts, ensuring their effectiveness and environmental safety. By understanding the chemical properties and interactions within materials, researchers can develop innovative, eco-friendly materials with reduced energy consumption and waste generation.

Xeriscaping (Water-Efficient Landscaping)

Xeriscaping, also known as water-efficient landscaping, is a sustainable approach to landscaping that aims to minimize the use of water while maintaining an aesthetically pleasing and functional outdoor space. It involves the careful selection of drought-tolerant plants, efficient watering techniques, and the use of mulch and other materials to promote water retention.

The practice of xeriscaping is based on the principles of water conservation, environmental stewardship, and sustainability. By reducing the amount of water needed for irrigation, it helps to conserve this valuable resource and protect freshwater ecosystems. Xeriscaping also minimizes the need for chemical fertilizers and pesticides, thereby reducing pollution and promoting the health of soil organisms and beneficial insects.

In addition to its environmental benefits, xeriscaping has several economic advantages. By reducing water consumption, it can lead to significant savings on water bills. The use of native or adapted plants in xeriscaping can also reduce maintenance costs, as these plants are generally more resistant to pests and diseases and require less attention and resources.

Furthermore, xeriscaping can contribute to a more resilient landscape by reducing the reliance on traditional irrigation systems and increasing the resilience of plants to drought and other environmental stressors. This is particularly important in regions prone to water scarcity, where xeriscaping can help create sustainable landscapes that thrive even in periods of limited water availability.

Xylitol As A Sustainable Sweetener

Xylitol is a sustainable sweetener that can be used as an alternative to traditional sugar. Derived from renewable plant sources such as corn cobs and birch trees, xylitol offers a lower environmental impact compared to other sweeteners, making it a more sustainable choice.

One key aspect of xylitol's sustainability lies in its production process. Unlike sugar, which requires large amounts of water, land, and energy to cultivate and refine, xylitol can be produced using less resources. The raw materials used in xylitol production, such as corn cobs or birch trees, are renewable, minimizing the strain on natural resources. Additionally, the production of xylitol generates fewer greenhouse gas emissions compared to sugar production.

Furthermore, xylitol's sustainability extends beyond its production phase. When consumed, xylitol has a minimal impact on blood sugar levels, making it suitable for individuals with diabetes or those concerned about their sugar intake. As a sugar substitute, xylitol can also contribute to reducing the prevalence of dental cavities, as it does not promote tooth decay like sugar does. This not only benefits individuals but also reduces the demand for dental treatments and associated waste.

In conclusion, xylitol offers a sustainable alternative to traditional sugar. Its production process utilizes renewable resources and generates fewer greenhouse gas emissions. By choosing xylitol as a sweetener, individuals can reduce their environmental impact, support sustainable agriculture, and promote better dental health.

Zero Waste International Alliance (ZWIA)

The Zero Waste International Alliance (ZWIA) is a global organization that promotes sustainable practices and the reduction of waste throughout the world. ZWIA is dedicated to educating and inspiring individuals, businesses, and governments to adopt a zero waste approach, which aims to eliminate the production of waste and instead focuses on resource conservation and the efficient use of materials.

With a focus on sustainability, ZWIA advocates for a circular economy where resources are used and reused in a continuous loop, rather than being disposed of in landfills or incinerated. The organization works towards achieving this by encouraging the implementation of strategies such as recycling, composting, and designing products with a focus on durability and repairability.

Zero-Emission Transportation

Zero-emission transportation refers to the use of vehicles and systems that produce no greenhouse gas emissions or other pollutants during operation. It is an essential component of sustainable transportation as it helps reduce air pollution, combat climate change, and promote environmental and public health.

This form of transportation includes various modes such as electric vehicles (EVs), hydrogen fuel cell vehicles, and sustainable public transportation systems. Electric vehicles are powered by electricity stored in rechargeable batteries, and they produce zero tailpipe emissions. Similarly, hydrogen fuel cell vehicles use hydrogen gas to generate electricity, emitting only water vapor as a byproduct. Sustainable public transportation systems involve the use of electric buses, trams, and trains that are powered by renewable energy sources.

In addition to reducing air pollution and addressing climate change concerns, zero-emission transportation also offers economic benefits. It decreases the dependence on fossil fuels, reducing fuel costs and vulnerability to oil price fluctuations. It also promotes innovation, job creation, and economic growth in the renewable energy and clean transportation sectors.

However, the transition to zero-emission transportation requires significant investments in infrastructure, such as charging stations for electric vehicles and hydrogen fueling stations. It also necessitates the development of renewable energy sources to provide clean electricity for the vehicles. Collaboration among governments, businesses, and individuals is crucial for the successful implementation of zero-emission transportation and achieving sustainability goals.

Zero-Emission Vehicles

A zero-emission vehicle is a type of vehicle that produces no tailpipe emissions of greenhouse gases or other pollutants during operation. These vehicles are designed to reduce the environmental impact of transportation and contribute to sustainability efforts.

Zero-emission vehicles are typically powered by electric motors that run on electricity stored in batteries or generated by hydrogen fuel cells. Unlike vehicles powered by internal combustion engines, which burn fossil fuels and emit pollutants like carbon dioxide, nitrogen oxides, and particulate matter, zero-emission vehicles produce no tailpipe emissions. This makes them an attractive alternative to conventional vehicles in terms of reducing air pollution and mitigating climate change.

By relying on clean and renewable energy sources to power zero-emission vehicles, such as solar or wind power for generating electricity or sustainable production of hydrogen, we can further enhance their environmental benefits. Additionally, these vehicles can contribute to reducing our dependence on fossil fuels and improving energy efficiency.

Zero-emission vehicles are an important component of sustainable transportation systems. They offer a viable solution to reducing air pollution, mitigating climate change, and promoting a cleaner and healthier environment. As efforts continue to develop and improve the performance and affordability of zero-emission vehicles, their adoption can lead to significant environmental and sustainability benefits for communities and societies as a whole.

Zero-Energy Buildings

Zero-energy buildings are structures that are designed and constructed to consume only as much energy as they generate over the course of a year. These buildings, also known as net-zero energy buildings or zero-net energy buildings, employ renewable energy sources to offset any energy they consume from non-renewable sources.

The sustainable design of zero-energy buildings incorporates various strategies to minimize energy consumption while maximizing energy production. These strategies include efficient insulation of the building envelope, optimized natural lighting and ventilation, energy-efficient appliances and equipment, and advanced control systems that regulate energy use based on occupancy patterns.

The primary goal of zero-energy buildings is to reduce greenhouse gas emissions and mitigate the effects of climate change. By generating their own renewable energy on-site, these buildings reduce their reliance on fossil fuels and decrease their carbon footprint. Additionally, zero-energy buildings contribute to energy independence by reducing the demand for energy from the electrical grid.

Advancements in technology have made zero-energy buildings more feasible and cost-effective. The integration of solar photovoltaic panels, wind turbines, geothermal systems, and innovative building materials allows these buildings to produce as much energy as they consume. Excess energy generated by zero-energy buildings can be stored for future use or fed back into the grid, further promoting sustainability.

In conclusion, zero-energy buildings represent a crucial component of sustainable architecture and urban development. By seamlessly blending energy efficiency and renewable energy generation, these buildings significantly reduce their environmental impact while providing comfortable and functional spaces for occupants.

Zero-Waste Cafe Design

A zero-waste cafe design refers to a sustainable concept that strives to minimize waste generation and promote responsible consumption practices within a cafe setting. It encompasses various strategies and principles that aim to reduce, reuse, and recycle resources, fostering an environmentally conscious and efficient operation.

At its core, a zero-waste cafe design incorporates principles such as conservation, resource efficiency, and waste reduction. This involves implementing practices that minimize the use of single-use items, opting for reusable alternatives instead. For example, the cafe may provide customers with ceramic mugs or encourage them to bring their own reusable cups to reduce the consumption of disposable cups.

Furthermore, a zero-waste cafe design involves a comprehensive waste management system. This includes setting up recycling stations for different types of waste, such as paper, plastic, and glass, to ensure proper segregation and recycling. Additionally, strategies like composting organic waste can be employed to minimize landfill contributions and promote nutrient-rich soil generation.

Energy efficiency is another aspect of a zero-waste cafe design. By utilizing energy-efficient appliances, incorporating natural lighting, and optimizing heating, ventilation, and air conditioning systems, the cafe can reduce its energy consumption and carbon footprint.

Overall, a zero-waste cafe design is a holistic approach to sustainability, encompassing various strategies to minimize waste generation, promote responsible consumption, and reduce environmental impact. It aims to create a space where customers can enjoy their meals or beverages while being mindful of their ecological footprint, encouraging a more sustainable lifestyle.

Zero-Waste Cafe Interiors

A zero-waste cafe is a sustainable establishment that aims to minimize waste and environmental impact by implementing various practices throughout its interior design. The concept of zero waste revolves around the principle of reducing, reusing, and recycling materials to avoid sending any waste to landfills or incineration.

In the context of cafe interiors, a zero-waste approach involves several key elements. First, the use of eco-friendly and non-toxic materials is prioritized. This includes furniture made from sustainable sources, such as reclaimed wood or recycled materials. Additionally, non-toxic and low-emission paints and finishes are chosen for walls and surfaces to ensure a healthy environment for both customers and staff.

Furthermore, zero-waste cafes focus on efficient space planning and utilization to maximize functionality while minimizing the consumption of resources. Design considerations may include the use of multifunctional furniture, collapsible or stackable fixtures, and modular layouts. This not only reduces waste during the construction and renovation process but also allows for adaptability and flexibility as the cafe evolves.

Zero-Waste Communities

A zero-waste community is a sustainable and environmentally conscious society that aims to minimize waste generation and eliminate the need for landfills or incinerators. It is based on the principle of "reduce, reuse, and recycle" and strives to approach a circular economy model, where all resources are used efficiently and no waste is sent to the landfill or released into the environment.

In a zero-waste community, individuals, businesses, and local institutions work together to prioritize waste prevention through various strategies. This includes minimizing packaging and single-use items, promoting reusable products, and encouraging composting. The community also implements comprehensive recycling programs to ensure that recyclable materials are collected, sorted, and processed effectively to be transformed into new products.

Furthermore, a zero-waste community actively seeks alternatives to conventional waste management practices. It fosters innovation and collaboration to find sustainable solutions for organic waste, hazardous materials, and electronic waste, as well as for hard-to-recycle items. This may involve establishing local facilities for composting, recycling, and eco-friendly disposal, or partnering with specialized organizations for the responsible management of specific waste streams.

By embracing the principles of zero waste, these communities strive to conserve natural resources, reduce pollution and greenhouse gas emissions, and promote sustainable consumption patterns. They recognize that waste is not a byproduct of human activities but rather an opportunity to create a more efficient and sustainable society. Through education, awareness campaigns, and community engagement, zero-waste communities inspire individuals and businesses to adopt behaviors and practices that contribute to a healthier planet for current and future generations.

Zero-Waste Event Decor

Zero-waste event decor refers to the use of sustainable and environmentally-friendly materials and practices in the design and execution of event decorations, with the aim of minimizing waste generation and promoting a more sustainable event industry.

This approach to event decor prioritizes the use of reusable, recyclable, and compostable materials, as well as incorporating principles of reduce, reuse, and recycle. It involves careful planning and consideration of the entire lifecycle of event decorations, from sourcing to disposal, with a focus on minimizing environmental impact.

Zero-Waste Event Planning

Zero-waste event planning is a sustainable approach aimed at minimizing waste generation and maximizing resource conservation throughout the planning and execution of events. This practice focuses on reducing the environmental impact of events by implementing various strategies to eliminate or significantly reduce waste that would otherwise end up in landfills or contribute to pollution.

Under the principles of zero-waste event planning, organizers prioritize waste prevention and reduction by implementing sustainable practices such as reducing single-use items, promoting recycling and composting, and encouraging the use of reusable products. This includes utilizing eco-friendly materials and minimizing excessive packaging. Incorporating sustainable alternatives for food and beverage service, such as compostable or biodegradable tableware, further contributes to waste reduction.

In addition to waste reduction strategies, zero-waste event planning also emphasizes resource conservation. This includes efficient energy management, utilizing renewable energy sources wherever possible, and implementing water conservation measures. Event organizers may also encourage attendees to use public transportation or carpooling options to minimize emissions and reduce the event's carbon footprint.

By adopting a zero-waste approach, event planners aim to create a more sustainable and environmentally conscious event that aligns with the principles of circular economy and responsible resource management. This not only contributes to a healthier environment but also sets an example for attendees, inspiring them to adopt more sustainable practices in their everyday lives.

Zero-Waste Events

A zero-waste event refers to an organized gathering or occasion that aims to eliminate waste generation and minimize its environmental impact throughout the entire event lifecycle. This concept aligns with the principles of sustainability by promoting resource conservation, waste reduction, and responsible consumption.

In a zero-waste event, organizers implement and follow a comprehensive waste management plan that emphasizes waste prevention, recycling, composting, and other sustainable practices. The objective is to divert as much waste as possible from ending up in landfills or incinerators, thereby reducing greenhouse gas emissions, conserving natural resources, and minimizing pollution.

Organizers employ various strategies to achieve zero waste at these events, including:

- Offering reusable or compostable food and beverage containers
- Implementing effective recycling systems with clearly labeled bins
- Encouraging attendees to bring their own refillable water bottles and utensils
- Partnering with local food vendors who prioritize sustainable practices
- Promoting clothing swaps or donation centers for used attire instead of discarding
- Collaborating with waste management companies to ensure proper waste sorting and disposal

By adopting a zero-waste approach, event organizers aim to inspire and educate attendees about the importance of waste reduction and encourage behavioral changes that promote a more sustainable lifestyle.

>

Zero-Waste Fashion

Zero-waste fashion is a sustainable approach to clothing design and production that aims to eliminate waste throughout the entire lifecycle of a garment. It is a response to the destructive environmental impact caused by the traditional fashion industry, which generates large amounts of waste through excessive production, overconsumption, and disposal of clothing.

In zero-waste fashion, designers strive to create garments that leave no fabric scraps behind during the cutting process. This is achieved through innovative pattern-making techniques, such as draping, folding, and interlocking, that utilize the entire fabric without generating any waste. Additionally, zero-waste fashion promotes a circular approach to clothing, focusing on longevity, durability, and recyclability.

This sustainable fashion practice also aims to reduce the use of harmful chemicals and synthetic fibers, replacing them with organic and natural materials that are biodegradable and less harmful to the environment. Energy-efficient production processes and low-impact dyeing methods are also implemented to minimize the carbon footprint of zero-waste fashion.

By embracing zero-waste fashion, individuals can contribute to a more sustainable future by supporting ethical and environmentally responsible clothing brands. This eco-conscious approach encourages consumers to make mindful choices when purchasing clothes, considering the longevity and recyclability of garments, and reducing overall consumption.

Zero-Waste Grocery Shopping Apps

Zero-waste grocery shopping apps are innovative digital platforms designed to promote and facilitate sustainable consumer behavior in the context of grocery shopping. These apps aim to combat the environmental impacts associated with traditional grocery shopping by encouraging users to adopt a zero-waste lifestyle and reduce their carbon footprint.

These apps provide users with a range of features and functionalities to support them in making environmentally conscious shopping choices. Firstly, they offer comprehensive databases of zero-waste products and sustainable alternatives, allowing users to easily locate and purchase eco-friendly items without the need for excessive packaging. By highlighting package-free options and offering suggestions for reusable containers, the apps enable users to minimize waste generation and contribute to the circular economy.

Additionally, zero-waste grocery shopping apps often incorporate features to help users track their waste reduction progress. They may include features such as waste tracking tools, which allow users to monitor the amount of waste they generate and provide insights on areas for improvement. These apps may also provide educational resources and tips on sustainable living, empowering users to make informed choices and adopt a more eco-friendly lifestyle.

In summary, zero-waste grocery shopping apps are digital tools that facilitate sustainable grocery shopping practices by offering comprehensive product databases, waste tracking features, and educational resources. By promoting package-free and eco-friendly alternatives, these apps contribute to the reduction of waste generation and the promotion of a sustainable circular economy.

Zero-Waste Grocery Store Design

A zero-waste grocery store design refers to a sustainable retail establishment that aims to minimize or eliminate the generation of waste throughout its operations. This concept is centered around the principles of reducing, reusing, and recycling, as well as adopting responsible and eco-friendly practices. In a zero-waste grocery store, the design considerations are focused on creating an environment that facilitates the adoption of sustainable practices by both the store operators and its customers. This includes designing the layout of the store in a way that encourages waste reduction and supports the use of reusable items. The store may feature bulk dispensers for various products, such as grains, nuts, and liquids, allowing customers to bring their own containers and purchase only the amount they need, thus reducing the packaging waste. Additionally, reusable containers or bags may be provided to customers for carrying their purchases, rather than relying on single-use plastic bags. Furthermore, a zero-waste grocery store design may incorporate waste management systems that prioritize recycling and composting. This can include clearly labeled recycling and composting bins throughout the store, along with staff training to ensure proper waste sorting. The store may also forge relationships with local composting facilities or recycling centers to ensure that all waste generated is disposed of in an environmentally responsible manner. By adopting a zero-waste grocery store design, retailers can contribute to the reduction of waste, conserve natural resources, and minimize their environmental impact. Such establishments play a crucial role in promoting sustainable shopping habits and inspiring customers to make conscious choices that support a circular economy.

Zero-Waste Grocery Store Layouts

A zero-waste grocery store layout refers to the arrangement and organization of a retail space that minimizes waste and promotes sustainable practices. It aims to reduce the consumption of single-use packaging, favoring reusable or refillable containers instead. The design of such a store prioritizes the efficient use of resources and encourages customers to make sustainable choices.

In a zero-waste grocery store, the layout typically includes various sections and features that support waste reduction. These may include bulk bins for customers to dispense dry goods like grains, nuts, and spices, allowing them to bring their own reusable containers or use provided ones. The store may also have refill stations for liquid products such as oils, cleaning supplies, or personal care items, where customers can replenish their own containers.

The layout may further incorporate dedicated areas for fresh produce, where customers can select loose items rather than pre-packaged ones. Additionally, the store may have a section for sustainable alternatives to commonly used disposable items, such as compostable or reusable packaging, eco-friendly cleaning supplies, or bamboo utensils.

By utilizing a zero-waste grocery store layout, retailers aim to create an environment that fosters a more sustainable and conscious approach to shopping. Such layouts encourage customers to actively reduce their waste footprint by making informed choices and embracing reusable solutions. Ultimately, the goal is to minimize the environmental impact of grocery shopping while still providing convenient and accessible options for consumers.

Zero-Waste Grocery Stores

A zero-waste grocery store is a sustainable retail establishment that aims to minimize waste and promote a circular economy.

Unlike traditional grocery stores that often rely on single-use packaging and generate a significant amount of waste, zero-waste grocery stores adopt a holistic approach towards sustainability. These stores prioritize the reduction of packaging materials by encouraging customers to bring their own reusable containers. They offer a wide range of products, including fresh produce, dry goods, and even personal care items, which can be purchased in bulk or by the desired quantity.

Zero-waste grocery stores typically operate on a self-serve model, with customers using dispensers to collect products such as grains, nuts, oils, and detergents directly into their own containers. This eliminates the need for single-use packaging, significantly reducing plastic and other waste. In some cases, these stores also provide reusable bags or offer alternatives, such as compostable or biodegradable packaging for items that cannot be sold in bulk.

In addition to reducing packaging waste, zero-waste grocery stores often prioritize sourcing products that are locally produced, organic, fair-trade, or sustainable. By promoting environmentally friendly and ethically sourced options, these stores contribute to a more sustainable food system that benefits both the planet and local communities.

Overall, zero-waste grocery stores offer consumers a sustainable alternative to conventional shopping, helping to reduce their ecological footprint and encouraging mindful consumption. By embracing the principles of waste reduction and resource conservation, these stores play a crucial role in working towards a more sustainable and circular economy.

Zero-Waste Hotel Planning

A zero-waste hotel is a sustainable accommodation facility that aims to minimize the generation of waste throughout its operations, with the ultimate goal of sending no waste to landfill. This concept incorporates various strategies and practices to reduce, reuse, recycle, and compost materials, leading to a significant reduction in the hotel's environmental footprint.

Such hotels implement waste management systems that prioritize waste prevention and reduction through careful planning, resource utilization, and efficient operations. They aim to eliminate single-use items and encourage the use of durable and reusable products. By promoting sustainable procurement practices, zero-waste hotels strive to minimize packaging waste and source environmentally friendly products.

Moreover, these hotels educate and engage their staff and guests in sustainable practices, encouraging them to actively participate in waste reduction efforts. They provide convenient and clearly labeled waste separation and recycling stations to facilitate proper waste disposal. Additionally, zero-waste hotels often collaborate with local recycling agencies or companies to ensure proper handling and diversion of recyclable materials.

The organic waste generated by these hotels, such as food scraps and yard trimmings, is typically directed towards composting or anaerobic digestion. By diverting these materials from the landfill, zero-waste hotels contribute to the production of nutrient-rich compost and renewable energy.

Zero-Waste Initiatives

A zero-waste initiative refers to a sustainable approach focused on minimizing waste generation and maximizing resource efficiency throughout various stages of production, consumption, and disposal. It entails implementing strategies and practices that aim to eliminate or significantly reduce the amount of waste sent to landfills or incineration facilities.

By adopting a zero-waste mindset, organizations and individuals strive to redesign systems and processes to prioritize waste prevention, reuse, recycling, and composting. This involves rethinking product design, packaging, and manufacturing techniques to minimize waste generation, as well as promoting the use of durable and recyclable materials.

Furthermore, zero-waste initiatives encourage the development of circular economies, where resources are kept in use for as long as possible through repair, refurbishment, and remanufacturing. This helps minimize the extraction of virgin materials and reduces the environmental impacts of resource extraction and waste disposal.

By embracing a zero-waste approach, businesses not only contribute to environmental conservation but also benefit financially by reducing costs associated with waste management and disposal. Additionally, these initiatives foster a culture of sustainability and responsibility within communities, helping raise awareness about the importance of waste reduction and resource conservation.

Zero-Waste Lifestyle Products

A zero-waste lifestyle refers to a way of living that aims to eliminate or significantly reduce waste production by adopting sustainable practices and utilizing products that are designed to be as waste-free as possible. In this context, zero-waste lifestyle products are items that are created with the intention of promoting sustainable and eco-friendly living.

These products are typically made from reusable, recyclable, or biodegradable materials, and are designed to have a minimal ecological impact throughout their entire lifecycle. For example, zero-waste lifestyle products may include reusable items such as cloth grocery bags, stainless steel water bottles, or bamboo utensils, which help to reduce the need for disposable alternatives.

Furthermore, zero-waste lifestyle products often prioritize durability and longevity, as well as being made from sustainable materials. This helps to reduce the overall consumption of resources and minimizes waste by preventing the need for frequent replacements.

Additionally, zero-waste lifestyle products may also include items that facilitate recycling and composting, as well as those that promote energy and water conservation. These products aim to inspire individuals to adopt sustainable habits and make conscious choices in their everyday lives, ultimately contributing to a more environmentally-friendly future.

Zero-Waste Manufacturing

Zero-waste manufacturing is a sustainable approach to production that aims to minimize or eliminate waste generated during the manufacturing process. It involves strategies and practices that focus on resource efficiency, waste reduction, and material reuse or recycling.

By implementing zero-waste manufacturing, companies strive to reduce the negative environmental impacts associated with traditional manufacturing methods. This approach involves the careful management and optimization of resources, materials, and energy to ensure that nothing is wasted or sent to landfill.

Zero-waste manufacturing involves the adoption of various principles and techniques. These include:

- Designing products with durability and recyclability in mind to avoid premature obsolescence and unnecessary waste.

- Analyzing and optimizing production processes to minimize material waste and energy consumption.

- Implementing efficient recycling and reclamation systems to reuse or repurpose waste materials generated during production.

- Encouraging collaboration and partnerships with suppliers, customers, and other stakeholders to promote sustainable practices and reduce waste across the supply chain.

By embracing zero-waste manufacturing, companies can achieve several benefits. These include the reduction of waste disposal costs, improved resource efficiency, and enhanced environmental stewardship. Additionally, companies can enhance their brand image and reputation among eco-conscious consumers who prioritize sustainable products and practices.

Zero-Waste Office Interiors

Zero-waste office interiors refer to the design and implementation of workspaces that minimize or completely eliminate waste generated during the construction, operation, and end-of-life phases. This approach emphasizes sustainable materials, efficient use of resources, and responsible disposal practices to create a workspace that has a minimal environmental footprint.

Zero-waste office interiors prioritize the reduction of waste at the source by using eco-friendly materials that are renewable, recyclable, or biodegradable. These materials are often sourced locally to reduce transportation-related emissions and support the local economy. The design also focuses on maximizing the lifespan of furniture and equipment, promoting repair and reuse rather than disposal and replacement.

Additionally, zero-waste office interiors aim to minimize energy and water consumption through the use of energy-efficient lighting, appliances, and fixtures. This includes incorporating natural lighting and ventilation to reduce reliance on artificial systems. Advanced waste management systems, such as onsite composting and recycling programs, are implemented to divert waste from landfills and recover valuable resources.

By adopting a zero-waste approach, office interiors can contribute to a more sustainable and circular economy. Not only does this approach reduce greenhouse gas emissions, waste generation, and resource depletion, but it also creates healthier and more productive work environments for employees. Ultimately, zero-waste office interiors exemplify the principles of sustainability by promoting responsible consumption and production practices within the business sector.

Zero-Waste Office Layouts

A zero-waste office layout refers to a design approach that focuses on minimizing waste generation and promoting sustainability within the workplace. This concept emphasizes the reduction, reuse, and recycling of resources to eliminate or significantly reduce the amount of waste sent to landfills.

By implementing a zero-waste office layout, organizations can take various measures to optimize resource efficiency and minimize their environmental impact. This includes incorporating eco-friendly practices, such as utilizing energy-efficient lighting, installing low-flow water fixtures, and promoting the use of recycled materials for office furniture and equipment.

Furthermore, a zero-waste office layout encourages the implementation of waste management systems, such as composting and recycling programs, to ensure that waste is diverted from landfills and properly managed. This involves educating employees on proper waste segregation and providing easily accessible recycling and composting bins throughout the office space.

Additionally, a zero-waste office layout promotes the reduction of paper waste by implementing digital document management systems and encouraging the use of electronic communication and file sharing platforms. This helps to minimize the consumption of paper products and reduces the need for physical storage space.

Overall, a zero-waste office layout aims to create a sustainable and environmentally conscious workplace by minimizing waste generation, maximizing resource efficiency, and promoting responsible waste management practices. By adopting such a layout, organizations can not only reduce their environmental footprint but also inspire employees and other stakeholders to prioritize sustainability in their daily operations and decision-making processes.

Zero-Waste Packaging Artwork

Zero-waste packaging artwork refers to a sustainable packaging solution that aims to eliminate waste throughout its entire lifecycle, from production to disposal. It is an innovative approach that prioritizes minimizing environmental impact by reducing resource consumption, promoting reuse and recycling, and preventing the accumulation of non-biodegradable materials.

As a form of sustainable packaging, zero-waste artwork follows key principles to achieve its goals. Firstly, it focuses on using materials that are renewable, biodegradable, or easily recyclable. This includes selecting packaging components made from responsibly sourced

434

materials such as recycled paper, cardboard, or plant-based plastics. Additionally, the packaging design should avoid complex layers or mixed materials that are difficult to separate and recycle.

Furthermore, zero-waste packaging artwork encourages packaging designers and manufacturers to adopt strategies such as minimalism and functional design. By reducing unnecessary packaging materials and optimizing the use of space, this approach aims to minimize the overall environmental footprint of the product. It also emphasizes the importance of considering the end-user experience, ensuring that the packaging is user-friendly and convenient to handle.

In terms of waste management, zero-waste packaging artwork promotes the concept of a circular economy. This means that at the end of its use, the packaging can be easily and efficiently recycled or composted, returning valuable resources back into the production cycle. Alternatively, it can be designed for reuse or upcycling, extending its lifespan and reducing the need for new packaging.

Zero-Waste Packaging Materials

Zero-waste packaging materials refer to sustainable materials that are designed to minimize or eliminate waste throughout their life cycle, from production to disposal. These materials are specifically engineered to have a minimal impact on the environment and are part of the broader effort to reduce the harmful effects of traditional packaging on ecosystems.

The concept of zero-waste packaging materials revolves around the principles of reusability, recyclability, and compostability. Reusable packaging materials can be employed multiple times without losing their functionality, reducing the need for single-use packaging. Recyclable materials can be processed and transformed into new products, diverting them from landfill and enabling a circular economy. Compostable materials can decompose naturally and return to the soil, minimizing their environmental footprint.

Examples of zero-waste packaging materials include glass, metal, cardboard, paper, and certain types of bioplastics. Glass and metal are highly reusable and infinitely recyclable. Cardboard and paper, sourced from responsibly managed forests or recycled fibers, are also recyclable and can be easily composted. Bioplastics, derived from renewable sources such as corn or sugar cane, offer an alternative to traditional plastics and can be composted under certain conditions.

By adopting zero-waste packaging materials, businesses and consumers contribute to reducing the amount of waste generated, conserving natural resources, and minimizing pollution. These materials promote a more sustainable and circular approach to packaging, aligning with the principles of a circular economy and the United Nations Sustainable Development Goals. Moreover, they serve as a tangible solution to address the environmental challenges associated with packaging waste, ultimately creating a more sustainable future.

Zero-Waste Packaging

Zero-waste packaging, within the context of sustainability, refers to a system of packaging that aims to eliminate or substantially reduce the amount of waste generated throughout the entire life cycle of a product. It is a holistic approach that considers the environmental impact of packaging materials, production processes, distribution methods, and end-of-life disposal.

The primary objective of zero-waste packaging is to minimize the use of non-recyclable materials, such as single-use plastics, and promote the use of sustainable alternatives, such as biodegradable or compostable materials. This approach encourages the redesign of packaging to optimize material usage, reduce energy consumption, and minimize pollution during production and transportation.

Zero-waste packaging also encompasses the concept of extended producer responsibility, which holds manufacturers accountable for the entire life cycle of their products, including the packaging. It involves implementing strategies to reduce packaging waste, such as designing packaging that can be easily recycled or reused, implementing take-back programs, and collaborating with consumers and recycling facilities to ensure proper disposal.

Furthermore, zero-waste packaging encourages businesses and consumers to adopt a circular economy mindset, where materials are kept in use for as long as possible, and the generation of waste is minimized through recycling, repurposing, and composting. It promotes sustainable consumption and production patterns, fosters innovation in packaging design, and supports the transition towards a more sustainable and regenerative economy.

Zero-Waste Practices

Zero-waste practices refer to a set of principles and strategies aimed at minimizing waste generation and promoting sustainable consumption and production patterns. It involves adopting systems and practices that prioritize waste prevention, reduction, reuse, recycling, and composting, while minimizing or eliminating disposal to landfill or incineration.

At its core, zero-waste practices recognize that waste is not an inherent part of the natural environment but rather a consequence of the linear model of consumption and production predominant in our society. By embracing a circular economy approach, zero-waste practices strive to close material loops and create a more sustainable, resource-efficient, and resilient system.

Zero-waste practices can be implemented at various levels, including individual households, businesses, communities, and governments. Strategies may include source separation for recycling, promoting the use of reusable products, designing products for longevity and recyclability, implementing organic waste management systems, and supporting extended producer responsibility schemes.

By adopting zero-waste practices, individuals and organizations can significantly reduce their environmental impact, conserve natural resources, mitigate climate change, minimize pollution, and protect ecosystems. Furthermore, these practices can contribute to the creation of green jobs, stimulate innovation, and foster a more sustainable and inclusive economy.

Overall, zero-waste practices represent a proactive and holistic approach to waste management and sustainable development, aiming to create a future where resources are used efficiently, waste generation is minimized, and the well-being of both present and future generations is prioritized.

Zero-Waste Restaurant Design

A zero-waste restaurant design refers to the concept and practice of creating a dining establishment that aims to minimize waste generation and promote sustainability throughout its operations. This design approach entails incorporating various strategies and techniques to ensure that all resources, including food, water, energy, and materials, are used efficiently and effectively.

This environmentally conscious design seeks to address the significant amount of waste typically generated by restaurants, including food scraps, packaging materials, and single-use items. It involves implementing a comprehensive waste management system that focuses on three main principles: reduce, reuse, and recycle.

Firstly, a zero-waste restaurant design focuses on reducing waste generation at its source. This can be achieved through careful menu planning and ingredient sourcing, ensuring that food and other supplies are purchased in quantities that minimize excess and spoilage. Additionally, the design includes measures to prevent food waste, such as proper storage and preservation techniques.

Secondly, the design emphasizes the reuse of materials to minimize the need for new resources. This can involve using durable and reusable tableware instead of disposable items, implementing systems for dishwashing and sanitization, and encouraging customers to bring their own containers for take-out orders.

Finally, recycling plays a vital role in a zero-waste restaurant design. This includes providing clearly marked recycling bins throughout the establishment, implementing efficient waste sorting and separation processes, and partnering with recycling programs and facilities to ensure proper disposal and processing of recyclable materials.

Zero-Waste Restaurant Interiors

A zero-waste restaurant refers to a dining establishment that follows sustainable practices in its interior design and operations, with the aim of minimizing waste generation and promoting environmental conservation. The concept of zero-waste in restaurant interiors revolves around implementing strategies to reduce, reuse, and recycle materials, while also considering energy efficiency and ecological principles.

In a zero-waste restaurant, the interior design takes into account the lifecycle of materials, ensuring that resources are used efficiently and waste is minimized. This involves selecting durable and recyclable materials, avoiding single-use items, and repurposing or upcycling materials whenever possible. The design also prioritizes natural lighting and ventilation systems to reduce energy consumption and enhance the dining experience by creating a visually pleasing and environmentally friendly space.

Furthermore, zero-waste restaurants aim to operate in a manner that reduces their carbon footprint and overall environmental impact. This includes using energy-efficient appliances and equipment, implementing effective waste management systems, and encouraging sustainable practices among staff and patrons. For example, these establishments may utilize composting systems to divert organic waste from landfills or offer reusable containers and utensils instead of disposable ones.

By adopting a zero-waste approach, restaurants contribute to the larger goal of creating a sustainable and circular economy. They demonstrate a commitment to sustainability by prioritizing responsible consumption and waste reduction, while also providing a unique dining experience that aligns with the values and expectations of environmentally conscious consumers.

Zero-Waste Retail Stores

A zero-waste retail store refers to a sustainable business model that aims to eliminate or minimize waste throughout the entire supply chain, from production to consumption. These stores prioritize the reduction of single-use packaging and the promotion of reusable and refillable containers. In a zero-waste retail store, customers are encouraged to bring their own bags, containers, or bottles to carry their purchases, thereby reducing the need for disposable packaging.

These stores typically stock a wide range of products, including cleaning supplies, toiletries, pantry staples, and household items. They source their items from local suppliers, organic farms, and responsible manufacturers to ensure the ecological and ethical integrity of their offerings. Additionally, zero-waste retail stores often prioritize the sale of sustainably produced, ethically sourced, and locally made goods to support local economies and reduce the carbon footprint associated with transportation.

Zero-Waste Store Layout

A zero-waste store layout refers to the arrangement and organization of a retail space that is designed to minimize waste and promote sustainable practices. It is a physical environment that encourages customers to adopt a zero-waste lifestyle by providing a range of package-free, bulk, and refillable products.

The layout of a zero-waste store typically incorporates various sustainable design elements. One of the key features is the placement of bulk bins and dispensers, which allow customers to bring their own reusable containers and purchase the exact quantity of products they need, reducing packaging waste. These bulk sections are often positioned prominently, making them easily accessible and encouraging customers to prioritize package-free options.

The layout may also include dedicated areas for refill stations, where customers can replenish household and personal care products from large containers, eliminating the need for single-use packaging. These refill stations are strategically located near related product categories, making

437

it convenient for customers to refill their supplies while shopping for other items.

In addition to these specific product-related features, a zero-waste store layout may prioritize natural lighting, energy-efficient fixtures and equipment, and sustainable materials in its construction and design. It may also incorporate thoughtful signage and labeling systems to guide customers towards eco-friendly choices and provide information on the store's sustainability practices.

www.ingramcontent.com/pod-product-compliance
Lightning Source LLC
Chambersburg PA
CBHW030859310526
45786CB00017B/3